# MORE OF THE BEST OF
# MILTON BERLE'S
## PRIVATE JOKE FILE

# MORE OF THE BEST OF
# MILTON BERLE'S
# PRIVATE JOKE FILE

*10,000 of the World's Funniest Gags,
Anecdotes, and One-Liners*

## Milton Berle
### Edited by Milt Rosen

WILLIAM MORROW AND COMPANY, INC.
*New York*

Library of Congress Cataloging-in-Publication Data

Berle, Milton.
    More of the best of Milton Berle's private joke file: 10,000
  of the world's funniest gags, anecdotes, and one-liners/by
  Milton Berle; edited by Milt Rosen.
        p. cm.
    ISBN 0-688-11879-8
    1. American wit and humor.    I. Rosen, Milt.    II. Title.
  PN6162.B47   1993
  818′5402—dc20                                              92-45031
                                                             CIP

Printed in the United States of America

First Edition

1 2 3 4 5 6 7 8 9 10

BOOK DESIGN BY PAUL CHEVANNES

This book is a tribute to the first teller of a joke. He was inventing the greatest gift given to the race and the world. Some people would vote for polyester, but my vote is solidly for the joke.

A nod also to the second comedian, who put two jokes together and invented the monologue. Polyester can't hold a candle to that.

# SPECIAL THANKS

To Mark Gompertz, Bob Shuman, Elisa Petrini, and
Lisa Considine, editors supreme
Arthur Pine, agent deluxe
Michael Glasser, who healed the computer
Ray Hoese, whose fingers made sparks fly from the keyboard,
and
Lorna Berle, for the sandwiches, the diet drinks, the coffee, the
Danish and, for some fast energy when we faltered, the pounds of
Hershey kisses and jelly beans

# CONTENTS

14

# CONTENTS

# INTRODUCTION

On the shelves of one wall of my den are several hundred books. Some of the books have as many as twenty-five hundred pages; one checks in at forty-two hundred onionskin pages. On each page of these precious books, there are between ten and twenty jokes. Many of the jokes are classics, others were written for me over seventy years, and still others, not a few in number, were lines I'd come up with on my own so that my writers wouldn't feel indispensable. Secure comedy writers work only sixteen hours a day. I like them full time.

What an army of writers there was serving my comedic crusade: Alan Jay Lerner, Paddy Chayefsky, Larry Gelbart, and a weird sexfiend named George S. Kaufman—to drop a name or two. I was given stories by Lyndon Baines Johnson and, when nobody was looking, by a young, handsome congressman named John F. Kennedy. A story I told for twenty years was handed to me by Flo Ziegfeld, who swore that it had gotten screams in Vienna. Flo could have handed me a few showgirls, but he chose the easy way out. Since then I've never trusted any man named Flo.

The material for my joke book of several years ago was culled from the files I kept, my private, under-lock-and-key, bonded files. To make an impression on the reader, I chose what I felt was the primest of this prime material. No smiles, no tiny chuckles, no whimsy; only, as W. C. Fields put it, jokes with a kick like day-old whiskey.

The book was received warmly and appreciatively. It sold well and continues to sell well. Even my brother Phil liked it. This was a true compliment, as Phil hasn't liked much of what I've done since he went off payroll. More significant, the book gave my accountant a few chuckles. He hadn't chuckled since the savings-and-loan scandal. I became a giant hit with my gardener too. To show his respect, he actually killed two weeds in my honor.

When approached to assemble a companion volume, I wondered if I could match the previous book. When in doubt, I go to the files. Perusing them—the first time I ever "perused" anything—I realized that I'd hardly tickled the surface with the previous book. There was more than enough material. It was just as prime, and, in some areas, much primer. Also, there were other books on other shelves and other walls from which I'd excerpted nothing. They reached out to me with leather-bound arms and begged to be exploited. And then there were my computerized files. The work of hardy electronic scanners and a dozen punch-line-drunk secretaries, these files contained jokes in three thousand categories. Moreover, the jokes were and are constantly being freshened. Each day, new jokes and stories find a home in one of those categories. Groups are constantly being added. Condoms became a lunchtime topic about a year ago. I now have a few gross of condom jokes. I have a gross of gross jokes too. Some of them may find their way into this book to show that man does not live by taste alone.

After a lot of perusing and the promise of a substantial check, I concluded: Yes, I could match my previous effort!

I started culling again. It was an enjoyable task. I ran into some old funny friends and many jokes I'd almost forgotten. It was, also, a difficult task. Which of the thirty pages of Adam-and-Eve jokes to include? How many ounces of parrot jokes? I only have a hundred and fifty. I managed to surge forward.

To make the deal stick to the wall, an advertising expression I fell in love with when I first heard it last year, I've included a special section on roasts. As a participant in two thousand of them, I feel that I have some clues worth passing on.

I chose roasts for the topic of the day as they have become one of the standard entertainment forms, yet still aren't fully understood. Because I love comedy and hurt when it's given warts, I want every roast to be perfect. And what better forum for the reader to try out some of the jokes in this book?

This second section is capped with an actual roast monologue: two, in fact, one normal and nice, the other naughty and not so nice. As a further premium, a pound and a half of extra roast material has been appended. For the money, you can't beat that.

First, however, there are the jokes. What follows, I believe, is a fine treasure lode of comedy. My mother would have liked it. That's all the seal of approval anybody needs.

# MORE OF THE BEST OF
# MILTON BERLE'S
## PRIVATE JOKE FILE

## AA

He just joined Alcoholics Anonymous. He still drinks but under an assumed name.

One AA group didn't quite get the idea. It applied for a liquor license.

AA has its own version of Russian roulette. They pass six glasses of tomato juice around, and one of them is a Bloody Mary.

At one AA meeting, a speaker waxed poetic about the evils of alcohol. When he got to a particularly sordid description of how alcohol ruins your life, a member yelled out, "I'll drink to that."

A friend of mine belongs to AA, but he's not a fanatic about it. He doesn't go to meetings—he just sends in the empties.

In AA you have to pray to your Higher Power. One fellow went home and prayed to his mother-in-law.

## AARDVARKS/ANTEATERS

An anteater is anybody who goes on a picnic.

A male and female anteater are snuggling nose-to-nose. The male asks, "Are you beginning to get a funny feeling all the way down to your toes?"

The female answers, "Don't rush me. It hasn't reached my nostrils yet."

An anteater tells a friend, "I ate four million ants today."

The friend says, "You're always dieting!"

"My uncle is in Africa hunting anteaters. He wants to bring one back alive."

"Why would he want to bring one back alive?"

"He hates my aunt!"

## ABSENTMINDED

A waitress was rather absentminded. At night, after sex, she'd turn to her husband and ask, "Will that be all, sir?"

One day he stopped his girl and went too far with his car.

Then there was the absentminded professor who unbuttoned his vest, took out his tie, and wet himself.

The absentminded biology teacher said to the class, "Today we are going to dissect a frog." He unfolded some paper and reacted as he saw a sandwich. He shook his head, puzzled, and said, "I distinctly recall eating lunch earlier."

My next-door neighbor is getting absentminded. The other day he kissed a woman by mistake and thought it was his wife. And it was!

One deadbeat was really absentminded. He parked his car in front of the loan company.

An absentminded gent came home, and his wife said, "Where's your umbrella?"

"I don't know."

"When did you first miss it?"

"Well, when it stopped raining, I reached up to close it, and it was gone."

The other day I left my wife at the bank and kissed my money good-bye.

My mother-in-law is absentminded. She can never find her glasses. She just leaves them where she empties them.

An absentminded soldier went on guard duty and shot himself. He had to. He forgot the password.

Absentmindedly, a man started to leave a restaurant with somebody else's umbrella. The owner, an elderly woman, grabbed it from him. He apologized and left. The next day he stopped off at a shop to pick up three umbrellas he'd left to be repaired. The elderly woman saw him as he walked home and sneered, "I see you did well today."

I'm getting so absentminded and forgetful. Sometimes in the middle of a sentence, I.

"I went out with an absentminded professor last night."

"How can you tell he's absentminded?"

"He gave me an 'F' this morning."

The absentminded professor walks in his bedroom and says, "Madam, what are you doing on my bed?"

"I like this room, I like the wallpaper. I like the lighting. And besides, I'm your wife."

The most absentminded of all absentminded professors was the one who forgot to write a thirty-dollar textbook to sell to his class.

## ACCIDENTS

Then there was the WAC who was discharged for being pregnant. It seems she'd been hit by a guided muscle.

I almost drowned the other day. I took an acupuncture treatment on my water bed.

A man sees his neighbor's car all banged up and asks what happened. The unfortunate says, "Yesterday I was in the country, and I hit a cow."

"Was it a jersey?"

"I don't know. I didn't see its license plate."

"Here, let me help you with that refrigerator."

"Okay, but don't drop it."

"Oops, it slipped. Let's get somebody to help us."

"No, John wouldn't like it left like this."

"Why?"

"Because he's under the refrigerator."

"Ma, I just knocked over the ladder in the garden."

"Tell your daddy."

"He knows. He's hanging from the bedroom window."

A man was run over by a steamroller. He was in the hospital in rooms 38 to 44.

A man was run over by a steamroller. His doctor told him to stay flat on his back.

A pedestrian stared at a lovely lady passing by, his eyes fixed on her shapely legs. Suddenly, he walked into a slowly moving car. Another pedestrian helped him up and said, "That was pretty close. Your eyes were almost on their last legs."

Two pirates are sitting in a grog shop having a few drinks. One of them has a peg leg, the other a hook for an arm and a patch over a bad eye. The first pirate explains his bad luck and the missing limb, saying, "We were attacking this vessel, and when we boarded, one of the enemy sailors took a swipe at me and severed my leg."

The second pirate explained his misfortune: "I got this when a sea gull let go of some droppings right into my eye."

The first pirate said, "That would be irritating, but it wouldn't cost you an eye."

The second pirate said, "Well, you see, it was my first day with this hook."

√ A man has a terrible accident and has to undergo surgery. When he awakens, the surgeon says, "I have bad news and good news for you."

"What's the bad news?"

"We had to amputate both of your legs."

"And the good news?"

"The guy in the next bed wants to buy your shoes."

A man with two sons directed them toward specific educations. One became a physician, the other an attorney. All went well for the father until he was involved in a terrible accident. His physician son wanted to cure him, but the attorney son wanted him to keep limping so they could sue.

I had a bad accident, but the doctor told me that he'd have me walking again in no time. It was true. I had to sell my car to pay his bill.

√ A husky lady lost her thumb in a car accident and sued for a fortune. The other lawyer asked her why she believed her thumb to be worth so much. The woman answered, "Because that's the thumb I kept my husband under."

This basketball player had just put on his aluminum cup when a shapely girl walked by the locker room. The basketball player died three hours later—shrapnel wounds.

A shin is a device used for finding furniture in the dark.

Sometimes it doesn't pay to pay attention. I saw a sign that said STOP, LOOK, AND LISTEN. I did, and a train hit me.

The head of a rescue team is telling his crew, "Look, we've got some dangerous work ahead of us. The roads are so slick, the tires can't get traction. There's a big forest fire heading for the area we're going into, flash floods, and there have been terrible avalanches reported. We leave at six A.M. But be on time. If you're one minute late, you won't get to go."

√ A gas leak caused an old woman's house to explode as she lit the stove one afternoon. Miraculously, she was unhurt. The claims adjuster handed the woman the only item that survived—a bottle of brandy. He suggested she take a nip to settle her nerves.

"Oh, no," she said. "I'm saving that for emergencies."

A man and his wife are on vacation in Europe. The wife gets hit by a car. It doesn't seem like a grave matter, so the man has his wife brought up to the room.

Sadly, the wife starts to fail and goes into a coma. The concierge calls and asks, "Sir, is there anything the hotel can do?"

"Yeah. Do you have a cheaper room?"

A policeman arrives at the scene of what looks like a bad accident. A pedestrian is lying, unmoving, in the crosswalk. The driver of the car under suspicion says, "I swear I didn't touch him. I saw him at the crosswalk. I came to a complete stop, motioned for him to cross, and he fainted."

I'll never forget the day I smashed into a police car and woke up two cops.

One masochist had a special bracelet that said, "I'm a masochist. In case of accident, please wait three hours before calling the paramedics."

An Irishman falls from the fourth-story scaffolding of a new building. When he hits the ground, a crowd rushes over. One of the group offers him a drink of water. The Irishman sits up and asks, "How far do I have to fall to get a shot of whiskey?"

This young man is assisting a roofer at work. The assistant reaches over for a stack of tiles, slips, and falls twenty feet to the ground. Picking himself up, he says "This is the damn part of the job I hate."

A man comes out of a shopping mall to find that the side of his parked car is rammed in. Seeing a note under the windshield, he reads it. On the paper is written: *As I'm writing this, about a dozen people are watching me. They think I'm giving you my name, phone number, and insurance company. But I'm not.*

## ACCOUNTANTS

A client gets his bill from the accountant and is stunned by the size. Furious, he calls the accountant and berates him for trying to squeeze him dry.

The accountant listens for a while and then says, "You're such an ingrate. And to think, I named my boat after you."

I knew I was in trouble with taxes when my accountant called me and asked if I knew anything about plea bargaining.

It's very hard to work with my accountant. Every time we're getting somewhere, the guard says, "Visiting time's over."

My accountant got into trouble last year—accounts deceivable.

I have a brilliant accountant. He can't count to twenty-one unless he's naked.

I have a considerate accountant. His office has a recovery room.

It's pretty scary when your accountant shows up on *Lifestyles of the Rich and Famous*!

My accountant has a lot of pull. If you go to jail for tax evasion, he can get you a job in the library.

When my accountant gets through cooking the books, eight people could eat.

Our new accountant can do triple-entry accounting. He has one set of books showing our real profits, one for my partner to show him that we just squeaked by with a few cents' profit, and the third for the government, showing the loss.

I let my accountant do my taxes because it saves time—sometimes as much as ten years.

My accountant is ready to deduct for my parrot if I can guarantee that it only talks business.

My accountant is going to put me in a fancy tax shelter—Leavenworth.

The boss comes in and asks a clerk, "Where's the accountant?"
    The clerk says, "He's at the track."
    "What's he doing at the track?"
    "Trying to make the books balance."

I have a wonderful new accountant— H&R Loophole.

## ACTORS & ACTRESSES

He's not doing well in his acting career. He's got more lines in his face than he does in the script.

An actor asked a young lady's father if he could have his daughter's hand in marriage. The father said, "Never. I would never let my daughter marry an actor."
    The actor said, "At least you could come see my play."
    The father went to the play, and the next day he called the young man and said, "Okay, you can marry my daughter. You're no actor."

An out-of-work actor applied for a job as a department-store Santa. He told the interviewer that he'd worked two weeks in the largest store in Newark.
    The interviewer said, "That would be okay for an off-Broadway store, but we need Broadway experience."

An actor opens in a Broadway show to a less-than-thrilling reception. Later, in a restaurant, he sits with a friend who commiserates with him, saying, "That was a terrible audience. So much booing."
    The actor says, "I don't feel that bad. There was also a lot of clapping."
    The friend says, "Don't kid yourself. The clapping was for the booing."

One actor had a stage name, a Swiss bank account, an unlisted phone, and a private fax number. One day, an agent got him a job, but couldn't find him.

An actor is a man who tries to be everything but himself.

Many actors have fan clubs. A fan club is a group of screaming kids who tell the actor that he's not alone in the way he feels about himself.

He acts in a lot of escapist plays. When he's on, you want to escape.

The best actors at an award show are the losers—the good losers.

One actor said, "I used to be the nastiest, most conceited, arrogant son of a bitch. Then I went to a shrink. Now you couldn't meet a nicer guy than me."

This actor was well known for being a great dresser. His suits were of fine Italian silk and handmade. Unfortunately, he never paid his tailor.

Another actor asked the tailor why he extended credit to the deadbeat.

The tailor said, "He must have money. Look at the way he dresses."

Samson must have been a great actor. He brought down the house.

When a normal man's house burns down, he calls his insurance man. When an actor's house burns down, he calls his publicity man.

I know an actress who's had so many tucks, she has a live-in plastic surgeon.

An actor runs into a friend and tells him he's appearing in an off-off-off-Broadway show. The friend says, "How much do they pay you?"

"No money," says the actor.

"Then why do you do it?"

"In the third act, they give us soup."

He's been in so many turkeys, he should be made an honorary Pilgrim.

Actors always speak in superlatives. The "best" meal I ever had, the "worst" outfit I ever saw. A perfect example is of this Broadway actor who finds himself in a real flop. Closing night, the take was only forty dollars. The actor leaves the theater and heads for a bar where many other actors hang out. Unable to lose the quality of talking in superlatives, he says to some of his peers, "Can you believe the take tonight? *Lowest* take in theatrical history. Twenty dollars."

One actor was in a one-man show, and the critics said, "There are too many in the cast."

A Broadway actor was auditioning for a part in a drama. The casting director told him, "In this play, you are a man who spent twenty years in jail. When you got out, you ended up on a desert island, and you don't see a woman for another twenty years. Then you're rescued. On the boat is a beautiful woman who beckons to you. She wants to crush you to her bosom and make love to you. So you take her in your arms. You start to kiss her. You—" The actor made a face and said, "What's my motivation?"

An actor gets a tiny part in Shakespeare's *Julius Caesar*. He plays a citizen of Rome. He doesn't have even one line to say. He tells a friend, who asks, "What's the play about?"

"Well, it's about this citizen of Rome . . ."

He's such a wooden actor, you could make a coffee table out of him.

An actor tells a friend, "I play this rat who goes around cheating, lying, and killing. I destroy my father and mother and end up ruining my kid. It's the first nice part I've had in years."

A famous actor's wife died. As her body was lowered into the ground, he broke down completely.

Later a friend consoled him: "You certainly cried your eyes out at the cemetery."

"That was nothing," the actor said. "You should have seen me at the funeral parlor."

Many a high-strung actor should be.

This one actor had a giant ego. He took along a makeup man when he went for passport pictures.

## ADAGES

Do unto others before they do unto you.

A hair in the head is worth two in the brush.

You can make both ends meet, but you can't make them like each other.

Never hit a man when he's down. Kick him. It's much easier.

Two is company. Three is bad birth control.

Dead owls don't give a hoot.

## ADAM & EVE

On their first night together, Adam warned Eve, "Stand back. I don't know how big this thing gets."

Adam and Eve must have been Irish. The first time he saw her, he looked at her crotch and said, "Oh, hair." Eve looked at his and said, "Oh, tool."

Adam had it good. He didn't have to listen to Eve talk about all the guys she could have married.

Came a time that Adam started to stay out all hours. He'd sneak back into Eden very late at night. Eve watched him for a few days, then one day while he was sleeping, she tiptoed over to him and counted his ribs.

Adam said to his wife, "Eve, I wear the plants in this family."

It was the day after they were created, and Adam looked at Eve and said, "You were only created yesterday, and already you have a headache?"

Eve was made from Adam's rib. There are a lot of men who wish that he'd kept his big rib shut.

As Adam and Eve cuddled for the first time and he cooed into her ear, Eve asked, "Why are we whispering?"

"What time of day was Adam created?" "A little before Eve."

Eve blamed the snake. The snake didn't have a leg to stand on.

"Adam, do you love me?"
    "Who else?"

Of course Adam lived in Paradise. He had no mother-in-law.

Poor Adam. He was the only man who couldn't say, "Haven't I met you before?"

Adam had a wife now, but he didn't quite know what to do with her. God said, "Study the birds and bees."
    The next day, Adam said to God, "It works okay when I fly out of a tree at her, but it hurts like hell if I miss."

Adam and Eve should have known about dieting. Then maybe they wouldn't have eaten themselves out of house and home.

This young boy in Sunday school swears that Adam played baseball. He'd heard that Adam fell from grace in the big inning.

Adam looked, and there was Eve. They went to bed. In the morning, a smiling Adam got up and said to God, "Lord, would you like another rib?"

"What did the serpent say to Eve?"
    " 'I'll bet you can't eat just one.' "

A relative asked Adam about the Garden of Eden. Adam explained, "It's a weird place. Eat one piece of fruit and you're out."

So Adam and Eve are sitting around Eden when a leaf floats down from a tree. Eve points and says, excitedly, "Adam, look—an invisible man."

Adam asked God, "Why did you make such a beautiful woman?"
    "To get you interested."
    "Why did you give her such a sweet personality?"
    "So you'd fall in love with her."
    "Then why did you make her so dumb?"
    "So *she'd* fall in love with *you*."

Adam is very lonely and asks God for a companion. God says, "Fine, but it'll cost you an arm and a leg."
    Adam says, "What can I get for a rib?"

You might say that creating Eve was the first splitting of the Adam.

Adam must have been in the army. He got an oak-leaf cluster.

As Eve said to Adam, "All right, but only the tip."

## ADVERTISING

**A** producer who had a clause in his contract for total control of a picture threw out fifteen different advertising campaigns and fired his entire creative staff. His new hireling brought in the latest effort. He lifted the placard and read it: "This movie is simply the greatest story ever told. It combines the drama of *Gone With the Wind,* the plot mastery of *Citizen Kane,* the tragedy of *King Lear,* and is more moving than the Bible!"

The producer nodded. "That's it. No exaggeration. The simple truth."

**T**hey have a dozen products that brag they're good for a headache. Who wants a headache?

**T**wo account executives meet. One says, "Hi, Jim, what's new and improved?"

**O**ne grocery chain advertises, "Our steaks are so tender, we don't know how that cow could walk."

**A** woman advertised for a husband. The following day she got fifty replies, all saying the same thing: "You can have mine."

**O**ne manufacturer says that he stands behind every bed he sells. To tell you the truth, I'd like a job like that.

**A** businessman was asked if he believed in advertising and said, "It works. Last Monday we put in an ad for a new watch-man, and that night the safe was robbed."

**T**hen there was the account exec who worked for an agency twenty-five years. When he retired, they gave him a golden ulcer.

## ADVICE

**N**ever play poker with a man named Ace!

**N**ever borrow money from a finance company whose president is named Nunzio or Vito.

**I**t's always better to give than to receive, especially if you're a fighter.

**W**hen you're a kid, you learn a lot at your mother's knee. The rest you learn at some other joint.

**A**dvice can be very good, especially if it doesn't interfere with your plans.

**A**lways pass it on, because you won't use it.

**I**f you know the difference between good and bad advice, you don't need advice.

**I** finally figured out why God made man before woman. He didn't want anybody standing behind him, telling him how to make a man.

Men, always aim high. That way you won't splash on your shoes.

Mark Twain was once trapped by a bore who lectured him about the hereafter. "Do you realize that every time I exhale, some poor soul leaves this world and passes on to the Great Beyond?"

"Really?" Twain replied. "Why don't you try chewing a mint?"

Don't hesitate to give advice. It makes the time pass, and nobody listens to you anyway.

A wise father offered his son two bits of advice the day before the son's marriage: "My first bit of advice is to insist on spending every night out with the boys."

"And what's the second bit?" the son asked.

"Don't waste it on the boys."

When arguing with a stupid person, make sure he isn't doing the same.

An elderly friend asked for advice. "I'm in love with a man, but he's very poor. And another man, who's very rich, wants to marry me. What should I do?"

I thought for a moment and replied, "Marry the rich—and be good to the poor."

I'm glad I ignore most advice. If I'd listened, most of the time I'd have been saved from some of my most enjoyable mistakes.

## AGE

You're aging if you remember when radios plugged into the wall and toothbrushes didn't.

You're aging when dialing long-distance wears you out.

You're getting old when the little old lady you help across the street is your wife.

You're aging when you worry because you don't have any symptoms.

You're aging if you're pushing sixty and it's pushing back.

A man is only as old as he looks—and if he only looks, he's old.

My sex drive was just turned into a putt.

You're aging when you have to light the candle at both ends to see the menu.

You're getting old when your children begin to look middle-aged.

You're aging when you start to look for your name in the obituary column.

You're getting old when you paint the town red and have to take a long nap before you put on a second coat.

You're getting on when you spend more time looking at the menu than you do the waitress.

You're getting on if you look around the market for a denture-flavored cereal.

An old man was walking down the street and saw a small boy sitting on the curb, crying. The old man asked, "What's bothering you, young fellar?" The small boy said, "I'm crying because I can't do what the big boys do." So the old man sat down, and he cried too.

Life isn't fair. The young don't know what to do, and the old can't do what they know.

You know you're getting old when you smoke only after sex, and it comes to a pack a year.

You're getting on in years when your telephone cord is kinky and your sex isn't.

You know you're getting old when you find a woman attractive because she can get three cups of tea from one bag.

You're getting on in years when a dripping faucet starts to cause an uncontrollable bladder urge.

Where can I go to sign a protest against having the good old days discontinued?

Nobody should get old without good reason, and I've never yet heard a good reason.

You finally reach the top of the ladder and then find it's leaning against the wrong wall.

I won't say he's old, but his car insurance covers fire, theft, and Indian raids.

Being eighty means getting up in the middle of the night as often as a handsome movie star. But not for the same reasons.

He's pretty old. When he was young, the Dead Sea was still alive.

Aging is when you can remember what you did yesterday only by what hurts today.

As I grow older, there are three things I have trouble remembering: faces, names, and . . . I can't remember what the third thing is.

Think of all the trouble we'd be in if sex hurt when we got older.

You're aging if you make love lightly and in self-defense.

By the time you learn to behave yourself, there's nothing else you can do.

The trouble with aging is that by the time we know what it's all about, we don't want to.

By the time a man can read a woman like a book, his eyes go bad.

I'm at that age in life where I lose my place during romance.

This elderly couple got married. The first night, the husband reached out, took his wife's hand, and fell asleep. The second night, the same thing. Again, the same thing on the third night. The wife looked at him and said, "What are you, some kind of sex maniac? Three nights in a row?"

A sure sign of getting old: When you pay for sex and you get a refund.

You're getting old when you can't fool chili at dinner.

Aging is when you consider weight lifting just getting on your feet.

You're getting on if everybody calls you Pop but your kids.

You're getting on in years if you're just as pretty as you ever were, but now it takes an hour longer.

You're aging when the partner you could have married looks like the one you did.

You're getting old if your favorite drink is Maalox and Perrier water.

You're aging when you feel your corns more than your oats.

You're aging when your actions creak louder than your words.

You're aging when the ice cream store on the corner cancels your annual free ice cream cone for your birthday.

You're aging if you celebrate your birthday with a magnum of Geritol.

You're aging when your wife says, "Let me slip into something more comfortable," and it's flannel.

You're aging if your figure is like the stock market—it's still there, but lower.

You know you're getting old when your toupee turns gray.

You're aging when you remember people being vegetarians because they wanted to be.

You're aging if you and your lover come up with headaches—at the same time.

You're aging when your eyes are still perfect but everybody is becoming blurry.

You're aging if you can remember when it took longer to fly across the country than it did to get to the airport.

You're aging if you feel terrible the morning after you've had no fun the night before.

You're aging if you can remember when you needed help to carry home five dollars' worth of groceries.

You know you're getting old when you suddenly become very moral. You don't believe men should fool around. You don't like them doing anything you can't do.

You know you're getting old when your wife gives up sex for Lent and you don't realize it until it's the Fourth of July.

Aging is the time of life when your get up and go did.

The bad part is that you have to grow old before somebody will tell you that you look young for your age.

Old age is when you wake up tired and lustless.

You're at that age when everything Mother Nature gave you, Father Time is taking away.

You know you're getting old when everything hurts, and what doesn't hurt doesn't work.

The trouble is—by the time you can read a girl like a book, your library card has expired.

You're old if you'd make the same mistakes with your sex life, only a lot sooner.

By the time we've made it, we've had it!

She's been pressing thirty-five so long it's pleated.

You know you're getting on in years when your knees buckle but your belt won't.

You know she's getting old if she orders a martini with a prune in it.

I'm old enough to know where it's at. I just forgot why it's there.

Anybody who thinks that old soldiers just fade away ought to watch one trying to put on his old army uniform!

You're old when you go to a carnival and the fortune-teller offers to read your face.

You're aging when it takes you two hours to undress and three to remember why.

You're getting on in years when you bend over to tie your laces and you look around to see if there's anything else to do while you're down there.

A young lady introduces her grandfather to another young and very beautiful girlfriend. The old man ogles the beautiful girl, so the granddaughter says, "This is my grandpa. He's in his nineties."

The grandfather says, "*Early* nineties."

How come the older we get, the later old age starts?

Anybody who can still do at seventy what he was doing at twenty wasn't doing much at twenty.

You're getting old when you can spell gastroenterologist.

I met this woman who claimed to be forty. She has no proof because the birth record was at a city hall that burned down sixty years ago.

There are two ways of keeping from getting old—lie about your age and drive while drinking.

I took my dog for a walk the other day, but he couldn't keep up with me. So I traded him for a turtle.

You know you're getting old when your kids and your clothes are the same age.

Growing older has its benefits. All the music you liked is in the bargain bin.

I know I'm growing old. I use tenderizer in my Cream of Wheat.

You're getting on when the happy hour is a nap.

It's not the good old days that some of us miss. It's the nights.

You know you're getting old when you have to take a nap before going to bed at night.

You know you're getting old when you're sitting in a rocker and you can't get it started.

The only good thing about old age is that you only go through it once.

One old gent said, "At my age, when a girl flirts with me in the movies, she's after my popcorn."

I don't mind becoming a senior citizen. I just don't look forward to graduation.

You're getting old when you remember the only people in blue jeans were workers.

I tell people I'm twenty years older than I am, just so they can tell me how good I look for my age.

I'm a father figure to most girls. They keep asking me for money.

When you get old, kissing may be dangerous. It can turn into mouth-to-mouth resuscitation.

I know I was getting old the last time I went to Las Vegas. I played a slot machine, and it came up three prunes.

One of the big problems with aging— every time I see a girl I used to know, it's her daughter.

A fellow at the Social Security office listens to a clerk tell him, "Feeling sixty-five isn't enough. You have to *be* sixty-five."

This elderly woman explains that she doesn't have wrinkles. They're laugh lines. I guess she did a lot of laughing in her time.

This old guy doesn't date women his age. There aren't any.

The terrible part about your past is the way other people can't forget it.

I don't have an enemy in the world. I outlived them all.

The only thing worse than being old and bent is being young and broke.

I never tell anyone my age. It keeps changing every minute.

It takes about twenty years to get used to how old you are.

Two old men are sitting on a bench in the park as a third man comes by with a woman. One old man says, "He's got a penchant for women."
     The other old man says, "I wish I'd worked for his company."

The older you get, the greater you were.

We're as old as we feel. Ain't that a shame?

They were both young. They said they'd grow old together. But then he went ahead without her.

He's so old, he has to go to topless shows through an interpreter.

I won't say he's old, but he got his new calendar, and it only goes as far as January 10.

"How old do you think I am?"
     "You don't look it."

My pal just reached eighty. I guess he's feeling his oat bran.

I'm at that age where my biological urge has become an occasional nudge.

You're getting old if you know what a balloon payment is.

## AGENTS

Two anthropologists are in the darkest jungles of the Pacific. They come to a native supermarket where many items are on sale: eyes, ears, feet. They see a special display offering agents' hearts for a million dollars a pound. One of the anthropologists asks the shopkeepers, "Why so much for a pound of agents' hearts?" The shopkeeper says, "Do you know how many agents we have to kill to get a pound of heart?"

A show-business agent was at a cocktail party when a beautiful young lady walked over to him and said, "You are a handsome young man. I'd love to grab you, throw you down on the couch, and make love to you for hours."
     The agent looked at her puzzled and asked, "What's in it for me?"

This theatrical agent has just signed a new female dancer. He raves about her to a possible customer, saying, "She has a sixty-inch bust."

"What kind of dancing does she do?"

"She doesn't exactly dance. When the curtain goes up, she's lying on the floor, and she spends the next fifteen minutes trying to get up."

The Devil appears before a theatrical agent and says, "I will give you five big clients and access to all the studios. But at the end of five years, you must give me your soul."

The agent says, "Okay, but what's the catch?"

An actor meets another actor, a friend, and notices that the man has an incredible tan. "How'd you get such a great tan?" the actor asks.

"Rotten agent," answers the friend.

A star, tired of the representation he's been getting, meets with a prospective agent and tells him, "Look, Epstein, you know I'm not a charity case. Studios want me. All you'll have to do is answer the phone."

"I know you're big."

"I make five million a picture. Since you get ten percent, there'll be bread on the table."

"I can see that."

"There's one more thing. Epstein, are you Jewish?"

"Not necessarily."

An agent is a man who hates you because you take 90 percent of his money.

"How do you say 'Screw you' in agent talk?"

" 'Trust me.' "

A man brings his poodle to an agent's office. The man cues the poodle, who starts to sing, doing impressions of the greatest female singers in the business. When she's finished, the man says, "Can you use her?" The agent says, "I don't know. Let me see her legs."

A man walks into an agent's office and takes a tiny pianist out of his pocket. The pianist is no more than ten inches high. The man takes a tiny piano out of another pocket. The tiny pianist plays a few songs beautifully.

The agent says, "Where did you find him?"

The man says, "I was walking on the beach, and I found this old bottle. I opened it up, and there was a genie in it. She offered me anything I wanted, and she thought I said ten-inch pianist."

## AGGRAVATION

To demonstrate aggravation to a troubled friend, a man says, "I'll show you real aggravation. It's about two in the morning, right? Watch this." After looking up a random number in the phone book, he dials. When connected, he asks, "Is Geller there?" A rain of expletives comes zooming through the phone. Ten minutes later, he repeats the call and asks, "Did Brewster get there yet?'' More expletives, even louder. Ten minutes go by. The man dials and says, "This is Geller. Any calls for me? Hear what's going on at the other end? That's real aggravation.''

**A** man and his wife are having their nightly tiff, with the husband waxing poetic about all the things his wife does that he finds irritating. The wife says, "I tell you what—make a list of all the things I do that bother you.''

About ten years later, as they are about to start watching television, the wife says, "Listen, ten years ago, you said you were going to make a list of all the things I do that aggravate you. Where's the list?''

The husband says, "I'm only up to the *M*'s.''

**A** man is going to baby-sit a friend's large dog and is given the instructions. "Just don't aggravate him," the friend says, "and it'll be fine.''

"How will I know when he's aggravated?''

"By the *whoosh* of air through where your crotch used to be.''

**A** man walks into a bar. As he sits down to have a drink, he takes a tiny object out of his pocket, a perfectly shaped man about four inches high.

The bartender says, "Gee, I had a customer who looked just like him.''

"It's him.''

"The guy who used to write for the *National Geographic*?''

"The same.''

"What the hell happened to him?''

"He made a little mistake. He told a witch doctor to screw off!''

## AIR-CONDITIONING

**I** know one air-conditioning repairman who's made so much money, he's stopped making house calls.

**I** like air-conditioning. Now I can have a cold at any time of the year.

**M**y air conditioner is terrible. In August it makes toast.

**I** have a great air conditioner. It's heat-resistant.

**I**n the office, we have an air conditioner that makes us all freeze. I think the repairman is Nanook of the North.

**T**he office air conditioner really keeps the office cool. It's the first air conditioner I ever saw that wears a sweater.

## AIRLINES

**I** know a real no-frills airline. It rents you oxygen.

**I** just came back from a trip on a real no-frills airline. Instead of movies, they show coming attractions of pictures that'll be shown on other airlines.

**O**ne airline must have terrible food. When you get in, the stewardess buckles your seat belt over your mouth.

This man was flying on one of those no-frills airlines, but the stewardess was first class all the way—a lovely figure, beautiful face, incredible eyes. When the stewardess came down the aisle mid-flight, the man beckoned for the stewardess to lean over. He whispered something in her ear. She smiled and answered, "You got that when you flew this airline!"

I was on a very considerate airline the other day. They served two meals. One on the plane and the other while you waited for your luggage.

It's good to check in early at the airlines. That way you learn about the delay faster.

A doctor was giving an airline pilot a physical. Taking his history, the doctor asked, "When was the last time you had sex?"

The pilot answered, "Nineteen fifty-five."

The doctor said, "That long ago?"

Looking at his watch, the pilot said, "That wasn't too long ago. It's only twenty-one-oh-five now."

One airliner went down in the Pacific. The sharks ate the crew and passengers, but they wouldn't touch the roast beef.

The airlines are really cutting back. I was on a flight the other day, they didn't offer coffee, milk, or tea. The stewardesses had their own lemonade stand.

I checked in at an airline and was told that the flight would go off at twelve-thirty. I told the clerk, "The timetable says eleven-thirty."

The clerk said, "So take the timetable."

There's a time when you can be reasonably certain if there'll be a delay in your flight. It comes five minutes after you buy your ticket.

My last flight was on a real no-frills airline. They didn't serve lunch. Instead, we landed at a McDonald's and they gave us fifteen minutes.

It was a small airline. If you wanted to get on a flight, you had to have the exact change.

Some airlines are now putting mistletoe at the baggage counter. That way you can kiss your luggage good-bye.

God must have loved airline fares. He made so many of them!

How come they can find one tiny fruit fly at the airport, but they can't find my luggage?

I went to the airport the other day, and when I got to the counter, I said, "I'd like two chances on your next flight to the Middle East."

So many airlines are going out of business. It's strange when your luggage is found, but the airline is gone!

One passenger had so many frequent-flyer miles, he forgot where he lived.

## ALASKA

It's no secret that Alaska can be cold. I sent my friend a birthday card, and my tongue was still on it.

They're still fairly primitive in Alaska. I saw a city bus that barked.

A young woman was walking near Juneau when a small plane passed overhead. "That's a mail plane," her boyfriend said. "How can you tell at that distance?" she replied.

Anxious to be admitted to the most exclusive club in northern Alaska, a tenderfoot asked what he'd have to do.

"Three things," he was told. "You've got to drink a quart of straight whiskey, hug an Eskimo girl for three hours without her parents catching you, and shoot a full-grown grizzly bear."

The tenderfoot immediately downed the whiskey and set out into the cold night with a wild look in his eyes. An hour later he was back, his clothes torn and scratches all over his body. "Okay, okay!" he reported. "Where's that Eskimo girl I'm supposed to shoot?"

I was in Alaska recently and saw some of the sights in the various parks. One park had giant boulders that had been brought down by glaciers. There were no glaciers. They must have gone back for more boulders.

Do you know what bugs Texans about Alaska? If you split it in half, Texas would be the third-largest state.

I know an Alaskan who's afraid to go to Texas. He's claustrophobic.

Then there was the Jewish Eskimo. He kept hitting his dogs and saying, "Moish, Moish."

Then there was this nearsighted Alaskan turtle. He kept trying to mount an igloo.

A man is on trial in Nome. The prosecutor says, "Where were you on the night of October twenty-first to May first?"

It gets so cold in Alaska, some of the people go to Siberia for the winter.

An appliance salesman is trying to sell a fan to an Eskimo. The Eskimo looks at him in disbelief, saying, "It's fifty below up here."

"Yeah, but what if it goes up to zero?"

Then there's the Alaskan traffic sign: MUSH AND DON'T MUSH.

## ALIMONY

Alimony is giving comfort to the enemy.

Alimony is always having to say you're sorry.

Alimony is the screwing a man gets for the screwing he got.

Alimony is the billing without the cooing.

I know a woman who won't get a divorce. She just can't stand the idea of sharing her husband's money with her lawyer.

Alimony is like paying for a subscription to a magazine that's stopped publication.

I pay my ex-wife her alimony on the button. I'm afraid that if I don't, she'll repossess me.

## ALLIGATORS

"What are alligator skins used for?"
"To cover alligators."

A professor is lecturing a biology class. "The female alligator," he says, "lays seven hundred thousand eggs at one sitting. The male eats up all but two or three of them."
Raising his hand, a student asks, "Why does the male alligator eat so many of them?"
The professor answers, "Because if he didn't, we'd be up to our asses in alligators."

A fellow says, "In Florida they use alligators to make handbags."
His friend says, "Isn't it amazing what they can get animals to do?"

A redcap asked this alligator if he could carry his luggage to the car.

The alligator answered, "Sure. But be careful, she's my wife."

## AMBITION

Henry Ford had millions, and yet he never wanted a Cadillac.

I have only one ambition. I want to meet a gorgeous woman who's looking to spite her husband.

Grass never grows under his feet. He's a sailor.

## AMERICA

America is truly the land of endless opportunity. One poor immigrant made a fortune and could speak only three words: Stick 'em up.

Putting Arabian oil into Japanese cars— that's what America is all about.

America is the only country where a housewife hires a woman to do her cleaning so she can do volunteer work at the day-care center where the cleaning woman leaves her child.

There's a lot of money in America. The trouble is that everybody owes it to everybody else.

I always spend more than I make. It's the American way.

Everybody in America is endowed with life, liberty, and some eight thousand dollars' worth of national debt.

## AMNESIA

Never lend money. It gives people amnesia.

A man slips while bowling, hits himself on the head, and gets amnesia. He disappears for ten years. A sudden shock brings back his memory. He returns home. After a tearful greeting, his wife goes to the phone and starts to call their friends. The husband says, "What are you doing?"

"I'm calling everybody. I want them to come right over. We'll have a party for you."

"Oh, no. Not on my bowling night."

A man was hit on the head by a falling plank and forgot his home, his wife, and kids. A year later, he was hit on the head again, and his memory returned. He sued.

Then there was the absentminded professor who got amnesia and forgot to forget.

Then there was the forger who got amnesia and forgot his name and everybody else's.

## ANECDOTES

George Washington Carver, the great scientist, liked to tell this story about himself. "I was having a dream one time," he'd say, "and I saw God. I asked Him to tell me all the great secrets of the universe. He told me that He was keeping that knowledge for Himself. Then I asked Him to tell me the secrets of the peanut. He told me, because that was more my size!"

Eleanor Roosevelt was famous for her travels. She went to most areas of the country. One day she was in a small tree grove in an Appalachian valley. On one of the trees was a sign: I BEEN HERE BEFORE ANYBODY. SIGNED, DAN'L BOONE.

Mrs. Roosevelt smiled and wrote a small note on the bottom of the sign: THAT'S WHAT YOU THINK. SIGNED, ELEANOR ROOSEVELT.

An actress who was unable to utter a complete sentence without adding two or three four-letter words to it was about to star in a brand-new play at a theater that had just been completed. A producer told Ethel Barrymore, "It's the largest theater you've ever seen. Worse still, the acoustics are dreadful."

Miss Barrymore said, "How nice. Now she can be obscene and not heard."

Eager to get some comments on a Shaw play that had just opened in New York, a reporter called the playwright the next afternoon. An unhappy Shaw said, "I do not accept phone calls after twelve noon."

The next day, the reporter called at eleven in the morning. Shaw responded,

"Sir, I do not accept phone calls before noon."

The reporter said, "Then I'll never be able to get you on the phone."

"Nice, isn't it?"

## ANGER

**A** bathroom scale is something you step on in the morning, and all it does is make you angry.

**H**e's real hostile. He even fakes premature ejaculation.

**M**y wife has an even disposition—always mad.

## ANIMALS

**A** Pekinese married a tomcat. Now they have a Peking Tom.

**"H**ow can you tell when an elephant is about to charge?"

"He takes out a credit card."

**W**e mustn't forget Tommy the Turtle. He was nearsighted and he fell in love with a German war helmet. He died of a broken heart.

**T**hen there was this mule with an IQ of 175. Nobody liked him, because nobody likes a smart-ass.

**S**cientists recently crossed a hyena with a porcupine. Now, instead of laughing, the hyena just needles you.

**A** camel can go five hundred miles without water. How far could it go *with* water?

**S**quirrels are destroying this woman's garden, digging up her flower bulbs and vegetables. The woman sets up two traps—one with apples and the other with nuts. The next morning she shows a neighbor that she's caught a squirrel.

The neighbor asks, "How did you catch him? By the apples?"

The woman smiles and answers, "Nope."

**R**abbits of the world—stop!

**A** studio is going through one of its periodic cleanups. A whole slew of old film is thrown out. A little later, some goats wander over from a nature picture being shot that day. One goat starts to eat the old film. The second goat asks, "How does it taste?"

The first goat says, "I don't know. I think I liked the book better."

**Y**ou can bet your wife is being unfaithful if your dog is taking your pipe and slippers to the house across the street.

**A**n old African proverb says, "When two elephants fight, the grass gets hurt."

**W**e all sprang from animals, but most of us didn't spring far enough.

**S**ome buffalo are grazing on the open prairie when a cowboy rides up. Making a grim face, he says, "God, you're the ugliest animals I ever saw. Look at that matted fur, that ugly hump on your back, the way you drool.''

One buffalo turns to another and says, ''I think I just heard a discouraging word.''

Then there's the little polar bear who sat on the ice and said, ''My tale is told.''

A rotten guy was with a cat under his arm. A neighbor says, ''Where'd you get the skunk?''

The rotten guy says, ''This is a cat.''

The neighbor says, ''I was talking to the cat.''

''How much does a psychiatrist charge an elephant?''

''Fifty dollars for the session and three-fifty for the couch.''

I just got a pair of alligator shoes. It took me an hour to get them off the alligator.

A mouse is making love to a giraffe. Every few moments, the mouse leans forward and asks, ''Am I hurting you?''

A lion walks over to a jaguar, growls, and asks, ''Who's the king of the jungle?''

''You are,'' the jaguar answers.

The lion walks on and sees a panther and asks, ''Who's the king of the jungle?''

''You are.''

The lion keeps walking and comes to an elephant. The lion roars and asks, ''Who's the king of the jungle?''

The elephant looks at him with disdain, picks the lion up with his trunk, dashes him against a tree trunk, drops him, steps on him, and kicks him twenty feet into a clearing.

The lion gets up, smooths his ruffled mane, and says, ''He just doesn't know. He just doesn't know.''

While she was doing a crossword puzzle, a woman asked her husband the word for a female sheep. He said, ''Ewe.''

He'll be out of the hospital Monday.

Noah says to two snakes when they finally reach land, ''Didn't I tell you to go forth and multiply?'' One of the snakes says, ''We can't. We're adders.''

Then there's the laughing hyena. He eats once a day, moves his bowels once a month, and mates once a year. What the hell does he have to laugh about?

An elephant doesn't watch where he's walking and steps on and flattens a gnu. A kid walking by with his mother asks, ''What's that under the elephant?''

The mother answers, ''There's nothing, son, under the gnu.''

Parrots are smarter than chickens. I mean, you've never heard of Kentucky Fried Parrot.

''Why do mice have such small balls?''

''Because there's so few of them who can dance.''

"I speak the language of the animals."

"Good. The next time you speak to a skunk, ask what's the idea."

A lady in Tibet rushed and looked in her stove and said, "Oh, my baking yak."

Then there were the three foxes—papa fox, mama fox, but the baby was too young to.

A farmer's wife was having trouble with a skunk in the cellar. She called the county agent and asked what to do. The county agent said, "Put a trail of crumbs from the cellar door to the outside. The skunk'll follow it and leave." Two days later, the farmer's wife called again: "It didn't work. Now I've got two skunks!"

While making love, the female porcupine says to her lover, "Pull it out deeper. It hurts so good."

A baby porcupine sees a hairbrush and asks, "Is that you, Mama?"

A frog goes to a Gypsy fortune-teller. The Gypsy fortune-teller says, "As I gaze into my crystal ball, I can see that you will meet a beautiful girl. She'll give you all of her attention. She'll want to know everything about you."

"Will I meet her at a party?"

"No. Bio One-oh-One."

Why do elephants drink? To forget!

A microbe is swimming around in a man's bloodstream when it runs into an-other microbe. The first microbe motions for the second to stay away, saying, "Careful. I think I caught a little penicillin."

"What did the boy octopus say to the girl octopus?"

"I want to hold your hand, your hand, your hand, your hand . . ."

A baby lion is chasing an explorer around a tree. The mother lion appears and shakes her head sadly, saying to her cub, "How many times have I told you not to play with your food!"

An elephant sees a naked man and says, "It's cute, but can you eat peanuts with it?"

"Why was the bluefish blue?"

"Because the blowfish wouldn't."

"So glad to meet you," said the Hindu politely.

"Charmed, I'm sure," said the snake.

"What's the best way to make a bull sweat?"

"Put him in a tight jersey."

Then there was the rabbit who had twelve little bunnies. Beat the record by a hare.

A puzzlement: If a sheep is a ram and a mule is an ass, how come a ram in the ass is a goose?

One day a duck was preparing to swim the Suez Canal. A scorpion appeared and asked to ride across on the duck's back. "Oh, no," the duck said, "my mother warned me about scorpions! How do I know you won't sting me midstream?"

"Silly duck," scoffed the scorpion. "In that case, wouldn't we both drown?"

It made sense, so the duck said, "Hop aboard."

Sure enough, midstream, the scorpion stung the duck. As they were going down for the third time, the duck gasped, "What made you do it?"

The scorpion gasped back, "What else did you expect? This is the Middle East!"

The epitaph on the gravesite of an army mule read: HERE LIES LUCY, WHO IN HER TIME KICKED TWO COLONELS, FOUR MAJORS, ONE CAPTAIN, TWENTY-FOUR LIEUTENANTS, FORTY-TWO SERGEANTS, FOUR HUNDRED EIGHTY-SIX PRIVATES, AND ONE BOMB.

As one deer said to another, "Man, I wish I had his doe."

It was Christmas Eve. Two pink elephants walked into a bar. The bartender said, "He ain't here yet."

A lion has just arrived at the Colosseum. A veteran lion tells him, "You won't like it here. All they give you to eat is Christians."

"Mama, why do elephants have such big trunks?"

"Well, they do have to come all the way from Africa."

When an elephant is in trouble, even a frog will kick him.

A very thin little man bought a ferocious tiger at an auction sale, outbidding several prominent circus proprietors. "What on earth are you going to do with that man-eating beast?" the tiny man was asked. "Going into competition with us?"

"Oh, no," said the little man. "My poor wife died last week, and I'm lonely."

*Centaur*—a man with a horse where his pants ought to be.

A lovely young lobster meets a young crab at the bottom of the sea. They fall madly in love and decide to marry. The lobster goes home to tell her parents. Almost fainting, the mother lobster says, "You can't marry a crab. Crabs don't walk straight like a lobster. They waddle. Their legs go in ten different directions at the same time."

The young lobster meets the crab that night and tells him that there'll be no marriage. The crab understands. No marriage.

A few days later, they meet again. This time the crab walks as straight as an arrow, no waddling, no flailing of legs, just straight.

The lobster says, "I can't understand. Most of the time you walk crazy. Now it's as straight as an arrow. How could this be?"

The crab answers, "Well, when we broke up, I started drinking."

Then there was the horny porcupine. She was in prickly heat.

"Now it all comes back to me," said the skunk when the wind changed.

There are giant mice where we live. Last week we lost the cat!

I found a fish that swims backward. It helps keep the water out of its eyes!

A snake is a head and a tail and there's nothing in between.

Elks have something no other animals have—parades.

### ANSWERING DEVICES

I met a doctor who recently underwent surgery. He had an ingrown beeper.

I have a telephone answering machine that never takes messages. It doesn't want to get involved.

An answering machine is great. You leave home, stay away all day, and when you come home, the machine lets you know that nobody has been thinking of you.

A voice-mail device called my house the other day and left an offer to buy some-thing on the answering machine. The bad part was that my answering machine bought two of them.

I have a terrible answering service. It keeps finding me.

One department store just put in a push-button answering gimmick. If you want to get the mail-order shopping service, you just push 1. If you want to know the price of an object, push 2. If you want to register a complaint, you just press 66609948847736363352552181818.

### ANTIQUES

I found out why they call it period furniture. Your wife drags you into an antique store and says, "I want that! Period!"

Rose admires Helen's furniture and asks about the period. Helen says, "It's Early Marriage. Some of it is my mother's, some of it is his mother's."

Lord Favisham, eighty-six, married a young lady of twenty. Among the many gifts he gave to her was an antique pendant.

An antique is what used to get in the way in the attic.

The other day I bought a copy of the Venus de Milo real cheap because it was an irregular. It had both arms!

I was in a museum in Genoa. It had two skulls of Columbus—one when he was a boy and one when he was a man.

An antique is something that's too old for the poor, but not too old for the rich.

If it's hard to dust, it's probably an antique.

The difference between antiques and junk is who's running the garage sale.

An antique is a household object that's made a round trip to the attic.

"What goes with Early French furniture?"
    "Late American payments."

"Helen, your furniture is so smart. What period is it?"
    "First marriage."

A poor man, he was never able to buy anything new. Everything was secondhand. He scrimped and saved for years. The savings enabled him to send his son to business college. The son graduated and became a rich financial wizard.
    One day the father ran into a friend and bragged, "My son just got back from London. He bought a hundred thousand dollars' worth of furniture that once belonged to Winston Churchill."
    The friend shook his head and said, "Some family you are. You keep buying secondhand."

## ANXIETY

You should feel a little anxious if there's a chair and an ashtray in your closet.

I'd be a little nervous if when I left for work, my wife was in an evening gown and opening a bottle of champagne.

I'd be anxious if my doctor botched my vasectomy and my wife told me to take him to small-claims court.

She's always as anxious as a hula dancer in a room full of lawn mowers.

You have a right to be anxious on a cheap airline if the oxygen mask has a meter on it.

If you're an astronaut, you have to be anxious when you see the ground crew bringing out jumper cables.

You should be anxious when you go to jail and your new roommate greets you with, "Care to dance?"

He once ran into a bar in the West and yelled, "Fire." Three men did.

You don't know what anxiety is until you see a guy with a sports car stop where there's a tall dog.

## APARTMENTS

Some apartments have strict rules against children. One lady apartment dweller is now in her fifteenth month!

I live in a security building, but it's got me worried. The other day I forgot my key, and a burglar lent me his.

The landlord gave me two days to pay up my back rent. So I said, "Okay, I'll take the Fourth of July and Christmas."

The world's greatest movers and shakers are those people who just moved into the apartment above you.

In the future, they predict, we'll be able to heat a building with one piece of coal. Big deal! I have a landlord who does that now.

Our apartment walls are so thin, the neighbors can hear everything we say. We'd put up drapes, but then we wouldn't hear what the neighbors say.

My landlord doesn't go too crazy with heating my apartment. This morning it was so cold, I had to jump-start my electric razor.

The walls of my apartment are very thin. I once asked my roommate a question, and I got four different answers.

We have a great super. This morning it was freezing, so he came up and helped me bang on the pipes.

We have a really small apartment. When the kitchen isn't being used, it folds right into the wall.

He told me he lived in a lush apartment. I didn't believe it until I tripped over a drunk.

## APPETITE

Could she eat? She was twenty before she found out what "chew" meant.

He's got a great appetite—his favorite food is seconds.

She eats a lot. She went to an Over-eaters' Anonymous session, and they made her a chapter.

I won't say she eats a lot, but she puts mayonnaise on Bufferin.

They say that people eat because they're disappointed in love. So how come there are so many fat sultans?

A man sits down at a table in a restaurant and tells the waiter, "I love food, but most of all I love bread. I must have bread."
    The waiter brings him two thick slices of bread, which the man devours. Finished eating, he says, "The food is good here and the service fine, but I must have more bread. More bread!"
    The next day the waiter brings him four slices of bread. The day after, five slices are put before him. The man still complains. Finally, the waiter takes a giant loaf of bread, cuts it in two, and puts it down before the man, who sneers

and says, "Why did you go back to two slices?"

## ARABS

A sheikh is in the maternity ward looking at the babies through the glass partition. The other sheikh asks, "Which one is yours?

The first sheikh says, "The first six rows."

Those Arabs are really loaded. The last time I was in Morocco, I saw a camel driving a Mercedes.

An archeological expedition returns to the capital of a Middle Eastern dictatorship with a mummy. The dictator insists on knowing how old the mummy is. The next day, the chief of the Secret Police goes to the dictator and tells him that the mummy is exactly 3,214 years old.

The dictator says, "How did you find out?"

"He confessed this morning."

"What's the difference between an Arab terrorist and a Jewish wife?"

"You can negotiate with an Arab terrorist."

Then there's this sheikh who had a hundred and fifty wives. He died waiting to get into the bathroom.

The sultan walked into his harem unexpectedly, and his harem let out a terrified sheikh.

They must have a baseball team in the harem. I heard one of the wives ask if she was in tomorrow's lineup.

Two Arabs meet in Baghdad. One spits. The other says, "Don't talk politics."

A sexy sheikh gets his pleasure down to a pattern. He hires a track star to sit at his feet. When the sheikh nods, the track star runs to the harem a mile away and brings him a wife. This happens four or five times a day. The track star dies at the age of twenty-four. The sheikh lives until he's ninety-five. The moral of that story is: Sex doesn't kill you. It's the running after it that does.

Everybody goes around wearing sheets in Arabia. It looks as if everyone in the country was taking a bath when the doorbell rang.

Then there was this Arabian kid who had to run around like crazy in the harem trying to celebrate Mother's Day.

An Arab is walking with his wife, the woman being five paces in front of him. Another Arab rushes over and says, "Why do you let your wife walk in front of you?"

The first Arab answers, "Mine fields."

One Arab says to another, "Saddam Hussein is his own worst enemy."

The second says, "Not while I'm alive."

An Englishman, an Arab, and an American are standing on a corner in the Casbah when a luscious Oriental beauty passes by.

The Englishman says, "By Jove."

The Arab says, "By Allah."

The American says, "By tomorrow night."

The Negev used to be hell. But the Israelis came along and irrigated the hell out of it.

You know what a harem is—that's a floor show with a husband.

An old Jewish man, Graber, boards a British plane bound for the Middle East. Two Arabs board and say, "Get out of that seat. We want to sit by the window."

Graber moves to another seat.

Five minutes later, one of the Arabs says, "Run up to the galley and get me some coffee."

Graber gets the coffee. Just as he sits down, the other Arab says, "Now I want some coffee."

Graber goes. Returning with the coffee a few minutes later, he sits down, exhausted. One of the Arabs says, "Jew, what do you think of the shape of the world?"

Graber says, "It's in terrible shape. In India, Sikhs are killing Muslims. In Ireland, Protestants are killing Catholics. And in airplanes, Jews are pissing in Arabs' coffee."

I wish the Arabs and the Jews would settle their differences in the true Christian spirit.

An oil sheikh goes into a department store, points to a rack of nighties, and says to the clerk, "I'll take them all."

"But they're all different sizes."

"So are my wives."

Sheikhs don't have it so good. By the time one of them gets through kissing his last wife good night, it's time to start kissing his first one good morning.

In Saudi Arabia, women aren't allowed to drive. It's real hard for them to get their kids to Little League in the camel pool.

"Why did the explorer pay a thousand dollars for a sheet of sandpaper?"

"He thought it was a map of Arabia."

## ARGUMENTS

Two gays are having a fight. One grabs the other, throws him down, and says, "Say 'Aunt'!"

My wife and I are inseparable. Sometimes it takes four people to pull us apart.

"I resent that."

"Do you deny it?"

"No, I just resent it."

Do you realize that Eve was the only woman who ever took a man's side?

There are two sides to every argument until you take one.

A couple of days before we were married, my wife and I had a big fight about going out with the guys for a stag party. But I figured if it meant that much to her, she could go ahead and do it.

"Whenever I have a fight with my wife, she becomes historical."

"You mean—hysterical."

"No, historical. She keeps bringing up the past."

The wife says, "I tell you what. I'll admit I'm right if you admit you're wrong."

A woman says to her husband, "Now that we're back on speaking terms, shut up!"

## ARIZONA

A city dweller came to a small town in the arid section of Arizona. He asked an old man sitting around whittling, "What's the death rate around here?"

The old man said, "Same as it is in most places—one to a person."

It was one of those typical Arizona windstorms, fierce and prolonged. A man driving by sees a cowboy's head in the sand. The man says, "Hold on, I'll dig you out."

The cowboy says, "Got a tractor? I'm sitting on my horse."

Out in Arizona, they're real dry. They've got water that's only wet on one side.

It can get real dry in Arizona. Sometimes you have to run a well through the clothes wringer to get enough water for coffee.

## ARMY

An army is a group of men sent out to fix up the work of diplomats.

No matter how much he begged, a soldier was unable to get more than a two-hour pass to see his wife. The officer of the day wasn't thrilled when the young man returned six hours later. "You've been AWOL for four hours. Explain yourself."

The soldier said, "Well, when I got home, my wife was in the bathtub, and it took four hours for my uniform to dry."

The company was on maneuvers. After a two-hour march, one of the men asked the sergeant, "How far to the bivouac?"

"About three miles."

Another hour's march, and a second soldier asked, "How far to the bivouac?"

"About three miles."

An hour and a half went by, and a third soldier asked the same question. The response was the same, "Three miles."

A fourth soldier smiled and said, "Thank God we're holding our own."

The thrill of a private's army career is to be taken on a twenty-mile hike by a sergeant who used to be the star of his school's cross-country team.

When my nephew got into the army, he had ten dollars to his name. Three years later, he came out and had five dollars. So the army can't be too bad. Where else can you live three years for five dollars?

I wouldn't say he's a coward, but he arrived at the draft board by ambulance.

A marine recruit was given a comb. The next day they shaved off all his hair. Later that day, they gave him a toothbrush. Ten minutes later, the dentist pulled his teeth. The next morning, the recruit was given a jockstrap. He's still AWOL.

A sergeant is telling his recruits about how noncoms happen, saying, "To be a noncom, a leader, a honcho, you can't learn it. You have to be born that way."

A soldier piped in innocently, "In or out of wedlock?"

A black infantryman in Italy during World War II wrote back home to his brother, "The drinkin's good. The gamblin's fine. The Italian gals are great. But the battles, they're damn dangerous."

Mess sergeants don't have an easy time of it in the army. They have enemies on both sides.

All the time I was in the army, my wife sent me nagging letters. I couldn't even enjoy the war in peace.

He was a paratrooper and spent three years climbing down trees he never climbed up.

The sergeant marched into the rookie barracks and said, "Fellas, I have good news and bad news for you. The good news is that you'll have a change of underwear tomorrow. The bad news is that Cohen will change with Jones, Smith will change with Brady . . ."

A rookie on leave walks into a recruiting office and says to the recruiting officer, "Can you give me that sales talk again? I'm getting discouraged."

Three officers were arguing about sex. The general insisted that sex was 60 percent work and 40 percent fun. The colonel felt that sex was about 80 percent work and 20 percent fun. The major said that sex was about 95 percent work and 5 percent fun. Since they couldn't agree, one said, "Let's ask the private who just came in."

The general asked the private about what percentages he gave the work and fun of sex. The private said, "Sex is a hundred percent work and no fun."

"How do you figure that?"

"Well, if it were the slightest fun, you wouldn't let me be doing it."

Digging foxholes was easy for me. I do the same thing when I'm playing golf.

The drafting officer asked me about my work experience. I told him that I'd been with Dr Pepper. An hour later I was in the Medical Corps.

One day I lost a rifle. They made me pay for it. They said I'd have to pay for anything I lost—a gun, a mortar, even a tank. Now I know why a captain goes down with his ship.

My base was nice. It was always knee-deep in mud . . . if you wore stilts.

The sergeant asked my cousin if he was fit for hard labor. My cousin answered, "Some judges have thought so."

One day I ran into a bowlegged private and asked him if he was in the cavalry. He said, "No. Short bunk."

I was in a big army camp. A three-day pass only got you to the front gate.

I was in World War II. I shot down six planes, captured ten officers, and blew up an ammunition dump. That may explain why I was shipped out of Cleveland.

One young recruit complained, "Twenty years ago I asked Santa Claus for a gun. Now, he gives it to me."

When she got to boot camp, they told her to mess with the men. It wasn't until four weeks later that she learned it was food.

A detachment of soldiers was withdrawn from combat and put in a zone where there was also a detachment of WAC. The colonel in charge of the men told the head of the women, "My men haven't seen any women for months. You better keep your ladies under lock and key."

Tapping her head, the officer in charge of the WAC said, "There'll be no trouble. My girls have it up here."

The colonel said, "It doesn't matter where they have it. Once my boys start looking, they'll find it."

The company was out on maneuvers. Rookie Pete was sent to fetch some water from the brook for the captain. Pete returned empty-handed. The captain said, "I thought I told you to get me some water from the brook."

"I intended to, but when I got there, there was a big alligator swimming around. I figured if that gator was half as scared as I was, the water wasn't fit to drink."

A potential draftee was told to bring a urine sample to the medical office at the enlistment station. Hoping to beat the enlistment, the young man filled the specimen bottle with urine from anybody around. It was tested, and the lab technician came over to the young man and said, "Your father has diabetes, your girlfriend is pregnant, your dog is in heat, and you're in the army!"

The drill sergeant barked, "All right, you dummies, fall out!" All the rookies fell out, except for Tommy Spencer. Puzzled, the sergeant looked at him. Tommy smiled. "There were a lot of them, weren't there, Sarge?"

The men complained about the bread being served during meals. The captain barked, "If Napoleon's men had had that bread in Russia, they would have eaten every last crumb!"

One soldier said, "Sure, but it was fresh then!"

**I** wasn't a hero in the army. In fact, I have the only medal for extreme caution under cover.

**My** army issue came close. The coat fit, but the pants were a little tight around my throat.

**A** soldier goes AWOL, is found by the MPs and brought back to his base. He joins some others who'd taken off without permission. The soldier is called before the lieutenant, who asks, "Any excuse?"

"No, sir."

"Into the stockade. Now sit down while I finish this up."

A second soldier stands up, and the lieutenant repeats his question.

"W-w-w-well, s-s-s-s-sir, I, I, I w-w-w-was . . . !"

The lieutenant says, "That's enough. Get this man out of here. Send him back to his unit."

The second soldier sits down, and the first one says, "That's weird. I go to the stockade, and you go free."

The second soldier says, "Y-y-y-y-you g-g-got-t-ta kn-kn-know h-h-how to t-t-t-talk to th-th-them."

**A** recruit, home for his first weekend pass, is telling his mother about his drill sergeant. "He stares me down and calls

me a dumb, fat, ugly, useless human being."

His mother says, "Why would he say those things?"

The recruit says, "I'd hate to tell you what he said about you."

**A** farm boy was drafted. On his first furlough, his father asked what he thought of army life.

"It's pretty good, Dad. The food's good, the work's easy, and best of all they let you sleep real late in the morning."

**I** got a medal for saving two women during the war—one for the lieutenant and one for myself.

**It** was during the war when men were being drafted. To make sure he escaped, Larry Daniels borrowed a truss from a friend of his and wore it to the recruiting office. The examining doctor took one look at him, smiled, and asked, "How long have you been wearing this truss?"

"Ten years, sir."

"Okay, you're in the tank corps. Anybody who can wear a truss upside down for ten years can stand a tank."

**The** boys in the squad have requested some whiskey, there being none on the small island where they'd been sent. So this hillbilly family hollows out a loaf of bread and puts a bottle of home brew in it.

The package arrives, and the boys send home a thank-you note: *Bottle was broke when it got here, but that was the best damn toast we ever had.*

One army outfit was late because of its camouflaged trucks. The soldier couldn't find them.

I just tried on my old army uniform. I guess I put on a few pounds. I had to let out the tie.

Then there's the Pentagon. That's a building that has five sides to it—on every matter.

Some people treat our soldiers like Christmas trees. They decorate them, and then they throw them out.

I joined the army for three reasons: I wanted to defend my wonderful country; I knew it would help me morally and physically; and they came and got me.

A father didn't know where his son was stationed, locations being classified during wartime. After a week, he got the first letter from his son. It read: *I can't tell you where I am, but yesterday I shot a polar bear.* A week later, another letter came: *I can't tell you where I am, but yesterday I danced with a hula girl.* Two weeks later, a third letter: *I can't tell you where I am, but yesterday a doctor said I should have danced with the polar bear and shot the hula girl.*

The young hillbilly soldier deports himself well in battle. He shoots about a dozen of the enemy. His captain says,

"You're a great shot. How come? You look too young to have been in battle for long."

"Oh, no, sir. This is the first public war I've ever been in."

During World War II, a young airman landed on an aircraft carrier. He jumped out of the cockpit and exclaimed, "What a day! I shot down two Zeroes, sank a destroyer, and torpedoed a battleship!"

"Very good," came the reply. "But you make one rittle mistake."

One soldier was a total foul-up. He would do nothing that was asked of him. They tried putting him on KP. That didn't work. They restricted him to the barracks while others went out on a pass. That didn't work. Finally, they came up with the only solution: They called his mother.

The prisoner, convicted of treason, is being marched to the firing squad in a downpour. He complains to his escort, "Look at this weather I have to walk through."

The escort says, "What are you complaining about? I have to walk back."

At the physical, the men stand around in the nude. Some don't know if they're being drafted or just fascinating.

During World War II, the mixing of British and American troops had a subtle effect on the Americans. They became more reserved. As one American officer was explaining to his British counterpart, "The GIs are so proper now. They have better manners."

Just then, a private came up and asked the officer, "Hey, can I take the jeep?"

Without waiting for an answer, the GI jumped into the jeep and took off.

"See what I mean?" the officer said. "A year ago, he wouldn't have asked."

My nephew pulled sentry duty one day. They told him to ask, "Who goes there?" and shoot. In two hours, he got three sergeants and a major.

A captain in an infantry unit made up for the most part of draftees summoned one of his lieutenants. "Better look up the pre-induction record of Private Spotts," he said. "I've noticed that every time he fires his pistol on the range, he wipes off the fingerprints."

## ART

Van Gogh painted 72 pictures. As of this morning, Americans have 423 of them.

An artist said to a girl at a party, "I'd like to put you on canvas."

The girl said, "You want to paint my portrait?"

"No, I have a camp cot in my studio."

The artist drew his nude model to him and started to kiss her, saying, "You're the first model I ever kissed."

"How many models have you had?"

"Three—oranges, grapes, and you!"

A man brings a family heirloom to an authenticator. Studying it, the art critic says, "I have good news and bad news for you. The good news is that this is an original Mastolacci painted in Venice in 1432. The bad news is that Mastolacci was a fish peddler."

An artist painted a rather unattractive dowager, who disliked the portrait and said, "It doesn't do me justice." The artist said, "Forget justice. Lady, you need mercy."

A girl goes to an artist and asks, "Can you paint me in the nude?" The artist answers, "Sure, but I'll have to keep socks on. I have no place for the brushes."

Modern art is where you paint on canvas, wipe off your brushes with a rag, and then sell the rag.

Graves, an artist who specialized in seascapes of ships tossed in wintry seas, was having his first showing at a big gallery. A dowager type studied his work and was impressed, saying, "You've got incredible technique and know how to use color, but it's a shame you didn't have better weather."

Modern art is like trying to follow the plot in a bowl of alphabet soup.

A store with a sign saying ART OBJECTS in the window displays a cross-section of avant-garde paintings. A man walks by, stops to look, and says to his companion, "I don't blame it."

One day Picasso was hit by a car, and the driver sped away. The police asked Picasso to draw a picture of the hit-and-run driver. The next day they went out and arrested three suspects—a priest, the Eiffel tower, and a T.V. set.

They're having a lot of trouble at one of the sport magazines. The photographers for their bathing suit issue just went on strike for longer hours.

An artist went to the gallery that represented him. The owner said, "I have good news and bad news for you."

"What's the good news?"

"A man came in earlier today and asked me if your paintings would go up in price if you were dead. I told him that they would, so he bought all I had."

"What's the bad news?"

"He was your doctor."

He was thrown out of art school. When they had a nude model in, he wanted to trace.

Two women are studying a modern painting in a museum. One says, "Why would they hang such a monstrosity?"

The second answers, "Maybe they couldn't find the artist."

Whistler came home one day and saw his mother washing the floor. He yelled at her, "Ma, you're off your rocker!"

A man goes to an artist's loft and, leaning back, says, "I admire your colors. I wish I could take them with me."

The artist says, "I think your wish is going to be granted."

"You're going to give me a painting?"

"No, you're sitting on my easel."

A wealthy celebrity amassed an impressive collection of modern abstract paintings. Quite proud of it, he hired a local woman to come in and design a custom-weaved rug. On scanning the many expensive paintings on the wall, she said, "Who's the artist in the family?"

Two archeologists are searching through Yucatán for artifacts and finally find two nude statues of men. One archeologist says, "This one is definitely Mayan."

The other says, "And I think that this one is Supermayan."

## ASTRONAUTS

An astronaut gets into a small capsule, flies miles into outer space, gets out on a strange planet and walks around, lands in an ocean at four hundred miles an hour, gets out, and lights a cigarette from a pack that says, "Cigarette smoking may be injurious to your health."

There are no Jewish astronauts. No Jewish wife would let him take a trip without her.

Two moon men watched astronauts collecting rocks, and one said to the other, "Well, there goes the garden."

If astronauts are so smart, why do they count backward?

This one astronaut is a real pain to the rest of his crew. He wants to ride with the top down.

Because of the dissolution of the Soviet Empire, a Russian astronaut had to wait six months for a space vehicle to bring him home, but the delay didn't bother him. He'd had a lot of practice, waiting for the number 4 bus in Moscow.

## ASTRONOMY

A man watches the astronomer line up his telescope with a distant star. Just as he has it in focus, a falling star zooms by. The man nods at the astronomer and says, "Good shot."

An astronomer is trying to get a good picture of the stars, but he can't. They keep moving.

A space probe sends pictures back from the other planets in six seconds. Now if you didn't have to wait three days to get them back from the drugstore . . .

The equipment on the Hubble telescope cost a billion dollars. Film is extra.

## ATLANTIC CITY

I didn't throw a coin into one of those one-armed bandits in Atlantic City. But I ran into a two-armed bandit in the parking lot.

In Atlantic City, the odds are that you won't get even.

A wino kept walking down the street in Atlantic City and putting money in the meters. Finally, he said, "I love this outdoor gambling."

No wonder Atlantic City is so crowded. Nobody has the bus fare to get out.

I have no luck in Atlantic City. Last month I lost fifty bucks in a gum machine.

I went to Atlantic City last week. Took the casino for everything I had.

Some people say that there's safety in numbers. Have you ever been to Atlantic City?

A man takes a bus to Atlantic City and loses every penny he has. Miserable, he feels that nothing worse can happen to him. He says to a stranger nearby, "I just lost every penny in the world. I cannot imagine Fate dealing me any lower blow."

The man says, "Don't bet on it. I just came from the station. The bus company went bankrupt."

## ATOMIC WARFARE

The next war will be over in two hours. That'll still give us our evening free.

I'll never get hurt in atomic warfare. I just bought a car, and the finance company will make sure nothing happens to me.

There was a scare at an atomic-bomb factory the other day. Because of a money crunch, they were told to drop everything.

They recently sent up an atomic missile, but it was unarmed—a Venus de Silo.

One Arab country contends that it has an atomic missile that could wipe out Cleveland. It also has some negative aspects.

## AVON LADY

One Avon lady has a great technique. After the door is opened, she says to the lady of the house, "You won't believe what I saw in your neighbor's bedroom. May I come in and tell you about it?"

Then there was the behavioral scientist who taught his Great Dane to come for food at the ringing of a bell. After the first experiment, the dog ate six biscuits, two steaks, and an Avon lady.

How does Avon do it? Where do they find so many women to take orders?

# B

## BABIES

She told him to change the baby, so he brought home a different kid.

At four in the morning, my wife used to nudge me. "Get up and see why the baby isn't crying."

Getting the baby to sleep is hard, especially when she's eighteen.

Little Tommy listened to his folks discuss the new baby. Both parents agreed that they'd have to move. Little Tommy chimed in, "It's no use. He'll just follow us."

Joseph was fishing way off the coast of Maine when Fred, another fisherman, pulled up to him and said, "Your wife had a baby this morning."
"How much did it weigh?"
"Four pound ten."
"Damn, hardly worth the bait."

Two new mothers are discussing a third, who had just given birth to triplets. One new mother said, "Do you know that happens only once every twelve thousand times?"

65

The other new mother says, "Really? When does she find time to do her housework?"

This woman turns pale when the doctor tells her she's pregnant again after six kids. The doctor asks her, "Does the idea of having another child bother you?"

The woman answers, "It's not the kids. I'm thinking of the PTA."

My wife did natural childbirth—no eye makeup, no lipstick, no rouge. . . .

Then there's this girl who sent her boyfriend a wire: BUY THREE RINGS—ENGAGEMENT, WEDDING, AND TEETHING!

A man was complaining about the cost of the baby. The nurse said, "Sure, but look how long they last."

He was a beautiful baby. His folks had him kidnapped just so they could see his picture in the papers.

My sister had a hard time breast-feeding her baby. She couldn't get my brother-in-law out of the way.

Two expectant fathers pace the waiting room. One of them complains, "Dammit, can you believe this is happening to us on the first day of our vacation?"

The other one said sadly, "What are you complaining about? This is our honeymoon."

A man and a pregnant woman get into a cab, and the man tells the cabbie, "City hall, then Doctors' Hospital, and go like crazy."

The baby looked just like me. Then they turned it right side up.

Carrying her baby, a woman rushed into a doctor's office and said, "Help me. Please help me. My baby swallowed a bullet."

The doctor said, "Give it some of this castor oil, but for the love of heaven, don't point it at anybody."

It was exactly nine months to the day that the Bronsons were married. A lovely afternoon wedding it had been, with the clock striking six as the newlyweds got into their limo and headed for their hotel suite.

The occasion now was just as thrilling as Mr. Bronson rushed his wife to the maternity ward and sat down to wait for the birth of his first child. At five after six, a nurse walked into the waiting room and said, "Congratulations, you are now the proud father of a baby girl."

At six-thirty, the nurse walked in again and said, "This one is a little boy." She started to rush out.

Mr. Bronson motioned for her to slow down and said, "Don't hurry. The third one isn't due for twenty minutes."

The first lesson a baby learns at its mother's knee today is to be careful of her stockings.

When you pick up a baby, everybody tells you to watch the head. That isn't the end that needs watching.

A new father visited his new family. Seeing a nurse coming out of his wife's room, he rushed over and looked at the child. Glowing, he said, "This little fellow is sure cute."

The nurse said, "It's not yours. It's a girl. And let go of my finger."

A hillbilly came into town carrying his new baby. A storekeeper said, "Is that your young one, Zeke?"

Zeke said, "I figure it is. It was caught in my trap."

"What a cute baby. Was his father redheaded too?"

"I don't know. He didn't take off his hat."

Some girls believe in long engagements. I know one who was seven months pregnant before she got married.

"Why does the doctor slap a baby so hard?"

"To knock the penises off the smart ones."

Two women meet and start to discuss children. One says, "I'm so happy. I'm seven months pregnant now."

"How? You had such a hard time conceiving."

"I went to a faith healer."

"My husband and I went to a faith healer for two months."

"Go alone."

When he was a baby, his parents could have eaten him up. Now, they're sorry they didn't.

The new mother is feeding the baby some strained fruit. Naturally, the food goes all over the infant. The father asks, "What are you doing?"

The mother answers, "I'm waiting to put on a second coat."

Here's a picture of me when I was only three hours old—in the background, you can see my mother arguing with the doctor.

How come the second baby isn't as breakable as the first?

If you live through infancy, all chances of being killed by kindness are gone.

The Jordans seemed to be running a baby factory. After their fifteenth, they went to a doctor who told Joe Jordan, "Come on, man. Use some restraint."

Six weeks later, Mrs. Jordan is pregnant again. The doctor is irate.

"Joe, I told you to use some restraint."

Joe says, "I am. But can I help it if in the middle of the night, I get up and the missus is helping herself?"

A new father was unhappy that his wife had given birth to a daughter. He was hoping for a son so he'd have somebody who could help him with the housework.

She's had fifteen kids. To her, birth control is making it to the hospital in time.

You can always tell which baby in the maternity ward is Jewish. He's the one with heartburn.

Having a baby takes a lot out of a woman.

Our baby just started eating solids—his crib, paint, pillows . . .

There's an easy way for nearsighted mothers to find their babies: Don't change their diapers.

A man with a black bag knocks on the door of a house. The proprietor, the father of fourteen children, opens the door and gulps, "I sure hope you're the piano tuner."

This couple brings the new baby home, and the father starts to practice diapering the child. He doesn't quite have the knack. Their other child says, "What's the matter? Didn't come with instructions?"

The world's greatest pickpocket married the woman who was known as the second-greatest pickpocket. Soon they had a baby. But it was the hardest delivery the doctor had ever been involved with. He couldn't get the baby's hand open. Try as he would, he couldn't pry open the tiny fingers. He shrugged his shoulders and left. The new father glowed at his infant son. He, too, tried to pry open the tiny hand. Finally, he got it open. There in the palm was the doctor's wristwatch.

A man goes into a department store and asks for a layette. The clerk says, "I see, you're expecting."

The man says, "No, we're damn sure."

More twins are being born than ever before. With the shape of the world, I think kids are afraid to come out alone.

A man goes to the doctor and complains, "Doc, we have sixteen kids, and you have to help me out."

The doctor says, "Well, I just received a book with the latest medical knowledge in it. Maybe that'll tell us something."

The doctor scans several pages and says, finally, "There's a new medicine from France called NB Thirty-four. You take a spoonful every night, and you won't have any more kids."

The man goes home, takes the medicine dutifully, but returns to the doctor several months later. "Doc, we're having another one."

The doctor says, "Let's look in the book."

He scans several pages and says, "The book says that it's possible you haven't been taking enough NB Thirty-four. After the baby is born, try taking two spoons."

The baby is born, the man takes his medicine and returns to the doctor. "It didn't work. She's having another one."

The doctor says, "Let's look in the book real good this time." He scans some more pages and says, "It says that if the woman is still having babies, the wrong guy is taking the NB Thirty-four."

## BABY-SITTERS

Our baby-sitter says that she's lost her appetite. I think she found a horse's to replace it.

It's thrilling when the baby-sitter calls you at the party and asks where you keep the fire extinguisher.

A baby-sitter is a girl you hire to fool around with her boyfriend on the couch while your kid cries himself to sleep.

My cousin took the baby-sitter home, and his wife is worrying about it. It's been four years.

## BACHELORS

They say that two can live as cheap as one, but it's worth the difference to stay single.

Years ago, a man who refused to fight was called a coward. Now, they call him a bachelor.

A bachelor is a man who can take a nap on top of the bedspread.

Then there's the bachelor who got thrown out of his apartment because the landlady heard him drop his shoes twice.

A bachelor is a man who loves home-cooking but has his choice of cooks.

A man calls himself a bachelor till he gets married. Then you ought to hear what he calls himself.

I was a bachelor so long, my favorite dish was a clean one.

There's one thing worse than being a bachelor—being a bachelor's son.

Show me a man who does what he wants, and I'll show you a bachelor.

Many a poor husband was once a rich bachelor.

I want a girl just like the girl that Daddy had on the side.

A young man walks into a posh fur salon with a girlfriend. He insists that he wants the finest fur coat in the shop. Money is no object. The girl picks out a ten-thousand-dollar mink. The young man nods and tells the salesman, "I'd like to pay by check. But you don't know me, so why don't you put through a credit check, and tomorrow I'll come back and pay. Meanwhile, of course, I understand you don't know me, so you can hold the coat."

The next afternoon, the young man goes to the shop and tells the salesman, "Thanks for a hell of a night."

A bachelor wants one single thing in life—himself.

It's easy to stay a bachelor. Just watch TV. All the women are sickly, fat, or have rough hands.

Bachelors know more about women than married men. That's why they're bachelors.

It's better to be laughed at for not being married than to be unable to laugh because you are.

A bachelor joins a dating service and asks for a perfect mate. He wants a companion who is small and cute, loves water sports, and likes group activities. The next morning the computer outfit sends him the address of a penguin.

A bachelor comes home, sees what's in the fridge, and goes to bed. A married man sees what's in the bed and goes to the fridge.

A bachelor is a man who comes to work every day from a different direction.

A bachelor is a man who makes mistakes, but not in front of a minister.

A bachelor is a guy who doesn't have to leave the party just when he's beginning to enjoy himself.

I have a bachelor nephew with a house full of garbage. There's nobody there to tell him to take it out.

His name was John Smith. He was descended from a long line of motel registers.

## BAD NEIGHBORHOODS

In my old neighborhood, when you made a reservation at a restaurant, you requested the "no shooting" section.

In my old neighborhood, the candy store had a bouncer.

In my old neighborhood, warrants were marked "Occupant."

Crime is so rough in my old neighborhood, our local bank keeps its money in another bank.

In my old high school, the class ring was a brass knuckle.

## BALD

Baldness can come in handy once in a while, especially when you're romancing a girl on the couch. When her folks come in, all the bald guy has to straighten out is his tie.

He's not bald. He's just taller than his hair.

He was so bald, he looked like a part with ears.

By the time I was ten, I gave my father gray hair. It thrilled him, because until then he'd been bald.

He's so bald—when he sleeps, his head keeps sliding off the pillow.

## BANKS

It was a bank that made you feel insecure. If you wanted to make a withdrawal, you had to stand around the tellers' cage and wait for someone to make a deposit.

**O**ne Texan drew a check on his local branch, and the bank bounced!

**T**he crooked teller was last seen leaving the bank. It was too heavy to carry.

**A** boy and his sister walked into a bank with a large sack of coins.

The teller asked, "Did you hoard all this yourself?"

The boy answered, "No, my sister whored. I pimped."

**F**or years it was so easy to borrow money from banks, I don't know why people robbed them.

**B**anks are for men who have everything, but can't afford to pay for it.

**A**ll banks are the same. They have one window at which ten people are standing. Then they have four windows called "Next Window."

**I** decided to start saving for a rainy day— I went to a savings and loan and deposited my umbrella.

**I**'d love a job in a bank. I think there's money in it.

**R**ates are so high in banks nowadays. I went into a bank the other day, and the loan officer was wearing a stocking mask.

**N**owadays, a dollar saved is a quarter earned.

**M**y banker believes in safe sex. That's where he takes the tellers after work.

**I** wish the guy who writes the bank ads about getting a loan was the same guy as the one that makes them.

**I**t used to be so great when we had folding money—instead of folding banks.

**A** banker was depressed because his bank was about to close. He sought solace in the Bible. He opened it only to see Chapter 11.

**T**he loan officer checks the application and says to Jones, "Your assets are in good shape. Tell me about your liabilities." Jones says, "That's easy. I can lie with the best of them."

**T**hings have really changed. Last year, the banks were putting their pens on chains. Now, it's the bank president.

**T**he old man was cleaning up in the branch bank at night when the phone rang. He answered, "Hello."

The voice at the other end said, "Can you tell me the penalty for withdrawing a five-year CD at the end of thirty-eight months?"

The old man said, "When I said, 'Hello,' I told you all I know about banking."

**T**hey now have a new S&L wristwatch. The little hand is on the ten, and the big hand is in the till.

A prospective employee was being interviewed. "What was your last job?"

"I cleaned out a bank."

"Janitor or president?"

My bank is in real trouble. I tried to make a withdrawal from an ATM, and an IOU came out.

Savings and loans are closing by the hundreds today. If you want to rob one, make sure you call first to see if it's still open.

I have printed checks that cover it all. They say three things—my name, my address, and "Insufficient Funds."

One robber with gall came into a bank, a stocking cap over his head, and asked for ten thousand dollars. With the money, he went to the next window and opened an account.

Banks have everything I love—money and holidays.

A joint account shows that many women are quick on the draw.

An elderly woman in a frayed cloth coat and carrying a large shopping bag walks into a bank. She goes to the vice president, puts the shopping bag on his desk, and says, "I'd like to deposit a million, seven hundred thousand, and thirty dollars." The vice president counts the money. When done, he says, "I'm sorry, but you only have a million seven hundred thousand, and eighteen dollars."

"Count it again," the elderly woman says.

After counting it again, the vice president says, "There's only a million, seven hundred thousand, eighteen dollars here."

The elderly woman says, "May I call my husband?"

"Certainly."

The woman dials. When her husband answers, she says, "Idiot, you gave me the wrong shopping bag!"

I don't understand banks. Why do they chain down a pen that doesn't write?

They have a new board game called S&L Monopoly. It's just like the original version, except now you build houses and hotels with other people's money.

An oilman was called in so that his loan position could be reviewed. The banker said, "We loaned you two million to revive your old wells, and they went dry."

"Could have been worse."

"Then we gave you five million to drill new wells, and they were dry."

"Could have been worse."

"Stop repeating that. How could it have been worse?"

"It could have been *my* money."

I went over to a loan officer at the bank and told him I was interested in a loan. He said, "That's great. How much can you give us?"

**B**anks are really in trouble nowadays. I opened an account the other day, and *I* had to give *them* a toaster.

**A** lady walks into a bank and says, "I'd like to open a joint account with somebody who has money in it."

**A** man trying to get some money in the bank says to the loan officer, "If I'm such a poor risk, how did I get so far into debt?"

**T**wo men robbed a bank and ran out to escape. But they were caught right away. While they were inside robbing the bank, the bank had repossessed their car.

"**D**id you get the check I sent you?"
"Twice. Once from you and once from the bank."

"**W**hat's the name of your bank?"
"Piggy."

**B**anks are feeling the financial squeeze. They're sending calendars one month at a time.

**A** joint account is never overdrawn by the wife. It's just underdeposited by the husband.

**M**y wife had an accident in the bank yesterday. She got on the wrong line and made a deposit.

**M**y bank just sent me a note that my account is overdrawn again. I'm going to try another bank. They can't all be overdrawn.

**M**y banker is an unhappy man. Nobody calls him except when they need money.

**T**he best investment the savings-and-loan industry made was in Congress.

**A**nybody who can pay the interest doesn't need a loan.

**M**y wife loves the bank. No matter how many checks she writes, the bank manages to get them all back for her.

**D**on't ever hit a bank loan officer in the heart. You'll break your hand.

**T**hen there was the bank robber with a hernia. He couldn't lift heavy bags of money, so he asked for a certified check.

*Cosigner:* A damn fool with a ballpoint pen.

## BARBECUES

**A** man was barbecuing a chicken over a spit in his backyard. His neighbor, a gentleman with a tendency to drink too much, looked over their mutual fence and said, "Not only can't I hear a note of what your organ is playing, but your monkey's on fire too!"

**I** finally got the knack of barbecuing. Yesterday I made something that was done exactly as I like it—charred on the outside and pink on the inside. Unfortunately, it was my thumb.

## BARBERS

I go to a barber shop that has five barbers—for panel discussions.

After being shaved, the customer wanted a glass of water. The barber asked, "Are you thirsty?"

The man answered, "No. I just want to see if my neck leaks."

A man walked into a barber shop and said, "Give me a shave. I don't have time to listen to a haircut."

My barber is prepared. He has a red styptic pencil.

I don't like my barber. He talks behind my back.

When a barber gives another barber a haircut, who does the talking?

A man rushes into a barber shop and asks, "How many ahead of me?"

The barber says, "Four."

"Thank you." The man rushes out. He returns a half hour later with the same question: "How many ahead of me?"

"Three."

The man leaves again. The barber says to the shoe-shine boy, "Follow him. I'd like to know where he goes."

The shoe-shine boy returns ten min-

utes later. The barber asks, "Well, did you find out where he goes?"

"To your house."

The barber asked me if I had ketchup on my shirt. I said no, and he dialed 911.

The customer sat down for a shave. When the barber, sharp razor in hand, turned to him, the customer could smell strong whiskey on the barber's breath. "Don't you know the evil of drink?" the customer said.

"Sure. It makes the skin mighty tender."

A complainer is having his hair cut and tells the barber, "I want my hair cut exactly in the middle."

The barber says, "I'm afraid that's impossible. There's an odd number."

"Are you the man who cut my hair the last time?"

"I don't think so. I've only been here a year."

The barber is certain that he can help the customer get rid of the dandruff that's been bothering him for years. All the customer has to do is wash his hair every day with a green shampoo the barber sells. Then the customer has to rub in some blue conditioner. Finally, he has to apply a yellowish lotion.

The customer returns four weeks later, a happy man.

"Obviously, it worked," the barber says.

. "The dandruff's all gone. Now, tell me—how do you get rid of confetti?"

## BARS

In the old days, when the whiskey flowed freely, a girl with curls would come to a drinker and say, "Daddy, Daddy, please come home with me." The man wouldn't pay attention to her. Nowadays, the girl says, "Daddy, Daddy, come home with me," and he does.

Sitting down at a bar, a man starts to stare at the young hippie type at the other end of the bar. The hippie type has long, scraggly hair and looks as if he hasn't washed in a year. Aware of being stared at, the hippie type strides over to the man and asks, "What the hell are you staring at, buddy?"

The man says, "Oh, I'm sorry. But you see—about twenty-five years ago I made love to a buffalo, and I was wondering if you could be my kid."

Some bars are weird. They make you wear shoes and a tie so you can go in and see a topless dancer.

A man walks into a swanky bar, sits down, and orders a drink. The bartender places the drink before him and charges him five cents. A second drink is another five cents. The third drink is free. The customer says, "I don't get it. Why are you doing this?"

The bartender says, "Well, the boss doesn't know I know, but he's upstairs with my wife. So I'm doing to him down here what he's doing to me up there."

I asked the bartender for something tall, cool, and full of gin, so he sent over his wife.

Most bartenders tend to cheat a little. There was one who, upon getting paid for a two-dollar drink, would put one in the cash register and one in his pocket. He did this for weeks. One day he got paid for a drink and put all the money in his pocket.

The boss happened to notice and said, "What's the matter? Aren't we partners anymore?"

A man goes into a bar, sees an attractive woman, walks over to her, and says, "Look, sweetheart, I don't like to waste time, so do you or don't you put out?"

The attractive woman says, "Well, normally I don't, but you've talked me into it."

A burly Texan walks into a bar and sees a man passed out on the floor. The Texan says, "Give me a double shot of that."

I know a bar with midget waiters—to make the drinks look bigger.

There's a great way to meet people at a bar—just pick up somebody else's change.

A big oaf storms into a bar and bellows, "I'm the toughest man in these parts. I'm as hard as nails and as ornery as a polecat." He keeps up the nauseating litany for fifteen minutes. Finally, a man sitting at the other end of the bar gets up, walks over, and hits the loudmouth with one shot in the stomach.

Gasping for breath, the loudmouth says, "Who are you?"

"I'm the guy you thought you were when you came in here."

A bouncer threw a drunk freeloader out of a bar for the fifth time in ten minutes, and sure enough, the man diligently marched back into the bar. A patron tapped the frustrated bouncer on the shoulder and said, "I think you put too much backspin on him!"

## BASEBALL

Then there was the baseball pitcher who was arrested for chewing tobacco. One day, he spit and drowned a midget.

Did you ever notice at a ball game, no matter where you sit, you're always between the seller with the beer and his best customer?

Some of these ballplayers get incredible amounts of money. One pitcher with a great fastball just signed for ten thousand a mile.

One pitcher caught a line drive on the fly. It ruined his sex life.

A rookie who thought he was God's gift to the game started to pitch his first game in the league. He walked nine batters in a row. The manager yanked him out of the game, and the rookie complained, "You can't take me out. I've got a no-hitter going."

A baseball player who was notorious for his inability to catch the ball was having a birthday, but his teammates seemed to be oblivious to the occasion. Finally, the ballplayer said, "Somebody should have given me a cake."

A teammate said, "We would have, but we were afraid you'd drop it!"

He couldn't make the team because he was too nice. He wouldn't even hit a fly.

Catching the ball is a pleasure. Knowing what to do with it is a business.

Little Freddy says to his father, "Watch me hit them out of the park. I'm the best batter on the team."

"Sure, Son."

Freddy throws up the ball and swings at it. Missing, he calls out, "Strike one." He throws up a second pitch and misses that too. "Strike two." He tries again, and again he misses. "Strike three. Boy, am I a great pitcher."

Do you want to see a baseball game in the worst way? Take your wife.

What's light field?

It's opposite left field in Tokyo.

There was one baseball player who was in a terrible batting slump. He even took a swipe at his beard with a razor and missed.

A turkey comes to spring-training camp and tries out for the team. He hits the ball a mile, fields like a natural, runs bases like the wind, and is at home in every position. The team owner says, "I'll draw a contract. A million a year with incentives."

The turkey says, "I just want one clause—we play through November."

This baseball player is carrying on the tradition of living it up on the road. The bellhop comes into his room and sees a woman's clothes strewn all over the place. Putting down the beverages he's brought, the bellhop says, "Is there anything I can bring for your wife?"

The ballplayer says, "Good idea. Bring me a dozen picture postcards."

The manager walks to the mound, ready to yank the pitcher. The pitcher protests, "I struck this guy out the last time."

"Yeah, but this is the same inning."

A baseball game is being played at the prison. It's the ninth inning, the score is tied, and the bases are loaded. The catcher goes up to the pitcher and says, "Take your time. You got thirty years."

"Why are baseball managers like diapers?"

"They're always on somebody's butt and full of crap."

Then there was the baseball player who cheated so much on the road, he was finally thrown out at home.

## BASKETBALL

A college basketball coach discovered a young high school prospect who was a dream come true. The youngster was 7'4" and never missed the basket. Unfortunately, he wasn't an academic whiz. The coach begged the academic dean to admit the young man. The academic dean agreed, saying, "I'll ask him three questions. If he answers them, he can be enrolled."

The young man was brought before the dean, who asked him the first question: "How much is two and two?"

His brow furrowed, the young man thought and thought and finally said, "Four."

The dean went on, "How much is four and four?"

The young man gulped, worked and worked, and finally said, "Eight."

The dean went on, "How much is eight and eight?"

Beads of sweat formed on the young man's forehead. After an eternity, he finally said, "Sixteen."

With that, the coach fell to his knees and said to the dean, "Give him one more chance!"

The coach gathered his team around him and said, "Okay, fellas, remember this is basketball, a game that develops initiative, your ability to lead, and individualism. Now go out there and do exactly as I say."

A famous basketball player is seven feet tall and got his height from his parents. Each one is 3′6″.

One college player negotiated his own pro contract for $10 million—ten dollars a year for a million years.

"What's the longest athletic contest in the world?"

"A white slam-dunk contest."

No one will ever forget when the whole basketball team showed in class. It was a sex-education class, and they'd heard there'd be an oral exam.

The three most popular sports in Indiana: pro basketball, college basketball, and high school basketball.

A true basketball fan is one who sits in the front row and later asks, "What cheerleaders?"

I finally found out what basketball players do during the off-season. They go to the movies and sit in front of me.

A basketball coach just came up with a terrific idea to get eight-foot players—seven-foot girls!

## BATHING

Two hippies are walking down the street when they see a Hare Krishna with a broken leg. They ask him what happened. He says, "I fell while I was taking a bath."

One hippie says to the other, "Man, what's a bath?"

The other hippie says, "Man, I don't know nothing about that Hare Krishna stuff."

Priests should wear trunks when they shower. Nobody should look down on the unemployed.

The doctor told me to bathe in some of the famous springs. So I took one in the spring of 1985.

I put my bathtub right in the living room. Now, when the front bell rings, I don't have so far to walk.

Every morning I take a cold shower. I eat a grapefruit.

## BATHING SUITS

I couldn't see her bikini. Her earrings were covering it!

Bikinis are something nowadays. I've seen more cotton in the top of an aspirin bottle.

Most new bathing suits look like they were turned out by one silkworm on a coffee break.

One company is having trouble with its new bikinis. It has no room to put the logo.

Nowadays, when a girl pays a fortune for a bathing suit, she has very little to show for it.

New bathing suits don't shrink. How could they?

The new bathing suits are nothing to speak of, but plenty to speak about.

Her bathing suit is smaller than the price tag.

A young lady modeled her new bikini for her mother and asked what she thought of it. The mother said, "If I'd worn that to the beach, you'd be six years older than you are."

## BEACHES

At the beach at Malibu, a young woman found out that the bra part of her bathing suit had gone out with the tide. Crossing her arms in front of her, she started to run for the house she'd rented.

A little boy, about eight, intercepted her and said, "Ma'am, if you're giving away those puppies, can I have the one with the pink nose?"

One day she went to the beach and lost her bathing suit. She spent the whole day going in and out with the tide.

You should see the bikinis they're all wearing. We've got more sun-kissed navels than Florida.

The lifeguard says, "Sir, I've just resuscitated your daughter."

The father says, "And the way you did it, you'll have to marry her."

It's nice to go out to the beach and watch the tide and men's eyeballs go in and out.

It must be great to be a girl in the summertime. You can go to the mountains and see the scenery, or go to the beach and *be* the scenery.

You never know how many friends you have till you rent a place at the beach.

I get a great color when I go to the beach—blue, from holding in my stomach.

My wife insisted on buying a new suit for the summer. The only thing wrong with the old one was that it had a hole at the knee.

The other day I saw two girls getting rescued and being given artificial respiration by the lifeguards. That was surprising, because neither of the girls had been in the water.

At the beach, you can't judge a woman by her clothes—insufficient evidence.

There's a new thing for girls who want to get to know the lifeguard at a beach—artificial drowning.

Then there was the girl at the beach whose bathing suit was ruined. It got wet.

It was crowded at the beach today. I had to dive in six times before I got wet!

I got a medal for bravery on the beach. I rescued a girl from a lifeguard.

These new ladies' swimsuits are something. A woman wears more in the bathtub than she does on the beach.

You know when it's summer. The beach chair gets up when you do.

There may not be anything new under the sun, but there's a lot more of it showing.

Do you remember when a girl with hidden charms hid them?

The beaches are so empty, lifeguards are saving one another.

A beach is a place where a woman goes today when she has nothing to wear.

The cute young girl tells her friend, "The water's great today. Filled with men."

The beaches in California are weird. They're always sun-drenched, but so cold you come home with a frostbitten suntan.

A little girl finds a seashell on the beach. It's early in the morning, and she listens, then she says, "Hey, somebody left this on all night."

She's a modest girl. She just bought a bathing suit with sleeves.

Her bathing suit fits her like a sunburn.

## BEARDS

Do you realize that Fidel Castro could rob a bank, shave, and nobody would know what he looks like?

His beard is very thick. For ten years, he's been kissing his wife through a straw.

## BEAUTY

This woman looks at herself in the mirror after her beautician finishes. Shaking her head sadly, she says, "I've been coming here thirty years, and I have to tell you—you're slipping."

She wears so much makeup, she has to talk through a straw.

When she leaves the beauty parlor, they make her use the back door.

She once entered a beauty contest, and they fined her a hundred dollars.

She's so ugly, she once left her beauty parlor as a P.O.W.

The key to being beautiful is to hang around with real ugly people.

Beauty is only skin deep, but ugly goes all the way down!

She looked prettier than a tax refund.

Every night she brushes her hair with five hundred strokes. Her hair doesn't look too good, but you should see the muscles in her arms.

Two women meet at a restaurant. One says, "Honey, what have you done to your hair? It looks like a wig."

The second says, "It is a wig."

The first one says, "Really? I never would have guessed it."

Beauty is when a woman looks the same after washing her face.

Figures don't lie, but girdles sometimes redistribute the truth.

She didn't have much upstairs, but what a stairway!

It's a good thing that Vegas chorus girls are women. Builds like that would be wasted on a man.

My wife's beauty parlor has a recovery room.

"She sure uses body language."

"She certainly has some vocabulary."

Nothing helps a woman's looks more than a nearsighted man.

A doll walked by, and one of the guys who hung around the corner whistled at her, asking, "Are you a model?"

"No," she answered, "I'm full scale."

My wife has been a blonde, a redhead, a brunette. She even has plaid dandruff.

My wife really does it with the makeup and style. The other day, she fell off her seven-inch Cuban heels. Luckily, her eyelashes broke the fall.

Some women go the beauty parlor to get a face full of mud and an earful of dirt.

"You're pretty dirty, Marge."

"I'm even prettier when I'm clean."

My wife wants to dye her hair back to its original color, but she can't remember what it was.

"Have you heard what they're doing with cosmetic surgery in California?" grumbled an indignant businessman. "They're making the world's most beautiful girl. They're using Elizabeth Taylor's eyes, Brigitte Bardot's mouth, Ginger Rogers's legs, and Raquel Welch's back."

"Boy, oh, boy," moaned his friend. "What I could do with the leftovers!"

"What is this: 10, 9, 8, 7, 6, 5, 4, 3, 2, 1?"

"A gorgeous woman getting older."

She's on the fiftieth day of a ten-day beauty plan.

Freckles would be a nice tan if they could get together.

I can't understand my wife. She spends two hours with a tweezer, plucking out her eyebrows. Then she spends another two hours with an eyebrow pencil filling them in.

Tell a woman she's beautiful, and she'll believe all your other lies.

The average girl needs beauty more than brains, because the average man can see more than he can think.

I was a handsome kid. Women chased me down the street. The fact that I snatched their purses had nothing to do with it.

Beauty is in the eyes of the beholder. The trouble is, so is ugliness.

A boss says to his gorgeous secretary, "Take the day off, dear. I want to think."

## BEHAVIOR

The way I feel is this—if I don't do something completely crazy once in a while, I'll go nuts.

When somebody does something for your own good, you can be sure you won't like it.

## BEVERLY HILLS

There's a new car wash in Beverly Hills. It not only washes your car, it irons it too.

I know a woman in Beverly Hills who has a split-level jewel box.

Two Beverly Hills businessmen were discussing their doctors. The first said, "My psychiatrist is the strongest guy in the world. He could beat up your psychiatrist with one hand tied behind his back."
    The second said, "Maybe, but my psychiatrist could cure yours of his aggressive behavior."

Beverly Hills is some town. The kids there play hide-and-go-shop.

In one Beverly Hills home, the carpets are so thick, nobody in the family has seen anybody below the neck for ten years.

In Beverly Hills, the police dogs are trained to smell out quiche.

I know a man in Beverly Hills with a house that has seven dining rooms—one for each course.

You don't get your car washed in Beverly Hills—dry-cleaned.

Last Christmas they went around Beverly Hills giving food packages to people with only one pool.

In Beverly Hills, even the bag ladies wear Gucci.

There's a great take-out place in Beverly Hills—Kentucky Fried Pheasant.

If you ask for water in a Beverly Hills restaurant, you can request the year.

When I found out how much my wife spent on dresses last year, I dumped her and proposed to the dressmaker.

Beverly Hills is so ritzy—women who breast-feed are having it catered.

Beverly Hills is incredibly rich. Where else can you look in the church collection box on Sunday and find credit cards?

They're rich in Beverly Hills, all right. The other day I saw a kiddie car with a phone.

They just finished an incredible mansion in Beverly Hills. One bathroom is so large, it can seat sixteen.

In Beverly Hills, they have traffic lights in decorator colors.

You can always tell a Beverly Hills widow. She's wearing a black tennis outfit.

There's a real shortage of water in Beverly Hills. Two Perrier trucks collided.

In Beverly Hills, they have a recipe for chicken soup. It starts: "Bring the Perrier to a slow boil. . . ."

Where else but in Beverly Hills can you find monogrammed garbage?

In Beverly Hills, you get picked up for wearing polyester.

In Beverly Hills, an underprivileged kid is one with only one set of parents.

A Beverly Hills poodle had an adorable doghouse near the pool. A visitor asked, "How do you keep it so clean?"

The owner of the pet answered, "We have a Mexican Chihuahua come in Monday and Friday."

"Why are there more housewives than housekeepers in Beverly Hills?"

"Because it's easier to find another wife."

In Beverly Hills, they use suede tennis balls.

One Beverly Hills husband told his wife, "This town ain't big enough for both your credit cards."

I know a Beverly Hills kid who won a school prize—he had the most parents at the PTA meeting.

In Beverly Hills, the bums on the street don't ask for handouts. They ask for tax-frees.

An out-of-towner comes into a plush Beverly Hills hotel, picks up the pen at the desk, and asks, "What have you for about fifty dollars?"

The desk clerk says, "You're holding it."

The Beverly Hills millionaire grabbed his heart as an attack hit him. Gasping, he said to his wife, "Quick. Buy me a hospital!"

Two women chatted while waiting for their hair appointments.

"How many bathrooms did you say your new residence has?" asked one woman.

"I can seat fourteen," the other woman replied.

They now have a psychiatrist in Beverly Hills who specializes in inferiority complexes. He takes only patients with less than ten million.

The son of a real estate baron sits down to breakfast and says, "Today I feel like a million dollars!"

His mother looks at him and says, "A million dollars? What makes you so depressed?"

Beverly Hills is special. Where else can you see money belts drying on the line?

There's one tycoon who has an unlisted telephone company.

Recently, a kid from Beverly Hills failed a test because he couldn't spell "poor."

I overheard two men at the Polo Lounge talking about their neighbor. "He says he's as rich as you are," one man says.

"Don't believe him," the other says. "He's never had more than thirty million dollars in his pocket at one time!"

This Beverly Hills citizen was audited, and the government claimed that he hadn't put down a quarter of a million dollars. He shook his head and said, "My kid has a newspaper route. Do you have to put everything down?"

Beverly Hills is famous for its fancy restaurants. One place even has a maître d' for the take-out counter.

A Beverly Hills couple are aghast because their son is dating one of the help—the butler.

The Beverly Hills millionaire shows his daughter the new house he built while she was away in school. It has huge servants' quarters, a tennis court, dog kennels, stables, cabanas, and an Olympic-size swimming pool. When they reach the pool, hanging around or swimming are some of the young rich men of the neighborhood. The daughter claps her hands gleefully and says, "Oh, Dad, this is a fantastic pool. And you've even stocked it for me."

## BIBLE

"Why did Moses wander in the desert for forty years?"

"Because even then a man wouldn't stop and ask for directions."

The Bible says you mustn't covet your neighbor's wife. But what about the wife of a guy who lives on the other side of town?

**D**avid must have been the first insurance man. He gave Goliath a piece of the rock.

**M**oses came down from the mountain and told his people, "I have good news and bad news for you. The good news is that I got it down to ten. The bad news is that adultery is still on the list."

"**I**f you read the Bible, you'll see that water has killed more people than whiskey."

"How can you say that?"

"Well, first off, there was the Flood."

**E**verybody hated Noah because he went around saying, "Into each life, some rain must fall."

**T**wo zebras stand outside in the rain while Noah moves the animals aboard the Ark. One zebra says, "Why alphabetically?"

**Y**ou have to understand—the Ten Commandments aren't multiple choice.

**I**t's very hard to believe in the story of Noah that there were only two asses on the Ark.

**M**oses was leading the Israelites out of Egypt and came to the Red Sea. His public relations aide was puzzled about the next step. It would be difficult to justify Moses' status if he failed to save his people.

Moses thought about the problem for a while and consulted with other leaders. One suggested a bridge. There was no time for that. Another suggested trying to find another way out. There was no time for that either.

Finally, Moses came up with an idea, saying, "I think I'll part the Red Sea and we'll walk across."

The public relations aide said, "If you do that, I think I can get you two pages in the Old Testament."

**C**onstipation figures prominently in the Bible. Cain wasn't able. Balaam had trouble with his ass. And Moses had to take two tablets.

**T**he message of the story of Jonah and the whale is clear—people make whales sick.

**T**he Flood was over. The animals were lined up as they left the Ark. The elephant turned to the flea and said, "Stop pushing."

**W**ho will ever forget the words of Noah's wife, who said to Noah, "I don't care what you say. I'm taking an umbrella."

**T**he Bible says, "Love thy neighbor." I did, and almost lost my wife.

**T**he pastor finished a forceful sermon on the Ten Commandments, and one parishioner was crushed momentarily.

"Anyway," he said to himself, "I have never made a graven image."

A Christian sees the lion coming, falls to his knees, and prays for the Lord to save him. The lion kneels too. The Christian says, "Saying your prayers too?"

The lion says, "No. Grace."

Noah tells the animals that the Ark is crowded, and he wants no multiplying during the period they are afloat. To oversee things, he appoints the giraffe. Comes the day the rain abates, and there is landfall. The animals start off two by two. Then two cats start off with a dozen kittens behind them. The male cat looks at the giraffe next to Noah and says, "Bet you thought we were fighting?"

The Bible class is discussing one of the old prophets. The minister tells about one who had a thousand wives and fed them ambrosia and nectar. One male parishioner says, "Never mind what he fed them. What did *he* eat?"

The Sunday school teacher asked, "Where was Christ born?"

Little Anthony said, "Pittsburgh or Lancaster."

The teacher said, "Christ was born in Bethlehem."

"I knew it was somewhere in Pennsylvania."

It was Sunday school during the Christmas season, and the teacher asked the class, "Who came to Bethlehem?"

"The three kings came," said little Margaret.

"The shepherds came," said little Norma.

"The donkey came," said little Grace.

Little Joey raised his hand and said, "Then the stork came."

## BIG MOUTHS

Her mind is always on the tip of her tongue.

She used to look like a siren. Now, she only sounds like one.

He's a man of few words, but he keeps repeating them.

He shoots his mouth off so much, he brushes his teeth with gunpowder.

After everything is said and done, she keeps on talking.

You can read her like a book. Too bad you can't shut her up the same way.

Her mouth is so big, she can whisper in her own ear.

Her vocabulary is limited in words, but what a turnover!

You couldn't get a word in with her even if you folded it in two.

She's an Amazon—big at the mouth.

He's getting a little tired. You can tell because he can hardly keep his mouth open.

Her tongue is her greatest weapon. It should be a secret one.

He not only holds a conversation, he strangles it.

When he says he wants to make a long story short, it's already too late.

Her tongue is so big, she can lick an envelope after it's in the mailbox.

She was sent from heaven just for him. They must like quiet up there.

## BILLIONS

The concept of a billion is too great for most people to understand. Just think of it as the number of times in one afternoon that a father tells his teenage daughter to get off the phone.

Think of a billion as the number of grains of beach sand in a man's wet bathing trunks.

A nervous salesman asked a statistician what the odds are of boarding a plane that has a bomb on it. The man checked the available data and told him, "The odds against you getting on a plane with a bomb are two billion to one."

"I fly a lot," the salesman said. "That doesn't sound very good."

"Well," answered the statistician, "If you really want to be safe, take a bomb with you. The odds are four billion to one against boarding an aircraft with two bombs on it."

A billion is the number of doughnuts eaten by traffic cops at doughnut stands each day.

A billion is the number of foreign cabdrivers during your vacation overseas who have a cousin who'll give you a discount.

A billion is the number of foods your wife found that are made with oat bran.

## BILLS

Some people pay their bills when due, some when overdue, and some never do.

Two men are discussing money, when one of them says, "I always manage to put some money away. I never pay my old debts."

"What about the new ones?"

"I let them get old."

Last night a bill collector came to my house. I gave him a stack about a foot high.

## BINGO

The plane was bouncing up and down in the turbulence. A frightened passenger said to the priest in the next seat, "Do something religious!"

So the priest called a game of bingo.

**A** woman comes home wearing a magnificent mink coat. Her husband asks her where she got it. The woman replies, "I got it playing bingo."

Several days later, the woman returns with beautiful large diamond ring. Again asked where she'd gotten it, she answered, "I got it playing bingo."

A week later, the woman drives home in a brand-new Rolls-Royce. Her husband inquires once more, and she answers, "I got it playing bingo. Now go upstairs and draw my bath."

The woman goes upstairs to find an inch of water in her tub. "I told you to draw my bath. Why only an inch of water?"

The husband replies, "I don't want you to get your bingo card wet!"

## BIRDS

**"I** spent five dollars on a canary."

"That's nothing. Last Saturday I spent fifty on a lark."

**O**ne of our neighbor's kids does bird impressions. He eats worms.

**T**hen there was this canary that was given a sip of whiskey. He ripped two bars out of his cage and chased the cat five blocks.

**A** woodpecker decides to take a long trip. On the second day, he lands on a tree and starts to peck at it. Just then lightning strikes the tree and splits it. The bird says, "Gee, a fellow doesn't know how hard his pecker is until he gets away from home."

**T**here was a male quail. He went off on a lark.

**C**ross an ostrich with a beer, and you get a beer with its head in the ground.

**T**wo pigeons were flying over a parking lot. Looking down, one said, "Hey, let's put a deposit down on that red car."

**T**he minister is explaining how smart his new bird is. "When I pull its right leg," he says, "it sings 'Onward Christian Soldiers.' When I pull its left leg, it sings 'Bringing in the Sheaves.' "

A listener asks, "What happens if you pull both legs?"

The bird says, "Dummy. I fall off my perch."

**T**hen there's the kee kee bird. It lives in the frozen north and has no feathers, so it just keeps flapping its wings and saying, "Kee kee Kee-rist, it's cold."

**T**wo chickens walk by a poultry store and see a roasting turkey in the window. One chicken says, "See where her gorgeous figure got her."

**W**hen turkeys mate, do they think of swans?

**C**ities are strange. New York is trying to get rid of its pigeons, and Las Vegas wants more of them.

A flock of geese is flying south. One goose asks, "Why do we always have to follow the same leader?"

The goose next to him says, "Because he's got the map."

Two eagles see a jet zoom by. One eagle says, "That bird is certainly in a hurry."

The other eagle says, "So would you be if your tail was on fire."

One penguin says to another, "Of course I'm frigid. Isn't everybody?"

A man goes in to buy a canary. He demands the best, saying, "I want a bird who sings like Sinatra, with the range of an opera star, with the tone of a Mario Lanza."

The clerk says, "That'll cost you five thousand dollars."

"If it does what I want, I don't care."

"But you'll also have to buy this other bird too."

"Why the second bird?"

"He's the arranger."

How do pigeons know you just polished your car?

A poultry dealer sends a crate of chickens to a friend in another town. The crate breaks, and the friend has to chase down the chickens. The brood caught, he calls up the poultry dealer and says, "The crate broke, and the chickens scattered all over everybody's yard. I managed to round up ten of them. Thanks."

The poultry dealer says, "Not bad. I only sent you six."

Smiling, the rooster asks the chicken, "How do you want your egg today?"

Two hens are running around the coop, being chased by a cross-eyed rooster. One hen says, "If we don't slow down, he's going to miss both of us."

Birds don't have it that easy. How would you like to pick up all your food with your pecker?

A carnival performer is aboard a train when the conductor asks what's in the wicker basket at his feet. "Pigeons," says the performer.

The performer's plea that they are specially trained pigeons is to no avail. It's against the rules, and the pigeons have to go.

"I hope you're satisfied now," the performer says as he eases the birds out the window. "Your superiors are going to hear about this as soon as we get to Cleveland!"

"Cleveland?" the conductor repeats. "This train goes to Cincinnati."

"Oh no!" the performer exclaims. He leans out the window and yells, "Hey, fellas! Cincinnati. CINCINNATI!"

A spotted owl says to his wife, "What do you mean you have a headache? No wonder we're an endangered species."

A camper has set up his camp in a national park. He's eating a slice from a bird roasting over a small fire he's lit. A Ranger comes by, says hello and then points to the roasting bird. "That's a condor, sir. It's a protected bird and you're not supposed to kill it. You could go to jail for a crime like that."

The camper says, "It was an accident. My gun happened to go off and this bird came crashing down."

"Well, in that case," the Ranger says, "I won't ticket you. But tell me—what does it taste like?"

The camper says, "A little like Spotted Owl."

A friend has a parakeet that won't eat anything but navy beans because he wants to be a Thunderbird.

A mother owl tells her youngster, "How many times must I tell you—it's *whooo* not *whoooom*."

Then there was the guy who taught his bird to talk dirty and was arrested for contributing to the delinquency of a myna.

## BIRTH CONTROL

If a girl doesn't learn how to cross her legs, she'd better learn how to cross her fingers.

There's a new birth control pill for men that's 100 percent perfect. In five years of testing, not one man has become pregnant.

Our neighbors have nine kids, and they practice birth control. They'd better

practice it, because they're not too good at it.

## BIRTHDAYS

By the time she finished lighting the candles on her birthday cake, the first one went out.

He's so old, they didn't bother with candles. They just built a bonfire in the middle of his cake.

You're getting on if the candles on your birthday cake set off the smoke alarm.

This seventy-year-old man married a twenty-year-old girl. For a gift, he gave her a string of pearls. She gave him the mumps.

You're aging if all you want for your birthday is not to be reminded of it.

My wife just got a gold bracelet. She gave it to herself for my birthday.

The best way to remember your wife's birthday is to forget it once.

I always remember my wife's birthday. It's the day after she reminds me.

I like it when he celebrates his birthday in winter. The candles on the cake warm up the house.

Her last birthday cake looked like a prairie fire.

Welcome to my surprise party. Well, it was a surprise until about four weeks ago when I came up with the idea.

A woman well on in years goes to her lawyer to work on her last will and testament. First, she orders that she be cremated. Then, she asks that her ashes be scattered all over the local mall. The lawyer asks, "Why do you want your ashes scattered all over the mall?"

The old lady answers, "That way I'll be sure my daughter comes to see me twice a week."

For his birthday, they gave him a solid gold lighter. He emptied it in one gulp.

They put a candle for each year on my birthday cake. I was glad. It was the only way I could read the writing.

## BLACKS

"What's the difference between a gay and a black man?"

"A black man doesn't have to tell his mother he's black."

"Can a black man ever become president of the United States?"

"Yes, if he runs against a Puerto Rican."

It's hard to understand the anger of blacks and their tendency toward race riots. You bring blacks over here in chains, give them jobs picking cotton and working car washes, and this is the thanks you get.

They finally found proof of black cavemen—they dug up two Cadillacs with four payments due.

A black man is in a graveyard and passes a headstone on which is written, NOT DEAD, JUST ASLEEP.

The black man says to a companion, "He ain't foolin' nobody but hisself."

A black man gets a call at the factory in which he does menial labor. "Are you Alexander Botley?"

"I am."

"Well, this is J. Adams, Jr., lawyer. I wish to tell you that your great-uncle died and left you a million dollars."

" 'Taint so?"

" 'Tis. And I notice that your factory is only five minutes from our offices. If you come over in the next few minutes, you can have your money right away."

About a half hour later, Alexander shows up at the lawyer's with his hand out and ready for his money.

The lawyer says, "How come it took you so long?"

Alexander says, "Well, first I had to stop and beat the stuffin' out of the foreman."

A black man asks his minister about Judgment Day, "Will everybody be in heaven on that glorious day?"

"Yes, brother."

"The Ku Klux Klan?"

"Oh, yes."

"And all the black folks?"

"Certainly."

"Well, the way I see it—there'll be precious little *business* going on there for the first couple of hours."

## BLINDNESS

He can't see a thing. He needs contacts to see his glasses.

Two men are sitting on a park bench. One says, "What do you mean, you can see perfectly? You're blind as a bat!"

The second man says, "Think so? I can see perfectly. See that cat coming? I can see he has one eye."

The first man says, "You are blind. That cat has two eyes. And he's not coming, he's going."

Then there was the blind man who went to a nudist colony. It was a touching sight.

Then there was the blind man who felt a piece of matzoh and said, "Who writes this stuff?"

## BLONDES

"Why do blondes have TGIF written on their shoes?"

"Toes go in first."

"How many blondes does it take to screw in a light bulb?"

"One. She holds it up to the socket, and the world revolves around her."

"What's the mating call of a blonde?"

"I'm sooooo drunnnk."

"What's a blonde standing on her head?"

"A brunette with bad breath."

"Why do blondes like tilted steering wheels?"

"More head room."

"What do you get when a blonde dyes her hair?"

"Artificial intelligence."

"What does a blonde say when you blow in her ear?"

" 'Thanks for the refill.' "

## BOATS

"They just dropped the anchor."

"I knew it. It's been dangling back there all day."

Then there was the little dinghy that committed suicide because it found out its mother was a tramp and its father a ferry.

"Do boats sink often?"

"Only once."

## BODIES

I think his name was Quasimodo. I'm not sure, but I had a hunch.

A little Protestant boy and a little Catholic girl are playing at the edge of a pond. The little girl says, "If I get my shoes and socks wet, my mother will yell."

The boy says, "Mine too."

They take off their shoes and socks.

Seeing some tiny fish farther in the water, the girl says, "I want to catch some fishies. But my mother will get angry if I get my clothes wet."

"Me too," says the boy.

They remove their clothes. As they stand naked, the girl says, "Gee, I never knew there was so much difference between Catholics and Protestants."

"Are you looking at my legs?"

"No, I'm above that."

Famous anchors on the TV news either know somebody or have some body.

She has no hips. It's uncanny.

She has an incredible body. A sculptor has been sculpting her, and he's run out of clay three times.

I saw her in shorts the other day, and she has a great body. She'd be a great companion to travel with, because she certainly can pack her trunks.

"Why do you scratch your face like that?"

"I have to. I'm the only one who knows where it itches."

A ten-year-old kid asks his father, "What's a penis?" The father whips his own out and says, "This is a penis, son. It's a perfect penis."

The next day, the ten-year-old is playing with a friend who asks if he knows what a penis is. The kid whips his out and says, "This is a penis. And if it were three inches shorter, it would be a perfect penis."

Then there was this mentalist's assistant whose heart was breaking. The mentalist didn't care about her body. All he wanted was her mind.

A young man is ashamed of being short. He goes to a physical therapist who literally puts people on a rack and stretches them.

A few weeks later, the young man runs into a friend, who asks, "How's it coming along?"

"I quit after the first week. I was confessing to too many crimes."

## BOOKS

He started out writing dime novels. Now, he gets fifteen cents a book.

I started to read a book last night about adultery, sex, orgies, infidelity. I just had to put the *Congressional Record* down.

"Have you read all of Shakespeare?"

"I think so, unless he's written something lately."

He writes a book a month and thinks nothing of it. Neither do the readers!

"Is your husband a bookworm?"
"No, just an ordinary one."

They just published a sure winner: *The Hypochondriac's Guide to Bad Health.*

In the old days, a hero didn't kiss the girl until the last page. Now, he does it on the cover.

I read his last book, and I say that it's not a book to be taken lightly. It should be thrown with full force.

Reading most books is like making love to your own wife—you want to get it over with as fast as you can without looking at it too much.

My problem is that it takes me six weeks to read the Book of the Month.

Never give a person a book for a gift. He may already have one.

I have hundreds of books, but no bookcase. Nobody'll lend me a bookcase.

I just took *The Joy of Sex* back to the library. I liked it so much, I was two hundred dollars overdue.

I never open a dictionary. Once you've read one, you've read them all!

A review of a new novel ended with: "In case of fire, throw this in."

Then there's the amateur writer who wrote the story of her life. They didn't buy the book, but the editor flew three thousand miles to take her out.

I just finished a book with a sad ending. The heroine dies, and the hero has to go back to his wife.

I must be getting old. I remember when romance novels had asterisks.

Nowadays, if you have nothing nice to say about someone, you can get a book deal.

## BORES

Bores are awful. They always talk about themselves when you want to talk about yourself.

A bore is a guy who, when you ask how he feels, he tells you.

A bore had trapped a man at a cocktail party. Finally, the man says, "Sir, my leg has gone to sleep. May I join it?"

A bore came over to me at a party the other day and said, "I passed by your house the other day."
I said, "Thank you."

A writer was boring various people at a party, talking about his cranking out book after book and article after article. Between nibbles at a canapé, he told a woman nearby, "I just finished writing for *The New Yorker.*"

The woman said, "That's wonderful. I hope they send it to you."

When there's nothing left to say, a bore is still saying it.

He has the gift of gab, but he doesn't know how to wrap it up.

Some people make you feel at home. Others make you wish you were.

The worst thing about a bore is that he won't let you stop listening.

## BORROWING

He doesn't borrow from everybody. You have to be reliable.

A man borrows fifty dollars from a friend, promising on his soul that he'll pay the money back the following week. Comes the following week, and the debt is paid. Some months later, the man is short again and once again borrows fifty. He repays it the following week as promised. Three months go by. Poverty strikes again. The man goes to his friend and says, "Lend me fifty."

The friend says, "Nothing doing. You fooled me twice already."

## BOSSES

It's no fun being a boss. You have to come in early to see who comes in late.

The kid asks his boss for a raise, saying, "My mother told me to ask you."

The boss says, "Okay, let me check with *my* mother to see if I should give it to you."

My boss is so mean, he's got a time clock that punches *you.*

Then there's the meanest boss in town. One of his workers came in early every day for a month. He charged him rent.

Three of my wife's relatives work for me. I have a payroll that just won't quit.

## BOSTON

Two Boston dowagers were talking. One said, "I heard you had face surgery."

The other said, "Only on my nose. It was getting so I could hardly talk through it."

A Bostonian couple drive to California. The hotel clerk asks, "Which way did you come?"

The Bostonian wife says to her husband, "Dear, didn't we go by way of Concord?"

A woman visits some people in an old section of Boston. The Bostonian women are all dressed sedately and wear lovely flowered hats. The woman asks, "Where did you ever get such lovely hats?"

One of the Bostonian women says, "We don't 'get' our hats. We 'have' them."

## BOWLEGGED

**S**he's not exactly bowlegged. It's just that her ankles are well turned up to the knees.

**I**t's not that she's bowlegged. It's just that her knees aren't on speaking terms.

**H**e was so bowlegged, his wife hung him over the door for good luck.

**S**he was so bowlegged, she could get out of both sides of a taxi at the same time!

**S**he had to quit her last job. Her boss was bowlegged, and she kept falling through his lap.

## BOWLING

**I** always wanted to be a bowler in the worst way. And I made it.

**I**t was Friday night, and Rabbi Goldman had sneaked off to the bowling alley to play a few games. On his second game, he scored a perfect three hundred. He looked up to heaven and started to cry: "A perfect game and I can't tell anybody."

**T**hen there was the girl who gave up bowling for sex. She found out the balls were lighter, and she didn't have to wear shoes.

**I**t's not that she's ugly, but she has been stood up more often than a bowling pin.

## BOXING

**I** depended on two things as a fighter— speed and artificial respiration.

**I** was knocked out so often, they sold advertising space on the soles of my shoes.

**I** was a crossword fighter—I came in vertically and left horizontally.

**H**e had a hundred and one fights and won all but a hundred of them.

**T**he other fighter hit me so hard, I was still in the air when they counted me out.

**T**he fight was over so fast, I got a refund on my hot dog.

**H**e wasn't too good a fighter. In his first six bouts, he never got to use his stool!

**H**e had to give up fighting. He wasn't making enough to meet his hospital expenses.

**H**is manager was sentimental. He had his teeth strung into a necklace.

**T**he favored boxer had been paid handsomely to throw this fight. His opponent, secure in a sure win, got a little cocky and threw some real doozies. The favored boxer scoffed, "Just wait till I get you outside, you runt!"

**T**he fight is supposed to be fixed. Mulrooney is supposed to go down after one left hook from Chavez in the second round. Unfortunately, Mulrooney lands one early in the round. Chavez goes down. He's groggy and won't make it too quickly. The referee counts, "One, two, three, four, five, six, seven, eight, nine, ten, jack, queen, king."

A fighter gets instructions in his corner. When he gets hit, he should stay down till eight.

The fighter says, "Okay. What time is it now?"

A club fighter of little talent is hit in the chin ten seconds into the first round of a fight. He falls to the ground. Knowing he's faking it, the referee doesn't stop counting at ten but goes on. At about sixty, the fighter looks up and says, "It doesn't matter how high you count. I'm through for the evening."

The fix was supposed to be in. Tank Farley was supposed to drop in the second round. Tank wanted no part of it. He'd never made it to the second round, and he wasn't going to start this time.

Then there was the bad fighter. The crowd always knew the result of his fights ten seconds before he did.

This one fighter had some reach. Before a bout, he'd shake hands with the opponent without leaving his corner.

## BOYS

Ma, can I help Dad put on the snow chains? I know all the words!

A youngster brags to a friend that he'd seen a sword swallower on television. The friend says, "That's nothing. My father eats light bulbs."

"Aw, come on."

"It's true. I went past the big bedroom and I heard my Dad say, 'Turn out the light and I'll eat it.' "

The school headmaster finds a young boy masturbating and says, "Young man, don't you know what the Bible says? A man shall save it till he marries."

A week later, the headmaster runs into the boy and asks, "How is it going, son?"

The boy says, "Not bad, sir. I already have a quart and a half."

## BOYS & GIRLS

"How about coming up to my room to see my etchings?"

"I'm afraid that the response is categorically in the negative."

"I don't get it."

"That's right."

"If I asked you to be my assistant at fifty thousand a year, would you say yes?"

"Ten times a day, if necessary."

"What do virgins dream of?"

"Beats me."

"Glad to hear that."

## BOY SCOUTS

My wife loves it when I go out nights with the boys. I'm a scoutmaster.

They keep telling him to get lost, but he can't. He's a Boy Scout.

When I was eleven, I tried to join the Boy Scouts, but they turned me down. I was prepared, but they weren't.

If you want to start a fire, better have two sticks and make sure one of them is a match.

Then there was the little old lady. The Boy Scout helped her across the street, and she was hit by a taxi.

## BRAGGING

Admit your faults. I would, if I had any.

He has a head like a doorknob. Anybody can turn it.

My brother-in-law: My brother-in-law finally hit the big time—ten to twenty in San Quentin.

A husband bragged to his wife, "I've taken you safely over the rough spots of married life, haven't I?"
   The wife said, "Yup, I don't think you missed any of them!"

A Texan visits California, picks up a watermelon, and says, "Is that the biggest grapefruit you've got?"
   The Californian nearby says, "Please, sir, you're crushing that raisin."

"Guess how much I've made so far this year?"
   "Half."

## BRAINS

"You have the brain of an idiot."
   "Want it back?"

He's so smart, he could find a way to get a massage from Venus de Milo.

"Do you think a man loves a woman for her mind?"
   "Of course, but her head is the last place he'll look for it."

Ignorance is strange. It picks up confidence as it goes along.

I found a girlfriend with the same name as my wife. That way, if I talk in my sleep, I'm safe.

One kid was very smart. He saved old magazines for years, and when he grew up, he became a dentist.

A man comes home from taking an intelligence test that will be used later in testing new employees. Sighing in relief, he says to his wife, "Thank the good Lord I own the company."

One small town figured out a way to keep cars from speeding across the town. It put up a sign that said NUDIST COLONY HALF-MILE AHEAD.

A smart guy is one who's smarter than he thinks he is.

A young man, seeing a girl he'd like to know, says, "Excuse me, miss. I'm writing a telephone directory. May I have your number?"

## BREASTS

A woman is unhappy about being flat-chested. She tells her husband that she plans to go to a plastic surgeon. The husband says, "Why don't you try this little remedy? Rub some toilet paper on your nipples three or four times a day."

"Will my breasts grow by rubbing on toilet paper?"

"Well, look what it did for your rear end."

A young man was fixated on women's breasts. A shrink said to him, "Maybe free association will help. I'll say a word, and you tell me the first word that comes to mind."

The patient says, "I'll try."

"All right. Orange."

"Breast."

"Nectarine."

"Breast."

"Grape."

"Breast."

"Ping-Pong."

"Breasts."

"How can Ping-Pong bring breasts to mind?"

"That's easy. First this way, then the other way."

She has incredible boobs. When you dance with her, you can't step on her toes.

Her bra is so small, it has to be put on by a jeweler.

This Hollywood actress was beautiful, but unfortunately, her bosom was tiny. To earn rent money, she became a bank teller. Her first day on the job, a robber came and said, "Stick 'em up!"

She went about her work.

The robber repeated his demand: "Stick 'em up!"

The actress said, "If I could stick 'em up, I wouldn't be working in a bank."

The space between her breasts was called Silicon Valley.

Like the Maidenform said to the hat— "You go on a head, and I'll give these two a lift."

She has a new bird-dog bra. It makes pointers out of setters.

One young lady said, "If I didn't have a bosom, I'd have one made."

She was big-busted. In fact, she was six-one—lying on her back.

"What do toys and women's breasts have in common?"

"They were both intended for kids, but it's the dads who keep playing with them."

## BRIBERY

Just before the election, Joe tells Burt that he's going to vote for the Democrats. Burt asks, "How come?"

"Well," Joe says, "The Republicans offered me ten dollars for my vote. The Democrats offered me five. I figure they're not as crooked."

## BRIDES

**S**he's been married so often, she should keep the bouquet and throw the groom away!

"**H**ow do you tell a bride at a Beverly Hills wedding?"
"I don't know."
"She's the one in the maternity gown."

**T**hen there was this bride who ordered a large lettuce salad for her husband because she wanted to see if he ate like a rabbit too.

**A** bride was showing her uncle around the new apartment. In the bedroom, she showed him around and said proudly, "You'll notice that we have twin beds. Harold and I are very shy, and we thought that this arrangement would be better." In the living room, she proudly showed him a magnificent Bible given to her by her parents.

Several weeks went by, and the bride couldn't find the Bible. She looked high and low, and there was no sign of it. Remembering that her uncle was the last to have seen it, she called him and asked, "Uncle, do you have any idea of what could have happened to that new Bible?"

The uncle answered, "Look in Harold's bed."

**S**he's been to the altar so often, she can walk it blindfolded.

**S**he's been to the altar so often, they want her to pay for the carpet.

## BRIDGE

**B**ridge is a great game. It gives women something to do while they're gossiping.

**F**our very deaf old ladies played bridge every Tuesday afternoon. A startled visitor heard the following bidding take place: The first lady bid four spades. "Three hearts," declared the second. "Two diamonds," said the third. "Well," said the fourth, "if nobody else has a bid, I'll try one club."

## BROTHELS

**A** madam, intent on making her place of business unique, arranged to have each of the three floors of the establishment set up with different kinds of young ladies. On the first floor, she had ex-models who were known for their looks and shapes. The second floor was replete with ex-secretaries, efficient and giving. The third floor featured ex-schoolteachers.

After a few weeks, the madam noticed that the third floor was doing the bulk of her business. She asked a customer why that was. He answered, "You know those schoolteachers. If you don't get it right the first time, they make you keep doing it until you get it right."

Leilani goes to the madam and says she's quitting. "Why?" the madam asks. "You're the most popular girl I've got. You seem to love your work. I know for a fact that you go in for any kind of action—whipping, S and M. Just today, you must have gone upstairs with fifty men."

Leilani answers, "That's it—the steps! My feet are killing me."

A brothel is like a circus, except that a circus is a cunning array of stunts.

A businessman goes to a brothel and engages a young lady for a hundred dollars. They have a merry old time, and the young lady is impressed by the gentleman's lovemaking. She offers him a second helping for free. This interlude completed, the girl says, "You are something. Let's make love again. I'll pay you a hundred dollars this time."

The businessman attempts to engage in another interlude, but the body isn't willing. He looks down at his limpness and says, "For spending you're great, but when it comes to making a buck . . ."

Then there was the madam who didn't want the IRS to know how much she earned, so she kept two sets of towels.

A man knocks on the door of an exclusive brothel. Through a small window in the door, the madam says, "What can I do for you, sir?"

"I'd like to get screwed."

"This is a very fancy private club. To join, you must slip a hundred dollars under the door."

The man does so, but the door doesn't open. The madam appears again. The man says, "Hey, I'd like to get screwed."

The madam says, "What, again?"

## BUSINESS

Business is so bad, the bankruptcy court just opened a drive-in window.

Business is pretty bad. A kid recently walked into a store and asked the owner if he had any empty boxes. The owner gave him the cash register.

A man's company needs an infusion of cash, and he's unable to get a bank to help him. When he returns home despondent, his wife says, "Why are you panicky? Look, every time we made love, I put a dollar in a jar. Take that money."

The husband says, "Really? You put a dollar in a jar for each time we had sex? If I'd known you were going to do that, I would have given you all of my business."

# C

## CABS

A man asked a cabdriver to take him to a sporting house. The cab driver took him to a Reebok store.

I finally met a man who didn't know the shortest distance between two points—a cabdriver.

It's kind of wild when you get a lady cabdriver and she asks you how far you want to go.

A cabbie picks up a lady fare who gives him an address that makes him go through a park. In the park, she asks him to stop and says, "I'm really a hooker. My price is fifty dollars."

The cabbie pays her and has himself a merry old time. Finished, he gets back behind the wheel and sits. The hooker says, "Aren't we going?"

The cabbie says, "I'm really a cabbie, and my fare back is fifty dollars."

A cabbie is driving this young couple to an area he doesn't know. After a while, the cabbie asks, "Do I take the next turn?"

A muffled male voice from the back says, "Like hell. Just keep driving."

**A** man walks out into the street and manages to get a taxi just going by. He gets into the taxi, and the cabbie says, "Perfect timing. You're just like Dave."

"Who?"

"Dave Bronson. There's a guy who did everything right. Like my coming along when you needed a cab. It would have happened like that to Dave."

"There are always a few clouds over everybody."

"Not Dave. He was a terrific athlete. He could have gone on the pro tour in tennis. He could golf with the pros. He sang like an opera baritone and danced like a Broadway star."

"He was something, huh?"

"He had a memory like a trap. Could remember everybody's birthday. He knew all about wine, which fork to eat with. He could fix anything. Not like me. I change a fuse, I black out the whole neighborhood."

"No wonder you remember him."

"You would, too, if you'd married his widow."

**I** saw a cab run into a pole the other day. The driver couldn't see it because of the safety stickers.

**A** New York cabbie is great. He'll take you any place he wants to go.

**A** fussy old lady got into a cab in New York. Determined not to let the cabbie pass her stop, she pestered him all the way up Fifth Avenue. Finally, she poked him vigorously with her umbrella as she saw a street sign go by.

"Isn't that Seventy-third Street?" she demanded.

"No, madam," said the enraged driver. "That is my behind!"

**T**he sweet young thing signaled a taxi and said to the driver, "To the maternity hospital, and never mind rushing, I only work there."

**A** fare asked the cabbie, "What's your average tip for a ride?"

"Two dollars."

At the destination, the fare tipped the cabbie two dollars.

The cabbie said, "Thanks, pal, you're the first average I've had today."

## CAJUNS

**T**here's a difference between a Cajun zoo and a regular zoo. The cage poster at a regular zoo gives the animal's common name and scientific name. The poster at a Cajun zoo gives the common name, the scientific name, and the recipe.

**C**ajuns don't spell too well. One paid a hundred dollars and spent the night in a New Orleans warehouse.

"**W**hat do they call a Cajun with an IQ of 6?"

"Mayor."

**T**hen there was this Cajun who didn't know what to do with his penis. It kept getting in the way when he made love.

"**W**hy don't Cajun women buy brooms?"

"They don't come with instructions."

**O**ne Cajun stopped taking his wife out. He heard she was married.

**A** Cajun is very puzzled. He keeps asking people the time, and everybody keeps giving him a different answer.

**T**he defendant in a case tells the judge, "I don't think I can get a fair trial here. The other guy is a Cajun. The jury is made up of Cajuns. How can I win?"

The judge says, "*Mon cher,* you got yourself a problem."

**A** Cajun was shopping, and the storekeeper said, "I'll give you all you want for a dollar."

The Cajun said, "*Bon.* Give me three dollars' worth."

"**W**hat is gross stupidity?"

"A hundred forty-four Cajuns."

"**H**ow does a Cajun counterfeit a dollar bill?"

"He erases the zero from a ten."

**T**his Cajun lost his job as a washroom attendant. He couldn't refill the electric hand dryer.

"**H**ow do you keep a Cajun busy for hours?"

"Give him a pack of M&Ms and tell him to put them in alphabetical order."

"**W**hy does a Cajun scale a glass wall?"

"To see what's on the other side."

**T**he newest drink for Cajuns: Perrier and club soda.

**C**ajuns find it hard to write the number 11. They don't know which number comes first.

## CALIFORNIA

**S**ister Rosalinda is a famous nun. She's spent her life ministering to the poor. To raise funds for her charity in the slums of Calcutta, she comes to California. She spends the whole first day praying silently for the success of her mission. The second day she goes out for a few hours but leaves on her answering machine. When somebody calls, the machine says, "A blessed day to you. May the Lord care for you. This is Sister Rosalinda of the Nuns for the Poor. Please leave a message."

The next day, the answering machine says, "This is Sister Rosalinda. I'm off doing the Lord's work."

The third day, the machine says, "Hi, this is Sister Rosie. I'm not in right now, but . . ."

**T**he weather was great in California. It was shining cats and dogs.

**I**t never rains in California. It's just that the sun drips perspiration.

**I**t's no secret that Californians have been known to brag as much as Texans. This one Californian is showing a visitor around. The visitor remarks, "Oh, look at those pretty grapefruits on that tree."

"The lemons are a little small this year."

A little later, they pass a field of three-foot-high gladioli. The visitor says, "What pretty gladioli."

"The dandelions are a little small this year."

They go on and arrive at a large lake. The visitor says, "Look, somebody's radiator must be leaking."

California has a hundred thousand palms. Six of them are trees, and the rest are on maître d's.

"Is California good for your health?"

"You're joking? When I first came here, I couldn't walk. They had to carry me around. I couldn't feed myself. Now look at me."

"How long have you been here?"

"I was born here."

You get real healthy in California. I have a friend whose weight was ninety pounds. Now, it's 195 and bulging muscles. Almost ruined her life.

There's a real drought in California. One fellow has to haul water to keep his ferryboat going.

"What happens when the smog lifts over the City of Angels?"

"UCLA."

## CANNIBALS

A cannibal returns home and tells his wife, "I just brought home an old friend for dinner."

The wife says, "Good. Put him in the freezer. We'll have him next week."

The head cannibal comes home and asks his wife, "What's for dinner?"

The wife says, "We're having two old maids."

He says, "Damn! Leftovers again!"

Some people are vegetarians, but a cannibal is a humanitarian.

This cannibal sees this lovely young girl being put in the pot. He says, "Stop that. I'd rather have breakfast in bed."

Then there was this crooked crematorium owner who sold the ashes to cannibals as Instant People.

A cannibal tells another, "My wife's not so hot."

The other says, "Boil her longer."

Then there was the hippie cannibal. He ate three squares a day.

One cannibal says, "My wife made a wonderful pot roast. And I'm going to miss her."

Two cannibal women are discussing their lives. One says, "I don't know what to make of my husband."

The other says, "Get a recipe book."

Then there was this cannibal who went to a shrink because he was fed up with people.

A man believes that he's a cannibal, so his wife convinces him to go to a psychiatrist. He returns home later, and his wife asks, "How was the psychiatrist?"

The man answers, "Delicious."

"I don't care for your friend."

"So just eat the vegetables."

A cannibal came home late one night, and his wife gave him a cold shoulder.

Two cannibals are talking. One says, "Did you see the dentist today?"

The other said, "Yeah, he filled my teeth at dinnertime."

I know of a cannibal who ate his mother-in-law, and she *still* disagreed with him.

Like the cannibal said to his son, "You are who you eat."

Then there was the cannibal who ordered a pizza with everybody on it.

The cannibal complains to the witch doctor, "I have terrible heartburn."

"What did you eat?"

"Just a couple of missionaries with hooded robes."

"How did you cook them?"

"I boiled them."

"No wonder you have heartburn. Those aren't boilers. They're friars."

Then there was this cannibal chief who was bragging about his daughter, saying, "I love every bone in her nose."

A man was shipwrecked and captured by cannibals. Each day one would take a dagger and puncture one of his veins, and some of the natives would drink his blood.

Finally, one day he said to the chief, "Look, I don't care if you eat me, but I hate to get stuck for the drinks all the time."

Then there're the cannibals who are flying to the United States. They saw a headline in a paper that said, FBI GRILLS SUSPECT.

"What happened when the young cannibal ate his whole class?"

"He passed the second grade."

The ultimate test of courage is two cannibals having oral sex.

Two women cannibals were discussing their marriage troubles.

"My husband has gotten so out of hand. I don't know what I'll do."

"Oh, don't worry," the other said, "I've got a great recipe I'll send you!"

Then there are the Catholic cannibals. On Fridays they only eat fishermen.

A cannibal is showing his new freezer to a member of the tribe.

"How much can it hold?" the member asks.

"A lot, but right now it only has the two guys who delivered it."

## CARDS

He's so got so many cards up his sleeves, he sends his suits out to be shuffled.

She was so ugly, the men wanted to play dress poker with her.

A cowboy who started the evening drinking and ended up playing cards is walking home. Over his shoulder is a saddle, but for the life of him, he can't recall if he lost a horse or won the saddle.

Two men are discussing their marriages as they sit at a bar. Talking about the weekly poker game, Phil says, "I always feel weird when I play late. I drive up as quietly as I can, I take off my shoes, I tiptoe into the house. But when I get upstairs, my wife jumps up and gives me hell."

Al says, "Wrong moves. I drive in and gun the engine in the garage. I bang the door when I walk into the house. When I walk upstairs, I sing at the top of my lungs. My wife thinks I'm loaded, and she pretends to be asleep."

"Let's play a friendly game of cards."

"No, let's play bridge."

I have a bridge date tonight, but I think it's the Golden Gate.

If looks could kill, an awful lot of people would die with bridge cards in their hand.

It's no sin to play bridge, but it's a crime the way most people play it.

A good bridge player is playing with a terrible partner. After an awful series of plays, the good player can't hold back and says, "When did you learn to play? And don't say—'This afternoon'. Exactly *what* time this afternoon?"

Strip poker is a strange game. The more you lose, the more you have to show for it.

A bridge game was in progress. One of the players had just butchered a hand. Shrugging his shoulders, he asked his partner, "How would you have played that hand?"

The partner replies, "Under an assumed name."

## CAREERS

The class is taking up careers. One youngster says proudly that his father is a bus driver. Another says that his father is a mailman. The third, Eddie Green, says, "My dad is a towel boy in a whorehouse."

The teacher is chagrined. She sends for Mr. Green and explains what Eddie had said. "Even if it's true, you shouldn't tell a child that you work in a whorehouse."

"It isn't true," Mr. Green says. "I'm really a lawyer, but you can't tell your kid that."

## CARS

The best time to buy a used car is when it's new.

I do use a little oil. Every time I go to a service station, Exxon goes up five points.

I bought so many extras for my car, I had to rent a trailer to keep them in.

My car couldn't go over twenty if it was spring and another car was chasing it.

My car has shock absorbers—me and the passengers.

My tires wouldn't be bad if I could teach my car to tiptoe.

My car works by push button. If the buttons don't work, I push.

I get good mileage. Three service stations to the gallon.

My car is very unusual. It has four headlights, two radiators, and the motor is in the back. It wasn't always like that. Only since the accident.

My car was filthy. I washed it, and it went from midsize to compact.

I just bought a new car and got a rebate check. The car is smooth, but the check keeps bouncing.

I just installed a car phone, but it's a pain in the neck having to run to the garage every time it rings.

I won't say my car is "used": The last time I drove up to a toll booth and the guard said, "Two-fifty," I said, "Sold!"

Owning a car wouldn't be bad except for two things—parts and labor.

The other day I saw a weird thing at a garage. The mechanic was wiping his hand on a rag when there was a brand-new seat cover in front of him!

The engine on my car sounded like maracas, so I went back to the dealer and asked him what I should do. He said, "Play 'The Girl from Ipanema'!"

After my last car checkup the mechanic told me, "Keep the oil and change the car."

She drives a convertible—everybody talks about how she got it.

My wife had a logical reason for banging up the car. She said, "Why have bumpers if you don't use them?"

I bought a fancy Japanese car. It's so fancy that before I can get in, I have to take off my shoes.

They just recalled 12 million Fords. So if you plan to cross the street, now's a good time to do it.

Some guy is going to make a fortune by inventing a windshield wiper that won't hold parking tickets.

They say that an Indy 500 pit crew can get the tires off a car in forty seconds. If they think that's fast, they've never been in Manhattan.

Cars have done a great deal for morality. They've completely stopped horse-stealing.

A young man went to a used-car dealer and asked to see a beat-up old jalopy. The salesman said, "Wouldn't you rather see a new model?"

The boy answered, "Oh, no. With a jalopy, my folks won't know whose fault the dents are."

The loudspeaker in the restaurant spoke up: "Will the owner of the red convertible with the beige fenders and the satin seat covers please go to the parking lot. There's no problem. The attendant only wants to see what you look like!"

Nowadays, you can get oil for your car just by going to the beach.

My new car is a collector's item—it was made entirely in America.

My car has an unlimited warranty on parts that don't break down.

She always says that I pay more attention to the car than I do to her. So the other day I decided to put her before the car. But she wouldn't stand there.

Some of those subcompacts present problems. Nowadays, when you want to be safe, you look left, right, and down.

You can always tell a good car company. They sell more cars than they recall.

If you think nobody cares, try missing a couple of car payments.

Sports cars are something. Most people who can afford them can't get into them.

I just read that Detroit can put a car together in seven minutes. I think I got one.

So far I've paid off three cars—my doctor's, my dentist's, and my shrink's.

My car is a religious experience. Every morning I pray that it starts.

Do you want to know how desirable your old car is? Just check out the prices of the new ones.

The way my wife drives, I wish they'd make a car with fenders on the inside.

My car comes with a lot of options—I have the option of pushing it, dragging it . . .

For an auto mechanic, hell is a pound of grease on each hand and no leather upholstery to wipe them on!

Cars are getting so high, one dealer has a showroom and a recovery room.

I get about five miles to a gallon. My son gets the other twenty.

I have a great car. It gets me exactly where I'm going—to the bank to pay the loan.

My car is a real lemon. It comes with a combination warranty and will.

I brought my car in for a checkup, and the mechanic told me, "Let me put it this way. If your car was a horse, I'd have to shoot it."

One fellow recently came up with a great excuse for stealing a car. He said, "I found it in front of the cemetery, and I thought the owner was dead."

My car has very low mileage. I drive it only when I can get it started.

I used to have a very small car, but last week it was stolen—by a pickpocket.

I saw an ad the other day. It was for a 1915 Stanley Steamer. The buyer just had to take over the payments.

I just got rid of my car phone. My phone bill was so high, I couldn't buy gas.

This woman brought her car into the mechanic. He told her, "You have a short circuit."

The woman said, "I don't care what it costs. Lengthen it."

I have an old car. It even has bifocal headlights.

Travel by car today is almost impossible. In New York, a man started to get on the Whitestone Bridge, and a cop stopped him. The man asked, "Was I doing something wrong?"

The cop answered, "No, I just wanted to know if you had a reservation."

The trouble with the bucket seats on the new cars is that not everybody has the same size bucket.

The good news is that every American family will soon have two cars. The bad news is that one'll be a Honda and the other a Toyota.

These gas-efficient cars kill romance. It takes too long to run out of gas.

Did you ever notice that cars always break down on the way home from work—never when you're on the way to.

"You keep your car so nice and clean."

"It's only fair. The car keeps me clean too."

I suffer from car sickness—every time I have to make a payment.

"Did you save anything for a rainy day?"

"Yup—washing my car."

"I just bought a set of balloon tires."

"I didn't know you had a balloon."

It's called a revolutionary car. I think George Washington bought the first one.

They've just come out with a new Japanese sports car. It has a low-cut grille, shapely fenders, long, sleek lines, and padded bumpers. They brought one to town, and three Chevies chased it into an alley.

Would the gent who owns the convertible with the cowhide covers please go to the parking lot? A bull is attacking your backseat.

A man takes his friend for a drive and says proudly, "Would you ever believe that I bought this secondhand?"

The friend says, "No. I thought you made it yourself."

A couple go to buy a used car. They find a nice car with only a thousand miles on it. The salesman swears it was driven only twice in two years by a little old lady. The couple get the name of the little old lady and call her. Is it true she drove the car only twice? And did it only have a thousand miles on it in two years?

The little old lady says, "It's true. I drove it twice in the Indy Five Hundred, that's all."

The loudest noise in the world is the first rattle in your new car.

I won't say I had a small car, but the glove compartment could only hold two fingers and a thumb.

My mechanic gave me a great report. He told me that my battery needs a new car.

I just bought a new car, and it's for the birds. At least they think so.

My car has very low mileage on it, and most of that was when it was being towed.

I just bought a new subcompact. They threw in a carrying case for nothing.

A friend of mine has two complaints about his car: The motor won't start, and the payments won't stop.

I bought a car the other day. With what the city charges, I can't afford the bus.

I saw a guy at the one-minute car wash the other day. He tipped the crew so they'd hurry it up.

I have a great car mechanic. I keep going back to him week after week.

The British just came out with a sub-subcompact. It's so small, the windshield is a monocle.

Dad says to his son, "Can I use the car tonight? I'm taking your mother to dinner, and I want to impress her."

## CATHOLICS

Mary found the man of her dreams. Unfortunately, he wasn't a Catholic. Mary's father forbid a marriage unless the young man converted. The young man, therefore, started to attend classes. Six months later, Mary came home shattered. Her father was aghast. "Your young man's stopped taking instruction, has he?"

Mary said, "No, but this afternoon he decided to become a priest!"

Catholics have really modernized. They now have a drive-in confessional. It's called Toot 'n Tell.

"Do you think the pope will ever allow priests to marry, Father Piero?"

"I don't know, Father Tomaso. Maybe in our children's lifetime."

## CATS

"What do you call a cat after he's four days old?"

"Five days old."

A tomcat is brought home after being altered. He sits around the house moping. Two other cats watch him sadly, and one says, "I think he misses himself."

They say that curiosity killed the cat. What the heck does a cat want to know?

Two kittens were watching a tennis game. One said, "My dad's in that racket."

A cat may have nine lives, but a bullfrog croaks every night.

Then there was this gambling cat. He put everything into the kitty.

A tomcat was heard running up and down the alley for hours. A neighbor called his owner and asked what was happening.

The owner said, "Well, I had him fixed today, and he's going around canceling all his engagements."

This rather inconsiderate gent has his tomcat fixed and tells his friend about it. The friend says, "I'll bet he just hangs around the house, eating and sleeping."

The inconsiderate gent says, "No, he still goes out every night, but now he's just a consultant."

A cat is an animal that never cries over spilled milk.

"Who sleeps with cats?"

"Mrs. Katz."

Gorman offers a thousand-dollar reward for the return of his wife's cat. Bronson says, "That's a pretty big reward for a cat."

Gorman answers, "Not after I drowned it."

Cats are a puzzlement. You never know how they're going to ignore you.

## CAUTION

They're a very cautious couple. They'll never fly in the same plane. In a department store, they won't even ride the same escalator.

A new executive is in a meeting with his boss. The boss tells about a new plan he has for the coming year and wants to know the new executive's feelings. Did he like the project?

The new executive said, "Look, you hired me because I shoot straight from the hip. You're paying me a fortune because I don't hedge. I give it to you straight. No hedging, no beating around the bush. Do I like the project? I do and I don't."

## CAVEMEN

A caveman is sitting around when another caveman rushes over. "A saber-toothed tiger is chasing your mother-in-law!"

The first caveman says, "What do I care what happens to a saber-toothed tiger?"

A young caveboy is drawing pictures of critters. His sister comes in and says, "Mom is going kill you for drawing on the walls!"

Times are changing. When a man gets mad at his wife now, he goes to his club. In the old days, he just reached for it.

Then there was the brilliant caveman. He was about fifteen thousand years ahead of his time.

## CHANGING TIMES

Remember when you got a real kick out of finding a quarter in the pocket of an old jacket?

Remember when a Saturday Night Special was a double banana split?

## CHARITY

If you make love to a married woman, that's faith. If you make love to a fiancée, that's hope. Make love to an old maid, that's charity.

He's very charitable. He donated $100,000 to a halfway house for girls who won't go all the way. He also donated $200,000 to a place for one girl who did.

I know of one charity that collected $3 million, and now they're going out in search of a disease.

A bum is standing outside of a fancy hotel when people who've just come from a fancy charity ball are emerging. The bum stops a woman and asks her for a few pennies. The woman says, "What is wrong with you? I just came from a fancy ball for the poor. I spent two thousand dollars for a dress, four hundred to have my hair done and nails polished, six hundred for shoes, the tickets for the affair cost fifteen hundred dollars . . . how dare you ask me for money after I've spent so much on you!"

I just gave a big contribution to a chain of homes for unwed mothers to be called "All-the-way houses."

Klein and Steiner met on the street. Klein was carrying two paper bags, and Steiner inquired about them. Klein explained, "I'm collecting for charity." Indicating a large knife he had in his pocket, he went on, "I see a restaurant, I go into the bathroom, and I tell the men there, 'Give me money or I use this knife.' So in this bag I have all the money I collect."

Steiner asked, "What's in the other bag?"

Klein answered, "Not everybody gives."

A young man was applying for a job as policeman. The interviewer asked, "How would you disperse a crowd?"

The applicant said, "I'd pass my hat."

Last week they had an odd occurrence. A car dealer raffled off a church.

I think men are more generous than women. The other day, a bum asked me for something. I was extremely generous. And so was she.

A stranger in town meets an attractive woman. He asks her if she'd join him for dinner. She'd be more than glad to, but she says, "I won't let you pay. We share."

## CHEAP

There's an old story about getting seven years' hard luck for breaking a mirror. He feels the same way about a buck.

One cheapskate called up a hooker and asked her what night she was free.

He got on a bus that had a sign, PAY WHEN YOU LEAVE. He's still riding.

He's very cheap. He feels miserable because he took out Blue Cross and didn't get sick.

He'd remarry his wife so he wouldn't have to pay any more alimony.

He looked for a wife who was born on February 29. That way he'd only have to buy her a birthday gift every four years.

He reaches for a check like it's a subpoena.

When he gives a check to charity, he doesn't sign it. He says he wants to keep his contribution anonymous.

He's tighter than the top olive in a jar.

He's so cheap, he'd shop for a discount artificial heart.

He's so cheap, the city has to repossess his garbage.

He's so cheap, his hearing aid is on a party line.

He's so cheap, he goes to the drugstore and buys one Kleenex.

He's so cheap, he takes off his glasses when he's not looking at anything.

If he'd been at the Last Supper, he would have asked for separate checks.

He's so cheap, he told his kids Santa doesn't make house calls anymore.

He's so cheap, he'll ride the subway during rush hour just to get his clothes pressed.

He tosses money around like a boomerang.

He'd marry a skinny girl so he could get a smaller ring.

He's so cheap that in his will he named himself as beneficiary.

But after all, a cheapskate is only a man of rare gifts.

I know a guy who's so cheap, he's waiting for the Bible to come out in paperback.

If he was hit by a liquor truck, it would be the first time the drinks were on him.

He bought his kid a dollhouse with a second mortgage on it.

He's carefree. He doesn't care as long as it's free.

He keeps divorcing his wives if they're ugly. It's cheaper than sending them to a beauty parlor.

He thinks nothing is too good for her, and that's what he keeps giving her—nothing.

This cheapskate puts on a mask, gets a gun, and goes in to rob a fancy men's store. He demands that the clerk bring him the most expensive suit in the establishment. The clerk brings him a magnificent black silk suit. The cheapie says, "How much is that suit?"

The clerk says, "Two thousand dollars."

The cheapie says, "Don't you have something a little cheaper?"

A cheapskate doesn't care how he's treated as long as he is.

The only thing he ever put on a bar was his elbows.

He throws money around like manhole covers.

This has to be the cheapest family of all time. One of them leaves to seek his fortune in another country. Twenty years later, he returns, and he sees that his brothers have beards just about down to the floor. He asks, "Why all this hair?"

One of his brothers says, "You took the razor with you."

He's so cheap, he won't even give his wife an argument.

A woman goes into a store and asks for a pair of cheap shoes.

The clerk asks, "To go with what?"

She answers, "A cheap husband."

The other day somebody broke into my brother's car. They put in a better radio.

He's so cheap, he won't even tip his hat.

He's so cheap, he recycles his belly button lint.

He came home and said to his wife, "Honey, you wouldn't want to go to the opening of that new Broadway show in that old gown of yours, would you?"

His wife said, "Of course not."

He said, "Great. That's why I only bought one ticket!"

He's cheap. He doesn't get a haircut every four weeks, he just gets his ears lowered.

He's a real cheapskate. He just bought his wife a fifty-piece dinner set—a box of toothpicks.

Money goes through his fingers like glue.

She wanted a foreign convertible, so he bought her a ricksha.

He takes the Bible literally. That's why they won't rent him a hotel room.

He doesn't care any more for money than he does for his right arm.

He's tighter than an elephant in a phone booth.

She kept complaining that her coat was too short, so he told her not to worry. It would be long enough before he got her another one.

He buys thermometers in the winter because they're lower then.

He's so tight, he saves money by eating his heart out.

He's so tight, when he winks, his kneecaps move.

He's the kind of guy who hates a nickel because it isn't a dime.

He gives no quarter. For that matter, he doesn't tip dimes either.

He's a charitable soul. When the Home for the Aged came to him for a donation, he gave—he gave them his father and mother.

He's so cheap, he once hypnotized his wife into thinking she was a canary so she'd eat birdseed.

He's a two-fisted spender. Both of them closed.

He's so cheap, he takes his kids to the airport, puts them on the luggage carousel, and tells them to play Valise.

He throws money around like a man without arms.

He borrows so much, his will is made out to the small-claims court.

He's so cheap—in his guest room he has a pay smoke alarm.

He saw an ad where coffins were on sale at half price. He tried to commit suicide.

He's so cheap—he's worn his suit so long, it's been in style six times.

He's so cheap—after he has dinner in a restaurant, he doesn't leave a tip. His wife helps clear the table.

He's so cheap—he puts soap flakes in his pockets and walks through a car wash once a week.

He's so cheap—his kid wanted a gum ball, so he told him the machine doesn't take credit cards.

He's not as cheap as people think. When he married, he and his wife honeymooned at a welfare hotel, but they took the bridal suite.

I'll give you an idea of how cheap he is. Last week, he and his wife went to the mall with the baby. His wife went in to shop, and when she got out, she looked and said, "It's not our baby in this carriage."

He said, "I know, but these wheels are better."

He's so cheap—he got married in his own backyard so the chickens could have the rice.

He's cheap—he got his wife pregnant so they could fly family plan.

He's so cheap—he eats everything in sight at a restaurant. By the time he finished dinner the last time, the ownership had changed place three times.

He always remembers the poor. It doesn't cost him anything.

He's so cheap he thinks "No Tipping" is one of the Ten Commandments.

He's real cheap. A few days ago he bought some secondhand shirts. He changed his name to fit the monogram.

When they got married, she didn't have a rag on her back. Now, that's all she's got.

A woman goes to a doctor. He examines her and charges her a hundred dollars. She says, "Can't you make it eighty?"

The woman comes for another visit, and it costs a hundred and forty. She asks, "Can't you make it a hundred and twenty?"

The doctor agrees and says, "Okay, come for your next appointment Tuesday at eleven."

The woman says, "Can't you make it ten-thirty?"

He's real cheap. When he finishes a cigarette, he has to wipe the ashes off his teeth.

I didn't know how cheap he was until one day I borrowed a vise from him. It had toothpaste on it.

He's so tight, he doesn't even breathe all the air he needs.

He's real cheap. When he was building his home, he called up the Masonic Lodge and asked them to send over a free mason.

### CHEATING

Two men meet. One of them has a shiner that covers half his face. The second man asks what happened. The first man says, "You know that cute lady who works as a checker at the supermarket?"

"You mean the one whose husband is overseas?"

"Well, he ain't."

A soldier at the front found a small but potent land mine and went to the post office to mail it home. The package was turned down. "Anyway," he was asked, "Why would you want a land mine?"

The soldier said, "Well, I'm suspicious about how my wife has been handling herself. So when I get home, I want to put this land mine at the back door of the house, then I'm going to run around, ring the doorbell, yell, 'Honey, I'm home,' and I'm going to sit down and wait for this big explosion."

"Is your wife entertaining?"

"Every time I go out of town."

Then there was the exterminator who came home and found a louse in his closet.

A man is telling his friend about some escapades, saying, "I feel so bad—I've been cheating on my wife."

"How many times?"

"How should I know? I'm a lover, not an accountant."

A woman runs into a friend and says, "I hear you caught your husband cheating, and you had a terrible fight."

The woman says, "Not exactly. It's true we had a fight, and I stabbed him three times, but that's as far as it went."

A man finds a naked man under his wife's bed and asks angrily, "What the hell are you doing down there?"

The naked man says, "I'm trying to kill a rat."

The man says, "From the looks of it, you're trying to screw it to death!"

Some men were sitting around, discussing marriage. One said that most men loved their wives and remained faithful. Another insisted that men loved to cheat. A third cut in, "I've never cheated."

The second asked, "How long have you been married?"

"Three days."

The men laughed and soon went their separate ways.

Some time later, one of the men went home and at the dinner table told his wife of the conversation. The wife looked at him sternly and points to the hat rack, saying, "Very funny. And where's your new hat?"

A man comes home to find his wife in the arms of his best friend. Upset, the man says to his friend, "Al, I have to, but you?"

One gal told her friend, "I don't mind his cheating, but I can't sleep three in a bed."

"Doctor, my son has herpes, and he told me today that he got it from the maid."

"Well, you know kids today."

"You don't understand. I've fooled around with the maid too. And worse still, I make love to my wife also."

"That's terrible. Now I'm going to get it!"

Maria Stone tells her friend Ann, "I'm having an affair with a man. He's stupid, slovenly, unkempt, and cheap as all hell, but I adore him."

Later that day when Ann's husband comes home from work, she accosts him at the door: "Are you having an affair with Maria Stone?"

I never found a stranger in my wife's closet. Just close friends.

When I first met my wife, she wasn't very social. In fact, she didn't start dating until after we were married.

A man returns home early and finds his wife in bed with a man. He pulls a pistol from a dresser drawer and is about to shoot when the wife says, "Don't. Who do you think gave us this house? And the car? And the silver service?"

The pistol comes down, and the husband says, "Cover him with a blanket. He might catch cold."

A man told his friend, "My girlfriend is such a cheat and a liar. I've been going with her for a year, and I never knew she was married until yesterday when my wife told me."

Two businessmen meet on a commuter train, and one says, "How's the wife?"

The other one says, "Fine. And how's mine?"

He finds his wife entertaining—every time he comes home.

A lot of couples break up because it looks like the marriage is going to last forever.

He looked at the woman he loved and said, "I'm sick. I saw you with another man yesterday."

She says, "Don't be silly. It was only my husband. You know there's nobody but you."

On the midnight-to-eight shift, Officer Brown managed to get off early one night and went home. He undressed and tried to get into bed without waking his wife, but she turned and said, "Honey, I have a terrible headache. Please run down to the all-night drugstore on the next block and get me some aspirin."

A nice husband, Brown got dressed in the dark, went to the drugstore, and asked for some aspirin. The clerk nodded, started to bag the purchase, and said, "I'm a little curious, Officer Brown, why are you wearing a fireman's uniform?"

Show me a man who kisses with his eyes open, and I'll show you a man who wants to make sure his wife isn't around to catch him.

A couple go out and have a wild time at a party. In the morning, the husband asks, "Was that you I made love to on top of the coats?"

The wife says, "About what time?"

A man is running through the street in his shorts. A jogger asks, "What are you in training for?"

The man says, "Who's training? Her husband came home early."

A man tells a friend, "My wife and I are incompatible, although I never actually caught her at it."

You know she's cheating when you move to another state and you still have the same plumber.

Guns don't kill people. Husbands who come home early kill people.

A man walks over to a lovely and well-endowed young lady at a party and asks, "Excuse me, but can I interest you in breaking up my marriage?"

A woman goes into a gun shop and asks for a pistol for her husband. The shopkeeper says, "Did your husband tell you the kind he wanted?" The woman says, "Oh, no, he doesn't even know I'm going to shoot him."

A wife berates her husband for cheating. He answers, "Hold on there. Don't I give you a great home? Don't I buy you cars? Don't I pay all your bills? I only use the others for lovemaking."

A woman runs into her husband's mistress and says, "My husband has told me so little about you."

A man returns home to find his wife in bed with another man. He rushes for his gun and starts to aim, when the man jumps up and says, "Don't shoot. Do you want to kill the father of your children?"

**T**wo friends meet. Joe looks very sad. Tom says, "What's bothering you?"

"I don't want to talk about it."

"Come on, what's up?"

"You want the truth? I've been fooling around with your wife, and I just found out she's cheating on both of us."

**A** lot of married men get a mistress just to break up the monogamy.

**A** minister announced from his pulpit, "There is a certain man among us today who is cheating with another man's wife. Unless he puts five dollars in the collection plate, his name will be read from the pulpit!"

When the collection plate came in, there were nineteen $5 bills and one $2 bill with a note attached: "Other three on payday."

**A** woman comes home and finds a young woman in bed with her husband. The wife demands an explanation. The husband tells her, "It's like this. I was driving home from work. I saw this young woman trying to get a hitch. Her clothes were torn. She had no shoes. She was freezing. I remembered that you had a lot of stuff you don't wear anymore, so I brought her home. I gave her that old dress over on the chair and those red shoes you hate and that little topcoat. Then she said to me, "Is there anything else your missus doesn't use?""

**A** man and a woman are in a restaurant having a great old time when suddenly the man slides from his chair down under the table. The maître d' rushes over and says, "Your husband just slid under the table."

"No," the woman says, "My husband just came into the restaurant."

**C**heating is two wrong people doing the right thing.

## CHIC & CLASSY

**A** woman found herself in a public toilet, but to her chagrin there was no paper on the roll. The woman called into the next booth, "Do you have any tissue paper?"

"No."

"Do you have any newspaper?"

"Sorry."

"Well, do you have two fives for a ten?"

**M**rs. Feldman tells her husband, Arnold, "Listen, Margie is bringing her new beau for dinner. For the love of heaven, use some table manners. Don't eat with your fingers or your knife."

Dinner comes, and Arnold is afraid to eat anything for fear of looking uncouth. Finally, the coffee is served. Arnold pours it into his saucer and says, "One word out of any of you and I'll make bubbles."

**I**t must be terrible to wake up and realize that all these years you've been eating with the wrong fingers.

He has class. He always takes off his shoes before he puts his feet on the table.

Chic is knowing which fingers to put in your mouth when you whistle for the waiter.

"I hope I haven't come too late."

"Oh, no. You couldn't come too late."

The guest asked, "Why does your dog keep staring at me?"

"I guess," the boy of the house answered, "it's because you're eating from his plate."

It's chic to hold the car door open for your wife, but not if you're going sixty at the time.

When a man holds the door open for his wife, it's either a new wife or a new car.

## CHICAGO

In Chicago on Election Day, it's no problem to get a man out to vote. The problem's in trying to get him to stop.

They discovered that half the prison guards in Chicago have prison records. That's good. When they get out, they don't have far to travel to get a job.

A New Yorker is bragging about how the Big Apple is the fastest place in the world. Its pace is incredible. "Why," he says, "on my way to work one morning, I saw them laying the foundation for a twenty-story building. By the time I headed home, it was finished."

The Chicagoan says, "That's cute, but not fast. Let me tell you about my Windy City. I went to work at seven in the morning, and they were laying the foundation for a sixty-story building. When I started home at four—"

The New Yorker cut in, "Don't tell me the building was finished."

"Finished, nothing. They were putting out tenants for nonpayment of rent."

They have a very smart police dog in Chicago. He can sit up and beg for graft.

## CHICKENS

The farmer brings a capon home to share his chicken coop. Later in the day, the family dog goes to the coop and asks through the wire meshing how things are going on. One of the chickens says, "Not too good. That darn capon keeps us from working. He does nothing but talk about his operation."

A rooster pushes an ostrich egg into the coop and says to the hens, "Look, I'm not telling you what to do, I'm just showing you what can be done."

We have the laziest rooster. In the morning, he waits for another rooster to crow, and then he nods his head.

A woman wrote the Department of Agriculture asking for advice on her chickens, who seemed to be suffering from a strange ailment. *Every morning for the past month,* she wrote, *I have discovered three or four of my hens lying on their backs with their feet in the air. What's the cause of this?*

A few days later she received a telegram. YOUR HENS, it read, ARE DEAD.

How about the chicken who sat on the ax? She was trying to hatchet.

## CHILDREN

Stop crime at its source. Join Planned Parenthood!

Strike your kid every day. If you don't know why, he does!

A minister was explaining the facts of life to his small son. The boy listened, entranced, as the minister explained about the birds and bees. Finally, the boy gasped. "Does God know about this?" he asked.

Some children learn a lot at their mother's knee, especially when they're bent over it!

A woman boarded a bus with nine children in tow. The conductor asked their ages, and the woman said, "Those three are ten, these are eight, and the last three are four."

The conductor said, "Do you always get three every time?"

The woman said, "Oh, no. Sometimes we don't get any at all."

Children are a great comfort in your old age, and they can help you get there faster too.

I wasn't too bright as a child. I used to sneak behind the barn and do nothing.

His folks weren't too thrilled with him. They used to wrap his lunch in a road map!

Little Timmy enjoyed nothing more than sucking his thumb. It tasted better than food. To break him of the habit, as he was almost six, his mother told him, "If you keep sucking on your thumb, your stomach will blow up. It'll become so big, you'll burst."

A few days later, it was his mother's turn to host the bridge club. The last to arrive was Mrs. Bronson, who was about eight months pregnant. Timmy looked at her and said, "I know what you've been doing."

A woman just had her fourteenth child and ran out of names—to call her husband.

Little Alvin is saying his prayers: "Dear Lord, bless us all. And please make the big kid on the next block stop hitting me. By the way, I've mentioned this to you before."

Eight-year-old Tommy comes home one day with a terrible report card and tells his father, "Mrs. Swanson, the teacher, is always picking on me." Naturally, Dad shows up at school the next day and berates the teacher, telling the teacher that he knows his son is smart. Smiling, Mrs. Swanson says, "Tommy, how much is four and four?" Tommy says, "See, Dad, she's always picking on me."

One eight-year-old boy has misbehaved and is grounded with no TV, no dinner. He has to go to his room. As he says his prayers a little later, he offers, "Dear Lord, please don't send Mommy and Daddy any more kids. They don't know how to treat the one they got."

One kid summed it up: A granny is an old lady who keeps your folks from beating you up.

Little Thelma came back from her first soccer game. Her father asked how it went. Thelma said, "Okay, but I wish the other team would learn how to share."

I want my kids to have everything I didn't have. So I'm moving in with them.

This mother tells her son to go play with his friends. The boy says, "I only have one friend, and I hate him."

Two little girls are looking at a picture of Mary and Jesus. One says, "Where's his daddy?"

The other says, "I think he's taking the picture."

What I like about modern times is the way parents obey their children.

A census-taker is greeted by cute little six-year-old Mary, who explains that her father, the doctor, isn't home. "He's performing an appendectomy."

"That's a big word for a tiny girl," the census-taker says. "Do you know what it means?"

Mary answers, "Five hundred bucks, and that doesn't include the anesthesiologist."

A mother says, "Son, we are in this world to help others."

The son says, "All right, but what are the others here for?"

Little Johnny asks his mother where children come from, and she says, "The doctor brings them."

Satisfied, Johnny goes out to play with his friend Willy. As they play, two beautiful little girls walk by. Willy asks, "Who are they?"

Johnny says, "They're the doctor's kids. He always keeps the best ones for himself."

A mother was lecturing her son on behaving properly and said, "My darling, you must live each day as if it were your last."

The kid said, "I tried that last week, and you grounded me."

If you ever feel like having a kid, go to a restaurant and sit next to one.

A child asks his mother, "Do all fairy tales begin with 'Once upon a time'?"

The mother says, "No, dear. Once in a while they begin with 'I'll be working late at the office tonight.' "

"Does Daddy tell you fairy tales like that?"

"He used to."

"What made him stop?"

"One day he told me he'd be working late, and I said, 'Can I depend on that?' "

## CHINA

Puzzled by an item on the menu in a Chinese restaurant, a customer asked the waiter to explain it—chicken fried-rice ding. The waiter said, "We take the different ingredients and put them in the microwave oven."

The customer asked, "What's the ding for?"

The waiter answered, "That's the timer."

Chinese Jews must have a hard time. What can they go out and eat?

The Chinese are sending us a lot of beer. It doesn't get you drunk, but after two bottles you get the urge to get undressed and iron your clothes.

I went to one Chinese restaurant where the food was real bad. In your fortune cookie, they had a get-well card.

Lying in bed, the lights out, a Chinese man says to his wife, "I want to have sixty-nine. I must have sixty-nine."

The wife says, "Go to hell. At this hour I'm not going to make beef and broccoli."

Why is a Chinese fortune cookie written in English?

I've always wanted to get a fortune in a fortune cookie that read, *Disregard previous cookie.*

The Chinese laundries of old are gone. The problem was that two hours after they cleaned your shirt, it was dirty again.

I got a fortune cookie the other day that said, *You will meet a beautiful dark-haired girl. She will smile at you. You will give her money. It'll be our cashier.*

A businessman hires a young Chinese fellow to be in charge of supplies for the company. At the end of a week, however, all of the section hands complain about a shortage of material. The businessman goes to the warehouse to find out why things aren't moving. As he walks in, the young Chinese jumps up from behind a crate and yells, "Supplies!!"

An optimist is a Chinese who stays up all night to see how the election came out.

"What do you call two thousand pounds of Chinese soup?"

"Won ton."

There's a meeting of the Central Committee, and Ling Po says, "We are supposed to be an advanced nation. Where are our automobiles? Where are our computers? Where are our VCRs? Where are our refrigerators?" Nobody responds.

A few weeks later, there is another meeting of the Central Committee, and Dao Chin says, "Where is Ling Po?"

## CHOICES

Just remember, a pretty girl can do anything, but an ugly girl has to do everything.

My neighbor's daughter told us, "My boyfriend and I are having a little disagreement. I want a big church wedding, and he wants to call off the engagement."

A woman doesn't know what kind of man she doesn't want until she marries him.

His wife says he's very versatile. He can do anything wrong.

One woman advised other women, "There's so little difference between husbands, you might as well keep the first."

A man walked into a bar and asked for a drink. The bartender said, "Sorry, sir. This is Election Day. We're closed."

The man said, "Sir, you're forcing me to vote sober."

The trouble with taking a middle-of-the-road position is that you can get run over from either direction.

Of two evils, pick the one you enjoy the most.

Two men sit in a fancy restaurant and discuss their preferences. One says, "I'd like to be out at the racetrack—betting horses and drinking juleps."

The second says, "I'd like to be reading a book and sipping wine."

Their black waiter smiles and says, "Have either of you gents ever tried women and watermelon?"

Why do service stations lock the rest rooms and keep the cash register unlocked?

Two men watch a new girl at the nudist colony. She's amply endowed, and one of the men says to the other, "Isn't she something? How would you like to see that in a sweater?"

When the horse is dead, get off.

Prisoner 924598 was given the right to go to Sunday services and could pick any chapel of his choice. When the other prisoners marched in to the different services, 924598 kept walking. He started to head out the gate, but a guard stopped him: "Where are you going?" Number 924598 said, "The Vatican."

Peebles went to the doctor, who examined him and said, "You're in awful shape."

"What should I do?"

"Go home and tell your wife to start cooking better meals for you. Let her worry about the family finances. Let her watch over and discipline the children. Let her stop nagging at you and forcing you to do things you don't want to do. If you don't make these changes, you'll be dead in three months."

"Look, could you do me a favor, Doctor? You call her and tell her what has to happen. When she hears it from you, it'll mean more."

"Of course."

Fred returned home in about an hour. As he walked into the house, his wife said, "I just spoke to the doctor. He says you have three months to live."

The trouble with politics is that it's too complicated. You can't sidestep one issue without stepping on another one.

## CHRISTMAS

The spirit of Christmas lives in Las Vegas. When a kid tells a department store Santa what he wants for Christmas, Santa gives him the odds on getting it.

Last Christmas I told Santa what I wanted, and he said, "Me too."

My kids get so many battery-operated toys during Christmas, they think the holiday celebrates the birth of Duracell!

My nephew got a soldier combat outfit, two guns, and a toy mortar. They were all wrapped in paper that said—Peace on Earth!

I gave my young nephew a book for Christmas. He's spent six months looking for where to put the batteries.

My wife loves to watch my kids with their stockings. It's the only time they ever hang anything up.

Santa has it real great. He has the addresses of all the bad little girls.

"Did you see Santa come down the chimney in the middle of the night, Johnny?"

"No, but I heard what he said when he stubbed his toe on the couch."

My family gave me a thoughtful gift: a calendar to remind me when the payments are due!

Some stores close early before Christmas so they can take all the stuff they've reduced for the holiday and mark it down.

I told my wife that the eggnog needed something alcoholic, so she threw in her father!

Christmas is the time of year kids get toys their fathers can play with.

Santa Claus must be a hippie. He never shaves and works one day a year.

Wanna bet the first Christmas card you get is from somebody you missed?

There are a lot of names for Santa . . . there's Kris Kringle, Saint Nicholas, Mastercharge.

Christmas is the season when you buy this year's presents with next year's money.

It's always better to give than to receive. Then you don't have to bother exchanging it.

Things aren't so good at the North Pole. The other day, Mrs. Claus said to Santa, "Big deal. Everybody you take care of—me you forget!"

For a Christmas gift, my kids always give a bottle of English Leather. It smells like my wallet.

My kids love to get money for Christmas because it's always the right size.

The holidays have become so commercialized. I heard a man reciting the great Christmas poem: " 'Twas the night before Christmas, and all through the house, not a creature was stirring . . . because they had a Cuisinart."

In the mall, Santa said to one kid, "And what can I bring you for Christmas?"
    The kid said, "Nothing, I'll use my credit cards."

The store Santa said to the little girl, "And what would you like for Christmas?" The little girl said, "Didn't you get my fax?"

I've been shopping all week, but I still can't find that one precious thing I'm looking for—a parking space.

Anybody who doesn't think Christmas lasts all year doesn't have charge accounts.

Two six-year-old kids were discussing the Christmas holiday. One said, "There's really no Santa Claus. It's just your parents." The other kid answered, "There must be a Santa. My parents couldn't afford to buy me all that junk."

My brother-in-law was disappointed last Christmas. I asked him if he wanted a large check or a small check. He didn't know I meant ties.

Santa keeps saying, "Ho-ho-ho." I'd laugh too if I only had to work one day a year.

I took my grandson shopping for Christmas. At the first place, he sat down on Santa's knee and mentioned what he wanted. We went to another store. Again he sat down on Santa's knee. When asked what he wanted, he told Santa, "I want a bike and a baseball glove." In the third store, he sat on Santa's knee, and Santa asked, "What do you want, little boy?" My grandson said, "I told you to write it down."

Do you think it's the thought that counts? Try sending someone a Christmas gift C.O.D.

My wife gave me a beautiful smoking jacket for Christmas. It took me an hour and a half to put it out.

Think of it this way—your Christmas presents of today are the garage sales of tomorrow.

My son swore he was going to give me something priceless for Christmas. He proved it—he didn't give me anything.

Last Christmas somebody gave me a bed warmer. But my wife wouldn't let me keep her.

I remember Christmas years ago, and the fat man who came around. He repossessed our car.

Alex, age ten, says to his father, "Who did you say gave me my bike?" His father says, "Santa."

"Well, could you get in touch with him and tell him some guy called today, and the last payment is overdue."

Every Christmas is described as the greatest ever. I always thought the first one was.

One department store had two Santas during Christmas—one was an express line for kids who wanted nine toys or less.

One chap came up with the perfect Christmas stratagem. He called up the secretaries of his friends and business associates and asked if their employers liked gold jewelry. The secretaries reported the inquiry to their bosses, who decided that a fancy gift was in order for the chap who'd called. Christmas came, and each of the people got a bottle of cheap wine, but it was addressed, *To a guy who has good taste in jewelry.*

I gave my wife the perfect Christmas gift—something she could exchange for what she really wanted.

Why does Christmas always come when the stores are so crowded?

One Christmas, they didn't get the catalogs out in time. Wisconsin was stuck with 15 million pounds of cheese.

Mother asks little Edward, "What would you like for Christmas?"

Little Eddie says, "I'd like a baby brother."

Mother smiles at him, kisses him on the cheek, and says, "I'm afraid there aren't enough shopping days left."

A wino staggered over to a depiction of the Crucifixion on Christmas Day and said, "Smile, boobie, it's your birthday."

The neighbors asked Santa for one thing—to bust my kid's drum set.

Christmas is one time you get homesick even when you're home.

They're planning to modernize the Christmas story. From now on, the three kings will bring gift certificates.

Three stages of man: He believes in Santa Claus; he does not believe in Santa Claus; he *is* Santa Claus.

Last Christmas, my son gave me something I've wanted for a long time—my car.

## CHURCH

A lady rushes toward the church door and says to the usher, "Is mass out?"

The usher says, "No, but your hat's on crooked."

The new reverend was waxing eloquent about purity, and ended by saying, "If there is a virgin in the congregation, let her stand." There was no response until in the back a young lady with a baby in her arms stood up.

The reverend said, "Didn't you hear the question?"

"I did," the young woman answered, "but the baby's only three weeks old. You don't expect her to stand by herself, do you?"

Pastor Johnson was noted for his long-winded sermons. One day he substituted for Pastor Brown at another church. Only ten parishioners showed up, and Pastor Johnson was disappointed. "Was the parish told I'd be here?" he asked the sexton.

The sexton answered, "No, but word must have slipped out."

You have to get to church pretty early to get a seat in the back row.

This minister is sermonizing on heaven and hell. His voice is monotonous, and one of the parishioners falls asleep. When the minister asks who in the congregation wants to go to heaven, all stand but the sleeping man. The minister then asks, "Who here wants to go to hell?"

The sleeping man comes to life and stands up. Then he says, "I don't know what we're voting on, preacher, but it looks like you and me are the only ones for it."

A newcomer to town is looking for a church to start attending. He drops in at the Fourth Street Church just in time to hear the minister say, "We have left undone the many things we should have done, and we have done many of the things we shouldn't have done."

The newcomer smiles and says to himself, "I found my group."

Carter never wore his hearing aid to church. This one week, the minister announced that there'd be three different collections for different causes. The first time the collection plate came round, Carter dropped in a quarter. The second time, a little puzzled, he dropped in a second quarter. When the collection plate came around again, Carter turned to the man in the next pew and said,

"What are they going to do next—frisk us?"

"Did you see that hat Mary wore to church?" one woman said to her husband.

"No," he said.

"Did you see that dress Louise had on?"

Again he replied, "No."

She shook her head. "A lot of good it does you to go to church!"

The Sunday school teacher is talking about the value of making things grow. She says, "Do you realize that even Father Adam was a gardener until Eve came along?"

Little Alex jumps in: "She sure cost him his job though."

The parishioners have nothing but praise for the new minister. You can tell when the collection plate is passed around.

This minister feels that the church atmosphere is a little too stodgy. He has a snack bar built, a jukebox put into the social hall, and pictures of famous music stars on one of the walls. At dances, he looks the other way when the youngsters dance close. Then one day the place turns into a morgue. Not one youngster shows up. The same happens the next day, and the next. Very puzzled, the minister checks around and finds that the parents won't let the kids go there because it's not a fit place for good religious children.

The church was holding a raffle to help with the building fund. Peterson wins third prize—a VCR with remote control. The second prize is won by Thompson, who comes to the stage to get his prize and is handed a box of cookies by the master of ceremonies. Thompson looks at them and says, "What is this—cookies for second prize?"

The master of ceremonies says, "They were baked by the minister's wife."

"Screw the minister's wife!"

"Ah, that's the first prize."

## CIGARETTES

My doctor told me to smoke only after sex. Now, I'm up to three packs a day.

A street bum passed another one, who was puffing away on a cigar. The street bum said, "I didn't know you smoked."

The other said, "Oh, it's just something I picked up."

Some people really miss smoking in restaurants. The other night I saw somebody trying to light a waiter.

A man is bragging that he smokes ten packs of cigarettes every day.

His friend asks, "Do you save the coupons?"

The man answers, "Where do you think I got this artificial heart?"

I gave up smoking because I was told it would help me get my taste back. So I found out what a bad cook my wife was!

An account executive with a cigarette-company client looks all over the country for a person who's been smoking for years but is still in fine health. One day he runs into an eighty-year-old man who smokes five packs of cigarettes a day. The executive asks, "Would you like to appear in a commercial?"

The man says, "Sure, but you'll have to shoot in the afternoon."

"Why?"

"Well, I don't stop coughing till two-thirty."

It takes a lot of willpower, but I've finally given up trying to quit smoking.

A man sees another leaning against the wall of a large building. The second man is puffing away, one cigarette after another. The nonsmoker says, "Sir, I couldn't help noticing how you chain-smoke. How many packs do you smoke a day?"

"Four."

"How long have you been smoking?"

"Thirty years."

"That's over six thousand packs. If you didn't smoke, you could have saved enough money to buy this building."

The smoker takes a deep puff and says, "Do you smoke?"

"Never."

"Do you own this building?"

"No."

"Well, I do."

You feel sorry you're a smoker when you're being chased by a mugger who isn't.

I have a friend who got a hoarse throat from cigarettes—not from smoking them, but asking for them.

Aunt Millie's been smoking for years, and her nephew says to her, "Did you ever think of what'll happen when you go to heaven and Saint Peter smells that ugly tobacco on your breath?"

"Nephew, when I go to heaven, I plan to leave my breath behind."

I owe an awful lot to cigarettes. Nowadays, I can puff on cigarettes, cigars, my pipe, and the stairs.

## CIRCUS

The two-headed man wanted a pay increase. After all, he had two mouths to feed.

Because of the many exciting acts at the circus, the elephant seems to have lost his glamour. His trainer is threatened with dismissal if he can't perk up the act. The trainer comes up with an idea. After building a booth on the midway, he offers a reward of ten thousand dollars to anyone who can get the elephant to lift all four of his heavy legs at one time.

Many people try but fail. One afternoon an old man takes on the challenge. Armed with a thick board through which protrudes a giant sharp nail, he whacks the elephant on the rump. The elephant jumps ten feet in the air. The old man collects his prize.

A few days later, the trainer has a second brilliant idea. Because of their muscular development, elephants can raise and lower their heads as if nodding. They are unable, however, to move them from side to side. Another reward is offered for anyone who can make the elephant shake his head.

Hundreds of people try and fail. Lo and behold, the old man shows up again, the board and nail in his hand. Then he asks the elephant, "Do you remember me?"

The elephant nods.

The old man goes on, "Would you like another shot in the ass with this board?"

Slowly, the elephant starts to shake his head from side to side.

There was a terrible mishap at the circus yesterday. The lion tamer needed a tamer lion.

An acrobat is a guy who goes around with a chap on his shoulder.

One day a man followed the bearded lady around. He must have been her five-o'clock shadow.

Being two-headed has some advantages. You can check your own cavities.

Being two-headed can be helpful. You can always tell if you have bad breath.

A roustabout was asked to look for a runaway lion. His friend said, "Do you want a shot of whiskey first?"

The roustabout said, "No, thank you. It gives me too much courage."

The lions in the circus act were real fierce. When the trainer walked into the cage with a chair, he didn't even get a chance to sit down.

A hillbilly goes to the circus and wanders down the midway. Seeing a poster advertising a knife-throwing act, he goes to the small tent where the act is to work, plunks down his money, and enters the tent. After a few minutes, there is a fanfare of recorded music, and the act appears. A beautiful girl stands erect against a wooden wall. The thrower takes aim, and zoom, his knife cuts through the air and lands an inch from the girl's head.

The hillbilly jumps up, saying, "I want my money back. He missed 'er."

The circus season was a dismal failure, so the owner calls over the whole troupe and says, "I don't have enough money to pay everybody, so I can only pay three of you: Joe the Bonecrusher, Phil the Strong Man, and Ben the Knife Thrower."

He was a real strong man. He lifted an elephant with one finger. But it took him twenty years to find an elephant with one finger.

A group of kids stood outside the circus, eager to get in but without any money. They begged the ticket-taker to let them sneak in. He sternly refused. Seeing this, a kindly old man put his hand in his pocket and said to the ticket-taker, "Count them as they go in."

One by one, the boys marched in. When the last one had disappeared into the audience, the old man said, "How many were there?"

The ticket-taker said, "Twelve."

The old man said, "Shucks, I guessed wrong again." And he walked off.

Then there was the contortionist. He made an *S* of himself.

He has a good job with the circus. He gets shot out of a cannon, fifty dollars a day and mileage.

A beautiful new recruit for the local circus asks the ringmaster, "I don't want to make the usual beginner's mistakes. Can you give me a few helpful hints?"

"Well, for one thing," the ringmaster says, "don't ever undress around the bearded lady."

A man applies for a job as a high-wire act with the circus. To demonstrate his skill, the man goes to the highest point of the tent and does a dozen twists and turns with one hand. The owner shakes his head. Too ordinary an act. The man blindfolds himself, ties his legs together, and does two dozen twists and a fifty-foot fall. The owner shakes his head again. Finally, the man opens a case he has with him, takes out a violin, climbs to the highest part of the tent, blindfolds himself, ties his legs together and, as he does his acrobatics with one hand, plays a classical selection. He returns to the owner and asks if he can have the job

now. The owner says, "Itzhak Perlman you're not."

The performer went to the owner of the circus and asked for a job, saying, "I do a sensational act. I catch knives between my teeth."

The owner said, "I don't believe it."

"No? I suppose you think I'm smiling."

How about the guy who got a job at the circus as the human cannonball? He was hired and fired the same night.

She said if I were half a man, I'd take her to the circus. If I were half a man, I'd be *in* the circus.

## CLEANING

I found a great new weed killer, but it stains the carpets!

The other day she cleaned her closet, and she found things she hadn't seen in ages—her vacuum cleaner, her iron. . . .

My wife and I do the dishes 50–50—I dry them and she sweeps them up.

No doubt you've heard of sunken living rooms. We have an elevated living room. My wife sweeps everything under the carpet.

## CLOCKS

When the clock strikes thirteen, it's time to get a new clock.

It's terrible. Every time I ask what time it is, I get a different answer.

A clock is something that wakes people who don't have kids.

## CLOSINGS (FOR SPEECHES)

Please drive carefully on the way home, because I'm walking.

I leave you with this hope: As you slide down the banister of life, may the splinters never point the wrong way.

As the Irish say: "Here's a long life to you, and may you get to heaven a half hour before the Devil finds out you're dead."

It's been a thrill to have participated in this evening's frivolities, and I wish you'd ask me again soon—like 2009!

## CLOTHES

A woman tries on an extremely low-cut gown. Worried, she asks the salesgirl, "Do you think it's a little too much?"
  "Do you have hair on your chest?"
  "No."
  "Then it's too much."

The husband says, "Honey, you look just like you looked the day we got married twenty years ago."
  The wife says, "Why shouldn't I? It's the same dress."

I won my wife on a quiz show. She wore a white dress, and I thought she was a refrigerator.

A manufacturer of hats found and married the girl of his dreams. Returning from his honeymoon, he told some friends, "I've never been so happy. I'm on Cloud Seven and an eighth."

Two young men are walking down Fifth Avenue. One says, "Look at that gorgeous redhead in that green suit."
  They walk on, and the young man says, "Wow! Take a gander at that blonde in those red slacks."
  They walk on, and the young man says, "Holy cow! Feast your eyes on that tall brunette in the—"
  The second young man says, "Is that all you do—just think of clothes?"

I surprised my wife with a mink coat. She'd never seen me in one.

A man walked into a clothing store and said, "I hear that my son has owed you for a suit for three years."
  The clerk said, "Did you come to take care of his account?"
  The man said, "No. I'd like to buy a suit on the same terms."

If a man can't see why a woman wears a strapless gown, she shouldn't.

My new suit is nice, isn't it? And so reasonable too—only two payments and one change of address.

How come clothes that are tight get tighter in the wash? And those that are loose get looser?

She was so embarrassed. She found out that the backless, frontless, topless gown she bought was a belt.

A smart man hides his money in clothes that need mending.

He has a suit for every day of the year and this is it.

A sure way to keep your wife from buying an outfit: When she tries it on, say, "I love that middle-aged look it gives you."

A man walks into a clothing store and orders a suit at the lowest price he can bargain for. A week later, he comes in for a fitting. The suit looks terrible. He yells, "This isn't a good fit."

The clothier says, "What do you want for that money—epilepsy?"

"Has the laundry made a mistake?" a man asks his wife. "This shirt is so tight, I can't breathe! It can't be my shirt!"

"Oh, it's your shirt," the wife says. "But you've got your head through a buttonhole."

Poor Victor Dabney. He can't wear monogrammed shirts.

After all, a girdle is only a device to keep an unfortunate condition from spreading.

A young man started working in his father's clothing store. One day he went to his father with a question: "A customer wants to know if those nonshrinking all-wool shirts will shrink?"

"Does it fit him?" the father asked.

"No, it's too big," his son said.

"Well," the father said. "Then it'll shrink."

## COLD

It gets a little cool in Minnesota. Last year I was there in December. I was cold in places I didn't even know I had.

It was cold this winter. It was the only time my frigid wife had an excuse.

It was real cold last winter. The termites didn't even have to chew. They just let their teeth chatter and leaned forward.

It was so cold the other day, I sneezed once and broke my Kleenex.

It was so cold the other day, Superman froze his *S* off.

It was cold in our neck of the woods last winter. Instead of storks, *penguins* were bringing babies.

It's been real cold. Yesterday I looked in my closet, and my coat was wearing a sweater.

It gets cold in these parts. If you look under my bed, you'll see some of last year's snow.

It's been freezing here, but I don't mind. I look great in blue.

It was so cold, flashers were walking down the street only describing themselves.

## COLLEGE

In Biology 101, the professor was explaining the spawning habits of fish, concluding, "The female fish deposits her eggs, the male comes along, fertilizes them, and then the little fish hatch."

One young coed raised her hand. "Do you mean to say that the male and female don't get together? I mean, nothing happens between them?"

The professor said, "That's right. And it also explains the expression 'Poor fish.' "

My nephew is taking so long to go through college, he's got ivy growing up his leg.

One young college girl got a letter in school. She deserved it because she made the team.

Some youngsters can't understand why they have to go to college for four years in order to be unemployed.

My nephew wants to quit college, but it's the only place he can sleep.

A student tells her friend, "I hear the faculty is trying to stop necking in school."

The friend says, "Gee, I hope they try to make the students stop too."

A university is a place with several thousand in the classes and fifty thousand in the stands.

An alumnus, visiting his alma mater, decided to take a look at the room he'd lived in while a student. Knocking on the door, he heard a voice from inside say, "Come in."

The alumnus walked into the room. Seeing no one, he figured that the present occupant was in the bathroom. Waiting, he looked around. The room was unchanged. He mused, "Same old bed, same old desk, same chair, same closet." Then he heard some shuffling noise in the closet. He opened the door to find the occupant of the room huddled up with a young lady. The young man explained, "This is my sister."

"Same old story," said the alumnus.

Two professors were talking about an undergraduate ballplayer. One said to the other, "That kid is great. He can do everything with a basketball but sign it!"

He was a two-letter man in college. On Monday and Friday, he wrote home for money.

He graduated from an agricultural college. In fact, he was chosen as the one most likely to sack seed.

The president of our college was John Smith, B.A., M.S., Ph.D. What a weird way to spell Smith.

The professor admonished his class, saying, "You'll have to study very hard because the final exams are in the hands of the printer. Any questions?"

One student asked about the specific subjects to be covered. Another asked if there'd be a lot of essay questions, but smart-ass Sam raised his hand and asked, "Who's the printer?"

Two fathers meet. One says, "My son just got his first job after college."

The second asked, "When did he graduate?"

"About fifteen years ago."

Junior wrote home from school begging for a food package, saying, "All they have around here is breakfast, lunch and dinner!"

My daughter came home from college last week with a little bundle in her arms. I was thrilled, because it was laundry.

It was one of those very proper colleges. All they gave a football player was room, board, and sixteen hundred dollars a week toward books.

My son, the college man, writes me, *Dear Dad, Please send me a check so I'll know you're all right.*

My son just got out of college, and not a dollar too soon.

My daughter started out as a psych major. Then she changed to English lit. After that she decided to try pre-law.

That was followed by international affairs, and now she's in philosophy. She may never get a degree, but she's a whiz at Trivial Pursuit.

A professor is somebody who talks while others sleep.

My kid is playing football in college. It's very difficult to have to write to him every few weeks for money.

My nephew was thrown out of college for cheating—with the dean's wife.

If I'm studying when you come back, please wake me.

Every time I go to class reunions, I find my classmates are so fat and bald they don't even know me.

The snow had fallen for hours and covered the whole area. The intercom said to the class, "Will those of you who parked on University Drive move your cars so the snowplows can get to work."

About ten minutes later, the intercom sounded again: "Will the two-hundred-fifty students who left to move six cars please return to class."

A college professor is talking to a group of coeds in a biology class and says, "Ask yourself: Is an hour of pleasure worth a lifetime of shame?"

One coed raises her hand and asks, "How do you make it last an hour?"

Two coeds are sneaking into the dorm at four in the morning. One says, "I feel like a burglar."

The other says, "Don't be stupid. Where can you get one this time of night?"

A professor was about to test his class and gave the students a clue, saying, "This first question is intended make you think."

A student yelled out, "Trick question!"

My son is going through college tossing a coin. If it comes up heads, he goes for a beer. If it comes up tails, he goes on a date. If it stands on edge, he cracks a book.

My son just made his first dollar since college. He sold the watch we gave him for graduation.

My son is having finals tomorrow. He's out now buying his books.

Peterson visits his son in college and knocks on the door of the youngster's dorm. "Does Tommy Peterson live here?"

A voice from beyond the door says, "Yeah. Bring him in."

My son has had a lot of trouble deciding on a career, but he's finally narrowed it down to two choices: genetic engineer or waiter.

My son has taken ten math courses, and all he knows is that the shortest distance between two points—is my car.

My nephew made a deal with his parents. He asked them to give him the money it would cost to send him to college. They did, and he retired.

The girls in Professor Albertson's class resent the way he keeps introducing sexual innuendo in his lectures. They agree to walk out the next time he says anything sexual.

The next day in class, Professor Albertson is discussing India and can't help but introduce sexually explicit material. "Indian men," he mentions, "are notorious lovers. Some of them are able to maintain an erection for days." With this, the girls jump up and start to march out of the room. The professor says, "Don't rush. The next plane to Calcutta isn't until tomorrow morning."

Margie comes home from college and tells her mother, "I'm pregnant."

"Who's the father?"

"Who knows? You told me not to go steady."

"How many basketball players does it take to change a light bulb?"

"One, but he gets three credits for it."

Couple applying for extension of son's student loan: "We had his board and tuition figured out right, but we didn't count on bail."

"What do college kids consider a balanced diet?"

"A beer in each hand."

## COMEDY

A comedian's wife has a baby. The new father meets a friend the next day. The friend says, "I see your wife has a better delivery than you."

He's so bad—even if he was playing the zoo, he couldn't have them eating out of his hand.

I worked at the biggest nightclub in town for months, but then they put in paper towels.

A comedian died and found himself in a room glowing with a pure white light. In walked a spirit in a magnficent robe who said, "We've checked out your life, and you deserve to have this."

The spirit handed the comedian some sheets on which were written the best jokes of all time. The comedian said, "I must be in heaven."

The spirit said, "Think so? Try to find an audience."

One comedy club was supposed to feature a sick comic, but he called in well.

## COMMUNISM

Under capitalism, man exploits man. Under communism, it's exactly the opposite.

Until recently, in Russia free speech wasn't dead—only the speakers were.

A communist is somebody who has nothing and is willing to share it with you.

A woman manages to avoid being hit by a Moscow car and says, "Thank the Lord."

A KGB agent stops her and says, "You shouldn't talk like that. You should say, 'Thank the Communist party'."

The woman says, "But what happens if the party disappears?"

The agent says, "*Then* you can say, 'Thank the Lord'."

## COMPLAINTS

This husband is a born crab. No matter what his wife does, he complains, especially at breakfast. If she poaches the eggs, he wants scrambled. Scrambled, he wants poached. Finally, the wife gives him breakfast with one egg poached and the other scrambled. The husband says, "You poached the wrong one."

A husband complained to his wife, "You always find fault with me. No matter what I do, you pick on me. I'm going nuts. I'll bet you that you can't go one minute without finding something wrong."

"You have a bet," the wife said.

A few seconds later, the wife blurted out, "It's freezing in here. I told you to fix the thermostat!"

The husband said, "Ah! I knew you couldn't last a minute."

The wife asked, "How long did I last?"

"About ten seconds."

"Ten seconds, my foot! I told you never to buy a cheap foreign watch."

A woman runs into a friend who asks how things are going. The woman says, "I'd complain, but how long would you listen?"

God has been good to you. God has been good to me. But He's been better to you than He's been to me.

## COMPUTERS

Our computer is really part of the office now. Last week it won the football pool.

A young man went into a dating service, and the clerk put his data in the computer. He was 6'1", handsome, had fifty oil wells and $10 million. On the way out, the computer mugged him.

They've just come up with computers that respond to the human voice. Now if they could only get telephone operators to do it.

My computer is just like a human. When it makes a mistake, it blames another computer.

We have fewer office parties nowadays. Who wants to kiss a computer?

The computer works faster than a human because it doesn't have to do its nails.

A computer salesman sold a computer to a customer who called him two days later. His computer wouldn't work. To assuage him, the salesmen went over to his house, bringing along a pamphlet, *1001 Things to Do with a Computer.*

After showing the customer the ins and outs, he started to leave. The customer called after him, "If I can't get this thing to work, I've got a thousand-and-second suggestion for you."

There's a benefit to computers. They keep everybody's hands up where they can be seen.

The newest kind of computer came out the other day. Somebody asked it, "What will the U.S.A. be like in 2020?"

The answer came back in Japanese.

A computer can do more work faster than a person because it doesn't have to answer the phone.

The information is put into the computer: Mary, the secretary, drinks and fools around. It looks as if she'll have to be fired.

The computer asks, "WHY?"

I had a terrible day at work. My computer broke down, and I had to think all day.

Nowadays, if a kid does a bad report, he has to bring a note from his computer.

Two computers got married and had a baby. The first word it said was "Data."

The Cubans came up with a brilliant computer. It defected to Miami.

Then there was the stockbroker who went to jail. His computer turned state's evidence.

For twenty years, the scientists slave over formulas and charts and build a giant computer. It stands six feet tall and has a hard drive that can hold a zillion bytes. It is programmed with all the knowledge and systems we know about. To celebrate its completion, the scientists gather and ask it, "Is there a God?"

The computer answers, "There is now."

They've just come up with a computer that does the work of a hundred men. They say it can even think. If it does the work of a hundred men, it can't.

Why do computers become obsolete the day before you learn how to use them?

A kid complained to his father, "Sure, arithmetic is easy for you. You figure in your head. I have to use a computer."

I knew it would happen. Our company computers are talking union.

I'm so glad we have a six-year-old in the house. We needed somebody who understands computers.

The computer really went wild at the company office party. He got zonked and tried to undo the printer's ribbon.

## CONCEITED

He's so conceited—when he turns away from his mirror, he thinks he's cheating!

He'd be broke if he had to pay taxes on what he thinks he's worth.

This guy plays Post Office by himself.

He's slightly conceited—he believes that if he'd never been born, people would want to know why.

He's really conceited—he joined the navy so the world could see him.

## CONFIDENCE

In a urinal, don't flatter yourself. Stand closer.

Confidence is a way of telling yourself that you can make it big. The IRS is a way of saying—Wanna bet?

## CONFUSION

Anybody who isn't confused doesn't know what's going on.

A Washington hostess throws a party for a visiting sheikh from the Middle East. The food is rich and makes the sheikh thirsty, so he is constantly sending his vizier out to bring him water.

On the tenth trip, the vizier returns without water. The sheikh demands to know why. The vizier explains, "Try to get water. But other guest is sitting on water hole in bathroom."

He comes from a very confused family. During the Civil War, his family fought for the East.

## CONGRESS

I wonder what congressmen do for a living!

God could never have enjoyed being a congressman. He'd have to rest on the first, second, fifth, and seventh day!

A congressman is a man who doesn't know where he's going, and he wants us to follow him.

Some pork-barrel bills are so blatantly stealing, some of the congressmen vote with a stocking on their heads!

On many issues, Congress is of one mind—five hundred congressmen and one mind.

Congressmen have stopped passing the buck. Now, they keep it.

Congress loves to adjourn and go home. I can't understand it. If I was my congressman, I'd be afraid to go home.

My congressman just changed his mind about a big issue, but only, he swears, after a big struggle. It was a fixed fight, I think.

They ran him for Congress. It got him out of town.

A candidate for reelection to Congress was firing off about his opponents when he was interrupted by "The only reason you're in politics is you're too lazy to get a decent job!"

"What do you do for a living?" the congressman challenged.

"I'm a garbageman, and it's a better job than my father had."

"What'd your father do?" the congressman asked.

The man said firmly, "He was a cheap politician!"

"What's the opposite of progress?"
"Congress."

Two congressmen came to yelling in a heated argument. One said, "You talk about the Constitution! Why, I'll bet you twenty-five dollars you can't recite the first words of the Preamble!"

"That so?" the other replied. Without hesitation, he began, "I pledge allegiance to the United States . . ."

The other congressman didn't give him a chance to finish. He said, "I didn't think you'd know it," and handed over the twenty-five dollars.

A new congressman, no matter how smart he is back home, is a babe in the woods his first year on Capitol Hill. One House member put it like this: "You feel like the young sheikh whose father has just given him a thousand concubines on his coming of age. 'It's not that I don't know what to do . . . I just don't know where to begin.' "

It doesn't take long for congressmen to size up a newcomer as a liberal, moderate, or conservative. Said of one new member: "He's so conservative, he doesn't even burn the candle at one end."

"A man should always vote with his conscience," the older congressman said. "Problem is, two thirds of the House didn't bring one with them when they were elected!"

An older congressman offered to the newcomer, "If you have the facts on your side, hammer them into your colleagues. If you don't have the facts on your side, hammer the hell out of your desk!"

A hooker decides to run for Congress. After making a few speeches, she suddenly starts to yearn for the old life. Puzzled, she tells her campaign manager, "How do you like this? I've only been in politics a few weeks, and already I feel like screwing somebody."

## CONSCIENCE

Conscience gets a lot of credit that really belongs to cold feet.

A conscience is that small inner voice that warns you someone is watching.

A conscience is what feels bad while everything else is feeling good.

## CONSIDERATION

One politician is a real considerate man. He recently went all around his district and visited every ghetto golf club.

Inconsideration is when a woman serves her boyfriend oysters right after his vasectomy.

A man gets up as a young lady boards the bus and stands before him. Smiling, she pushes him back into his seat gently. At the next block, the action is repeated. After the fifth time, the man says, "Lady, you better get out of my way. I'm five blocks past my street already."

A man boards a commuter train and sits down next to another man. Looking out the window, the new arrival sees somebody he knows at the station. Asking the man in the window seat to forgive him, the new arrival leans out the window and says, "Charlie. Charlie, I'm in here."

On the platform, Charlie sees his friend and waves.

The man in the train calls out, "Charlie, I want to thank you for last weekend. It was terrific. That Mary of yours is a great hostess. She's a fantastic cook. And she's the best sex partner I ever had." Then he sits down, and the train takes off. After a few minutes, the man near the window is unable to contain himself and says, "Sir, how could you talk like that? Here these people host you and wine and dine you, and you tell the husband that his wife is a great sex partner. You should be ashamed of your-self.''

The loudmouth says, "What could I do? Charlie's such a good friend I didn't want to hurt his feelings.''

Then there was the woman who wore black garters in memory of those who passed beyond.

The new nurse was eager to please. As she made her first rounds, she said to a very sick patient, "The doctor is very worried about your case. He doesn't think you'll make it. So when he makes rounds this morning, be cheerful and put on a happy face.''

He says, "Let's go out and have some fun tonight.''

She says, "Great idea. But leave the front light on if you get home before I do.''

A man called 911 because his car was on fire. They told him the shortest route to the firehouse.

## CONTRACEPTIVES

Two fellows are discussing condoms. One says, "You know, they have the name of the manufacturer at the start of a condom.''

The other says, "I didn't know that.''

The first fellow says, "That's because you don't have to unroll that much.''

The new bride rushes to the doctor and tells him, "I'm frightened. I don't want

any children, but the birth control pills you gave me keep falling out.''

A condom comes with a guarantee. Of course, if the condom breaks, the guarantee runs out.

Joey goes to the drugstore and is baffled to see such a large display of condoms. He finally chooses a blue packet. About five months later, Joey returns to the drugstore and asks for a maternity bra.

The druggist says, "What bust?''

Joey says, "One of those damn blue ones.''

A man comes into a drugstore to buy some condoms. He's unsure of what size he needs, so the female pharmacist says, "Look, we're used to men not knowing their size. Why don't you go out in back where we have a board with several holes in it. That way we'll know your size.'' The man goes in back and puts his peter in one of the holes. Unbeknown to him, the pharmacist has slipped behind the board, and as he works his way into different openings, she toys with him. When he learns his size, he goes inside. The pharmacist asks, "Did you find your proper size?''

The man says, "To hell with the condoms. How much do you want for that board?''

Trying to show off, a Russian company ordered a hundred gross of condoms from an American outfit. Each condom was to be three inches wide and fifteen inches long. The Americans shipped out the order, and on each box was written, MEDIUM.

A lover is having a nice time with the lady of the house when they hear the sound of the husband's car pulling up. The lover doesn't have time to dress or even take off his condom. Grabbing up his clothes, he jumps out the window and starts to run to his car down the block. A man watering his lawn reacts as he sees the lover and asks, "Do you always wear a condom?"

"No," the lover answers. "Only when it looks like rain."

They're giving out condoms at high schools now. Pretty soon, the school yearbooks will have centerfolds.

They're giving out condoms in school today, with the students allowed to pick from regular, large, and "Miss Brown thinks you should stay after class."

I wonder if they call a rubber for midgets a condominium.

There's talk of our sending $10 million worth of female contraceptives to the Third World. I can save them money. Let them just send over my wife, and she'll teach the women how to pretend they're asleep.

A man goes into a drugstore and complains, "I bought a gross of condoms three days ago, and there were only eleven dozen in the pack."

The druggist says, "Gee, I hope it didn't spoil your weekend."

A young couple go out on a date. After a nice meal and movie, they start to head toward her house. On the way, the young man tells the girl that he has to make a necessary purchase. He does so, and they head to her house. As they sit and neck, the door opens, and her father enters. Immediately, the boy sits up and tries to look innocent. The girl says, "Why didn't you tell me you only go so far?"

The young man says, "Why didn't you tell me your father was a druggist?"

Gwendolyn is a rather ugly, dumpy woman in her fifties, but she goes into the pharmacy three times a week and buys a dozen condoms. Her friend Irma says, "You haven't had a date in ages, yet you keep buying condoms."

Gwendolyn says, "Another dozen and I think the pharmacist is mine."

## CONVERSATION

A tourist was spending the night in a small New England town. After walking around for three minutes and seeing all the sights, he found that the general store was open. Seated comfortably around a stove were four men. They seemed to be lost in reverie, just rocking back and forth. When ten minutes had gone by, the tourist asked, "Is there a law against talking in this town?"

One of the men said, "Nope. But we

have an understanding. Nobody speaks unless he's darn sure it can improve on silence!"

It's good to hold a conversation. Just let go of it once in a while.

## COOKING

Men love home cooking. Women hate cooking home.

She used to serve me cold boiled ham. That's ham boiled in cold water.

I told my wife I wanted to be surprised at dinner, so she soaked all the labels off the cans!

The other day, my wife decided to cook a meal for us with her new microwave oven. An hour went by, another went by, and no food. Finally, I went into the kitchen and asked, "What's keeping dinner?"
My wife said, "I'm letting the microwave preheat."

My wife is not the best cook in the world. We have Mylanta on tap.

I never go out for junk food. My wife makes her own.

A husband said to his wife, "Where am I when you serve the meat that we always have for leftovers?"

We have a new cook. She's a doll. Steak, chicken, turkey, casseroles—it makes no difference to her. She eats everything.

My wife makes heavy pancakes. We have the only bow-legged stove in town!

My wife made us a picnic lunch the other day. I felt sorry for the ants!

Dinner was a little late at my house yesterday. The pizza truck broke down.

My wife feeds the birds with her heavy homemade bread. Poor things had to walk south for the winter!

"I cooked a sponge cake for you, darling," says the young bride, puckering for a kiss, "but it didn't turn out right. I think the grocer sent me the wrong kind of sponges."

My wife used to make me breakfast in bed, but it got the sheets all greasy.

The other day, my wife apologized to me about dinner being burned. She told me, "Before I made up my mind what to have, there was a fire in the take-out restaurant."

"Beans again?" the husband asked.
"I don't understand it," the wife replied. "You liked beans on Monday, Tuesday, and Wednesday, and now all of the sudden you don't like beans?"

Wanting to surprise her husband, the wife bathes, puts on her sexiest perfume, and lies down on the couch in the nude. When the husband walks in, the wife says, "Guess what you're having for dinner?"

The husband says, "How do you know I didn't have it for lunch?"

The wife smiles and says to her husband, "How do you like this for a coincidence? You forgot my birthday, and I forgot how to cook."

## COSMETICS

My wife puts on eye shadow, eyeliner, eyelashes, mascara, toner, and turns to me: "Do I look natural?"

In a panic, a man goes to a doctor. The man is worried to death about a livid red rash in his groin. He explains that he has been to see a half-dozen specialists who have charged him a fortune, but with no results.

After a brief examination, the doctor says, "Just go home and wash the red off. On the way out, give the receptionist a check for ten dollars."

The man says, "But the other doctors charged a lot of money."

The doctor says, "They don't know much about lipstick, that's why."

My wife puts on a dozen creams and oils at night—elbow oil, shoulder oil, neck oil, face cream, eyelid cream, crow's-foot oil. If she caught fire, the guys who quenched the Kuwaiti wells couldn't cap her.

She uses a rejuvenation cream to make herself look younger. She must be using too much, because this afternoon she called me from her Brownie meeting.

## COURTS

Judge Brown studied the defendant and asked, "How is it you can't get a lawyer to defend you?"

The defendant said, "As soon as they found out I didn't steal the million, they quit!"

The bailiff held up the Bible and asked the defendant to tell the truth, the whole truth, and nothing but the truth. The defendant nodded and said, "Heck, I'll try anything once!"

Once there were two gay judges. They tried each other.

He was so relieved when the judge gave him a hundred and ten years. He was afraid he'd get life.

Tom was on trial for armed robbery. The jury came to the conclusion that he wasn't guilty. Tom jumped up: "Does that mean I can keep the money?"

A man was picked up for walking in the street without a stitch of clothes on. The judge asked him, "Is it true you had no clothes on?"

"Yes, Your Honor."

"You should be ashamed. Are you married?"

"I am."

"Do you have children?"

"Fourteen of them."

The judge banged down with his gavel. "Free this man. He was in his work clothes."

The truth will make you free—unless you're a criminal . . . then the courts will make you free.

A woman brings her husband to court for beating her. All day and night he beat her. The judge asks the husband, "What have you got to say about that?"

The husband says, "Don't listen to her. She's punch-drunk."

A lady applied for a divorce because she said that her husband wasn't faithful. The judge asked, "How do you know he wasn't faithful?"

The woman said, "Well, I just had a baby, and it doesn't look like him."

A court is a weird place. They lock up the jury and let the prisoner go home.

A man told the judge, "My doctor says I can walk, but my lawyer says I can't."

They're speeding up criminal justice in my hometown. They have a special court for people with eight crimes or less.

A lawyer is addressing an all-male jury: "Gentlemen, shall we cast this beautiful young lady into a dank, dim cell, or shall we return her to her lovely apartment on Park Avenue, telephone 555-0540?"

A speeder was brought into court. His records revealed that he had a hundred parking tickets, many moving violations, and improper vehicle-registration papers. The judge said, "I'm going to fine you fifteen hundred dollars. I'm also considering taking away your license."

The speeder said, "You can't do that. I never had a license."

A defendant stands up and says, "I want to change my plea to Guilty." The judge says, "Why didn't you do so at the start of the trial?" The defendant says, "Well, until I heard the D.A., I didn't know I was guilty."

The judge says to the defendant, "I told you I didn't want to see you again."

The defendant says, "I told that to the cop. He wouldn't believe me."

A convicted felon jumps up in court and says, "How do you like that? Twelve people out of two hundred fifty million find me guilty. And you call that justice. As God is my judge," he yells out, "I'm not guilty."

The judge says, "He's not. I am. Six years!"

Just think of it this way—when you're on trial, your fate is being settled by twelve people who weren't smart enough to get out of jury duty.

A man is brought in for stealing a pair of shoes. The judge says, "Weren't you here last year for the same charge?"

The man says, "Your Honor, how long can a pair of shoes last?"

A felon is charged with forgery. He says, "I can't even sign my own name."

The judge says, "You're not charged with signing your *own* name."

**A** bigamist is hauled before a judge for marrying a third wife who had only a dollar to her name. The judge says, "How could you marry a woman for one dollar?"

The bigamist says, "You know how it is, Judge—a dollar here, dollar there, it adds up."

**A** judge with almost no legal experience is hearing his first case. As soon as the plaintiff makes his case, the judge says, "Plaintiff wins."

The defense attorney jumps up and says, "Your Honor, at least let me present my case."

The judge nods. That's okay with him.

The defense attorney presents his case eloquently. The judge listens and then says, "Ain't that something? Now the defense wins."

**P**hil's lawyer makes an impassioned plea to the judge in which he proves that his client, Will, hadn't stolen the chickens as charged. The case dismissed, Phil says to Will quietly, "You did steal those chickens, didn't you?"

Will says, "I thought I did, but after hearing you, I'm not sure anymore."

**I** wanted to tell the truth, but my lawyer wouldn't let me.

**T**he judge asked, "What possible excuse can you have for freeing this defendant?"

A juror said, "Insanity."

The judge said, "All twelve of you?"

**A** judge hears a juvenile case involving three boys. The first says, "All I did, Your Honor, was break a window, ruin somebody's bike, and throw peanuts in the lake."

The second says, "Me too. All I did was break a window, ruin somebody's bike, and throw peanuts in the lake."

The third says, "All I did was break a window and ruin somebody's bike."

The judge asks, "Didn't you throw peanuts in the lake?"

The boy says, "I'm Peanuts."

**T**he defense attorney says, "Mr. Collins, do you mean to say that my client went at you with a knife in his hand? But didn't you have something in your hand?" Collins says, "His wife. Nice, but not much good in a fight."

**A** woman is being questioned about jury duty, but says, "I don't believe in capital punishment."

The judge says, "This is a case about a woman whose husband took some money she was saving for a new dress and lost it at the track."

The woman muses and then says, "Maybe I can change my mind about capital punishment."

**O**ne very socially conscious jury brought in a verdict of "We're all guilty."

**T**he jury didn't exactly call it murder. They just said it was an act of God under very suspicious circumstances.

## COWBOYS

**A** cowboy is riding along when he gets thrown off his horse. Quickly, the horse drags his rider to a shady spot, props him against a tree, and runs off to town to get help. An hour later, several people ride up, one of them obviously a doctor. The cowboy is saved.

A few weeks later, the cowboy relates the story to a friend who says, "My Lord, that's the smartest horse in the world."

The cowboy says, "He's not so smart. He came back with a vet."

**T**he dude, up at the dude ranch for a week of roughing it, watched a cowhand roll a cigarette. Shaking his head in awe, the dude said, "It's amazing how you roll a cigarette with one hand."

The cowhand said, "That's nothing. The hard part's getting the filter in."

## CRAZY

**A** loonie is praying in a room, and another loonie asks, "What are you doing?"

"Keeping the elephants away."

"There are no elephants here."

"See."

**T**wo crazies were looking for a way to get out of the funny farm. They came to a high wall, and one asked, "How can we get over this thing?" The other crazy said, "Tell you what—I'll shine my searchlight up there, and you climb up the beam."

The first crazy said, "Oh, sure. I know you. When I get halfway up, you'll turn it off."

**T**hen there was this man on the train who everybody thought was a nut. He kept saying he was George Washington. But everybody got shook up when he got off at Mount Vernon.

## CREDIT

**E**ven though I owe a fortune, I have a lot to be grateful for. At least I'm not one of my creditors.

**Y**ou have to give my wife a lot of credit. She can't get along without it.

**A** man went into a store and asked for credit. The clerk asked, "Do you have any credit references?"

"Sure. I owe every store in town."

**I**f you don't think that anybody cares whether you're living or dead, try missing a few car payments.

**C**redit cards are a great way of spending money you wish you had.

**C**redit lets you start at the bottom and then dig yourself into a hole.

**T**he other day I wanted to pay somebody cash, and he demanded to see my driver's license.

**M**y wife just underwent plastic surgery. I cut up her credit cards.

Why ask me to live within my income? I can't even live within my credit.

Money doesn't buy everything. But then, with credit cards, who needs it?

I tried to use my credit card in a health food store. They said they only accept natural cash.

The other day I called a store and asked a clerk, "Do you honor credit cards?"

He answered, "We not only honor them, we love and obey them."

I'm so used to paying by credit card. The other day I paid cash and signed all the dollar bills.

My credit cards need some help—cash transplant.

There's one bad point about credit cards—Visa and Mastercharge don't accept American Express.

My wife has the world at her feet. I have the creditors at my throat.

A credit card is what you use to buy today what you can't afford tomorrow because you're still paying for yesterday.

A credit card is what you use after you learn that money can't buy everything.

I couldn't afford to go on a trip this year, and my wife was upset. She said, "Why not charge things?"

I said, "I'm not taking a trip on borrowed money."

My wife said, "It was good enough for Columbus."

## CRIME

Recently, a crook wore suede gloves to rob a safe. The police went to work on the case, and two weeks later, Interpol arrested a goat in the Alps.

Who will ever forget the poor pickpocket who washed his hands and couldn't do a thing with them?

A crook's kid brings his report card home for his father to sign. His father says, "Aren't you getting old enough to forge my name?"

Joe and Fred are in a store when it is held up. As the holdup man searches various customers for valuables, Joe whispers to Fred, "Take this."

"Take what?"

"The twenty I owe you."

A kleptomaniac is somebody who helps himself because he can't help himself.

In my hometown, you don't have to worry about crime in the streets. They make house calls.

Crime is growing. When you call local cops, there's a three-week waiting list.

There's one thing about kleptomania— you can always take something for it.

One burglar came home to his wife and said, "Honey, I wanted to bring you a diamond today, but the store was still open."

The other day a guy in a mask took all my money. I was in surgery at the time.

Then there's the one about the one-fingered pickpocket. All he could steal was Lifesavers.

Recently, I was mugged by a guy in Chinatown who stabbed me forty times. He didn't get much money, but my bad back went away.

I don't know what he does for a living, but when he tunes the TV set, he has to sandpaper his fingers.

The attorney asked his client what his assets were. The client said, "All I have in the world is a 450 SL." The lawyer said, "All right, I'll defend you. What were you charged with?" The client said, "Stealing a 450 SL."

Organized crime takes in about $50 billion a year and doesn't spend much on office supplies.

A criminal told the man next to him in the courtroom, "It's not fair. By the time you pay off your lawyers, there's nothing left to pay off the judge."

One day I was arrested for statutory rape. If I'd know she was a statue, I would have passed on it.

Then there's the efficient hitman. He sends get-well cards a month before they're needed.

He only robs banks so he'll feel wanted.

My house is really secured. On my windows, I have six-inch steel bars. On the front door, I have four locks, three sets of bars, an electric alarm system, and eight beepers. I never worry about getting robbed when I'm not home. I can't get out of the house.

Crime doesn't pay, unless, of course, you're good at it.

A crook comes back from a robbery, and a friend asks, "What did you get?"
    The crook says, "It was a lawyer's house."
    The friend says, "Oh, then what did you lose?"

If crime doesn't pay, how come so many people want to be lawyers?

One of these days, there's going to be as much crime on the street as there is on TV.

A robber stuck a gun in a man's rib and asked for his watch. The man said, "This watch has only sentimental value."
    The crook said, "Thank you. I'm sentimental."

A cat burglar and his new partner are on their first job, cracking a safe. Lying down on his back, the cat burglar starts to dial the combination with his toes. The new partner says, "Stop fooling around."

The cat burglar says, "This always works. It drives the fingerprint guys crazy."

I don't know where we're going to put all the crooks today. The prisons and Congress are full.

I was in this town the other day, and they made me feel at home. They mugged me.

I know a crook who deals in furniture. He just tried to sell me a hot water bed.

I come from a larcenous family. The day after Bell invented the telephone, my great-great-uncle invented the slug!

There's a criminal whose rap sheet is a page long. He was first arrested for mugging someone, then for stealing a car, then for burgling a house, and after that, six times in a row for sexual assault. I guess it took him a little time to find out what he was good at.

A bank robber shoves a note under the cage gate to the teller. It says, *Put the money in the bag, and don't try anything funny.* The teller sends back a note: *Straighten your tie. They're taking your picture.*

My uncle Vinny from Chicago once walked to the middle of the field during halftime at the Rose Bowl, pulled out a gun, waved it at the crowd of ninety thousand, and said, "Nobody move. This is a stickup."

"What do you call a midget fortune-teller who escapes from the police?"

"A small medium at large."

A man felt a strange touch in his pocket and turned around swiftly to see a pickpocket. The pickpocket explained, "I'm getting so absentminded. I used to have a pair of pants just like that."

An ugly girl had been stopped by a mugger who frisked her quickly then stopped, saying, "You don't have any money."

The ugly girl said, "Keep doing what you're doing, and I'll write you a check!"

A bank clerk describes a robber who has robbed the bank four times: "I noticed one thing about him—he seemed to dress better each time."

The burglars tied and gagged the bank cashier after extracting the combination to the safe. Then they herded the other employees into a separate room under guard. As they were leaving, the cashier made desperate pleading noises through his gag. Moved by curiosity, one of the burglars removed the gag.

"Please," whispered the cashier, "Take the books too. I'm eighty-five hundred dollars short!"

Crime doesn't pay. Eventually, every murderer will get a parking ticket.

A robber stuck a gun in a man's back. The man suddenly turned, applied a judo grip, threw the man ten feet, and kicked him in the head, breaking the man's jaw and bruising his ribs. Then the man punched the robber, gave him two black eyes, and broke his arms.

"Hey," the robber finally yelled. "Ain't you ever gonna call a cop?"

He committed the perfect crime. He got caught and sold the rights as a miniseries for 2 million.

## CRITICISM

Criticism shouldn't be allowed to bother you. If it had any power to hurt, the skunk would be extinct.

One theatrical critic said that he saw a play under unfortunate circumstances—the curtain was up.

## CROSS-EYED

She has pedestrian eyes. They look both ways before crossing.

Then there was this teacher who was cross-eyed. She had trouble with her pupils.

He's really cross-eyed. They once found him in Alabama looking for the Northwestern Mounties.

## CROSSINGS

I once crossed a bee with a doorbell, and I got a humdinger.

I once crossed a rooster with a rooster and got a pissed-off rooster.

I'm crossing barley and soap flakes. It doesn't taste too good, but it makes dishwashing easy.

I once tried to cross a kidney bean with a pea pod so I could get a plant that waters itself.

He crossed a crocodile with some sausages and ended up with a crockabaloney.

I once crossed a chicken and a parrot. It not only laid an egg, it came over and told me about it.

## CRUISES

The food on the cruise was nice, but all day long people kept bringing it up.

One day we were signaled by a tramp steamer. They wanted a quarter for a cup of coffee.

"Did you pick up any Italian on your cruise?"
   "I sure did."
   "Let me hear some words."
   "Oh, I didn't learn any words."

A spinster is taking a sea cruise. As she stands at the railing, she sees a whale approach. Lying on its back, it suddenly spouts. The spinster starts to turn away and says, "I hate show-offs."

Seasickness on a cruise is terrible. The first day you think you're going to die. The second you're afraid you won't.

It was his first sea cruise, and he was spending it in his cabin, a victim of intense seasickness. The steward knocked on the cabin door and asked, "May I bring you some dinner, sir?"

"No," was the answer, "just throw it overboard directly!"

Jones was a victim of the most violent attack of mal de mer in history, the condition resulting from a storm that buffeted the ship from stem to stern. As giant waves slammed onto the decks, the captain assured some of the passengers, "There's no need to worry. We won't give up the ship!"

From his perch at the rail, Jones said, "I couldn't. I haven't eaten it yet!"

It was a classy ship. The smokestacks had filter tips.

A man is on a cruise that he isn't taking too well. As he leans over the railing and lets out his lunch another voyager says, "You're not doing too well."

The man says, "What do you mean? I'm heaving as far as anybody else."

We were on a real expensive cruise. It cost three thousand dollars to be a stowaway.

We were on a giant ship. You had to start for the rail at eight in the morning to get there by dusk.

A small cruise ship sinks, and a number of passengers find themselves on a lifeboat being tossed in an angry sea. At the front of the boat, the skipper says, "I'm in charge of the rations. Each of the nineteen people aboard will get an equal share. It'll be small portions, but they should sustain all fifteen of us until we are rescued. We're a little short of liquids, so there'll only be half a cup for each of the ten of us. Now all six of us will have to exercise great discipline. I'm sure the four of us can do it. Let's hear it from the two of you. Great, let's you and me chow down."

The Rosses were on a cruise. But Mr. Ross was very unhappy. Every which way he turned, there was a palm out. He had to tip a fortune. On the sixth day out, he received a note from the captain asking the Rosses to join him at dinner. Mr. Ross blew up. "How do you like this?" he said. "First, I have to tip everybody in sight. Now they want us to eat with the crew."

## CURES

A man was having trouble in bed and imparted that to a co-worker. The co-worker told him that oysters were a natural aphrodisiac and could make him perform like a porno star.

The man went out, bought a whole bushel of oysters, and ate them at one sitting. Unfortunately, that night he still couldn't perform.

But the next morning, he crapped six pearls.

A man has a terrible headache. One of his co-workers tells him, "When I have a headache, I go home. My wife massages my neck and then we make love. In ten minutes, my headache is gone. You ought to try it."

The man with the headache starts to put on his coat and says, "Good idea. Is your wife home now?"

## DAKOTA

"When do Dakota girls start to look good?"

"Five minutes before closing time."

Some Dakotans buy blank bumper stickers. They don't want to get involved.

"What do you call a North Dakotan with half a brain?"

"Gifted."

A Dakotan once walked into a restaurant and said, "I'm in a hurry. Just bring me the bill."

The Dakota fire chief bought a new fire engine. Somebody asked him, "What are you going to do with the old one?"

He answered, "Oh, we'll just use that for false alarms."

## DANCE

I don't like the ballet. I can never tell which side is winning.

Today, kids dance funny. They don't speak, they don't look at one another, and they don't touch. They look as if they've been married for twenty years.

"What's a chimp doing at a singles' dance?"

"Are you kidding? Have you ever been to a singles' dance?"

I saw some couples doing the lambada. I tried to cut in, but I didn't have a chain saw.

I'm a great dancer, but how many bands play the Virginia reel today?

A country gent came to the big city, and while there visited a nightclub. He watched the people dancing and said to someone next to him at the bar, "Why are they doing that standing up?"

Some girls have a rough time at a dance. They always meet guys who are all feet when they dance, and when they stop they're all hands.

The rumba is where the front of you goes along smoothly like a Mercedes and the back of you is a Jeep.

I hate to go to dances. I have two left feet, and it's hard to find a girl with two right ones.

It's easy to do the new dances. Just watch popcorn over a hot fire.

Then there was the miserable ballet master. He was rotten to the corps.

Then there was the stripper with a tan who peeled for nothing.

My wife once said, "Waltz a little faster, dear, this is a rumba."

She once auditioned to be a topless dancer. They hired her as a busboy.

## DATING

A bachelor was bragging that he loved variety. Monday he'd gone out with Irma, Tuesday with Alice, Wednesday with Fido.

His friend said, "Fido sounds like a dog."

The bachelor said, "You should see Irma and Alice."

Twenty-year-old Marie received a diamond engagement ring, but nobody seemed to notice it. She waved her ring finger all around like a baton. Nobody seemed to care. She displayed it, she modeled it, but no responses were forthcoming. Finally, she blurted out, "I don't know how I can stand it. I'm so warm in my new ring!"

One girl broke up with her boyfriend because he wanted to get married, and she didn't want him to.

A friend of mine signed up with a dating service but quit when they matched him up with his wife.

Her father asked me, "Could you support a family?"

I said, "Of course."

He said, "Are you sure? There are eight of us."

I once got a black eye fighting for a girl's honor. She wanted to keep it.

A man at a singles' bar sees a beautiful woman with a great shape come in. The man leans over to the bartender and says, "Did you ever see such tight jeans? How does somebody get into those pants?"

Overhearing him, the woman strides over and says, "Well, for starters, you can buy me a vodka martini."

He took this girl to a fine restaurant, and she ordered everything on the menu—caviar, wine, pheasant, mousse. Watching her, he said, "Does your mother feed you like this?"

She said, "My mother doesn't want to take me home later and screw me."

The girl said, "Aren't the stars lovely tonight?"

The boy said, "I'm in no position to see."

After a heck of a night, he asked her, "Do you tell your mother everything you do?"

She said, "My mother doesn't care. It's my husband who keeps asking questions."

Her girdle was so tight—when we had dinner, she got three inches taller.

I have a lot of trouble with women. Not long ago I met a girl. She liked me, but her father didn't. Then I met another girl. Her father liked me, but she didn't. Finally, I met a third girl, and she liked me, her father liked me, but her husband couldn't stand me.

I've always looked for a certain kind of girl—she has a fur coat already, and her appendix is out.

Every time this young man brought a young lady home to meet his mother, the mother turned up her nose. She never liked any of the women in whom he became interested. One day he brought home a girl who looked like his mother, sounded like his mother, and even walked like his mother. It did him no good. His father didn't like her!

She was the kind of girl he could have brought home to his mother, but he couldn't trust his father.

One girl told her friend, "He not only lied to me about his yacht, but I had to do most of the rowing."

A man works hard for years to keep the wolf from his door. Then his daughter grows up and brings one right into the living room!

A girl went to a computer dating service and told them she didn't care about looks or wealth. She just wanted a man of upright character. Then a man came in and told them he didn't care about anything in a girl but intelligence. The computer put them together because they had a lot in common—lying.

**I** told my girl I was taking her out royally, so we ate at the Burger King and the Dairy Queen.

**One** girl tried to break down his door. Of course, she was in his room at the time.

**I** know a guy who dated a girl named Phyllis with a fake fur. Then he found out it was Philip, a fake her.

**I** have no trouble making dates with women. My problem is they never show up.

**Phil** is having trouble meeting women. His co-worker, Danny, says, "Here's a surefire way to meet women. On your day off during the week, take the train and get off at Belmont. You'll see a lot of women who've just sent their husbands off. The women get lonely, and you can have a great time."

Phil is desperate, so on his next weekday off he takes the train and gets off at Carterville, a nearer station. Sure enough, in ten minutes he meets a lovely married woman. They have a bite to eat, then she invites him over to her house.

They cavort all day. As they are about to try again, the door opens, and Danny stalks in. Danny says, "You rat! I told you Belmont!"

**This** young man climbs a ladder and taps at his girlfriend's window. They are plan-

ning to elope. The girl comes to the window and whispers, "Don't make so much noise. You'll wake my father."

The boy says, "You don't have to worry. He's holding the ladder."

**"Dearest,** will you marry me?"

"No, but I'll always admire your good taste."

**When** it comes to dating, there are problems with men. Either they're so slow, a girl could just scream, or so fast, a girl has to.

**I** found out this girl wasn't old enough for me. I started to talk about rumble seats, and she didn't know what they were.

**A** woman and man meet at a party. As they talk, the woman asks, "How long have you been in town?"

The man says, "About a month. Until then I was away."

"Where were you? Europe? The Far East?"

"I was in jail."

"Really? And why were you in jail?"

"I hacked my wife to death twenty years ago."

"Oh, that means you're single."

**A** young man returned from a date that had obviously not turned out too well. His friend asked what the problem was, and the young man answered, "She used too many four-letter words all evening."

"I can't believe that."

"Oh yeah. All night she kept saying, 'Don't' and 'Stop' and 'Quit that'."

"And if I turn you down, you'll just go out and kill yourself, right?"
"Well, that's what I usually do."

This teenage girl discovered that she was pregnant. She moaned to a friend, "I should have gone to the movies with my folks that night."
The friend asked, "Why didn't you?"
The teenage girl said, "I couldn't. It was an *X*-rated movie."

Girls, don't look for a husband. Just date single men.

A passionate kiss is like a spiderweb. Sooner or later, it leads to the undoing of a fly.

He finishes a romantic interlude and says, "If I'd known you were a virgin, I would have taken more time."
She says, "If I'd known you had time, I would have taken off my pantyhose."

There they were in Lovers' Lane. As he groped her, she said, "Don't do that. I'll go to pieces." He said, "Go ahead, I got the part I want."

"Are you familiar with Judy Smith?"
"I tried to be, and she belted me."

She has a slight impediment in her speech. She can't say "No."

I don't believe in running around with married women. That's why I always leave my wife at home.

A middle-aged man of forty-five hits on a pretty girl of twenty and asks her, "Where have you been all my life?"
The girl answers, "Teething."

This young man has been dating a young lady for a while, and one day he shows up with a diamond ring. "Marry me," he says.
The girl says, "I can't. I love somebody else."
The young man says, "Who is it? I'd like to sell him this ring."

This young girl went out with a cheapskate. He spent about five cents on her. When he took her home, she said, "I'd invite you in, but I'm sure you want to get back to your money."

A man takes a girl out for dinner, and on the way home, to settle the food, they walk around a fancy neighborhood. As they pass an attractive lingerie shop, the girl says, "Oh, I'd love to have some of those frills."
At that, the man takes a brick out of his pocket, heaves it through the window, and collects many goodies for the lady.
They walk on. At a fur salon, she says, "Oh, I'd love to have one of those mink coats."
The man takes out another brick, heaves it, and in five minutes the lady has a lovely dark mink coat.

At a jeweler's, the girl says, "Oh, I'd love to have that diamond."

Another brick, and soon the girl is wearing a lovely diamond ring.

They walk on. At a Rolls-Royce dealer, the girl says, "Oh, I'd love to have a Rolls-Royce."

The man looks at her and says, "What is this with you? Do you think I'm made of bricks?"

A cute young lady was heard saying to a friend, "I wish I could combine the attributes of Tom and Fred."

"What are they?"

"Well, Tom is handsome, bright, and rich. And Fred wants to marry me."

The young couple was smooching in the darkened living room, and the girl's father was becoming a little concerned. He called down, "Honey, is that boy there yet?"

The girl called back, "No, but he's getting there."

A girl tells her roommate about her latest beau: "You won't believe this, but we met in the strangest way—we were introduced."

How about the good girl who had been saying no so long, she almost loused up her wedding.

Dating is that period of time during which a girl decides whether she can do any better.

A young couple go out on a date. As they drive in his car, the pretty miss cuddles up to the young man. After a while, he gets excited and says, "I'm going to pull over so we can have some fun."

"People will see us."

"We'll get under the car. I'll have my feet out so people will think I'm fixing the car."

They get to the top of a hill. The young man pulls the car to a stop. They get out and under the car. As they make love, a traffic cop appears. Coughing, he bends over and taps the young man's shoes. The young man says, "We don't need any help. I'm fixing the engine myself."

The traffic cop says, "Shame you didn't fix the brakes first. Your car rolled down the hill."

"It'll be perfectly simple for us to get married," the guy tried to convince his girl. "My father's a minister."

"Well, let's give it a try anyway," the girl said. "Mine's a lawyer."

Some car rides put a girl on her feet.

"Listen to all these crickets in Lovers' Lane."

"They're not crickets—they're zippers."

A wolf is like a good dry cleaner—he works fast and leaves no ring.

The difference between a popular girl and an unpopular one is yes and no.

A young man puts a ring on his girl's finger. Thrilled, she says, "Isn't that your mother's engagement ring?"

"It sure is. She fought like a crazy woman, but I finally got it away from her."

Henry and Phoebe are in Lovers' Lane. As they start to embrace, Henry sees a policeman approach. He says, "Oh, God. Fuzz."

Phoebe says, "What'd you expect— an Afro?"

A young fellow complains to his live-in girlfriend, "I'm not against your mother moving in with us, but she could have waited until after we were married."

She promised her mother she'd be in bed by ten. We almost didn't make it.

The girl I took out the other night looked good enough to eat and did she.

## DAUGHTERS

A girl comes home and tells her father she's pregnant. The father looks at her, stunned, and asks, "Are you sure it's yours?"

She's only a stockbroker's daughter, but the guys all get their share.

She's only a realtor's daughter, but she sure gives lots away.

She's only an Indian's daughter, but she sure can say—How.

She's only a plumber's daughter, but she sure makes the most of her fixtures.

She's only a philanthropist's daughter, but she keeps giving things away.

She's only a senator's daughter, but she sure can advise and consent.

She's only a cabbie's daughter, but she sure can take you for a ride.

She's only a coin collector's daughter, but she shows all the guys her quarters.

She's only an actor's daughter, but she'll make a play for anybody.

Never believe your daughter's boyfriend if he says he didn't take her to a motel, especially if the Bible he swears on is a Gideon.

It's not what my daughter knows that bothers me. It's how she found out.

She's only a boxer's daughter, but you should see what she can do in the clinches.

She's only a dentist's daughter, but she always has her cavity filled.

She's only a salesman's daughter, but she gives out plenty of samples.

She's only a surgeon's daughter, but she can operate.

She's only a doctor's daughter, but she's ready to make house calls.

**S**he's only a mechanic's daughter, but she sure can fix your wagon.

## DEADBEATS

**H**e always walks around with big bills in his wallet—unpaid ones!

**H**e's a born deadbeat. If you reminded him that a bill was a year old, he'd send it a birthday card.

**H**e loves to borrow money from a bank. At least he knows that somebody is going to call him.

**H**e was a real deadbeat. Even his bills came postage due.

**A** deadbeat shopkeeper doesn't pay his bill for a previous order but has the gall to ask the company to send him more stuff. The company tells him, "We can't send you anything until you pay your last bill."

The deadbeat says, "Cancel the order. I can't wait that long."

## DEAFNESS

**A** man stops his car and asks a farmer in a field, "Can you tell me the way to Porterville?"

"Ehhh?"

"Porterville," the man says, a little louder. "Can you tell me the way to Porterville?"

"Ehhhh?"

By now, the man is screaming. "Por-terville! Tell me the way to Porterville!"

"Ehhhh?"

The man is furious, starts his car, and drives on. About five miles away, he stops at a farmhouse and rings the bell. A woman comes to the door.

The man says, "Excuse me, but—"

The woman says, "I heard you before. It's about five miles if you turn left at the crossroads."

**I** have a friend who was deaf but tried one of those new hearing aids. An hour later, he heard from his brother in Akron.

**H**is wife talked so much, it was two years before he found out he was deaf and dumb.

**J**ohnny's birthday is coming up, so he starts to say his prayers, but very loudly as he asks for a bike. His mother comes in and says, "The Lord isn't deaf, Johnny."

"I know, but Dad is."

**O**ld George was the deafest man in town. The other day he was near the railroad tracks, and he heard the loco-motive's shrill whistle. Old George said to Old Al, the second-deafest man in town, "First robin I've heard this spring."

**T**wo men are sitting on a bench at the shore. One says, "I'm so grateful I have all my faculties. Take hearing, for ex-ample. I'm eighty-two, and I can hear the birds in the morning, the breeze in the trees. I can hear a pin drop fifty feet away. I can even hear my watch tick.''

The other man says, "What kind is it?"

The first man says, "Eleven-thirty.''

## DEATH

On her knees graveside, a woman is weeding her husband's grave. A breeze comes up and rustles some of the grass beneath her. She says, "Easy, Mike. Don't forget you're dead.''

Two friends meet. One says, "Where's Benny? I've been looking high and low for him.''

The friend says, "Those are the places to look. He died last month.''

A young woman is brought to the morgue to identify the body of her boyfriend, who perished in a terrible car collision. The attendant pulls the sheet from the corpse's face. The woman shakes her head. She isn't sure. The attendant lowers the sheet more and more until the groin is revealed. The woman says, "It's not him. But I'll tell you one thing. Somebody lost a very good friend.''

There's a loud knock at the door, and a woman answers it. A man says, "Be you the widow Murphy?''

"My name's Murphy, but I'm no widow," she says.

"You're not, huh?" says the stranger. "Wait till you see what they're bringing up the stairs!''

A salesman died recently and left an estate of 300 towels and 180 hotel room keys.

Care in our coffins drives the nails no doubt,

But Mirth with merry fingers plucks them out.

## DEFINITIONS

*Archives*—where Noah kept his bees

*Alabaster*—an illegitimate Arab

*Chiropractor*—a slipped disc jockey

*Hangover*—a toot ache

*Jonah*—the man who spent three days in the stomach of a whale. At least that's what he told his wife

*Realist*—a guy who gives electric blankets for wedding presents

*Toastmaster*—the man who starts the bull rolling

*Virginity*—a big issue about a little tissue

A *wife*—somebody you make love to so you can get the cooking and cleaning done

## DELINQUENTS

Three delinquents saunter into a coffee shop and see an old lady at the counter, drinking a cup of coffee. Deciding to have fun at the old lady's expense, one of the delinquents tells the others, "You know, my mother and dad never got married."

The second delinquent said, "My mother didn't even know who my dad was."

The third said, "Tell you true, I don't even know who my mother was."

The old lady smiled and said, "Will one of you bastards pass the cream?"

He used to bring the teacher an apple, then turn her in for taking stolen goods.

We used to send our kid to school with his bail money pinned to his coat.

One delinquent was too young to drive, so he only stole cars with chauffeurs.

My son got a job parking cars at a restaurant. The first day he made two hundred dollars—he sold a Buick!

Ours was a rough school. We had the only class with a lookout.

My friend has a son who just graduated from law school. He also has a younger son who may be the new lawyer's first client.

## DEMOCRATS

In a certain Mississippi town many years ago, a Republican vote kept cropping up election after election. Everybody fig-

ured it was cast by an old Union soldier who had been wounded and left behind during the War Between the States. When the old-timer died, the town gave him a fine funeral. Everybody then breathed a sigh of relief that its one Republican vote had been eliminated.

But that fall, when the presidential election votes were being counted, a sudden commotion arose.

"That Republican vote has showed up again!" one of the tabulators yelled. "We buried the wrong man!"

A granite-solid Democratic minister was cornered by one of his parishioners one day.

"Reverend, you are so partisan, I believe you'd vote for the Devil himself if he were a Democrat," the man said.

The reverend thought for a moment and said, "Well, not in the primary, I wouldn't."

## DENTISTS

I used to think I had long white teeth. Then I found out I had short gums.

I just got bad news from my dentist. My teeth are okay, but my gums have to come out.

My dentist put in a big gold filling and told me, "Don't chew on that side, don't eat caramels, and don't smile at a mugger."

There are three rules for good teeth: Drink milk, brush your teeth often, and mind your own business.

A man goes to a dentist. During the examination, the man says, "My teeth are great. But let me tell you something. I never brush my teeth. I never use a rinse on my teeth. I never use a breath mint. I eat garlic all day long. And I've never had bad breath."

The dentist says, "You need an operation."

"What kind of operation?"

"On your nose."

My dentist told me to try dental floss, but it hasn't helped. I've been chewing some for a year, and I still get cavities.

My dental bill is huge. My bridge cost more than the one they put over the River Kwai.

My dentist just put in a crown for me. From the price, I think it was the Crown of England.

A woman went to her dentist complaining for the tenth time that her teeth didn't fit. The dentist examined her and said, for the tenth time, "These fit your mouth perfectly."

The woman said, "The glass. They don't fit in my glass."

This patient complained, "My teeth are turning yellow. What should I do?"

The dentist replied, "Wear a yellow tie."

My dentist just put in a tooth to match my others. It has two cavities.

When a dentist says, "Open wide," he could also be talking about your wallet.

I never go to a dentist who's had his office soundproofed.

My dentist isn't really painless. He screamed like mad when I bit his finger.

I've got so much bridgework in my mouth, I have to go to my dentist every six months to check for metal fatigue.

Nothing gets an old bill paid like a new toothache.

This patient says to the dentist after the examination, "I know you're a painless dentist, but this is going to hurt a little. I have no money."

I have very bad teeth. Even my wisdom teeth are retarded.

She goes to the dentist twice a year— once for each tooth.

The other day, I had such a deep cavity my dentist sent me to a podiatrist.

My dentist relieved two swellings—one in my gums and one in my wallet.

An old man returns to the dentist and complains, "I don't like these teeth. I have to use tenderizer."

The dentist says, "A lot of people use tenderizer."

The old man says, "On soup?"

I just paid my dental bill. Now there's a cavity in my bank account.

You can be philosophical about everything but a toothache.

I was in a strip joint once that had a lady dancer who climaxed her act by bending over backward and picking up a handkerchief with her teeth. For an encore, she bent over backward and picked up her teeth!

Mrs. Carter sits down in the dental chair, her face contorted with pain. The dentist says to his assistant, "I can take care of this alone." As soon as the assistant is gone, the dentist embraces the patient, whose pain has disappeared in a flash. As they kiss, the dentist says, "Darling, I'm afraid we can't keep meeting like this much longer."

"Why not?"

"Because you're down to your last tooth."

Only when you see your kid's braces can you really understand the meaning of a million-dollar smile.

## DEPARTMENT STORES

Where do you go in a department store to complain about the complaint department?

I go to a very fancy department store. The salesclerks there ignore you by appointment only.

I almost was waited on in a department store the other day, but luckily the salesclerk caught herself in time.

Business is so bad in department stores. I heard of one that just laid off three mannequins.

## DESERT

There hasn't been rain here in ten years. At a funeral last Saturday, they had to prime the mourners.

In this part of the country, when they say the river is up, they mean we've had a dust storm.

At a small desert gas station in the middle of nowhere, there's a sign: DON'T ASK US FOR INFORMATION. IF WE KNEW ANYTHING, WE WOULDN'T BE HERE.

It's so dry here that for baptisms, they're only using a damp cloth.

## DIET

They now sell a nicely packaged empty box in supermarkets for people who want to diet. It's called Hunger Helper!

She just went on a liquid diet—Lake Superior.

**H**e's lost a lot of weight recently. Last week he put on his winter underwear and fell through the flap.

**I** have a great way to stay on a vegetable diet—I let the cow eat it.

**Y**ou can lose a lot of weight by giving up only two things—a knife and a fork.

**M**ary was a hundred pounds overweight and in very bad shape. She'd tried every kind of regimen, but nothing had worked. Finally, her doctor came up with a sure cure, saying, "I want you to be home this evening at six."

"Why six?"

"Just be there."

At exactly six, the doorbell rang. Mary opened the door to find the handsomest young man she'd ever seen standing there. He smiled and whispered, "If you catch me, you can have me." He wheeled and started off. Mary tried to follow him but he was soon lost in the distance. She huffed and puffed as she shut the door.

The next evening at six, the same ritual took place. Again, Mary took after the young man. Again, he distanced himself. This went on daily for a month. At the end of that month, Mary had lost some weight but was in much better shape. She'd almost caught the young man the evening before. She was sure she'd catch him this evening.

The usual knock on the door, and Mary flung open the door only to find the fattest, ugliest, most bepimpled young man standing in the doorway.

Through black teeth, he said, "I'm going to make love to you if I catch you!"

**I**'m working on a Playboy diet—I'm trying to get rid of my centerfold.

**S**how me a girl with a good figure, and I'll show you a hungry girl.

**Y**ou're ready for a diet if you need a bicycle for two and you're only one.

**I**f you can imagine the future, you're halfway there.

**Y**ou need to lose weight if you look like the Odd Couple and you're alone.

**I** have a brand-new diet—you eat only when the news is good.

**I**t took a lot of willpower, but I finally gave up dieting.

**A** friend of mine has a great diet—you drink booze all day and eat anything you want. You don't lose weight, but you forget you're fat.

**I** hate calories. They keep hitting below the belt.

**S**he helps men with their diets. When she takes off her clothes, they lose their appetites!

**T**he toughest part of dieting is not watching what you eat. It's watching what your friends eat.

I never go to a health spa. It feels funny to spend a thousand to get rid of what it cost ten thousand to put on.

My sister has a new diet that allows her to eat anything that comes from a blender. For dinner yesterday, she drank three chickens and a roast beef.

I used to get tired when I went on a diet, so my doctor gave me pep pills. I gained weight—I ate faster!

My wife claims she keeps young by dieting, exercising, and lying about how good she feels.

They're carrying the diet fads a little too far. One mortuary is advertising that they're using formaldehyde-lite.

They now have an eat-everything diet. It's for fat people who want to stay that way.

Did you ever notice that they never advertise celery on TV?

He's even tried the garlic diet. You eat nothing but garlic. You don't lose weight, but people stand farther away, and you look thinner.

She's on a rotation diet. Every time she turns around, she eats.

I have a great new diet. I just cut out baked goods, anything sweet, or any dessert. I can't wait to start it. It's a piece of cake.

I have a great new diet. It's called a food bill.

Give up those intimate dinners for two—unless you have a date.

You can lose food through acupuncture. The stuff leaks out.

A woman told a friend, "I never eat anything with preservatives or additives. I never take a bite of anything that's been sprayed or given chemical grain."
The friend asked, "How do you feel?"
The woman moaned, "Hungry."

I am on a new Valium diet. It doesn't curb my appetite, but the food keeps falling to the floor.

There's a great new pasta diet—walk past a bakery, walk past a candy store, walk past an ice-cream shop. . . .

I went on a great diet recently. I don't eat while my wife is on the phone.

You should start dieting if you eat a Chinese dinner and the manager has to send out for more rice.

This young lady tells him that if it wasn't for this one diet drink, she wouldn't be able to get into her jeans. So he's been drinking it ever since.

We live in a strange country. We spend half our money on food, and the other half trying to lose weight.

A woman meets a friend for a cup of coffee and starts waxing eloquent about her husband. "He's a cheap bastard," the woman says. "He doesn't even leave me enough money for food. Last month I lost ten pounds."

The friend says, "Why don't you leave him?"

The woman says, "I will as soon as I lose ten more pounds."

Nothing tastes better than the stuff you're eating when you're cheating on your diet.

I know what I'm doing. I just traded in my diet and workout tape for one on self-acceptance.

The best way to diet: Take your scale out of the bathroom and put it in front of your refrigerator.

I just bought a great bathroom scale. It takes off for good intentions.

I went on a diet where you eat a lot of fish, but I quit. I was starting to breath through my cheeks.

I went to a spa where the portions are so small, the guests fight over the food. Each dinner table comes with a waiter, a busboy, and a referee.

My wife just went on her second diet. There isn't enough for her to eat on the first one.

A grossly obese man was sent to the hospital to lose weight. To ease the woes of a very strict diet, his employees sent him a beautiful flower arrangement to show their support. The fat man acknowledged the gift with a note: *Thank you for the flowers. They were delicious.*

My friend Tom bought a home exercise gym. Now he's starving to keep up the payments.

## DINERS

A trucker orders a bowl of soup. When the waitress brings it, he points to several suspicious spots. "Aren't these foreign objects?" he asks.

The waitress says, "No, these things live around here."

At Mom's Diner, you don't need a menu. To find out what's available, just look at Mom's apron.

It was a real greasy spoon. There was so much grease on the counter, the bugs thought it was a ride.

Do you know what a thrill it is to go into a diner and learn that the catch of the day was just swatted?

## DISAPPOINTMENT

Do you know what a disappointment it must be to find out you were voted the Eleventh Best-Dressed woman in the country?

Do you know how disappointed Columbus was when he asked the natives if they knew any good Chinese restaurants?

## DISCOMFORT

I feel terrible. I've got so much gas, I'm being followed by Arabs.

Oh, am I feeling that dinner. I wish I had this much gas when I was on the freeway!

## DISTANCE

A young man goes to a doctor and complains about his stomach. He hasn't been able to go to the bathroom in days. Taking a bottle from his cabinet, the doctor says, "Did you walk or drive here today?"

"I walked."

"How far is it?"

"About half a mile."

With this, the doctor poured a small amount of the bottle's contents into a glass and went on, "About how far is it from your front door to the bathroom?"

"Thirty feet, give or take a foot."

More liquid. "About how many feet is it to the toilet seat?"

"I'd say about six feet."

More liquid. The doctor stirred the mixture and said, "Drink this and go right home."

A half hour later the patient calls the doctor and says, "Hey, you're a great doctor. But you're a lousy engineer!"

## DIVORCE

I was happily married once. Now I just lease!

A marriage license is very important. Without one, you can't get a divorce.

Marriage is a knot tied by a minister and untied by a lawyer.

A wife lasts only as long as the marriage. But an ex-wife lasts forever.

I know a fellow who got a divorce because he lived in a two-story house. One was, "I got a headache." And the other was, "This isn't the right time of the month."

Divorce is the future tense of marriage.

In the old days, a gal married a guy for his money. Now, she divorces him for the same reason.

One woman told her divorce attorney, "My husband always said that everything he has is mine. Now, I want it."

Divorce starts with the engagement.

My mother-in-law broke up my marriage. One day my wife came home and found us in bed together.

Alimony is like not reporting a lost credit card.

**D**ivorce provides security for your wife's next husband.

**O**ne woman got a divorce after twelve kids—for compatibility.

**W**hen we divorced, my wife and I split the house. She got the inside.

**M**any women think it's okay for a man to leave them, as long as he leaves them enough.

**O**ne woman recently got a divorce because of the housework. She didn't like the way her husband was doing it.

**I** know some couples who have separate bedrooms, drive different cars, take separate vacations, and use different names—anything to keep their marriage together.

**Y**ou can't buy love, but you can pay through the nose for it.

**M**y wife would love to divorce me—if she could only find a way of doing it without making me happy!

**M**any divorces start with a separation. That's a smart way of giving a man time to hide his money.

**T**here are so many divorces today. That proves that there are more adults running away from home than children.

**D**ivorce laws can make you crazy. One state says you can't get a divorce un-less you can prove adultery. That's weird. The Ten Commandments say you shouldn't, and the state says you have to.

**A** woman is explaining her bad marriage to the judge and says, "That's my side of the story, Your Honor. Now, let me tell you his."

**A** man goes to court to get a divorce, explaining, "There are always crumbs in bed."
    The wife says, "Your Honor, make him stop talking that way about my gentlemen friends."

**H**e's been divorced so many times, he thinks his wife's name is "Plaintiff."

**I**t was a friendly divorce. He got to keep everything that fell off the truck as she drove away.

**A** couple goes to court after a brief attempt to reconcile. The husband says, "In the six weeks we were together, we haven't been able to agree on one thing."
    The wife says, "Seven weeks."

**W**e would have gotten divorced long ago if it wasn't for the kids.
    Neither of us want them.

**T**his woman got a divorce because her husband was careless about his appearance—he hadn't shown up in two years.

**H**is wife sued for divorce and asked for custody of the money.

Then there was the magician and his assistant who got a divorce. It was amicable until she wanted everything divided in half.

A fair divorce is when each party thinks he or she got the best deal.

All divorce proves is whose mother was right.

They ask one woman if she was planning to get a divorce. She says, "What for? I'm getting all I need on the side anyway."

The lawyers for a husband and wife are battling out a financial settlement. After hours and hours of negotiation, the husband's lawyer says, "Look, we upped our offer. Up yours."

There are 2 million divorces a year in America, so there must be something nice about it.

I know a man who'd love to divorce his wife, but he doesn't know her that well.

## DOCTORS

My doctor finally found out what I had—and took it.

My doctor told me I had low blood pressure, so he gave me his bill and raised it.

A man visits his doctor and complains about groin pains. After examining him, the doctor decides the muscles are strained. He asks the patient how often he makes love. The patient says, "I make love every Monday, Wednesday, and Friday."

"Well, you'll have to cut out Wednesday."

"I can't do that, Doc. It's the only night I'm home."

A patient called his doctor in the middle of the worst storm of the year and begged him to come out to the house because his wife was ill. The doctor said, "Why don't you make an appointment to come in and see me?"

The patient said, "In this weather?"

My doctor is a very busy man. He can only be contacted through his caddie, the skipper of his yacht, or his answering service.

He's a great doctor. He can tell what's wrong with you just by listening to your wallet.

Doctors are brilliant. They cure poor people faster.

A specialist is a doctor with a smaller practice and a bigger house.

An elderly physician went on a vacation and left his son in charge of the office. The elderly physician asked, "How did things go?"

The son said, "I cured Mrs. Jones of that stomachache she's had for twenty years."

The elderly physician said, "That was crazy! That stomachache sent you through medical school."

Two doctors found themselves on the beach at a resort in Hawaii. As the beautiful girls walked by in their scanty outfits, one of the doctors said, "Look at that. Those girls have great legs, don't they?"

The other doctor said, "I'm sorry, but I'm a chest man."

A patient came in for an office call. The doctor examined him and said, "It's a good thing you dropped in to see me."

The patient said, "Why? Are you broke?"

A good doctor can add ten years to your life—just waiting in his reception room.

When a doctor wants a consultation, it means that he's calling in an accomplice.

My doctor charges forty dollars for a house call—more if he has to dial the number himself.

A couple of kids were playing in the house, and one of them took some money out of his father's wallet. His friend said, "Come on, let's play doctor."

The kid said, "I am playing doctor."

A doctor's fiancée broke off their relationship. The next day he billed her for eighty-five house calls.

A doctor is a man who acts like a humanitarian and charges like a TV repairman.

My doctor says I have the body of a twenty-year-old—a twenty-year-old Chevy.

A man went to his doctor and reported, "I take a look in the mirror, and I think I'm looking at a dead man. My face is thin, my cheeks are hollow, my skin is sallow, my hair is falling out. What is it?"

The doctor said, "I don't know. But I can tell you one thing—your eyesight is perfect."

A doctor tells a male patient, "You're okay, but remember that your body is your home, so keep it neat and clean."

The male patient says, "Okay. I'll call in a woman twice a week."

I have a great doctor. If he treats you for kidney trouble, that's what you die from.

I found a way of getting my doctor to make a house call. I bought a place on a golf course.

The doctor told the pretty young girl, "Go into the other room and take off your clothes."

The pretty young girl said, "It's my aunt here who's sick."

The doctor said to the aunt, "All right, lady, stick out your tongue."

Doctors believe that the best things in life are fees.

**A** man hears the report from his doctor and says, "Can I get a second opinion?"

The doctor says, "Sure. Come back tomorrow."

**O**ne doctor told a patient, "Let me know if this medicine works. I'm having the same trouble myself."

**I** once asked my doctor, "How can I ever repay your kindness?"

He said, "Check or cash."

**A** man goes into a doctor's office and complains of being very tense. The receptionist says, "The doctor isn't in yet, but if you come in back with me, for fifty dollars I can relieve your stress."

They go in back, and his stress is relieved.

A week later, the man returns and makes the same complaint to the doctor. The doctor says, "Here's some pills. That'll be twenty-five dollars."

The man says, "If you don't mind, I'd just as soon have the fifty-dollar treatment."

**A** patient runs into his doctor at a party and starts to describe his symptoms: "I get dizzy, I have no appetite, and I haven't slept in a month."

The doctor says, "Make an appointment to see me."

The patient says, "I will. As soon as I feel better."

**M**y doctor told me I had two weeks to live. God, I hope they're not in August.

**T**he receptionist said, "Let's get your medical history. Do you pay your bills on time?"

**A** man goes to his doctor and complains of terrible gas, saying, "I've got a gas pocket like a rock. I haven't been able to get rid of it for three days."

The doctor gives him two pills and says, "These should give you relief. Just go home and take them. If they don't help, I'll give up my practice."

The man goes home and calls back in two days. "Doc," he says, "you're a genius. Those pills were fantastic. I feel great."

The doctor says, "That's good to hear. Where are you calling from?"

The man says, "I'm in a phone booth right next door to where the town hall used to be."

**A** patient walked into a doctor's office and asked, "Is the doctor in?" The receptionist said, "No. When he saw his malpractice insurance, he decided to become a lawyer."

**I**f laughter were really the best medicine, doctors would have found a way of charging us for it.

**A** patient tells his doctor, "I did what you told me to do. I slowed down and I lost my job, so now I can't pay your bill."

**A**n old lady comes into the doctor's office. He tells her, "Go into that small room and get undressed."

A few minutes later, the doctor walks

into the small room and sees the old woman sitting with all her clothes on. He says, "I told you to take off your clothes."

The old lady says, "You first!"

**A** bent-over man walks into a doctor's office. Opening the door to the examining rooms, the nurse leads him, saying, "Walk this way."

The man says, "If I could walk that way, I wouldn't need a doctor."

**My** doctor believes in shock treatments—his bill.

**My** doctor is doing so well, he can occasionally tell a patient there's nothing wrong.

**My** doctor never passes the buck. He keeps it.

"**Did** you recover from your operation?"

"No, I still have three more payments."

**A** man limps into a doctor's office and says that he was just bitten by a dog. The doctor says, "Didn't you see the sign on my office door? My visiting hours are only until four."

The man answered, "I'm sorry, Doctor, but the dog couldn't read!"

**A** shapely woman goes to her doctor. He asks her to undress. When she does so, he starts to feel her thighs, and asks, "Do you know what I'm doing?"

The woman says, "Yes. You're check-

ing to see if there are any abrasions or abnormalities."

The doctor starts to feel her breast, asking, "Do you know what I'm doing now?"

The woman replies, "Yes. You're trying to feel for any lumps that would indicate a problem."

Then the doctor pushes her back against the examining table and starts to make love to her, asking, "Do you know what I'm doing now?"

The woman answers, "Yes. You're getting herpes!"

**A** woman visited her doctor and complained, "This morning I went to the bathroom, and five pennies came out. This afternoon I went again, and dimes and quarters fell out. I couldn't wait to get here!"

The doctor said, "Take it easy. You're just going through your change."

**The** doctor's nurse called a patient: "Your check came back."

The patient said, "So did my arthritis!"

**I** know a doctor who's making real money. He bought his own cemetery.

**I** always wanted to be a doctor. I had the handwriting for it.

**Doctors** have it so good. They get a woman to take off her clothes, then they send the husband a bill.

**A** man brought his wife into the doctor's office, complaining that she was fading away. After a thorough examination, the doctor said, "She needs more sex. She should have sex every day." The man said, "Okay. Put me down for Tuesday and Thursday."

A couple walked into a doctor's office. The husband said, "My wife seems to be having trouble with sex." The doctor examined the patient carefully and found nothing. Then, to check on a thought he had, he started to have sex with her. The husband happened to come into the room as the pair were in the throes of activity. The husband asked, "What are you doing?"

The doctor said, "I'm taking her temperature."

"Okay," the husband said, "but that better have numbers on it when you take it out."

A woman walked into a doctor's office. Leaning against a cane, she seemed to be about four feet tall, her back being bent so much. The receptionist asked if any of the other waiting patients minded if the woman was treated first. There were no objections.

Ten minutes later, the woman emerged, walking as if she were ten feet tall. Another patient asked, "What kind of shot did he give you?"

The woman said, "He didn't give me a shot. He gave me a longer cane!"

I know a doctor who charges two hundred dollars a visit—more if you're sick.

Acupuncture is nothing new. My doctor has been sticking me with the bill for years.

I know a great doctor. He's trained his patients only to become ill during his office hours.

A patient walked into a doctor's office and was told he needed an operation. He asked, "What are you operating for?"

The doctor said, "Two thousand dollars."

The patient said, "No, I meant, what's the reason?"

The doctor said, "I told you—two thousand dollars!"

A patient tells her doctor, "I've consulted a fortune-teller, a palm reader, Tarot cards, and a faith healer."

"And what dumb advice did these quacks give you?"

"They told me to go see you."

A patient is terribly overweight, and the doctor tells him, "Look, I want you to eat normally for two days, then skip a day. In a month, you'll lose forty pounds."

The patient returns in a month, gets on the scale, and the reading shows that he has lost the required forty pounds. Congratulating him, the doctor says, "You lost all that weight just from following my diet?"

"That's right, although I have to tell you, I almost died that third day."

"From hunger?"

"No, from skipping."

A woman accompanies her husband to the doctor and waits while he gets a physical. After the examination, the doctor comes out and says to the wife, "I don't like the way your husband looks."

The woman says, "Neither do I, but he's good with the children."

A man goes to his doctor for an examination. After a battery of tests, the doctor says, "I have good news and bad for you."

"What's the good news?"

"My son has been accepted to Harvard."

"And the bad news?"

"You're paying for it."

Who will ever forget that immortal day when Stanley found the man he'd been searching for throughout Africa. "Dr. Livingstone, I presume." The doctor said, "Do you have an appointment?"

A young woman comes into the doctor's office and says, "I'd like a contamination."

The nurse says, "You mean an examination."

"That could be it. I hope that this doctor is a fraternity doctor."

"You mean maternity."

"Look," the girl says, "the heck with the big words. I just know I haven't demonstrated for two months, and I think I'm stagnant."

The doctor finishes his examination and tells the shapely young patient, "You're ill, young lady. Go home, get undressed, and lie down in bed. Take a few of these pills, and you'll get drowsy. Don't answer your phone. Don't let anybody into your apartment until you hear three short knocks."

I have a modern doctor. If you call with a complaint, he says, "Take two aspirins and fax me in the morning."

A teenager goes to a doctor for a checkup. When she removes her blouse, he checks her breathing and says, "Big breaths." The teenager says, "Yeth and I'm only thickteen."

An orthopedist and a tree doctor met and started to discuss business. The orthopedist said, "Oh, by the way, yesterday one of my patients ran into one of yours."

My doctor gave me an infallible cure for insomnia: Get lots of sleep.

With a bushel of apples, you can have a heck of a time with the doctor's wife.

The doctor tells the new patient, "Here's exactly what's wrong with you. You don't eat right, you don't exercise, and your eyes are weak. My sign says I'm a veterinarian."

"Doc, every time I drink coffee, I get a stabbing sensation in my eye."

"Take out the spoon."

This woman went to a plastic surgeon to have her breasts enlarged. After the surgery, she fell in love with the doctor, and they were soon married. Six months later, the glow was off, and a divorce followed. All the woman had left were her mammaries.

A doctor examined a patient with bruises all over his legs and asked, "Are those from horseback riding or softball?"

"Neither," the patient answered. "Bridge."

I know a patient with great guts. He told his doctor, "I don't have any money, but I'll pay you out of the malpractice suit."

A woman goes to a doctor, who tells her, "Take off your clothes."

She says, "You're not going to take me to dinner first?"

"You should see my doctor. He's great."

"But there's nothing wrong with me."

"Don't worry. He'll find something."

The average patient goes to the doctor four times a year. The average doctor goes to Europe five times a year.

A wrestler plunks himself down on the doctor's examining table. The doctor asks what bothers him. The wrestler explains, "Last night I was wrestling the Terrible Titan, and he had me pinned, so I figured there was only one way out.

His rear end was staring me in the face, so I took a big bite."

"Isn't that against the rules?" the doctor asks.

"Worse still, it was my own behind."

O'Connell wheeled his way into the doctor's office for his first physical since his accident. The doctor said, "I just don't know about whether you'll ever walk again."

O'Connell said, "Why don't you put a shot of whiskey on that table over there? If I can't make it, I'm helpless."

A doctor had taken his family to the seashore for a well-deserved vacation. They walked down to the beach, and the doctor almost fainted when he saw a fin sticking up out of the water. His wife saw his reaction and said, "My dear, that was just a shark. You've got to stop imagining there are lawyers everywhere."

An elderly couple go to the doctor for a physical. Most of the tests are perfect, but the man has a problem. He tells the doctor, "The first time I make love with my wife, everything is fine. But the second time, I sweat like crazy."

The doctor asks the wife, "Can you explain that?"

The wife says, "Certainly. The first time is in December, the second in August."

Why shouldn't I be coughing more easily, Doctor? I practiced all night.

Then there was a doctor who failed as a kidnapper. Nobody could read his ransom notes.

"I feel terrible, I have a high fever, and every bone aches. Please come to see me."

"Ma, you know I don't make house calls."

You should consult my doctor. You'll never live to regret it.

The doctor tells his elderly patient, "You'd better stop drinking or you'll go blind."

The patient says, "I'm ninety-one. I think I've seen just about everything I want to."

The husband says to the doctor, "Have you got something for my wife's laryngitis that'll cure it in a couple of months?"

Then there was the patient who told the doctor he was a kleptomaniac and wondered if there was something he could take for it.

The nurse rushes into the doctor's inner office and says, "The patient you just gave a clean bill of health to dropped dead outside the door. What should I do?"

The doctor says, "Turn him the other way, so it'll look like he was just coming in."

I told my doctor my nose was sore. He told me to stay off it for a few days.

"Doctor, I have trouble breathing."

"Don't worry. I'll give you something to stop that."

I don't know why they say that a doctor treats you.

"I'm the doctor's nurse."

"Gee, I didn't know he was ill."

"Doc, do you think I'll live?"

"Yes, but I don't advise it."

He was a lonely proctologist, so he looked up a few friends.

I know a doctor who's so independent—he won't even make hospital calls.

It's about eleven at night, and the doctor has just come in from making his rounds at the hospital. He's so bushed, he falls asleep as soon as he sits down on the couch. A moment later, the phone rings. His wife answers. As she listens, he signals her to say that he isn't home yet. His wife tells the caller that. The caller says, "Have him call me as soon as he comes in. My husband has the hives."

Now half-awake, the doctor forgets himself and mumbles to his wife, "Tell her he should take a Benadryl and call me in the morning."

The wife repeats his message to the caller, who says, "Is the guy with you qualified to give medical advice?"

A really smart doctor is one who can diagnose the problems of a patient who doesn't smoke, drink, or overeat.

An older man goes to a doctor and gets examined. The doctor says, "I think you ought to cut your sex life in half."

The older man says, "Which half: talking about it or thinking about it?"

The pretty patient says, "Doctor, I'm afraid I'm a nymphomaniac."

The doctor says, "Don't worry. I have just the thing for you."

The doctor tells the lady patient, "Go into the other office and lie down on the couch." The lady patient says, "My boyfriend said that a month ago. That's why I'm here."

A young woman comes into the doctor's office and complains of some symptoms. The doctor says, "Stop smoking, eat better, and go to sleep early. In fact, have dinner with me, and I'll see that you're in bed by nine."

A girl walks into the doctor's office, feeling listless. The doctor says, "You've either got a cold or you're pregnant."

The girl says, "I must be pregnant. I don't know anybody who'd give me a cold."

"Doctor, you charged me fifty dollars, and all you did was paint my throat."

"What do you want for fifty—wallpaper?"

I have a very neat doctor. He always washes his hands before he touches my wallet.

The doctor tells one patient, "You'll be up and complaining about my bill in no time."

I have a buddy who's always being consulted by doctors. He's a caddie.

A man goes to a doctor for a physical checkup. The nurse starts with certain basic items. "How much do you weigh?" she asks.

"One-seventy."

The nurse puts him on the scale. It turns out that his weight is 183.

The nurse asks, "Your height?"

"Five-eleven."

The nurse checks and sees that he's only 5' 8½".

She then takes his blood pressure, and it's very high. The man explains, "Of course it's high. When I came in here, I was tall and wiry. Now, I'm short and dumpy."

Can anybody explain why the scale in the doctor's office is always five pounds more than the one at home?

At the end of her seventh month, a pregnant circus performer seeks out a leading doctor in Boston and asks how much longer she can safely continue to do her act.

"The circus!" exclaims the doctor. "What do you do in the circus?"

"I walk the tightrope," she says.

"Holy smoke!" he says. "You do your act tonight, because I have tickets, but tomorrow you quit!"

**M**y doctor has real problems. Tomorrow he's operating on a malpractice attorney!

**T**hen there was the woman doctor who had a problem. She wanted to paint a patient's throat, but she couldn't decide on the color.

**A** man complains to his doctor about his inability to perform sexually. The doctor gives him some pills. A few hours later, the doctor calls the man, asking, "Did the pills help?"

"You bet. I've already had three orgasms."

"Your girl must be happy."

"She didn't get here yet."

**H**e's a miserable doctor. I called him because I was constipated, and he put me on hold.

**O**ne doctor became a psychiatrist and a specialist in proctology. Now, he can fix both odds and ends.

**A** woman told her doctor, "I don't feel good, and I'm constantly constipated."

"Tell me," the doctor says, "do you take anything?"

"Yes," the woman says, "I always take my knitting."

**A** doctor was called out to a house in a blizzard. The snow was so thick, he had to walk the last half-mile of the journey. After examining the man, he ordered, "Get your lawyer, your family, and your friends over here on the double!"

Once everyone had assembled, one of the man's friends asked, "Is he really that sick?" The doctor grinned. "He'll be fine in forty-eight hours—I just didn't want to be the only one out on a night like this."

**A** man goes to a doctor for a vasectomy. The doctor says, "This is a rather important matter. You should discuss this with your wife."

"I did. She told me to ask the kids."

"Did you?"

"They voted for it, twelve to six."

**A** man goes to a doctor with a strange complaint. The man has a giant penis that pulls down on his vocal cords, causing him to stutter badly. The doctor says, "I can cure you, but I'll have to amputate and take six inches from your member." The man agrees. The operation is a success. The man can return to a pleasant sex life. After a while, however, the man starts to miss the part of him that made him the talk of the town. Returning to the doctor, he asks that the missing piece be grafted on again. The doctor says, "I'm-m-m af-f-f-raid t-that-t's-s imp-p-posible."

## DOGS

**T**hen there was this neurotic bloodhound. He thought that people were following him.

**"W**hat do you do if a Great Dane starts to make love to your knee?"

"Fake an orgasm."

A blind man walks along with his new seeing-eye dog. When they reach a corner, the dog lifts a leg and wets down the blind man's shoe. The blind man reaches down and pats the dog's head. A passerby says, "I don't understand that. The dog just misbehaved and relieved himself on your shoe. Why are you patting him? I'd give him a good swift kick in the rear end."

The blind man says, "First, I find his goddam head, then I kick his rear end!"

A company is making a fortune with a new dog food. It tastes like the mailman.

Seeing a puppy she adores, a woman asks the pet shop clerk, "Does that dog have a pedigree?"

The clerk answers, "Lady, if that dog could speak, he wouldn't say a word to either of us."

A woman is walking along with her dog and is stopped by a wino who asks, "Lady, can I throw your dog a bit?"

The woman says, "Certainly."

So the wino picks up the dog and throws him thirty yards.

"I got a dog for my wife."

"No kidding? I wish I could make a trade like that."

Two dogs met. One asked the other, "What's your name?"

The other answered, "I'm not sure but I think it's Down, Boy."

A dog saw a sign, WET PAINT, and he did.

A man told his friend, "I shot my dog last night."

The friend asked, "Was he mad?"

"Well, he wasn't too happy about it."

A woman lost her dog, but she wouldn't put an ad in the paper. She said her dog couldn't read.

He calls his dog Handy because he's always doing odd jobs around the house.

One day a man bought a bulldog. In no time at all, he had him eating out of his leg.

This man had seventy-two dogs in his house. The doctor told him to stop whistling in his sleep.

A man walks into a bar with a small dog. The bartender shakes his head and says, "Sorry, sir, you can't bring a dog in here." The man says, "You don't understand. This is a talking dog." The bartender says, "Oh, sure he is. Please leave."

"I'll ask him some questions, and you'll see."

"Okay. I'll give you about a minute."

The man turns to the dog and asks, "What's on top of the house?"

"Roof," says the dog.

"What's a bad place to be on the golf course?"

"Ruff."

"Who's the greatest baseball player in history?"

"Ruth."

The bartender says, "You must think

I'm some kind of dummy. Get out of here."

The man and the dog exit. In the street, the dog turns to the man and says, "Do you think I should have said Ted Williams?"

**A** kid explains to a friend, "My dog must have had a flat today. I saw another dog blowing her up."

**T**he town idiot was elected dogcatcher. He knew that he was supposed to catch the dogs. But at what?

**H**e called his dog Seiko. It was a watchdog.

**A** man tried to board a bus with his giant Saint Bernard. Naturally, the driver refused him entry. The man told the driver what he could do with the bus. The driver answered, "If you can do that with your Saint Bernard, you can get on the bus!"

**I** took my dog to obedience school. I learned how to fetch two hours before he did.

**I** never realized that a dog is man's best friend until I started betting on horses.

**A** dog is better than a wife. The license is cheaper, there are no in-laws, and he already has a fur coat.

**I**t's a school for hunting dogs. A man is watching a demonstration. The hunting dog he's interested in is being put through its paces. It runs into a clump of bushes and returns and wags its tail once. The teacher explains, "There's one bird in that clump." Sure enough, a bird flies up and out of the bush. The teacher points to a second clump. The dog returns and wags its tail twice. Sure enough, two birds fly out. After two other clumps, the dog returns from a fifth with a stick, which he shakes and drops at his teacher's feet. The customer says, "What does that mean?"

"It means that clump has more birds than you can shake a stick at."

**A** dog's affection increases in direct proportion to how wet and sandy he is.

**I** bought a lapdog last week, but every time I try to sit in his lap, he bites me.

**M**y dog is a Doberman pinscher. He goes around all day pinching Dobermans.

"**I** want you to keep that dog out of the house. It's full of fleas."

"Rex, don't go in the house. It's full of fleas."

**A** ventriloquist walks into a bar with his small dog. Putting the dog on the top of the bar, he asks for a scotch and soda. The dog says, "I'll have a ginger ale."

Another customer looks up, amazed. "Does that dog talk?"

The dog says, "I certainly do."

The customer says, "Wow! I must have that dog. Sell me that dog. I'll give you anything."

The ventriloquist says, "How about a hundred dollars?"

"Done." The customer whips out his bankroll and manages to come up with the money. The ventriloquist pushes the dog over to him.

The dog says, "Just for that, I'll never say another word for the rest of my life!"

My dog is taking an advanced course at obedience school. He knows how to fetch, heel, stay, and now he's learning how to fax.

A woman calls the doctor and says, "My dog just swallowed fifty aspirins. What should I do?"

The doctor says, "What else? Give him a headache."

Did you ever hear of the gay attack dog? If you come near it, it'll scratch your eyes out.

We just got a Great Dane. I think the house'll be broken before he is.

The way I see it is: When a Doberman licks your face, he's not being friendly. He's just basting you.

## DREAMS

I know a lawyer who charges you if he dreams about you.

A man had a terrible nightmare. He dreamed that he'd jumped from a plane, pulled his parachute rip cord, and the chute didn't open. Then he looked down, and waiting on the ground to catch him was an outfielder for the Dodgers.

I got double rest last night. I dreamed I was sleeping.

"In my dream last night, I dreamed you bought me a fur coat."

"When you dream tonight, wear it well."

Dreaming is the only place you can meet a better class of people.

A middle-aged woman went to her doctor complaining of a recurring dream in which she's constantly pursued by a young man intent on having her sexually. The doctor sent her home with sleeping pills.

A few days later, the woman returned. "Aren't you sleeping any better?" asked the doctor.

"Oh, I'm sleeping fine," the woman said, "but I sure do miss that young man."

## DRINK

They have a new support group called Teetotalers Anonymous. If you feel like going on the wagon, you call a certain number and two drunks come over to talk to you.

He drank so much, he was officially declared a beverage.

She told me she was the cream of society, and I believed her. Whenever I saw her, she was at the top of a bottle.

My doctor says that my wife'll go home to her mother if I keep drinking. I wish she would, because this booze is killing me.

He had to give up those three-martini lunches. They were cutting into his cocktail hour.

My uncle tried to stop drinking recently. Two bars sued him for nonsupport.

My nephew just had a baby. Now, his wife has to have two bottles ready at night.

I always know when I've had too much to drink—somebody steps on my tongue.

If she takes a drink, she can't feel it. If she takes two drinks, she can feel it. If she takes three drinks, anybody can feel it.

I recently went on the drinking man's diet. I lost twenty pounds and my driver's license.

A man who'd had a little too much to drink looked to the gentlemen seated at the bar near him and asked, "Did you spill a drink on me?"

"Certainly not."

"That's what I figured. It's an inside job."

A man without arms walked into a bar, sat down, and ordered a drink. When the bartender brought it over, the armless man said, "Will you please hold it up to my mouth?"

When the bartender had done so, the armless man said, "Could you reach into my pocket, please, and take out my handkerchief so you can wipe off my face? I seem to have spilled a bit of my drink."

When the bartender had wiped off the moist face and replaced the handkerchief, the armless man said, "By the way, where's your john?"

The bartender pointed off and said, "About six blocks down."

He just got a new job—in an auto repair shop. He breathes off the old paint.

Nobody ever drove me to drink, but they sure had to drive me back.

He drank a fifth of whiskey every day of his adult life. When he died, they cremated him, and it took four days to put out the fire.

A drunk staggered out of a bar, staggered the two blocks home, staggered into the house, fully expecting to get the usual lecture from his wife. The wife, however, had decided to try kindness. She smiled and said only, "You've had a long day. Let's go up to bed and make love."

The drunk said, "We might as well, because I'm going to get hell from my wife when she gets back!"

I won't say he's a boozer, but the other day he cut himself, and the blood had a head on it.

A social worker visited the jail and asked one dejected man, "Was it liquor that brought you here?"

The dejected man answered, "Nope. You can't get any in here."

Joe Paysock came home all snockered, but managed to undress and get into bed without waking his wife, except for one small accident. Turning the wrong way in the living room, he walked right into the bar and the shelves of whiskey bottles displayed there. He had a few nicks on his face, so he rushed into the bathroom and did a little first aid on himself. In the morning, he came into the kitchen as if all was well. His wife said, "You were drunk again last night."

"Heavens no," he answered. "I just got hurt at work."

His wife said, "Okay, then explain the bandages all over the bathroom mirror."

There's a wonderful remedy for a hangover—just take the juice of two martinis.

A man should learn that martinis and a woman's breasts have a lot in common. One isn't enough, and three are too many.

Drinking gets rid of pimples—not on you, but on the girl you picked up at the bar.

It only takes one drink to get pie-eyed. It's either the fifteenth or the sixteenth.

The other day he took a blood test, and they found an olive in it.

He isn't really a boozer. He willed his body to science, and he's preserving it in alcohol until they need it.

They're thinking of closing bars earlier, but the way I see it is—if you can't get drunk by midnight, you're not trying.

Although many people have tried, nobody has found a way to drink for a living.

A drinker has a hole under his nose that all the money goes into.

I don't know why people accuse me of not being sober. I've been sober three times today already!

A wino was explaining his drinking to a friend who thought he was stupid. The wino said, "Oh, yeah? If you put a bucket of booze and a bucket of water in front of a jackass, which would he drink?"

The friend said, "The water, of course."

"I rest my case."

Whiskey drinkers get more cavities than milk drinkers. But they go to the dentist in a better frame of mind.

I know a bar with midget waiters—for patrons who like to drink themselves under the table.

One old boozer loves this one bar. He says, "They're very considerate. After I drink for a while, they always serve me coffee on the floor."

I read so much about the bad effects of drinking, I've decided to give up reading.

He has two olives in his martinis. The doctor told him to eat more vegetables.

Lost in a blinding snowstorm, Joe sees a Saint Bernard approaching him. Joe jumps up and says, "Thank God! Man's best friend. And a dog too."

Then there was the guy who poured margaritas in the birdbath. It was enough tequila mockingbird.

My uncle still has his baby habits. He gets his two o'clock bottle, his three o'clock bottle . . . his . . .

"Drinking makes you look beautiful," he said.
   "I haven't been drinking," she said.
   "I know, but I have," he said.

He's been drinking all his life. In college he was voted the most likely to dissolve.

I won't say he drinks, but this year's New Year's resolutions started out: "First thing I'm going to do is find out what year this is."

A wino comes out of a bar and goes right into a lamppost. He circles it for a while, then says, "It's no use. I'm walled in."

A drunk is driving home when he runs into a telephone pole. He comes up with a handful of wires and says, "Thank God, it's a harp."

I knew it was time to quit drinking when I started to read the handwriting on the floor.

Two drunks staggered into the lion's cage at the zoo. The lion roared, and one drunk said, "I'm getting out of here."
   The other said, "Not me. I'm staying for the movie."

A lush got into a cab and said, "Take me to Grogan's Bar."
   The cabbie said, "You're there."
   The lush said, "Thanks, but next time don't drive so fast."

Two men were drinking in a bar. After the fifth shot, one of the men fell off his stool, passed out, and was dead to the world. The other one looked down and said, "That's what I like about Joe. He always knows when he's had enough."

You know you're drunk when your hiccups are slurred.

He drank to people's health so often, he ruined his.

A man was walking along when he saw a cluster of people around an evangelist. The evangelist was fuming about the evils of drink, pointing out that the city was filled with lushes, that men couldn't go a day without getting drunk, that some spent their last pennies on liquor.

The encounter changed the man's life. Right after the sermon, he went out and bought a bar.

My brother drinks occasionally—and at every one, too.

Water kills more people than booze. Remember the Flood?

Two boozers are walking down the block, and one asks, "Who has horns, a tail, and carries a pitchfork?"

The other one says, "I don't know. Why?"

"Because he's been following us since we had that last drink."

Congress is smart. They put a big tax on booze, then they drive you to drink.

He's a big drinker. He's the only one who blows on birthday cakes to light the candles.

This woman has had a hard day, so before she puts Junior to sleep, she makes herself a martini. As she kisses the kid good night, he looks up and says, "Mommy, you're wearing Daddy's perfume."

Downtown they have a zillion winos. Liquor stores have to sell milk under the counter.

Some drunks feel sorry for the rest of us who don't drink. When we get up in the morning, that's about as good as we're going to feel.

My brother-in-law won't eat breakfast unless it has ice in it.

His idea of frozen food is scotch on the rocks.

He only drinks because he's cautious. He's afraid Prohibition will come back.

He does drink some. He hasn't had a drink in two months, and he still has a hangover.

Jones is wandering around feeling no pain at five in the morning. A cop asks him, "Do you have an explanation for this?"

Jones says, "If I had an explanation, I would have gone home to my wife."

A man who has obviously had too much to drink drives his car into a lamppost. An officer rushes over, and the drunk says, "Thank God, an officer. Can you tell me where I am?"

The officer says, "Fifty-ninth Street and Maple."

The man says, "Forget the details. Which city?"

I can tell when my girl drinks too much. Her face gets blurred.

This drunk flows into his house at about four in the morning. His wife says snidely, "Why do you come home at four in the morning?"

The drunk says, "It's the only place open."

This man is at a bar. Every time he takes a drink, he shuts his eyes first. The customer next to him asks, "Why do you close your eyes when you drink?"

" 'Cause I love this stuff so much. If I look at it, my mouth waters, and that dilutes it."

A drunk sits down in the park and starts to throw bread to the pigeons, calling at them, "Here, pigeon, pigeon, pigeon."

Cackling, all but one pigeon rush over and start nibbling at the bread. The drunk looks at the pigeon off to the side and says, "How do you like that? A deaf-and-dumb pigeon."

He makes a great martini. The secret is in the dust.

Liquor may be slow poison, but who's in a hurry?

I'm sore at my wife. The other day she was cleaning the attic, found a bottle of twenty-year-old scotch, and threw it out. She figured it was stale.

A drunk staggers into the house at three in the morning. His wife looks at him and sums up her feelings in one word: "Swine!"

The drunk says, "No, sweetheart. Swhiskey."

In the Ozarks, where the homemade whiskey is a little stronger than in the rest of the country, they have a different definition of intoxicated. A man was lying in the middle of the street in a hot noonday sun.

"He's drunk," the sheriff said. "Guess I'll run him in."

"No, he's not," the man's friend said. "I saw his fingers move."

A banker got slightly loaded at a party but was determined to maintain his dignity when the hostess showed him her newborn twins.

He said, "Ah, what a beautiful child."

A drunk looks up from his tenth drink and says, "Bartender, I have to go. Which way is the bathroom?"

The bartender waves off toward the bathroom and, as the drunk staggers off, adds, "While you're there, go for me too."

The drunk leaves, returns in a few minutes, sits down on his stool, then suddenly looks up, saying, "I forgot something."

Once again he staggers off to the men's room, returning a few minutes later and saying to the bartender, "You didn't have to go."

My uncle was a souse. At Christmas we used to stand him in the window because he was more lit up than the tree.

Holding a gun in one hand and a bottle of cheap wine in the other, a wino stopped a well-dressed man and said, "I don't want your money or your watch, pal. Just take a swig of this."

The well-dressed man took a sip of the wine and spit it out. "This is rotgut!"

"I know," said the wino. "Now you hold the gun and make me take a swig!"

One tonsil was talking to the other: "It's so dark in here, I can't tell where we are."

"It must be Capistrano," said the other tonsil. "Here comes another swallow!"

A few drinks of moonshine, and you're eight feet tall and bulletproof.

I staggered home one night and told my wife we had a drinking contest.

"Oh, yeah?" she said. "Who came in second?"

You know you're drunk when somebody tells you to go fuck yourself and you ask for the phone number.

You know you've had too much when you try to play a pizza on the stereo.

He's of mixed heritage—half Scotch, half soda.

## DRIVE-INS

There are people who go to see a movie at a drive-in and love every minute of it.

One thing about a mystery movie at a drive-in. Even when it's over, nobody knows who did it.

## DRIVING

One lady driver said, "The thing I hate most about parking is that noisy crash."

"I'm afraid your wife fell out of your car about a mile back."

"Thank God! I thought I'd gone deaf!"

A truck driver tried to edge his semi past the lady driver on the road ahead of him as she was obviously having difficulty deciding which lane she wanted to be in. Finally, her mind made up, the woman veered into the truck driver's lane and jammed on her brakes, which resulted in a slight collision.

Unhurt but obviously harried, the lady driver rushed over to the truck driver and started to bawl him out, barking, "You knew I was going to do something idiotic. Why didn't you stop to wait and see what it was?"

A little girl asked her father, "Daddy, before you married Mommy, who told you how to drive?"

A drunken driver was heading up a one-way street the wrong way. A policeman stopped him, pulled him over, and asked, "Where the heck do you think you're going?"

The drunken driver answered, "I

don't know. But I must be late, because everybody else is coming back."

When a woman gives you half of the road, it's usually on both sides of her.

A careful driver is one who just saw the guy ahead of him get stopped by a motorcycle cop.

If you don't like the way women drive, get off the sidewalk.

You don't need manners if you're a five-ton truck.

I got a puncture in a tire the other day. I didn't see the fork in the road.

She's a bad driver. When we were on vacation, we went to Egypt. She came back from the Pyramids with a dented camel.

The guy who drives like he owns the road generally doesn't even own the car.

A motorcycle cop stops a driver and starts to write a ticket because the man was going fifty-five miles in a thirty-mile zone. The driver looks at it nicely and says, "Could you make that eighty? I'm trying to sell the car."

Be careful of children. They're terrible drivers.

Bad driver? She once got a ticket for making a U-turn in the Lincoln Tunnel.

The little girl is crying and yelling at her mother because she backed the car over the doll. The mother said, "Don't come crying to me. I told you not to leave it on the porch."

Driving while drunk today is almost as dangerous as walking sober.

The fastest way to get the light to turn from red to green is to look for something in the glove compartment.

How come when you're driving, anybody going slower than you is a moron, and anybody driving faster than you is a maniac?

A married couple pull into a service station for gas. As part of the service, the attendant starts to wipe the front window. The husband says, "Just wipe her side. That's where all the driving's being done."

What this country needs is a set of brakes that will stop the car behind us.

She's pretty good. She gets twenty-two miles to a fender.

A couple is stopped by a traffic cop who starts to write them a speeding ticket. The man says, "I wasn't going over forty." The wife chimes in, "I was watching. He never went over twenty." The man added, "Fifteen at tops."

The cop says, "I'd better give you a ticket for illegal backing up."

How about the woman driver who went to heaven? She drove through the Pearly Gates and took one of them with her!

## DRIVING WIVES

A motorcycle cop stopped my wife the other day for going too fast. As he started to write out the ticket, he said, "Ma'am, you weren't going ninety in a twenty-mile zone, but I'm giving you a ticket for trying."

When my wife has an accident, it's never her fault. Two days ago, a building backed into her.

A man went out for a spin in the country. For hours, his wife showed why she had a black belt in backseat driving. Finally, the man couldn't take it anymore and barked, "Look, who the hell is driving this car—you or your mother?"

My wife is going to England. She wants to see what it's like to drive on the left side of the street legally.

The other day my wife called me. "The car's stalled."
    "Where are you?"
    "In a phone booth on the corner of Walk and Don't Walk."

My wife backed out of the garage this morning, but she forgot she backed in last night.

"How did the accident happen?"
    "My wife fell asleep in the backseat."

The cops stopped my wife so often they finally gave her a season ticket.

Wife to husband: "I put a little scratch on the bumper, dear. If you want to look at it, it's in the backseat."

I let my wife drive the car the other day, and she only hit one thing—Nevada!

My wife's car wouldn't start this morning. Her fuel line was clogged with pedestrians!

## DRUGS

Then there was the man who mixed his wife's ashes with marijuana. It was the first time she ever made him feel good.

They now have a new soap for drug dealers. It launders your money.

The other day, the cops broke into an old man's house and found him snorting prunes.

They'll never get around to legalizing pot. Too many people keep forgetting where they left their petitions.

A dog was responsible for a big marijuana bust. His handlers knew they had something when the dog started sniffing the bales and then sat down and wrote a rock song.

Two college kids are planning an evening. The first says, "Tonight we're going to do every drug they've come up with."

The second says, "Are you sure that's what you want to do?"

The first college kid replies, "Man, you'll forget all your concerns and problems. Everything will be great, and if you're real lucky, you'll want to die!"

Miracle drugs are great. They keep you alive until the bill is paid.

My wife takes a lot of pills. If she breathes at you, you go limp.

They're incompatible. He's on Xanax and she's on Valium.

Two druggies are tearing down the boulevard. One says, "Okay, another two blocks and then you make a left."

The other druggie says, "Why tell me? You're driving!"

They have a great new drug now. It doesn't make you relaxed. It just makes you enjoy being tense.

There used to be only one drug problem—where to get a prescription filled on Sunday.

"Why is sex like marijuana?"

"Because the quality depends on the pusher."

A man goes to his doctor for something that will cure his impotence. The doctor says, "Okay, I have a new pill. Take it right now and run home. It only works for two hours."

The man runs home only to find a note in the kitchen from his wife. She's gone shopping and won't be back for three hours. The man calls the doctor and asks if there's something that can be done.

The doctor says, "Isn't there any woman who can help you?"

"The only woman around is the maid."

"Then go have fun with the maid."

"You don't understand, Doc. For the maid, I don't need a pill."

## DRUGSTORES

"Do you have Prince Albert in a can?"

"We certainly do."

"Better let him out, he's suffocating."

A man walked into a drugstore and was rather embarrassed about making a purchase because the clerk was a woman. The man asked for the owner. The clerk told him that she and her sister owned the drugstore and were qualified pharmacists. What was his problem?

After hesitating for a moment, the man finally said, "I need some kind of pill to help me with my sex life. I can't seem to get enough sex. What can you do?"

The clerk said she'd discuss it with her sister, went in back, and returned a few moments later. "I talked it over with my sister, and the best we can do," she said, "is a thousand cash and the drugstore!"

A pharmacist is a man in a white coat who stands behind a soda fountain selling you a cheap watch.

**A** kid walked into a drugstore and asked the druggist, "Do you fit diaphragms?"

"I do."

"Okay, wash your hands and get me an ice-cream cone."

**T**he whole neighborhood shook from the explosion. As shopkeepers ran outside to see what happened, they spotted the pharmacist staggering out of his smoldering building.

His white uniform was now scorched black. He went up to a woman standing nearby.

"Lady!" he said, "Would you please ask your doctor to write that prescription again. And this time, PRINT IT!!"

**A** Scot goes into a drugstore and buys a baby bottle. The druggist says, "Ian, that's a mighty extravagance."

The Scot says, "Not this time, Brian. She's had triplets."

**A** lady went into a drugstore and bought two packages of invisible hairpins. As she paid for them, she asked the clerk, "Now, are you sure these hairpins are really invisible?"

"Lady, I'll tell you how invisible they are," the clerk said. "I've sold fifty bucks' worth of those pins today, and we've been out of them for weeks!"

## DRYNESS

**T**here hasn't been a drop of rain around here for months, and there's an incredible water shortage. Old ladies don't know what to throw on two dogs in heat!

**I**t hasn't rained in so long, people are putting stamps on letters with thumbtacks.

**O**ne day in this part of Texas, a few drops of rain fell. One man fainted. They had to revive him by throwing a bucket of sand in his face.

**T**urn on a faucet in some parts of Nevada, and you get hot or cold dust.

**T**here are fish in Nevada that haven't learned how to swim yet.

**I**t was so dry, they had female dust-wrestling.

## DULL

**H**e's so dull, he couldn't even entertain a doubt.

**H**e's so dull, he could be the sex symbol for Women Don't Care Anymore.

**H**e's really something—when he walks into an empty room, he blends right in.

**I** won't say he's dull, but he puts more people to sleep than ether.

**H**e asked his wife what he could do to improve their sex life. She said, "Get out of town."

GUEST: This is a dull party. I think I'll leave.

HOST: That might help it!

He has the personality of a dial tone!

Philadelphia isn't as dull as people say it is. It just seems dull because it's right near thrilling Camden, New Jersey.

He's the kind of guy who'd notice that there was a horse under Lady Godiva.

If his life were a movie, he'd spend his time at the snack bar.

His life is so dull, he looks forward to dental appointments.

His life is so dull, he has to count sheep to keep awake.

## DUMB

"Why is he such an imbecile?"
"The hours are good."

"Are you positive?"
"Only a nut case is positive."
"Are you sure?"
"I'm positive."

He was real dumb. He tried to raise eggplant by burying a chicken.

He was the dumbest burglar in town. When he robs a house, he breaks two windows—one to get in and one to get out.

Great inventions by dumb people: parachutes that open on impact; the waterproof sponge; the waterless shower; the artificial appendix; onion-flavored mouthwash.

He's real dumb. He likes to finger-paint, and it took him two years to do the kitchen.

He once bought a suit with two pairs of pants, but he didn't like it. It was uncomfortable wearing two pairs of pants.

She's really dumb. She has a twin sister, and one time she forgot her birthday!

She's real dumb. When she eats alphabet soup, she needs an interpreter.

They were so dumb. They adopted a Korean kid and went to school to learn how to speak Korean. They wanted to understand the kid when he grew up.

Somebody stole his car, but he wasn't worried. He got their license-plate number.

He walks around with his fly open all the time. That's in case he has to count to eleven.

He was pretty dumb—he once turned down a cruise around the world because he didn't have a way of getting back.

He's so dumb. The other day the Mafia made him an offer he couldn't understand.

He's pretty dumb. He signs his checks with a typewriter.

Dumb? He'd commit suicide on his vacation.

They told him his ship would come in someday, so every day he waited at the bus station.

She's not too bright. I gave her a calendar watch. She nailed it to the wall.

One day he went out and bought a toupee. The ad said he could swim, ski, and even wrestle in it. He didn't need a toupee, but he wanted to become good in sports.

He won a gold medal at a track meet and had it bronzed.

He was a dumb pharmacist who quit his job because he couldn't get the little bottles in the typewriter.

The sergeant told the new recruit that he'd have to put on new underwear every day. After a week, he couldn't get his pants on.

He went to a doctor to get a hernia transplant.

She's very dumb. She just signed a medical card that in case of death allows the hospital to use her kidneys for heart transplants.

He's pretty dumb. He'd put a ZIP code on the Gettysburg Address.

She's so dumb, she felt she had to study for a blood test. She didn't, and she flunked.

He's real dumb. He picked a guy's pocket in an airplane and made a run for it.

He was a dumb kid—his folks went to PTA meetings under an assumed name.

The Dummies were having their nightly brawl. Mr. Dummy said, "You don't have a brain in your head. I bet you think that Dun is married to Bradstreet."

Mrs. Dummy answered, "What's the difference? As long as they love each other."

He's not a big brain. He once froze in a drive-in because he went to see a movie called *Closed for Winter*.

He heard that most accidents take place within five miles of the home, so he moved.

Then there was the dummy who got a ticket for speeding while on the way to his mother-in-law.

He's not too bright. He once opened a breakfast shop in Niagara Falls.

He's real dumb. I saw him this afternoon, and he was soaking wet. I asked him why, and he said, "Those are the instructions. It says 'Wash and Wear.' "

He's so dumb—his pencils have erasers at both ends.

How about the gardener who went to work for a golf club? The first day, he filled in all the holes.

## DYING

Life is great. Without it, you'd be dead.

Did you ever look at an obituary column? Everybody dies in alphabetical order.

He died a natural death. He was hit by a car.

A woman has been carrying on with the family's boarder for years. One day the woman dies. The boarder goes to pieces. He can't eat, he can't sleep, he just sits around the house and mopes. Finally, the husband goes over to him and says, "Don't worry, Joe. I'll get married again."

The dying old man says to his wife, "When I'm gone, let Phillip run the store."

The wife said, "Phillip? He can't run a store. Let Harold run it."

"Okay, let Harold run it. But give Seymour my car."

"Willie needs it."

"Okay, give it to Willie. But let Marsha have the bungalow at the lake."

"Marsha hates water. Let Ann have it."

"Look, who's dying—you or me?"

A widow should be grateful for one thing. She knows where her husband is.

## DYSLEXIA

There was once a dyslexic who was an atheist. He didn't believe in Dog.

A bumper sticker: DYSLEXICS OF THE WORLD, UNTIE!

There's a new organization called the DCO—the Organization to Cure Dyslexia!

In Israel the poor dyslexic has to start at the beginning of a book!

A dyslexic took an eye test and found out he had 02-02 vision!

I know a guy who was dyslexic, but he was also cross-eyed, so everything came out right.

# E

## EASTER

Easter morning, the rooster took a little walk and saw a whole lawn full of colored eggs. He wheeled and ran down the block to knock the hell out of the neighbor's peacock.

I like Easter Sunday. That's the day my wife gets home from her office Christmas party.

The class is discussing Easter, and the teacher asks little Johnny to explain about the holiday. Johnny says, "Well, I think it's where Jesus dies and they put Him in a cave for a while and they pray and then Easter morning He comes out and . . . and . . . and if He doesn't see His shadow, He goes in again."

## ECONOMICS

The United States keeps losing money every year. Somebody must be fooling around with the books.

The cost of living is like a miniskirt. Neither can go much higher.

It's not the purchasing power of the dollar that has me worried. It's the purchasing power of my wife.

The trouble with economics is that there are more ways to go into debt than there are ways to get out of it.

A recession is when your pal loses his job. A depression is when you lose your job. A panic is when your wife loses hers.

You know there's inflation if you save up to buy something and it isn't enough.

I can't pay as I go. I haven't even paid for where I've been.

They say you can't take it with you. I can't even afford to go.

You know times are bad when couples get married because they need the rice.

It's awful. Today money doesn't buy as much as when I didn't have any.

Things must be real bad. The president walked into a room, and the Marine Band played, "Brother Can You Spare a Dime?"

I won't say we're in a recession, but I put two dimes in a phone booth, and the operator said, "God bless you."

Remember the good old days when students, not teachers, went after the summer jobs?

No matter how bad things become, I hope they never get as tough as my wife's roast beef.

I wish people would stop talking about a recession. I'm still forty grand in the hole from the boom.

The president said that inflation has been arrested. He should check—I think it's out on bail.

I've got a lot of frozen assets—four TV dinners.

I won't say inflation is rampant, but the other day a man gave out dollar bills, and he was arrested for littering.

That's our big problem—you can't take it with you, but where can you go without it?

With the shape of today's economy, if pessimists aren't happy, they never will be.

The good news is that we see a light at the end of the economic tunnel. The bad news is that it's a homeless man looking for food.

Inflation is when it costs so much to make a thing, you can't afford to sell it.

The best time to buy something is a year ago.

There's one basic problem with our economy. We all work five days a week, but the government spends seven.

They say that a dollar doesn't go far nowadays. Mine goes all the way to Washington.

In the good old days, I could live beyond my means for half as much as it takes today.

An economist is a guy who knows a thousand ways to make love, but doesn't know any girls.

Nobody will ever invade us. Who can afford to live here?

I tell you, prices are high. The other day I saw an Arab sending home for money.

Nowadays, I eat only political meals—fifty dollars a plate.

Business is so bad, lobbyists are using food stamps to bribe congressmen.

I found a great way to make inflation go down. I'll buy stock in it!

Everybody has to chip in today in the house. I just found a part-time job for our parrot.

We're a wasteful people. We have ten times as much inflation as we need.

Depressions come at the wrong time. They show up just when everybody's out of work.

Inflation is being broke with lots of money in your pocket.

All my friends kept telling me, "Cheer up. It could be worse." So I cheered up. And things got worse.

Living in the past has one thing going for it—it's cheaper.

"What's the difference between a pigeon and the average farmer?"
"The pigeon can still make a deposit on a tractor."

Business is so bad, one big hotel chain is stealing towels from the guests.

I know a lot of men who are very stressed—from underwork.

I found out why it's so hard to keep up with the Joneses. They're on welfare.

## EDUCATION

I've been studying trade relations. That's what I'd love to do—trade relations.

Education is important. After all, if you couldn't sign your name, you'd have to pay cash.

You can lead a horse to water, but if you can teach him to float on his back, then you've really got something!

Then there was the man who cut classes in correspondence school. He sent in empty envelopes.

He has a B.A., an M.A., a Ph.D. but no J.O.B.

## EFFICIENCY

The expert has it all worked out, telling the boss, "Get rid of the clutter. Throw out all the old bills and letters and invoices."

The boss says, "Good idea. But first we'll make copies."

An efficiency expert is a guy who puts unbreakable glass on all the fire alarms.

## EGO

A man explains to a friend, "I used to be a selfish, conceited, overblown pain in the ass. I went to a shrink for six months. Now, you couldn't meet a nicer, more considerate guy than me."

She's so self-involved, she has a special place in her heart for herself.

I know a fellow who's so egotistical, he believes that God only gave *him* the Ten Suggestions.

Some people fall in love with themselves, but he just filed for self-adoption.

He hates to read books or go to movies. They take his mind off himself.

A conceited person never gets anywhere. He thinks he's there already.

A man told a friend, "You know, I'm not fair. I don't love myself as much as I should."

If you fall in love with yourself, you have no rivals.

You can always tell an egotist by the faraway look in his eye when the conversation goes off him.

He's really self-centered. When he walks down the street, he holds his own hand.

An egotist is the kind of guy who doesn't go around talking about other people.

I won't say he's egotistic, but he found his better half in a mirror.

"What does a man have that gets bigger when you stroke it?"
"His ego."

He's such an egotist. When he hears thunder, he takes a bow.

The most difficult secret for an egotist to keep is his opinion of himself.

It's a good thing he doesn't have to pay taxes on what he thinks he's worth.

He's such an egotist. When he says his own name, he takes off his hat.

When somebody asks him to name the Seven Wonders of the World, he makes the list twice.

I know a guy who's so egotistical, he collects his own autographs.

He's such an egotist. At a funeral, he's sorry he's not the corpse.

God didn't give me looks, but he gave me an absolute monopoly on brains and talent.

He's not egotistical. He just admires brilliant people.

His marriage was an eternal triangle—his wife, him, and him.

An egotist is a guy who just happens to be everything you think you are.

An egotist is a man who tells you tons of stuff about himself that you were going to tell him about yourself.

His idea of being unfaithful is to turn away from his mirror.

He's one of the most egotistical men in the world. When he has a climax, he screams his own name.

He never takes a hot shower. It clouds his mirror.

I like egotists. Under duress, they'll concede they're wonderful.

He's got such an ego, his head is getting too big for its toupee.

People who think they know everything really bug those of us who do.

"What does your new girlfriend think of you?"
"She thinks I'm wonderful and terrific."
"What do you like most about her?"
"That she thinks I'm wonderful and terrific."

## ELECTRICITY

I didn't know what to get our electrician for Christmas, so I just got him some shorts.

He bought his wife an electric toaster. Then he bought her an electric mixer. Then he bought her an electric typewriter. He's working his way up to a chair.

## ELEPHANTS

The elephant was taking a drink in the river when a crocodile bit off his trunk. The elephant said, "Veddy funny. Veddy funny."

Then there was the elephant who went away to forget.

Then, as the river said when the elephant sat down in it, "Well, I'll be dammed."

"How do you make an elephant fly?"
"Well, you take a zipper about three feet long . . ."

This elephant decided to make love to a female mouse. The female mouse says, "I'm a little afraid."

The elephant says, "Don't worry. I'll wear a golf bag."

"How do you find an elephant?"

"An elephant is so large, he's hardly ever lost."

A cop sees a man walking with an elephant and asks, "Where are you going with that beast?"

"To have her bred."

"Where?"

The man raises the elephant's tail and points, saying, "Right there."

"Why do ducks have flat feet?"

"To stamp out forest fires."

"Why do elephants have flat feet?"

"To stamp out burning ducks."

"How does an elephant get up a tree?"

"He sits on an acorn and waits for a squirrel to carry him up."

"Where would you find an elephant?"

"That depends on where you left him."

## EMBARRASSMENT

Tom is visiting the Adlers. During the evening, Tom has to go to the bathroom, so he saunters in and locks the door. Unfortunately, he's in the wrong bathroom and has sat down on a seat that had been painted an hour before. He finds himself stuck to the seat. He makes a terrible racket, and his host and hostess arrive. They force the door open and see Tom's terrible condition. The host rushes for a screwdriver. He manages to separate the seat with, of course, Tom's bottom still glued to it, from the rest of the unit. Tom says, "Did you ever see anything like this?"

The host says, "Yeah, but this is the first time I ever saw one framed."

A man knocked on Marsha's door as she sat relaxing in the bath. The knocker persisted, so Marsha called out, "Who's there?"

The man answered, "Blind man."

Feeling secure, Marsha didn't bother to put on even so much as a towel when she went to the door to find out more. She opened the door, and the man said, "Okay, where do you want me to install these blinds?"

This woman and her son are in a nice restaurant. There's quite a bit of food left over, so the woman tells the waiter, "Please put the meat in a bag for the dog."

The son jumps up. "Wow, Ma, are we getting a dog?"

## ENEMIES

I've learned to love my enemies. It drives them up a wall.

Be nice to your enemies—remember, you made them.

He has no enemies. His *friends* hate him.

## ENGLAND

An American is invited to go on a hunt with an English duke. After an hour out, the American rides over to the duke and says, "I just shot the strangest creature. It had a huge nose and big fat ears and the widest ass I ever saw."

The duke says, "Old boy, I think you got the duchess."

"They say that one out of every six Englishmen is a homosexual."

"Are you sure there'll always be an England?"

During World War I, the skipper of a small British ship runs into a large German warship. He looks through his binoculars for a while, then whirls and orders, "Battle stations."

The small ship heads right for the warship, arrives at its side, and proceeds to attack it with the few small guns it carries. Hour after hour, the small ship keeps attacking. Finally, the warship sinks.

The small ship returns to port and a cheering populace. The town mayor asks, "How could you take on a battleship like that?"

The skipper explains, "I didn't mind when it shot at some of the ships we were escorting. I didn't mind when it started to loft giant shells at our coast. But when one of their sailors spit in our ocean, I became frightfully angry."

A tourist was asked what he thought about warm English beer. He said, "I think they ought to pour it back into the horse."

This American goes on his first English fox hunt. When it's over, his host explains, "Look, when we first see the fox, we say, 'Tallyho,' not 'There goes the little son of a bitch.' "

There was a big spelling bee in England recently. For a while, it looked as if a young farm boy from the countryside would win, but they asked him to spell "auspice."

This Englishman comes home unexpectedly and finds his wife in bed with another man. The Englishman gets his hunting rifle from the gun rack and shoots the man.

Seeing this, the butler says, "Good hunting, sir. You got him on the rise."

During the London Blitz, a wife screamed at her husband to come with her to the bomb shelter.

"I'm not going until I find my false teeth," came the reply.

"Are you balmy?" she asked. "They're not dropping sandwiches!"

A cockney hobo comes into a pub called the George and Dragon. He asks for a free drink. The lady behind the counter comes forward, spits at him, and tosses him out of the pub.

Getting up, the hobo says, "Okay, can I also talk to George?"

This couple comes out of the hotel, and the doorman signals a cab. The people get in, and the doorman says, "Waterloo."

The cabbie says, "The station?"

Icily, the doorman replies, "Well, it's a bit late for the bloody battle."

## ESKIMOS

I have a great recipe for Eskimo pies. First, take two Eskimos . . .

Once there was an Eskimo girl who spent the night with an Eskimo boy. The next morning she found out she was six months pregnant.

A bishop discovered a tribe of Indians in the Yukon who had never recorded a baptism, confirmation, or marriage. The bishop soon rectified the situation by baptizing and confirming everyone. He also married every beaming couple that walked by.

Later, the tribal chief told the bishop the tribe had never had so much fun. The bishop asked the chief which part they enjoyed the most.

"The marriage service," the chief said, smiling. "We all got new wives!"

When Eskimos meet, they rub noses. The rest of us rub fenders.

Eskimos always teach their kids not to eat the yellow snow.

Wrong! A snowbank is not where Eskimos keep their money.

## ETERNITY

Eternity is the second hour of Trivial Pursuit.

Eternity is waiting for the rabbit to die.

Eternity is waiting for the AAA in the rain.

Eternity is the second ten minutes of aerobics.

Eternity is somebody reloading the projector for more home movies.

Eternity is jogging back.

## ETHNICS
### (You Fill in from Your Own Bigotry)

The sign on the ——— dance hall reads: MEN AND WOMEN WELCOME, REGARDLESS OF SEX.

"Why don't they have ice cubes in ———?"

"The lady who had the recipe died."

They have a new ——— abortion clinic. There's a two-year waiting period.

Have you ever seen a ——— firing squad? They form a circle.

"**W**hat do you call a pretty girl in ———?"

"A tourist."

**T**he other day sixty ———s died. They tried to push-start a submarine.

**T**wo ———s almost drowned. They tried to build a cellar in their houseboat.

**I** know this ——— who was in the army. During a battle, he ran out of ammunition. So he kept on firing. That way the enemy wouldn't know.

**T**hen there was this sixty-year-old ———. She went on the pill so she wouldn't have any more grandchildren.

**T**he ——— water-polo team had very bad luck. The horses drowned.

**A** ——— policeman answered a call to a bank where half a million dollars had been stolen. He spent weeks trying to find a motive for the crime.

——— don't buy balloons. They don't come with instructions.

**A** ——— is chopping away the cross beam over his front door as a friend comes by. The friend says, "What are you doing?"

The ——— says, "I figure the cold weather's coming, so I'm making it so that my horse can get into the house."

"Why ruin your door? Just dig up a little earth at the bottom."

"You're a fool. It's not his feet, it's his head can't get in."

"**W**hy did the ——— proctologist use two fingers?"

"He wanted to get a second opinion."

**A** ——— climbs a tree to catch a parrot. Higher and higher they go. When they reach the top, the bird says, "What are you after?"

The ——— says, "Sorry, pal. I thought you were a parrot."

**A** ——— airplane crashed into a cemetery. Immediately, an investigative committee went to work. In less than two days, they'd already found a hundred thousand bodies!

"**W**hat is the last thing a ——— stripper takes off?"

"Her bowling shoes!"

**T**wo ——— were at the beach. A nude girl walked by, and one of them said, "I'll bet she looks great in a bathing suit."

"**W**hy don't ——— throw dinner parties?"

"Because they can't spell RSVP."

**I**n ——— they just opened a massage parlor. It's self-service.

**A** ——— doesn't act stupid. It's the real thing.

**T**he ——— have finally done something about the population explosion. They've started to sterilize storks.

A nurse approached an impatient —— in the maternity-ward waiting room. "Congratulations," she said, "you have twins."

The —— said, "Don't tell my wife. I want to surprise her."

A group of ——s are hired to work with another gang to put telephone poles into the ground. At the end of the first day, the boss asks the foreman of the ——gang how many poles they put in. The foreman says proudly, "Three."

The boss says, "You're not serious. That other gang put in twenty-one poles."

The —— foreman says, "Sure, but look how much of them they left above ground."

A —— left the theater after the first act because he read in the program that Act Two was a week later.

"Why did the —— lose his job at the M&M factory?"

"He kept throwing away the *W*'s."

Some ——s tried to climb Mount Everest. They almost made it, but fifty feet from the top they ran out of scaffolding.

Then there was the —— athlete. He defected to ——. That raised the IQ of both places.

Two ——s are at the zoo. They come to a large cage in which there are several kangaroos. A sign in front of the cage identifies the marsupials and says that they're Australian. One of the ——s says, "It's a shame. My sister married one of them."

"How can you tell a —— on the slopes?"

"His skis have chains."

"What do you do if a —— throws a hand grenade at you?"

"Pull the pin and throw it back."

The —— clothes designer came up with new uniforms for the team. Aghast because they were transparent, the coach said, "You can see right through these uniforms."

The designer answered, "Not while they're wearing them."

A —— arrives in America and is asked, "How did you get here—plane or ship?"

The —— says, "I don't know. My brother bought the ticket."

"How does a —— pilot navigate?"

"He reads street signs."

A —— had a used-car lot. He spent most of his time turning back the fuel gauges.

Once upon a time, two ——s went ice-fishing. They drowned frying their catch.

A —— bought his wife a washing machine, but it had to be sent back. Every time his wife got into it, she came out black-and-blue.

## ETIQUETTE

A young woman should wait in the car until her escort opens the door for her. However, she shouldn't wait too long. If he's already in the restaurant and is ordering his entrée, she shouldn't wait much longer.

Etiquette is when you make your guests feel at home when you wish they were.

## EUNUCHS

Then there was the eunuch who got his job in the harem by accident.

A eunuch is a man just cut out to be a bachelor.

## EXERCISE

If exercise makes you lose weight, how come my wife's mouth is over a double chin?

The only exercise he gets is pushing his luck.

The human body has thousands of muscles just to tell us we shouldn't have jogged so much.

Why does anybody who jogs ten miles a day go crazy when he can't find the TV remote control?

I hate those body-builders. I met one the other day—he had muscles on his breath.

The only exercise I get is bending to my wife's will.

They tell me swimming is great exercise. Did you ever see a whale?

My wife has a brand-new exercise. She shops faster.

No matter how much I exercise my body, it refuses to go away and leave me alone.

I get winded winding up a conversation.

If he didn't raise his eyebrows, he'd get no exercise at all.

They say exercise kills germs. How do you get them to exercise?

I have a special way of falling down— it's called skiing.

A man trained for two years to run the Boston Marathon. He had to quit after twenty-five miles and went home to find his wife in bed with a guy who'd quit after one mile.

My wife doesn't have to go to exercise class. She's had enough just by trying to get on her leotard.

I really don't need hours of exercise and running. I can fall down without any help.

I get winded reading the paper.

I didn't pay anything for my body, but the maintenance costs are rather high.

## EXPERIENCE

The trouble with experience is that it teaches you stuff you don't want to know.

Experience is what you have when you are too old to get a job.

Experience is what you get when you don't get what you want.

## EXPLORERS

Two explorers meet on a remote mountain high atop the Himalayas. One says, "I came here to get away from the clutter of the city, the dirty air, the panic of city living, and the sickening pace. I wanted to be where the air was clean, where I could see a lone eagle soaring above, and watch the sun set behind snowcapped mountains. Why are you here?"

The second explorer says, "Because my son is taking violin lessons."

The explorer returns from a trip to the frozen north and runs into the bootmaker who had made his weatherproof boots. "How were they?" the bootmaker asks.

"Best boots I ever ate," says the explorer.

## EYES

My wife makes love with her eyes closed. It gives her a chance to think about shopping.

"I've been seeing spots before my eyes."
"Did you see a doctor?"
"No, just spots."

When he took his eye examination and the doctor showed him the eye chart, he kept answering True or False.

"Doctor, when I drive on sunny days, I get the sun in my eyes."
"Drive on cloudy days."

"I wear sunglasses on rainy days. They protect me from umbrellas."

## FACES

She has a face with everything, including some things that I never saw on a face before!

While she's strolling through the park, an old maid is attacked by a man. She rushes home and tells her sister, who says, "Come into the kitchen immediately." In the kitchen, the sister cuts a lemon in half. Offering half, she says, "Suck on the lemon."
　"What'll that do?"
　"For one thing, it'll get that grin off your face."

He has some face. He has to sneak up on the mirror to shave!

She always cleans her mirror. Who wants to see dirty wrinkles?

"She had her face lifted the other day."
　"No kidding? Who took it?"

She had the face of a saint—a Saint Bernard!

"He must use an electric razor. He has a face only a motor could love!"

He had a face like a dog's dinner.

"She has a face only a mother could love."

"Not necessarily. I'm her mother!"

She looked like death warmed over—in a waffle iron!

She had a natural complexion—oatmeal!

He had so many pockmarks on his face, he shaved with an echo!

She always kept her mouth closed. She was afraid they'd put an apple in it!

## FAILURE

Two bums were sitting leaning against a tree in the fields. One said, "I'm sick and tired of this life. I'm sick and tired of sleeping in the cold and rain, begging for food, wearing torn clothes. I'm sick of it."

The second bum said, "If you feel like that, why don't you get a job?"

The first bum sat up and said, "And admit I'm a failure?"

For years, he was an unknown failure. Now, he's a known failure.

## FAIRY TALES

Snow White had twins. That proves only one of the dwarfs was dopey.

Jack's mother told him to take the cow to market and sell it because they needed money badly. Taking a shortcut across the railroad tracks, Jack was unable to move the cow along, and it was hit by the train, knocking its tail off. When Jack got to town, he had to sell the cow wholesale because he couldn't re-tail it.

## FAITH

A man is driving, skids off the road, and lands at the edge of a cliff. His car totters. One slight move and it will go over the precipice. As he sits there, sweating, waiting for some divine help, he hears a voice, "Open the door and grab the big branch of the tree near you."

"Who is this?"

"This is God. Do what I tell you. Open the door and grab the big branch."

"But, God, I'd never make it. If I sneezed, I'd be dead."

"Do what I tell you. Open the door and grab the big branch."

"Maybe You can help me."

"I can't leave heaven. Do what I tell you."

"Wait a minute, God. Is there anybody else up there I can talk to?"

I'm losing faith in my doctor—all his patients seem to be sick.

## FAME

Lyndon Baines Johnson was a senator and already well known. In a fancy Washington restaurant one afternoon, a man ran into him at the entrance and said, "Senator Johnson, I admire you. I respect you. I'm having lunch with some buddies, and they'd flip if you came over to my table and made some small talk with me."

The senator smiled and went off to join his party. A few minutes later, he rose and strolled over to the man's table. "Hi, Freddy," he said. "Introduce me to your friends."

The man said, "Later, Lyndon. Can't you see we're having lunch?"

## FAMILY

Every morning I come down to breakfast and have coffee with two lumps— my wife and her brother.

A family with ten kids returns from a car trip. The father is asked, "Where did you stop?"

He answers, "At every service station."

A widow with sixteen children was asked what she was looking for in a second husband. Without hesitating, the lady answered, "Moderation."

I'm having my will changed to read, *I leave all my relatives all the money they owe me!*

He took after his mother who took after her father who took after the maid.

My nephew was in the sixth grade so long, they thought he was the teacher.

The boss's son returned to his office from a two-week vacation. A co-worker asked, "How was it?"

"Great. But it's terrific to be back. There's nothing like the feel of a desk under your shoes again."

A family is a group of people who each like different breakfast cereal.

My mother broke a leg. Now, my dad can't work. It was his leg.

People complain about nepotism. But let's face it—the queen of England got her job through family.

The reason grandparents and children get along so well is that they have a common enemy.

Nowadays, parents pray that the youngest child will get married and move out of the house before the oldest gets divorced and moves back in!

In some parts of West Virginia, incest is in wide practice. The people are relatively happy.

You can always tell when a guy grew up with a big sister. One eye is shaped like a keyhole.

Two sisters had been fighting and feuding all of their lives. One day Mary becomes ill. She calls Tessie over and says, "Tessie, I want to let you know that if I die, you're forgiven for all you've done to me. But if I get well, things remain just like they are."

A mother and her young son are washing the dishes while the father and the daughter watch television in the den. There is, suddenly, a crash of breaking glass. After a moment, the daughter says, "It was Mom's fault."

"How do you know?" the father asked.

"Because Mom didn't say anything."

Two Hollywood kids are talking, and one says, "My mother is going to court tomorrow to sue my father."

The other kid says, "Boy, you're lucky. My mother doesn't know who my father is."

A pedestrian is a man with two cars, a wife, and a son.

"Ma, where does fire go when it goes out?"

"That, my child, is one of the great mysteries about fire and your father."

I come from a stubborn family. They didn't know the meaning of the word "quit" until I was born.

My son took a bath yesterday. My wife spent half the night dredging it.

We have two daughters, but they don't live with us. They're not married yet.

My brother-in-law hangs around the house so much, we're having slipcovers made for him.

I have a very independent son. He lives alone at our house.

My daughter used to think I was a dreamboat. Now, she thinks of me as a supply ship.

A woman goes to court and complains that her husband deserted her and their ten children.

The judge asked, "When did he desert you?"

"Ten years ago."

"How come all those children?"

"He kept coming back to apologize."

My brother-in-law likes to fix things around the house—like drinks, sandwiches . . .

My brother-in-law must be a great pool player. We had meatballs last night, and he ran fifteen before I got one.

My brother-in-law is a fast eater. I've seen him eat a minute steak in twelve seconds.

Sometimes I wish my wife was my mother—then I could run away from home.

A young man gets off the train as it stops for a few minutes in Pottersville and asks the stationmaster, "Does Al Brody live here?"

"Nope."

"You ever hear of Al Brody?"

"Nope."

"Anybody ever mention Al Brody?"

"Nope."

Heading back for his luggage, the young man says, "Then this is where his new son-in-law is getting off."

Grandma comes to visit the family for the first time. Little Margie, age eight, says, "You're my grandma, huh?"

"Yes, my dear. On your father's side."

"Gotta tell you—you're on the wrong side."

## FAMOUS LAST WORDS

This is General Custer speaking. Men, don't take prisoners!

This'll be a short meeting.

There'll be zillions of good-looking girls.

You can put it together yourself in five minutes.

Believe me, nobody'll dress up.

We'll only stay five minutes.

My folks'll be home late.

Why put the top up? It won't rain.

One hot dog won't blow my diet.

Of course there's film in the camera.

You'll housebreak him in no time.

They'll feel terrific once you break them in.

When it says empty, there's always a gallon or two left.

If you knew anything, you wouldn't be a traffic cop!

Gimme a match, I think the gas tank is empty.

You can make it! That train isn't coming fast.

Of course, bring the kids.

That's not poison oak.

Me? Why would the army take me?

I don't burn, I tan.

Take off your clothes, the doctor will be with you in a minute.

Your table will be ready in five minutes.

Of course they're mushrooms. Toadstools come to a point.

We have plenty of room.

We service what we sell.

Is there anything I can do?

## FAMOUS QUOTES

Achilles' mother: "Stop whining! There's nothing wrong with your heel."

The great Mahatma Gandhi said, "If you don't let my people go, who'll run the Seven-Eleven stores?"

Custer said to Sitting Bull, "Hold it. I thought we were playing two out of three!"

King Kong said to Fay Wray, "Not right now. I have to catch a plane."

Sigmund Freud's mother: "Stop pestering me, I told you a hundred times, the stork brought you!"

Jack the Ripper's mother said to Jack, "How come you never go out with the same girl twice?"

To Franz Schubert: "Take my advice, never start anything you can't finish."

Let's take Amelia Earhart, who said, "I don't go all the way."

## FARM LIFE

A farmer owes his life to udders.

The crops were bad this year. In order to mow the wheat, they had to lather it.

A farmer was bragging: "I put up a scarecrow, and I didn't lose an ear of corn."

The second farmer said, "That's nothing. My scarecrow was so scary, the birds brought back the corn they stole a year ago."

A city girl is wandering around in the fields when a bull rushes at her. She runs off and manages to climb up a tree. Laughing, a farm boy helps her down and asks, "Can't you use a little good loving?"

The city girl says, "Sure, but what am I going to do with a calf in the city?"

A census-taker comes to a ramshackle cabin in the hills of Missouri. The roof is a sieve, the walls are crumbling, and the floors give with every step. The census-taker says to the farmer, "I finally found you—the poorest man in the state."

The farmer says, "Don't bet on it. I live here, but I don't own the place."

This farmer has a cow he adores, but his pasture runs through some railroad land, and at the same hour daily, a train whizzes by. One day the cow is missing, so the farmer sues the railroad. Before the case goes to the judge, the farmer agrees to settle for half. The railroad lawyer says, "You had us worried. You could have held out for it all."

The farmer says, "You had me worried too. The cow came home this morning."

A tourist in New England stopped at a small service station and asked directions to a certain town. Given the directions, the tourist drove on. An hour later, he found himself at the same service station. "What the heck's going on?" the tourist roared.

The service station owner answered,

"Just wanted to see if you could follow directions."

**A** gentleman farmer is one who has whitewall tires on his manure spreader.

**A** farmer is munching on a cookie as he watches the rooster chase a hen around. Playfully, the farmer throws a piece of cookie to the ground. Seeing it, the rooster stops chasing the hen and runs to the piece of cookie. The farmer shakes his head slowly and says, "Gosh, I hope I never get that hungry."

**T**hings aren't going too well on the farm. There's not much money in milk and eggs, so many a farmer is sitting around, trying to figure out something else the cows and chickens can do.

**T**his city slicker comes on a farmer in an orchard. Holding a goat in his arms, the farmer has climbed a ladder. The goat nibbles at some shiny red apples. The city slicker says, "What are you doing?"

"Feeding my goat."

"But doesn't it take longer that way?"

"Sure, but what's time to a goat?"

**T**here's something great about living on a farm. Where else can you find people who get up to watch the Late Late Show?

**I** met a farmer who was an absolute magician. He turned a cow into a field.

**A** stranger noticed that there were children all over this town. They numbered many times the average. The stranger asked a clerk in the drugstore why there were so many children.

The clerk said, "It's on account of the train."

"What does the train have to do with it?"

"It comes by at about five in the morning and gives the darndest whistle. Wakes everybody up. Well, it's too early to get up, and it's too darn late to get back to sleep."

**M**y wife and I were in the country a few weeks ago. We were standing in front of a wishing well, and she fell in. I never dreamed those things worked.

"**W**hat's that I smell?"

"Fertilizer."

"For land's sake!"

"Yes, ma'am."

**A**n IRS man asks a farmer, "How much is your prize bull worth?"

The farmer says, "For tax purposes, or has he been hit by a train?"

**O**ne farmer couldn't keep his hands off his bride, so he fired them.

"**I**s this milk fresh?"

"Fresh? An hour ago, it was grass."

**S**ome of our cattle were so thin, we put carbon paper between them and branded two at a time.

**B**ronson, a visiting farmer, can't help but admire the efficiency of Taylor's farm. "How do you get your bulls to breed so well?"

Taylor says, "I give them potency pills."

"No kidding? What are they made of?"

"Darned if I know, but they taste a lot like a saltine."

**A** farm is a parcel of land on which, if you get up early enough in the morning and work late at night on, you'll make a fortune—if you strike oil.

**A** farmer won $10 million in a lottery. Asked what he was going to do with the money, he answered, "I guess I'll just keep farming till it's gone."

**A** farmer put an ad in the papers that said, *Need wife who owns her own tractor. Please send picture of tractor.*

**F**armer Brown and Farmer Stone were always trying to outdo one another. One day Farmer Brown told his son to go over and borrow Stone's cross-saw. "Tell him," Brown said, "that I want to cut up one of my pumpkins."

The son returned a short time later and said, "He can't let you have his saw just yet. He's in the middle of cutting one of his potatoes."

**T**he Farm Bureau sent a young investigator out to check a farm area. About a week later, he called in and said that he'd found a strange creature on a lot of farms. It was haggard, scraggly, had a thin frame and a pained look. Was it some new kind of animal? His supervisor said, "That's the farmer. Be nice to it. It votes!"

**A** real estate man applied some pressure to make a sale of some poor farmland. "All this land needs is a little water, a cool breeze, and some good people to settle here."

"Maybe so," said the prospective buyer, "but that's all hell needs too."

**A** salesman asks a farmer where he can find Farmer Peterson. The farmer says, "Drive down about six miles, turn at the crossroads, and it's a mile up. But don't honk your horn."

"Why not?"

"Well, Peterson's wife ran away with some dude six months ago, and every time Peterson hears a honk, he's afraid it's the dude bringing her back."

**T**his farmer experimented for years and finally came up with a new kind of chicken soup. But he couldn't get his chickens to eat it.

**T**his farmer's eyes went bad. One day he milked the same cow twelve times. She didn't give milk all the time, but she tried.

**W**e tried mating cows and mules so we could get milk with a kick in it.

**T**hen there were the two shepherds who merged. It was shear and shear alike.

**A** young commuter late for his train asked a farmer, "Do you mind if I cut through your field to catch the six forty-five?"

"Not at all," the farmer said, "but if my bull sees you, you'll catch the six-fifteen!"

A dude from the city goes to a ranch for a vacation. While there, he sees a fierce-looking bull snort and charge a cowboy in the pasture. The cowboy takes off like a bat out of hell and jumps into a large hole. After a moment, he jumps out of the hole and starts running as the bull comes after him again. The dude says, "Why didn't you stay in the hole?"

The cowboy says, "Because there's a snake in it."

Then there's the farmer's daughter who was sent home from the state fair because she couldn't keep her calves together.

I can't understand the guys from the country who go to the city so they can make enough money to move to the country.

A farmer is hammering away when a neighbor comes by and asks, "How's the missus, Henry?"

"Not well."

"That her coughin'?"

"No, this is a new shed."

A city boy who hasn't been within a hundred miles of a farm before arrives and is bewildered. Noticing a jar of honey on the table, he says, "Gee, you folks have a bee."

The farmer's daughter suffered a fate worse than death so that she could pay the villain who held the first mortgage on the farm. She must have enjoyed it, because the next day she went out and looked for the guy who held the second.

The government sent a farmer a notice that an adviser was coming to the country to teach the farmers how to farm better. The farmer wrote back, *I won't be at your meeting. I'm not farming half as good as I know now.*

This city slicker goes to a small hillbilly town where he rents some dogs for hunting. He comes back to the general store and asks for more dogs. "What happened to the others?" the storekeeper asks.

"I shot them already."

A farmer is talking about his neighbor, known for his playing loose Molly with the truth. The farmer says, "I won't say he lies, but when it's time to fetch the hogs for slop, he has to have somebody else call them."

When a farmer plans to get a cow with calf, the process is called "serving the cow." No wonder a lot of farmers shiver when they hear a candidate say he wants to "serve the public."

Silas had a smart dog. It knew how fast to run after coyotes so it wouldn't catch up to them.

The farmer has his bull attached to his plow and works the animal up and down a rocky field. Another farmer, passing by, says, "You got a tractor. Why don't you use that?"

The first farmer answers, "I'm trying to teach this bull that there's more to life than romance."

A farmer's cow got out of his grazing field and found its way to another farmer's still. The cow proceeded to drink up about five gallons of home brew. By morning the cow was dead. The farmer sued.

The defense attorney put him on the stand and proved it wasn't the whiskey that got the cow. It had started to give eggnog, and the farmer had milked the poor thing to death.

When you hear the farm prices and it says, "Slaughter cows weak," it doesn't mean that some cows are taking it worse than others.

What this country needs is a lie-detector test that seed catalogs can take.

## FAT

She's pretty fat. In fact, she's taller lying down than she is standing up.

You know you're fat when you're sitting in a chair and rock yourself to sleep trying to get up.

She was real fat. One day I was at her side hugging her and kissing her. Then I saw a guy on the other side doing the same thing.

One day when she was wearing a blue dress, she yawned as she stood on the street. Somebody shoved a letter in her mouth!

She's so fat, she was the front row in her high school graduation picture.

You know you're fat when you can donate your pants as a shelter for the homeless.

Two women meet and one says, "My husband just bought me something, and I'm so ashamed. I can't get into it."

The other woman said, "Change it for another outfit."

"What outfit? I'm talking about a Mercedes."

A heavy woman walked into a department store and said to the clerk, "I'd like to see a bathing suit in my size."

The clerk said, "So would I."

One fat woman says to another, "My husband loves to make love to skinny women."

The second says, "What's wrong with that?"

The first one says, "He likes to do it when I'm at Weight Watcher's."

She's so fat—when she sits at a bar, she doesn't have to drink to have a hangover.

She's so fat—a phone booth fits her like a girdle.

I won't say she's fat. She's just living beyond her seams.

She's getting a double chin. I think it was too much work for just one.

I won't say she's big, but cars won't pass her on the right.

A rather obese man is in a car showroom and is being shown a Jeep by the salesman. The obese man says, "It's nice. What would it take to get me into one of those?"

The salesman says, "A crowbar might do it."

She's real fat—she and the Statue of Liberty wear the same size dress.

You know you're fat when you qualify for group insurance.

I won't say she's fat, but if it had rained during her wedding, they would have held the ceremony under her gown.

She's so fat—she has to wear a girdle to put on a muumuu.

She's real fat. The other day she wanted drop earrings and had to have her ears harpooned.

She's so fat, she has to wear a six-piece bikini.

She's so fat, she has to wear prescription underwear.

His wife is the only investment he ever made that doubled.

I won't say she's fat, but I saw her this morning putting on sunscreen with a roller.

"What have you got in my size?"
"Try the freight elevator."

I'll say she's fat. She hung out a pair of her pantyhose to dry, and a Gypsy family moved in.

I asked this store clerk if he had anything that would make me look thinner, and he said, "How about a weekend in Ethiopia?"

She's so fat—she was voted Miss North *and* South Dakota and a little piece of Montana.

She used to have a little fat on her chin, but it's all over now.

Their wedding cake was nice, but during the ceremony the bride ate the groom.

I suppose it's not nice to make jokes about fat people, but it doesn't make any difference. They can't catch you.

She was even a fat child. Her father had to put truck tires on her bike.

She's so fat—when she went to a séance, she didn't have a medium. She had to use a large.

She eats a lot. She walked into a 7-Eleven, and when she came out it was only 6-Two.

He was fat from the very first. In fact, he was born on the fifth, the sixth, and the seventh.

She's so fat—she went to the doctor the other day, and he said, "Open your mouth and say 'Moo.'"

I won't say she's fat, but this afternoon a cop drove by where she was standing and said, "Break it up."

She's so fat, they had to let out her garment bag.

She was thrown off the beach the other day. People were complaining she made too much shade.

I'm a 38 with gusts up to 40 and 42.

She's a good-natured girl. She has to be. It would take hours to get her mad through and through.

I don't know if she's putting on weight, but she has to buy a girdle with blowout patches.

They say there are three women for every man in this town. I didn't expect to get all of mine in one lump.

"My girl once weighed a hundred-ten pounds."

"When you first met her?"
"No, when she was born!"

She's a little plump. But she'd look good in something flowing—like the Nile.

I got her a wristwatch for Christmas. She didn't like it. Now, her sister wears it for a belt.

She's so fat, at the wedding three relatives had to give her away!

## FATE

Imagine a guy who plays the harp all of his life, and when he dies, he doesn't go to heaven.

A successful man is a guy who works like the dickens to become rich, and then spends the rest of his life sitting on the veranda of a sanitarium looking at the healthy poor people strolling by.

## FATHERS

Every father was a kid once, and every mother keeps trying to prove he still is.

I've got TV, cable, a satellite dish, two phones, one in my car, a fax machine, and my kids tell me I'm out of touch.

A man went to a fortune-teller who looked in his crystal ball and said, "I see you are the father of two children."
The man said, "Three."

The fortune-teller said, "That's what you think."

**A** father is a banker provided by Nature.

**A** father is a man with pictures in his wallet where his money used to be.

## FATHER'S DAY

**I** knew Father's Day was coming when my kid came over and asked me what size cologne I wear.

**T**he kids in Hollywood have a big problem on Father's Day. They know what to buy, but they don't know who to give to.

**F**or Father's Day, I wanted breakfast in bed, so my kids put a cot in the kitchen.

**O**n Father's Day, I can always count on getting one thing—the bills from Mother's Day.

**F**ather's Day scares me. I'm afraid they'll get me something I can't afford.

## FATIGUE

**T**hey recently scheduled a seminar on Chronic Fatigue Syndrome. But it was a failure. Everybody was too tired to go.

**T**hen there was the tired hooker. As soon as she stopped hitting the pillow, she hit the pillow.

## FAX MACHINES

**A** man goes to an office-supply store to update his office equipment. The clerk says, "Would you like to see some of our two-way phone systems?"
   "No, just the fax."

**A** mother complains to her son, "You never call me, you never write to me, you never fax me."

**Y**ou have to be careful with your fax machine. I got my tie caught in one, and four minutes later I was in Chicago.

**W**ant to drive a friend crazy? Send him a fax saying, "Disregard first fax."

## FBI/CIA

**C**IA chief to new recruit: "Your first job is to take your target, tie him up, gag him, shoot him six times, put him in a barrel of cement, and drop him in the river. Oh, and be sure to make it look like an accident."

**I** visited the CIA headquarters in Langley, Virginia, and saw a dog chasing a cat—and they were both blindfolded.

**I** found out my mailman was a CIA agent today, so I told him, "You took a chance—my pit bull is trained to attack strangers."
   The mailman said, "Don't worry about your dog, he's one of us."

## FIGHTING

**T**wo crooked managers are discussing the upcoming battle between their men. One says, "Look, your boy'll drop mine in the second round. Okay?"

The other manager says, "Make it the fourth round. The people did come to see a fight."

**A** fighter dies and goes to heaven. After a while, he's given a chance to call his best friend back on Earth. He makes the call, and his friend is beside himself with joy. After a little small talk, the friend asks, "What is it like up in heaven?"

The fighter says, "It's fantastic. All the great fighters are up here: John L. Sullivan, Jim Corbett, Jack Dempsey. And you're not going to believe this, but next week Marciano fights Joe Louis, and you and I have ringside seats."

**M**y grandfather was an old Indian fighter. My grandmother was an old Indian.

**I** had a piece of a fighter with a great rabbit punch. Unfortunately, they only matched him with people.

**A** heavyweight champ is walking down the street with a girl when a runt of a mugger accosts him and demands his money. Without a sound, the champ hands over his wallet. The mugger runs off. The girl asks, "Why didn't you put up a fight?"

The champ says, "I only had ten grand in my wallet. I never fight for less than two million."

## FINANCE

**T**he government just strengthened the dollar overseas. So I'm moving overseas.

**I** think all Americans should invest in America. But how do we get the Japanese to sell it back?

**I** dialed a 900 number to get some advice on finances. It told me not to dial a 900 number.

**I** worked out the family budget the other day. One of us will have to go.

**I** don't know how much I have in the bank. I haven't shaken it lately.

## FISH & FISHING

**A**n oyster is a fish that's built like a nut.

**T**he dogfish in Tennessee are big and mean. People report that they've seen two of them tree a bear.

**T**he only way a fish can take a shower is to jump up when it rains.

**T**wo little fish meet. One asks, "Does a whale have a big nose in its back?"

"No."

"Oh, Lord. I'm engaged to a submarine."

"What's the difference between a game warden and a flu shot?"

"Nothing. They're both a pain in the ass."

"Why do some women prefer fishing to sex?"

"It's not as boring."

Then there were these fishing buddies. They didn't get any bites, but they sure got plenty of nips.

There are two types of fishermen: those who fish for sport and those who catch something.

A man is hauled before a judge for catching twenty large fish. The judge fines the man a hundred dollars. The man says, "Can I throw in another hundred for some copies of the court report to show around?"

Al and Greg go on a fishing trip. The first day, Al catches his limit. Greg gets nothing. Greg can't understand it. Maybe it was just dumb luck. The second day, Al can hardly get his line into the water before he snares a fish. All day long, Al keeps pulling them in. Greg decides to go out alone the third day.

He gets up at dawn, sneaks out, and is on the lake at sunrise. He drops his line into the water, feels a tug, pulls up the line, and there's a note attached to the hook. It says, *Where's Al?*

"What's the difference between a hunter and a fisherman?"

"A hunter lies in wait, while a fisherman waits and lies."

Two old codgers went fishing one morning. Sitting in the boat, neither of them said a word for hours. Then one shuffled his legs a little, trying to work out a cramp. He shuffled his legs again about two hours later. His buddy looked up and said, "Did you come to fish or to practice your dancing?"

This dude is in the country and goes fishing. The fish get away with every worm he puts on his hook. He turns to a farmer fishing nearby and says, "Isn't that something, the way they get the worms?"

The farmer says, "Ain't so amazing. They do it for a living."

A man returns from a weekend fishing trip and is a little upset with his wife, asking, "Why didn't you pack my warm pajamas?"

His wife says, "I did. I put them in your tackle box."

The cruelest thing you can hear on a party fishing boat: "That's a nice fish. Can I use it for bait?"

A woman goes fishing with her husband, and after about an hour she asks, "Do you have any more of those small plastic floats?"

"Why?"

"The one I'm using keeps sinking."

I got a lot of bites while I was fishing last week. One of them was even a fish.

**A** fisherman in a small boat sees another man get another small boat, open his tackle box, and take out a mirror. Curious, the fisherman asks what the mirror is for.

The other man says, "That's how I catch fish. I shine the sunlight on the water, fish come up to the top, and I nab them."

"Does that really work?"

"You bet it does."

"Well, I'll give you ten dollars for that mirror."

"Sure."

The transaction is completed. The fisherman says, "By the way, how many fish have you caught this week?"

"You're the sixth."

**T**wo city slickers went ice-fishing in Minnesota. When they got back to camp, the man in the bait shop asked, "Did you catch many fish?"

One city slicker said, "Heck no, it took us six hours to get the boat into the water."

**S**ome of the ten-inch crappies caught in the pond last summer are now six feet long.

**I** caught a fish so big, the Polaroid weighed nine pounds.

## FLORIDA

**I**n Boca Raton, there's a very fancy hotel that caters to the extremely wealthy. However, people not registered at the hotel can, for a fee, use the pool. One dowager from up North asked a Boca matron, "How in the world do you keep out the riffraff?"

The matron said, "My dear, in Boca, all the riffraff have their own pools."

**I**t would be great if Moses were alive today. He could part some of the retirement land I bought in Florida!

**I** feel great. They just found land on some of my Florida property!

**I**t was so hot in Miami Beach the other day. Women weren't carrying their minks—just the appraisals.

**I**t was so hot in Miami Beach that one woman almost died. Luckily, a lifeguard saved her—he opened her coat.

**I**n St. Petersburg, Florida, they brag that they have 365 days of sun a year. And that's only a conservative estimate.

**F**lorida is flat. In fact, the center of the Orlando Magic basketball team is the highest point of elevation.

## FLOWERS

**I**f a man brings home flowers for no reason, there's a reason.

"**W**hat's the use of reindeer?"
"It makes the flowers grow."

## FLYING

Some stewardesses can actually make love in airplane johns. That's what I call *real* flexible flyers.

Salesman to airline clerk: "How can anything that goes eight hundred miles an hour be late?"

A giant plane is crossing the Atlantic, when the captain goes on the intercom and says, "Ladies and gentlemen, I have an announcement to make. We have lost one of our engines. But we can certainly get to our destination with the three we have left. Unfortunately, we'll be an hour late."

A few minutes later, he goes on the intercom with a second announcement: "We have lost another engine, but we can still reach our destination safely with two. Of course, we'll be several hours late."

A half hour goes by, and a third announcement is made: "We have just lost a third engine but will still reach our destination. We'll be six hours late."

One of the passengers turns to the man sitting next to him and says, "If we lose another engine, we'll be up here all night."

I won't say it was a small airplane, but we had to make a detour to dust some crops.

Times are really rough for some airlines. Just the other day, the president of one hijacked one of his own planes to bankruptcy court.

A jet was in trouble. It had one engine out, and the other was running poorly as the plane limped to the nearest airport. One passenger noticed the priest beside him didn't seem bothered at all.
"You think we'll get down safely?"
"Oh, yes," said the priest.
"What if the other engine goes out?"
"I can't answer that," the priest said. "You see, I'm not up in administration—my department has always been sales!"

Somebody'll have to explain this to me. When you're at forty thousand feet, the pilot tells you to roam as you will through the plane. But when you're on the ground, the pilot tells you to remain in your seat while you taxi.

At the counter, a woman was complaining about the departure time, saying, "Young man, I could stick a feather in my ear and get there faster."
The clerk smiled and said, "Madam, the runways are clear."

A journey of a thousand miles begins with a delay of about three hours.

I didn't know where to go, so I just asked for a ticket to where my luggage was going.

We had a terrible stewardess. Every time you asked her for champagne, she popped her cork.

The pilot got on the intercom and said gently, "Ladies and gentlemen, please sit back and relax. Don't worry about a thing. If anything goes wrong, you'll know immediately. The co-pilot will become hysterical."

You always know when a plane is about to fly into turbulence. The stewardess is right next to you, serving coffee.

"Where do you think atheists pray?"
"In the airport baggage-claim area."

A stewardess explains to the passengers on this second-rate airline, "In case of emergency, your oxygen mask will fall down. If it doesn't, open the window."

When I fly, I think about three things: faith, hope, and gravity.

I just flew on the cheapest airline. To save money, they use student drivers.

I just took the cheapest no-frills flight where the airline cut every corner it could. As soon as I was strapped in, I heard, "Our airline has experienced a few cuts and some layoffs, but our service remains normal. . . . This is your automatic pilot speaking."

The Wright brothers experienced all the thrills of flying but one—they never lost their luggage.

"I hate to be up there in a plane."
"I'd hate to be up there without one."

"Can you telephone from an airplane?"
"Sure, anybody can tell a phone from an airplane."

If the world is getting smaller, why are plane tickets costing more?

There's a terrible risk in flying—the cab ride home from the airport.

I never go by plane. The long ride to the airport makes me carsick.

They say that you won't get killed in a plane unless your number is up. But what if the pilot's number is up?

The way I see it is this: Nobody has ever complained because his parachute didn't open.

It was a cheap airline. When it had engine trouble, we all got out and pushed.

It's no fun to go to the airline desk to complain about lost luggage only to see the clerk wearing your clothes!

If the good Lord really intended for us to fly, He would have made it easier to get to the airport.

A little old lady called over the stewardess and told her, "Please tell the pilot not to turn on that red light. Every time he does that, it gets bumpy."

My last flight was really no-frills. Instead of showing films, we just buzzed the drive-ins!

One airline pilot had a great way of getting the attention of the passengers. As his plane sat on the runway, he spoke over the intercom, saying, "We'll take off in a few minutes. First, I have to work up the nerve."

With the way they're putting people closer and closer together on some flights, the airlines will have to do something—either put saltpeter in the drinks or mirrors on the ceiling!

The pilot tried to sound cheerful when he turned on the intercom and told the passengers, "I've got some bad news, and I've got some good news. The bad news is that we're lost. The good news is—we've got a strong tailwind!"

The pilot sounded confident when he told the passengers, "Two of our engines are out, and the other two are on fire. But don't worry. I'm putting on my parachute and going for help."

I always use this one airline. For two years, I've been a member of their frequent-waiters club.

Lindy was the last guy who flew to Europe the same time as his luggage.

## FOOD

A mushroom is like love. You never know if it's the real thing until it's too late.

With all the preservatives they put into food today, it's a thrill to know that a maraschino cherry will live longer than I do.

After a meal with an entrée that was fairly tough, a soldier walked over to his mess sergeant and said, "Gee, Sarge, I'm darn sorry your hippo died."

Last night we had incubator chicken. It had to be. Nothing with a mother could have been that tough.

One hillbilly family ate so many rabbits, when they heard the dogs bark, they'd run under the porch.

I saw in the paper last night a man went thirty-eight days without food. He really should have ordered from another waiter.

I worry about hospitals. How can you expect to be cured in a place that called what you had for lunch Swiss steak?

Then there's the vampire who wanted to become a vegetarian. But he couldn't get blood out of a turnip.

"Did you enjoy the food, sir?"
"I could get more nourishment biting my lip."

Nowadays, there are three basic food groups: canned, frozen, and takeout.

A rustic finds himself in New York at a fancy delicatessen. He points at the Limburger cheese and asks, "Will that hold till I get back home?"

The counterman says, "Can't nothing else can happen to that cheese."

There's a new Japanese-Jewish restaurant in town. It's called So-sumi.

An Englishman visits America and finds himself in a restaurant. He takes a sip of tea and says to the waiter, "Really, your tea wasn't worth going to war for."

The quickest way to make a tossed salad is to give it to a two-year-old kid in a restaurant.

One thing about liver is that you can always get enough of it.

I never eat anything in which the list of ingredients covers more than half the package.

How come you never see a recipe for leftover lobster?

Nowadays, we're kept alive by half of what we eat, and killed by the other half.

The company has just come out with a new cat food. The company executive vice president is trying to get his salesmen excited about the product. "Which cat food is the result of ten years of research?"

"Ours," the salesmen yell.

"Which cat food has been tested in fifty markets?"

"Ours."

"Which cat food has the highest nutritional content?"

"Ours."

"So how come it isn't selling?"

One salesman says, "Because cats hate it!"

Did you ever realize—the artichoke is the only food you have more of after you finish eating it?

A gourmet—that's a glutton with a tux.

A man goes into a country diner for breakfast. He orders some eggs. The cook has to heed the call of nature, so the hillbilly dishwasher has to do the cooking. He puts in a little of this and a little of that, but by mistake adds some Limburger cheese.

The customer looks at his eggs and gets a whiff of the Limburger. He calls over to the cook, "You ought to keep an eye on your henhouse. Some skunk is diddling your chickens."

On a flight, the pilot announces over the intercom, "Our menu today is baked chicken, roast beef, or lasagna. If you don't get your first choice, you'll never know."

A smashed gent comes into a bar, sits down, and orders a drink. While he waits, he sees a dartboard on the wall. He asks if there are any players. The bartender says, "That's not for regular playing. That's for the contest. Anybody who gets three darts in a row in the center wins a prize."

The smashed gent picks up a dart, aims as best he can, and throws the first dart. It lands smack-dab in the bull's-eye. Hardly able to sit up, he throws the second dart. It, too, hits the center, as does the third. "Gimme my prize."

The bartender, who'd been having fun with the drunk, doesn't have the faintest idea what to give as a prize. His eyes land on the turtle in a small terrarium. That'll be the prize.

The drunk walks out with his prize gleefully.

A week later, smashed again, the drunk returns and wants to enter the contest. He's even more blotto than the first time, so the bartender hands him three darts. The drunk tosses the darts—right in the center. Three bull's-eyes. "Gimme my prize."

The bartender hands him some cigars. The drunk says, "I want what you gave me last time—a roast beef on a hard roll."

## FOOTBALL

Then there's the fan who drank bottle after bottle of beer. Unfortunately, when the cheerleaders yelled, "Go, go, go," he went.

One southern cheerleader said to her chum, "You know, honey, horny players are all alike."

The other smiled and said, "Horny ones are all *ah* like too."

One football team goes on its game trips with a gorilla. If anything goes wrong with a lineman, they have spare parts.

This man bought a used car with a New Orleans Saints sticker on the back. One day he scraped off the sticker. In ten minutes, the car ran and passed better.

"What do you get when you cross our quarterback with an octopus?"

"A quarterback and he'll still fumble."

Angered at what he felt was a bad call, a pro player yelled at the referee, "You stink to high heaven."

The referee picked up the ball, walked off fifteen yards, and said, "Can you still smell me?"

Tom Taylor lived for football. He spoke about nothing but football. About to accompany his wife to her firm's Christmas party, he's warned, "Don't you dare say one word about football. Don't you dare."

They go to the party. For hours Tom stands around, not saying a word. One of his wife's employers saunters over to him and asks him if everything is all right. Tom nods. The employer says, "Are you sure?"

Unable to hold back, Tom blurts out, "Tell me, do you think Joe Montana believes in God?"

Mrs. Johnson storms into the den and stands in front of the set so that her husband can't see the game. "I swear," she says, "I'd drop dead if you said once that you'd rather be with me."

Mr. Johnson says, "Don't tempt me."

"What do Notre Dame coaches write on their players' uniforms?"

"Helmet, jersey, pads, shoes . . ."

It's football time again—the players get on the field, I get on the couch, and my wife gets on my back.

"Why do football players wear helmets?"

"So they don't wipe the wrong ends."

Women will never play football. Imagine eleven women in public wearing the same outfit.

The halfback gets the ball and starts around right end only to be clobbered by half of the other team. Knocked out, he finally comes to and looks around. He sees the eighty thousand fans cheering. Puzzled, he asks the quarterback, "How did all those folks get back to their seats so fast?"

Notre Dame travels to California to play Southern California. When they arrive, the Southern California coach says to the Notre Dame coach, "I hear you travel with a priest for the team. I'd like to meet him."

The Notre Dame coach says, "Which one—the defensive priest or the offensive?"

The day after the big game in which Morgan had run a hundred-yard touchdown, Coach Flores was analyzing the play. "Morgan," he said, "you carried the ball too closely and in the wrong hand. You ran to the inside when you should have run to the outside. You ran ahead of some of your blocks. It was just a lucky run."

Morgan said, "How was it for distance, Coach?"

An irate alumnus asks the football coach, "How many male students are there in this school?"

"About ten thousand."

"Is it too much to ask for a couple of them to be in front of the ball-carrier?"

A college coach is berating his team during halftime: "What the hell is wrong with you guys? You're playing like a bunch of amateurs."

## FRENCH

"You French have this strange habit of kissing a woman's hand when you meet her. Why?"

"Well, *mon ami,* you have to start somewhere."

A Frenchman was asked, "What's more important—sex or wine?"

The Frenchman said, "Burgundy or Bordeaux?"

A Frenchman went to a wild party that lasted until the early hours of the morning. When he went to bed, he fell asleep the minute his feet hit the pillow.

**P**aris—where men are men and women are women. You can't beat that combination.

**T**hings have changed in Paris. Now, they're *writing* on postcards.

## FRIENDSHIP

**I**f you make one new friend a day, at the end of the year you'll be stuck with 365 new friends.

**A** friend is a guy who's got the same enemies you do.

**I** always dump friends who do me a favor and then say, "Hey, what are friends for?"

**S**how me a friend in need, and I'll show you a pest!

**N**ever try to keep up with the Joneses. Drag them down with you!

## FRUSTRATION

**M**y wife keeps trying to demand the last word with an echo!

**F**rustration is trying to find your glasses without your glasses.

**I** have a frustrated pet. It's a turtle that chases cars!

## FUNERALS

**M**y uncle died. My aunt was all broken up about it. She and her boyfriend cried all during the funeral.

**A**t the funeral, Jim was carrying on as if he'd lost ten wives instead of one. No matter how many people tried to console him, he was inconsolable. His brother Ted said, "Look, Jim, I know things look grim, but in a year from now you'll meet another woman and you'll fall in love, and life will look great again."
Jim said, "Yeah, Teddy, but what am I going to do tonight?"

**J**im Hoskins asks Al Clark if he's going to the funeral for Gerber's wife. Al says, "I'm not sure. I went to the funeral when he buried his first wife. I was there again for his second wife. Now, it's his third. It doesn't seem fair I should accept all his invitations without having anything to invite him to."

**W**hile out of town, a man gets a call from a mortician. The man's wife has died, and the mortician wants to know what his orders are. "Shall I embalm, bury, or cremate her?"
The man says, "All three. Let's not take any chances."

**A** man has his wife cremated, and as he watches the smoke come out, he says, "That's the first time I ever saw her hot."

**A** man walked into an undertaking parlor in Las Vegas and saw corpses all over the place. He said to the owner, "Hey, business must be great."

The owner said, "Business is lousy. They're all shills."

Her father was a southern planter—an undertaker in Atlanta!

This man left no instructions for his funeral. He just wanted his wife to surprise him.

A hooker dies, and her girlfriends gather to pay their respects. Doing the eulogy, one says, "Jeannie was something special. She could go through fifty men a night, she could do tricks nobody else knew, there wasn't a perversion she wouldn't cater to."

A hooker in the crowd says to another, "Isn't it terrible? You have to die before somebody says something nice about you."

"My family follows the medical profession."

"Doctors?"

"No, undertakers!"

It is toward the end of a funeral. Mrs. Elkin, the widow, is obviously distraught, but this doesn't seem to bother Harry Cooper, who says, "I must confess something—I've loved you for years and wanted to possess you."

Mrs. Elkin says, "You pervert. How can you talk like that?"

Harry says, "I can't help it. I'm overwhelmed by your beauty."

Mrs. Elkin says, "You should see me when I haven't been crying."

Never argue with an undertaker. Sooner or later, he'll have you dead to rights.

His family couldn't afford a stone, so they just left his head out.

As the old man lies dying in the bedroom, out in the parlor the family discusses funeral arrangements. Son Gary says, "We'll make a real big thing out of it. We'll have five hundred people. We'll order fifty limos."

Daughter Grace says, "Why do you want to waste money like that? We'll have the family and maybe a few friends. One limo just for us."

They proceed. Grandson Jeff says, "We'll have lots of flowers. We'll surround him with dozens of roses and lilies, dozens and dozens."

Daughter Alice says, "What a waste! We'll have one little bouquet, that's enough."

Suddenly, the voice of the old man is heard, wafting weakly from the bedroom: "Why don't you get me my pants? I'll walk to the cemetery."

The funeral is almost over. Kellogg, the mortician, turns to an old man nearby and asks, "Are you a relative?"

"Yup. Cousin."

"How old are you?"

"Ninety-six."

"Hardly pays you to make the trip back to town, does it?"

A movie-theater owner died, and he was buried at 2:15, 4:40, 6:30, and 8:40.

Jeff Peterson, the town wastrel, dies. He'd never held a job for more than an hour, drank like a fish, and was mean to his family. But at the funeral, the reverend extols the virtues of this sainted man, so beloved and such a model for others.

Mrs. Peterson turns to Jeff, Jr., and says, "Take a peek in that coffin. See if it's really your old man."

They're thinking of putting a tax on funerals. I'd die before I'd pay that.

The dying woman calls over her husband. With great difficulty, she says, "Dear, I have one final request. Please ride in the first car with my mother at the funeral."

The husband says, "All right, but it'll spoil my whole day."

My family thinks that a high-priced funeral is a waste. When I go, they're just going to wet the ground and let me sink in.

## FURNITURE

I bought a love seat the other day, but I returned it. It kept getting fresh with me.

If God had intended for us to walk around naked, why did He invent wicker furniture?

## FURS

She loves animals. She'd do anything for a mink.

"I will not take that mink coat. I'm not that kind of girl."

"What kind of girl are you?"

"A size twelve."

A girl I know came up to me bragging about her new mink coat.

"How do I look?" she said.

"Guilty!"

When a woman turns around to look at another woman—that's real mink.

I bought my wife a mink outfit—two rifles and a trap.

## FUTURE

I don't know if there's an afterlife, but I'm taking along a change of underwear.

The trouble with the future is that it keeps getting closer and closer.

## GADGETS

Civilization is held together by three things—the staple, the paper clip, and the zipper.

Some gays are now making a strong kind of condom—it's called Seal-a-Meal.

They are now selling strobe lights for bedrooms. That'll make it look as if your wife is moving during sex.

My cuckoo clock is broken—all it does is come out and shrug.

The Mafia invented acupuncture. Only they used an icepick.

She has the perfect kitchen gadget—an oven that flushes.

They now make a battery-operated battery. But the batteries aren't included.

A woman working in a department store as a clerk is showing her a new electrical gadget. "I guarantee you," the clerk says, "this'll pay for itself."

The woman says, "Good. When it does, send it over."

**I** bought her an Indian washing machine—a rock.

**I**'ve come up with a new pushbutton. You push it and it pushes back. Makes you feel wanted.

**H**er hair is a mess, and her roommate asks, "Did you get caught in the rain?"

"No. My vibrator shorted out before."

**A** tourist saw his first country windmill and asked the farmer what it was. The farmer said, "It's an electric fan for blowing the flies off my cows."

**A** woman in Denver stabbed her husband 280 times. She didn't know how to turn off her electric knife.

**A**t the airport, a man who was going to take the next plane to Dallas saw a scale. He put in a quarter, and a message came: *You weigh 175 and you're on the way to Dallas.*

Puzzled, the man put in another quarter, and the same message came out.

Really addled, he went into the men's room, combed his hair in a different way, and changed his sport jacket. He returned and tested the machine with another quarter.

This time the message was: *You still weigh 175, and you just missed your plane to Dallas.*

**I** just found a machine that could do half my work for me. I bought two.

**A** flashlight is a great gadget for storing dead batteries.

**W**e have a zillion built-ins in our new home. Everything has a button on it— except my shirts and my shorts!

**I** don't understand—why do people stay up day and night working so they can get some labor-saving gadgets?

**T**hings that have to be in the works: battery-operated paper clips.

**M**y wife loves her self-cleaning stove. Now if they could come up with a purse like that . . .

**N**ot all gadgets work. I bought a hot-water bottle last week, filled it, and it still isn't warm.

**I** read recently that the air is so polluted, skywriters are using Wite-Out.

## GALL

**G**all is when you borrow your pal's new car and call him a half hour later, saying, "Your air bag works."

**A** guy with gall is a fellow who goes to the gift-wrapping counter to get them to wrap stuff he shoplifted.

## GAMBLING

**H**e loves animals. He gives half of his money to the horses.

An inveterate Atlantic City gambler took a vacation with his wife. While in Asia, they saw the Taj Mahal. The gambler said to his wife, "I don't see the casino."

I only make mental bets. Last week, twice I lost my mind.

His gambling brought his family together. He lost the house, and they had to move into one room.

My brother has no luck. He played with phony dice and won a bunch of counterfeit twenties.

Gambling is a great way of getting nothing for something.

A friend of mine told me about a system he had: "One day I lose and one day I win."
　　I told him, "Play every other day."

Americans spend 80 billion a year on games of chance, mostly weddings.

Pretty soon, 90 percent of the world will be desert. We'll go crazy having to build all those gambling joints.

I hate to win a jackpot at a slot machine in a gambling joint. It takes so long to put the money back in.

I don't believe in games of chance. That's why I'm a bachelor.

I have enough money for gambling. I just wish I had some for food.

It's weird. You take your own money out of the bank, then you pay your own transportation to a gambling town so you can bring it to them.

## GARAGE SALES

A woman picks up a piece of junk at a garage-sale table and asks how much it is. The man of the house says, "A penny."
　　"That's too much."
　　"Okay, make me an offer."

I like garage sales. You get a chance to see what people bought at garage sales a year ago.

I was at a garage sale and wanted to buy an item that was marked three dollars. I said, "Fifty cents."
　　The seller said, "Two-seventy-five."
　　"Sixty."
　　"Two-fifty."
　　"One."
　　"Two-twenty-five."
　　"One-twenty-five."
　　"You know, this is a good game," the seller said. "Let's play a nickel a hundred."

A garage sale is a device for moving a plate that says, WELCOME TO PUMPSWITCH, IDAHO from one garage to another.

I went to a four-family garage sale once and bought a grandmother.

## GARDENING

**I** am not a born gardener. I once killed a century plant when it was six.

**T**his year I did real well with the garden. My tomatoes were almost as big as my blisters.

**H**e was talking to his plant, and the plant answered, "Not tonight, I've got a headache."

**I**f God intended us to rest on Sunday, why did He create weeds?

**A** weed is a plant with nine lives.

**T**hey had it wrong. Trees grow on money.

**I** had great luck with my zucchinis this year. They didn't come up.

**G**ive the weeds an inch, they'll take a yard.

**T**he grass is greener on the other side of the fence, but I'd hate to have his water bill.

## GARMENT CENTER

**T**hey have a brand-new religious sect in New York's garment center: Seventh Avenue Adventists!

**A** garment manufacturer runs into a friend and starts to tell him about his recent vacation. "We had a great week in Paris. It was terrific in Geneva. The last week, we went to Rome and had an audience with the pope."

"What's he like?"

"A thirty-eight long."

**T**wo garment-center men meet, discuss politics, and finally start talking about their families. One says, "I can't stand it. My son comes in every day and spends eight hours grabbing and kissing the models."

The second garment-center man says, "What's wrong with that?"

The first one says, "I'm in menswear."

**A** manufacturer retired to a home in the country where he spent his leisure time puttering in the garden. A friend came to see him, and the manufacturer took him into the garden to show off his many flowers. Impressed by one bright red flower, the friend asked, "What kind of flower is this?"

The manufacturer shrugged his shoulders and answered, "How should I know? I wasn't in the millinery business!"

## GAYS

**A** homosexual is just somebody who doesn't believe in mixed marriages.

**I** knew a guy who didn't drink, smoke, curse, and never made a pass at a girl. He also made all his own gowns.

A gay walks into a gay bar, and the bartender asks, "Where's your companion? I haven't seen him around."

The gay explains, "He joined up to fight for Aunt Sam."

Being gay kept him out of the army. So he became a major in the WACs.

The police in West Hollywood are so polite. I put my hand out to make a turn, and a cop kissed it.

Two Englishmen of the old school are discussing old friends in their club.

One asks, "Whatever happened to old Chumley?"

The other says, "Didn't you hear? Chumley went to Africa on a safari and took up with an ape."

"An ape? Is the old chap queer?"

"Of course not. It was a female ape."

Two gays are walking down a street along the San Francisco shoreline. In the distance, one sees a ship and says, "Look at that ferry."

The other gay, an innocent, says, "Really? We also have a navy?"

A gay is only a man who likes his vice versa.

Last month a gay won the Golden Gloves. And they came all the way up to his elbow.

The gays in West Hollywood want to be able to elect their own mayor, police chief, and homecoming queen.

Two gays are breaking up, and they are dividing their possessions. One insists that he get all the CDs. The other wants some of them. They argue for an hour, and the second gay says, "All right, keep the CDs, and you know what you can do with them."

The other gay says, "Oh, now you want to make up."

The insurance salesman was putting the finishing touches on a policy. "Let's see, you want monthly payments on a straight life, right?"

"Well," said the customer, "I'd like to mess around a *little* on Saturday nights."

Then there was the gay who developed a goiter on his neck and started to knit baby clothes.

Then there was the gay who'd been in so many fights, he had a cauliflower wrist.

A man comes home and announces to his wife, "I have a gay lover."

The wife says, "I can't believe it. What's he got that I haven't got?"

They have a new gay doll. You wind it up, and it ignores Barbie and asks Ken if he wants to go to the movies.

One of the top dons is gay. With him, the kiss of death includes dinner, dancing, and champagne.

A temporary resident of San Francisco starts to pack. A friend asks him why he's leaving. He explains, "They've made homosexuality legal."

"So why leave?"

"I want to get away before they make it compulsory."

A gay is really just a man's man.

A gay walks into a rough-trade bar and orders a drink. Swallowing it with one gulp, he says, "I feel like a bull."

From the other end of the bar, a voice says, "Mooooo."

Then there was the gay contortionist who got a heart attack and died in his own arms.

Then there was the gay Australian who left Victoria to go back to Sidney.

Two middle-aged women are walking down a street in Hollywood when two gay men go by, rudely pushing them aside. One woman says, "They should shoot men like that."

The other says, "If they did that, my beauty parlor would be self-service."

Then there was this gay decorator who committed suicide. After an accident in which he'd been bruised black-and-blue, he went home and found he clashed with his drapes.

A trucker has made some nasty remarks to a gay who runs to him and starts beating him up. Two other gays walk by and see the mayhem.

One says to the other, "That Bruce. Once a tomboy, always a tomboy."

There was a big fight at the drag races. Two gays showed up in the same dress.

A gay man develops a crush on his doctor and uses the slightest pretext to make an office call. He comes in this one day and asks the doctor to examine him. The doctor looks up his rear end and says, shocked, "You have a dozen roses in your rear."

The gay says, "Read the card! Read the card!"

One gay had to come out of the closet. His mother needed the space.

A man complains about a gay, "Why does he lisp like that?"

The man next to him says, "How do you want him to lisp?"

I took my girl to Greenwich Village the other night. She got three propositions. I got four.

Two gays are walking down the street when they see a man standing, leaning against a wall. One gay says, "Oh, what a beautiful profile."

The second gay says, "I'll bet that's just his keys."

The other day I was mugged by three gays. For an hour, two held me down and the third one did my hair.

I know a gay who belongs to a motor-cycle club called Hell's Hairdressers.

They now have a gay hotel in town. The room-service waiter is on the menu.

The Mounties just got their first gay trooper. He not only gets his man, he's allowed to keep him.

A bisexual is a guy who likes girls just as well as the next guy.

## GENIUS

A genius is a nephew who can do everything but make a living.

Every family should have three children. If one turns out to be a genius, the other two can support him.

A genius is anybody who can describe how an accordion works without using his hands.

One brilliant ex-railroad executive got a job with the New York subway system. The first thing he did was try to eliminate the passenger trains!

## GEORGE WASHINGTON

When George Washington chopped down the cherry tree, his father was angry. But not as much as the family dog.

Washington's birthday is February 22, but it was celebrated on the eighteenth. Which means that George's mother was in labor for five days.

"What did George Washington say just before he got into the boat to cross the Delaware?"
" 'Fellas, get in the boat.' "

If George Washington never told a lie, how'd he get elected?

## GERMANS

An American couple are traveling in Germany. While they are in a shop looking at souvenirs, the wife sneezes. The shopkeeper says, "Gesundheit."
The husband says, "Thank God. Somebody who speaks English."

A typical German weather report: Tomorrow will be nice. That's an order!

## GIFTS

For a wedding gift, some people gave us towels marked His and Hers. My brother-in-law gave us a blanket marked Us.

I bought my son a spacesuit last week. Now, he won't go.

My wife has wedding gifts she hasn't used yet—a vacuum cleaner, a mop, a broom.

His wife was a little loaded, and she said, "My gift to you is that tonight you can do with me whatever you want."
The husband thought it over and then sent her home to her mother.

A man brings a dyed skunk coat home to his wife. She says, "How can such a pretty coat come from such a foul-smelling beast?"

The husband says, "I don't expect gratitude, but I do want some respect."

My birthday gift to my wife will be a real surprise for her. I'm getting her a toaster. She's expecting a Mercedes.

A man showed his friend a ring with a giant diamond in it and explained that it was his wife's birthday present. His friend said, "I thought she wanted a Mercedes."

The man answered, "I know, but where can you get a fake of that?"

A man goes into a gift shop and sees a strange necklace. "What's this made of?" he asked the clerk.

"Alligator teeth."

"But it's so much more expensive than a pearl necklace."

"Well," the clerk says, "anyone can open an oyster."

The other day he bought his wife a clothes dryer—fifty feet of clothesline.

A gift shop is where they sell things you wouldn't have as a gift.

She wanted something for her neck, so I bought her a cake of soap.

I recently made a donation to the Home for Unwed Mothers. Next time I'll give money.

You can't make a silk purse out of a sow's ear, but lots of women can get a mink out of an old goat.

They recently found a pearl that weighed sixteen pounds. Somewhere down deep is an oyster with a hernia.

He knew she loved antiques, so he gave her an Early American washing machine—a tub and a bar of soap.

Brady had been drinking pretty good. Hoping that his wife wouldn't be upset, he went into a candy shop to buy her a little something and asked, "Do you have those chocolates with the whiskey in the middle?"

The clerk said, "Oh, yes, sir."

Brady said, "Give me a fifth of middles."

I have a great way of shopping for my wife. I buy anything marked "Petite," and I save the receipt.

I have a tough time buying things for my wife. I like to get something she'd never think of buying for herself. But that eliminates almost everything.

My kid loves music. All he wanted for his birthday was a CD player with a Porsche attached to it.

For her birthday, I gave my wife money. She tried to exchange it for a different color.

This man didn't know what he could get his wife who had everything. So he got her a husband who could afford it.

My brother gave us a beautiful silver tray. It even has something engraved on it: HILTON.

## GIRLS

A man can burn his fingers trying to grab the toast of the town.

A young man calls up the Salvation Army and asks, "Do you save girls?"

"Of course we do."

"Great. Save me one. I'll be there at eight."

It's strange, but when a girl gets old enough to go out alone, she doesn't have to.

Gorgeous women don't bother me. I wish they would.

Some men like tall girls. Others like little lasses.

A mother once asked her pregnant daughter, "Are his intentions honorable?"

The daughter answered, "Of course. He's going to let me keep the baby!"

Then there's the poor girl who doesn't have any dates because she's sixteen . . . where she should be thirty-eight.

Her heart belongs to me, but the rest of her goes out with other guys.

The only thing young girls don't do nowadays is premarital cooking.

"What's the first thing you notice about a girl?"

"That depends on which way she's walking."

She's like a flower. Grows wild in the woods.

"I have a friend who wants to marry a girl who doesn't drink, smoke, neck, curse, or tell risqué stories."

"Why?"

## GOD

God created the earth in six days because He didn't have to wait for a legal opinion.

A visitor to a Jersey truck farm admires the farmer's tomatoes and says, "Look what you did with God's help."

He moves on to fat green heads of lettuce in row after row. "With God's help, you certainly made this a paradise."

Wherever he goes on the farm, the visitor repeats his being impressed with what the farmer and God have done.

Finally, the farmer says, "I don't want to shake you up, but you should have seen this place when God was working it alone."

A neighborhood preacher is notorious for his swigging down the bubbly. One night, after a record-setting session, he starts for his car. A parishioner says, "Reverend, you oughtn't to drive in that condition."

The preacher says, "Don't fear. The Lord is with me."

The parishioner says, "The way you're soused up, maybe He ought to drive with me."

A golfer is playing a round and gets his first tee shot two inches from the first cup. A golfer in the foursome behind says to another player, "He must think he's God."

The other player says, "He *is* God. Once in a while, he thinks he's Arnold Palmer."

Think of it—God said, "Let there be light." And there was night.

Some people say they just found God. I never knew He was lost.

The God who invented laughter can't be all bad.

God created the world in six days. On the seventh day, He rested. On the eighth day, he started getting complaints.

## GOLD DIGGERS

Some gold diggers only make a few dollars with each marriage. But it's steady work.

Marsha's new beau was one of the dullest men around. Cynthia asked her, "What does he have going for him?"

Marsha answered, "He inherits."

A reporter asks a Hollywood starlet why she is so frequently seen with a wealthy octogenarian.

She explains, "He possesses that rarest of masculine virtues, about fifteen million dollars."

She has a great way of getting a new wardrobe. She starts by taking off the old one.

You can tell a girl is a gold digger if she asks you, "How much did you say your name was?"

She likes him because he's tall, dark, and has some.

I have a friend who went broke last year. He put all his money in junk blondes.

One sexy girl who loved to sleep in the nude woke one morning to find that she was completely dressed. "Oh, God," she said. "I've been draped!"

They asked a gold digger, "Why are you having an affair with a man of ninety?"

She answered, "Listen, sweetheart, if somebody handed you a check for a million, would you look at the date?"

She likes only two kinds of men—domestic and foreign!

She was a wild girl. She had thirty towels in her hope chest, each one from a different hotel.

Two models are walking down the street and come to the window of a fur salon. They stop to admire a gorgeous sable coat in the window. One model says, "Beautiful, isn't it? But who would be fool enough to pay ninety thousand for it?"

The second model says, "I don't know, but I'll find him."

It doesn't take much to soften her up—just soak her in money.

I know this chorus girl who got a mink coat. She spent the next month describing it to her friends and explaining it to her parents.

They say she married him because his father left him a fortune. That's a lie. She would have married him no matter who left him a fortune.

You know she's been around if she can do more things with leather than Gucci.

She's really been around if she met her husband at a Lamaze class.

She's been around if she knows more tricks than Houdini.

She's the kind of girl who drives home from a walk.

When some women say they'll go through anything for a man, they usually start with his bank account.

"What's the first thing a gold digger does in the morning?"

"She gets dressed and goes home."

Girls with flat heels catch only flat heels.

The young man was attempting to worm his way into the affections of this young lady. "I don't have as much as an Arabian sheikh," he said. "I don't have expensive houses or cars like an Arabian sheikh. I can't afford to buy you fancy diamonds and pearls like an Arabian sheikh. But I love you."

The young lady said, "That's nice. Now tell me more about that Arabian sheikh."

She doesn't care if you're a cad as long as you own one.

She never wanted practical gifts. She just wants things with sentimental value—money, stocks, a BMW.

I don't know what she does for a living, but her phone number is listed under "Entertainment."

A modern playgirl is known by the company that keeps her.

I think she's a gold digger. When they get married, she wants a home near a jeweler.

She's looking for a meaningful one-night stand.

## GOLF

A couple met while at a resort. They fell madly in love and decided to marry immediately. But the husband-to-be cautioned, "I have to warn you, honey. I'm an avid golfer. I live golf. I sleep golf. I eat golf. I never come home."

The wife-to-be said, "Thank you for being so open about things, dear. Let me confess something too. I'm a hooker."

"That's all right. Maybe you're not keeping your wrists straight."

One golfer finally told the truth on the golf course. He called another player a liar.

One pretty lady I know says, "Give me my golf clubs, the fresh air, and a young handsome golf partner, and you can keep my golf clubs and the fresh air."

The Royal Crest Golf club was the most exclusive in the world. It didn't have one minority member, one member whose money didn't go back generations, one actor or professional athlete; it was utterly fancy.

One day, Cabot Lodge, a proper Bostonian, tried to get into a game, explaining, "My family came over a week before the *Mayflower* arrived. No member of my family has ever lifted a finger to work. And the fact is, we can trace our ancestry back to William the Conqueror."

Almost impressed, the club secretary said to the starter, "Let Mr. Lodge play. But only nine holes."

Every golf club has its grouch. In this one club, the grouch managed to hit a hole-in-one. He threw his club down and said, "Just when I needed the putting practice."

If you think it's hard to meet new people, just try to pick up the wrong golf ball.

They say that golf has replaced sex. Of course, the men over sixty are saying it.

This golf fanatic took a lot of time from work to play golf, instructing his secretary to tell all callers that he was away from his desk.

One of the members of his foursome one day forgot which club they were meeting at and called the office. The secretary said, "Mr. Thompson is away from his desk."

The player said, "Tell me, is he ten miles away or twenty?"

The caddie master walks over to a golfer and says, "You're almost a foot past the tee-line. You'll have to move the ball back."

The golfer ignores him. The caddie master repeats his instruction. Again he is ignored. This goes on for ten minutes until the golfer turns to another player in his foursome and says, "Will somebody tell this clown that it's my second shot?"

A fine player waits around for a decent game, but all he can find is a new man whose practice shots identify him as a duffer. The duffer agrees to play but insists on an edge. "I just want a couple of gotchas handicap."

The fine player, eager for a game and confident of his own ability, doesn't even bother to ask what a gotcha is. The duffer must have meant a gimmie.

The fine player gets set to drive from the first tee, but just as he brings his arms back, the duffer rushes up and grabs him about the waist, saying "Gotcha!"

This shakes the fine player's concentration. He proceeds to shoot the worst game of his life, going ten over par on the very first hole.

Later, in the clubhouse, another player asks the fine player, "How could you shoot such a terrible round?"

The fine player says, "Did you ever shoot a round waiting for a second gotcha?"

Two men are trying to start the fourth hole, but ahead of them are two women who seem to be having a great time. They walk into the woods, giggle, take a sip from a water container, trudge through the grass, and talk as if they didn't have a care in the world. One of the men walks up to them and says, "For the love of heaven, use another ball."

One of the women says, "We have the ball. We're looking for her club."

"I'll bet there are people worse at golf than me."

"Sure, but they don't play."

A caddie has terrible hiccups. Every time his player is about to swing, the caddie hiccups. By the tenth hole, the player is a frazzle. He drives for the eleventh hole, and the ball goes fifteen feet. Angrily, he says to the caddie, "You've really screwed up my game."

"I didn't hiccup on that one."

"I know, but I allowed for it."

The duffer ended up shooting 135 for nine holes. He asked the caddie, "Am I the worst golfer you ever saw?"

The caddie answered, "I can't say that, but you've taken me to places I never knew were on the property!"

An employee of the country club saw ex-president Gerald Ford stepping off the green and asked "Do you notice anything different since you left office?"

"Yes," was the rueful answer. "A lot more golfers are beating me."

Golf—that's flog spelled backward!

In a golf game, it's always easy to tell the boss from the underlings. When an underling makes a hole-in-one, he says, "Oops."

Golf is a great game. You can spend your whole life with hookers, and your wife doesn't say a word.

It was ladies' day at the golf club, and some of the women were sitting around.

Down the corridor, the locker room was partly open, and they couldn't help but see a nude man whose head and shoulders were covered with a bath towel.

One lady said, "That's not my husband."

The second said, "That's not my husband either."

The third one said, "He's not even a member of the club."

"**W**hat do you think I should give to my caddie?"

"How about your clubs?"

**G**olf has made more liars of Americans than the IRS.

**O**ne golf widow got sick of her husband's obsession with the game. One day he came home and found a note that said, *Went shopping. Your dinner is in the dog.*

**L**adies, when your husband comes home with pine needles in his hair, don't ask him what his golf score was.

**A**fter three sets and ten lessons, I finally got some fun out of golf. I quit.

"**W**hat goes putt-putt-putt-putt?"

"A bad golfer."

**A** terrible golfer slices the ball into a treacherous trap. He asks his caddie, "What club do I use now?"

The caddie answers, "It doesn't matter which club you try. But be sure to take along lots of food and water."

**A** visitor to Tokyo is playing golf with a young Japanese lady. When he holes out after a very bad lie on the first hole, the young lady says, *"Shimubu."*

Hole after hole, the man manages to outdo himself. Each time, the young Japanese lady says, *"Shimubu."*

The next day, the visitor plays golf with an executive from a company that could do much business with him. At the first hole, the executive hits a fantastic five-iron and holes out for an eagle.

To show his appreciation of the shot, the visitor nods and says, *"Shimubu."*

The executive looks at him and says, "What you mean—wrong hole?"

**A** handicapped golfer is anybody who plays with his boss.

**A** six-year-old boy watches his father on the golf course and finally asks, "Daddy, why don't you want to put that little ball in the hole?"

**I**'m doing great with my golf game. This morning I hit a ball in one.

**T**he club pro is giving a lesson to a duffer. Demonstrating the grip and stance, the club pro says, "In this first lesson, let me see you grip the club and swing. But don't hit the ball."

The duffer says, "I can do that already. Let's go on to the second lesson."

**A** new man joins the golf club and takes his first lesson from the golf pro.

"What am I supposed to do?" the new man asks.

"Hit the ball toward the flag down on the green."

The new man swings, and the ball loops into the sky, heads down the fairway, onto the green, and lands an inch from the cup.

The pro says, "You're supposed to hit the ball into the cup."

The new man says, "*Now* you tell me."

A duffer is playing with a friend. After an unusually bad shot, the duffer says, "This is the toughest club in the world."

The friend says, "How would you know? You haven't been on it yet."

My wife is thrilled with her golf game. Her score just came down to her weight.

Then there was the golfer who was going to be hanged. He wondered if he could get in a few practice swings.

I finally discovered why golf is the name of the game. It's the only four-letter word that hadn't been used.

Crane sees a player in the sand yelling wildly. Crane runs over as the player sinks farther and farther into the sand. "I'll save you," Crane yells.

"Forget that. Just hand me my wedge."

I almost made a hole-in-one today. I just missed it by nine strokes!

My kid cousin is such a good golfer, he's been offered a scholarship to medical school!

There was a fellow who always cheated at golf. One day he got a hole-in-one, and he put a zero on his golf card.

This lady is one of the great duffers of all time. She comes off a game, and a man asks her what her score was. She answers, "I'd rather tell you my age and weight."

This avid golfer finishes a round and unhappily starts home. En route he sees an attractive young lady at the side of the road. It's obvious that she has a flat and can't fix it. The man pulls over and repairs the damage. The young lady is grateful and invites him over to her house for a drink.

After some soft music and a few drinks, they have a little romantic interlude. As they sit back to relax, the man notices the time. He'll get hell if he doesn't scoot home.

He arrives at his house, and there waiting to greet him is an irate wife. The wife demands to know where he was.

The man explains, "I helped a young lady with her car, and she asked me over for a drink and then we became friendly, but then I noticed the time and rushed home."

The wife looks at him bitterly and says, "You bum! You played thirty-six holes, didn't you?"

A golf nut played a championship course after a big tournament. On the first tee, he asked his caddie what club the tournament winner used there. The caddie said, "A three-wood."

The golf nut took out his three-wood, swung, and pummeled the ball straight down the fairway. "What club did he use now?" the golf nut asked.

"A three-iron."

The golf nut used his three-iron, and the ball went over the green into a water trap. The golf nut turned to his caddie and barked, "You said he used a three-iron. Look where I landed—in a water trap."

The caddie said, "So did he."

Nothing counts in golf like your opponent.

The trouble with golf is that by the time you can afford to lose a few balls, you can't hit them that far anymore!

A man does a favor for an Indian potentate. To thank him, the potentate asks what gift he can bestow. The man says, "Just get me a couple of golf clubs."

Two weeks later, a note arrives at the man's house. It says, "Bought the golf clubs. One is in Palm Springs, the other in Florida. But I have to apologize. Only one of them has a swimming pool."

Jones was one of the worst golfers of all time. One day, on the first tee, he sent a high drive way off to the right. The ball went through an open window. Kissing the ball good-bye, Jones went on playing.

A few holes later, a policeman showed up and said, "Did you hit the ball that went through the open window?"

"It was probably me."

"Do you know what it did? It knocked over a vase. The noise scared the dog who ran out of the house onto the highway. To avoid hitting him, a driver rammed into a wall, sending six people to the hospital. All because you slice the ball."

"Is there anything I can do?" Jones said.

"Well," the cop said, "it might help if you kept your head down and closed up your stance."

Men are strange. They'll walk thirty-six holes of golf, but at home they won't get up to get a glass of water.

A duffer took three swings with his driver, missed, and finally hit the ball about ten feet from the tee. Turning around, he happened to see a man watching and said, "Hey, only golfers are allowed on the course."

The man said, "I know that, but I won't say anything if you don't."

The golfer hits his drive right into the middle of the woods. Then he smacks it into a deep trap and, a moment later, into the lake. He stands, trying to figure out how to get the ball back.

The caddie says, "Why not forget it?"

The duffer says, "I can't. It's my lucky ball."

Golf is great exercise, especially climbing in and out of the cart.

I'm such a bad golfer. I can't even break 90 when I cheat.

## GOSSIP

My wife just joined the women's club. That's where you knock after you enter.

A gossip can't believe everything she hears. But she can repeat it.

Four women were playing canasta. One said, "I've been holding this in for ages, but I'm a kleptomaniac."

The second said, "I'm a nymphomaniac."

The third said, "I'm a dipsomaniac."

The fourth said, "I'm a gossip, and I can't wait to get to the beauty parlor."

A gossip always believes much more than she hears.

Every woman should have two good friends—one to talk to and one to talk about.

Gossip is something that goes in one ear and in another.

One gossip was overheard saying to a friend, "You know I only say good things about people. Well, this is good. . . ."

At a party, don't talk about yourself. It'll be done when you leave.

Two women are lunching, and one looks off to see a friend. She says, "Oh, there's Ruth. Do you believe that awful story about her?"

The other woman says, "Of course. What is it?"

My wife can keep a secret. It's the woman she tells it to who can't.

"Mary told me that you told her the secret I told her not to tell you."

"Gee, and I told her not to tell you that I told her."

"Well, I wouldn't tell her I wouldn't tell you that she told, so don't tell her I told you."

She's such a born gossip. She always says, "If you have nothing good to say about somebody, sit near me."

The only thing she spills at dinner is her girlfriend's secrets.

## GOVERNMENT

How times change. When Columbus came over, all of his men were in three boats. Now, we're all in the same boat.

Most people would love to attend to their own business, but the government won't give it back to them.

Why do men take up a life of crime when there are so many legal ways of being dishonest?

A young man applied for a government job. When asked what he could do, he said, "Nothing."

He got the job immediately. They wouldn't have to break him in!

In Washington they have a new motto: Eliminate waste no matter how much it costs.

I don't mind the government living beyond its means, but it's also living beyond mine.

They say talk is cheap. Do you have any idea what a session of Congress costs?

After all is said and done in Congress, more is said than done.

If you think you can be happy by letting the government take care of you, just think of what happened to the American Indian.

"Why did the Defense Department just cancel the missile program and hire two hundred economists?"

"Because they're the most destructive force in America."

It thrills me to know that my bank account is protected by a government that's four trillion in debt.

I figured out a way this country can save money. All we have to do is close thirty-two states.

A constituent asks the congressman, "Why don't you cut spending if the revenues are down?"

The congressman answers, "That'd be stupid. This is government, not real life."

In Congress a man gets up to speak and says nothing. Nobody listens, and then everybody disagrees.

Government is the art of making possible things impossible.

A small town had some problems with a sign over the highway. It spent several thousand dollars to raise the sign. An out-of-towner commented, "It's a good thing this was a local job. If the federal government had done it, they would have lowered the highway."

They have a new organization called Workaholics Anonymous. When you get the urge to put in an eight-hour day, you call them up and they send over two government workers to talk to you.

They just named a new space missile after government workers. It can't be fired, it won't work, and it costs the taxpayer a fortune!

The government is so nice to us. It has something called Social Security. That's making sure you get a steak when your teeth are gone.

## GROCERIES

This woman says to the butcher, "I'd like a steak but no fat and no bone."

The butcher replies, "We've been trying to grow them like that for years, ma'am, but they keep falling over."

A woman goes into a grocery store and asks for an avocado. The clerk tells her that there aren't any. She insists. She wants an avocado.

"They're not in season. There are no avocados."

"I'd like an avocado."

"Lady, can I ask you something?"

"Certainly."

"Are you a good speller?"

"I'm a fine speller."

"Good. Tell me how many *F*s are there in avocado?"

"There is no *F* in avocado."

"That's what I've been trying to tell you. There are no effing avocados!"

## GROSS JOKES

"What happens when you soul-kiss an epileptic?"

"She might swallow *your* tongue too."

"Why were Helen Keller's hands purple?"

"She heard it through the grapevine."

"What's the function of a woman?"

"She's the life-support system for a vagina."

"What's the last thing that goes through a bug's mind when it hits a windshield?"

"Its ass."

## GYPSIES

One Gypsy family won ten million in the lottery. They took the first payment and moved into an empty store.

A man went to a Gypsy for a reading, but he noticed that her crystal ball had two holes in it. The man asked, "Why the two holes?"

The Gypsy answered, "When business is bad, I give bowling lessons."

A Gypsy walked over to me and whispered, "Would you like to buy a diamond ring?"

I said, "Where is it?"

He said, "Sssh. The man next to you is wearing it."

## HABIT

**A** man calls his shrink in the middle of the night, saying, "Doctor, my wife's driving me crazy. She keeps sitting in front of the TV set with nothing on." The psychiatrist asks, "Why doesn't she put something on?"

The man says, "She can't. The set's broke."

**I** spent two years teaching my dog to sit. Now, he forgot how to stand.

**A**n actor reads that his ex-wife is getting married for the fifth time.

He sighs. "I guess I got her into a bad habit."

**T**hen there was the man who was arrested for making obscene phone calls. In jail, he was given one free call. He made an obscene phone call.

**A** newly married man finds that his sexuality is fatigued to the point of extinction. He and his wife are told by a doctor, "You need to start practicing control. For the next six months, I want you only to make love on days that have an *R* in them."

257

A week goes by, but hormones start to rise in the bride. In the middle of the night, she taps her groom on the shoulder.

Sleepily, he says, "What day is this?" She says, "Sundray."

**A** lovely rich girl falls in love with a poor beggar. She's willing to marry him, but he's stubborn. "How do I know you really love me?" he asks.

"I'll do anything," she answers.

He says "To prove your love, come with me, we'll travel the world, begging from house to house."

The woman objects, but sees that her love is adamant.

Soon they're married and start off on their begging tour of the world.

When the trip is over, the beggar turns to his wife. "Well, darling, at last it's over and done. Now we can go home and live a normal life. No more begging."

"Fine," says his wife. "But first, let's finish this row of houses."

**W**hile visiting a national park, the Parkers' little boy, Ellis, wandered off into the woods. For a week, the family and park officials looked for him with no luck. Meanwhile, Ellis was found by a pack of wild dogs, who raised him.

Some years later, Ellis was accidentally discovered. He walked on all fours, ate raw meat, and barked. Not discouraged, the Parkers took him back into the fold.

Within one year, he had caught up in school. He went on to college, where he graduated at the top of his class. The day after the graduation ceremony, he was killed—chasing a car.

**B**en had been having half a grapefruit for breakfast every day of his thirty-five-year marriage. One day, his wife neglected to go shopping and had no grapefruit to serve. She was almost in tears as she made the announcement.

Ben smiled and said, "It's all right, my dear. I never really liked it anyway."

**A** man is sick and tired of being dominated by his wife. He takes a course in assertiveness and goes home. He stares into his wife's face and says, "I'm going out on the town tonight. And do you know who's going to button up my shirt and even put on my tie for me? You! Yes, you! And who's going to help me get into my coat?"

The wife looks at him, amused, and says, "The undertaker!"

**A** man sitting in the airport asks another man nearby, "Could you pass that ashtray stand over?"

"Certainly," says the second man.

"Do you have a cigarette to spare?"

"Sure."

"Do you have a light?"

"Buddy, you don't have anything but the habit, do you?"

**M**yrna the manicurist is complaining to Martha the hairdresser: "Every night it's the same thing. Out for dinner, some drinks, then into bed for sex and more sex. Believe me, I'll be thrilled when I've had enough of it."

A man comes into a butcher shop for steaks. As he waits, he brags, "My wife just had an eleven-pound baby."

The butcher says, "Including the bones?"

The girl next door flunked her driver's test. When the car stalled, out of habit she jumped into the backseat.

Two men are walking through Central Park. As they stroll, they see two dogs making love. One man says, "Did you ever try that with your wife?"

The other man says, "Are you kidding? I couldn't get her in the park."

A scientist taught his dog to go for food when he heard the bell. One day, the dog ate a door-to-door salesman.

## HAIR

"Where do women have the curliest hair?"

"The answer, wise guy, is Africa."

A man comes home from work one evening, and his wife hands him a bottle of hair tonic.

"What's this for?" he asks. "My hair's fine."

"It's for your secretary. Her hair keeps coming out badly on your shoulder."

She gets her hair done in a place that picks up and delivers.

My girl wanted me to raise a mustache. I said, "Must we do everything together?"

She has a weird hairdo. It looks as if her head fell in the cheese dip.

The barber gave me a tonic and swore that my hair would grow in heavy. I now have one hair, but it weighs twelve pounds.

Eventually, you get what you pray for. When I was a kid, my mother used to comb my hair with a vengeance. I kept praying that I'd get up one morning and have no hair. It worked. Now I don't have any.

The young lady tapped a taxi driver gently on the shoulder. "Could you put your window up?" she asked. "It's blowing Papa's hair too much."

"How far can a little wind blow a man's hair?" sneered the driver.

"The last gust,' she informed him, "blew it about three miles!"

## HALLOWEEN

The most embarrassing thing at a Halloween party is to ask one of the guests to take off her mask and find out she isn't wearing any!

The jack-o'-lantern should be the symbol for a politician—a head with nothing in it!

For politicians, every day is Halloween—they always put on a false face!

One kid went to a deadbeat's house, and the deadbeat said, "Honest, kid, your candy is in the mail."

Thanks to our political candidates, we have trick-or-treat all year!

The vice president is very upset. He found out they won't let him go trick-or-treating this year!

She's so ugly—on Halloween her folks send her out as is!

Halloween is the day when kids put on strange outfits to startle the adults. In my house, that would be a clean shirt.

## HAPPINESS

My wife always starts the day with a smile and gets it over with.

Happiness is when you see a double chin on your husband's old girlfriend.

Everybody you know can make you happy—some by arriving and some by leaving.

Happiness is a No Tipping sign.

Happiness is seeing your girl in a two-piece outfit—slippers.

A woman gets married to make two people happy—her and her mother!

Ecstacy is what happens between the second drink she sips and the bacon and eggs!

Happiness is offering a helping hand, and maybe the rest of your body too.

Columbus must have been happy when he saw the New World. There, staring him in the face, was a shoreline with a tree. But *his* happiness was nothing compared to his dog's.

Happiness is parking on what's left of the last guy's quarter.

A man packs up and starts to leave his house. His wife yells at him, "You'll be back. How long do you think you can stand happiness?"

A lot of us are poor and unhappy until we're forty. Then we get used to it.

When a married man looks happy, we wonder why.

Did you ever have one of those days when you didn't give a damn what's deductible?

Even if you could buy happiness, some folks would try to chisel down the price.

Happiness is good health and a bad memory.

A businessman drops in on a friend and asks about the state of the friend's affairs.

The friend says, "Business is awful. I don't think I can make it through the year. I may have to sell this house, my car, everything."

The businessman leaves a little later. The wife of the friend says, "You've never had it so good. Why did you tell him you were in such bad shape?"

"Look, does it hurt to make him happy for a couple of minutes?"

The only really happy people are married women and single men.

Happiness is when your girl sees you out with your wife and forgives you.

## HAREMS

Then there's the story of the sheikh who liked to get up early. He left a call for seven in the morning.

Two harem wives are talking. One says, "I'm scheduled for this coming Monday."

The other says, "Don't count on it. He's way behind."

Bulletin board in the harem day room: ALL LOVEMAKING FOR NEXT TWO WEEKS OFF. THE SHEIKH HAS A HEADACHE, AND THAT'S NOT ALL THAT HURTS.

## HAWAII

They've checked into the fanciest hotel on the Islands. As they walk on the beach, the wife picks up a shell and holds it to her husband's ear. "Can't you hear the roar of the ocean?" she asks.

"Nope. All I can hear is—three hundred a day and no meals."

Two Hawaiian dancers meet. One says, "Your skirt is lovely. Who's your gardener?"

I went to Hawaii and got a beautiful tan. Then I saw the bill, and I turned white again.

Those new Hawaiian hotels are huge. If you want to get the desk, you have to dial long-distance.

I just came back from Hawaii with a gorgeous tan. It only cost me thirty dollars a square inch.

What a weird state Hawaii is. There, the Japanese have the money, and the Americans carry the cameras.

In Hawaii, the girls wear grass skirts and the guys love to hit the hay.

## HEADACHES

"Have you got some aspirin?" the man asked his wife. She pulled out a small tin box and handed him two.

"Thank you, thank you," he said. "But why did you slam the lid?"

Today's my day for my semiannual affair with my wife. It's also her day for her semiannual headache.

## HEALTH

I've been to plastic surgeons, orthopedic men have given me plastic hips, and I had a heart transplant. The other day I realized that my teeth were fifty years older than the rest of me.

In one restaurant, they're really health-conscious. They have a nonsmoked-fish section.

You're getting old when your get-up-and-go depends purely on whether you had prunes for breakfast.

"Why do rodeo cowboys chew tobacco?"

"To sweeten their breath."

My acupuncturist filled me with needles. He said I need the iron.

I knew I needed glasses the day I started to dial the pencil sharpener.

A friend of mine went to a health spa recently, but didn't take part in any of the activities. He didn't take one hike. He didn't do one aerobic exercise. He just sat around eating.

In the lobby on checkout day, my friend paid his bill and was about to summon a bellhop to take his bags out when the operator of the spa came over and said, "Sir, you were here for a week and didn't move a finger. Could you just try one tiny exercise before you go?"

My friend's a sport and said, "Sure."

"Good. Let me see you bend over just enough to touch your big valise."

My friend leaned over and touched the big valise. "Is that it?"

"No, one more thing. Reach into the valise and give us back our towels."

I've got so many aches and pains right now that a new one would have to wait about a week before I could feel it.

An older couple die and go to heaven. Looking around, the wife says, "Isn't it gorgeous up here? It's beautiful. The air is so clean, the sky so blue. It's perfect."

The husband says, "If it wasn't for your damn oat bran, we could have been here ten years ago!"

His doctor told him to play thirty-six holes a day, so he went out and bought a harmonica.

You can tell whether a man is healthy by what he takes two at a time—pills or stairs.

In the United States, we spend $50 billion a year on health. That could explain all the healthy doctors.

I'm as sound as a ruble!

I know this couple who are really involved with physical health. Whenever they have an argument, she jogs home to Mother.

I'm in great health. In fact, there's only one thing harder than my muscles—my arteries.

I must be in great shape. Ten years ago, I used to huff and puff bringing home twenty dollars' worth of groceries. Now, I don't even know I'm carrying it.

Fred takes a physical. The doctor examines the reports and says, "You have the highest cholesterol level I ever saw."

Fred says, "How high is it?"

The doctor drags him to the window. "See that oat field there?"

"Sure."

"Well, *bon appétit.*"

A man is walking on the beach when he sees an old bottle. Opening it, he is stunned when a genie appears and says, "I'll grant you any three wishes you want."

The man says, "Okay, I want something that'll bring me health, and then I want a date with a famous movie star."

The man arrives home, and there is a knock on the door. On the mat is a fifty-gallon drum of chicken soup. A second later, the phone rings. It's Lassie.

I never worry about my health. Eventually, it'll go away.

Two old friends run into one another. The first asks how the second friend feels.

The second friend answers, "Lousy. I've got arthritis, a bad back, I'm always tense, I have insomnia. Miserable, I'm miserable."

The first friend says, "And what kind of work are you doing?"

"Same thing—still selling health foods."

## HEAT

My dog's nose got so hot, it burned a hole in the back door.

My wife loves to have me around during a heat spell. I leave her cold.

It's been so hot, politicians won't even put their hands in your pocket.

It was so hot, a panhandler didn't ask for money. He just wanted me to spit on him.

It was very hot today. I bought some steak in the market, and by the time I got home, it was well done.

It was so hot today, my water bed perked.

It was so hot, even my wife thawed out.

It was so hot today, we were all praying for the Cold War to break out again.

## HEAVEN

**A** fancy Boston dowager died and arrived in heaven to be greeted by Saint Peter. Saint Peter indicated the wide expanse beyond the Pearly Gates and said, "Come in."

The dowager said, "I don't think so. Any place where a stranger can get in without a reservation isn't my idea of heaven."

**T**he fence between heaven and hell fell down. Appearing at the broken section, Saint Peter called to Satan, "Look, since you've got all the engineers on your side, why don't you get some of them to repair this fence?"

Satan said, "Are you kidding? My men are much too busy."

"I'll have to sue you."

"Think so? Where are you going to get a lawyer?" Satan asked.

**A**fter a thousand years at the Pearly Gates, Saint Peter wants to take a day off. He asks Jesus to cover for him, saying, "It's easy. When a new arrival comes in, just ask him his name, his occupation, and other simple pertinent questions."

Saint Peter is gone about ten minutes when a gray-haired man arrives at the Pearly Gates. Jesus asks, "What is your name?"

"I suppose in English it would be Joseph."

"What kind of work do you do?"

"I'm a carpenter."

"Any children?"

"One boy."

"Anything unusual about him?"

"Well, he wasn't born in the normal way, and he had nail marks in his hands and feet."

Jesus throws out his arms. "Daddy!"

The gray-haired man says, "Pinocchio?"

**A** wonderful man passes away and goes to heaven. His first meal is served. It turns out to be a tuna sandwich. The man starts to eat but looks down, and there below the clouds, in hell, people are feasting on lobster, steak, the fanciest desserts. The man says, "Saint Peter, I've been an angel all my life. How come I get tuna? Down in hell, they're eating steak and lobster."

Saint Peter replies, "To tell you the truth, it doesn't pay to cook for just two."

**A** man enters heaven and sees a group of people chained to a heavy post. He asks another heavenite to explain. The other heavenite says, "They're Texans. We have to keep them chained or they'll run back home."

**M**y greatest fear is that I'll be on line behind Mother Teresa at the Pearly Gates, and I'll hear Saint Peter tell her, "You didn't do enough."

**"D**o you know the quickest way to get to heaven?"

"Stand in Dublin and say, 'To hell with the pope.'"

Heaven and hell—one's bliss; the other, blisters.

I had a dream about heaven. To get there, you had to climb a ladder and mark each rung with chalk for every time you had sinned. As I was going up, I passed my wife coming down.

"Where are you going?" I asked.

"For more chalk," she said.

Three men die and go to heaven. Saint Peter asks the first, "Were you faithful to your wife?"

The first says, "Well, I must admit I had two affairs back on Earth."

"Just for that," St. Peter says, "you'll have to drive around in a compact."

The second man says that he was unfaithful only once. Saint Peter gives him a midsize car.

The third man swears that he never cheated. Saint Peter gives him a magnificent big car.

About a week later, the big-car man runs into the other two men. On his face is a very unhappy expression. The others want to know what's bothering him. He says, "I just ran into my wife."

The first man says, "What's wrong with that?"

"She was on a skateboard."

A Hollywood lover had quite a way with the ladies. He finally got killed in a hunting accident. It's said, Saint Peter turned a little pale when the man showed up at the Pearly Gates.

"Just a minute, my boy," Saint Peter said, and disappeared for some time.

"What's the idea?" the man asked. "Don't I rate in this place?"

"Of course," Saint Peter replied. "I was just locking up all the women before I let you in!"

## HECKLE LINES

Keep it up, honey, and I'll tell your date your real age.

Well, if it isn't a bicarbonate cowboy—Wild Bill Hiccup.

I like that outfit. Do you always wear seconds?

You're like an umbrella after the rain—all wet but you can't be shut up.

That must be a face. It's got ears on it.

That's a nice suit you've got on. Didn't they have one your size?

Do me a favor. Take a nap under a falling ax.

## HELL

A meek gent arrives in hell and makes himself right at home there. Another occupant says, "Hey, you act as if you own this place."

The meek gent says, "I should. I got it often enough from my boss and my wife."

Where do the people in hell tell each other to go?

The Devil is showing a new arrival around. Everywhere they go, in one room after another, there are nothing but stunning naked women and kegs of beer. The new arrival is ecstatic: "This is better than heaven."

The Devil says, "Not quite. You see, the kegs all have holes in the bottom, but the women don't."

"Hell, yes," said the Devil, picking up the phone.

Henry dies and goes to hell. Satan gives him a choice of two doors to go through for eternity. Henry thinks and thinks and finally points to the door on the right. The door opens. Henry smiles as he sees a group of people standing up to their waists in garbage. They seem to be having a good time as they sip their coffee. Henry thanks Satan and goes through the door. Just as he enters, Satan says, "Okay, gang. Coffee break's over. Everybody on their heads again."

## HENPECKED

He's so henpecked, he's still taking orders from his first wife.

He's so henpecked, his wife makes him wash and iron his own aprons.

I know a really henpecked man. He's sterile, and he just doesn't dare tell his pregnant wife.

At home his parakeet gets to talk more than he does!

## HIJACKING

People on flights are so scared today. On my last flight, I got up to go to the bathroom, and the whole crew surrendered.

A skyjacker jumped up from his seat, pulled out a gun, and said, "Take me to Los Angeles."

The pilot said, "This plane goes to Los Angeles."

The skyjacker said. "I know. But this is the third time I've tried, and each time we end up in Havana."

## HILLBILLIES

A hillbilly entered an elevator, pushed the button, and spent the next five minutes waiting for gum.

A hillbilly goes to a doctor and says, "I wants you to castrate me."

"You're not serious."

"I sure am. If you don't do it, I'll get me a doc who will."

Shrugging his shoulders, the doctor ships the hillbilly off to the hospital. The next morning the operation is performed successfully.

As soon as the hillbilly is out of the recovery room, the doctor visits him and says, "You know, while we were getting you ready, I think I should have asked you if you wanted to be circumcised too."

Weakly, the hillbilly looks up, "Darn. *That* was the darn word I was looking for."

**A** young hillbilly came home one night and told his father, "Pa, I'm fixing to get married with a new girl from the next town. Her name's Margie Bronson and she's—"

The father interrupted, "Son, you can't marry with that girl. I don't know how to tell you this, but I'm her pa and she's your half-sister."

The young hillbilly was heartbroken. When his mother came home and saw how sad he was, she pried the story out of him.

She smiled and said, "No need to cry. He ain't even your paw."

**T**hen there was this hillbilly who complained because the new schoolteacher was teaching his kid how to spell taters with a *P*.

**A** hillbilly has to go into the big city for some business. He leaves the farm chores to Zeke, saying, "Take care of things. I want it to be like I was there myself."

A week later, the farmer returns and asks Zeke how things have been going.

Zeke says, "The chickens have been laying eggs like mad, and the vegetables are big and tasty, and as for those monthly spells your daughter's used to having, I've even got those stopped."

**P**appy sees Elmer walking with a lantern and asks, "Where you going, boy?"

"I'm going courtin'."

"When I went courtin', I didn't need a lantern."

"Sure, and look what you got."

**T**his young hillbilly went over to his father and said, "Paw, I'm planning to get married, and I'd sure like to know how you proposed to Maw."

The father said, "There wasn't much to it, Son. Your maw and I were setting on the porch swing when she leaned over and whispered something in my ear, and I said—'You're what?' . . . and that's how we got married."

**"W**hat does a hillbilly groom call an old rusty pickup truck?"

"The bridal suite."

**O**ne hillbilly married a girl of thirteen and didn't like it. He had to come in from the fields five times a day to see if she was home from school yet.

**A** hillbilly went to the hospital where his nineteen-year-old son was undergoing surgery. Baffled by modern medicine, the hillbilly watched every move the doctors made.

Seeing something puzzling in the operating room, he asked one of the surgeons, "What's that dang thing you're doing?"

The surgeon answered, "We're giving him an anesthetic so he won't know anything."

The hillbilly said, "Might as well save your time, Doc. He don't know anything now."

A middle-aged farmer married an attractive widow with a ten-year-old brat. Soon after the wedding, the farmer remained home with the boy while the new wife went into town to buy some flour.

Returning home, she asked her son, "How'd you get along with your step-dad?"

The boy said, "We had fun. Twice today he took me out in the lake and let me swim back."

"That's a mighty long swim."

"I didn't mind that. It was easy once I worked my way out of the burlap bag!"

A revenue agent, hot on the trail of a West Virginia moonshiner, suddenly heard a shot and something grazed his sleeve. Undaunted, he continued the pursuit, and a shot grazed the agent's coattail. When a third bullet grazed his hat but still failed to halt him, a voice from the woods sounded.

"One more step, mister, and I'll start takin' aim!"

Two hillbillies run into each other at the general store. Zeke says, "Ain't seen you around, Luke. Where you been?"

"Wasn't here," Luke answered. "Went to the city for a spell."

"Have a good time?"

"Sure did. Went to a whorehouse."

"That must have cost some."

"Nope, kinfolk."

The hillbilly checks into the big-city hotel and tracks in a ton of mud as he crosses the lobby. The desk clerk says,

"Sir, I'd suggest you clean off your shoes next time."

"What shoes?"

A doctor comes to the hillbilly's cabin, and the hillbilly says, "Doc, you've got to fix up my son-in-law. I shot him."

The doctor says, "How could you shoot your son-in-law?"

"Well, he wasn't my son-in-law when I shot him."

A hillbilly goes to New York for a few days and returns home. Neighbors ask him, "Did you see the city?"

The hillbilly says, "Tell you the truth, there was so much going on at the bus depot, I never got into the city."

This hillbilly brings his new bride to the new cabin he's been building. The bride admires its spaciousness, but asks, "Where's the door?"

The hillbilly says, "Door? You aimin' to go someplace?"

This hillbilly's will gave his wife everything in trust. But she couldn't touch it till she was fourteen.

A tourist loses his way. After hours of stumbling around, he sees a hillbilly. "I'm glad to see you. I was lost," he says.

"There a reward out for you?"

"Not that I know of."

"Then you're still lost."

A tourist pulls up to a rural gas station and asks, "Do you have a rest room here?"

The hillbilly owner says, "Nope, but we got a mighty comfortable rocker on the porch."

A hillbilly is told that his old jalopy needs tires and shocks. He says, "No, thanks. When I'm driving, I want to know it."

"What do you call a hillbilly's index finger?"
"A handkerchief."

## HIPPIES

I knew he was a hippie. I saw him carrying his medicine cabinet in a brown paper bag.

His long hair used to come in handy. He didn't have to wear a shirt.

Being a hippie had its advantages—you never missed an important phone call because you were taking a bath.

During the hippie days, I couldn't stand watching the teenagers at a restaurant combing their shoulder-length hair during the meal. And the girls were just as bad.

Definition of a hippie: He with a she haircut.

I know a masochistic hippie. He takes baths.

Then there was this hippie girl. Came in every morning and dirtied up a little.

This cop pulls the hippie over and asks, "Did you see the red light you just went through?"
The hippie says, "Man, I didn't even see the house."

This little old lady walks over to a hippie in Greenwich Village and asks, "Crosstown buses run all night?"
The hippie replies, "Doo dah, doo-dah."

## HISTORY

"General Lee wore his Confederate uniform. What did Grant wear?"
"His Union suit."

They asked General Grant what his favorite songs were. He answered, "I only know two songs. One of them is 'Yankee Doodle' and the other isn't."

When Columbus came to America, there were no taxes, no debts, the women did all the work, and the men hunted and fished all day. How did Columbus expect to improve on a system like that?

The accountants suggested to Nero that he close down the Colosseum. "We're not making a drachma," they told him. "The lions are eating up all the prophets."

"What did Paul Revere say at the end of his ride?"
"Whoa."

Columbus said the world was round like an egg. He was wrong. From the looks of it, it's scrambled.

Lady Godiva tiptoes into the house at midnight. Lord Godiva is waiting for her. "Where the hell have you been? Your horse came back two hours ago."

A young man arrives in California and says to no one in particular, "It says: Go West, young man. I did. Now what?"

## HOBBIES

Hobbies can be a lot of fun, especially if your wife doesn't find out.

A hobby is something you do that you'd be ashamed to do for a living.

A hobby is something you do for free you wouldn't touch if you got paid for it.

My wife has two hobbies. She swims and knits. . . . It makes the wool a little soggy, but it keeps her happy.

## HOCKEY

They asked a great hockey player, "Did you ever break your nose while playing?"

He answered, "No, but eleven other guys did."

Annoyed, the hockey player yelled at the interviewer, "You know, I'm not as dumb as I look."

The interviewer said, "Nobody could be."

A girl says to her hockey-playing boyfriend, "I'd like to talk."

He says, "I can't. I'll get in trouble if I miss this period."

The girl says, "I did and I am."

## HOLLYWOOD

An actor works all of his life for recognition, then he puts on a pair of dark glasses so no one will know who he is.

A casting director told a starlet, "I'm sorry, but you won't do."

The starlet answered, "Did I say I wouldn't?"

A Hollywood producer decided he wanted a portrait of his wife. Somebody suggested that he contact one of the better local artists. The producer said, "That's stupid. I'm sending her to Europe so she can be painted by one of the Old Masters."

Hollywood is a real wild town. They even play strip Monopoly there.

Two Hollywood stars just got married. It was just as well. They weren't getting along anyway.

Stars love to show off. One I know has a small car to drive him to his big car.

In Hollywood, stars don't live in sin. They just have unlisted lovers.

One Hollywood star was furious because one of the tabloids had said she was engaged to the man she was dating. She said, "That's the trouble nowadays. A girl can't make love to a guy without somebody saying she's engaged to him."

I know a female movie star who is forty-six this week. She was also forty-six twelve years ago.

Then there was this Hollywood star who would follow anyone who whistled at her. Her name was Lassie.

One day Lassie went to Denmark and came back a cat.

Where else but Hollywood can you go out on a blind date and end up with your own wife?

Most Hollywood dogs don't bite. That's because their teeth are capped, and they're up for a series.

Hollywood couples have strange relationships. Many couples live together but don't get married. Others get married and don't live together.

Hollywood stars are very lucky. Can you imagine if they had to pay taxes on what they claim they make?

A newly married star walked into her new home and asked, "John, this house looks so familiar. Haven't we been married before?"

Hollywood has everything under the stars—including the starlets.

They have a new holiday in Hollywood: Unwed Mother's Day.

Hollywood is where you stab your best friend in the back and then tell the cops that he's carrying a concealed weapon.

In Hollywood, you automatically get four contact lenses. That's because everybody is two-faced.

I met an actress whose life is a Cinderella story. Every other night at the stroke of midnight, she turns into a motel.

One Hollywood actor was out of work two years before he found out that his agent had died.

One Hollywood star just hired three press agents to let the world know how modest he is.

She's on the Hollywood diet—three males a day.

Many visitors to Hollywood are impressed by all the women who don't wear bras, and all the men who do!

One Hollywood star just took pictures of her honeymoon. It'll soon come out as a workout video.

An associate producer gets his job in Hollywood because he's the only one who'll associate with the producer.

**A** Hollywood couple just broke up. They found out that a mutual hatred isn't enough for a successful show-business marriage.

**O**ne actor complained that his wife was into group sex: "I'm tolerant to a point, but I wish they'd let me into the group."

**A**rafat is walking down the street in Cairo when he spots a timid-looking elderly man. Arafat barks, "What's your name?"

"Stein."

"You're in Arab country now. When you speak to me, I'm Arafat of the PLO. Remember that, Jew. And what kind of work do you do?"

"I'm a producer."

"Really? Stein, do I have a script for you!"

**O**ne new Hollywood player complained, "I've got more film with my doctor than I have with the studios."

**T**wo actresses meet in a restaurant. One says, "You're awfully pretty to be such a bitch."

The other says, "I'm not the biggest bitch in Hollywood."

The first one says, "No, but you run me a close second."

**I** know a big star who produced a movie. To get the leading role, she had to sleep with herself.

**I**t was so cold in Hollywood the other day, two stars almost got married.

**O**ne Hollywood star was so embarrassed at a party the other night. She and her dressmaker were wearing the same outfit, and he looked better in it than she did.

**A** man calls a friend of his, a producer, and asks how things are going. The producer answers, "Things are going great. I've got three picture deals, I just signed to produce a twelve-hour miniseries, and tomorrow I will sign a fifty-million-dollar deal with Paramount."

The caller says, "Good. Listen, I'll call you back when you're alone."

**A** starlet's mother picked up the phone to find a struggling young actor at the other end of the line. He wanted to talk to her daughter. The mother said, "She doesn't live here anymore, and I don't have the faintest idea of where you can contact her unless you're a producer or a director!"

**T**wo actresses, both a little long in the tooth, met at a party. One said, "Do you know that my boobs are insured with Lloyd's of London for ten million dollars?"

The other actress said, "No kidding? And what did you do with all that money?"

**H**alf the men in Hollywood want to marry one actress. The other half has.

**T**hey have a new game now called Sex Roulette. You get your choice of six starlets, but one of them is writing a book and will sue.

In Hollywood, they sit down to a bottle of water, a bran muffin, and decaf coffee and call it a power breakfast.

The most foolish thing you can do in Hollywood is buy a newlywed movie actress a set of monogrammed towels.

This producer met and was smitten by a young actress. In addition to setting her up in a nice condo, he also paid to have plastic surgery done on her so that she'd be perfect. A short time later, the couple broke up. The producer ran into the actress at a cocktail party. She snubbed him. He turned to a friend and said, "How do you like that? She's lifting my new nose at me."

A starlet comes back from a trip with a gorgeous mink coat. Her manicurist says, "Where did you get that beautiful coat?"

"I met a gentleman who had ten thousand dollars."

Later in the year, the manicurist comes back from her own vacation with an equally exotic coat. The starlet asks how she got it.

The manicurist says, "I met a thousand guys with ten bucks apiece."

I know a Hollywood director who's so conceited, he has a stretch director's chair.

A Hollywood star had a secretary who kept terrible records. The star had two more divorces than she had marriages.

A producer is having difficulty convincing a young actress to go back to his house to see his new Jacuzzi.

"Look," he says, "how long have I known you?"

"About three-quarters of an hour," she says.

"All right then," he storms, "have I ever lied to you?"

An actress is taking a demo ride in a car. After a block, she says to the salesman at her side, "I don't like the rearview mirror. I can't see myself in it. I can only see the cars behind me."

Then there was this beautiful movie star who appeared in all the epic adventure pictures. She was mounted more times than the horses.

One actress made it to the top by wearing clothes that didn't.

A producer comes home and finds his wife in bed with an actor. The producer says, "What are you doing?"

The actor says, "Well, this week, I got two days on a picture, and next week . . ."

I know a sentimental actress. She saved a piece of the wedding cake for her divorce lawyer.

They had a real weird party in Hollywood the other night. Everybody brought his own wife.

One Hollywood producer loved *The Ten Commandments* so much, he hired a team of writers to come up with ten more.

A cameraman is asked how he has remained just a cameraman after so many years. He explains, "When you start a picture, there are all kinds of meetings. One day I was so sick of going, I got a monkey, put some of my clothes on him, and let him go to the meeting. Now that monkey is running a studio, and I'm still a cameraman."

I know a Hollywood actress who's dating a producer. Every time he makes a move, she makes a movie.

A young starlet walks over to an actor at a party and asks, "If I were a genie and could grant you three wishes, what would the other two be?"

In Hollywood, friendships don't last. They usually end up in marriage.

Someone asked a big executive how he got into motion pictures.

"It's a simple story," he said. "My father was in pictures, you know. One day he bumped into me on the studio lot and took a liking to me!"

One star complains, "Every time I meet a gorgeous girl, either she's married or I am."

A writer returns from a meeting to find a commotion on his block. He sees that his house has burned down. He asks a cop what happened.

The cop explains, "Your agent came over to your house before, beat up your wife, stole your kids, and then burned your house to the ground."

The writer says, "My agent? Came to my house?"

One Hollywood studio is really in jeopardy. Even the yes-men aren't too sure.

Pietro's is one of those fancy Hollywood restaurants in which many famous stars are photographed by paparazzi with the accompanying publicity. Naturally, out-of-towners flock to the restaurant to see names. One out-of-towner sits in Pietro's for four hours running up a huge tab, but sees nobody famous.

He says to the waiter, "How come I haven't seen one star?"

The waiter says, "I've been here fifteen years, and I haven't even seen Pietro."

One Hollywood starlet got her start in a unique way. She was discovered sipping soda in a drugstore by a producer who happened to be sharing her apartment at the time.

A producer is concerned with the cost of the movie he has in production. He goes to the set and wanders around. He's stunned by the expensive props. Calling over the set decorator, he says, "What is this expensive stuff doing here? Look at that bottle. It's hand-blown and must cost a fortune."

The set decorator says, "I never saw it before." Picking it up, he runs his fingers over it, and there's a *poof!* A genie appears. The genie says, "What do you want?"

The set decorator says, "I want to be in Tahiti, painting like Gaugin."

*Poof!* and the set decorator is gone.

The genie turns to the writer nearby and asks, "What do you want?"

"I'd like to be in Paris, writing like Hemingway and Joyce."

*Poof!* and the writer is gone.

The genie turns to the producer and asks, "What do you want?"

The producer says, "I want those two idiots on the set at nine o'clock tomorrow morning!"

## HOLLYWOOD DIVORCE

Hollywood is a town where movies have happy endings but marriages don't.

In Hollywood, the expression goes, "Always a bride, never a bridesmaid."

One Hollywood actress ran out of husbands to marry and had to start all over again with those she'd already had.

That's the only town where the bride tossing the bouquet is just as likely to get married next as the girl who caught it.

One Hollywood star was happily married for twenty years. Of course, it took her six marriages to do it.

Hollywood now has a group called Divorce Anonymous. If a star gets the urge to get a divorce, they send over an accountant to talk him out of it.

In Hollywood, a successful marriage is when the couple leaves the church together.

A Hollywood marriage is a great way to spend a weekend.

In Hollywood, if you don't go to a shrink, people think you're crazy.

Some Hollywood actresses have signed more marriage certificates than autographs.

One Hollywood marriage ended very quickly. The bride sued for the wedding cake.

One Hollywood star has towels marked "Hers" and "Next."

## HOLLYWOOD KIDS

Two Hollywood kids are playing house. One says, "I want to have a big family— three mothers and four fathers."

A Hollywood kid was asked to bring his mother to school the following Monday but said he couldn't, explaining, "Next Monday I don't know who she'll be."

One Hollywood kid talks back to his father. The mother says, "Don't you dare talk back. You hardly know the man."

Some Hollywood lawyers charge fifty thousand for a divorce. Or three for a hundred.

One Hollywood star was very sentimental. She got a divorce in the same dress her mother got a divorce in.

One couple finally ironed out their divorce settlement, so they went ahead and got married.

Where else but in Hollywood do they have a jewelry store that rents engagement rings?

When Hollywood actresses think about a family, they have to consider one thing. Is this the man they want their children to spend weekends with?

One Hollywood star got married recently, and her folks didn't know what to give her for a gift; so they promised to pay for the divorce.

One Hollywood couple is about to get married, but neither of them can figure out who to invite. They've already married all their friends.

Hollywood marriages break up so fast, they just throw Minute Rice.

## HOMES

They made a movie once called *The Invisible Man*. I think it was about the guy who built my house two minutes after the end of escrow!

They must have used real cheap lumber on my house. The termites eat out.

He has a Japanese gardener and a German cook. Last month they got together and captured his house.

A carpenter puts up an outhouse for Mrs. Bronson. After a week, she makes him return to do some repairs. He checks out the structure and can find nothing wrong. Mrs. Bronson says, "Try putting your head near the darn seat."
  The carpenter does so and gets one of his whiskers caught. As he yells, "Ouch," Mrs. Bronson says, "Happens to me every time."

Our builder wasn't too good at it. Where else do you have to walk downstairs to get to the attic?

Split-level homes are a big thing nowadays. Years ago, if you lived over a garage, you kept quiet about it.

We have the lowest ceiling in town. You can't even yawn up and down.

We have a waterproof house. Do you remember that big rainstorm recently? Three days later, not one drop had leaked out!

We had some trouble with our furnace last night. It went out—right through the roof.

I built my own home from prints in the magazines. It came out great except for one thing—the picture window is in the john.

Prices of homes are incredible nowadays. A man won a million in a lottery and was asked what he planned to do with the money. He said, "Well, I think I'll put a payment down on a one-bedroom house. Then, if there's anything left . . .

I borrowed five thousand from my uncle, sixty thousand on a first mortgage, forty thousand on a second, another thirty on an equity loan, and they have the nerve to call me a homeowner!

I have the feeling that my house isn't too strong. The other day I saw termites wearing hard hats.

I live in a subdivision. It got that name because the basement is always under water.

I finally saved something for a rainy day—a leaky basement.

We've got a ten-room house, and it's not to be sneezed at. The walls couldn't take it.

I hate my new house. It has all the latest computerized gadgets. How can you live in a house where the appliances are smarter than you are?

We lived in a trailer for a while, but it was terrible. Every time my wife and I had a scrap, she went home to her mother, and she took the house with her.

The easiest way to find something you lost around the house is to buy a replacement.

In the middle of the night, a man comes down from the upstairs bedroom and finds a burglar halfway out the window.

The man says, "Don't panic. I'm not armed, and I won't call the police. I'd just like to bring my wife in to meet you because she's been hearing you downstairs for ten years."

I'm pretty handy around the house. If something can be fixed, I can break it.

A man moves into a new house. Within two weeks, he has to call the electrician, the water man, the roofer, the plasterer, the carpenter.

One afternoon he returns from work early and sees a plumber's truck in the driveway. He looks to the sky and says, "Lord, please let her be having an affair."

## HOMETOWN

If we didn't have bowling in my hometown, there'd be no culture at all.

My hometown is very clean. Even the birds fly upside down.

My hometown isn't exactly a gourmet haven. One restaurant has a sign in the window: SORRY, WE'RE OPEN.

The food is bad in my hometown. There are only two restaurants, but no matter which you go into, you're sorry you didn't go to the other one.

I come from a real friendly town. Everybody wants to help you carry your wallet.

In my hometown, the hotel had a sign—WASHINGTON WOULDN'T SLEEP HERE.

My brother just came back from our hometown. He visited the grammar school he'd entered when he was six. Everybody remembered him. They should. He just got out last year.

In my hometown, they once outlawed sex. They were afraid it might lead to dancing.

My hometown isn't much. It's the only town I know where both sides of the track are wrong.

My hometown is the healthiest place in the world. They had to kill someone to start a cemetery.

## HONESTY

Vote for the incumbent. When he runs for reelection, it means he's honest. He hasn't laid his hands on the loot the first time.

Honesty is the best policy, but keeping your mouth shut sometimes is even better.

Most people know that honesty is the best policy, but the trouble is that too many people don't want the best.

## HONEYMOONS

The honeymoon's over when you stop living on love and start living on a budget.

One bride was so tired on her honeymoon, she couldn't stay awake for a second.

Carl was unlucky enough to be in a terrible car crash on the eve of his honeymoon. In the hospital, the doctor examined him and told him that a very special part of his anatomy had been badly hurt and would need a special bandage.

Assembling a special bandage made from tongue depressors and strips of bandage, the doctor stepped back, admired his handiwork, and told Carl to do the best he could on his honeymoon.

In the honeymoon suite, Carl's bride started to take off her clothes. Her bosom bared, she said, "Carl, these have never been touched by any other man."

Taking off her skirt, she went on, "No other man's eyes have ever seen this."

Carl opened his robe and said, "Look at this. It's still in the original crate!"

On the first night of the honeymoon, she appeared—a vision in white silk. The groom said, "My darling, you look so beautiful I wouldn't dream of touching you." The second night, the bride was a vision in blue silk. The groom said, "You look so beautiful I wouldn't dream of touching you."

He didn't touch her through orchid and pink either. On the fifth night, he came in to find her in black and asked, "Why are you wearing black?"

The bride said, "I'm in mourning. Something's dead in here."

Two couples met in Niagara Falls. They decided to share the same suite. Going into the room after dinner, they found themselves in darkness, a power shortage having hit just then. After a while, the lights went on and one of the newlywed brides saw the other husband kneeling at the foot of the bed, praying.

Seeing that this wasn't his wife, the praying husband jumped up and said, "My Lord, my wife is with your husband."

As he rushed to the door, the new bride said, "You don't have to hurry. My husband never prays."

A bellhop and desk clerk were discussing some arrivals of the day before. The bellhop said, "That Mrs. Moore was something."

The desk clerk said, "We don't have any Moores here."

The bellhop said, "We must have. Every time I passed the room, I heard her saying, 'I want Moore. Moore.' "

"Does your husband snore in his sleep?"

"I don't know. We've only been married three days."

A football player went on his honeymoon. As he started to get into bed to consummate the marriage, he slipped and hurt his back. So he sent in a substitute.

The Yukon is a great place to honeymoon. The nights are six months long.

My wife kept a diary of our honeymoon. Forty pages of ditto marks.

The young couple come down to the kitchen to eat after their first night together. The husband looks at the runny eggs and the burned toast and says, "Don't tell me you can't cook either!"

A new bride looked at the sign in the honeymoon hotel coffee shop. It read: BREAKFAST 7–10. LUNCH 10–3. DINNER 3–9.

She turned to her groom and said, "Honey, we'll be so busy eating, we won't be able to get anything else in."

A newlywed couple arrive at a hotel and ask for a suite. The clerk says, "How about a bridal?"

The groom says, "Forget that. I'll just hold on to her ears till she gets the hang of it."

The honeymoon is over when he takes her off a pedestal and puts her on a budget.

This couple don't have much money and start their honeymoon in the bride's house. The nuptial chamber is right next to the bedroom of the bride's parents. As the youngsters start to make love, the bed creaks. The bride is perturbed, so they decide to go to a motel. They start to pack up their clothes but have a little trouble closing the valise. In the next bedroom, the father hears the bride say, "Let me sit on it." A moment later, the groom says, "Let's both sit on it."

Jumping out of bed, the father heads for the door, saying to his wife, "This I gotta see."

You could tell they had a bad honeymoon. When they came down for breakfast the next morning, he asked for separate checks.

They married late in life. In fact, Medicare paid for the honeymoon.

An intermission is when a honeymoon couple goes out for lunch.

Nowadays it isn't easy to go on a honeymoon. It's hard to find a baby-sitter.

Bill gets married to a woman he hasn't known too long. On the honeymoon night, she takes off her hair, she removes a glass eye, she removes her hearing aid, she removes her falsies. She starts to unscrew her wooden leg, and Bill says, "Look, you know what I want. Unscrew it and throw it into the bed!"

A new bride goes to a psychiatrist. He tells her to lie down on the couch. She says, "Doctor, I just came back from my honeymoon. Do you mind if I stand?"

A bride-to-be goes into a specialty shop and asks the clerk if she has a red-white-and-blue-striped nightgown. The clerk is puzzled and asks why such a garish outfit. The bride-to-be says, "On the honeymoon, I'd like to surprise my husband with something."

"Sweetheart," he asked, "will I be the first man to sleep with you?"

"You will be if you doze off."

On their honeymoon, a bride kneels and says a prayer: "I need Thee every hour."

On the other side of the bed, the groom kneels and says, "God give me strength."

## HOOKERS

Two hookers meet on the way out of court. One asks, "Where do you work?"

The other one answers, "Sunset Boulevard. It's fantastic. Business is incredible."

The first hooker says, "You don't have to tell me. I'm sold on it myself."

He's so ugly, a hooker told him, "Not on our first date."

One hooker went to a plastic surgeon on her lunch break and asked if he could make it snappy.

Hookers should make good auto mechanics. Same position, better prices.

You can be suspicious of her if there's a sign over her bed that says—GROUP RATES.

I know a man who gives hookers money just to get them back on their feet.

She was on a diet. She took nothing but greens—tens, fifties, hundreds.

Three prostitutes are arrested and brought before a judge. As the first prostitute stands before him, the judge asks, "What is your defense, young lady?"

The first prostitute says, "I was arrested by mistake. I'm a secretary and just happened to be standing on the street when this officer arrested me."

"Sixty days or two hundred dollars."

The second prostitute explains her arrest: "I'm also a secretary, and I also happened to be on the street."

"Sixty days or two hundred dollars."

The third prostitute says, "Your Honor, I'm a hooker, and I don't care who knows it."

"How's business?"

"Lousy, especially with all these secretaries around."

This fancy southern family learns that one of its twenty-year-old girls has become a hooker in a big city. The head of the family starts to cry, and somebody asks, "Why are you so upset?"

The head of the family answers, "Because she's the first one in the family who ever worked."

A man picks up the ugliest hooker in the world. He takes her into an alley where he has sex with her. Finished, he comes up with a dollar bill and says, "This is all I have."

The hooker says, "I don't have any change. Let's do it again."

A very high-priced call girl brings a customer to her fancy apartment. The customer admires the furnishings and the art. He asks the prostitute how she amassed such splendor. She says, "Oh, these things belonged to my father when he was an ambassador."

The customer says, "Well, how did you get to be a prostitute?"

She answers, "Pure luck."

There was one prostitute who'd finish a job by saying, "It's a real business doing pleasure with you."

She's a hooker if she carries a change-maker in her pantyhose.

Three young boys were playing in a park when a Rolls-Royce pulled up and an expensively dressed blonde got out. She hugged one of the boys and gave him a bag full of toys and some money.

"Golly, John, was that your fairy godmother?" one asked.

John looked at him with scorn and replied, "Nah! That wuz my sister what was ruined."

The way I see it is that a hooker with a three-hundred-pound customer will be pressed for cash.

A man calls for a hooker to come to his room at a hotel, but he has special demands: "I want the tallest, skinniest dame you can come up with."

A half hour later, there's a knock on the door, and a hooker walks in. She's about 6'10" and weighs eighty pounds soaking wet. She gets undressed. The man motions for her to remain standing. Then he goes into the other room of his suite and returns with a Great Dane. Pointing to the girl, he says, "If you don't want to look like this, eat your kibble!"

She was one of the busiest hookers in town. When she quit, the phone company retired her number.

I know a seventy-year-old hooker who's got her number in the Yellow Pages. She's the oldest trick in the book.

A beautiful girl of only nineteen or twenty years stood before a judge. He reviewed her extensive arrest record and asked, "How does one so young come to a point like this?"

"Well, Your Honor," she said, "when I was about ten, a little boy my age told me what little girls were for. And do you know, Judge, of all the grown-up men I have met since then, not one has told me different!"

A man picks up a cheap hooker who says that she'll make love to him as often as he wants for twenty dollars. The man takes her to a cheap motel. They put out the light, and the man makes love to her. A minute's rest and he's at it again. After the sixth time, the girl turns on the light and sees a total stranger. "You're not—"

The stranger says, "No. He's outside selling tickets."

I don't know what she does for a living, but she got thrown out of one hotel because she didn't have a permit for a parade.

Then there's the new breakfast cereal called Hooker. It doesn't snap, crackle and pop. It just lies there and bangs.

I knew a streetwalker who was so exclusive, she had an unlisted telephone booth.

Two women are talking. One says, "My daughter lives in a gorgeous condo. She has designer clothes, a mink coat, a sable, she eats out in the fanciest restaurants and has dozens of boyfriends."

The second woman says, "It's amazing. My daughter is a hooker too."

## HORMONES

Two women meet and start to discuss their sex life, or lack of it. One of them says, "I'm not pessimistic. Yesterday we went to the doctor, and he gave my husband monkey-gland injections."

The second woman says, "Did it help?"

"Not yet. But it might when he stops swinging from the chandelier."

After delivering a woman's tenth child, the doctor took the husband aside and said, "Next time you feel like propagating, you might ask yourself if you can support another child."

"Doc," said the husband, "when I feel like propagatin', I feel like I could support the whole state of Georgia!"

A woman is losing her hair. She goes to a doctor who tells her that there's a brand-new male hormone that grows hair. Its one serious side effect is that there's no way of knowing how much hair it will grow.

The woman risks the side effect and returns to the doctor a few weeks later. He asks, "How's it coming along?"

The woman says, "Fine, except that it makes my testicles itch."

## HORSE RACING

I bet on a good horse today. It took eleven other horses to beat him.

A tout is a guy who has nothing to lose and makes sure you do too.

The other day at the track, I beat them in the first seven races. If I'd had any money left, I would have beaten them in the next two also.

I wouldn't have bet on this horse if I'd gone down to the paddock area. He was so old, they had to dunk his hay for him.

They told him the horse would win in a walk. Unfortunately, the other horses ran!

It would have been a photo finish, but by the time my horse finished, it was too dark to take a photo.

Then there was the jockey who ate too much. He kept putting à la carte before the horse.

I bet on a horse the other day that ended up in a photo finish with the wagon that waters the track.

Taken to the track for the first time, a very conservative old lady was persuaded to bet five dollars on the daily double. And she won!

Collecting her money at the collection window, she pointed her finger at the payoff clerk and said, "Young man, I hope this will be a lesson to you!"

I bet on a terrible horse the other day. He came in seventh in the race and tenth in the instant replay.

At our local racetrack they have a sign: KEEP OFF THE GRASS. IT MAY BE YOUR DINNER.

The horse was so slow, the jockey carried a change of saddle.

The owner berates the jockey, "I told you to come out of the gate fast and take the lead."

The jockey says, "I know, but I didn't want to leave the horse behind."

My horse would have won the race easily, but he kept looking around to see if his plow was on straight.

## HORSES

A man says to a veterinarian, "My horse walks perfectly at times. At other times, he's got a decided limp. What should I do?"

The vet says, "The next time he walks well, sell him."

Harrison showed up at the general store and started to tell everybody around about his horse Lightning. "Lightning," Harrison said, "gets up first thing in the morning, scoots down to the bakery to get me some fresh bread, runs over to the dairy for fresh milk, heads home, brings in the paper, starts a fire, and makes coffee. Then he takes me to work, hangs around, and is waiting at quitting time."

One day, a man from the neighboring town heard Harrison's words and bought the horse for a lot of money. After all, a horse like that was worth a fortune.

After a week, the new owner returned. Seeing Harrison, he walked over and said, "What kind of cock-and-bull story did you give me? That horse doesn't lift one finger. It eats and sits around. It doesn't do a thing."

Harrison said, "If you don't stop talking that way about your horse, you'll never sell him."

A country parson bought a horse, and the owner warned him, "This here horse was brought up in a very religious atmosphere. You don't say giddyap to make him go, ya gotta say 'Praise the Lord.' And likewise, 'Whoa' won't make him stop. Ya gotta say, 'Amen!' "

This only added to the horse's value in the parson's eyes, and he gladly paid the man and took the horse.

Heading home, the parson commanded, "Praise the Lord," and the horse took off. A few minutes into their gallop, the parson saw the bridge ahead had been washed out. Starting to panic, he yelled, "Whoa, horsey! Whoa!" to no avail. Finally, he remembered and yelled, "Amen!" and the horse stopped right at the edge of the chasm.

All was fine, until out of habit the parson mumbled, "Praise the Lord!"

The county fair is in full swing. At the horse barn, Farmer Thompson is offering a hundred dollars to anybody who can make his horse laugh. One of the hands, hanging around, takes him up on it. He whispers something in the horse's ear, and the horse laughs as if he were watching a funny movie.

Farmer Brown is ready to pay off but thinks he has a way of coming out even. "Double or nothing. Bet you can't make my horse cry."

"You got yourself a bet."

The hand goes over and gets close to

the horse and does something nobody can make out. The horse starts to cry a river. His tears won't stop flowing.

The farmer asks the cowhand how he'd managed to work his magic. The hand says, "Well, first I told him my penis was bigger than his. That got him laughing. Then the second time I showed him."

"Why did the rodeo rider marry the horse?"

"He had to."

"What's a wrench?"

"A place where Israeli cowboys hang out."

This happened during the good old days. A horse pulling an ice wagon runs into a friend of his, another horse. The second horse asks, "How is it going, Walter?"

Walter says, "Terrible. This guy makes me drag this wagon all day, uphill, downhill, in the rain, in the cold. I'm miserable."

The second horse asks, "Why don't you bawl him out?"

"You're kidding. If he knew I could talk, he'd have me yelling, 'Ice.' "

"What do you get if you cross a rodeo cowboy with an ape?"

"You still get an ape."

Then there was the stallion who hated his life. All day long, it was nag, nag, nag . . .

## HOSPITALS

I only had one concern when I was in the hospital. I just wanted to make sure the doctors didn't go to the same school as the cooks.

A doctor walks over to his patient and says, "Congratulations, Mr. Smith. Our team of doctors think you're well enough to see your bill."

You know you're getting better in the hospital when they give you an enema and you ask for seconds.

Then there was this nurse who made the patient without disturbing the bed.

A patient listened to the surgeon explain his rates and said, "Look, I can't afford the whole thing. Just cut out fifty bucks' worth."

Always guard your rear in the hospital. You're in enema country.

As her doctor was unable to find the cause of her ailment, a woman was checked into a hospital. As she lay on the gurney in the hall so that a room could be prepared, the woman looked up and saw a man in white raise her sheet and nod slowly. A second man in white did the same. Frightened, the woman said, "Will I live?"

One of the men answered, "We don't know, lady. We're the painters."

I didn't have any surgery this year, so it looks like I'll have to talk about my old one for another year.

The operation is going on full swing. Reaching a certain point, the surgeon breathes a sigh of relief and says, "Another half inch and I'd be out of my specialty."

My hospital had semiprivate accommodations—two to a bed.

The nurse walks over to a man in the waiting room and says, "You're a bouncing father. We just tried to cash your check."

Doctors are really getting younger. Last week I saw a surgeon with his operating gloves pinned to his shirt.

Nowadays it costs more to go to a hospital than it does to go to medical school.

I asked this nurse for a bedpan, and she wouldn't give it to me. She was the head nurse.

Hospitals are really cutting corners. One just put in coin-operated bedpans.

I was in the hospital for a few days last week, and I didn't want to check out. Compared to my wife's, the meals were so good.

A prominent citizen was confined in a Carolina hospital for several weeks and was served so faithfully by a young orderly that he gave him an unusually big tip when he got out. The orderly was overwhelmed and felt he must pay a compliment in return.

"We're goin' to miss ya around here, Mr. Walker. You sho' does take a good enema."

A patient is waiting to be brought into surgery. After a few hours, an orderly comes in to get him ready. All flustered, the orderly says, "Sorry to be so late, but it's murder down here."

They move patients around today. On my last hospital trip, I was on the fourth floor. Then, as soon as I finished paying for it, they moved me to the fifth.

Most hospitals have one rule for safety: Don't leave the hospital until you've seen the cashier.

A doctor told his patient: "We believe in getting the patient on his feet as soon as possible after an operation. So the first day, I want you to walk around your room for five minutes. The second day, I want you to walk around for ten. On the third day, I want you to walk around for a full hour. Okay?"

"Sure," the man replied. "But for the operation, do you mind if I lie down?"

In surgery, the anesthesiologist always tells you, "Breathe in, breathe out."

Is there any other way?

A cute nurse is walking along a hospital corridor with one of her breasts exposed. The resident sees her and berates her for showing her endowments. The nurse shakes her head sadly and says, "Those darn interns never put anything back after they're through with it."

They have an alcoholic hospital in Los Angeles that's really unusual. The nurses drink, the doctors drink, the patients drink. They don't cure many alcoholics, but the time sure does fly.

## HOT

It was so hot, a holdup man put a gun to my chest and said, "Put 'em up and down real fast a hundred times."

It was so hot, the thermometer read, "Continued on next thermometer."

It was real hot. I saw a midget buy a quart of ice cream and get in.

Heat can do some nice things. I know a couple who are remaining together for the sake of the air conditioner.

It was so hot, a guy got into a cab and said, "The Yukon and step on it."

It's real hot. Yesterday, I saw a tongue in a delicatessen window panting.

I wouldn't say it's been hot, but if somebody tells you to go to hell, you stay where you are.

## HOTELS

He was born with a silver spoon in his mouth, but it had a hotel's name on it.

He's so ugly, he could be a desk clerk at a Roach Motel.

Because of big convention business, a salesman is forced to share a room with a Texas cowboy. The first morning, the Texan is shaving when the salesman comes in and sets the bathroom seat so he can use it. The Texan looks at it and starts to shake his head. "Darn," he says, "I've been riding the damn thing bareback all week."

We just came from the worst hotel in the world. Room service was 911.

Then there's this hotel room. It was so small, the mice were hunchbacked.

Then there was this hotel room. It only looked small because the mice were so big.

It was the smallest hotel room ever. You couldn't get in unless you were born there.

Some hotels have towels so soft and fluffy, you can hardly get your valise closed.

This hotel had a very small swimming pool. I've had more water with an aspirin.

Hotels ask you to be out by noon. How come the room isn't ready when you check in at 7:00 P.M.?

I was in this hotel room with a hard mattress. I had to get up three times to get some rest.

The bellhop finally arrives. "Did you ring, sir?"

"No," the guest says, "I was tolling. I thought you were dead."

A man walks into a hotel and says, "Do you take children?"

The clerk replies, "No, only cash and traveler's checks."

Hotels cost a fortune nowadays. You can go broke sleeping.

Why are walls in hotel rooms so thin when you're trying to sleep, and so thick when you're trying to listen?

A tourist at a hotel calls down for room service. Connected, he says, "Please send up a badly wilted salad with watery salad dressing, a chicken sandwich on burned toast, and a pot of tepid coffee."

Room service says, "I'm afraid we can't do that."

The tourist says, "Why not? You did it yesterday."

## HOUSES

You know your house isn't properly insulated when you have to put snow tires on your vacuum cleaner.

You know your house is in bad shape when the termites start calling it "junk food."

When I first moved into my house and undertook a twenty-five-year mortgage, I wondered if I'd last that long. Now, I keep wondering if the *house* will last that long.

It's a real thrill to send in your property taxes while off in a corner the termites are betting which way the house will fall.

The trouble with owning your own home is that no matter where you sit, you're looking at something that has to be done.

## HUNTING

Returning from a hunting trip, a man tells his friend, "The last night out, I ran into a giant bear. He indicated he wanted my gun."

"Did you give it to him?"

"You bet. Then he pointed it right at me."

"What did you do then?"

"What could I do? I married his daughter."

Two hunters bed down at their campfire and were about to fall asleep when a giant bear loomed in front of them. One hunter started to put on his sneakers. The other said, "What good'll that do? You'll never outrun that bear."

The first one said, "All I have to do is outrun you!"

Joe took his girlfriend Mary hunting for the first time, warning her, "If you get a deer, make sure you guard it from other hunters. They all try to claim it was their prize."

During the excitement of the hunt, Joe and Mary were separated. He managed to find her a little later. She was standing in front of her catch. Her gun was pointed at another hunter. Mary said, "This is my deer, and you can't take it from me. I'll shoot if you try."

The hunter said, "Okay, lady. He's yours, but let me get my saddle off him!"

I once took twenty shots at a deer. Finally, he came over to me, gave me a dollar, and said, "Here, pal. I don't want to see you go hungry."

A man is packing a hunting knife as one of his companions watches and asks, "Why do you need that knife?"

"In case I get bitten on the arm by a rattler. I make a cross and suck out the blood."

"What if you get bitten on the ass?"

"Then you find out who your true friends are."

Two dummies go on a hunting trip. Each bags a moose. Returning to the plane, they are told by the pilot, "Those moose are too heavy. The plane will crash."

One of the dummies says, "We brought two of them in the plane last year."

The pilot shrugs his shoulders and they take off. In ten minutes, the heavy load causes the plane to go down in the woods. One of the dummies says, "This is something. The same place we crashed last year."

It was dawn. The morning was bitter cold and ugly. The hunters waited in their blind, their hands blue even under their gloves and their teeth chattering. Finally, one hunter stood up and said, "I don't think I can take much more of this fun."

Then there was the guy who was hunting elephants and got a hernia from carrying the decoys.

Some men go on a hunting trip. During the day, they separate into pairs. That evening, Willy returns with a twelve-point buck slung over his back. A hunter asks, "Where's Jimmy our partner?"

Willy says, "He tripped a couple of miles back and couldn't move another foot."

"You left him there and brought back the buck? How come?"

Willy says, "Well, I figure nobody's gonna steal Jimmy."

Two hunters had just arrived at their camp and hadn't even had time to load their guns. Suddenly, a giant bear reared up twenty feet away. One hunter asked, "What are we going to do?"

The other said, "Don't know about you. But I'm about to start spreading the news to the rest of the country."

Two hunters were lost in the woods. One was all set to give up the search for a

way out. The other said, Tell you what—
let's just shoot us an extra deer. The
game warden'll be here in two minutes."

"Why are hunters the best lovers?"
    "Because they go into the bush, shoot
a lot, and eat everything they get."

## HUSBANDS

At the dinner table, as the husband
studies his racing form, the wife says,
"Dear, I went to see the doctor today."
    The husband says, "Really? How is
he?"

He's a good husband. He's spouse-
broken.

A few years ago, my wife started to wear
jeans. I bought a VW. The year after
that, my wife dyed her hair red. I took
vitamin shots. A few months ago, she
got her face lifted and her breasts enlarged. I got a transplant. That's the way
it's been for the two of us—side by side,
just growing young together.

A good wife always forgives her husband
when she's wrong.

"Honey, will you love me when my hair
has turned to gray?"
    "Why not? I've loved you through
those six other colors."

In response to a whim, a man was married in a cage filled with lions.

Years later, a friend asked, "Did it feel
exciting?"
    The first man said, "It did then. It
wouldn't now."

His wife lets him run some things
around the house—errands!

A man should always keep an eye out
for little hints that his wife isn't satisfied,
like when she vacuums up his stamp collection.

We've been married for thirty years,
and it feels like just yesterday. And you
know what a lousy day yesterday was.

A woman hired a private eye and told
him, "Follow my husband. I don't want
to know who the woman is, but I'd certainly like to know what she sees in the
idiot!"

A man was accused of making love to
his wife after she died. His only defense
was that he didn't know she was dead.
She'd been like that for years.

"Did you hear about my wife? She ran
off with my best friend."
    "I thought *I* was your best friend."
    "Not anymore!"

One bright guy dressed his wife in
leather, checked her in at the airport as
luggage, and never heard of her again.

I came up with a great place to hide
money. I put it in a stocking that needs
darning.

Two women were discussing marriage, and one said, "We've been married twenty-five years, and every night my husband has complained about the food. Not one night without complaining about the food."

The other woman said, "That's awful. Doesn't it bother you?"

The first one said, "Why should I object if he doesn't like his own cooking?"

It's weird about men sitting at bars. They have only one of two reasons to be there—they have no wife to go home to . . . or they do.

He liked to make things around the house—the maid, the babysitter . . .

A man was putting on a pair of trousers when they ripped along the fly. The man said to his wife, "I know you'd think it was an imposition, so I'll just wear them this way. It'll give the guys an idea of what I have to put up with."

The wife said, "No, I'll repair them. I don't want them to know what *I* have to put up with."

"People say that you married me for my money."

"I had to give them *some* reason."

I told my wife that men become better with age. So she made me sleep in the wine cellar.

"John, I've changed my mind."

"Thank the Lord. Does it work better now?"

In the middle of the night, a wife nudged her husband and said, "I can't sleep. I keep thinking there's a mouse under the bed."

Wearily, the husband said, "Start thinking there's a cat under the bed and go to sleep!"

They'll never forget the first time they met, but it's not for lack of trying!

A husband complained, "My wife likes to use the rhythm method. That's why there's always a drummer in the bedroom."

A man was asked who was the boss of the house. He replied, "My wife is in charge of the kids, the maid, the pets, and the canary. But I can say anything I want to the guppies."

I just moved near a pawn shop so my wife could be near her jewelry.

Joe Baker read in the paper that there was a terrible shortage of men in Washington, D.C. He packed his clothes and started to write a farewell note to his wife when she walked in. "Where are you going?" she asked.

"I'm heading for Washington. Men are at a premium there. A gigolo could get fifty dollars a night there."

His wife laughed. "Really?" she said. "How are you going to live on a hundred a year?"

One married bartender shows where the real power is. On the bar he has a sign reading, THE OPINIONS EXPRESSED BY THE BARTENDER ARE THOSE OF HIS WIFE.

A husband explains to the guys at the bar, "Do you know why I left her? She started to use four-letter words like: Find work!"

A woman accosts her erring husband at the door: "Ah-ha! I know everything now."

The husband says, "Really? When was the Battle of Gettysburg?"

The murderer was holed up in his house, and the SWAT team was trying to get him out. A cop got on the bullhorn and said, "Come on out, or I'm going to come in there and drag you out."

The murderer called back, "I'm warning you. If you don't wipe your feet when you come in, my wife'll kill us both."

I take my troubles like a man—I blame them on my wife.

A woman visits a new friend at home, and seeing a beautiful vase on the mantel says, "That is gorgeous."

The hostess says, "Those are my husband's ashes."

"Oh, I didn't know he was deceased."

"He isn't. He's too lazy to look for an ashtray."

The wife says, "I'm getting tired of sex."

The husband says, "I know it. You've been sleeping through it for years."

He bought a book on how to become the boss of the family. But his wife won't let him read it.

Then there was the husband who grew a mustache. He was tired of his wife calling him a barefaced liar.

This wife screams at her husband, "I'm tired of your shenanigans. Two days ago you came home yesterday. Yesterday you came home today. If you come home today tomorrow, I won't be here."

He feels that there's nothing too good for her, and that's what he gives her.

Disguising his voice, Joe Smith calls his ex-wife and asks for himself.

Nancy, the wife, says, "We're not married anymore."

The next day, Joe calls again, and again Nancy says, "We're not married anymore."

Joe calls the third time, and Nancy, exasperated, says, "I told you we're divorced. Why do you keep calling?"

Joe says, "I know. It's just that I can't hear it often enough."

Then there was the husband who took his wife to a witch doctor because she was.

At about four in the morning, Mrs. Bronson woke her husband. "I think there's a burglar in the house. Tiptoe downstairs and hit him over the head. But if there's nobody there, bring me a glass of orange juice."

One husband complained to his wife, "How can you say I'm responsible for our marital problems? I'm never home."

Some husbands are hard to understand. They don't go near their wives for a year, but they'd shoot a guy who did.

I try to make my marriage more exciting. But my wife always finds out.

A man came home in the wee hours and found a burglar picking the lock on the door. He said to the thief, "I'll open it if you'll go in first!"

The wedding is in full swing. Joe, who has had a couple of martinis, walks up behind a woman he thinks is his wife and pinches her. The woman turns. Joe says, "I'm sorry. I thought you were my wife."

The woman says, "You're a poor excuse for a husband."

"Gee, you even *talk* like her."

I hate to fix things around the house. That's why everything works.

A smart husband thinks twice before saying nothing.

"A husband like yours must have been hard to find."

"He still is."

A man tells a buddy, "Our sex life has really improved since my wife and I got twin beds."

"How does that happen?"

"Well, we have them in different apartments."

## HYPOCHONDRIACS

One hypochondriac received a Valentine's Day card and assumed it was from his cardiologist.

He's such a hypochondriac, they can't operate on him. He's taken so many pills, he keeps rolling off the table.

"How's your mother?" a friend asked.

"Not good," I answered. "She's got chronic frontal sinusitis."

"My goodness," the friend said. "Where did she get that?"

"*Reader's Digest.* Last month's issue."

# I

### IDEAS

How about the guy who put a hole in a Lifesaver and made a mint?

The trouble with mental notes is that the ink fades so fast.

Ideas are great, but most of the time they degenerate into work.

### ILLNESS

Then there's the glassblower who got the hiccups. He made eight thousand crystal balls before they cured him.

A man is told that he has a rare disease for which mother's milk is the only treatment. Luckily, he finds a wet nurse who can help him for a fee. After about five minutes of the treatment, the wet nurse forgets her purpose and starts to hear her hormones calling. Purring, she says, "Can I offer you something else?"

The man says, "A couple of cookies would be nice."

Do you know how you get a headache? You just take some liquor the night before.

A sign over a display of allergy products said, BUY NOW AND AVOID THE RASH.

Forget about your doctor's fees. Just check the price of get-well cards today.

"How does a leper laugh his head off?" "Heh, heh, heh, *THUMP.*"

My feet hurt. I've got to stop biting my nails.

You've probably heard the one about the woman who had water on the knee. She got rid of it by wearing pumps.

And it must have been her father who suffered from water on the brain. One cold night he fell asleep, and the water froze. When he awoke, he couldn't remember a thing. Everything had slipped his mind!

He used to get up out of bed every morning with a headache. And his wife kept telling him, "Honey, it's *feet* first."

If he's still got his appendix and his tonsils, twenty to one he's a doctor.

I know a real hypochondriac. He arranged to be buried next to a doctor.

The other day, an executive I know was found to have made an awful mistake. The boss said, "You're fired. Turn in your ulcer."

They've discovered that the common cold is really caused by two germs—a boy germ and a girl germ. There's no difference between the two. That's what makes you sick.

## INCOME

My wife can live on my income. Now, I have to get one for myself.

It's getting silly. Last year I spent all the money I'm going to make this year.

## INDIA

In India, the people pray in the streets. We have the same thing here, but only when crossing the streets!

The two fakirs were sleeping on beds of nails. All went well until they decided to have a pillow fight.

Then there was the snake charmer's son who was just beginning. He played to a worm.

## INDIANS

This Indian goes to a shrink and describes his symptoms. Several times a week, he lives in a wigwam. The other days he lives in a tepee. The shrink says, "I see your problem. You're two tents."

Custer couldn't understand what was going on at Little Big Horn. The night before, the Indians were so nice at the dance.

Then there was the Indian who put electricity in the outhouse—the first time an Indian wired a head for a reservation.

Indians have a new way of playing sex games. Instead of wife-swapping, they call it, "Passing the buck."

Once there was an old Indian named Short Cake. He died, and squaw bury Short Cake.

An Indian was sending smoke signals back home when behind him they set off an atomic blast. The family signaled back, "Don't yell."

An Indian checked into a hotel. Ten minutes after getting to his room, he showed up at the desk with the blanket from his bed and said, "Last customer leave overcoat."

It happened a long time ago. The Indian chief and his brave looked off in the distance and saw the smoke rising. The brave asked, "What does that smoke signal say?"

The chief answered, "A Mrs. Leary is having trouble with her cow."

That must have been some rain dance. Everybody drowned.

The Indians decided to buy back Manhattan. A delegate was sent to talk to the authorities. Returning a week later, the delegate said, "I have good news, bad news, and sensational news."

The Indian chief asked, "What's the good news?"

The delegate said, "They want to sell the island back for twenty-four dollars, the exact price they paid for it."

"What's the bad news?"

"The bad news is that the island isn't worth the money. It's filled with blacks and Puerto Ricans."

"The sensational news?"

"They taste just like buffalo!"

The battle was in full swing. In counterpoint to the exploding shells of the artillery and the gunshots, the Indian drums kept up a steady beat. Custer leaned over to his aide and said, "I don't like the sound of those drums."

From across the arroyo, the Indian chief yelled, "He's not our regular drummer!"

Then there was this Indian who drank cup after cup of tea. The next day they found him dead in his tepee.

An Indian once summed up a speech by a politician: Big wind, high thunder, no rain.

## INFERIORITY

I hear you're kind to your inferiors. Where do you find them?

My brother has a terrible inferiority complex. He met somebody who's as good as he is.

I asked a salesman in a haberdashery to show me something cheap. He said, "Look in the mirror."

## INSECTS

Jersey mosquitoes are giants. One mosquito came to earth at the Newark airport, and they filled it with two hundred gallons of gas.

"What's the difference between a mosquito and a fly?"
"Try sewing buttons on a mosquito."

Two ants were watching a duffer tear up the golf course. One ant said to the other, "Let's get on the ball before he kills us!"

A mother moth admonished her baby moth, "If you don't eat all your cotton, you won't get any satin."

Then there was the religious moth who gave up woolens for lint.

Then there was the centipede who was late for a date. She explained, "I was playing 'This Little Piggy' with baby."

Two mosquitoes are buzzing around when they see a drunk. One says, "You bite him. I'm driving."

A seven-year-old girl writes a composition about ants for school. It reads, "Ants sometimes live in the ground, sometimes on trees, and sometimes with their married sisters. That's all I know about ants."

A flea jumps in over the swinging doors of the saloon, drinks three whiskeys, and jumps out again. He picks himself up from the dirt and, brushing himself off, says, "Okay, who moved my dog?"

Scientists have just crossed a termite with a praying mantis. Now they have a termite that says grace before it eats your house.

Will somebody please explain why Noah didn't swat those two flies when he had the chance?

A centipede tells the doctor, "When my feet hurt, I hurt all over."

Two boll weevils came from the country to the city. One became rich and famous. The other remained the lesser of two weevils.

You can catch more flies with honey than you can with vinegar. But who wants a lot of flies?

The mosquitoes are pretty tough around here. If you slap them, they slap you back.

A man comes into the kitchen and swats the life out of a dozen flies. Six, he tells his wife, were male and six female. She asks, "How do you know the males from the females?"

"Six were at the sugar and six on the mirror."

Two Jersey mosquitoes see a man walking. One mosquito says, "Let's carry him to the swamp."

The other Jersey mosquito says, "Nah. If we do that, the big mosquitoes will take him away from us like they always do."

## INSULTS

She's here incognito—no leash.

There's nothing wrong with him that reincarnation wouldn't cure.

The cost of living is so high. Why do you bother?

Nice girl. If she had two more legs, she could star in westerns.

Honey, how many Peeping Toms have you cured?

He was the last one born in his family. He's enough to discourage anybody.

There's a girl who could set sex back fifty years.

She's a good friend of mine. I've known her ever since we were the same age.

I'd like to say something nice about him, but I can't think of anything.

She sent him a Dear John letter because that's where he got her phone number.

He's trying to pass for Jewish. He has clip-on foreskin.

She gets along with people. Even her diseases are social.

She has a lot of time on her hands and the wrinkles to prove it.

They call him a saint. His wife is always crucifying him.

He'd like to get into her pants, but she has an asshole there already.

She's not in *Who's Who,* but she did make *What's That.*

One thing I can say about him—in all the years I've known him, never once has he lapsed into good taste!

He knows a lot—too bad he can't think of it.

I like him very much, but then I've never had any taste.

He's a monument to the human race, and you know what pigeons do to monuments.

He eats in the finest restaurants. I can tell from his silverware.

They made a movie about his sex life— *The Night of the Living Dead.*

When the sexual revolution broke out a few years ago, she was a casualty.

She's not pushing forty. She's dragging it.

He's got a lot of degrees. The police gave him three of them.

He's not too popular. His answering machine hangs up on him.

He has a photographic mind. Too bad it never developed.

"Are you trying to make a fool of me?"
    "Never! I don't interfere with nature."

She's so narrow-minded, she only has to wear one earring.

He's the kind of friend you can depend on. He's always around when he needs you.

He has three companies after him— Visa, American Express, and the Electric.

Well, there's always room for one bore.

They say man developed from the monkey. What happened in this guy's case?

I don't mind a guy being born again, but does he have to come back as himself?

Every time he opens his mouth, his foot falls out.

Everybody says she's a ten. But I know some guys she charges twenty.

He's the kind of guy who'd buy his wife a swimming pool and put a shark in it.

He's unlucky. He spent five hundred dollars getting his bad breath cured, and then he found out nobody liked him anyway.

He reminds me of a toothache I once had.

You're not yourself today. Enjoy it while you can.

He ought to go to a dentist and have some wisdom teeth put in.

She's going to lose her looks when she's older, but then she was always lucky.

He's as memorable as Whistler's father.

I'd tell him to eat his heart out, but he'd break his teeth on it.

He leaves his listeners openmouthed. They all yawn at once.

I think his incubator blew a fuse.

He has a split personality, and everybody hates both of them.

She's nearsighted. She can't even tell her friends until they're right on top of her.

He's terrible. I didn't even like him when I did.

He's a heck of a guy. Let's all stand and give him a round of ammunition.

He could be brainwashed with an eye-dropper.

He's very versatile. He can do anything wrong.

He wants to divorce himself. He's tired of living together.

Making love to her must be like playing handball against a blanket.

Those who don't know him said he was a bum. Those who did could swear it.

If she'd been alive during Sodom and Gomorrah, they'd have had to name a street after her.

People give her a constipated greeting: They say, "How are you?"—but they don't give a shit.

He doesn't have ulcers. He's just a carrier.

If he had his life to live over, he'd still fall in love with himself.

He doesn't act stupid. It's the real thing.

She looked like an undertaker had just started to work on her and was called away.

There are people you wouldn't give two cents for. His type is six for a nickel.

## INSURANCE

An agent convinces a customer that he needs insurance, telling him, "You should have about fifty thousand for a straight life."
The customer says, "Can't I fool around a little?"

I knew a girl so ugly, she could collect on insurance even if she didn't have an accident!

I have Fire and Theft. They pay me if I get robbed during a fire.

Allstate Insurance has the hands—my insurance company gives you the finger.

We should have national health insurance. The government is making us sick, why shouldn't it pay for it?

A rabbi who specializes in circumcisions applies for malpractice insurance.
The agent promises to try to get some. A week later, the agent returns and says, "I got lucky with Lloyd's of London. They're willing to insure you. The premium isn't too high either. But there's one catch—you'll have a two-inch deductible."

Insurance keeps you poor all your life so you can die rich.

It seemed like a great group insurance plan until I found out that to collect, the whole group had to be sick.

Blue Cross, what an outfit. They dock your pay so you can pay your doc.

Health insurance is just like wearing one of the hospital gowns. You only think you're covered.

The agent for one insurance company handed a life-insurance check to a widow from her late husband's policy. He then advised her to take out a policy on herself.

"Why, I do believe I will," she said. "My husband had such good luck with his."

Why do life-insurance brokers always talk of death benefits? Growing old has its benefits. You get fewer calls from insurance salesmen.

The problem with a policy is that the big print giveth and the small print taketh away.

A dry-goods proprietor took an insurance policy out on his store the same day it burned down. The insurance company was suspicious, but an investigation failed to find any signs of fraud. The only thing the company could do was write the policyholder a note: *Sir: You took out an insurance policy from us at 10:00 A.M. and your fire did not break out until 3:30 P.M. What took so long?*

I carry a ton of insurance. If anything happened to me, Lloyd's would have to get out of London.

## INTRODUCTIONS

Our next speaker will not bore you with a long speech—he can do it with a short one.

Recently, our speaker had to discontinue several of his long talks on account of his throat. Several people threatened to cut it.

You have heard it said before that this man needs no introduction. Well, I have heard him, and he needs all the introduction he can get!

Our next speaker is a fine man. It's hard to exaggerate his accomplishments, but I'll do my best.

If I thought that I'd be eulogized so much, I'd have done the decent thing and died first!

Please don't make a fuss over me. Treat me the way you would treat any brilliant speaker.

## INVENTIONS

Somebody ought to come up with a set of car brakes that become tight when the driver does.

I have a friend who just came up with a new screen for drive-ins. You fit one around each car.

They now have nonalcoholic wine. The only trouble is that cops can stop you for nondrunk driving.

There's a great new surgical tool on the market for surgery in the house. It's called Suture Self.

Build a better mousetrap, and the world will beat a path to your door. Build a better door, and the mice can't get in.

They have a new solar-powered car. It not only runs on sunlight, but when it hits a pedestrian, it also gives him a tan.

How about a one-piece jigsaw puzzle for idiots?

A friend of mine is compiling an index for the dictionary.

I'm looking for inventors. I want to come out with a waterproof tea bag.

How'd they ever come up with that great plastic wrap that sticks to the roll but not the bowl?

One soft-drink company used to advertise that it hit the spot, so some smart man mixed it with cleaning fluid. That not only hit the spot, it removed it too!

My uncle just came up with an invention that takes a car apart in six seconds. It's called a sixteen-year-old nephew.

It's tough being an American with ideas. You invent something—then two weeks later the Russians invented it before you, and the Japanese can make it cheaper.

Ben Franklin may have discovered electricity, but the guy who made all the money was the fellow who invented the meter!

## IRISH

Liam and Sean are working on the excavation for a new building. By mistake, Liam kicks at some of the plastique used as an explosive. There's a huge explosion, and both men disappear.

About an hour later, the boss of the project arrives and, noticing the absence of the men, asks James, a third worker, "Where are Liam and Sean?"

"They're gone."

"Do you know when they'll be back?"

"Well, if they come back as fast as they went, they should have been here yesterday."

I know an Irishman who went to Switzerland just to raise Saint Bernards for the brandy.

An Irishman comes over from the old country, gets a job with a demolition crew, and happily writes to his relatives in Dublin. *America is wonderful. I'm working with a grand bunch of Irish boys, there's a saloon across the street, the money is good, and I'm tearing down a Protestant church.*

O'Malley dies and is lying in his bier at home. Mrs. Finnegan comes over to

Mrs. O'Malley and says, "You know, I happened to touch the body, and he's still warm."

Mrs. O'Malley says, "Hot or cold, he goes in the morning."

O'Ryan is walking down a country lane when he meets Sweeney, who asks him where he's going. O'Ryan answers, "I'm going to Waterford."

"You mean, you're going to Waterford, God willing."

"I'm going to Waterford, God willing or not."

At that blasphemy, there's a puff of smoke, and O'Ryan is changed into a frog.

Confined to a pond, he prays and prays for forgiveness. It is granted, and he heads home to pack again. Sweeney comes by and asks, "Where are you going?"

"I'm going to Waterford."

"You mean, God willing."

"No, I'm going to Waterford or back to that damn pond!"

The Irish ignore anything they can't fight or drink!

Then there are two Irish gays—Gerald Fitzpatrick and Patrick Fitzgerald.

One Irishman says, "My wife drives me to drink."

The second says, "You're lucky. My wife makes me walk."

Irish foreplay: "Mary, brace yourself."

An English cleric visits New York. After checking into a hotel, he summons a cab and asks to be taken to Christ's Church. The cabbie, Paddy Murphy, takes him to St. Patrick's Cathedral. The cleric is upset and says, "I told you to take me to Christ's Church."

The cabbie says, "Well, this is where He stays when He's in town."

Poor O'Connor. He broke a bottle of whiskey on the floor, and he still has a dozen splinters in his tongue.

Connick is dying. His wife sits mournfully at his side. Connick says, "Remember, my love, O'Malley owes me twenty dollars."

"I'll write it down."

"Finnegan owes me thirty dollars."

"I'll write that down."

"Sean Kennedy owes us a tenner."

"I'll write that down, never fear."

"I owe Willie Joyce two dollars."

"Oh, just listen to the man rave!"

McGee has himself too much brew and passes out. He's so stiff, the crowd at the bar calls the undertaker, and McGee is put in a coffin.

A few hours later, he wakes and says to himself, "If I'm alive, why am I in this coffin? And if I'm dead, how come I have to go to the john?"

### IRS

If her face is her fortune, she'll never have to pay income tax.

He had untold wealth, and that's what the IRS got him for.

The IRS now has an express lane for people with ten loopholes or less.

An IRS agent stormed into a tiny delicatessen on a side street. Calling over the owner, he said, "I have your returns right here. How can you justify your travel expenses? Four trips to Europe?"
The owner answered, "We deliver."

My accountant came up with so many deductions, I had enough left over for bail.

Last year I saved so much money on taxes, my wife wants to go to Europe. I want to go to Rio. The government wants us to go to jail.

I went up to the IRS last week, and I really let them have it. Every penny I had.

Every time my ship comes in, the government unloads it.

A man rushed into the IRS and said indignantly, "What did you do with all the money I gave you last year?"

It takes more brains to make out the income tax than it does to make the income.

The tax man must have been part wolf. He huffed and he puffed and he blew my shelter down.

I think it would be nice if the IRS offered us our money back if we aren't completely satisfied.

Success used to go to your head. Now it goes to the IRS.

Somebody just bought my tax returns for last year, but then works of fiction do sell easily.

The IRS recently got a letter: *I cheated on my taxes last year, and it's kept me awake at night. Here's five hundred dollars. If I find I still can't sleep, I'll send you the rest.*

I told my IRS auditor, "You can't get blood out of a turnip."
He answered, "No, but we can send the turnip to jail."

The IRS has a new deal. A hundred percent down and nothing a month.

A man walked into a bar with an alligator on a leash. He asked the bartender, "Do you serve IRS agents?"
"We sure do."
"Good. I'll have a beer, and my gator'll have an IRS agent."

Then there was the IRS agent who had to go to a shrink because he thought people liked him.

I went down to the IRS the other day. There was some fight. Hundreds of people battling to be last in line.

## ISRAEL

The Israelis have just developed a brand-new car tire. It not only stops on a dime, it also picks it up.

A visitor came to Israel and saw the Wailing Wall. Not being too versed in the religious aspects, he inquired of another tourist about the significance of the wall. The other tourist explained, "This is a sacred wall. If you pray to it, God may hear you."

The visitor walked close to the wall and started to pray. "Dear Lord," he said. "Bring sunshine and warmth to this beautiful land."

A commanding voice answered, "I will, my son."

The visitor said, "Bring prosperity to this land."

"I will, my son."

"Let the Jews and Arabs live together in peace, dear Lord."

The voice answered, "You're talking to a wall!"

The Israelis finally deciphered the last Dead Sea Scroll. It was the bill for the Last Supper.

"Why did the Israelis win the Six-Day War?"

"Because the equipment was rented."

The prime minister of Israel visits the White House. On the desk in the Oval Office, he sees several phones. The president explains them. Pointing to the red phone, he says, "That's a direct line to Tokyo."

"How much does it cost for a call?"

"About fifty dollars a minute." Pointing to the white phone, the president adds, "That's a direct line to God. It costs ten thousand a minute."

"We have a direct line to God too. It only costs a quarter."

"How could that be?"

"Maybe it's because from us it's only a local call."

A gigantic ocean liner heads for the dock in the harbor at Haifa. A quarter of a mile from land, the ocean liner collides with a huge yacht.

Naturally, an inquiry is held. The captain of the ocean liner takes the stand and swears that he had observed protocol to the letter. He turned when he was supposed to, he went as slowly as was required, and he signaled with every international sailing signal.

The captain of the Israeli yacht, a short, chubby, balding man, then took the stand. He was sworn in and asked for his version of the tragedy. The captain said, "First of all, I want to tell you—a sailor I'm not. . . ."

A typical El Al flight is about to take off. Over the intercom, we hear, "Ladies and gentlemen, welcome aboard. Your hostesses are Mrs. Sarah Klein and Mrs. Esther Schwartz, and, of course, my son, the pilot."

### ITALIANS

"Why do Italian women wear panties?"
"To keep their ankles warm."

When Italian kids grow up, they marry and move in with the folks. Before long, the house is pretty crowded. I know one Italian kid who didn't see linoleum until he was fourteen.

In keeping with the new peace so prevalent in Europe now, Italy is selling off all its rifles from World War II—they've never been used and only dropped once.

"Why does an Italian man have his hands in the air?"
"He's on war maneuvers."

Italian girls are just like a cold engine—when you really need them, they won't turn over.

"Why don't Italians have freckles?"
"They slide off."

They now have an Italian airline that flies out of Genoa. It's called Genitalia.

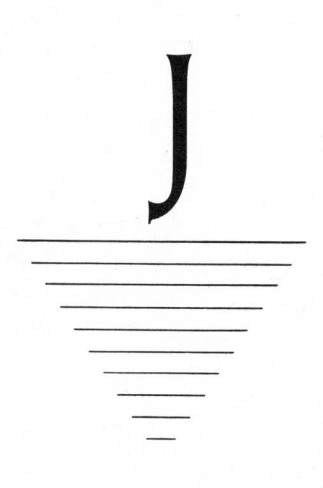

## JAIL

They have two children. The first is the president of a savings and loan, and the other one is in jail too.

Henry had been in the penitentiary for ten years and had never had one visitor. Feeling sorry for him, the guard said, "Don't you have any family?"

Henry said, "Sure do, but they're all in here."

My uncle knew the exact day he'd die. A judge told him.

A first-time hustler gets thrown in jail and rooms with a burglar. The hustler decided to make something of himself, so he says, "I'm going to spend my time in here learning. When I get out of jail, you'll still be a common thief. I'll be an embezzler!"

A new social worker was interviewing a prisoner and asked him if he watched television.

The prisoner said, "Only in the daytime. At night we get locked in our cells."

The social worker said, "That's not

too bad. It's nice of the warden to allow you to watch in the daytime."

The prisoner said, "Nice? That's part of our punishment."

**M**y uncle is popular in prison. He's the lifer of the party.

## JAPANESE

**A** GI and a Japanese soldier were indulging in hand-to-hand combat when the GI muttered, "What a fight you're putting up. Where the hell are you from?"

The Japanese soldier said, "Yokohama."

The GI said, "We ought to be buddies. I'm from Tulsa."

**T**he Japanese are really buying up New York. They own so much of Manhattan that when you come through the Holland Tunnel, you have to take off your shoes.

**O**ne Japanese woman had a white baby, which proves that Occidents can happen.

**P**eople all over Japan drive subcompacts. It's been fifteen years since any pedestrian got hit above the waist.

**T**he Japanese have been buying everything in sight. One traveler saw something he liked, and now he's stuck with an indoor volcano.

**I** don't know why people complain about the Japanese. They're buying American.

"**W**hat's a Japanese girl's favorite day?"
"Erection day."

**E**verything is being made in Japan. There may be delinquents in the United States who've never stolen an American product.

## JEALOUSY

**T**his general left the army and joined a large typewriter company. But a week later, he quit out of jealousy. They had more ribbons than he did.

**H**e was so jealous—his wife had twins, and he swore that only one looked like him.

**H**e's incredibly jealous. His wife bought him some underwear, and he keeps looking for a man with the initials—BVD.

**T**he knight is about to take off for a dragon hunt. Handing his chief servant a key, he says, "You know how jealous I am of my wife. You know I'm so jealous, I die at the thought of another touching her. Therefore, you must take care of this key to her chastity belt. It must never leave your hands."

The knight takes off. He's about two miles down the road when the chief servant, out of breath, rushes to him and says, "Sire, you left the wrong key."

## JEWELRY

**A** black man is walking along the beach when he comes to a strangely shaped bottle. He uncorks it. A genie rushes out and says, "You have freed me. I'll grant you any wish."

The black man says, "I want a hundred thousand dollars."

*Poof,* and he has $100,000 in his hand. He walks on.

Right behind him is another man. The genie sees him and says, "I feel so good about being free, I'll grant you a little wish too."

The man says, "Okay. Give me about twenty dollars' worth of fake jewelry and let me catch up to the black guy."

A woman is showing off a beautiful diamond ring, saying, "I got this from my husband just for a little kiss."

Her friend says, "You got that just giving your husband one little kiss?"

The woman says, "No, I'm talking about the one I saw him give to the maid!"

Gertie the receptionist comes into the office and proudly displays a diamond bauble on her finger. Grinning, she says, "It's a boy—six foot one and a hundred eighty-five pounds."

I gave my wife a gold pin with forty diamonds on it, one for each year she's been thirty-five.

He handed her the engagement ring and said, "Be careful you don't drop it. You'll get seven years' bad luck."

A robbery occurs at Tiffany in New York. The police question an old man who saw the entire theft. He tells them, "I was standing around when I saw this truck pull up. The back came down, and an elephant walked out of the truck. With one leg, he shattered the window. He reached, scooped up all the jewels, went back into the truck, and they took off."

One of the policemen says, "Was it an Indian elephant with big ears or an African elephant?"

The old man says, "I couldn't tell. He was wearing a stocking mask."

## JEWS

Jews are real optimists. They cut some off before they know how big it's going to be.

One Jewish mother had a terrible dilemma. Her gay son was dating a doctor.

Then there's the Jewish kid who flew to Tijuana for a quickie bar mitzvah.

A Jewish couple is traveling across the country and get to a small picture-postcard town. They stop for a bite. In the diner, the waitress makes small talk and finds out that they're Jewish. She says, "You know something? We've never had one Jewish person arrested in this town."

The Jewish wife says, "Really? Is the jail restricted?"

Two bees were buzzing around when one of them reached under his wing, came up with a small yarmulke, and put it on his head. The second bee asked what he was doing with a yarmulke. The first bee said, "I don't want to be taken for a WASP."

"What do you get when you pick up a Jewish frog?"

"Schwarts."

I know one Jewish girl who read Exodus and was so impressed, she had her nose changed back.

Mrs. Goldfarb couldn't stand getting expensive gifts from her son Alvin. One day he brought her a mink coat but told her it only cost a hundred dollars.

He came around two days later, couldn't find the coat, and said, "Ma, where's the coat?"

Mrs. Goldfarb said, "I sold it to Mrs. Klein for a hundred and fifty dollars. Could you get me three more?"

"Why are there so few Jewish alcoholics?"

"It dulls the pain."

Then there's something called the bar mitzvah. That's when a Jewish boy realizes that he has more of a chance to own a ball club than play on one.

A Jewish girl dreams of her perfect home—a house on a cliff, ten living rooms, a pool, and no bedrooms.

They just started a Jewish sperm bank. When you go there, it has a headache.

Many a young Jewish girl is single. She just hasn't met Dr. Right.

The president of the United States is concerned about our intelligence. He goes to the president of Israel and asks him to share the secrets of Mossad, the Israeli intelligence agency. The Israeli president is unable to help him but suggests something. He tells the president, "If you want to know anything, just go to synagogue. The Jews there know everything."

The president dresses up in skull cap, beard, and all the accoutrements of the religious Jew and goes to a temple. He sits down next to an old Jew and says, "What's happening?"

The old Jew says, "The president is going to be here."

A man walks into a delicatessen and points to the ham, saying, "Give me a pound of that corned beef."

The clerk says, "That's ham."

"Did I ask you?"

On the Day of Atonement, religious Jews are supposed to observe a strict fast until the sun goes down on the day known as Yom Kippur in Hebrew.

This one Jew felt unable to maintain the fast, so he sneaked out of the temple during the midday services and headed for a restaurant. A friend of his happened to walk by and, looking in the window, saw the culprit chewing away. The friend walked inside and accosted him, saying, "Shame, shame on you. You pretend to fast and look at you slurping down the food. And what's even worse, look at what you're eating—oysters!"

The culprit said, "What's wrong with oysters? Yom Kippur has an *R* in it."

Jews have firm beliefs about birth. They believe that a fetus is a fetus until it graduates from medical school.

The biggest Jewish dilemma—ham at half price.

"What's the difference between a chess player and a Jewish wife in bed?"

"Every once in a while, the chess player moves."

This young gentile lady married a Jewish lad and was invited to his parents' house for a pleasant dinner. One of the courses was matzoh-ball soup.

The following week, another dinner, and again matzoh-ball soup.

This went on for months.

One day, as they drove home, the gentile wife said, "Honey, doesn't your mother know how to make any other part of the matzoh?"

One time a Jewish mother was on jury duty. They sent her home. She insisted *she* was guilty.

Two women met on a stroll in Miami Beach. One bragged about her sons. One was a lawyer, another an accountant, and a third, a doctor. She asked the other woman if she had any children.

The woman replied, "I have one boy. He's a rabbi."

The other said, "A rabbi? What kind of business is that for a Jewish boy?"

In Israel, the weather forecast is always, "You can't complain."

A Jewish youngster asked the boy next door to play with him. The boy answered, "My father says I can't play with you because you're Jewish."

The Jewish lad answered, "Oh, that's all right. We won't play for money."

## JOBS

He's an upholsterer, but he specializes. He analyzes psychiatrists' couches.

I knew a guy who lost his job because the weather didn't agree with him. He was a TV forecaster.

"I see your application says you're twenty-five. If you join our company at the bottom, what will you be in three years?"

"Twenty-eight."

They've just come up with a great thing for people on unemployment insurance. You chip in fifty cents from every check. Then, if you get a job, they hire a lawyer to fight it.

One Italian refused to take a job as an underwater demolition expert. He refused to work in a place where he couldn't spit on his hands.

## JOGGING

Since jogging came along, more people are collapsing in perfect health.

Anybody who says they run twenty miles a day with their muscles stretching, their legs pounding, their hearts beating like a drum, and their lungs on fire because it makes them feel great will lie about everything else too.

The average Joe will jog ten miles for exercise, then take the elevator up to the second floor.

A jogger is a pedestrian who's going down a dark street.

I don't jog too fast. The other day I was jogging and got arrested for loitering.

Millions of people have bought books about jogging. They're smart. Reading is easier than running.

A boss told his friend, "Jogging is doing me a lot of good. I caught my secretary this morning."

You use as much energy jogging a mile as you do making love. Only after you jog, you don't light up a cigarette and ask the runner next to you, "Was it good for you too?"

## JOKES

"Did you hear my last joke?"
	"I hope so."

Some women know their husbands' jokes backward, and that's how they tell them.

A girl laughs at her boyfriend's jokes not because they're clever, but because she is.

## KIDS

**T**wo little girls are looking at a book of fairy tales. One asks, "Who's that on the cover?"

The other says, "Cinderella."

"Why is she crying?"

"Because her wicked grandmother won't let her go to the mall."

**A**n ugly man and woman are walking down the street with their two beautiful children. They overhear a passerby tell another passerby, "How could two such ugly people have such gorgeous kids?"

The ugly man said, "Idiot, we didn't make them with our faces!"

**A** kid says to his mother, "Hey, Ma, the milkman is here. Do you have the money, or should I go to the park and play for a half hour?"

"**M**y father can beat your father."

"Big deal, so can my mother."

**A** kid was obviously the boss of the house. Walking with his father, he said, "I want an ice-cream bar."

The father said, "What else do we say?"

The kid said, *"NOW!"*

**H**ow come the man who wasn't good enough to marry your daughter is now the father of the smartest kids in the world?

**T**hey have two children. The first is a college graduate, and the other one isn't working either.

**M**y kid went to a progressive nursery. You didn't realize how progressive it was until you saw two of the kids getting married.

**T**he coach talks it over with his Little Leaguers: "We have to use sportsmanship. No temper tantrums, no yelling at the umpire, and no being bad losers. Do you understand that?"

The kids nod.

The coach goes on, "Good. Now explain that to your mothers."

**I** hid my son's Christmas gift where he'd never find it—the bathtub.

**I** wonder what my kid is going to be if the neighbors let him grow up.

**Y**ou know a kid is growing up when he stops asking where he came from and won't tell you where he's going.

**B**y the time a couple can really afford to have children, they're having grandchildren.

**T**hen there were these strict Roman parents. The kids had to be home from the orgy by ten.

**O**ne kid complained to his friend, "I don't know what's going on in the house. They spell everything."

**O**ne kid came home from school all upset and reported, "I'm so tired. The computer went down, and we had to write."

**T**he quickest way for a parent to get a kid's attention is to sit down and look comfortable.

**A** woman with a half-dozen kids goes to a movie. There, the kids make a terrible racket, talking, jumping up and down, throwing things. A man sitting behind them says, "Madam, you should have left half your kids home."

She says, "I did."

**M**argie is seven and a terrible child. One Sunday morning as the family gathers to eat breakfast, Margie pushes away her food and says, "I don't want cereal. I want a worm."

Her father walks out. Muttering, he goes into the garden and gets a worm. He brings it in and puts it on Margie's plate. She makes a face. "I only want half," she says.

The worm is cut in half. Margie goes on, "I want you to eat half."

Dad makes a face but manages to down half of the worm. But Margie starts to cry, saying, "You ate the the half I wanted."

**A** man buys his kid a gerbil. The next day, the man returns from work to find his son in tears because the gerbil is dead. The man goes to the cage and sees that the gerbil is only sleeping. He nudges the cage, and the animal comes to life. The man says, "See, your gerbil is alive."

The kid says, "Good. Let's kill it."

**M**y nephew brought home a report from school that said he was doing well for a six-year-old. The trouble is—he's twelve.

**S**ome youngsters are at play during lunch recess. The teacher hears one of them crying and rushes over. "What's the problem?" she asks. Little Tommy says, "George took Tony's apple."

"Where is the apple?"

"I ate it. I'm the lawyer."

**A** man loads his kids into the car—four in back and three in front. As he tries to squeeze into the driver's seat, he mutters, "You know, I almost screwed myself out of a seat."

**L**ast month I told my kid about the birds and the bees. Now I can't get him out of the garden.

**"T**here will be a very small PTA meeting tomorrow night," the little tot sheepishly told his mother. "It's just you, me, and the teacher."

**A** five-year-old studied his new baby brother, who was now six hours old. The young boy turned to his dad and said, "Ugh, no wonder Mom hid him under her coat so long!"

**A** seven-year-old came home from school a bit teary-eyed one afternoon. He told his mother, "Agnes broke off our engagement. She returned my frog."

**A** young boy watched a movie where a man ripped off a woman's blouse and said, "I want what I want when I want it!"

The boy thought that looked like fun and rushed home to try it on the girl next door. He ripped off her blouse and said, "I want what I want when I want it!"

The girl looked at him and replied, "You'll get what I got when I get it!"

**J**immy's old aunt Mary asked if he'd take a nickel to let her kiss him.

Jimmy answered, "I get more than that for taking medicine."

**M**other was thrilled to see little Mildred sitting so quietly and said, "Millie, I'm so proud of you sitting like a little doll while your dad takes a nap."

Millie said, "I'm watching his cigarette burn down to his fingers."

**K**ids have it so good today. A kid's mother drives him everywhere—to school, to karate lessons, to Little League, the movies. . . . One kid told his mother, "I hate it here. I'm going to run away from this home."

His mother said, "Wait. I'll drive you."

A kid said to his father, "I didn't ask to be born."

The father replied, "If you had, the answer would have been no."

Mary was four and was just beginning to peel from her very first sunburn. As she looked in the mirror, tears filled her eyes, and she said, "Look at me. I'm four and I'm starting to wear out already."

An allowance is what you pay your kids to live with you.

Two small boys watched big sister get dressed in a low-cut formal gown. One kid said to the other, "Aren't you glad you're not a girl? Look at all the neck they have to wash."

"Honey, did you put fresh water in the fishbowl?"

"Nope. They haven't drunk what I gave them yesterday."

Joey's teacher sent a note home to Joey's mother, saying, "Joey is bright, but he spends all of his time thinking about girls."

Joey's mother wrote back, "If you find a way to cure him, let me know. I have the same trouble with his father."

One rotten kid brought an apple for his teacher and then turned her in for taking a bribe.

Two kids are talking, and one says, "Boy, my old man works twelve hours a day to give me a nice home and good food. My old lady spends the whole day cleaning and cooking for me. I'm really worried."

The other kid says, "What have you got to worry about?"

The first kid says, "What if they try to escape?"

I don't teach my kids the meaning of a dollar. Why fill their heads with useless information?

"Why didn't you go to Johnny's party?"

"The invitation says three to six, and I'm seven."

A man comes to dinner at a new friend's house. While they eat, the new friend's small son keeps staring at the guest. Finally, the guest says, "Why are you staring at me like that, young fellow?"

The kids says, "Well, Daddy told me you were a self-made man."

"I am."

"Well, why did you make yourself like that?"

My son's room is so dirty, he just got an EPA grant to clean it up.

Never hit your kids. They may be armed.

Kids can't understand. Parents teach them to walk, send them to school to learn how to talk, and then say, "Sit down and shut up."

## KISSING

A kiss that speaks volumes is never a first edition.

"Who told you that you could kiss me?"
    "Almost everybody."

She gave him a kiss that would cost five bucks in a taxi.

## KU KLUX KLAN

How about the polite Klanner on the bus? He offered his sheet to a lady.

A Klan klaxon had a formal dance last week—top hat, white tie, and sheets.

Then there was the Klansman who checked into a hotel and the maid wanted to change his sheets—while he was still wearing them.

A Klanner is a fellow who gets up in the middle of the night and goes out, taking the bedsheet with him.

In one small town in Georgia, they have a Klan bank. If you open an account, they give you a free '65 pickup truck, unless you'd rather have the ballpoint pen.

One Klan klaxon was so poor, the men had to ride out three to a sheet.

# L

## LANGUAGE

Two men are walking down the street in Calcutta when a woman goes by. One says, "I think that's Mother Teresa."

"You're nuts."

"I'm telling you."

They walk over to the woman and ask, "Are you Mother Teresa?"

Scornfully, the woman looks at them and says, "Go to hell, you god-damn perverts." She strides off.

Stunned, the first man says, "Now we'll never know."

My mother-in-law came home and said, "I almost ran over a man, and I think he was from Florida. When he got to the curb, he yelled something about the sun and the beach."

A man returns from a long overseas trip. Seeing his wife waiting for him as he comes down the steps of the plane, he yells, "FF."

The wife yells back, "EF."

"No, FF."

"EF."

Another passenger asks, "What's that all about, buddy?"

The man says, "She wants to eat first."

**A** dog went to college and came home for the summer. The dog next door asked how he was doing, and he answered, "I'm doing great at math and economics, but I'm really terrific in foreign languages."

"No kidding? Say something in a foreign language."

"Meeow."

**A** synonym is a word you have to use because you don't know how to spell the other one.

**A**t the weekly club meeting, a lady lecturer was defending the rights of women, pointing out that women allowed themselves to be abused. "Is there a man in this group who would dare to let his wife be slandered?" she asked.

One man jumped up, saying, "I would."

The lecturer said, "Can you honestly tell me you'd stand there without raising a finger if your wife were slandered?"

The man said, "Oh, I'm sorry. I thought you said 'slaughtered.' "

**T**o some women, the sexiest word in the world is "cash."

**A** hump is the thing on a camel's back. Unless it's another camel, and then it becomes a verb.

**T**he other day I overheard two Iranians at the airport. One was speaking in Ira-nian, and the other jumped in: "Look, you're in America now. Speak like an American—Spanish!"

**H**ow come "fat chance" and "slim chance" mean the same thing?

**"Y**ou see, we all have an id and an ego."

"Stop using such big words."

**A** genius—that's an average student with a Jewish grandmother.

**"M**arsha, I've been invited to go to Monaco for the Grand Prix."

"Claire, that's not the way it's pronounced."

**A** man brings his pants to a tailor and says, "Eumenides."

The tailor says, "Euripides?"

**A** professor was discussing the difference between adultery and fornication. After his lengthy description of the variance, a young coed stood up and said, "Professor, I've tried both, and they seem the same to me."

**H**e was a Yankee with a real nasal twang. She was a southern belle with a soft drawl. He used to love to get his twang into her drawl.

**I**t was Ladies' Day at the golf club, and once again, Rose Maddox was telling her usual off-color stories, the telling sprinkled with more than a few four-letter words. The other ladies were offended, so while Rose was out on the practice tee, they agreed to walk out if she came in and started one of her racy stories.

After a few swings, Rose returned to the other ladies and said, "Did you hear—they're rounding up all the hookers in town at noon?"

At this, the ladies started to make a fast exit.

Rose said, "Why are you rushing? It's not even ten yet."

A very proper young lady is overwhelmed when she hears a new immigrant say to his companion, "Emma comma first, I comma next, two assa comma together, I comma again, two assa comma again, I comma one more time, pee-pee twice, then I comma for the last time."

Blushing, the young lady calls over a cop standing nearby and demands that he arrest the immigrant.

The cop looks at her, puzzled and says, "For spelling Mississippi?"

Finally, we've learned why Webster compiled the dictionary. Every morning at breakfast, he'd sit down and talk to the wife for a few minutes. As soon as he said something, she'd say, "Now what's that supposed to mean?"

You can only find a butt in three places—at the end of a line, at the end of a rifle, and at the beginning of insky.

A reporter rushes into the editor: "It just came over the wire. There's just been an earthquake in Splskbknvwi, Poland."

The editor says, "Find out the name of the place before it happened."

The other day, a truck delivering ten thousand Roget's Thesauruses ran into a pole. The driver was shocked, startled, taken aback, thunderstruck, and caught unaware.

Add five words a day to your vocabulary. In six months, your friends will wonder who the heck you are.

A deaf person is talking to a person who understands sign language but isn't totally fluent in it. After a few signs, the hearing person says, "I don't quite understand." The signs are repeated with more flourishes. "I still don't understand." The deaf person tries again, making giant moves. The hearing person says, "You don't have to holler."

An American visitor went into a small London restaurant and asked the waitress what was good. She said, "You'll like our roast. It comes with rice and rhubarb."

The visitor says, "Miss, you sure roll your *R*s."

The waitress said, "Could be these new high heels I'm wearing."

A candidate for state office once ran on this simple platform: He didn't want any foreign languages taught in school. If English was good enough for Jesus, he felt, it was good enough for the state.

"What's the definition of 'macho'?"

"Running home from your own vasectomy."

## LAS VEGAS

Las Vegas is a wild town. An hour after I checked into a hotel, the house detective knocked and asked, "Do you have a woman in there?"

I said, "No."

So he threw one in.

I played 21 for ten hours and didn't get hit with a blackjack till I got to the parking lot.

The price of transportation to Las Vegas keeps going up. That's because half the people there couldn't afford to leave.

Las Vegas is a strange town. There, a blessed event is getting three of a kind on a slot machine.

I went to Vegas recently. I lost my car, my watch, my money. I lost everything but my good-luck charm.

There's a new group called Gamblers and Alcoholics Anonymous. During the Gamblers Anonymous meetings, they drink up a storm, and on Alcoholics Anonymous nights, they have an all-night poker game.

I was in Las Vegas last week. I just hope the hotel has more luck with my money than I did.

What a wild place Las Vegas is. I dropped a dime in a meter, and I lost my car!

When he was in Las Vegas, he played roulette, putting every penny on number 8. Number 8 never came up. A stranger asked, "Why don't you play another number?"

"Are you kidding? Eight's my lucky number!"

Las Vegas is one of a kind. You can't beat the sun, the clean air, the cool nights, the slot machines. . . .

Las Vegas is loaded with all kinds of gambling devices—dice tables, slot machines, wedding chapels. . . .

One weekend, this man goes to Las Vegas and loses a fortune at dice. Three in the morning, he stops a dealer who has just gone on a break and says, "What's the secret?"

The dealer says, "Buddy, this is Saturday, it's three in the morning, and I'm working. And you ask *me* for the secret?"

If anybody attacks us with an atom bomb, I'm going to hide under a slot machine in Las Vegas. It's never been hit yet.

There's a new classy hotel in Las Vegas. You have to wear a tie to lose your shirt.

This one hotel used crooked dice. I mean, I never saw dice leave skid marks before.

In Las Vegas, money isn't everything. If you stay long enough, it's nothing.

Did you hear about the man whose Las Vegas vacation was interrupted by severe abdominal cramps? He went to a doctor who examined him briefly before offering, "I'll give you five to one you have acute appendicitis!"

One of the chorus girls at a Vegas hotel fainted. It took six men to carry her out—three abreast.

A Brooklyn baker worked so hard and turned out such superior goods that at age fifty-five he was able to sell out his bakery for $100,000. With the cash in his pocket, he and his wife boarded a plane for California, set on living the rest of their lives in peaceful retirement.

The plane developed engine trouble over Nevada and had to land in Las Vegas.

The pilot announced, "We'll have a four-hour layover. You may dine at any hotel you like at the airline's expense." He also cautioned, "This is Las Vegas, and as far as gambling goes, you're on your own."

"Gamble," scoffed the baker to his wife. "Anybody who plays against the odds ought to have his head examined."

On a whim, the baker put down a five-hundred-dollar bet. Soon the lure was too much for him, and he had lost everything at the roulette table. The poor man headed for the washroom and found he didn't even have the quarter for entry.

A fellow passenger pressed a quarter into his hand and smiled knowingly.

"You're very kind. I've never borrowed a cent in my life, and I'll pay you back as soon as I'm able," the baker said. He took the man's name and address. When the baker got to the bathroom, he found the door ajar. Walking back through the lobby after he'd taken care of nature, he passed a slot machine. On a whim, he put the quarter in, and the rest is history. The baker won over $200,000 in the next hour and a half.

In California two days later, the baker and his wife soon discovered the life of idleness was not for them. They started another bakery and, because they knew their business so well, prospered from the start. A few years later, the baker was worth millions. One day the baker told his well-satisfied sales staff the Las Vegas story. "I owe it all to one man, and I will leave no stone unturned until I find him," the baker said.

"I thought the man who loaned you the quarter gave you his name and address?" one man asked.

"I don't care about him," the baker replied, "I'm looking for the guy who left the bathroom door open!"

I asked a clerk for two aspirin. He said, "I'll bet you double or nothing."

I ended up with two headaches.

I told a friend of mine that you can't beat the climate in Las Vegas. He wants to know where I bet on it.

The best way to beat the slot machines is with a hammer.

The busboys in Vegas hotels look so important. Why not? A week ago they were customers.

I go to Vegas once a month—to visit my money.

The most common statement made by husbands to wives in Las Vegas: "Give me the money I told you not to give me."

## LATIN AMERICA

"How do you get twenty-five Latin Americans in a phone booth?"
    "Tell them they own it."

This dictator is lying ill in the hospital when he receives a visit from his deputy. The deputy keeps telling the dictator about how much the people miss him. The dictator responds only with gasps and choking sounds. Finally, the dictator beckons weakly for the deputy to come close. The dictator gasps, "Take your foot off the oxygen tube."

In some of the Third World countries, life is very unsettled for youngsters. In one place, they even have Little League rioting.

Some leftist Latin-American countries have their share of problems. The country is south of our border. The government is in Russia. And all of the people are in Miami!

There's a new Latin-American restaurant. First you eat, and then you overthrow the chef.

You don't need alarm clocks in Latin America. They're not needed because a bomb goes off every morning at six.

A Latin dictator throws one of his former aides in jail. Arriving there, the aide meets another former companion of the dictator. The companion asks, "How long are you in for?"
    "Thirty years."
    "What did you do?"
    "Nothing."
    "You must have done something. For doing nothing, you only get ten years."

A traveler asks a Latin American what the most popular sport is in that country. The Latin American says, "Bullfighting."
    "Revolting."
    "No, that's second."

Some Latin-American presidents are real optimists. One of them even had personal stationery made.

This one country in Latin America has had so many revolutions, the government meets in a revolving door.

## LAUNDRY

It's the worst laundry in the world. They even lose buttonholes.

A man storms into a laundry and throws a small piece of lace on the counter. "You've got a lot of nerve advertising that you're a specialist in fine things. Look at this!"

The clerk examines the lace and says, "It's a very nice piece of lace."

The man says, "When I brought it in, it was a curtain!"

They opened a new laundry in our town, and the mayor was there to tear off the first button.

I get my laundry back the same day. They keep refusing it.

## LAWYERS

My lawyer borrowed five grand from his father to go to law school. His first case was when his father sued him to get the five thousand back.

I had a great malpractice suit going. I ended up owing the doctor a liver and a kidney—and I owed my lawyer an arm and a leg.

I had two great lawyers in a recent case, but I lost. The other guy had one good witness.

A lawyer called his client and said, "Justice has been done."

The client said, "Then we'll sue."

The other day a lawyer got a guy off for robbery. But then the guy had to go out and commit robbery so he could pay the bill.

"What's the difference between a dead skunk and a dead lawyer in the middle of the road?"

"There are skid marks in front of the skunk."

Did you ever see a lawyer's brief that was?

Ignorance of the law doesn't keep a lawyer from collecting his bill.

"What's the difference between God and a lawyer?"

"God never thinks He's a lawyer."

"I'll take this case on contingency."

"What's contingency?"

"If I lose, I get nothing."

"And if you win?"

"*You* get nothing."

A bystander asked the victim of an accident, "Are you hurt?"

The victim answered, "How do I know? I'm a doctor, not a lawyer."

"What's a damn shame?"

"That's when a busload of lawyers go over a cliff and there's two empty seats."

A lawyer is an expert on justice—the same way a hooker is an expert on love.

My cousin Alvin is a criminal-defense attorney. He's very reasonable. He charges a hundred down and the rest when you get out of prison.

A man asked a lawyer, "Is it true that you'll answer two questions for a hundred dollars?"

"Yes. Now what's the second question?"

"Why do medical labs use lawyers instead of rats?"

"Because lawyers breed faster. And they do things rats won't do."

I met a lawyer at a party and asked him about a problem I was having and did I need a lawyer. He billed me for a hundred bucks the next day. I asked another lawyer friend if he could do that, and this lawyer billed me for two hundred.

A judge decides to impanel twelve lawyers to hear a controversial case. The testimony is given, and the jury retires. Day after day goes by, and there is no verdict. Finally, the judge sends in the bailiff. The bailiff returns, and the judge asks, "Are they close to a verdict?"

The bailiff says, "They're still working on their nominating speeches for foreman."

Three surgeons are discussing their work. One says, "I love to work on poor people. They're so grateful for the least thing you do for them."

The second says, "I like to work on accountants. You do your job, there's a figure, and you get paid."

The third says, "I like it easy. I just want to operate on lawyers."

The first surgeon says, "Why are they easy?"

The third one replies, "Because they only have two parts—a mouth and an asshole. And they're interchangeable."

"What's the difference between a catfish and a lawyer?"

"One is a scum-sucking scavenger. The other is a fish."

"What's the difference between a lawyer and a hooker?"

"There are some things a hooker won't do for money."

He's a great lawyer. Right now, he's suing 7-Up. He insists he drank seven but only six came up.

The lady client asked the lawyer, "Should I bare everything?"

"No," he said, "just cross your legs."

Some lawyers have the gift of gab. One of them got the jury so mixed up, they convicted the judge.

"How do you get a lawyer out of a tree."

"Cut the rope."

He was a brilliant attorney. He used to keep giving his closing arguments until the statute of limitations ran out.

Lawyers are good for you. They prevent someone else from getting your money.

The jury finds the defendant guilty. He asks his attorney, "What do we do now?"

The attorney says, "You go to jail. I go to my office."

Nobody likes a crooked lawyer until he needs one.

He's such an unlucky lawyer. The other day, he chased an ambulance for ten blocks, and there was a lawyer in it.

The tooth fairy, a low-priced attorney, and a high-priced attorney were in a room. On a table was a thousand-dollar bill. Who ended up with it?

The high-priced attorney. The other two were merely figments of his imagination.

Laws protect everybody who can hire a good lawyer.

A client complained to his attorney, "You're overcharging me. I brought you the case, and you're taking half of the damages."

The attorney said, "I happen to be providing years of law-school training, and a knowledge of all the legal codes."

The client said, "Yes, but I'm the one who came up with the case."

The lawyer said, "Big deal. Anybody can get hit by a bus."

"You are on a deserted island with Hitler, Stalin, and a lawyer. You have a gun with only two bullets. What do you do?"

"Well, you take one bullet and shoot the lawyer. Then with the other bullet, you shoot the lawyer again."

An attorney, a banker, and an accountant were fishing together. In deep waters, the oars became loose and fell into the water. Unable to retrieve them, the men agreed that one would have to swim to shore for help. Unfortunately, by now the boat was surrounded by sharks. The accountant volunteered to go but was told that the sharks would gobble him up. The banker volunteered but was also discouraged. Saluting his friends, the lawyer jumped into the water and started to swim ashore. Instead of attacking him, the sharks backed up and gave him room to swim. The accountant was stunned. "I believe we're seeing a miracle."

The banker said, "No, it's just professional courtesy!"

## LAZY

We had the laziest rooster. He never crowed. He'd wait for the rooster next door to crow, and he'd just nod.

The first thing he does when he gets up in the morning is take a sleeping pill.

He's so lazy, he bought his wife a yacht for her birthday, so he wouldn't have anything to wrap.

He hates to get up in the morning. It keeps him awake the rest of the day.

"My brother is out of work."
"How long?"
"Look at his birth certificate."

He's so lazy, he went and married a widow with five children.

He likes to relax over a cup of coffee, sometimes for three or four months.

He's like a blister—doesn't show up until all the work is done.

It's not that he's lazy. It's just that he went to sleep in 1970 and forgot to leave a wake-up call.

My uncle tripped on a broken curb and went to the hospital. After examining him, the doctor said, "I have some good news and some bad news for you. First of all, you'll never be able to work again."

My uncle said, "Okay, now what's the bad news?"

The doctor gave him medicine and told him to take a teaspoon before going to bed. He used eight bottles last week.

He doesn't even walk in his sleep. He hitchhikes.

His wife doesn't know how tall he is. It's been years since she saw him standing up.

The other day he retired from his job, and nobody knew.

A boss comes over to his sleeping night watchman and says, "I wouldn't wake you unless it was for something really important—you're fired!"

He's really lazy. He gets into a revolving door and waits.

A man is preparing to go fishing in the lake. He asks the clerk in the fish store to put on a hook for him. The he asks the clerk to put on the bait. Once outside, he calls to the clerk and asks him to untie the rowboat he's rented. In the boat, he asks the clerk to push him out about a foot.

He starts to fish and gets a bite. He calls to the clerk again and asks him to bring in the fish. The clerk reels in a ten-ounce crappie.

His fishing urge satisfied, the man in the boat says, "Had enough. I'd like some female companionship now. Any pregnant women around here?"

He's been on his back so much, he hasn't seen his shadow in years.

## LESBIANS

They're now putting special pool tables in lesbian bars—no balls.

Some women are becoming the men they wanted to marry!

I just found out my wife is a lesbian. But I don't want a divorce. I'm crazy about the girl she's going out with!

Two girls go on a vacation together. When they get to the room they'll share, one says, "I have to explain a few things about myself. To be frank—"

The second girl jumps in, "Oh, no. Let me be Frank."

You can always tell a butch lesbian. She's hung like a doughnut.

"What's the difference between a bull dyke and a rhino?"
"A hundred pounds and a plaid shirt."

## LIBRARIES

The librarian comes over to Tommy and says, "Please no noise. The kid next to you can't read."
Tommy says, "That's a shame. I've been reading since I was five."

We have a tough branch library. I owed them five cents, so they attached my salary.

How can you whistle while you work if you're a librarian?

## LIES

A woman is in a gambling casino. At the roulette table, a man suggests that she play her age. She puts her money on twenty-eight.
Number thirty-six comes up, and she faints.

He keeps trying to pull the wool over his wife's eyes, but it's always the wrong yarn.

I know of one farmer who was such a liar, his *wife* had to call the hogs.

He doesn't lie. He just rearranges the truth in his favor.

If his tongue were notarized, I still wouldn't believe him.

I don't mind when people talk about me. I get worried when they tell the truth.

Most lying should be blamed on women. They insist on asking questions.

All right, so George Washington never told a lie. For those of us who don't have cherry trees, it's become a way of life.

It's hard to belive a man is telling the truth, when you'd lie if you were in his place.

The two biggest liars in the world: the guest who keeps saying, "I must be going" and the host who asks, "What's your hurry?"

Old Ben Carter went hunting with his friend Jim Frazier. Jim was surprised to see Ben come out with his two dogs and a monkey. "What's the monkey for?" Jim asked.
"I saw Jake McClonkey hunt with him, and he's good. He gets right into the tree when the dogs have the quarry cornered and shoots him close range. He hates raccoons. I paid a fortune for him."
The men take off. About an hour

later, the dogs take off. When the men catch up, they see that the dogs are barking up a storm at a big oak tree. No doubt there's a coon up there.

Ben hands the gun to the monkey, who takes off and is up the tree in a minute. A minute later, the monkey comes down. Without hesitation, he picks up the gun and shoots the dogs dead.

"What the heck is this?" Jim asks.

Ben says, "There was nothing up that tree. If there's one thing he hates worse than coons, it's liars!"

The person who agrees with you will lie about other things too.

## LIFE

Living life is great. Don't miss it if you can.

If life had a second edition, how would you correct the proofs?

Just when you think you see your life clearly, somebody changes the channel.

In spite of the cost of living, it's still popular.

I think our number-one problem is that nobody wants to take responsibility for anything, but don't quote me.

We have two choices: ruin the environment with plastic, or use a paper bag and kill a tree.

Life isn't always worth living, but what else can you do with it?

You get out of life what you put into it—minus taxes!

If the meaning of my life doesn't become clear soon, I may have to ask for an extension.

I know a fellow who gave up drinking, smoking, and sex. He was the picture of health until the day he killed himself.

Life is full of disappointments. Nothing ever comes off but buttons.

I'm not in a hurry. Please tell God He can take His time disposing of my case.

You shouldn't go through life looking for something soft. You might find it under your hat.

## LIGHT-BULB JOKES

"How many nuclear scientists does it take to screw in a light bulb?"

"Nine. One to screw it in, and eight to figure out what to do with the old one for the next twenty thousand years."

"How many government employees does it take to screw in a light bulb?"

"Two. One to insist that it's being taken care of, and the other to screw it into a water faucet."

"How many paranoids does it take to change a light bulb?"

"Why do you want to know?"

"How many gays does it take to screw in a light bulb?"

"One, if he uses K-Y jelly and goes real slow."

"How many physicians does it take to change a light bulb?"

"That depends on the kind of insurance the bulb has."

"How many psychiatrists does it take to change a light bulb?"

"What does the questioner mean by that?"

## LINCOLN

Lincoln showed you can become somebody in Washington even if you're poor. George Washington proved that being rich doesn't hurt either.

I've saved a five-dollar bill for sentimental reasons. My wife looks like Lincoln.

Lincoln was a captain during the Blackhawk War. He knew next to nothing about giving orders. His troops came to a high fence, the only way through it being a very narrow gate. Not knowing the kind of command to give, Lincoln said, "Company dismissed for one minute. Then reassemble on the other side of this fence!"

I celebrate Lincoln's birthday. For a day, I don't beat my slaves.

Abe Lincoln wouldn't have any trouble getting an education today. He'd be a cinch for a basketball scholarship.

Lincoln and General McClellan didn't get along. The general just didn't want to engage the enemy. One day, there was a brief skirmish, and the Union troops captured six cows. McClellan wired a report and mentioned that he'd captured six cows. Facetiously, he added, WHAT SHALL WE DO WITH THE SIX COWS?

Lincoln wired back, MILK THEM.

Abraham Lincoln once took a sack of grain to a mill whose miller was known to be the laziest man in twelve counties. After watching him for a while, Lincoln wearily remarked, "I could eat that grain as fast as you're grinding it."

"Indeed," said the miller, "and just how long do you think you could keep that up?"

"Until I starved to death," answered the future president.

When General McClellan, pursuing his campaign of "watchful waiting," finally exhausted Lincoln's patience, the president replaced him with "Fighting Joe" Hooker. Wishing to create an impression of activity and speed, Hooker sent a dispatch to Lincoln that read, HEADQUARTERS IN SADDLE.

Lincoln remarked, "The trouble with Hooker is, he's got his headquarters where his hindquarters should be."

## LINGERIE

Old age is when a woman buys a see-through nightgown and can't find anybody who can still see through one.

A man walked into a smart specialty shop and asked the saleslady for a bra as a gift to his wife. The salesgirl said, "What size is she?"

"I'm not sure."

"Is she as large as grapefruits?"

"Smaller."

"Apples?"

"Smaller."

"Eggs?"

"Yeah—fried."

Some silk negligees are so sheer, it makes me feel sad. Eight thousand silkworms died for nothing.

I had an uncle who worked in ladies' lingerie. Unfortunately, he was with the shoe department.

I had a niece who was so thin, she kept slipping through her pantyhose.

## LOGIC

The way I see it, a fool and his money were lucky to get together in the first place.

Two men are discussing their lives. One says, "I'm getting married. I'm tired of a messy apartment, dirty dishes, and no clothes to wear."

The other one says, "I'm getting divorced for the same reasons."

I can't understand why funerals are allowed to go through red lights. What's the hurry?

People who live in glass houses shouldn't throw parties.

A man observed, "Look at this suit. The wool was grown in Australia, the cloth was woven in New England, and the thread comes from India. The suit was made in Baltimore, and I bought it in Buenos Aires."

"What's so remarkable about that?" his friend asked.

"I just think it's wonderful that so many people can make a living out of something I haven't even paid for!"

He didn't have a penny to his name. So he changed his name.

A man is applying for a job as chauffeur. The potential employer asks, "What would you do if another car with armed men in it came at us doing seventy miles an hour? Exactly what would you do?"

"Eighty."

"What do you call a boomerang that won't come back?"

"A stick."

If the good die young, why make New Year's resolutions?

A wife says to her husband, "I couldn't agree with you less even if you were twice as wrong."

## LONE RANGER

There he was, the Lone Ranger with Tonto off somewhere. The Lone Ranger looked to the right and saw a thousand savage Indians preparing to attack him. He looked to the left. Another thousand bloodthirsty Indians. Behind him, more Indians. In front of him, more Indians. So he did the best thing—he became an Indian!

**I** know a guy who got into trouble for playing Lone Ranger in a bank.

## LOOKS

**If** you want to look handsome, hang around with ugly people.

**He** made a terrible goof the other day. He told a woman her stockings were wrinkled, and she wasn't wearing any.

**I** like my mirror. Even though it never lies, it never laughs.

**It's** funny, but when you tell two people they look like each other, both of them get sore.

## LOS ANGELES

**They** have a weird way of committing suicide in Los Angeles. You stand in a safety zone.

**In** ten years, there will be 25 million cars in L.A. If you want to get across the street, you better go now.

**A** tourist, visiting the City of the Angels, stops to watch a deep hole being dug. He asks someone nearby, "What are they building?"
"A subway."
"When will it be done?"
"About ten years."
"The hell with it then, I'll take a cab."

**I** love L.A. in the fall. I go outside, and I see the birds change color and drop out of the trees.

**"What's** the difference between Los Angeles and yogurt?"
"Yogurt has an active living culture."

**"Country** air?" questioned the Los Angeles resident. "I like air you can sink your teeth into."

**God** created heaven and earth in six days. But L.A. still isn't finished.

**A** passenger on a jet explained to his seat-mate that he was from upstate New York. "How far are you from Manhattan?" the other passenger asked. "About two hundred fifty miles," the man answered.
"In Los Angeles, where I live, *uptown* is farther away than that!"

## LOSERS

**A** guy is a loser if you show him a porno film, and his bride-to-be is in it.

**He** took a course on how to be your own best friend and flunked.

He's got to be a loser when he calls up a 900 number and the girl says, "Not tonight, I have an earache."

He's such a loser that once in Las Vegas, the stamp machine beat him.

He's a real loser—he called his answering service, and it told him it was none of his business.

You're a loser if your twin forgets your birthday.

You're a loser if you get married and you're not in the wedding pictures.

A real loser is a woodpecker in the petrified forest.

He was a real loser. When his ship came in, he was waiting at the train station.

He once got a letter from one of those magazine sweepstakes outfits. It said that he owed *them* a million!

He's a real loser. When he tells somebody he's thirty-two, they ask him how much that is in people years.

You're a loser if your office door says MEN.

You know she's a loser if you throw her a Frisbee and she catches it with her teeth.

You know you're a loser when your girl leaves you for a Death Row inmate because his future is brighter than yours.

## LOTTERIES

In the basement of a warehouse in the most squalid part of town, a tailor slaved day in and day out. At that, he still barely made enough to stay in business. He allowed himself one indulgence. He'd save twenty-five cents a week, and at the end of the month he'd spend it all on lottery tickets. After fourteen years of slaving, he finally won $250,000.

The tailor locked his shop and threw the key into a river. He bought himself a wardrobe fit for a king and rented a floor on the fanciest hotel in town. Soon he found himself supporting half the chorus girls and models in town. Night after night he caroused until dawn, throwing his money around like a drunken sailor. At the end of a year he had squandered the entire $250,000.

The tailor had no choice but to go back to his shop and his grindstone. He continued to save twenty-five cents a week and buy lottery tickets. Three years later, two men came to his door.

"An amazing thing has happened," one of the men said. "You've won the sweepstakes a second time."

"My God," the tailor said. "Do I have to go through that again?"

A man wins millions in a lottery. The clerk says, "What's the first thing you're going to do?"

The man answers, "Tell my friends it wasn't me."

Love, some say, is a lottery. Baloney! Love is no lottery. A lottery you can win once in a while.

A Scotsman buys two lottery tickets. One of them hits for a million dollars. Sadly, the Scot says, "Now why did I have to go for that other ticket?"

## LOVE

A modest girl never pursues a man. Just like a mousetrap never pursues a mouse.

He can look at a girl and tell what kind of past she's going to have.

They just came up with a new statistic. Seven out of eight women can't express love, but that eighth one . . . wow!

Any woman can live on love—if he's rich.

"I love you terribly."
  "You certainly do."

You know you're not a great lover if you make mad love to a girl and your self-winding watch stops.

All the world loves a lover except people who are waiting to use the phone.

For most women, love is being with the man they love, except when they're out using his credit cards.

Love has its compensations—alimony, for example.

He loves her like anything, and he'll love anything.

I took my wife on a cruise, and I fell in love all over again—with the redhead in the next compartment.

He used to date a schoolteacher. Every time he wrote her a love letter, she sent it back corrected.

The national pastime of Bali is making love. And *we* picked baseball!

The only people who make love all the time are liars.

Love doesn't make the world go round, but it sure makes the ride worthwhile.

## LUCKY/UNLUCKY

He had absolutely no luck. He went out and bought a fancy watch. It was shatterproof, breakproof, and waterproof. He lost it!

He once made love to an inflatable doll, and her inflatable husband came in and beat him up.

I have no luck. I'd have taken General Custer and points!

My cousin is very unlucky—the other day he got a kidney transplant from a bed-wetter.

I have no luck. When I came to the big city, I hid my money in my sock and a midget picked my ankle.

He once went on a guilt trip and lost his luggage.

I don't only have bad luck—I'm a carrier!

If my ship was about to come in, there'd be a dock strike.

He has no luck. His inflatable doll just ran off with his airbag.

He's real unlucky. He brought a girl back to his apartment and told her to make herself at home, so she invited her boyfriend over.

Serendipity is like looking for a needle in a haystack and finding the farmer's daughter.

I broke a mirror some time ago. But I didn't get seven years' bad luck. My lawyer got me off in five.

She had plastic surgery from top to bottom, then her husband left her for an older woman.

If it was raining soup, he'd be standing outside with a fork.

I bought a new watch the other day that was waterproof, dustproof, shockproof, and guaranteed against theft. It burned.

He has absolutely no luck. If he fell into a barrel of tits, he'd come up sucking his thumb.

He's very unlucky. Last week his swimming pool burned down.

He had no luck. He spent years paying off a funeral plot, then he died at sea.

A man lay dying, his wife at his side. In a voice a little more than a whisper, the man said, "Dear, you've been with me through everything. Remember when I tripped on the rake and broke my ankle? You were there. When I lost the business, you were there. Now I'm weak and ill, here you are again. You know, dear, I think you're bad luck!"

He's very unlucky. One day his bookie's joint burned down. The only thing the firemen saved was his IOUs!

The unluckiest man in the world was the guy who from birth never had anything nice happen to him. He was abandoned by his parents. Growing up, he had every childhood disease known to man. No matter how hard he worked, he never advanced at work and never got a single raise in pay. He died the day after his insurance lapsed. The city had to bury him, so a hearse was sent over. It picked him up, but on the way to the cemetery, the hearse got a flat tire. By the time the flat was repaired, there was a terrible snowstorm. Eventually, they got him to a cemetery where the ground was too hard to be dug, so he was cremated. On the way back from the crematorium, a blizzard struck. The hearse was caught in the cold muck. And in order to get it going again, they had to use his ashes for traction. That was an unlucky man.

He's got no luck. He once put a seashell to his ear and got a busy signal.

He's so unlucky, aspirin gives him a headache.

He was the unluckiest man I ever knew. He spent five years perfecting somebody's signature on checks. When he had it down pat, the check came back marked INSUFFICIENT FUNDS.

I know a fellow who was sued by his wife for sterility. He went out and hired a lawyer. Then a girl sued him for fathering her child. He got another lawyer.
    He lost both cases!

Then there's the unluckiest guy in town. He had a wet dream and contracted a social disease.

He was real unlucky. He joined the navy to see the world and spent four years in a submarine.

The unluckiest man in the world was this lightning-rod salesman who got caught in a big storm with ten samples in his hands.

He's real unlucky. He was once shipwrecked on a desert island with his wife.

Luck is when you marry a woman for love, and you find out later she has money.

Feeling romantic, he carried his bride over the threshold. He got a kiss, a warm feeling, and a hernia.

## LUGGAGE

I have luggage that's traveled twenty thousand miles more than I have.

A grizzled old miner comes to a fairly large city and checks into a hotel. The clerk asks, "Where's your luggage, sir?"
    The old miner says, "What fer? I'm only staying a week."

There's a sure way of not losing your luggage on a flight—go by bus!

It's always a long walk from the terminal to the boarding area at most airports. They do that so your luggage can get a head start!

Last week, the luggage handlers at the airport were going to go out on strike, but they couldn't. Somebody lost the picket signs.

## MAGIC

An old man is strolling on the beach when he discovers a magic lamp. He rubs it, and a genie appears. "You have freed me," the genie says. "I'll grant you any wish you want."

The old man says, "Let me tell you. About forty years ago, I had a big fight with my brother. We haven't spoken since. I'd like to make up with him."

The genie says, "Is it because you're old and dying?"

The old man says, "No way. But my brother is, and he's a millionaire."

I have no luck. If I sawed a woman in half, I'd get the part that eats.

## MAIDS & SERVANTS

The wife told her husband that she couldn't do it all—cook, clean, work, take care of the baby, all of the chores. So the husband hired a lady to be his wife.

A woman points to a painting in her dining room and says to a friend, "This painting is so lifelike. Would you believe that my maid once spent an hour trying to get rid of that cobweb painted in the corner of the painting?''

The friend says, ''That's hard to believe.''

''You can't believe that an artist can paint that lifelike an image? Artists have been doing that for centuries.''

''Artists, of course. But maids?''

We just hired a new cook, and it's terrific. We pay her so much, she doesn't have to cook. She can afford to take us out to eat.

We have a great maid. Every two weeks she comes in and changes the topsoil on the table.

Mrs. Wilson is sick of the maid's work. When she's had enough, she says, ''Marie, no more. You are fired!''

Mrs. Wilson goes out to do her daily shopping and returns to the house in the evening. Marie is still there, dusting. Mrs. Wilson says, ''Didn't I fire you?''

''Yes, ma'am, but I forgave you.''

Two maids are talking about their jobs. One says, ''The lady of the house insists on having warm plates for meals.''

The second says, ''That's a lot of extra work.''

The first says, ''No. I just warm hers, and she never knows the difference.''

This maid was unable to walk two steps without running into something. If she exited the kitchen, she'd trip the lady of the house. Opening another door, she slams it into one of the children. She would often push the man of the house. Eventually, she gave notice. ''I can't work here,'' she said. ''I'm in the family way.''

The lady of the house called over Jamison, the butler, and said, ''Jamison, you remember when we hired you, we wanted you to take care of our son.''

''I recall that, madame.''

''Well, my son moved out twenty-two years ago.''

''Then what would you like me to do next?''

## MALENESS (MACHISMO)

Then there was the elephant who saw a man in the nude and asked, ''How the hell does he eat with that thing?''

A man has been concerned for years because of the insufficient length of his pride and joy. Finally, he musters up enough courage to explain his problem to a doctor. The doctor tells him, ''There's a wonderful new treatment you might consider. We graft on part of the trunk of a baby elephant and increase the size of your member substantially.''

The man agrees and undergoes the surgery. A few weeks later, he returns to the doctor, who asks, ''How's it coming along?''

The man says, ''The sex is great. But I don't think my rear end can take another peanut!''

"What do they call the useless piece of meat at the end of a penis?"

"A man."

"What's a swinger?"

"A well-built guy in the nude."

One actor in Hollywood is so well endowed, they had to hire somebody to play his penis as a young boy.

He was so well endowed, his penis applied for statehood.

"What does a male have that proves he's a man?"

"His birth certificate."

My nephew had his vasectomy done at Sears. Now, every time he makes love, the garage door opens.

"What's got a thousand teeth and holds back a monster?"

"My zipper."

Harvey is extremely well endowed, and the boys in the frat are proud of him. Jim, one of the boys, gets a visit from his older brother. A few minutes after they start to talk, through the wall from the next room both hear the sound of a woman's voice. The woman is obviously in ecstacy, oohing and aahing, gasping deliriously. Jim's older brother asks what's going on.

Jim explains that Harvey the mightily endowed has a girl in the next room.

"Oh, he must be putting it to her with a vengeance."

"No, not yet. For the next ten minutes, he'll just be *showing* it to her."

**MARRIAGE**

This man married. In no time at all, his wife cured him of drinking, smoking, and staying out till all hours. She also introduced him to the finer things like art and music. She taught him to dress well and to master the rules of etiquette.

One morning he took a look and decided that she wasn't good enough for him.

This young beau falls in love with a showgirl and lavishes everything on her. He buys her clothes, jewelry, a car, and then, one day, proposes.

The showgirl answers, "Me marry you? The way you throw your money around?"

Your marriage is in trouble if your wife says, "You're only interested in one thing," and you can't remember what it is.

You know you've got a rotten marriage if you go to a wife-swapping session and have to throw in the maid.

One morning a husband looks up from the breakfast newspaper and says to his wife, "I've been holding this in for years, but you're the worst cook in the world, a terrible slob, a miserable wife, and the world's worst lover."

The man comes home from work

early and finds his wife in bed with another man. The husband says, "What the heck are you doing?"

The wife says, "I'm getting a second opinion."

A typical couple were driving in their car, both rather quiet after they'd had a screaming session. En route, they passed a jackass in a field. The husband asked bitterly, "A relative of yours?"

The wife answered, "Yes. By marriage."

You know the honeymoon is over when you start to go out with the boys on Wednesday night and so does she.

Marriage is the most expensive way of discovering your faults.

Marriage is a romantic story in which the hero dies in the first chapter.

A woman decided to lose weight by wrapping herself in Saran wrap and sweating it off. Her husband came home, took one look, and said, "Leftovers again!"

My wife and I were happy for thirty years. Then we met.

This woman's husband said he wanted more space, so she locked him out of the house.

Marriage is making a comeback. Even couples who are living together are getting married.

Marriage is the only war in which you sleep with the enemy!

They had it real good, then one day they went broke. The husband said to his wife, "If you learn to cook, we can fire the maid."

The wife said, "If you learned to make love, we could fire the chauffeur!"

My wife wanted to be kept in the manner to which she was accustomed, so I let her keep her job.

A man told his wife that he'd been invited to a friend's bachelor party. The wife asked to go along. The man explained, "This is a stag party. There won't be any women there."

At the party, when the cake was brought in, four naked women popped out.

The man went to the phone and called his wife, saying, "Honey, I was wrong. There are four naked women running around. What should I do?"

The wife answered, "If you think you can do anything, head right home."

My wife laughs at everything I do. That's why we have no kids.

I don't know why they're making such a big deal about celibacy. My wife took it up two weeks after we got married.

She's been to the altar so often, she just got ordained.

We have an open marriage. I open her mail, and she opens my wallet.

The great thing about marriage is that you can say anything you want around the house and nobody pays any attention to you.

As soon as we were married, I let my wife know who was the boss. I looked her in the eye and said, "You're the boss."

My wife complained that she didn't have any outside interests. So I bought her a lawn mower.

I want a girl just like the one Grandpa married. Grandpa got married last week.

My wife suffers in silence louder than anyone I know.

My wife never tells me what to do. She just points.

Marriage is terrific. A man can sit home, wear his slippers, drink a beer, and watch his wife's favorite TV shows.

She lied to me. She told me that her father was a banker, and his health was failing. After the marriage, I found out his health was fine. It was the bank that was failing.

I like to run my home like a captain. Too bad I'm married to an admiral.

My wife does bird imitations. She watches me like a hawk.

Marry in haste, and everybody starts counting the months.

When we were first married, we got along beautifully, but as we left the church . . .

One man was too good to his wife. To show her feelings, the wife said, "Honey, if you ever divorce me, I'm going with you."

For house repairs, there's nothing like having a man around the house with a checkbook.

A woman yelled at her husband, "What do you mean you have nothing to live for? You have plenty to live for! The house isn't paid for, the car isn't paid for, the TV isn't paid for . . ."

It's easy to tell the difference between a newly married couple and one that's been married a long time. The new bride says, "Oh, no. Not already?"
The old wife says, "The ceiling needs painting."

This one fellow I know runs his wedding pictures backward. That way, he can watch himself walk out of church a free man.

A man says to his wife, "Let's change jobs."
The wife says, "Fine. You go get the children dressed, and I'll go out and honk the horn for ten minutes."

Our marriage is run on a 40–60 basis. I make forty, and she spends sixty.

It doesn't matter who wears the pants in the family as long as there's money in the pockets.

I have the feeling that it's better to have loved and lost than to have loved and won.

"I hear your husband is in the hospital. What's his problem?"

"His knee. I found his secretary on it."

Joe walks into the house, and his wife says, "Oh, dear, you must be so exhausted. How about a nice juicy steak, some *au gratin* potatoes, a salad, and some nice wine?"

"No, thanks," the husband says. "I'm too tired to eat out."

I got four invitations to dinner out last week—all from my wife.

You haven't nagged me all evening, dear. Is there someone else?

A couple comes home from an evening out. John, the husband, goes into the bathroom and comes out a moment later with two aspirins and a glass of water.

His wife, Loretta, says, "I don't have a headache."

John says, *"Gotcha!"*

They have a perfect relationship. They both like to nap during sex.

The private eye reports to Mrs. Brown, saying, "Your husband went into four bars on Main Street, a saloon on Third, and then into a motel on Maple."

Mrs. Brown says, "I wonder what he was doing."

"I think he was trailing you."

He owes his success to his first wife, and his second wife to his success.

You know it's the beginning of the end when you start to make love to your wife and she leaves a wake-up call.

I asked a recently divorced friend if she planned to get married again.

She replied, "I have a dog that growls and sleeps all day, a parrot that swears, and a cat that stays out all night. What do I need a husband for?"

While making love, the married man always fantasizes that his wife isn't fantasizing.

A little boy is playing around the sculptures at the Rockefeller Center and he looks up at one and asks his father, "What's that?"

"That's the image of a woman," his father says.

The boy takes a look at the statue and asks, "Is Mommy a woman?"

Before the father can answer, a large, square woman walks up to him and says, "Hello, darling," and picks up the young boy.

After considering the question for a

few more seconds, the father turns to the son and answers, "Fundamentally."

The bad thing about marriage is that both sides think they're management.

This husband tells his wife, "You did get the last word, dear. This is a new argument."

There are two ways to handle a woman, and nobody knows either one of them.

A woman was reading a magazine when she looked up and said to her couch-potato husband, "It says here that paying attention to one's mate is a sign of true love."

The husband said, "What?"

The washing machine wasn't working, so Mrs. Brown asked her husband to fix it. He made a face and said, "Who do you think I am—the Maytag man?"

An hour later, Mrs. Brown said, "My car isn't working. Will you fix it?"

Mr. Brown said, "Who do you think I am—Mr. Goodwrench?"

Later that night, Mr. Brown returned from his usual bowling game and asked his wife, "Did you get everything repaired?"

Mrs. Brown said, "The next-door neighbor did it."

"No kidding. How much did it cost?"

"Nothing. He just wanted me to bake a cake for him or make love to him tomorrow when you're at work."

"What are you going to do?"

Mrs. Brown answered, "Who do you think I am—Betty Crocker?"

If it weren't for marriage, men would go through life thinking they had no faults at all.

A young man and woman come to a small town to be married by a justice of the peace. The JP looks at their marriage license and says, "This isn't dated. Run back to city hall and have the clerk date it."

The young man rushes to city hall and returns a little later with a dated license.

The JP looks at the license again and says, "You don't have the bride-to-be's maiden name. Run back to city hall and get it put in."

Once again, the young man runs off and returns with the maiden name written in.

The JP now says, "There's no county seal on this license."

For a third time, the young man rushes off and returns with the license.

The JP says, "I can marry you now." But then, for the first time, he notices a small girl sitting in back. "Who's that?" he asks.

"That's our daughter."

"Oh. In that case, I can marry you. But she's a bastard."

The young man says, "Funny, but that's what the clerk said you were."

"I want to marry a smart woman, a good woman, a woman who'll make me happy."

"Make up your mind."

A young married woman comes up with a great way to get some extra house money. When she and her husband start to go to bed, she demands that he pay her fifty dollars. The husband says that he only has forty. The wife says, "For forty, I'll only give you a taste of what you can get."

They start to neck. After a while, the wife gets turned on. Finally, she says, "Why don't I lend you ten dollars until tomorrow?"

A woman is very suspicious of her husband. Each night she checks his coat for a woman's hair. Finding none one night, she says, "Now it's bald women."

They're inseparable. Sometimes it takes ten people to separate them.

Give my wife an inch and she'll redecorate it.

"Did you ever marry the girl you liked in college, or do you still do your own cleaning and cooking?"

"Yes."

I'm celebrating my silver anniversary. I like to think of it as twenty-five years of détente.

A man calls into the police station and says, "My wife is missing."

The officer says, "How long has she been gone?"

"A month."

"Why are you reporting it now?"

"Well, until yesterday I thought it was just a dream."

A man tells his lawyer, "I leave my wife everything on condition that she get married six months after I die."

The lawyer asks, "Why six months?"

"I want somebody to be sorry I'm gone."

## MARTIAL ARTS

He was a karate expert, but one day he joined the army, saluted, and killed himself.

In kung fu, your feet can become deadly. The same with my son's. He never changes his socks.

In kung fu, you fight with your feet. I always fight with my feet. The minute somebody gets tough, I run like hell!

## MARTIANS

The Martian kid complained to his mother, "Finish making my sandwich. I'll be late to school."

The Martian mother said, "Don't rush me. I only have four hands."

Then there's the Martian who landed in San Francisco and said, "Take me to your queen."

Two Martians landed in front of a traffic light. One said, "I saw her first."

The second said, "Sure, but I'm the one she winked at."

A Martian looked at UNIVAC and said, "She's not only gorgeous, she's also got brains."

Two Martians landed in Chicago. One said, "This doesn't look like Washington, D.C."

"You better ask someone," the other said. So his friend asked a fire hydrant and got no reply.

"Stupid," the first one said, "Can't you see he's only a kid?"

Two Martians land on a dark country lane. One asks, "Where do you think we are?"

The second Martian says, "We must be in a cemetery. See that gravestone? That man lived to be one hundred and six."

"What was his name?"

"Miles from Toledo."

A woman is sitting in a bar. Every few minutes, various men come over and try to strike up a conversation. Each man is obviously after a little fun-and-games. The woman lets each man know that he's barking up the wrong lady.

A Martian walks in and sits down at the bar. He ignores the woman, who after a while is puzzled by his manner. She says, "Every man in this place has tried to get into my pants. Why not you?"

The Martian says, "Because we Martians have sex in a different way."

"Really? That sounds interesting."

"Our sex is too powerful for people. But if you'd like a sample, here it is."

With that, the Martian extends his index finger, places it on the woman's brow, and starts to chant. In five seconds, the woman starts to feel an ecstacy she has never known before. Her loins seem to be melting. Her whole pelvic area is quivering. Finally, she reaches the utmost climax of her life.

Not satisfied, she says, "Let's do it again. Please, again."

The Martian holds up his bent index finger and says, "In about a half hour."

A Martian lands in a big city just as a garbage truck zooms by. Because the truck hits a bump, a trash can falls off and rolls to the Martian. Picking it up, he rushes after the truck, yelling, "Wait, lady, you dropped your purse."

A Martian walking through the lobby of a hotel in Las Vegas sees a slot machine hit the jackpot. As the silver dollars spray the floor, the Martian pats the machine on top and says, "Say, buddy, you better do something for that cold."

Martians keep asking to be taken to our leaders. What do they expect to learn?

A Martian lands in a piano store. "Wow," he says, "do these guys have dentists."

This neurotic Martian walks into a piano showroom. He looks around, finally walks over to a Steinway, and says, "Okay, wipe that smile off your face."

Two Martians land on a golf course and watch a hacker work away. First, he gets into the middle of the woods. He then gets caught in a sand trap. Another two swings and he's at the edge of a water hazard. He manages to chip the ball, and it goes right into the hole. One Martian says to the other, "Oh, boy, now he's really in trouble."

## MASTURBATION

Then there was the dull guy who was masturbating. His hand fell asleep.

Then there was the masturbator who had an offbeat sense of humor.

Most people masturbate because they know that if you want something done right, you have to do it yourself.

This poor soul has been on a desert island all by himself for ages. One day he looks out toward the sea and says, excitedly, "Look, there's a ship coming. And on the deck there are six beautiful women walking around topless. And there's one with the most luscious face and lips."

As he rants on, he gets himself all hot and bothered. Finally, he grabs at his erection and says, "Fooled you. There's no damn ship."

## MEAN

He'd dab ice cream behind his ears and go to an Overeaters Anonymous meeting.

When she went to see the Wizard of Oz, she rooted for the witches!

He was so mean, his first nursery rhyme was about Jack and Jill being pushed down the hill.

## MEDICINE

Medicine is impossible today with all those specialists. When my sinus infection went to my throat, I had to change doctors.

Americans spent more money on doctors last year than ever before and it's working. More doctors are feeling better.

Why are all arthritis pills in bottles that say "Twist to open"?

Why is healing such hard work when getting sick takes so little effort?

A doctor told Mrs. Stone to give her husband one pill a day and one drink of whiskey to improve his stamina. A month later, when Mrs. Stone came in for another visit, the doctor asked, "How are we doing with the pill and the whiskey?"

Mrs. Stone answered, "Well, he's a

little behind with the pills, but he's about six months ahead with the whiskey."

At Johns Hopkins, they put the heart of a dog into a human patient. The surgeon can't collect, because the patient keeps burying the bills in the backyard.

At Columbia University, they put the heart of a turtle into a man. A month later, that man left the hospital. The following month, he got to his car.

My wife has really changed with her new tranquilizer. She's beginning to be pleasant to people she doesn't even speak to.

Malpractice insurance is what allows people to be ill at ease.

Money, in medicine, still talks. It's what the doctor hears through his stethoscope.

By mistake, my druggist gave me a bottle of bust developer instead of hair restorer. It didn't hurt me, but what am I going to do with those two little bumps on my head?

Medicine can be summed up this way: ill, pill, and bill.

Time is a great healer. With the cost of a doctor today, that may be the best arrangement.

An elderly man goes to a specialist because of his deafness. In no time at all, the doctor has him hearing perfectly.

During a checkup, the doctor says, "How does your family feel about your new hearing?"

"I haven't told them yet. And it's been great. I've changed my will six times."

I know a girl who hitches everywhere and is never molested. She just tells the driver she's going to pick up some AZT.

A lot of men were incurable romantics. Then antibiotics came along.

By mistake, a man swallows a whole bottle of aspirin. Rushing to the phone, he calls his doctor. "Doc," he says, "I swallowed a whole bottle of aspirin. What should I do?"

"Take two aspirin and call me in the morning."

A man goes to his doctor and says, "I have a date with a girl who wants to stay over. She's an incredible sexpot, so give me something that'll enable me to keep up with her."

The doctor gives him an experimental drug.

Two days later, the man returns and says, "Doc, you have to give me some liniment. I need liniment."

"You're crazy. Liniment'll burn."

"It's for my arm. The girl never showed up."

I have a new expensive medicine. I take one a day when I can afford it.

They now have an amazing new antibiotic. It's so powerful, you can't take it unless you're in perfect health.

Medicine has made great strides in recent years. What used to be an itch is now an allergy.

Since doctors have stopped making house calls, lots of patients now have to die without their help.

A man is having terrible rectal pains. A friend suggests that tea can be medically helpful in such matters. Nothing else having worked, the man places a tea bag on his anus and waits for relief. The pains, however, become even more intense, so he rushes to Emergency in the hospital. The doctor, an intern from India, studies his rear end, then concludes, "I don't know what the problem is, but you are going to take a long trip."

Then there was this lady who called her doctor frantically: "Doc, you must rush over here for my husband. When he got up today, he took his vitamin pills, his heart pills, his liver pills, his antihistamine pills, his appetite-depressant pills, and then his enzyme drink—then he lit up a cigarette, and there was this incredible explosion."

## MEMORY

Harry Gramapolis decides to change his name for business reasons. He goes to court and becomes Harold Graham. To celebrate the event, he invites some people over to his fancy apartment for a little party. His eighty-year-old father is also invited. However, the old man never arrives. Hours go by. No old man. Finally, the party breaks up, and Harry bids his guests good night. A little concerned, because no one answers the phone at the old man's place, Harry decides to go over and see what's happened. When he comes downstairs, he sees his father sitting in the lobby. Rushing over, Harry says, "Dad, why didn't you come upstairs?"

The old man says, "To tell you the truth, I forgot your name."

I used to suffer from senility, but I forgot all about it.

You know you're getting old when you walk into a room and can't remember why you're there—and it's the john.

The teacher asks, "Who built the Pyramids?"

Little Albert says, "I knew, but I forgot."

The teacher says, "That's a shame. You're the only person alive who knows and you had to forget."

An old man married a young girl, and they went off on their honeymoon. Returning a week later, the old man looked a little down, and a friend asked him what was wrong. The old man answered, "I'm in trouble with my bride."

The friend said, "Look, sex isn't everything."

The old man said, "Oh, the sex is great, but after each time I have trouble remembering her name."

My wife says I have a terrible memory. So far this year, I've forgotten her birthday, our anniversary, Valentine Day, and who's boss.

"Did you forget you owed me ten dollars?"
"No, but give me time."

There are three kinds of memory— good, bad, and convenient.

Memory is what tells a man his anniversary was yesterday.

## MEN

Whatever a man sews—will rip.

Nowadays, when you see a man and his son, the one with the beard is the son.

One guy was accused of being wishy-washy, and he retorted, "Maybe I am and maybe I'm not."

Even if a man understood women, he still wouldn't believe it.

For some men, life is just wine, women, and song. I concentrate on women. I can drink and sing when I'm old.

I finally figured out why they call it the mother tongue. Father never gets a chance to use it.

Why is it nobody ever asks a man how he combines marriage with a career?

A happily married man has a wife who cooks, a wife who makes love like a rabbit, and a wife who works while he stays home. And if he's lucky, the three of them will never meet.

When Nature designed men's knees, she didn't have walking shorts in mind.

Some men start out in the best circles and end up in the worst triangle.

A recent survey tried to determine why men get up in the middle of the night. Five percent, the survey concluded, got up to go to the bathroom. The other 95 percent got up to go home.

I never look at another woman. I'm too faithful. I'm too honest. I'm too near-sighted.

My uncle didn't exactly like his wife, so he had eighteen kids and lost himself in the crowd.

"Women have PMS. What do men have?"
"ESPN."

The man who says he can understand women is either a psychiatrist or in need of one.

A food faddist was lecturing on the evils of junk food. He asked a bored-looking man in the back, "What's the worst food you'll eat in your life that will affect you the most?"

"That's easy," the man said. "Wedding cake."

The weaker sex is the stronger sex because of the stronger sex's weakness for the weaker sex!

Big men make docile husbands. So do big women.

## MENTAL HEALTH

A nurse picks up the phone. On the other end is an agitated man who asks, "Did one of your loonies escape today?"

The nurse said, "I don't think so. We check every day."

The agitated man said, "Check again. Somebody ran away with my wife."

A visitor asked a patient what he was doing at the mental hospital, and the patient explained, "I'm here because I'm not all there."

The whole staff spent months working on Flint, who believed that he was Napoleon. Finally, the head psychiatrist said to Flint, "You're all better."

Flint said, "Can I make a call? I want to tell Josephine the good news."

A minister went to a hospital to provide for the religious needs of the patients. While there, he heard of a patient who thought he was God and thought it would be nice to talk to the man. One of the nurses brought over a dignified patient with a long, flowing white beard who had been walking around blessing other patients. The minister engaged the patient in conversation and said, "There's a subject I'd like to discuss with you—the Creation. When the Bible says you created the world in six days, does that mean a literal six days or some other time measurement?"

The patient said, "Please forgive me, but I don't like to talk shop."

A farmer was coming back from town with a load of fertilizer. When he passed the local mental hospital, a patient called through the fence, "What you got there?"

The farmer said, "A load of fertilizer. I put it on strawberries."

The patient said, "You should try them with sugar and cream."

The doctor was interviewing a patient who was about to be dismissed and asked what career plans the man had made. The patient said, "I think I may go back into accounting. Since I have a master's, I may even try to become an economics adviser to the government. There is also an opportunity to become an efficiency expert."

The doctor said, "That is terrific. You have so many potential career moves."

The patient said, "Yes, I do. Of course, if any of those don't work out, I could always become a microwave oven."

A man told his friend, "My wife doesn't understand me, but she charges me fifty an hour to listen to my problems."

## MEXICANS

"What is matched Mexican luggage?"
"Two shopping bags from the same store."

Then there's the Mexican girl who told the producer she wanted to be a Hollywood harlot.

You can always tell a Mexican doctor. He writes his prescriptions with spray paint.

There is a man who smuggles Mexican midgets into the United States by hanging them from the rearview mirror of his Chevy truck.

I just got back from Mexico. I went down there for the Kaopectate Festival.

They say that all our troubles began when Adam ate a piece of fruit in Eden. That was nothing compared to what can happen if you do the same thing in Mexico.

Choo-choo is an old Mexican expression—if you don't leave my wife alone, I'm going to choo-choo!

I think I'm getting old. I drank some bad water in Mexico and got a bad case of the walks.

How about the Mexican lady who named her first son José and her second Hose B.

A wide-eyed little girl from the barrio was taking her first vacation away from home. Her aunt took her to the guest room and pointed to the freshly made bed. "My dear, this is all yours."
The little girl cried, "I wanna sleep in a regular bed. One with five or six people in it!"

## MIAMI

It's the senior citizens' dance. One woman says to the man she's dancing with, "Why are you undressing me with your eyes?"
He answers, "Because I have arthritis in my hands."

My cousin in Miami Beach just went through a real trauma. The shrink he's been going to for ten years told him the other day, *"No hablo inglés."*

A woman dashed excitedly around the pool of a nice Florida hotel shouting, "Help! My son Clarence, the lawyer whose office is at 381 Park Drive, is drowning!"

Two women meet in Miami. One says, "I just came from my doctor. It's the most awful thing. I've got these bumps on my forehead, and they keep growing and growing like horns. I also have this growth on my back that's getting bigger and bigger like a tail."
The other woman says, "Oh, so what else is new?"

In Miami Beach, a young man felt that his eighty-five-year-old mother was spending too much time alone and arranged for her to meet a man of ninety. The couple went out on a date. Anxiously, the son waited for his mother to return and report on the evening out. Finally, she returned and told him, "I had to slap his face three times."

"He got fresh?"

"No, I thought he was dead!"

Miami Beach has had very uncertain weather the last few years. The other day I saw a pair of mittens pinned to a bikini!

In Miami, you hear conversations like this: "Max, was it you who died or your brother?"

Two elderly ladies are sitting on chairs at the beach, discussing their lives. One says, "You know, I went out with Gus Paley last night. He was a regular Don Juan."

The other elderly woman said, "Such a great lover?"

"No, he's been dead a hundred years."

Two elderly men are sitting and one says, "TGIF."

The other says, "What does that mean?"

"Thank God, it's Friday."

The other one says, "SHIT."

"What does that mean?"

"So Happens It's Thursday."

Two older Jewish men are sitting on the boardwalk, discussing their friend Stein, age eighty, who'd just married a twenty-year-old girl in one of those May-December marriages. The first one said, "I know what December is going to find in May—looks, charm, excitement—but what is May going to find in December?"

The second man says, "Christmas."

In Miami, you're not legally dead until you lose your tan.

A little girl was visiting her grandmother in Miami Beach. The little girl ran into the water. The grandmother called out, "Stop! You're tracking sand into the ocean."

Mildred was in her eighties and was having a hard time impressing some of the old bachelors at the retirement home. One day she hit on a scheme. Taking off all of her clothes, she ran naked through the porch where the men sat. As she went by, one man said, "What was that?"

The man next to him said, "I don't know. But whatever it was, it needed pressing."

## MIDDLE AGE

You're middle-aged if your crowd considers you a sex symbol because you still have hair.

You're getting on if you remember when it cost more to buy a car than park it.

You can tell she's forty. Just count the rings under her eyes.

They say that life begins at forty. But after fifty, it's only from the waist up.

You're middle-aged when you look forward to a dull evening.

It's a little sad to reach your September years and find out you blew the best of July and August.

You're getting on when your favorite part of the paper is "Twenty-Five Years Ago."

You can tell when you hit middle age by the way it hits you back.

How did I reach the other side of so many things that were once in the future?

Aging is at work when your kids study in history what you used to study as current events.

You've reached middle age when you notice that kids are getting noisier every year.

You're middle-aged when you remember when "boobs" meant the dumb kids.

You're middle-aged when you start thinking that sixty isn't so old.

You're middle-aged when your idea of unwinding on a Friday night is to go to bed and read.

Middle age is when you don't care where you go, as long as you're home by eight-thirty.

Middle age is no fun because you have to set a good example for the kids.

## MIDDLE EAST

During one of the wars for which the Middle East is notorious, an Arabian regiment was retreating. A soldier asked his company commander if he could go on leave. The company commander looked at the private in amazement, saying, "We're in the middle of a big battle. Are you crazy?"

The private said, "But I'm up for leave."

The commanding officer said, "I tell you what—we'll try to retreat through your hometown!"

During Operation Desert Shield, an Iraqi officer told his men, "Don't fire at the Yanks. It pisses them off."

## MIDGETS

Then there was this midget who walked into an undertaker and asked for a short bier.

A midget married a woman 6'2" who weighed almost two hundred pounds. On their honeymoon, the midget looked at his new bride and said, "So much to do and so little time to do it!"

A female midget went into a bar, and just to prove she was friendly kissed everybody in the joint.

A midget is accused of attacking a woman and using a bucket to have sex with her. His attorney stands the midget on the bucket and shows that the woman could have pushed him over with one finger. The case is dismissed.

Afterward, the judge calls the midget over and says, "Look, you've been tried and found innocent. You can't be charged again. Tell me how you did it?"

The midget says, "The bucket."

"But your lawyer showed you couldn't stand on it."

"I didn't stand on it. I put it over her head and swung from the handle."

## MINISTERS

The new minister seemed to be looking for something. When Joey came by, the minister said, "Son, can you tell me where the post office is?"

Joey said, "It's about three blocks up Oak Street and left until you get to Maple."

The new minister thanked the boy and said, "I'll make a point of mentioning how nice you were when I preach in church Sunday."

Joey said, "I don't go to church."

The new minister said, "That's terrible. Come by Sunday and I'll tell you how to get to heaven."

"Don't think you can. You couldn't even find the post office!"

The minister passed a group of young boys and stopped to watch them. They were sitting around in a circle with a dog in the middle. The minister asked what they were doing. Little Alex said, "Nothing much. We're telling lies, and the one that tells the biggest gets to have the dog."

Shocked, the minister said, "When I was your age, I never would have thought of telling a lie."

Little Alex said, "Guess we have to give him the dog, fellas."

A minister was visiting the wife of a member of his congregation. As he sipped a cup of coffee, the door burst open and the husband burst in, carrying a dead possum over his back. He started to tell his wife, "Finally got the varmint who's been at the chickens. I shot him twice and stomped at him and clubbed him until . . ." He saw the minister, and went on, "Till the Good Lord called him home!"

The minister explained to his wife that his sermon about the rich giving to the poor was half-successful. He'd convinced the poor!

The sermon was endless. The minister droned on and on, just about going through the Bible word by word. As he started to wind down, he said, "Yes, my friends, what can I say? What can I say?"

From the rear, a voice yelled out, "How about 'Amen'?"

Ministers are known for being tight-fisted. One minister showed up at a convention in Las Vegas with the Ten Commandments in one hand and a ten-dollar bill in the other. At the end of the week, he hadn't broken either one!

A very foul-mouthed man met the local pastor on the street. "Now where in the hell do I know you from?" the man asked.

The pastor replied, "From where in hell do you come, sir?"

## MIRACLES

A man sued and won a fortune from the insurance company of the bus that had hit him. The insurance investigator believed that the man wasn't as crippled as the doctors had reported to the jury. On the way out of the courtroom, the insurance investigator said, "Pal, you're not going to get away with this. You may be in a wheelchair now, but one day you'll forget to play crippled, and I'll pounce. I'm going to watch you like a hawk twenty-four hours a day, and I'll see you goof yet. Wherever you go, whatever you do, I'll be watching."

The man said, "I'll tell you what you'll see. For a few months, you'll see me in the house. Then one day, a nurse is going to push my chair out of the house and into a taxi. We'll go to the airport, and there I'll be wheeled onto a plane. That plane will fly me to Lourdes. Then I'll be wheeled to the church, where you'll see me pray. And then, are you going to see a miracle!"

The doctor tells his patient, "Your recovery was a miracle."

The patient replies, "Thank God. Now I don't have to pay you."

Two nuns driving in a car run out of gas. One nun says, "I saw a gas station about a half-mile back."

The other one says, "We have nothing to carry gasoline in."

"Well, we have this bedpan we keep in case of emergencies. I'm sure we could put some gasoline in it."

They take the bedpan out of the trunk and walk to the service station. They get two gallons of gas and return to the car. As they start to empty the contents into the gas tank, a man drives by and sees what they're doing. He shakes his head and says, "These gals really believe in miracles!"

Mrs. Klein returns from a doctor's exam and tells her husband she doesn't want any children. She explains, "The doctor says if I have a baby, it'll be a mackerel."

Baffled, Mr. Klein calls the doctor, who says, "I told your wife if she had a baby, it would be a *miracle*."

## MISERY

Misery is putting something in a safe place and never being able to find it.

Misery is seeing your car keys through a locked car window.

Misery is a VCR that works perfectly when the repairman comes.

## MISTRESSES

A mistress is something between a master and his mattress.

One Manhattan mistress had to give up her beautiful apartment. Her louse had expired.

## MODERN LIFE

A lot of people think we're nothing but a bunch of numbers now—Social Security number, credit-card number, ZIP code, area code. I don't happen to agree with them. Just this morning, I was telling that to my wife—702-10996-04!

Have you noticed that all the things you used to do when you were a kid are now being done by batteries?

We've really come a long way. You can leave your air-conditioned office at five-thirty, get into your air-conditioned car, drive to your air-conditioned club, so you can take a steam bath!

What this country needs is something that will outlast the box it came in.

## MODESTY

He once failed a lie-detector test. He couldn't get past the first question that had to be answered with, "In my humble opinion . . ."

Modesty is the feeling that other people will discover how great you are.

## MONEY

Money can't buy happiness, but it sure goes a long way toward a down payment.

A man goes to the doctor and says, "Doc, I swallowed three quarters last month. Can you get them out?"

"You swallowed them last month and you didn't come in until today?"

"Well, I didn't need the money till now."

He earns roughly three hundred. When you smooth it, it comes to about twenty dollars.

How did a fool and his money get together in the first place anyway?

The other guy's wallet always looks greener.

There are three ways to become a billionaire nowadays: Inherit it, earn it, and sue.

He brings his wife his pay envelope every Friday. If she saves up a whole year, she'll have fifty-two envelopes.

How come people miss two payments on their cars and still have enough for a down payment on a giant-screen TV set?

I'd gladly participate in any experiment to test the effect of sudden wealth.

Money can't buy you happiness, but it can take you to more places to look.

Somebody said that money can't buy happiness, money can't buy respect, money can't buy love. That guy must be a terrible shopper.

Money talks—in Japanese.

Now I know why I could never keep up with the Joneses. They were just indicted for tax evasion.

He knows money can't buy happiness, but he doesn't care. He likes money more than happiness anyway.

I've been rich and I've been poor, and it's real obvious why Rockefellers laugh and I don't.

The art auction is going at full swing when an usher walks up to the auctioneer and whispers something to him. The auctioneer turns to the audience and says, "I've just been informed that a man has lost his wallet. If anyone finds it, he'll give him a five-hundred-dollar reward."

From the back of the room, a voice says, "I'll give six."

I'm losing the war on poverty because my wife keeps fraternizing with the enemy.

There are more important things in life than money. The trouble is they all cost money.

There's one reason you can't take it with you—it leaves before you do.

A wise man once said, "You can marry more money in ten minutes than you can earn in a lifetime."

Money isn't everything. Sometimes it's not even 99 percent.

The way I see it is: When the rich have money, they invest. When the poor have money, they eat.

A very, very, very big broker was having financial difficulties as a result of his gambling. He and his secretary were discussing various debts.

"You owe the tailor three hundred dollars," she says.

"Promise him two hundred dollars," he says.

"You owe your bookmaker five hundred dollars," she says.

"Promise him three hundred dollars," he says.

"You owe your partner one thousand dollars," she says.

"Promise him six hundred dollars," he says.

As the broker gathers up his racing forms, he turns to his secretary and says, "And promise yourself something, too."

If you see a dollar on the sidewalk, pick it up. There might be something valuable under it.

My wife loves checkbooks. She's already finished 185 of them.

I couldn't reduce my bills even if I put them on microfilm.

There's one thing about my wife. Once she starts a checkbook, she can't put it down until she's finished.

It's better to give than to lend, and it costs just about the same.

A man left his hotel without paying the bill. The hotel sent him a letter saying, *Please send the amount of your bill now.*

He wrote back, *The amount of my bill was $165.14. Regards.*

A shopkeeper had been trying for months to collect on an overdue bill to no avail. Finally, he sent a tear-jerking letter with a picture of his young daughter. Under the picture, he wrote, *It is because of this little one that I must have money.*

A few days later, he received a reply. The man had sent a photograph of a voluptuous blonde. Underneath it read, *It is because of this little one that I have none!*

A young man stopped into a clothing store and asked the price of a shirt in the window. "Ah," the owner said. "You've chosen the nicest shirt here. And to show I respect good taste, I'm not going to ask sixty-five dollars, I'm not going to ask fifty-five dollars. I'm not even going to ask forty-five dollars. My price for you, my friend, is thirty-five dollars!"

The customer replied, "I wouldn't give you forty-five dollars, I wouldn't give you thirty-five dollars. I wouldn't give you twenty-five dollars. I'll give you fifteen dollars for the shirt."

"Sold!" said the owner. "That's the way I like to do business. No chiseling."

There are a lot of things you can't bank on nowadays—like my salary.

I was going to join this anti-inflation group, but they raised their dues.

The darkest hour is just before you're overdrawn.

Money isn't everything, but it's way ahead of the competition.

The door-to-door salesman tries to convince the lady of the house to buy a double freezer. She'd save enough on her food bills to pay for the freezer. The lady of the house says, "That sounds nice, but we're paying for the house on the rent we save, and we're saving on movies with the cable TV, and we're saving on laundry with the new washer. And we just can't afford to save any more right now."

They say that you can't take it with you. I don't even have enough to get me there.

Money may not be the key to happiness, but if you have enough, you can get a key made.

All my life, people have told me it is better to give than to receive. But you know, when I think about it, receiving isn't so bad.

In the plush dining room of a private Wall Street club, several portly gentlemen were discussing who the greatest inventor was. Edison, Morse, Ford, Whitney, were some of the names mentioned.

Finally, an imperious financier broke in, "Well, the man who invented interest was no fool."

At twenty, a man thinks he can save the world. At forty, he's lucky if he can save part of his salary.

MAID: "Madam, the installment man is here again."
MISTRESS: "Tell him to take a chair."

## MONSTERS

"Why did the doctor tell the zombie to get some rest?"
"He was dead on his feet."

"How can a monster count to thirty-one?"
"He takes off his shoes."

"What's more invisible than the Invisible Man?"
"His shadow."

Three vampires come into a bar and order. Two ask for a glass of blood. The third asks for a cup of plasma. The waiter calls to the bartender, "Two bloods and a blood lite."

FIRST MONSTER: Have an accident?
SECOND MONSTER: No, thanks, I just had one.

"What does a boy monster call a girl monster with four green heads, brown fur, and eight clubfeet?"
"Cute."

Then there was the vampire who became a vegetarian but couldn't make it work. He kept trying to get blood out of a turnip.

MONSTER KID: Mommy, can I eat Pittsburgh?
MONSTER MOM: Wash your hands first.

## MORMONS

There's recent proof that Brigham Young wasn't a polygamist. He had only one wife, but she had forty-seven wigs.

A Morman husband knows which wife he wants for the night. He throws water on all of them and picks the one that sizzles.

A Morman wedding was in progress. The minister got to the final part and said to the assembled brides, "Do you take this man to be your lawfully wedded husband?"

He paused and went on, "Some of you girls in the back better talk up if you want to be included in this thing."

## MOTELS

It was one of those hotels for a quickie. The other night, a car backfired, and twelve guys ran out in their shorts.

The motel I was in had air-conditioning. The trouble was that I never saw air in such a condition.

I'd say it was a shoddy motel. No paper towels, just loose wallpaper.

I never stay in a motel that has a paper strip around the bed.

## MOTHERS

Women who miscalculate are called "mothers."

My mother was brilliant. She saved more than my dad earned.

This mother got a letter from her son in the army telling her he'd grown another foot. So she knitted him another stocking.

My mother is so proud. I go to a psychiatrist five times a week and just talk about her.

A statement that breaks a mother's heart: "Ma, I missed the school bus."

## MOTHER'S DAY

He was an incubator baby. On Mother's Day, he sent candy to an oven.

On Mother's Day, he sends her something to put in water—his laundry.

I can't understand it—I saw a gun shop having a Mother's Day sale.

Give your mother something she can be grateful for on Mother's Day—move out!

God couldn't be everywhere at once, so He created mothers.

Mother's Day and Father's Day are alike except that on Father's Day, you buy a cheaper gift.

Then there's this sad alligator. Every year she lays a thousand eggs, and on Mother's Day, not one lousy card!

## MOTHERS-IN-LAW

For a wedding gift, we got a perfect present from my mother-in-law: a dozen towels marked HERS and ITS.

My mother-in-law never liked me. At the wedding, she bit the head off the groom on the wedding cake.

A man heard his mother-in-law wanted to come for a visit and said, "I won't have her in my house and that's semi-final."

Behind every candidate, there stands a proud wife and a flabbergasted mother-in-law.

"Your dog bit my mother-in-law this morning."

"I guess you're going to sue me for damages."

"Not if you'll sell me the dog."

Want to know what mixed emotions are? A state of mind occasioned by seeing your mother-in-law drive off a cliff in your new car.

They say that every woman has her price. I've got a mother-in-law I could let you have dirt-cheap.

I keep telling my wife, "I like your mother-in-law much more than I do mine."

Do you think you have a problem? My mother-in-law has a twin sister.

I don't have it so good. My wife left me last month, but my mother-in-law didn't.

My mother-in-law sent me two sweaters for Christmas, so when she arrived on her visit, I was wearing one.

She glared at me. "What's wrong, didn't you like the other one?"

Mothers-in-law are a lot like seeds. You don't want them, but they come with the tomato.

A mule kicks a farmer's mother-in-law in the head so hard the poor woman dies. At the funeral, the crowd is the biggest ever assembled in the county. The minister says to the farmer, "She must have been a special lady."

" 'Taint that," the farmer says. "Most of the crowd is here to buy the mule."

Out half the night playing poker, a man sneaks into the house, undresses, and hops into bed. Feeling sexy, he turns to the sleeping beauty next to him and makes love to her. Afterward, feeling hungry, he goes downstairs for a snack. His wife is in the kitchen drinking coffee. Puzzled, the man says, "Who's in our bed?"

"Oh, that's my mother. She dropped in, so I made her stay and gave her our bed."

Shocked, the husband returns to the bedroom, nudges his mother-in-law and says, "Please forgive me. Tell me you forgive me."

The mother-in-law says, "I haven't talked to you in twenty years. I'm not going to start now."

Margaret sees a gray hair on her husband's coat. Her eyes flashing, she says, "You've been over at your mother's again, getting sympathy!"

If the theory of evolution works, how come a mother still has only two hands?

Ten-year-old Tony takes over another kid's paper route. At the end of the first week, Tony brings home his pay—six dollars. The second week, he brings home $5.90. The third week, he walks into the house and hands his mother $5.80. His mother looks him in the eye and says, "Tony, tell me true—you gotta girl?"

The mother cat was nagging the heck out of its kitten. Finally, the kitten couldn't take it anymore and said, "Can't I lead one of my own lives?"

## MOVIES

Go figure Hollywood. If there's a scene where a man kisses the bare breast of a woman, that gets an *X* rating. But if he cuts it off with a chain saw, that's an *R*.

They just made a great movie that combines sex and violence. It's called *Chain Saw Vasectomy*.

It was dark in the theater when suddenly a woman yelled, "Is there a doctor in the house?"
    A man rushed over. "I'm a doctor."
    The woman said, "Nice. Would you like to meet my daughter?"

Just think: What would a drive-in be called if there was no movie?

These new mini-movie houses are great. You get to see one picture and hear three.

In westerns, the cowboy never gets the girl. That's because he's always riding his horse or eating with his horse or sleeping with his horse. After twenty-four hours of that, what girl would go near him?

In a *G*-rated movie, the hero gets the girl. In an *X* movie, *everybody* gets the girl.

A novelist recently got the idea for a new novel. It came from the movie version of his previous novel.

I saw a movie so bad, people were waiting in line to get out.

This is the worst movie of all time. When it plays the drive-in, people ask for their gas money back.

They just made a terrific British sci-fi picture. All the Martians carry umbrellas.

A man is waiting in line for a hit movie. Behind him are two women. The usher comes along and says that he has two seats together. Seeing the problem, the usher says to the man, "Let them go first. You wouldn't want to separate a woman from her mother, would you?"
    The man says, "No, sir. I did that once, and I've been sorry ever since."

In a movie theater, you can still find the cops on the screen. But the crooks are behind the refreshment stand.

I saw a movie that was real sexy. In one love scene, the ushers had to throw a bucket of water on the screen to break it up.

One western star says he keeps on making oaters because: Out West, men were men and women were women, and there's not much of that going on nowadays.

I saw a real stinker the other day. I should have been suspicious. They gave people their money back on the way in.

They just made a modern western. It doesn't take place in Dodge City, but in a shopping mall three miles out of town.

The producer of a movie about the poor white trash of a southern state invites a director to a screening. After the movie ends and the lights go up, the producer says, "Do you think the South will find it offensive?"

The director says, "Also the North, East, and West."

If you wipe off the windshield in a drive-in, you're married and with your wife.

There's always the story of the kid whose father was the Invisible Man. The kid wanted to follow in his father's footsteps, but he couldn't find them.

Everyone in the theater gleefully watched a young couple make love through the entire movie. As soon as the credits rolled, the theater manager came over.

"We're letting the picture go tomorrow, but we'd like to hold you kids over for another week."

John Wayne was fantastic during the earthquake. The first thing he did was draw all of the houses into a circle!

There's so much nudity in films this year that the Oscar for Best Costume Design will probably go to a dermatologist!

I went to one of those new movies last week that was so bloody it was rated "O-positive!"

## MUGGERS

I was mugged by an unemployed bus driver the other day, but he wouldn't take my money. I didn't have the exact change.

I live in a wild part of town. If you want to shake hands, you have to reach in your wallet pocket.

An American, a Frenchman, and a Pole were walking down the street when a mugger jumped out of a dark alley. In his hand, he held a syringe and said, "Give me your money or I'll inject you with this AIDS virus. The American and Frenchman didn't hesitate. They handed over their wallets and walked on.

The Pole said, "I won't give you a nickel. Inject away."

The mugger injected him and ran off.

The Pole caught up with friends. The American said, "Are you crazy? How could you let him inject you?"

The Pole said, "Nothing'll happen. I'm wearing a condom."

A team of three muggers catch a man on a dark street. He resists with the fury of a dozen men. Finally, they wrestle him to the ground. Going through his pockets, they find he only has a dime on him.

One of the muggers shakes his head and says, "Good thing for us he didn't have a quarter."

## MUSEUMS

Two youngsters were in a museum with their class. When they reached an Egyptian exhibit, they stopped to look at a mummy and the card in front of it. One kid said, "It says, 2328 B.C. I wonder what that means."

The second kid said, "Must be the license number of the car that hit him."

Then there was the mummy who went to jail. He got a bum wrap.

## MUSIC

He was a musician. He emptied jugs for hillbilly bands.

A struggling musician went to a doctor and reported on his condition, saying, "Doc, I can't go to the bathroom."

Writing out a prescription, the doctor said, "These pills will do the job."

The musician left but returned a week later. "Doctor, I still haven't gone to the bathroom."

The doctor wrote out a second prescription. "These are stronger. They should do the trick."

A week later the musician came back, still with bad news. The doctor looked at him and said, "What do you do for a living?"

"I'm a musician."

"Why didn't you tell me before?" With that, the doctor wrote out another prescription—for food.

"Did you notice how my voice filled the hall?"

"I even noticed people leaving to make room for it."

I go to the opera whether I need the sleep or not.

Some people think a harp is a nude piano.

The mother beamed as her young daughter auditioned with a great love song. Another mother nearby murmured at the strange notes the daughter was coming up with. The proud mother said, "She got her voice from me."

The other mother said, "You were damned lucky to get rid of it."

Two people told me not to sing—a doctor and a musician.

"I used to play violin in the orchestra, and each time I played, I got bumps in the back of my head."

"Music inspires you that much?"

"No, I used to sit in front of the trombone player."

My nephew just went to Europe to study violin. The neighbors sent him.

"What can I do with my voice now that it's trained?"

"Hang around, and if there's smoke you can yell, 'Fire.' "

I know a big-band leader whose wife keeps his books. And also his male singer.

A young composer says to a music critic, "What's your opinion of my work?"

The critic answers, "I believe it will be performed long after composers like Bach and Beethoven are forgotten."

"Really?"

"Yes, indeed, and not a minute before!"

The greatest war song ever written: "Here Comes the Bride."

She brought a record player home last night. A six-foot disc jockey.

She's a terrible singer. A frog makes the same noise, and you can also eat its legs.

My wife has a terrible voice. She sang around the house the other day, and the canary threw itself to the cat.

A terrible violinist finishes a composition, and someone from the audience yells up to him, "Play Tchaikovsky's Violin Concerto."

"Again?"

The local reverend runs into a parishioner who hasn't attended church for a while. The reverend asks for an explanation.

The parishioner says, "About three months ago, my daughter started taking harp lessons. Now I'm not as eager to get to heaven as I once was."

It was the Irish who invented the bagpipe. A couple of years later, they gave it to the Scots and told them it was a musical instrument.

A hillbilly and his bride went to Pittsburgh for their honeymoon and bought tickets for the performance of a touring musical show. At the end of the first act, the hillbilly presented himself at the box office and paid five dollars extra to have his seat changed from the balcony to the orchestra floor. Ten minutes after the second act started, he was back at the box office. "Give me my money back," he demanded. "That's the same damn show that's playing upstairs!"

An older man who enjoyed his retirement by reading in his garden hours on end returned with a complete drum set borrowed from a neighbor boy.

"I had no idea you played the drums," his wife said.

"I can't," said the man, "and now, neither can that boy!"

Every morning Mrs. Feldz practiced piano for an hour. She played with great enthusiasm. Unfortunately, she still played terribly.

One day, a piano tuner showed up.

"I didn't order a tuner," she said.

"No," he answered, "but your neighbors did."

A teenager comes home from a rock-and-roll concert, and his mother asks him how it went. The teenager says, "It was great, Mom. You would have hated it."

A henpecked husband arrived late with his nagging wife. "What are they playing?" she asked.

"The Fifth Symphony," he replied.

"You dummy!" she said. "We've already missed four of them!"

A piano teacher addressed a problem student: "If you don't behave, I'm going to tell your parents you have real talent!"

The neighbors must really like my piano playing. Just last week, they broke my front windows so they could hear better.

## NAIVE

He tricked her into marriage. He told her she was pregnant.

He's really naive. He has a connect-a-dot sex manual called *The Joy of Tracing.*

When she serves breast of veal, it wears a bra.

She heard a rumor that Procter and Gamble were going to split and felt terrible. They'd been together so long.

He's pretty naive. He was invited to a pot party, and he brought Tupperware.

## NAMES

Emily Brown comes back from her honeymoon all bright and glowing. Mabel asks her, "What's your married name?"

Emily says, "I'm Mrs. Peter Zgfrdslapaska."

Mabel says, "Gee, you must really love the guy."

A woman who was expecting twins ended up with quadruplets. Asked about the name problem, she replied, "No problem. I just added two names. Now it's Adolph, Rudolph, Getoff, and Stay-off."

"Isn't that Hortense?"
"She looks relaxed to me."

I know a couple named Mr. and Mrs. Smith. They never went on a honey-moon. They were too embarrassed to sign a hotel register.

I know a guy named Zybkqrst. He made a fortune renting it out to eye charts.

There was a man named Kissinger. He hated the name, so he changed it to Can-trell. After a while, Cantrell bored him, so he became Stevens. Then he became Baker. Before long, his friends were confused. They didn't know who was Kissinger now.

## NAVY

Two sailors are talking about their fu-tures after the war. One says that he plans to live in California.
    The other says, "Not me. I'm going to put an oar on my shoulder and keep walking until somebody says, 'What's that you're carrying?' and that's where I'm going to settle down."

The captain tells his men, "This isn't your ship. This isn't my ship. This is our ship."

One of the crew yells out, "Good, let's sell it!"

He was a toadman in the navy. That's like a frogman, but he also gives the enemy warts.

He had a big job on a submarine. When it wanted to dive, he held its nose.

We've just come up with a submarine that can submerge in ten seconds. You have to take your hat off to the sailor boys, especially those still on deck.

The chief petty officer is teaching some new sailors about naval nomenclature. To explain the difference between fore and aft, he asked one of the rookies, "If you're walking toward the stern, in which direction are you going?"
    "Aft."
    "Good. Which direction would you be walking if you were walking toward the bow?"
    "Aft backwards."

## NEAT/SLOPPY

One woman complained, "My husband has everything, and I wish he'd hang it up once in a while."

He only kisses his wife when he has no napkin.

He's a real slob. There's so much dirt under the rug, it's uphill to the coffee table.

She's real neat. She puts newspapers under the cuckoo clock.

She's very neat. When she's having company, she runs around putting in fresh light bulbs.

He carries his neatness too far. Who else irons shoelaces?

## NEIGHBORS

This man has had it up to his throat with his wife, so he packs some clothes and moves out into the garage. However, he continues to do little chores around the house—mow the law, repairs, weed. The wife, meanwhile, brings him food a few times a day, cleans up for him, and so on.

One day, a friend asks the man, "Why don't you just pack up and move?"

The man says, "Well, to tell you the truth, she makes a pretty good neighbor."

I live in a tough but quiet neighborhood. All night long in the streets, you can hear people whispering for help.

Summer must be over. My neighbors just returned my lawn furniture.

## NERVOUS

He's so nervous, he can thread the needle on a sewing machine when it's on.

A man runs into an old friend who says, "Gee, Tom, you look very stressed."

"Stressed? You're kidding. Look how slowly I'm twitching."

Nervousness is when you open your cedar chest to get your winter clothes out, and you hear the moths burp.

I'm so used to being tense that when I'm calm, I get nervous.

"What's the difference between worry and panic?"

"About twenty-eight days."

## NEWLYWEDS

"What's the most common cause of death for newlyweds?"

"Eating at home."

He carried his bride into the new home. When he put her down, she smiled and said, "Pick a room you want me to be good in."

## NEW YEAR'S

The only thing more depressing than staying in on New Year's Eve is going out.

As they were getting dressed for their New Year's party, she accused him of being a procrastinator. So he stopped addressing the Christmas cards and left.

The masquerade is going full swing. At the stroke of midnight, the guests cheer and kiss their partners. Later, the Bronsons start home. Mr. B. says, "When you kissed me at midnight, did you know it was me?"

"I certainly did. Did you know it was me?"

"Yup. It's a shame too. We might both have enjoyed it."

You know it's been a wild New Year's party when you wake up with tinsel in your shorts.

## NEW YORK

Two pigeons fly over New York. One of them releases some droppings, which float downward and spread out. The other pigeon says, "Boy, a little crap goes a long way in this town."

If you go to a fancy Manhattan restaurant, you'd better tip the maître d' when you ask for a corner table. I didn't, and got one at Oak and Maple in Cleveland.

There's a pothole on Sixty-fifth Street in New York that hasn't ever been repaired. The crews can't get close enough to fix it because they're afraid of the bends.

She's from Buffalo and you see the resemblance.

Two sardines decide to take a trip to Manhattan. One says, "Let's take the train."

The other says, "What, and be squeezed in like people?"

This young actress misses Hollywood so much when she's in New York, twice a week she has a man come in and expose himself.

There's a snazzy new restaurant off Park Avenue where prices are so outrageous that when you find a pearl in your oyster, you break even.

"How was the limbo invented?"

"A Haitian sneaking into a pay toilet."

In New York, when you make up your budget, you have to put aside a certain amount for holdups.

New York is a really crooked town. I saw a man paying off a cop with counterfeit money.

In New York, cabs are very expensive. It's cheaper to get slugged by a mugger and wait for an ambulance.

Some New Yorkers are complaining. They wish the city would collect the garbage as often as it does taxes.

New York has a great snow-removal system. One snowplow pushes it to the next block. The snowplow from that block pushes it to the next block. This goes on until the snow is worn out.

**A** New Yorker claims he went eighteen days without water. I once had the same waiter.

**A**nybody in New York who speaks good English must be a foreigner.

**H**er arms loaded with packages, a woman boards a New York bus. No one offers her a seat. But one gent proves to be amazingly chivalrous, whispering to her, "Be alert. I get off at Twenty-third Street."

**A** New Yorker is uncomfortable in the subway and turns to another passenger nearby and says, "Damned foreigners!"
   Another passenger behind them reacts and says, "Lady, I don't see you wearing an Indian blanket!"

**T**he subways are getting better. This morning, I had a strap all to myself.

**"W**hat do you think of Flushing, New York?"
   "Great idea."

**A** self-styled street preacher is haranguing a crowd in the park. "You are faced with hell," he says. "Heat, nothing but heat. Bodies pressed together so you can't breathe. That's hell."
   A voice says, "Hell, nothing. That's Coney Island."

**T**hings bad in New York? Today the Statue of Liberty traded in her lamp for a cup and pencils.

**M**anhattan is an island about thirteen miles long and five hours wide.

**H**alf of New Yorkers dream of having their own apartments. The other half dream of breaking into them.

**A**mazing city, New York. Where else can you buy mutual funds with your welfare check?

**N**ew Yorkers aren't very warm. If it weren't for the muggings, there'd be no personal contact at all.

**A** mugger stopped a man in a New York side street and demanded money. The man had no cash, but afraid that he'd get hurt, he said, "Let me give you a check."
   The mugger answered, "You're nuts. Why would I take your check? I don't even know you."

**M**any years ago, New York was the site of a caveman colony. One of the cavemen invented the wheel. Two days later, somebody stole his hubcaps.

**N**ew York is the only city in the world where friendliness is a felony.

**T**here's no trust in New York. Muggers are now demanding identification.

**T**hey keep the animals in the Central Park Zoo behind bars. It's for their safety.

They say that New York is not governable. That's just a rumor started by people who live there.

In New York, they don't give you the key to the city. They just send over a guy who shows you how to pick the lock.

Keep New York clean—throw your trash in New Jersey.

New York is the only town in the world where you can park your car, walk two blocks, and find your hubcaps for sale.

In New York, people from all walks of life—run.

New York is a great town where something happens every minute. Most of the time, it goes unsolved.

New York muggers are up-to-date. They've even started taking credit cards.

If you ask a cop directions in New York, he says, "Well you go to Seventy-ninth Street, and if you make it . . ."

In New York everybody runs—you're either a jogger running to keep your figure, or a pedestrian running to keep your wallet.

## NIGHTLIFE

It was an Indian nightclub. They charged twenty-four dollars for a Manhattan.

Business was so bad, the B-girls were dancing with the chairs.

This nightclub had the nicest table I was ever under.

A customer listens to the pianist and asks, "Have you always been a pianist in a piano bar?"
  The musician says, "No, I used to play the violin."
  "Why did you stop?"
  "The tip glass kept falling off."

The other day they had the ropes up. The boss was trying to hang himself.

I can't understand why cabaret owners make you wear a shirt and tie to go in and watch a topless-bottomless dancer.

## NOSES

When I kissed her, I knew it was puppy love. Her nose was cold.

I wouldn't say her nose was long, but she had to wear her glasses sidesaddle.

Most people have tiny noses. They have to breathe all day. Not him. He takes one breath, and it keeps him going.

He's got a huge nose. Birds going north perch on it.

He had a crooked nose. One time it got caught in his ear, he sneezed and blew out his brains.

## NOUVEAU RICHE

A couple, recently the beneficiaries of an inheritance, go to a very posh resort for a weekend. As the bellhop takes their luggage, the man says to the desk clerk, "Can you change a hundred for me?"

The clerk says, "At this hotel, a hundred *is* change."

This couple who have made it big move into their new forty-room house. After dinner the husband says, "Let's have dessert in the library."

The wife says, "We can't. It closes at seven."

## NUDISTS

Lady Godiva rode down the street side-saddle. And on the left, people kept yelling, "Hooray for our side."

Then there was the midget who entered a dancing contest at a nudist colony and almost got clubbed to death.

These two nudists decided to break up. They'd been seeing too much of each other.

It's great to be a nudist. You don't have to sit around all day in a wet bathing suit.

Nudists are so relaxed. They just let it all hang out.

You can always tell a nearsighted man at a nudist colony. It isn't hard.

There they are, lolling on the grass. He says, "I love you."

She looks down and says, "I don't have to ask you how much."

Nudists have the right idea. There's nothing like a day in the sun to put color back into your cheeks.

A salesman knocked on the door of a house. When the door was opened, he saw the lady of the house completely nude. At his puzzled look, the lady said, "I'm a nudist."

She opened the door fully and invited the salesman in. As he started to make a pitch for his wares, he also started to fill out a questionnaire. He came to a line and asked, "How many children do you have?"

"Eight."

"How come?"

"Not all salesmen are as dumb as you."

I went to a party at a nudist colony, but it was no fun. Everybody got so drunk, they started to put on their clothes.

A young male nudist introduced himself to an attractive and curvaceous young lady. As they started to stroll through the grounds, the young man said, "Don't look now, but I think I'm in love with you."

They don't like midgets at nudist colonies. They have their noses in everybody's business.

On Saturday night, at a nudist colony, they had a masquerade ball. I didn't have time to get an outfit, so I backed in and went as a Parker House roll.

At the nudist masquerade ball, the first prize was won by a young lady who put on black gloves, black shoes, and went as the five of spades.

For a man, the first day at a nudist colony is generally the hardest.

"Why don't women wear clothes in a nudist colony?"
"Nothing looks good on them!"

A husband allowed his wife to talk him into going to a nudist colony. Once there, the husband became even more timid than he usually was. In their room, the wife kept insisting that they undress and walk around the colony. The husband refused. Eventually, the wife prevailed, but the husband demanded one compromise.
When they came out into the grassy fields of the colony, he had on no clothes, but in front of his personal treasure he held a newspaper.
Another couple passed by, and the man of the couple looked and said, "Gee, I wish I had one that could read!"

I'd say that the fastest thing in the world is a nudist who spills coffee.

Think of the advantages of nudism. You don't have to put out your hand to see if it's raining.

What's wrong with being a nudist? I was born that way.

They had a nudist convention in town last week, but there wasn't one mention in the news. But then nudists always get little coverage.

I think I'm a nudist. My wife wears the pants, my son uses my suits, and the IRS took the shirt off my back.

She went to a nudist colony and found out that no matter what Lincoln said, all men aren't created equal.

One nudist was bashful, so he had his hand enlarged.

I saw this girl at a nudist colony. Nothing looked good on her.

### NUMBERS

A man went to a brothel and was told that he was in luck. This week, they were having a contest with a big prize for the man who could satisfy all ten girls. Proud of his sexual prowess, the man makes love to eight of the women. When he is done with the eighth, the madam nods and says, "Okay, move on to number seven."
"Wait a minute. I'm on number nine."

"No. You just finished number six."

The man started to complain and demanded his money back.

The madam said, "Tell you what. Because there's a doubt, you can start at number one again."

---

A woman is in court, and the judge asks her about her age. She hems and haws. The judge says, "You must tell me, and you must tell me the truth, because you're under oath."

The woman says, "I'm thirty-two and a few months."

"How many months?"

"Sixty."

---

"Honey, rate me on a scale of one to ten."

"Can I use fractions?"

---

He was the unlucky victim of the number 13—twelve jurors and a judge.

---

One and one could make a dozen—if they got married early enough.

---

A wife kept nagging her husband about his past. "How many women have you gone with in your life? How many?"

One day he answered her. "You'll get mad."

"I won't get mad."

"All right. Let's see. One, two, three, four, five, you, seven."

## NYMPHOS

They have a brand-new club for nymphomaniacs. The meetings are great. All you do is examine new applicants.

---

A nymphomaniac decided to write a book about her illness. She never got to page two because the research kept getting in the way.

---

"How can you tell a Jewish wife is a nymphomaniac?" ·

"She's willing to have sex on the day she has her hair done."

---

"How does a nympho turn on the light after sex?"

"She opens the car door."

---

"What does a nympho say after a night of really good sex?"

"So, are all you guys on the same team?"

---

"What's the difference between a nympho and *The Titanic*?"

"We know exactly how many men went down on *The Titanic*."

---

A nymphomaniac finds she's out of change, so she puts in a collect call. The operator says, "Name, please?"

"Bonnie."

"I can't hear you."

"Bonnie—*B* like in breast, *O* like in orgy, *N* like in nut, *N* like in the other nut . . ."

"**W**hy did the nympho call off her trip to Scandinavia?"

"She found out a fourteen-inch Viking was only a TV set."

"**H**ow many nymphos does it take to screw in a light bulb?"

"None. They only screw in hot tubs."

"**H**ow can you tell a Jewish wife is a nymphomaniac?"

"She wants sex every month."

"**H**ow does a nympho practice safe sex?"

"She locks the car door."

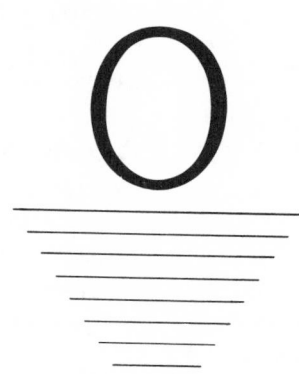

## OFF-COLOR JOKES

"Why did the pervert cross the street?"
"His thing was in a chicken."

A nun and a priest are in the desert on a camel heading for Mecca. In the hot, blistering sun, the camel soon stops, whinnies, and falls down. The nun panics. She rips off her clothes to make a shelter of some sort. Seeing a woman in the nude for the first time in many years, the priest finds his manliness soon becomes erect. The nun asks, "What is that?"

The priest says, "That is the stuff that brings life."

The nun says, "Well, shove it up the camel's rear end and see if we can get to Mecca."

A laborer gets a note from his shift boss, asking him to bring in a sample for testing. Not certain of what is meant by "sample," the laborer asks another laborer what it means. An hour later, the first laborer comes home, sporting a big black-and-blue shiner. His wife asks what had happened. The laborer explains, "You see, I asked this guy something, and he told me to piss in a jar. So

I tell him to crap in a box. And that's how it started."

A man points down to a barrel of apples and tells his friend, "I'm going to patent these."

The friend says, "Apples? You're nuts. You can't patent those."

"Taste one."

The friend obliges and says, "Amazing, this tastes like a pear."

"Try the other side."

"This side tastes like a peach."

"Take another apple."

"Hey, this one tastes like a banana."

"Try the other side."

"This side tastes like cherries. But I'll tell you something. You should have one that tastes like pussy."

"Try the dark one."

"Jesus! This tastes like crap."

"Try the other side."

One brothel closed for a holiday, so a sign was put up on the front door—GO SCREW YOURSELF!

It is the honeymoon night. The bride rubs a half-dozen sweet-scented lotions all over her body, saving an especially oily one for her private grotto. Her husband watches her for a while, then says, "Sweetheart, can I borrow that string of pearls I got you for your birthday?"

"Why on earth do you need them?"

"Because I ain't going into a mess like that without chains!"

Then there was this woman who spent a weekend in a fishing camp with five guys. She came back with a red snapper.

A man walks into a doctor's office with a frog on his head. The doctor asks, "What's the problem?"

The frog says, "My ass."

"What about your ass?"

"You gotta do something." The frog points to the man and goes on, "Two weeks ago, this was just another wart!"

A corpse is brought into the funeral parlor. The mortician is stunned by the size of the penis. It measures a foot. The old assistant says, "I have one just like that."

"Twelve inches?"

"No. Dead."

Tommy had always loved Sally's boobs. He saw them everywhere he went. He dreamed about them. Finally, he ran into Sally at the coffee machine and said, "I'll give you a thousand bucks if you'll come into the supply closet and let me suck on those gorgeous things for five minutes."

Sally agreed. They went into the closet, and Tommy feasted. With each suck, he moaned, "I don't know . . . I don't know . . . I don't know."

Finally, Sally said, "What don't you know?"

Tommy said, "Where I'm going to get the thousand dollars."

"If you're in the jungle and you come upon a gorilla, what should you do?"

"Wipe it off quick and run like hell."

"Why does a cannon roar?"

"Wouldn't you if one of your balls was shot off?"

"How do you get five pounds of meat out of a fly?"

"Unzip it."

"Why is a Catholic priest like a Christmas tree?"

"Both have balls that are purely ornamental."

"Do you know how I make mine twelve inches long? I fold it in half!"

"How did the poor girl become a countess?"

"She went down for the count."

"How did the Statue of Liberty get VD?"

"It was either from the mouth of the Hudson or from the rear of the Staten Island Ferry."

"Why is a cheap whore like an elephant?"

"Both will roll on their backs for peanuts."

"What's the difference between having a job for ten years and a wife for ten years?"

"After ten years, most jobs still suck."

"How come Popeye's tool doesn't rust?"

"He dips it in Olive Oyl."

"What do you get if you cross an uptight girl and a computer?"

"You get a computer that never goes down on you."

"What do you get when you cross a computer with a hooker?"

"A fucking know-it-all!"

"Is a circumcised penis a good deal?"

"Certainly. It's about twenty percent off."

"What's the ultimate sign of trust?"

"Cannibals doing sixty-nine."

"What's the difference between light and hard?"

"You can sleep with a light on."

"What's more embarrassing than when your doctor tells you that you've got a venereal disease?"

"When your dentist tells you."

"What has a cow four and a woman only two?"

"Feet, you horny bastard!"

## OFFICE

A boss came in one morning and found his accountant embracing his secretary. The boss asked, "Is this what I pay you for?"

The accountant answered, "No, I do this for free."

This office had a Xerox machine that was always breaking down. The boss put up a sign: PLEASE DON'T BREAK MY REPRODUCTIVE EQUIPMENT.

A boss asked his new secretary, "Would you like to come out to my beach house on the weekend and we could have some fun?"

The secretary said, "I'd love to. And I'll bring along my boyfriend in case your wife wants to have some fun too."

Sadly, the boss said to the employee who was leaving, "We'll never be able to replace you, especially at the salary we've been paying you."

The new employee couldn't understand what all the fuss was about his coming in late. "After all," he mused, "I do leave early!"

The new secretary can't touch-type. She's a-huntin' pecker.

The boss wasn't pleased when Bronson came in and asked for the afternoon off as it was his fiftieth wedding anniversary. An angry look on his face, the boss said, "Bronson, don't expect me to put up with this every fifty years!"

I had to fire my secretary yesterday because she lacked experience. All she could do was take shorthand and type.

The boss called in a young executive who was leaving the company and said, "I'm really sorry to see you go, Smith, because you've been like a son to me: lazy, fresh, arrogant!"

The morning after the annual office party, the accountant asks his wife, "Did I do anything dumb last night?"

The wife says, "Did you ever! You tried to make love to the boss's wife, and he fired you."

The accountant says, "Who cares? Screw him!"

The wife says, "I did. You go back to work Monday."

The inspirational message on the bulletin board read: TODAY IS THE TOMORROW YOU WORRIED ABOUT YESTERDAY.

Under it, somebody had penciled in, AND NOW YOU KNOW WHY.

One man was given the form for all new job applicants. Where it said, *Marital Status*, he wrote, *Not speaking*.

The boss is the only one who watches the clock during a coffee break.

"How can you tell the new secretary has been using the computer?"

"There's White-Out on the monitor."

The new girl is standing in front of the paper shredder, looking very confused. Another secretary, walking by, says, "Do you need some help?"

The new girl says, "Yeah, how does this work?"

"It's simple."

The secretary takes the important report from the new girl's hand and starts feeding it into the shredder.

The new girl says, "Thanks, but where do the new copies come out?"

I asked my new secretary to take some dictation. She said, "Where to?"

He used to break his neck working. He hired a cute secretary. Now he breaks his work necking.

The smart boss always has staff meetings at four in the afternoon on Friday. That way, nobody disagrees with him.

The office manager heard a noise coming from the supply closet. Opening the door, he found one of the secretaries in an embrace with the shipping clerk.

The office manager asked brusquely, "What's this?"

The secretary said, "We're both on a break, and we don't drink coffee!"

An employer approached the young lad in the stockroom and asked, "Do you believe in life after death, young fellow?"

"No. I'm sorry I don't."

"Well, then maybe you can explain your grandfather coming into this office an hour after you went to his funeral."

Jeff, a nice young man, came to work for a large company. There were many pretty women around, and the young man found them disconcerting. He went to his supervisor, who heard him out and said, "Jeff, my young friend, don't yield to temptation. Resist and you'll get your reward in heaven."

Jeff went back to work. He was good-looking, however, and some of the girls indicated with smiles and a swagger or two that they'd like to get to know him better. The supervisor happened by a little later, and Jeff stopped him, saying,

"It's really hard. The girls are so pretty."

"Resist and you'll get your reward in heaven."

"And what will that reward be?"

A co-worker nearby yelled over, "A bale of hay, jackass!"

I found the secret of a clean desk—a giant wastepaper basket.

Our office is on edge all the time. We have a computer with ulcers!

An enterprising boss put up a sign saying DO IT NOW! The next day, the cashier absconded with the contents of the safe, the secretary ran off with the boss's son, the office boy urinated in the coffee machine, and the rest of the staff went to a ball game!

## OLD

You know you're aging when a cute girl goes by and your Pacemaker makes the garage door go up.

He just turned eighty and found out why he's constipated—cobwebs.

The worst thing about growing old for a man is that he has to sleep with a grandmother.

He doesn't have an enemy in the world. They're all dead.

She's so old, undertakers send her estimates.

You're old if you need an orthopedic tuxedo.

A ninety-year-old man was arrested for rape, but he won his case easily. The evidence wouldn't stand up in court.

Nobody lives forever, but she's trying.

She knew Howard Johnson when he had only two flavors.

The ancient Greeks had a word for it—and she was there to hear it.

He's so old, he has an autographed Bible.

This man went out with this older lady who drank, smoked, and danced all evening. He told her to act her age, so she died.

He's at the age where all the numbers in his little black book are urologists.

Two old men are sitting on a bench in the park. One says, "I just married a beautiful girl of twenty-two. She adores me. She can't get enough sex. She thinks I'm a great lover."

The second man says, "What's bad about that?"

The first one says, "I can't remember where I live."

I won't say he's old, but the picture on his driver's license is by Rembrandt.

I don't know how old she is, but when Cain killed Abel, she was on the jury.

I don't know how old she is, but when she and her husband got divorced, she got the cave.

He's real old. He reads *Playboy* for the same reason he reads *National Geographic*. It shows him places he'll never get to visit.

When you get to be ninety-five, you don't have to worry much about peer pressure.

What's all the hullabaloo about getting older? I know men who can do the same things at ninety that they could do at eighty-nine.

A lot of older men go into retirement. For his wife, retirement means twice the husband and half the income.

He's so old, his first job was parking covered wagons!

"What does an old woman have between her breasts?"
"Her navel."

A grandmother was delighted to baby-sit her two very young grandsons. On the way to the park, she ran into a friend who looked at the two youngsters and said, "These must be your grandchildren. How old are they?"

The grandmother said, "The doctor is four, and the lawyer is two."

He may be getting old, but he's still in there pinching.

There are so many wrinkles on his forehead, he has to screw on his hat.

They asked a man how he'd managed to live to a hundred and five.

He answered, "I stopped smoking last year."

He looked like a million—every year of it!

I don't know how old she is, but she has antique jewelry she bought when it was new.

As Confucius said—and she was there when he said it!

You know you're getting old when you sit down in a rocker and can't get it started!

"What's the most useless thing on Aunt Phyllis?"

"Uncle Howard."

Ruth is ninety-one and goes to the doctor, complaining of terrible stomach pains. After an examination, the doctor tells her she's with child.

"How's that possible?" she asks. "Max is ninety-three. We still fool around, but he's ninety-three."

The doctor says, "I'm sure you're pregnant."

As soon as she's out of the doctor's office, Ruth goes to a public phone and calls her husband, saying, "You rotten bastard, you knocked me up."

Max says, "Really? Who is this calling?"

My ninety-year-old uncle just went to a flower show in the nude. He won first prize for best dried arrangement.

## OLD-FASHIONED TOWN

"I come from an old-fashioned town. In my town, people voted for Calvin Coolidge."

"That's nothing. A lot of people voted for Calvin Coolidge."

"Last year?"

There's a town in Iowa that's really old-fashioned. You can get arrested there for running a red traffic candle.

My hometown is old-fashioned. The local paper didn't come out last week. The quill broke.

## OLD MAIDS

Then there was the old maid who saw a wanted poster in the post office and offered two hundred dollars more than the police.

Then there was the old maid who heard about a Peeping Tom in the neighborhood. So she cleaned every window in the house.

A woman who swears that no man has ever made love to her has a right to swear.

A mugger stopped a spinster and said, "Don't worry. I just want all your money."

The spinster says, "Get out of here. You're just like all the other men."

Loretta, an old maid, wakes up in the middle of the night to find a young man trying to burgle her apartment. Holding a gun on him, she demands that he make love to her. If not, she'll call the police.

The young man tries to become aroused, but Loretta is wrinkled and has a sallow complexion and matted hair. No matter how long the young man tries, he can't get into shape to perform. When Loretta tries to smile encouragement, he sees that she has no teeth.

Sighing, the young man says, "What's the number? I better call the police."

I saw this old maid go through the detection area at the airport fourteen times to be frisked. And she wasn't going anywhere.

She wanted to be a calendar girl, but she couldn't get any dates.

She was so far gone, not even a Doberman would pinch her!

She was two-thirds married once. She and the preacher were there.

She used to drive through red lights so cops would whistle at her!

She's so eager to get married, she pays a judge fifty dollars a week to tell her which couples are breaking up!

I won't say she's untouched, but when she went to the Virgin Islands, they gave her a hero's welcome.

Cucumbers are three for a dollar. An old maid takes three, saying, "I suppose I can always eat the other two."

## OLD NEIGHBORHOOD

My old street has so many potholes, it looks like a pinball machine with curbs!

There are so many holes and breaks in my old street, anybody whose car has its wheels aligned is from out of town!

## OPERA

The opera is a place where when a guy gets stabbed, he doesn't die—he sings.

*Pagliacci* is a terrible opera. It only has one good laugh.

When the tenor finished singing the aria, the applause from the audience was deafening. To a man and woman, the audience insisted that he sing the aria again. After he obliged, the reaction was just as strong. "More, more, more," the audience roared. Eight times he sang the aria.

Indicating that the applause be withheld, he stepped forward and told the audience, "This is the greatest moment of my life. Eight times you have made me sing this one aria."

A voice from the balcony yelled out, "And we're going to make you keep singing it until you get it right!"

One opera singer was so bad, she was charged for mutiny on the high C's.

A famous opera star is touring the Wild West with her company. She's captured by a bandit and says, "You must let me go immediately. I'm a prima donna."

The bandit says, "Prove it. Sing for me."

The prima donna says, "Without an orchestra? Without being paid? And in front of a scraggly crowd like yours? Never!"

The bandit says, "Let her go. She's a prima donna all right."

## OPPORTUNITY

The trouble with opportunity is that it looks bigger coming than going.

A soldier married a girl in the service who happened to be a master sergeant. He had the opportunity to do what GIs since time began have wanted to do.

This young man takes a date for a drive. As they reach a small wooded area, the engine starts to act up. The young man says, "I wonder what that knocking is."

The young lady answers, "One thing I can tell you—it's not opportunity."

When the door to opportunity doesn't open to polite knocks, kick it in.

Opportunity knocks only once. Temptation bangs on the door for years.

## OPTIMISTS & PESSIMISTS

Did you ever hear a pessimist count his blessings? Five, four, three, two . . .

It's a sad fact, but pessimists have more experience than optimists.

He's a real optimist. He has a burial suit with two pair of pants.

He's a real optimist. He brings a fifth to a New Year's Eve party and saves the cork.

An optimist believes that after he marries his secretary, he'll still be able to dictate to her!

A pessimist is a man who thinks that God created the earth in six days and then was laid off.

An optimist is a guy who goes down to city hall to find out when his marriage license expires.

An optimist refuses to believe that he's unpopular. He merely believes that his answering machine is.

An optimist is a fellow who grabs a fishing pole when he discovers his basement is flooded.

An optimist thinks the glass is half-full. The pessimist thinks it's half-empty. The realist knows that before long he'll have to wash the glass.

A pessimist believes that women are bad. An optimist hopes so!

An optimist is a eighty-year-old bridegroom who asks the landlord of a potential apartment if kids are allowed.

I saw a real optimist today—a man whistling at girls through his false teeth.

A pessimist believes that life is a car wash, and he's on a bike.

A pessimist is a guy who's afraid that someplace someone is having a good time.

An optimist is a man who'd go into a restaurant flat broke, order oysters, and expect to pay the bill with the pearls he'll find inside.

An optimist stays up on New Year's Eve to see the new year in. A pessimist stays up to make sure the old year left.

## ORGASMS

"How can you tell when a woman who's been married five years has an orgasm?"
"She says, 'Myrna, I have to hang up now.' "

God created orgasms so teenage boys would know when to stop screwing.

"What's the difference between a married woman and a volcano?"
"A volcano never fakes an eruption."

"How does a macho man know when a woman's having an orgasm?"
"He doesn't care."

The other day I had such a loud orgasm, it almost woke my wife.

A man goes to his doctor and complains that he has been unable to realize an orgasm more than three times a day during sex with his wife.
The doctor says, "It's probably a temporary condition."
The man says, "Good. For a while there, I thought it was the masturbation in between."

## ORGIES

Never tell your mother you're going to an orgy. She'll make you take a sweater.

I think I was invited to an orgy today. The letter came RSBVD!

You're aging if group sex is when a second person shows up.

I'd never go to an orgy. Do you know what they do to crush the grapes?

At a wild resort, a man happens to walk into a room and sees an orgy in full swing. At his stunned look, one of the participants says, "What's the matter? Haven't you ever seen seven people in love before?"

Then there was this sexpot who went to an orgy. She was the good time had by all.

## OVERSEXED

If you're oversexed, get married. It'll help you taper off.

What do you give somebody who's had everybody?

She was so innocent, she wouldn't molest a fly unless it was open.

She doesn't run after men anymore. She bought skates.

He always had sex on his mind. Every thirty days, he'd get a nosebleed.

He has a water bed with whitecaps and a lifeguard.

She must be a napkin. She's always on somebody's lap.

In high school sex classes, she used to be the homework.

To attract men, she puts something behind her ears—her legs.

She's been coupled and uncoupled more than an Amtrak locomotive.

She just came down with a rare ailment—an ingrown mattress!

She was twenty-five before she found out cars had front seats.

Her phone number is 555-3109. If the line's busy, that means the fleet's in.

Men like her because of her vocabulary. "Yes" is the greater part of it.

Every time she asks a man to say good night, he winds up saying good morning.

She's been picked up so often, she's beginning to grow handles.

He's really horny. His medic-alert bracelet reads—I'M A SEX FIEND. IN CASE OF ILLNESS, SEND FOR A BROAD.

She needs a man real bad. On her hotel-room doorknob, there's a sign that says, PLEASE DISTURB.

**M**en like her because she doesn't "no" much.

She had a great time in Acapulco. Somebody told her "*sí*" meant no.

She had a lot of trouble at the 4-H Club. She couldn't keep her calves together.

**S**he must be a debutante. She came out in 1950 and hasn't been home since.

**M**y girl hates to move. She'd have to change her phone number in a zillion phone booths.

**S**he just got fired from her job at the furniture factory. She kept losing her drawers.

# P

## PAIN

A man is in need of gum surgery, but he is afraid of the potential pain. The dentist tells him, "I have a patient who underwent the same surgery six months ago. Call him and find out about the pain."

The man places the call and asks the previous patient about the pain.

The previous patient says, "Let me put it this way. Two days ago, I fell off the roof and landed on some boiling tar. It was the first day in six months my gums didn't hurt."

I'm very sensitive to pain. I have to take Novocain for haircuts.

The pains of childbirth are indescribable. If men had babies, there would have been one.

## PARENTS

Half of the fun of fatherhood is getting there.

Never lend your car to anyone you gave birth to.

Parents are people who thought that the deductions would come in handy.

A parent is somebody who thinks he has dibs on the family car.

## PARKING

A man walked into a downtown car showroom and paid cash for a brand-new car in the window. The salesman said, "Shall we deliver it?"

The man said, "Leave it where it is. I'll never get a better parking place."

The trouble with the straight and narrow is that there's no place to park.

It's not so easy to get a parking ticket nowadays. First, you have to find a place to park.

Parking is real tough. If I squeeze into a parking place, I'm usually sexually satisfied for the week.

I parked in front of my office. Ten minutes later, another car pushed mine up and got into the space. Then a third car pushed the second car up. Five minutes after that, a fourth car pushed the third car up. My car got home an hour before I did.

Those meter maids are getting a little eager. Last week I got two parking tickets, and I don't even own a car.

I always wonder—do parking-lot attendants have licenses?

Do you remember when it cost more to buy a car than to park it?

The parking at this place is unique. A lot more compacts leave than ever came in.

A parking space is what disappears when you make a U-turn.

Parking is such a problem today. You even have to wait in line to get in a tow-away zone.

## PARROTS

A man buys an exquisite and expensive parrot for his mother. He comes to visit his mother a week later and is invited to dinner. His mother serves him a delicious bird. When he asks her what kind it was, she explains that she'd baked the parrot he'd sent her.

The man explodes, "How could you do that? That was a rare parrot. It cost two thousand dollars. It could talk ten languages."

The mother says, "If it could talk so many languages, why didn't it say something?"

A man goes to an animal auction. One parrot excites him, and he bids on it. Every time he makes a bid, there's another bid to top him. He finally wins. He goes over to the parrot and asks, "Can you talk?"

The parrot answers, "Who the hell do you think has been bidding against you for the last half hour?"

A man owns a parrot who has the run of the house. One day, however, the parrot won't return to his cage. The man puts out a special plate of sunflower seeds. The parrot swoops down, but his wings knock over a glass of whiskey. The parrot licks a little whiskey, chews a sunflower seed, licks some more whiskey, and flies up to the rafters again. The owner offers him fruit. The parrot says, "Want booze. More booze. More booze."

The man pours a little whiskey in the sunflower plate. Zooming down, the parrot empties the plate.

This goes on for hours. Finally, the parrot staggers into his cage and goes to sleep.

The next morning, the parrot wakes up with a giant hangover and says, "If I live to be a hundred, I'll never touch another sunflower seed again."

I know that birds talk. I bought a parrot last month. My telephone bill tripled.

I bought a South American parrot recently. I stood in front of his cage and tried to get him to say, "Good morning. Good morning."

The parrot answered, "NO HABLO INGLÉS."

So now he's teaching me Spanish.

A man feels that his bird isn't feeling well, so he puts the little bird into a carrier and goes to a veterinarian. The vet asks what the problem is. The man starts to answer, "I'm not sure, but—"

The parrot cuts in, "Listen, I'm not like your cat. I can talk for myself."

A man goes into a pet shop to buy a parrot. The clerk says, "We have three for sale. The red one speaks three languages and costs fifteen hundred dollars. The yellow one knows five languages and costs three thousand. The blue one over there costs ten thousand, but doesn't speak at all."

"Ten thousand? Why so much?"

"Well, we don't know what he does, but the other two call him 'Boss.' "

A parrot that had belonged to a hooker is being auctioned off. The auctioneer says, "What's the first offer on this gorgeous bird?"

A man raises his hand. "I'll give ten dollars."

A second says, "Twenty-five."

"Fifty," says a third.

The parrot says, "Make it a hundred, honey, and I'll be real nice to you."

I bought a parrot for fifty cents the other day. He doesn't talk, but he's a hell of a listener.

A woman buys a parrot and gets a very good price because the bird uses some curse words. When she gets the bird home, she covers it for a week so that it'll forget them. Finally, the woman takes the cover off, but her husband happens to come home from work at that exact time. The bird starts to screech and then says, "New madam. Same old customers."

A burglar breaks into a house and hears a voice say, "I see you. The saint sees you."

The burglar shrugs and heads for the bedroom. At the steps, he hears, "I see you. The saint sees you."

The burglar looks around, and in the corner of the den he sees that it's the voice of a parrot. He snickers and goes back to work. At the steps, he looks up to see a giant dog staring down at him. He hears the parrot say, "Sic 'im, Saint."

A man runs into an old friend who is carrying a parrot in a cage.

The man says, "Isn't that bird a lot of trouble?"

The friend says, "I use him for an alarm clock to get me up in the morning."

"How can that be?"

"I never hear the alarm on my clock, so I hang it right next to his cage. When it goes off, he says a few things that would wake anybody."

## PARTIES

I have an infallible way of getting my wife to leave a party. I start flirting with a good-looking woman.

You can always tell the host at a party. He's the one watching the clock.

"Did you have a nice time at the party?"
"So they tell me."

Why make your guests feel at home? If they wanted that, they would have stayed there.

Recently, they held a Reincarnation Ball. You came as you were.

I wouldn't say it was a dull get-together, but the dip was the life of the party.

"Didn't you hear me pounding on the wall?"
"That's okay. We were making a lot of noise ourselves."

What a party! First the ice was broken, then the glasses, then the dishes, then . . .

Was last night's party crowded?
Not under my table.

## PATIENTS

A patient calls his acupuncturist and says, "I have a terrible pain in my side."

The acupuncturist says, "Take two thumbtacks and call me in the morning."

The surgeon discussed the coming operation with a patient, asking, "Do you want a local anesthetic?"

The patient answered, "I can afford the best. Give me something imported."

## PENTAGON

The Pentagon just ordered a new tank for sixty million each—radio and heater extra!

Tanks, bombers, air-to-air missiles, submarines—to us, they're all military hardware. To the Pentagon, they're Toys-R-Us!

A young officer was assigned to a desk job at the Pentagon. At the end of a week, he was utterly confused by the red tape. He started to spend much of his time in the men's room. Noticing that he spent so much time there, a colonel asked him why. The young officer said, "Well, this is about the only place where anybody knows what he's doing!"

Our newest defense system has two hundred thousand moving parts. It also has nonmoving parts—like the Pentagon.

It must be very hard to buy a tank. Have you ever kicked a tread?

## PEOPLE

The trouble with human nature is that there are too many people connected to it.

There are more kids born in China than in India. And in India there are more kids born than in Turkey. I guess that proves more people talk turkey in India than in Turkey.

If you don't enjoy your own company, you're probably right.

## PERFUME

She has a new perfume. It doesn't make a man surrender, but it puts the girl in a darn good negotiating position.

They just came up with the world's greatest perfume. It can even compete with the Super Bowl.

At a store counter, the salesgirl is telling a customer that their newest perfume is irresistible.
    The customer says, "How come *you're* still working here?"

A salesgirl tried to sell me a perfume for two hundred dollars an ounce. That's four thousand a fifth!

My niece is looking for a perfume that'll overpower a man. She's tired of kung fu.

They have a new perfume that drives women crazy. It smells like credit cards.

They have a very powerful new perfume. On the bottle, it tells you not to use it if you're bluffing.

## PERSISTENCE

If you think nothing is impossible, try getting your name off a mailing list.

The store buyer says, "You salesmen are something. I've thrown fifteen of them out today."

The salesman says, "Yeah, and I was twelve of them."

## PETS

**A** man tasted some of his dog's pet food and liked it. The doctor told his wife that it would kill him. And it did. After he'd eaten it for a week, he got to chasing cars and ran himself to death.

**A** man told his wife, "I love my dog, but a man needs two friends."

His wife went out and bought him another dog!

**A** woman comes into a pet shop and asks for a dog to keep her company. The shopkeeper shows her a tiny dachshund. The woman says, "Aren't his legs too short?"

The shopkeeper says, "How can you say that? They all touch the ground at the same time."

**A**l had nothing to do, and being lonely, he went into a pet shop and looked around. Suddenly, from a small tank filled with rocks and greenery, he heard a voice say, "Take me home. Please take me home."

Al was stunned because the sound came from a tiny frog on a small rock. Naturally, Al had to buy the small frog. He brought it home and made a place for it in a small aquarium he had in the house. At midnight Al turned out the light to go to sleep when he heard the voice speak again. "Can I sleep with you?" the tiny voice asked.

Al shrugged his shoulders and allowed the frog into the bed. After a few moments, the frog said, "Can you kiss me good night?" Al didn't think that was too much to ask, so he leaned over and kissed the tiny green lips. Suddenly, there was a shimmering in the air, and the frog turned into a lovely naked sixteen-year-old-girl.

"And in summation, Your Honor, that is my client's total defense in this case."

**T**hen there was the pet-shop owner who made a fortune. He kept teaching his parrots to say, "I miss my brother."

**M**rs. Bronson's kitty isn't feeling well—a bad case of constipation. She takes it to the vet, who gives her a new kind of laxative. "Give her about six teaspoons of this, and she'll be better in no time."

Mrs. Bronson does as she's told and returns a week later. The vet asks, "How's your calf?"

"I don't have a calf. It was my cat who wasn't feeling well."

"Well how's your cat doing?"

"I'm not sure. The last time I saw her, she was heading toward the north end of town with ten other cats. Five were digging, three were covering, and two were scouting for new territory."

**A** man walked into a pet store and complained, "This cat you sold me is no good. You told me that it would be good for mice, and it hasn't caught one yet."

The clerk said, "Isn't that good for the mice?"

## PHILOSOPHY

We praise heartily only those who admire us.

You can't shake hands with a closed fist.

The philosopher finished his lecture by summing up with his favorite adage, "Happiness is the pursuit of something, not the catching of it."

A voice from the rear yelled out, "Have you ever tried to run after a bus on a snowy night?"

A hypocrite is a person who—but who isn't?

Men are like pay toilets. Either they're taken or they're full of crap.

## PHOTOGRAPHY

He took a lot of pictures, most of them with numbers underneath.

Two photographers, Henry and Felix, are in the woods of Canada shooting an essay on bears. The first morning out, they arrive at a stream and see a giant grizzly munching on salmon. The grizzly detects their presence, drops his fish, growls angrily, and starts after the lensmen. They take off. As they run, they see a tree ahead. Henry says, "There's only one tree. What's going to happen?"

Felix says, "I don't know for sure, but one of us is going to take a hell of a picture."

A friend invites a neighbor to his house for a drink. When he gets him there, he makes the unlucky soul sit down and watch his slides of Hong Kong. About two hours into the display, the neighbor says, "How many people are there in Hong Kong?"

"About ten million."

"Isn't that nice? You're going to show me all of them."

Do you have any religious views?

No, but I've got some great shots of the Grand Canyon.

## PLASTIC SURGERY

I know a plastic surgeon who made $2 million. He could have made more that year, but he didn't want to work full time.

A woman comes to a plastic surgeon for her fifth face-lift. The surgeon says, "All right, Lucille, but I want to warn you—another face-lift and you'll have an unexpected dimple and hair on your chest."

She went to a plastic surgeon for a face-lift. It was too much work, so he just lowered her body!

The plastic surgeon couldn't do much for her looks, but he performed one nice thing—he tattooed "Beware" on her forehead!

If one of those tucks in her face came loose, in five minutes she'd be a rug!

My wife isn't gorgeous. She came from the plastic surgeon last week with her leftovers in a doggie bag.

She got her looks from her father. He was a plastic surgeon!

The plastic surgeon just couldn't help this one woman. He gave her a face-lift, and there was another one just like it underneath!

A plastic surgeon's office is the only place where it's okay to pick your nose.

A friend of mine borrowed a thousand dollars from me so he could go in and get plastic surgery. Now I can't get my money back. I can't recognize him!

She's had her face lifted so many times, it's out of focus!

The plastic surgeon wouldn't give her a boob job because there'd be nothing left in her shoes.

If she gets one more face-lift, her ears are going to meet.

Plastic surgery really does wonders today. I followed a girl for two hours the other day before I found out she was my grandmother!

## PLUMBER

Show me a man who laughs when things go wrong and I'll show you a plumber.

She married a plumber. She liked seeing a man with a pipe.

Plumbers are always supposed to forget things. My sister went out with one, and he didn't forget a thing.

It's always better to call the plumber. A flush is better than a full house.

## POLITICS

This one senator is going to retire, and in his honor they're going to have a testimonial probe.

Today you can rent everything but a politician. You have to buy those.

Politicians didn't invent crime. They just improved on it.

"What's the difference between crime and politics?"
   "In crime, you take the money and run."

A nice politician will never lie about an opponent—if the truth will do more damage.

A statesman is a politician who didn't get caught.

The guy who says that crime doesn't pay never met a politician.

One year a politician is sworn in, the next year at.

A salesman, a doctor, and a politician got lost in the woods. They wandered about, and finally came to a farmhouse. The farmer said, "I only have room for two of you. The third one will have to sleep in the barn with the animals."

The salesman said, "I'll sleep in the barn."

A few minutes after they all went to bed, there was a noise outside.

The salesman had slammed the barn door shut and was standing outside. "I couldn't stand the smell."

The doctor volunteered to sleep in the barn. But no sooner had they started to go to sleep than he, too, stormed out of the barn. "I couldn't stand the smell."

The politician volunteered to trade places. One minute after he went to bed, there was again noise from the barn area. There in the moonlight, standing just outside the barn door, were all the animals.

There's so much scandal in politics today that a lot of people go to the convention under an assumed name tag!

Politics is a great profession because there are great rewards. If you disgrace yourself, you can always write a book.

A politician is someone who believes you don't have to fool all the people all the time. Just during campaigns is enough.

Nowadays, when you hear that a politician is starting a new term, you're not quite sure where.

He's a real politician—he can say absolutely nothing and mean it.

Most politicians have three hats: One they wear, one they toss into the ring, and a third they talk through.

Politics is like sex. You don't have to be good at it to enjoy it.

Some candidates are called favorite sons. Why doesn't anybody finish the sentence?

The Democrats say the Republicans are crooks. The Republicans say that the Democrats are crooked. Funny, but they're both right.

He's a great politician. That's because he looks ahead and plans his mistakes carefully.

Isn't it a shame that all the people who know how to run the country are driving cabs?

One important politician wanted to join the others on Mount Rushmore, but they don't have room for two more faces.

A politician comes home late, and his wife is angry. "Where have you been?" she bellows.

He explains, "I was with Senator Munson. We're working on a new tax bill."

His wife says, "All right, come in, but first wipe the senator's lipstick from your collar."

The best position to take is one to the left of the Conservatives, the right of the Liberals, and in front of the camera.

Our politicians really know how to handle our money—when they're not passing the buck, they're pocketing it.

Elections should be held on Christmas. That way, if you don't like who we elect, we can exchange them.

In Eastern Europe, most of the politicians spend a lot of time in jail before they are elected. In America, it's the other way around.

He's an honest politician. When you buy him, he stays bought.

A politician is a man who can straddle the fence while he keeps both ears to the ground.

A young Washington secretary, pretty but flat-chested, dies and goes to heaven. Asked what she'd like, she says, "Two of the biggest boobs in the world."

There is a puff of smoke and two senators appear at her side.

A Washington table setting: forks on the left, knives in the back.

I know a politician who ran for office. Six months later, he had to run for the border.

He's a candidate, ready and willing. Now if he were only able.

The governor of the state was an all-around chap, so often he would do the driving while he let his chauffeur sit in the backseat. One day the governor happened to forget himself and started speeding, only to be stopped by two highway patrolmen on motorcycles. One officer said, "Who's that sitting in back?"

The other officer peered in and said, "I don't know, but he's got to be mighty important. The governor is his chauffeur."

In some cities, you can vote ten times—more, if you're a citizen.

I don't make jokes. I just watch the government and report the facts!

Some politicians can't understand about crime. There are so many legal ways to be dishonest.

Most politicians really belong to both parties—they eat like elephants and think like donkeys.

When you dodge a car, you're a pedestrian. Dodge taxes, and you're a businessman. Dodge responsibility, you're an executive. Dodge everything—you're a politician!

You can always tell a good politician by the way he answers. He makes you forget the question.

The ideal candidate claims everything, concedes nothing, alleges fraud, and demands a recount.

One candidate has an identity problem—everybody knows who he is.

I just realized something. In an election, most people pick the winner.

A conservative is a liberal who got mugged.

A candidate stops off at a farm to shake hands with the family. In the barn, he finds the farmer's daughter milking the cow. The farmer, hearing something, calls out from the house, "Sue, what's going on out there?"

"There's a politician out here, Pa."

"Well, get right in the house. And bring the darn cow with you."

Most politicians make speeches that are like horns on a steer—a point here, a point there, and a lot of bull in between.

I always vote for the candidate who's on the take, carouses with women, and drinks like a fish. That way, we won't have to break him in.

There are three candidates for the office. Two of them are veterans who brag about how they were in combat. One was shot in the leg and twenty years after the war still feels the pain, limping after standing a few minutes. The second was hit on the arm and now has almost no feeling in his fingers. He has only partial use of the arm, he swears.

The third candidate stands up and says, "I was never in the war and I was never touched by a bullet, but let me tell you, I got the worst goddam hernia in this county!"

People always keep saying, "Things can't go on like this." And that's how it ends up. Things get worse.

This politician addresses a group of farmers. After the speech, he asks one for some comments. The farmer says, "Pal, you and I could cross up and down this state and tell more lies than any two men, and I wouldn't have to say a word."

A candidate is making one of his typical endless speeches and saying, as he plunges on, "I'm not speaking to this group. I'm talking for posterity, for future generations."

A voice from the back of the room says, "If you don't stop talking soon, they'll be here."

I've decided to run for office next year, but first I'll change my name to "None of the Above."

I finally won an election bet. I bet my candidate to place.

He was born a politician. As a baby, he wriggled out of everything they put him in.

A lot of candidates brag they started life as a barefoot boy. Who didn't?

## POLLUTION

I was in Cleveland last summer. I had a rough time. I got my foot stuck in Lake Erie!

It was so smoggy out that when I stuck out my hand to make a left turn, I broke two of my fingers.

The water around here isn't too polluted. You can hardly tell if you just add a little tenderizer.

Pollution is way out of hand nowadays. The other day a dam gave way, but the lake didn't.

Pollution is affecting everything. Did you hear about the ninety-eight-pound weakling who took his girlfriend to the beach—and a bully kicked oil in his face?

The drought situation is getting better in the West. They just found water in the rain.

You can always tell when it's spring in New York City. The garbage goes up the Hudson River to spawn.

## POPE

"What do you think happened when the pope went to Mount Olive?"
"Popeye got pee'd off."

The pope just addressed a thousand people. It must have been a great speech, because he got a kneeling ovation.

"What's the difference between your boss and the pope?"
"The pope only expects you to kiss his ring."

## POPULAR/UNPOPULAR

When he was three, he said he was going to run away from home. His father wanted him to put it in writing.

I was an unloved baby. For my first gift, when I was taking a bath, they gave me a toaster shaped like a rubber duck.

I was really unloved. My folks gave me a going-to-the-army party, and I was only two.

In a recent campaign, one candidate ran unopposed and came in third!

I must have been unloved. My dad bought me a bike and said, "Come up to the roof, and I'll give you a lesson."

When I was a kid, one day my folks played hide-and-seek with me. Six years later, I found them in a motel room five hundred miles away.

When I was a kid, my father used to throw me in the air—and walk away.

I won't say he was an unwanted baby, but when he was born, there was a coat hanger sticking out of his ear.

I was such an unwanted child, I had to take a cab home from the hospital!

The most popular girl is one who knows how to play tennis, piano, and dumb.

He tried to be his own best friend and was rejected.

I was in surgery once, and I heard the doctor say, "I'll take all calls!"

He never pays any of his bills. Otherwise, nobody would ever call him.

When you play hide-and-seek with your father, is he supposed to hide in another town?

I wasn't too well liked as a kid. My parents kept trying to send me to winter camp.

I used to belong to a social club that loved to have wild parties at my house. But they'd never invite me!

I once took my girl to the Tunnel of Love. She asked me to wait outside.

He had a paternity suit against him from his kids.

When she asks a man what he wants out of a relationship, he usually says—her.

I wasn't too popular. At Club Med I used to room at the lost-and-found.

She's been turned down so often, she looks like a bedspread.

He just joined a new group—Sex Without Partners.

She's really unloved. She was stood up at the Father-Daughter Dance.

My parents didn't like me. They bronzed my baby shoes while my feet were still in them.

When he was a kid, he was kidnapped, and the kidnappers sent back a piece of his ear. His parents wanted more proof.

When he was five, he ran away from home. The police came to the house, but his parents couldn't describe him.

I had a rough childhood. I had to share my sandbox with the cat.

He couldn't get laid if he walked into a brothel with a handful of hundreds and tears in his eyes.

When I was a kid, I wanted to play in the school marching band—so they gave me a piano.

I was an unloved kid. When I was three, my folks took me to an orphanage and told me to mingle.

I was not a joy to my family at birth. When I was born, my father gave out cigar butts.

I was an unwanted child. My folks used to give me my allowance in traveler's checks.

I was unloved. My parents used to sit around telling me, "We're seeing another kid."

He knew he was in trouble right off. His bride came to the wedding with a date.

He really was unloved. His mother didn't want to breast-feed him. She just wanted him for a friend.

When he was a kid, he went hunting with his father, and his father only gave him a two minute head start.

When he was born, his mother asked, "What shall we call it?"
His father said, "Quits."

When he was an infant, he found out his mother was nursing another baby on the side.

A friend of mine swallowed a bottle of sleeping pills and called 911. They told him to take a few drinks and get some rest.

## PORNOS

You're getting on in years if you come out of a porno and only remember the credits.

One porno star got tired of doing sex scenes, so she hired a lie-in.

If you're not an adult when you go into an adult movie, you certainly are when you come out.

I saw a really strange Danish movie last night. The voices were natural, but the sex was dubbed in!

I went into one movie that was so wild, the only one wearing clothes was the projectionist!

They just made a western porno. The only things covered are the wagons.

I went to a porno theater the other day. The movie must have been very emotional, because by the time it ended, there wasn't a dry fly in the house.

Then there was the porno murder mystery. Everybody did it.

## POST OFFICE

Like the letter said to the stamp, "You stick with me, and we'll go places."

If the world is getting smaller, how come they raise the postal rates?

Old mailmen never die. They just lose their ZIP.

The post office would like to raise the price of stamps. They need to buy new signs that say, THIS WINDOW CLOSED.

A man wrote to a mail-order house, "Please send me one of those kitchen tools you advertise. If it's any good, I'll send you a check."

A week later, he received an answer, "How about one of your checks first? If it's any good, we'll send you the kitchen tool."

The post office has increased its efficiency by one third. They now lose your letters one-third faster.

Letters are getting so expensive, some college kids can't afford to write home for money!

"My brother went for a job in the post office."

"What is he doing now?"

"Nothing. He got the job!"

My mailman even loses letters marked "Occupant."

Why is it that bills travel through the mail three times as fast as checks?

Bill Marx retired after twenty years in the post office. Twenty-one, if you counted the time it took them to mail him his check.

A mailman took his girl to a motel one afternoon and registered as Mr. and Mrs. Occupant.

"What do a shoe store and a branch post office have in common?"

"About a hundred loafers."

The post office guarantees that it'll deliver the mail anywhere within three days. Those days are Thursday, a week from Thursday, and a month from Thursday.

The new postal rates will guarantee that the post office will get new machines. That way your stuff can get mangled faster.

I know why the post office charges so much for mail. They include storage.

My postal delivery is real slow. I still get V-mail.

My cousin just went to that eternal resting place. He's with the post office.

With the cost of stamps nowadays, we get more of a licking than they do.

## POVERTY

I've still got the first dollar I ever made. Nothing else, just the first dollar!

We were so poor, we couldn't give my sister a sweet-sixteen party till she was thirty-two.

Most politicians know what it was like to be poor, and they want us to learn too.

I'll tell you how poor we were. I had so many brothers and sisters that when I came home late, I got to sleep on the top of the pile.

He was so poor that if somebody threw the dog a bone, the dog had to signal for a fair catch.

In my old neighborhood, we've got garbage that's been there so long, it's become a landmark!

My neighborhood was so poor, you could only buy alphabet soup with one letter in it.

We were so hungry, after a meal my mother had to count the kids.

I lived in a real poor neighborhood. Only one family had garbage.

We were so poor, our ZIP code only had one number.

We were so poor, we mailed our Christmas cards with food stamps.

We were very poor. When my rich uncle died, in the will we owed *him* fifty thousand.

Money can't buy you poverty!

I came from a poor town. We didn't even have a pay toilet—a pay bush!

Show me a man with no money, and I'll show you a bum!

He used to have the wolf at his door. Now, he has no door.

When I was a kid, we were evicted so often, my mother made shades for the street lamps.

Did you ever notice that when a family is fighting to keep the wolf from the door, the stork usually comes down the chimney?

We were so poor, the tooth fairy used to leave IOUs!

Poverty is no disgrace, but it's mighty inconvenient.

I sold my house the other day. There'll be hell to pay when the landlord finds out!

The easiest way to become poor is to pretend you're rich.

I lived in such a poor neighborhood, rainbows came in black-and-white!

Blessed are the poor. The more things you have, the more you have to dust.

We were so poor, we could only buy one shoe at a time.

I come from a real poor family. We couldn't even afford underwear. My mother painted buttons on us.

He came to this country fifty years ago as a poor boy. Now, fifty years later, he's a poor man.

## PRAYER

A good crisis can get our faith back on track. Nobody prays to Blue Cross!

Every day this man prays to God to let him win the lottery. He keeps promising all kinds of things if God will only let him win the lottery. But he never wins. One day he asks God, "I'm such a good man. Why can't I win the lottery?"

God answers, "You gotta buy a ticket!"

Sometimes children don't really understand prayers. I hear a couple of them saying, "Our father who art in Seven-Eleven!"

If your prayers aren't answered, the answer is no.

When football players pray together before a game, they always win . . . if the line outweighs the other one by fifty pounds a man.

## PREGNANCY

The man was complaining. "Why can't you look like you did when we got married?"

"Because I'm not pregnant, that's why!"

This young girl came home and announced to her mother that she had become pregnant in college. The mother asked her who the father was. The young girl shrugged her shoulders. She had no idea. The mother said, "Didn't they teach you anything in that college? Didn't they even teach you to ask, 'With whom am I having the pleasure?' "

A young woman goes to a doctor and tells him she's pregnant.

He asks, "Who's the father?"

She says, "How do I know? My mother would never let me go steady."

The young man skipped town. The next day, the pregnant girl went to the police and had him arrested for leaving the scene of an accident.

We got a dog from the pound. We figured if we couldn't have one naturally, adoption was in order.

When he found out she was pregnant, he told her, "It's all a mistake."

She said, "Yeah, but what are we going to do with the mistake?"

This woman goes to a doctor and says, "My water broke. What should I do?"

The doctor says, "Get off my rug."

The new mother sat up in her hospital bed, poring over a thick phone book. The nurse said, "We have a book that lists hundreds of first names for babies."

The new mother said, "I'm looking for a last name!"

## PRESIDENTS

It's tough being president. Everybody knows where you live and what you make.

"In America, everybody can become president of the United States."
"It's a risk you have to take."

When it comes to electing a president, we get our pick of two candidates. For Miss America, we get our choice of fifty.

An ex-president was asked whether he thought it was right for a man of his seventy-five years to be president. The ex-president answered, "In this country, that's about the only job an old man can get."

Two journalists listened to the president speak on the economy.
"How can he do this?" one said. "He's murdering the truth!"
"I wouldn't worry about it," the other said, "He'll never get close enough to it to do bodily harm."

## PRICES

The cost of living is always the same—everything you have.

Prices are going out of control. Yesterday my supermarket tried to buy back the groceries I bought last week.

Prices are so high, I'm using my refrigerator to store clothes.

I just heard that the gas shortage was delayed by high prices.

I was in this very fancy restaurant. The prices were so high, only the chef ate there.

The other day, I was in a restaurant and ordered a steak. I told them to put it on my credit card, and it fit.

All you can do on a shoestring today is trip.

Do you know how much bus fare is today? Starting next week, I'm going to mail myself to work.

The cost of lumber is so high, it's hard to believe it grows on trees.

It used to be that only death and taxes were inevitable. Now, there's shipping and handling.

Prices were really high this last Christmas. I bought a tree for fifty dollars, and my wife wore it as a corsage.

Things aren't too good. It costs as much to heat the house in winter as it does to go south.

I went into a restaurant that had stratospheric prices. When I got the check, I fainted. They threw water in my face, and that was another five dollars.

## PRIESTS

Priests know more than rabbis because their parishioners tell them everything.

If they allow priests to marry, their kids will have to call them "Father Daddy."

A priest found himself in a restaurant. As he ate, his eyes drifted to a stunning woman at a nearby table. Her gentleman escort was rather embarrassed by the priest's ogling and walked over to him, saying, "You're a priest. You shouldn't be staring at a pretty woman."

The priest said, "Just because I'm on a perpetual diet doesn't mean I can't study the menu!"

## PRISON

We can improve our prisons. Let's send a better class of people there.

The condemned man is brought before the firing squad. The officer in charge asks him if he'd like a cigarette. The man shakes his head no. The officer is surprised and says, "You've refused everything. You refused a last meal and a priest. Isn't there something important that we can do for you?"

The condemned man says, "There's one thing. I love singing. I'd like to sing my favorite song before I die."

The officer says, "That's not too much to ask. Go ahead and sing."

The condemned man starts singing, "Ten million bottles of beer on the wall, ten million bottles of beer . . ."

Two convicts were going at it hot and heavy when a guard stopped them and asked, "Why are you fighting?"

One convict said, "The son of a gun called me a dirty number!"

The warden was interviewing a politician's nephew for a job as a guard and said, "We have a tough bunch of prisoners. Do you think you can handle them?"

The nephew said, "No problem. If they act up, out they go!"

Prisons are so crowded nowadays, prisoners have to take a number to escape.

One man didn't mind being sent to jail. He knew he'd get out quickly, because his wife never let him finish a sentence.

A few years ago, one prisoner got the electric chair. Now, once a year his family lays a wreath by the fuse box.

Prison has its advantages. You don't have to get up in the middle of the night to see if the door is locked.

My cousin is having a hard time in San Quentin. They say he's a disgrace to his uniform.

## PROBLEMS

The chief cause of problems is solutions.

If a man can see both sides of a problem, you can bet he doesn't have any money on it.

Mrs. Taylor meets Mrs. Garber, who looks extremely agitated. Asked if she has any problems, Mrs. Garber says, "Problems? You don't have any idea of what problems are. Last week, my husband ran off with his receptionist. Five days ago, my son was arrested for selling dope. Yesterday, my daughter told me she was pregnant. And tomorrow morning, the painters are coming."

## PROCRASTINATION

"All you do is procrastinate."
"Oh, yeah, just wait."

Procrastination is a habit most people put off trying to correct.

I know some real procrastinators in politics. They just got up a Stop Coolidge movement!

There was supposed to be a convention of procrastinators next month, but it's been delayed!

That's when you decide to procrastinate but never get around to it.

Procrastination has its good side. You always have something to do tomorrow.

## PRODUCTS

Last week I bought one of those collapsible pools for my kids. Two days later, it did.

A housewife was showing her friend around. All the little extras had been furnished with soap coupons—the microwave oven, the toaster, the blender, the roaster. "Everything," she boasted, "came from soap coupons."

The friend indicated a door and said, "I'll bet you have a dozen more things in that room."

The housewife said, "Oh, no, that's where we keep the soap!"

## PROMISES

A bride-to-be resists making love to her intended until after they are married. He agrees.

On their honeymoon night, the groom says, "I'm so glad you made me wait. If I'd found you easy, I never would have married you."

The bride says, "I know. That's how the last four guys fooled me."

He promised her that her hands would never touch dishwater, and he kept his promise. When they got married, he bought her gloves.

It's useless to hold anybody to his word if he's in love, drunk, or running for office.

A young woman agrees to let her beau make love to her, but only if he uses a minimum part of his male endowment. He agrees.

A little later, as they make love, the young lady is overwhelmed with passion and yells, "Give it all to me."

The beau says, "No. A promise is a promise."

## PROVERBS

**A** lawyer and a wagon wheel must be well greased.

**H**e who marries a widow will have a dead man's head thrown in his dish.

**A**ny fool can make a rule.

**O**nly the shallow know themselves.

**T**here is no sweeter sound than the crumbling of one's fellow man.

**A** little inaccuracy sometimes saves a ton of explanation.

**V**irtue is its own revenge.

**T**alk is cheap because supply exceeds demand.

**I**f God lived on Earth, people would break His windows.

**I**f you want an audience, start a fight.

**N**ature has given us two ears and but one mouth.

**T**he two hardest things to handle are failure and success.

**B**ed is the poor man's opera.

**A**fter three days, fish and guests stink.

**I**t is easier to stay out than to get out.

**I**t is better to be a coward for a minute than to be dead forever.

## PRUDES

**O**ne senator is a real prude. He wants to put a fig leaf over the Washington Monument.

**M**y brother-in-law is such a prude. Last month he pulled his daughter out of school because he'd heard that the boys and girls matriculated together.

## PSYCHIATRISTS

"**D**octor, my wife throws dishes at me, curses at me, yells at me, and calls me dirty names."
  "That's an easy case. I think she doesn't like you."

**T**here's nothing wrong with a person that a good psychiatrist can't exaggerate.

**M**y psychiatrist goes in for group therapy. Instead of a couch, he has bunk beds.

**T**hree out of five people go to psychiatrists. The other two *are* psychiatrists.

**M**y wife's first visit to the psychiatrist was a real failure. She spent fifty minutes rearranging the couch.

**S**he'll never go in for psychiatry. She doesn't trust any man with a couch in his office.

A young man complains to his shrink, "I'm always thinking of food. Nothing but food. Always food."

"Don't you ever think of girls?"

"A lot, but I'm always putting mayonnaise on them."

A man goes to a psychiatrist and says, "Doc, I have a morbid fear of thunder."

The psychiatrist says, "That's pretty silly. You shouldn't be afraid of a thing like thunder. Why don't you just think of it as a drumroll from heaven?"

"Will that cure me?"

"Well, if it doesn't, do what I did: Stuff cotton in your ears, crawl under the bed, and sing 'Zippety-Doo-Dah' like I do."

The way I see it is this: I don't care if you have an Oedipus complex. As long as you love your mother.

The psychiatrist was matter-of-fact, saying, "After listening to you for so many hours, I must tell you that you are really crazy."

The patient said, "I think I'd like a second opinion."

"All right. You're ugly too!"

A man returned from his thousandth visit to his psychiatrist and told his wife, "I'm cured, honey, I no longer believe that I'm a dog."

The wife asked, "And you're not anxious or anything like that?"

"No, I'm perfectly calm. Just feel my nose."

The psychiatrist helped him get rid of his inferiority complex. He proved that he was really inferior!

A woman goes to the doctor and complains that her husband thinks he's the Lone Ranger. The doctor tells her that he can cure her husband in no time. The woman says, "Not too fast. Tonto is so good with the children."

A psychiatrist is a man who never has to worry as long as his patients do.

A psychiatrist is a man who'll listen to you as long as you don't make sense.

If you wonder why a psychiatrist is called a "shrink," check your bank account after a month.

The psychiatrist was ecstatic as he told his patient, "Mr. Klein, your kleptomania is cured."

"You mean I won't shoplift anymore?"

"Test yourself. Walk through a department store after you leave here. You'll see you're cured. But if you happen to have a relapse, I need a travel alarm."

A man complains to his psychiatrist, "I'm always talking to myself."

The psychiatrist says, "A lot of people talk to themselves."

"I know. But I'm such a bore."

A woman complains to a shrink, "My husband keeps emptying ashtrays. All day long, he empties ashtrays."

"That's not a big problem, emptying ashtrays."

"In his mouth?"

---

A wife called a psychiatrist and said, "My husband thinks he's Moses."

The doctor assured her that these delusions of grandeur were only a passing fancy.

The wife said, "I hope so. But meanwhile, how can I keep him from parting the water when I take a bath?"

---

Two patients meet in the drugstore under the medical building in which their shrinks have offices. One says, "Are you coming or going?"

The other answers, "If I knew that, would I be here?"

---

A man tells his new psychiatrist, "I love boxer shorts."

"That's not terrible. I prefer boxer shorts myself."

"Really? With mustard or mayonnaise?"

---

I had insomnia for a while, and my psychiatrist suggested sex for it. I asked him, "Will that help me sleep?"

He said, "No. But you'll have more fun while you're awake."

---

I paid a shrink fifty dollars to cure my inferiority complex. Then it cost me a hundred because I talked back to a traffic cop.

---

You can go to a shrink slightly cracked, and before you get done, you're broke.

---

A lady psychiatrist and a girlfriend went to a movie. While they were sitting there, the man sitting next to the doctor started to grope at her. Seeing this, the girlfriend said, "Why don't you tell this creep he's sick?"

The lady psychiatrist said, "Why should I? He's not my patient."

---

A shrink is a man who, when a gorgeous woman is lying on his couch, just talks to her.

---

A patient went to his doctor and said, "I'm feeling very schizophrenic today."

The doctor said, "That makes four of us."

---

A psychiatrist was behind the wheel of his brand-new sports car, tooling away on the highway. As he slowed down near his off-ramp, he felt a terrible jolt. His pretty car had just been rear-ended.

Jumping out, the psychiatrist ran to the driver of the other car and was about to curse him out when he realized his calling, so he faced the man down and asked, "Why do you hate your mother?"

---

My brother has been going to a shrink lately. He thinks his inferiority complex is bigger and better than anybody else's.

---

Klein goes to a shrink and identifies himself as Napoleon. "I have the love of my people, a great army, and whatever I want."

The shrink says, "Why did you come here?"

The man says, "For my wife. She thinks she's Mrs. Klein."

A patient told his doctor that he could be made better in two or three visits. The psychiatrist said, "Buddy, if you think you'll walk out of here healthy, you're insane."

Anybody who believes we practice free speech in America never went to a shrink.

The psychiatrist said to the IRS agent, "Don't be a fool. The whole world isn't against you. Maybe the people in the United States, but the whole world? . . ."

A shrink costs a fortune. I asked one what he could do for me for fifty dollars. He said, "Send you a get-well card."

This psychiatrist told me to speak freely. I did, and he charged me a hundred bucks.

A patient said to his doctor, "When you say that I should forget the past, does that also mean what I owe you?"

Freud was visiting a mental institution. After checking out all the facilities, he boarded the bus to town. A minute later, the keeper brought in some patients who were going on a little field trip to the city. When they were in their seats, the keeper started to count, "One, two, three, four, five, six." He got to Freud and asked, "Who are you?"

Freud said, "I'm Sigmund Freud."
The keeper said, "Seven, eight, nine . . ."

"I bet you're a psychiatrist."
"What makes you ask?"
"I was right. You're a psychiatrist."

Brown rushes to his shrink and says, "Doc, I'm not a loser anymore. I dropped an English muffin on the floor, and it landed with the butter side up."
The shrink said, "You're not there yet. You buttered it on the wrong side."

A man complains to a psychiatrist that he goes around biting his nails all the time. The psychiatrist says, "That's not so bad."
The man says, "But I'm a carpenter!"

A patient went to the doctor and asked if the doctor could give him a split personality. The doctor asked him why. The patient answered, "I'm so lonely."

A psychiatrist had to leave his profession because of a physical handicap—he couldn't help blushing.

My psychiatrist has two baskets on his desk. One is "Outgoing," the other "Inhibited."

A man goes to a shrink, lies down on the couch, and doesn't say a word for an hour. At the end of the hour, the psychiatrist says, "That'll be a hundred dollars, and I'll see you next week." This goes on for months. The patient comes in, lies down, and says nothing. A hundred dollars each nothing.

Finally, at the end of six months, the patient sits up on the couch.

The shrink says, "Don't tell me you finally have something to say?"

The man says, "Yeah. Do you need a partner?"

A man goes to a psychiatrist and explains his problem. For months his wife has been imagining she's a lawn mower. The shrink said, "Why didn't you bring her in to see me?"

The man answers, "I can't until the neighbor next door returns her."

I stopped going to my shrink. He kept asking me the same question my wife does—"Who do you think you are?"

He's a very strict psychiatrist. If you're five minutes late, he makes you stand.

A patient says, "Nobody listens to a word I say."

The psychiatrist says, "Next."

One New York psychiatrist is very lucky. He has a client with a split personality, and they both pay.

A patient complains to a shrink about his wife: "Look, I don't care if she thinks she's an octopus, but in the last three months I've been going broke buying her elbow-length gloves."

My cousin, a window washer, went to a shrink recently. He's tired of being on the outside, looking in.

A patient lies down on the couch, and the shrink says, "Okay, tell me what you dreamed last night."

"I didn't dream."

"How can I help you if you don't do your homework?"

I better get to my shrink. If I'm not there on time, he starts by himself.

A man comes into a psychiatrist's office, lies down on the couch, and starts to go to sleep. The psychiatrist asks, "What's your problem?"

The man says, "I don't have a room."

A woman complains to the shrink, "My husband is always washing the car."

"A lot of men wash the car."

"In the bathtub?"

A patient tells his shrink not to worry about payment, saying, "I'll pay you every penny I owe you, or my name isn't Julius Caesar."

"Doc, I have these dreams every night. Beautiful women, redheads, blondes, and brunettes, appear, and one by one they try to kiss me, and I keep pushing them away."

"What would you like me to do?"

"Break my arms!"

A shrink led a group of people into a restaurant and spoke to the manager, saying, "Sir, I'm leading this group from the local mental hospital, and they're completely fine, but they will insist on paying you in bottle caps. If you'll be so kind as to humor them and take the bottle caps, I'll take care of the bill later."

A considerate man, the manager happily collected all the bottle caps.

The shrink returned with gratitude and said, "Thank you so much. I'll pay the bill now. Do you have change for a hubcap?"

I asked my psychiatrist, "How soon will I know I'm cured?"

He said, "The day you run out of money."

"You've got to help me," a man pleaded. "It's my son!"

"What's the matter?" the psychiatrist asked.

"He's always eating mud pies. I get up in the morning, and he's in the backyard eating mud pies. I come home for lunch, he's eating mud pies. I come home for dinner, and he's back there eating more mud pies!"

"Give it time," the doctor says, "he'll grow out of it."

"Well, I still don't like it," the man says. "And neither does his wife!"

## PUNCTUALITY

Being punctual is no fun. There's nobody there to appreciate it.

"When is the time-management seminar?"

"Fivish, sixish."

## PUNS

"What do ghouls eat for breakfast?"
"Scream of wheat."

The chief of the tribe was beside himself with pain from a bad stomachache. The witch doctor told him, "Take the tanned hide of an animal, cut it into long, thin thongs, and swallow one every day."

After twelve days, the chief returned to the witch doctor, still in terrible pain, saying, "Doctor, it's no use. The thong is gone, but the malady lingers on."

BABY CORN: Mommy, who brought me?
MOMMY CORN: The stalk did.

## PUT-DOWNS

If we gave you a going-away present, would you?

You can go home now—your cage is clean.

He's okay in my book, but then I only read dirty books.

He's a good egg, and you know where eggs come from.

I can see he has an open mind. It's a shame he had to close it for repairs.

He has no equals—only superiors.

Hey, let's play Post Office. You become a letter that's lost.

They just threw him a big dinner, but it missed.

Can I drop you off somewhere later—like the Golden Gate Bridge?

You've got a lot of humor in you. Too bad you can't let it out.

In his case, brain surgery would be a minor operation.

Is that a chip on your shoulder, or is that your head?

This man just had a bright idea. Beginner's luck.

He's the only person who enters a room mouth-first!

Why are you trying to prove that your father was bad in bed?

I wish I had a lower IQ, so I could enjoy your company.

A man with the courage of his convictions. I think he's had six of them.

If brains were dynamite, he wouldn't have enough to blow his nose!

I don't mind your interrupting. Three heads are better than one.

Did you heckle at your mother's wedding?

Do you do imitations? Great—act like a human being.

He had an extremely high IQ when he was five. Too bad he grew out of it!

For a yawning audience: "I don't mind you falling asleep, but at least you could say good night!"

Why don't you head for a hospital and your annual autopsy?

Was the ground cold when you crawled out this morning?

I can't place your face, but I never forget a breath.

## QUIZ SHOWS

**A** young man has been on a quiz show for several weeks and is set to play for the big money. Because the questions will be about sex, he brings along a French friend as an expert. The quiz master asks, "If you were going on a honeymoon with a movie star, what three parts of her anatomy would you be expected to kiss?"

The young man thinks and says finally, "Her lips and her neck."

"Correct," says the quiz master. "Now come up with the third answer."

Unable to come up with the third response, the young man turns to his French expert. The French expert says, "Don't look at me, *mon ami*. I got ze first two wrong."

**I** won my wife at a quiz show. She was wearing a white dress, and I thought she was a refrigerator.

## RABBIS

**A** rabbi goes off on a European vacation. While there, free from restraint, he decides to sample the cuisine of the country, so in Paris, he orders roast pig.

An hour later, the waiter wheels out a cart on which is a succulent pig with an apple in its mouth. But as luck would have it, a member of the rabbi's temple happens into the restaurant. Seeing him, the rabbi shakes his head sadly. "Can you believe that this is how they serve a baked apple over here?"

**A** priest and rabbi were debating their callings. The priest waxed eloquent about his chances for improvement. "I could become a bishop in no time," he said. "Then I could become a cardinal."

"So?"

"After that I could become pope."

"Big deal."

"You're something, Rabbi. What do you expect a man to become—God?"

"Why not?" the rabbi said. "One of our boys made it!"

**A** man approached the rabbi and said, "Rabbi, help me. I have fifteen kids. What should I do?"

417

The rabbi said, "Haven't you done enough?"

Rabbi Gelber from Chicago and Gus Greenbaum, a businessman from Mount Vernon, met at Miami Beach and became fast friends after just a few days. On the plane back to New York, Greenbaum insisted that his new friend spend a weekend with him in Mount Vernon before returning to Chicago.

They had a grand time together, lots of good food and drink, but when Monday morning came, Gelber was amazed to find a bill for forty dollars on his breakfast tray. He was outraged.

"How could you do this?" Gelber demanded.

"You didn't think I was going to give you all this for nothing?" Greenbaum said.

The argument waxed fast and furious. Finally, Greenbaum said, "I tell you what, how about letting the rabbi here decide who is right in this argument?"

So they went to the rabbi, who quickly made his decision. "Gelber must pay the forty dollars."

Gelber was furious but handed over two twenty-dollar bills. Greenbaum refused to take them. "I don't want your money, I just wanted to show you what a terrible rabbi we have here in Mount Vernon!"

## RABBITS

If rabbits were smart, they wouldn't run away from the dogs. They'd just stop for forty seconds and outnumber them.

Papa Rabbit took a look at his first children and said, "Well, as I live and breed."

## REAL ESTATE

Things aren't too good in the real estate business. I know one house that's been up for sale so long, the For Sale sign needs to be repainted.

The real estate agent told me that my house would bring more if I fixed it up. I put in new wallpaper, painted, redid the bathrooms, put on a new roof, and resodded the lawn. I got one offer—from the city, for slum clearance!

The real estate agent told us, "There are a lot of little things about this house you don't notice at first." He was right—termites!

We finally found a house we can afford. Right now, it's owned by a German shepherd named Rover.

A real estate salesman showed us a shack one day that looked as if it was falling apart. My wife said, "The only thing keeping this house together is the termites holding hands."

I put my house up for sale for $200,000. The termites wanted to chip in a buck apiece.

Nowadays, a town house costs more than the town used to.

When the real estate agent says that the house has no flaw, he could mean the one you walk on.

The agent says, "Would you like to see our model home?"

"Sure, but I'd like to take her for a few drinks first."

A real estate agent shows some property way out of town to a prospective sucker, saying, "The climate here is perfect. Nobody dies here."

Just then, a funeral procession passes by. The prospective customer says, "Well, what's that?"

Quick as a wink, the real estate agent says, "Our local mortician. Starved to death."

A real estate agent was showing us a place that was for sale. I mentioned to him that the place was a little damp. He said, "That would come in handy in case of a fire."

He specializes in two-story houses—one before you buy, and the second afterward.

An agent is showing a house to prospective buyers. He shows the large yard and says, "Your children will love it here."

As they start in, a mouse runs across the patio. Unfazed, the agent adds, "And think what a great time your cat will have."

## RELATIVES

I solved my problem of too many visiting relatives. I borrow money from the rich ones and lend it to the poor ones. Now none of them come back.

I think of my wife's family as pearls. They're always hanging around my neck.

## RELIGION

The Baptist revival is under way. All the new members have been dipped, but along comes Joe Hardy, the rowdiest man in town. Joe says, "I'd like for you to dip me."

The preacher says, "If you're sincere about becoming a Baptist, a dipping won't do it. We'll have to anchor you out here overnight."

The guru proposed marriage to one of his attractive followers. He reached a point in his life where he wanted to contemplate someone else's navel.

There's a new religion called Jehovah's Bystanders. That's a Witness who doesn't want to get involved.

An archeologist is digging in the Dead Sea area and comes up with an exciting find. He rushes back to the university and tells his colleagues, "I just found the skeleton of a man four thousand years old who died of a heart attack."

"How do you know he died of a heart attack?" a colleague asked.

"He had a paper in his hand that said, 'A hundred shekels on Goliath.' "

A priest recently came up with a list of 823 sins. In one week, he received two thousand requests for the list.

A visitor to the nunnery asked a sharp, modern young nun, "Do you think the pope will ever allow nuns to marry?"

The nun answered, "Someday she might."

In the repository where the Mint keeps old bills, two of the bills were talking. A twenty said, "I've had some life—the best restaurants, the finest shops. How about you?"

A one-dollar bill said, "All I ever did was go to church, go to church, go to church."

A priest and rabbi are sitting on a park bench. The priest asks, "Rabbi, have you ever had ham?"

The rabbi says, "I have to confess, I tried it once. But tell me, Father, did you ever have sex?"

The priest says, "I tried it once."

The rabbi says, "Beats ham, doesn't it?"

Three ministers are discussing prayer, while in the background a telephone repairman is working on the phone line. One minister says, "The best way to pray is kneeling."

The second says, "I find it more satisfying to pray with my arms out to heaven."

"Both of you are wrong," the third minister says. "The best way to pray is when you're lying down prostrate."

Unable to control himself, the repairman says, "I don't know about any of that. But the best praying I did was when I was hanging on upside down on a thin telephone wire."

This man got into a terrible fight with his wife over religion. She worshiped money, and he wouldn't give her any.

I know a Reform Jewish temple that's so reformed, it does a twenty-four-hour fast in thirty minutes.

I know a drive-in Catholic church. It's called Toot 'n' Tell.

A minister called out to the congregation, "What must we do before we can expect forgiveness of sin?"

A voice from the back yelled, "Sin!"

The preacher listened as the businessman swore that he'd gotten religion and asked, "Are you sure you're going to set aside all sin?"

"I certainly am."

"And are you going to pay all your debts?"

"Hold on a minute. You're not talking religion now, you're talking business."

A bishop was approached one lovely morning by a priest. "Your Eminence," the priest said, "there's a young lad outside who claims to be seeing a vision of our Savior in the chapel. What should I do?"

The bishop said, "Look busy."

**M**y church welcomes all denominations, but prefers fives and tens.

**T**here's a church in my town that has bingo every Tuesday night. The priest calls the numbers in Latin, so Jews and Protestants can't win.

**S**ome people are very liberal in their religion. They believe in the Ten Commandments, but they insist you can pick five.

**A** synagogue and church are across the street from one another. The priest and rabbi have been in friendly competition for years. Then, one day, the members of the church buy the priest a brand-new car. The priest blesses the gift with holy water. Undaunted, the members of the synagogue buy the rabbi a brand-new car. But he is unable to match the rite of the holy water, so he goes out and cuts six inches off the tailpipe of the car.

**I** used to be an atheist, but I gave it up. No holidays!

**P**ARISHIONER: Do you think practicing birth control is a sin?
PRIEST: I hope not. I've been practicing it for years.

**A** man retired to a monastery after taking vows of silence. For five years, he wouldn't be allowed to speak. Then he would be allowed two words. After another five years, he would be allowed two more words.

Five years passed, and the man said to the abbot, "Hard beds."

Five more years passed, and the man spoke again, saying, "Bad food."

After the fifteenth year, he said, "I quit."

The abbot said, "It's a good thing. All you've done here is complain!"

**A** tourist touring South American jungles was a bit nervous when he returned his rental car. "Do you have any cats three feet long?" the man asked.

"Sure," the clerk said.

"Do you have any cats four feet long?"

"Yeah, I think so," the clerk said.

"What about cats six feet long?"

"Could, be, I'm not really sure," the man answered.

From the backseat of the car the clerk could hear the man's wife say, "I'm telling you, you dope, you've run over a priest!"

**O**ne day, God calls Father Valenti, the pastor of St. Catherine's.

"Valenti," God says, "I'm tired of religious bickering. Starting next Monday, I've chosen one religion to take over. All the others will disappear."

"Where are you calling from, Lord?"

"Salt Lake City."

**A** candidate is running in an area that has a mix of Catholics and Baptists. To make sure he doesn't have any problems, he tells every audience, "Come Sunday morning, I'd drive over to my Catholic grandparents and take them to church. In the afternoon, I'd drive over and take my Baptist grandparents to church."

A local politician says, "I didn't know you had any Catholic grandparents."

The candidate says, "Heck, I didn't even have a car."

Times have really changed. Years ago, a minister's only black book was the Bible.

I believe in all religions. I don't want to blow heaven on a technicality.

Call on God, but row away from the rocks.

An elderly tiny Quaker lady is driving along when a truck comes up behind her and tries to zoom out of the way but can't. The lady's car is totaled. She manages to control her Quaker temper and says, "Sir, when thee gets to thy home tonight, I hope thy mother bites thee."

A man goes to the races and sees a priest making the sign of the cross over a horse. The horse goes on to win the first race. The man continues to bet each horse the priest blesses. When the last race comes up, the man bets his whole fortune on the horse over whom the priest had made the sign of the cross.

The race goes off. The horse drops dead as it leaves the gate. The man rushes to the priest and wants to know what went wrong. The priest says,

"That's the trouble with you Protestants. You don't know the difference between a blessing and the last rites."

The best test of your faith is when the collection plate comes around and the smallest you have is a twenty.

"What happened in A.D. 13?"
"Jesus was bar-mitzvahed."

## REMEDIES

A good home remedy is orange juice and horseradish. No matter what you've got, you'll be up in ten seconds.

My grandfather drank three glasses of prune juice every day. He was a regular guy.

Everybody has a home remedy for something. My uncle takes prune juice and vodka. It's called a pile driver.

Some pills are huge today. There's one that cures a headache. But it gives you a hernia.

My doctor gave me a weird remedy. He told me to take a laxative and stay in bed.

## REPORTERS

A world-famous figure is hospitalized. To ensure him some peace and quiet, the man is isolated. Only medical personnel are allowed into his room. To obtain an interview, a young female reporter dresses up like a nurse and goes to the hospital.

A few hours later, she returns to the paper, and the editor asks, "Did you get an interview?"

The female reporter says, "No. The doctor from the *Herald* had me thrown out."

## RESTAURANTS

They have a new chain of African restaurants now. You walk in, and they eat *you*.

In Manhattan, they have real chic restaurants with tables and chairs outside. We used to have that years ago. It was called eviction.

After a long wait, the customer looks askance at the waiter, who walks over and says, "Sir, "I'll have your fish out in a minute."

The customer says, "Meanwhile, just tell me what bait you're using."

The restaurant was so crowded, twice I put silverware in somebody else's pocket.

A waitress explains that the special of the day is tongue. The customer makes a face and says, "I won't eat anything that comes from an animal's mouth. Just bring me some eggs."

A lady diner accidentally gives in to a little flatulence at the table. Wishing to save face, she says to the waiter, "Stop that immediately." The waiter says, "Certainly, madam. Which way was it headed?"

A man is in a restaurant. He tastes his food and calls over the waiter, saying, "This sauerkraut isn't sour enough."

The waiter says, "It's noodles."

"Oh. For noodles, it's sour enough."

A customer says to the waiter, "What's my offense? I've been on bread and water for almost an hour."

I asked a waiter in a restaurant for a suggestion. He said, "Don't wear that color tie with that suit."

Think about it—the worse the restaurant, the bigger the pepper mill.

Never eat in a restaurant called Mom's unless the only other place in town is called Eats.

There's one rule in a French restaurant: If you can't pronounce it, you can't afford it.

I was in the cheapest restaurant the other day. It even had a substitute for margarine.

A diner asks, "Do we have to sit like this until we starve?"

The waiter says, "No, we close at eight."

A waiter comes back to a patron and says, "Congratulations on your discernment. The chef says it *was* dishwater!"

A patron asks the maître d', "How long do I have to wait for a table?"

The maître d' answers, "Two hours or a twenty, whichever comes first."

A man walks into a restaurant and says, "Give me a table near a waiter."

A customer says to the waiter, "There's dirt in my soup. What does this mean?"

The waiter says, "If you want your fortune told, go to a gypsy!"

This restaurant had the hottest chili in the world. I ate a spoonful, burped, and set fire to the curtains.

"Waiter, there's a fly in my soup."

"Now that fly knows good soup."

The chef tells the waitress, "Push the soup du jour. It's a week old."

I went to an authentic Mexican restaurant the other night. You weren't supposed to drink the water.

I went to the worst restaurant the other day. If it wasn't for the salt and pepper, I would have starved.

This man stops off at a small diner in a little town and orders breakfast. The waitress brings his order, but the toast is extremely well done. The man says, "That toast is a little too dark, isn't it?"

The waitress says, "Man, you can scrape it any shade you want."

It has to be a bad restaurant if it features the wines of Tunisia.

I was in a restaurant one day last week, and a waiter dropped dead.

It took God to catch his eye.

A waitress brings a man his order, but the toast is burned, the eggs runny, and the coffee like dishwater. The man gulps it down. Watching him, the waitress confides to another waitress, "I finally found a man I can cook for."

A man sits down in a restaurant and tells the waiter, "You know, I first came into this place in 1952."

The waiter says, "I only have two hands. I'll be with you in a minute."

A minister was at a banquet when a careless waiter dropped a steaming-hot plate of pasta into his lap. The minister looked around the room with agony in his face and finally whispered, "Would some layman kindly say something appropriate?"

A man dipped his shrimp in Tabasco sauce for the first time in his life. After biting it, he jumped up and screamed. The manager ran over. "Hey, now!" he said, "Keep quiet or I'll put you out!"

"I wish you would," the guy said. "I'm on fire!"

It's strange, but whatever the person next to you orders is always better-looking than what you order.

The house specialty is *poulet à la chewy*—that's a chicken who was run over by a pickup truck!

It's a great restaurant. Their catch of the day is fish sticks!

Then there was the cook who got his hand caught in the dishwasher, and they were both fired.

One restaurant had a neat sign: OUR SILVERWARE IS NOT MEDICINE. DON'T TAKE IT AFTER MEALS.

The customer calls the waiter over and says, "Didn't I say well done?"

The waiter says, "Thank you. I very seldom get a compliment."

I can't stand going to fancy restaurants. It bothers me when the napkin has better material than my suit!

I went to the fanciest restaurant in town. It used solid silver knives and forks, Lumbagos china, crystal glasses, and if you wanted a napkin, the waiter brought over two silkworms and a whip.

I went to a terrible restaurant the other day. I was going to complain to the manager about the food, but I wouldn't stand in line.

I get a strange feeling in a restaurant, because today's tip is tomorrow's dinner.

A man comes into a very fancy French restaurant. As he looks at the menu, a fly lands on it. It doesn't seem to disturb him as he orders. "I'd like some oysters Rockefeller for an appetizer. And bring me a 1976 Médoc sauterne." He looks at the various entrées, all of which are in glowing French—*le boeuf de poeuf de roi de rôti, mignonettes de croix à la pume de rume*. He orders a rare pigeon dish but flambé.

"Will that be all, sir?"

The man starts to shake his head no, but stops. "Oh, yes," he says, "bring a turd for the fly."

A new waiter in a posh restaurant was standing at a table, waiting for a couple to order. The woman sighed at the extensiveness of the menu and, in doing so, heaved a little too much. Her breasts popped out on the table.

A little later, the maître d' called the waiter over and said, "Pierre, this is a very fancy restaurant. In the future, will you please use two warm spoons?"

A man takes some friends to a restaurant. All order. When the entrées are brought, one of the guests tastes his and says, "This is terrible duck."

Angrily, the host calls over the waiter and says, "Do me a favor, please. Go into the kitchen and tell the chef to shove this duck up his ass."

The waiter returns a minute later and says, "The chef told me to tell you that there are two steaks and a veal cutlet ahead of you."

Then there was the busboy who was fired. They caught him pinching the waitress's tips.

## RETIREMENT

An old man in a retirement home says to a nurse, "Take it off."
The nurse says, "Take what off?"
The old man says, "I forget."

Mr. Stoner, sitting outside on the patio of the retirement home, kept leaning over to the left. Each time he started to lean, the nurse rushed over and straightened him out again. A little later, Mr. Stoner's son came to visit and asked about the service at the home. Mr. Stoner said, "The food's okay, the rooms are nice, but the goddam nurse won't let me fart!"

## REVENGE

Two couples were neighbors, friends for twenty-two years, partying together, vacationing together, wrapped up in one another's lives. Suddenly, the husband of one woman runs off with the wife of his best friend.
The cuckolded couple can't believe what their spouses did. "Your husband and my wife . . . running away together. They've left us."
She says, "Come up to my place, we'll have a drink, it'll calm us down." While they're cheering each other up, she gets an idea. "Why stop at drinks? Let's get revenge. Let's go to the bedroom."
So they go to the bedroom and get revenge. They come out, have a couple of more drinks, and start commiserating again.
"How could two people deceive us that way? You know what we should do? We should have another revenge."
So they go to the bedroom and get revenge again. They come out and start drinking and commiserating again. By midnight they've reached a grand total of five revenges, and the man is still wallowing in remorse.
"Can you imagine my best friend doing that to me? And your best friend doing that to you?
She says, "Come on. It's time we had another revenge."
He looks at her wearily and says, "Good God, haven't we held a grudge long enough?"

Pierre is standing in the gents' room when Raoul comes in and notices that Pierre is gripping his penis tightly. Raoul asks about the cause of this strange behavior.
Pierre says, "It is for revenge. Last night it wouldn't work. Today it wants to urinate, and I won't let it. Revenge! Revenge!"

One airline is finally getting even with its passengers. It's serving larger portions of food.

I have no luck. If I came back as a dog, my wife would come back as a flea.

A truck driver is having a bite to eat in a diner when three leather-clad bikers parade in. One grabs his coffee, a second his pie, and a third takes his cigarettes. Without a word, the truck driver gets up and walks out. One of the bikers walks over to the cook and says, "He's not much of a man, is he?"

The cook answers, "He's not much of a driver either. I've been looking out the window, and he just drove his truck over three bikes."

## RICH

He's so rich that he has a gold tooth . . . but his grew in.

Most of us hate to see a poor loser—or a rich winner.

Their town is rich. The high school mascot is a mink.

He made so much money betting on the Democrats, he became a Republican.

He got rich by a lucky stroke. His rich uncle had one.

He collects Old Masters and young mistresses.

I wouldn't say they're rich, but even their paper plates are sterling silver.

In my rich neighborhood, the girls go around selling Girl Scout croissants.

He's so rich, he buys *TV Guide* in the hardcover edition.

I think that a four-room Rolls is a little ostentatious.

I never wanted much out of life—just to be born into a family where filet mignon was soul food.

This kid is so rich, he has a chauffeur for his sled.

He has music in his elevator—a live band.

When a man becomes rich, there's only one change. Instead of his wife telling him to move the couch, it's the decorator.

"He's real rich—he flies his own Cessna."

"A lot of people fly their own Cessna."

"In the living room?"

This little kid wanted a set of trains, so his father bought him Amtrak.

He was so rich, his nurse had a maid.

He was so rich, his piggy bank had two vice presidents.

There's only one problem with living in the lap of luxury. You never know when luxury is going to stand up.

**A** rich man often speaks with the courage of his investments.

**H**e's so rich, his kid has an air-conditioned baby carriage.

**H**e's so rich, he has no parking problems. He buys cheap cars and leaves them.

**H**e's so rich—in his kitchen, his crumbs have their own mice.

**H**e's got money—he has a split-level 350 SL.

**H**e lives in a real rich town. The station wagons there are bigger than the station.

### RIDDLES

"**W**hat is pigskin used for?"
"To hold the pig together."

"**W**hy is a helicopter good to take along fishing?"
"Because the whirlybird gets the worm."

"**H**ow did the rocket lose its job?"
"It got fired."

"**W**hat's the best way to keep a skunk from smelling?"
"Hold his nose."

"**W**hy is grass dangerous?"
"It's full of blades."

"**W**hat's pink and moist and split in the middle?"
"A grapefruit."

"**W**hat are two things you can never eat for breakfast?"
"Lunch and dinner."

"**W**hat's a Grecian urn?"
"Depends on his line of work."

"**H**ow do you make gold soup?"
"You put in fourteen carrots."

"**D**id you hear about the man who ran over himself?"
"No, how did he do that?"
"He couldn't get anybody to go, so he ran over himself."

"**W**hy can't you drive a golf ball?"
"It doesn't have a steering wheel."

"**W**hat has a foot on each side and another foot in the middle?"
"A yardstick."

"**W**hy is the figure 9 like a peacock?"
"Because without its tail, it's nothing."

"**W**hat starts with *T* and ends with *T* and is full of *T*?"
"A teapot."

"**W**here do you find a turtle without feet?"
"Exactly where you left him."

"What's the best way to make a coat last?"

"Make the pants first."

"Why does Santa love his garden?"

"Because he likes to ho, ho, ho."

"Why did twenty-five men walk out of a restaurant?"

"They were finished eating."

## RITZY

She won't even buy ladyfingers unless they're manicured.

He's so ritzy, he has an unlisted Social Security number.

When he went to jail for embezzlement, they had to give him an unlisted uniform.

This rich man went on a diet. He hired somebody to swallow for him.

So I made a lot of money, and I can afford to buy champagne and beluga caviar. Now if I could only learn to like them.

Two newly enriched men plan a golf game. One says, "I have to warn you—at my club they don't let you use caddies."

The other man replies, "That's okay. We'll use Buicks."

## ROBOTS

Then there was this robot that said to the gas pump, "Take your finger out of your ear and listen to me."

"What's the difference between a male robot and a female robot?"

"Lug nuts."

One robot asks another, "Read any good books lately?"

The second robot says, "Nah, books are all the same. Boy meets girl, boy loses girl, and then boy builds girl."

Two robots find a way out of the lab and go out on the town. They separate in hopes they can escape notice. They meet after a while. One of them is standing in front of a mailbox and a fire alarm.

The new arrival says, "Who are your two friends?"

The waiting robot says, "Forget them. The short, fat one with the big mouth just stands there, and if you touch the redhead, she screams."

## ROCK & ROLL

I went to a rock-and-roll concert last week along with thirty thousand others—two thousand kids and twenty-eight thousand cops.

Then there was the rock-and-roll star who wore a hearing aid for years. Then he found out all he needed was a haircut.

Some groups are so loud, they make my ears water!

**A** nice thing about playing rock and roll is that if you make a mistake, nobody notices.

**D**ad sticks his head into Junior's room and yells, "Turn off that darn radio of yours!"

Junior says, "I turned it off an hour ago, Dad."

**T**here's a great advantage to a rock-and-roll song. Nobody can whistle it.

**I**'m getting scared. Rock is beginning to sound like music to me.

**Y**ou can't tell me that rock isn't a lot of noise. I was in a restaurant the other night, and a waiter dropped a tray of dishes. Three young couples got up to dance.

**T**he only problem with rock and roll is that you can't tell when the record is worn out.

**"W**ho's your favorite rock group?"
"Mount Rushmore."

**A** rock-and-roller went to a doctor for a wrenched knee, and his first question was, "Doc, will I still be able to sing?"

### ROMANCE

**"S**ir, I am seeking your daughter's hand," said the young man hesitantly. "Have you any objection, sir?"

"None at all," said the father. "Take the one that's always in my pocket!"

**A** man ran into his ex-wife at a party and, after a few drinks, said to her, "Why don't we go out to dinner, a little music, candlelight, and then maybe we can make love?"

"Over my dead body!"

"I see—you haven't changed a bit."

**A** young man came home and told his father that he'd just gotten engaged. The father said, "Well, tonight you'll find out if you're a man or a mouse. If you make love tonight, you're a man. If you hold off until you're married, you're a mouse."

The young man said, "I guess I'm a rat. I made love to her last night."

**A**ll the world loves a lover—except the lady's husband.

**T**hree young people met at a lecture. One, a young man, said, "My name's Paul, but I'm not an apostle."

The second, also a young man said, "My name's Peter, but I'm not a saint."

The last of the trio, a young lady, said, "Gee, my name's Mary, and I don't know what the heck to say."

**A** couple went out on a blind date and visited a carnival. "What do you want to do?" the young man asked.

"I'd like to get weighed," the girl answered.

The boy took her to the midway, and a beturbaned weight-guesser looked the lady over and said that she weighed about a hundred and ten.

As they walked away, the young man asked, "What do you want to do now?"

"I'd like to get weighed."

Back they went to the midway. This continued for an hour, until the young man figured he'd had enough. He took the girl home and exited quickly.

As she entered her house, the young lady was welcomed by her mother, who asked, "Did you have nice time, dear?"

The girl said, "Wousy."

This young man was trying to find out the score with the young lady, so he asked her to have breakfast with him. The young lady agreed. Then the young man went on, "Shall I phone you or nudge you?"

I was in love with the girl next door. I walked my dog in front of her house so often, her tree died.

Many a man with money to burn has gotten a girl to start playing with fire.

The married boss says to his secretary, "Will you ever forget this weekend in Palm Springs?"

"Possibly. What am I offered?"

I tried everything on my wife—flowers, candy, jewelry, mink—and they all worked.

An old-timer is somebody who remembers when the only problem you had

parking your car was getting the girl to agree to it.

A lovely lass gave her analysis of the difference between "like" and "love," saying, "If I like them, I let them. If I love them, I help them."

The office Christmas party was in full swing. Off in a corner, on the couch in the outer reception room, their breathing was inspired. "Alex," she said, passionately, "Alex, oh, Alex. You've never given me so much before. Do you think it's because of the holiday spirit?"

"No," he breathed softly, "I think it's because my name is Phil."

Not too many things cost more than a girl who is free for the evening.

If all the world loves a lover, how come Lovers' Lane is crawling with cops?

In the old days, a young girl used to say, "Stop it or I'll scream." Now, she says, "Make it snappy or I'll scram."

The young lady says to her beau, "You asked my father for my hand in marriage. What did he say?"

"Nothing," the beau answered. "He just threw his arms around me and sobbed."

He invited her to his apartment to look at his etchings. When she walked into the apartment, she saw that he had no etchings. Nor did he have one piece of furniture. She was floored.

For everything you give, two come back to you. Last year I had my daughter at home, and two weeks ago she and her husband moved in with us.

He finally got his girl to say yes. Next time they may even talk about marriage.

A cute girl fended off her boyfriend by telling him, "Nothing goes in until the ring goes on."

### ROTTEN

He's a real mean guy—he showed his kid a picture of Santa's funeral.

He's so rotten, he'd get a hammer and flatten out Braille.

He's the kind of guy who'd take a Polaroid of somebody with nine seconds to live!

He'd go to a blind man's house and rearrange the furniture.

He's the kind who goes over to the widow after the funeral and says, "Have a nice day."

### RUNNING

A candidate is going from door to door, giving out some campaign literature. When he reaches a corner house and rings the doorbell, he is set on by a large dog. Discretion being the better part of valor, he starts to run, with the dog in pursuit. Opening the door, the lady of the house yells, "What are you running for?"

The candidate yells back, "Alderman, Fourth District."

There's a critical spot in marathon running. Just before you get to it, you're afraid you'll die. When you pass it, you're afraid you won't die!

### RUSSIANS

A Russian dies and goes to hell. Asked which section he'd like to stay in, he answers, "Put me in the Russian section. There, I know, the heater won't work."

A Russian scientist calls IBM and says, "I have one of your computers, but I can't make heads or tails out of the instructions."

The IBM man says, "We can't help you. We don't read Japanese either."

A Russian's a guy who sits on nothing and dances.

During World War II, a Russian pilot was describing one of his exploits to some American pilots, saying with a heavy accent, "Over Stalingrad, two German fuckers attacked me. I get away and into the sun, but the fuckers come after me. I try to shake them, but it was hard to shake the fuckers."

An American pilot said, "You mean Fokkers. F-O-K-K-E-R-S. They were flying Fokkers."

The Russian said, "No, these fuckers was flying Messerschmidts."

A Russian family owned a parrot, and one day they came home to find it was gone. They rushed to the local office of the KGB. The agent in charge asked them, "If you lost a parrot, why come to the KGB?"

The owner said, "Well, they might bring him here, and I want you to know we don't share his opinions."

A Russian commissar was talking to another and wondered what would happen if the border were open, saying, "We'd be the only two Russians left."

"Really?" the other commissar said. "You and who else?"

A Russian asked another one, "What would you do if they opened the border to the West?"

The second said, "I'd climb a tree."

"Why a tree?"

"So I wouldn't get trampled by the mob."

In the United States, everybody talks and nobody listens. In Russia, everybody listens and nobody talks.

What's a Russian string quartet?

A symphony orchestra on the way back from an American tour.

A dissident was tried and sentenced to Siberia. He said to the judge, "Look, if America is so bad, why don't you send me there?"

Some of the Baltic republics show absolutely no gratitude to Russia for all those years of Soviet oppression.

There are two questions about Lithuania—why do the Russians want to keep it, and why do the Lithuanians want it back?

When you're in a Russian hotel, never put out your cigarettes in the potted plants. It could damage the microphones.

In Russia, a man can really talk his head off.

A Russian looked at an American mail-order catalog and said, "Whoopee! Look at all the great new things to invent."

We just worked out a great trade treaty with the Russians. We're sending them fifty thousand cars, and they're sending us a hundred thousand parking spaces from Siberia.

A Russian was bragging about his sons. One was a physician, a second a lawyer, a third, a scientist, but the son he was proudest of was the one who had emigrated to the United States. "There," the father explained, "he doesn't have a job, he's on welfare, and gets food stamps, but if it wasn't for the money he sends home, the rest of us would starve."

A German and Russian were fishing on opposite sides of a small river. The German kept reeling in fish after fish. Puzzled, the Russian said, "I can't understand it. I'm not even getting a nibble."

The German said, "Maybe on your side, the fish are afraid to open their mouths."

**A** Yank and a Russian were discussing travel. The Yank said, "I take a Caddy to go to my office, my wife takes the BMW to go shopping, and when we go to Europe, we rent a Fiat."

The Russian said, "I go to office by subway, my wife walks to do her shopping, and when we go to Europe, we go by tank."

**In** Russia, there's a shortage of everything but shortages.

**The** Russians have just come out with a reinforced bra. It supports and lifts the masses.

# S

## SAFARIS

**A** man on safari lost his guide, and the native bearers ran away. Suddenly, he was surrounded by fierce-looking natives. Remembering a trick he'd seen once in a movie, he whipped out his cigarette lighter, flicked it, and pushed the flame toward the leader of the natives.

The leader jumped back and said, "It's a miracle. I've never seen a lighter that worked the first time."

**A** hunter's wife said, "I spotted a leopard."

Her husband said, "They come that way."

**The** Bronsons were on safari in Kenya. As they walked through the jungle, a lion jumped out from behind some trees and grabbed Mrs. Bronson. She screamed to her husband, "Shoot! Shoot!"

Mr. Bronson said, "I can't. I'm out of film."

**The** Brickmans decide to have a very special bar mitzvah for their son. Instead of the usual luau or lawn party, they hire a special caterer who puts together the most unique bar mitzvah of all time. The guests will be taken on a safari to Africa. There, under a jungle canopy, the young Jewish boy will take the vows that help a youngster become a man.

The Brickmans charter a plane, entertain their guests aboard the flight, take over a section of the most modern hotel in Nairobi, and start out on safari.

Two days into their journey, the jungle guide orders the procession to stop. Mrs. Brickman says, "Why are we stopping?"

The guide explains, "They're backed up today. There are two bar mitzvahs and an engagement party ahead of us."

While on safari, Mrs. Mislin wakes up from a light sleep to see a cobra slithering across the ground. Mrs. Mislin screams, "Get out of here!"

The cobra says, "As soon as that mongoose goes."

## SAFE SEX

The Polish mother asked her son if he had any protection for his date that night. "You don't have to worry, Ma, I've got a knife."

They have a new definition of safe sex— don't go to the office party.

I'm always concerned about safe sex. The first thing I ask a girl is, "When will your folks be home?"

He practices real safe sex—he gives the girl a phony name.

In high school, they're teaching courses in safe sex. If you don't get a pass, you're in for more tests.

My girl and I have taken safe sex to heart. We never see one another.

My wife and I really practice safe sex. We go right to the cigarette.

My girl really believes in safe sex. She makes me floss after it.

## SALARIES

Some fast-food companies are starting to hire older people. Now you can make as much at eighty as you did when you were fourteen!

There are so many deductions on my paycheck, if I cash it, I lose money.

The salary we dreamed of ten years ago, we can't live on today!

The assistant clerk asked the boss for a raise. The boss answered, "Young fellow, I worked five years for six dollars a week in this shop, and now I own it."

The assistant said, "I'm not surprised. Any man who treats his help like that is gonna lose his business!"

The train conductor had it good for years. He'd never told his wife what he earned. One day he was sick, and she picked up the check, discovering that he made a lot of money. She accosted him:

"I never dreamed that you made so much money."

The conductor said, "There's really not that much left after I pay the engineer, the fireman, the brakeman . . ."

## SALESMEN

The greatest salesman in the world is the guy who brought a girl up to his apartment to see his etchings, and he sold her four etchings.

The greatest salesman in the world is the guy who sold a milking machine to a farmer with only one cow, and then he took the cow as a down payment.

A customer asks, "What can you suggest for a man of fifty?"

The salesgirl answers, "How about a girl of twenty?"

A salesman in a haberdashery sells a customer a cheaply made tie.

The customer goes home and tries to hang himself by the tie. But it rips, and he doesn't get hurt.

Hearing about this the next day, the salesman says, "He owes me his life. Can you imagine if we carried good ties?"

I ran into a real dumb salesgirl. I tried to buy some invisible ink, and she wanted to know what color.

One car salesman told me, "Of course I'm an honest man. It's one of the conditions of my parole."

I knew a traveling salesman who died and left his wife $65,000 in towels.

I know the greatest salesman in the world. He actually made his wife feel sorry for the girl who lost her panties and bra in his car.

The boss gives Sindon an impossible route—fifteen cities in nine days. When Sindon returns, the boss says, "All right, where are the orders?"

Sindon replies, "I've been too busy traveling. Who had time to take orders?"

"This is the greatest medicine in the world," said the street vendor. "Look at me, for example. Purely by use of this medicine, I have lived to the healthy, hearty age of three hundred."

"Hey, is that true?" a listener asked the man's young assistant.

"Can't say," said the assistant. "I've only been with him a hundred years."

A prominent midtown salesman entertained an out-of-town buyer lavishly one week. The very next day, he got an order for three hundred more girls.

A manufacturer says to a friend, "I feel miserable. This morning, my best salesman died."

"What did he have?"

"New England and upstate New York."

A man goes into a department store to buy some perfume for his wife. The salesgirl has her nose buried in a book and doesn't even bother to look up. The man tries to get her attention a half-dozen times, but she pays no heed. Finally, the man manages to get her to look up and asks, "What book are you reading?"

"A new one called *How to Sell.*"

---

"George is so forgetful," the sales manager complained to his secretary. "It's a wonder he can sell anything. I asked him to pick me up some sandwiches on his way back from lunch, and I'm not sure he'll even remember to come back!"

Just then the door flew open, and in bounced George. "You'll never guess what happened!" he shouted. "While I was at lunch, I met Old Man Brown, who hasn't bought anything from us for five years. Well, we got to talking, and he gave me this half-million-dollar order!"

"See," sighed the sales manager. "I told you he'd forget the sandwiches."

---

Two passengers lolling in deck chairs on the *Queen Mary* were boasting to each other of their sales abilities.

"I'm from Schenectady," one said, "and you may not believe it, but the day before we sailed, I sold General Electric one million dollars' worth of cardboard boxes."

"That's nothing," the other said. "I run a clothing store in Glens Falls. The day before we sailed, a woman came in to buy a suit to bury her husband in, and I sold her an extra pair of pants!"

## SANTA CLAUS

Santa has the right idea. He knows how to make himself welcome—he comes around once a year.

One Santa went to a shrink and said, "Help me, Doc. I don't believe in myself."

Then there's the kid whose father hadn't been home since his mother caught Santa Claus kissing the maid.

Many Santas who work in department stores suffer from water on the knee, some of them ten times a day.

Two kids are dragging and kicking at a big bulky sack. A passerby says to them, "If you keep doing that, Santa won't come around to visit you."

One of the kids says, "No? Who do you think we got in this sack?"

## SAVINGS & LOANS

A woman recently broke up with a man because she found out he wasn't a construction worker. He was really the president of a savings and loan.

They now have a new game called S&L Monopoly. Most of the rules are the same, but now you buy houses with other people's money.

Now we know what Robin Hood was doing in the forest—running a savings and loan.

The government expects to spend $400 billion to bail out the savings and loans. Wouldn't a large pail do it just as well?

The ex-president of a savings and loan was just sent to jail. If he acts up even once, he'll lose golf and tennis privileges.

## SCATOLOGICAL JOKES

My doctor gave me a powerful laxative last week. It may not cure me, but it will sure give me a run for my money.

A man is severely constipated. His doctor gives him a powerful laxative.

The next day, the man's wife calls the doctor and explains that her husband had died that morning.

"Did the laxative work on him?" the doctor asks.

"Yup," says the wife. "Three times before he died and twice afterward."

"What's the difference between a rectal and an oral thermometer?"

"Taste."

A deer and a rabbit are both relieving themselves in the forest. The deer asks the rabbit, "Listen, I'm curious—does crap stick to your fur?"

The rabbit says, "Of course not."

"Great," the deer says, and he wipes his rear end with the rabbit.

## SCHOOL

A teacher told her friend, "I have one child in class who's impossible. He's loud and nasty. He talks all the time. And the worst thing of all—he's got a perfect attendance record."

Little Billy brought home his report card. His mother took him to task for all the low grades. Little Billy responded, "It's got its good side too. You know darn well I'm not cheating!"

Miss Brown was very upset with Jimmy, saying, "This composition about the puppy is exactly like your brother's."

Jimmy said, "Why not? It's the same puppy!"

Little Jimmy brought his report card back to school and told his teacher, "Look, I don't want to scare you, but the next time I bring home a report card that bad, somebody's gonna get whipped!"

The teacher says, "If any of you have to go to the bathroom, please raise two fingers."

From the back, little Johnny says, "How's that going to stop it?"

Little Joey complained about school: "I'm not going back tomorrow. I can't read yet. I can't write. And they won't let me talk!"

The teacher asked the class where God lived. Many ventured different opinions.

Finally, it was little Peter's turn. He said, "The Lord lives in my bathroom."

The teacher said, "How could you say a thing like that?"

Little Peter said, "It's true. In the morning, my father gets up, knocks on the bathroom door, and says, 'Good God, are you still in there?' "

The kids in my old neighborhood never drop out of school. There'd be nobody to drive the teachers crazy.

The teacher reproached a student, "You can't sleep in my class."

The student said, "If you didn't talk so loud, I could."

There are no more little red schoolhouses, but there sure are a lot of little-read youngsters.

The singing teacher asked if anyone in the class could sing "The Star-Spangled Banner." Little Joey stood up and sang, "And the home of the brave, play ball. Is that the one?"

He went to school one day a year. That was to find out when vacation started.

A teacher asked her class to make a list of the five greatest Americans. One youngster seemed to be having a great deal of trouble. The teacher asked him what his problem was. He answered, "I can't decide about the center."

My son was out of school for three days last week. His teacher sent home a thank-you note.

I had a terrible time in school. Everybody hated me because I was so popular.

Our local high school just figured out a way to save money. They're going to teach driver ed and sex education in the same car.

This schoolteacher got married, but she couldn't forget her training. Every time her husband sent her a love letter, she sent it back corrected!

My nephew thinks school is stifling. They teach you to spell a word only one way.

Some people are against sex education in school and have a good reason. When they learned math, math started to bore them.

The teacher asked the class to write a composition on where the elephant was found. One kid wrote, "The elephant is so big, he's hardly ever lost."

The teacher checked Johnny's math and shook her head. Johnny said, "But I added it up ten times. You can see my ten answers if you want to."

Mixed emotions is when your kid gets an "A" in sex education.

The human brain is special. It starts working as soon as you get up, and it doesn't stop until you get to school.

My son always complained that he'd never learn to spell in school. The teacher kept changing the words.

A second-grader is heard saying a terrible four-letter word by his teacher. She admonishes him, "You shouldn't use a word like that. You don't even know what it means."
The second-grader says, "Sure I do. It means that the car won't start."

A school custodian can tell how far the semester has progressed by the size of the crayons on the floor.

A youngster comes home from school with a note from the teacher that says he doesn't have an inquiring mind. The mother is furious. "You're going to have an inquiring mind. I'm going to make you have an inquiring mind. If I have to beat you, you'll have an inquiring mind."
The youngster says, "What's an inquiring mind?"
"Shut up and don't ask so many questions!"

It costs more nowadays to amuse a kid than it used to cost to educate his father.

"Did Mary's lamb follow her to school every day?" a young boy asked his father.
"That she did," his father said.
"How'd it all end?" the inquisitive boy asked.
"They finally separated," the father said. "The lamb graduated."

A school kid asks his teacher, "Is it true that the Law of Gravity keeps us on Earth?"
The teacher says, "Yes."
"What kept us before the law was passed?"

A student is reprimanded for not having written a book report on a Dickens novel. The student says, "I couldn't help it. We couldn't get the video."

I must be missing something. Parents drive kids to school, and then the kids go to a physical-education class where they learn how to exercise.

My kid must have a Chinese teacher. She's always giving him homework to take out.

I once fell in love with my public-school teacher. It didn't work out. She was twenty-four, I was thirty-eight.

## SCIENCE

One of these days, scientists are going to discover why a kid can't walk around a puddle.

For ages, uranium cost pennies—then scientists found out that you could kill people with it.

In a movie house, two chemists watch a picture in which a girl fights like the dickens for her virtue. One chemist says to the other, "What's she making a big fuss over? She's only worth a dollar and a quarter."

The Theory of Relativity is like an erection. The more you think about it, the harder it gets.

If scientists were any good, they could come up with a lying bathroom scale.

"How far does light travel?"
"I don't know, but it gets here real early in the morning."

Albert Einstein received a call from an acquaintance one night at 3:00 A.M. In a drunken voice, the friend asked him, "Can you explain to me the relationship between positively charged electrons and antimatter?"
"I can't possibly explain that to you over the phone, but if you'll come down to the lab tomorrow, I can clear it up for you."
"I can't wait for tomorrow," the man said.
"Why can't it wait until tomorrow?" Einstein asked.
"Because tomorrow I won't give a damn!"

Scientists used to wonder how old the world was. Now, they're just wondering how long it's going to last.

I always had a scientific bent. I once tried to build a woman with my Erector Set.

## SCOTS

A Scot was walking down the street when a cute young lady tourist said, "I've always wondered what you men had under your kilts."
The Scot said, "I'm a man of few words. Give me your hand."

A Scot came to America by ship. As they docked, he saw a deep-sea diver come up from studying the hull. The Scot said, "If I'd known about an outfit like that, I would have walked over too."

You can tell what a Scot is by what he has under his kilt. If it's a quarter-pounder, then he's a McDonald.

In spite of the long line behind him, the Scotsman at the Radio City Music Hall box office counted his change very carefully three times.
The ticket seller watched him for a while and finally grew impatient. "What's the matter?" he asked. "Isn't the change right?"
"Oh, it's right," the Scotsman said, "but only just right."

One Scot went crazy trying to shoot off a cannon a little at a time.

A wealthy Scot died and left no instructions about his ample estate. His two sons started to quarrel about the division of the estate. The local minister solved the problem, saying, "Why doesn't one of you become the executor of the estate, divide it, and let the other one have first choice?"

A young American lady tourist asks this handsome kilted Scot, "Is there anything worn under your kilt?"

"No, miss," he says, "it's as good as it ever was."

An innkeeper in Scotland acknowledged cheerfully at breakfast that the family's pet ghost paid him a visit last night. "But he didn't stay very long," he added. "He vanished the moment I asked him for a small contribution to the community fund!"

"What did the Scotsman do with his first fifty-cent piece?"

"He married it."

Then there was this Scottish terrorist. He lit a bomb but hated to let go of it.

A Scotsman is on the way home from a night on the town. Being in no shape to make it, he lies down in a meadow to take a nap. Two lasses come by and see him. One says, "Now's the time to see whether he's got anything under his kilt."

They look and find the usual. To play a trick on the poor man, they tie a blue ribbon around it and go off.

The Scot awakes later and looks down. Smiling, he says, "I don't know what you've been up to, but I'm glad you took first prize."

A Scottish chemistry professor dropped two shillings into a glass of acid and asked his class to explain why the coins wouldn't dissolve.

"Because," one student offered, "if they would, you wouldn't have dropped them in there!"

## SECRETARIES

My wife fired my secretary the other day because she felt she was a security risk—hers!

Three secretaries got together for the morning coffee break. One whispered, "Last night I left a condom on Mr. Baker's desk."

The second secretary said, "I saw it, and I poked a hole in it."

The third secretary fainted.

The personnel manager said to the curvaceous applicant, "You've got the job. Now would you like to try for a raise?"

The new secretary wasn't the brightest. Coming to work the first day, she walked into the boss's office and saw him putting golf balls. She asked what they were, and he told her they were golf balls. About a week later, the secretary came in and saw him putting again, and said, "Gee, I see you shot another golf."

My secretary is well trained. The other day she told her boyfriend, "Stop and/or I'll scream!"

The sudden arrival of the boss's wife has made many a secretary change her position.

The old man was being sued by his secretary for breach of promise. Somebody said, "You're eighty-five. What could you promise her?"

The secretary forgot to order the sofa for the new executive suite. So the boss had her on the carpet.

The pretty secretary was late coming back from lunch and explained to the boss, "I couldn't help it. A tall, gorgeous man was following me, and he walked very slowly."

She's some secretary. She can't type well, but she erases fifty-five words a minute.

This one secretary resigned a few days ago. She found the boss being too friendly with his wife.

A secretary tells another in the office, "I knew I couldn't trust the boss. He went home to his wife."

One boss confided his great way to treat secretaries, saying, "I don't mess with them. If at first I don't succeed, they're fired!"

Eager to make a good impression on his new boss, a young man showed up at his job promptly at eight. He found the boss's curvy blond secretary sitting on the boss's lap.

The next day the young man arrived at eight-fifteen to find the boss and secretary kissing. As he tiptoed out, the boss called after him, "If you get here tomorrow at eight-thirty, you're fired!"

She's a very efficient secretary. She hasn't missed a coffee break in two years.

My secretary can write shorthand, but it takes her longer.

The boy in the shipping department asked the secretary, "How'd you get your raise?"

She said, "I'll tell you, but it wouldn't do you much good."

I only give my secretary a half hour for lunch. If she took longer, she'd have to be retrained.

Johnson hired three voluptuous women as his secretaries. His partner asked, "How do you expect to get anything accomplished?"

Johnson said, "It's easy. I'll give two of them the day off."

The boss says very sweetly, "Your typing has really improved. I can only see four mistakes. Now type the second word."

Two secretaries are chatting by the water cooler. One says, "Marge, I'm telling you, this time it's the real thing—sex!"

A new woman being interviewed for a job as secretary asks, "What will I earn?"

"How much do you expect a day?" the boss asks.

"Fifty dollars."

"I'll give you that with pleasure."

"With pleasure, it'll be seventy-five."

---

"Excuse me, but I'm Mr. Troy's wife."

"I'm Mr. Troy's secretary."

"Oh, were you?"

---

Hilda, the secretary, rushes in to see her boss and says, "Mr. Cooper, I have good news and bad news for you."

"What's the good news?"

"You're not sterile."

---

My last secretary quit because, after all the coffee breaks, she couldn't sleep at night.

---

For her first week's pay, I gave my new secretary a gorgeous negligee. For her second week's pay, I gave her some jewelry. For her third week's pay, I raised her first week's pay.

## SECRETS

There are some people who can keep a secret except when telling the truth will cause more damage.

---

My nephew has been going to private school for three years, and it's driving his parents bonkers. He won't tell them where it is.

---

Make someone happy today. Mind your own business.

---

My wife can keep a secret. It's the women she tells it to who can't.

---

They had fallen madly in love while vacationing, but the day of departure had arrived. He said, "It can't end like this. I know we're both married, but we must go on meeting."

She said, "Would you really want us to sneak around, meet in out-of-the-way places? Would you really want me to join you in cheap hotel rooms? Would you?"

He said, "It was only a suggestion."

## SEDUCTION

The hooker reports to her procurer about the assignment she'd been on. "He was a strange cat," she says. "He wanted to make love in a coffin."

"That must have made you sick."

"It did, but the pallbearers seemed to like it."

---

The great Norse god Thor prided himself on seducing a different woman each night. One conquest pleased him so much, he decided to marry her.

Early in the morning, he tapped her on the shoulder and said, "Darling, I'm Thor."

The woman said, "Tho am I, but it wath worth it."

## SERVICE STATIONS

I went into a service station the other day. The attendant asked, "How can I help you?"

I said, "Gas."
So he burped me.

I hate self-service. It's always so bad!

## SEX

A coolie is a quickie in the snow.

You can't take sex with you, so you might as well wear it out here.

A young man has a prodigious sexual appetite that is matched by his ability to deliver. An impresario signs him for a tour. On their first engagement, showtime arrives. The young man polishes off the first woman volunteer, the second, the third, but on the fourth, he falters and is unable to perform. The impresario rushes to him and asks, "What's the matter?"

The young man says, "I don't know. This afternoon the rehearsal went great."

A young woman meets a young man at a church social. The young man asks her if he can get her a drink. The young woman says, "I don't drink."

He offers her a cigarette. Again she declines. Then she says, "Come with me, I want to show you something. She leads him to a small room off the vestibule, where she proceeds to throw herself on him and make the most passionate love.

Finished, she says, "See how much fun you can have without drinking or smoking?"

A group of refugees arrived in the country and were taken to the town church. There, townspeople like Mrs. Peterson were to pick those they'd take care of.

Indicating an old man and woman, Mrs. Peterson said, "You two will come home with me."

Arriving at her house, she showed them to a guest bedroom and told them they'd sleep there.

A little later, the old woman came down to Mrs. Peterson and said, "I think you are very nice, lady, but who is this old guy I'm going to sleep with?"

A woman says to her husband, as she clasps her hands together, "Guess what I have here and you get some loving tonight."

The husband says, "An elephant."

The wife says, "That's close enough."

A man joins the Foreign Legion. In the evening, he asks where the other fellows get their fun. They explain that there's a camel and a big waiting list. His turn finally comes, and he starts to unzip his fly. The Legionnaire next to him says, "I don't know what you're planning to do, but the rest of us get on the camel and he takes us to the girls."

After forty years of marriage, my wife and I finally reached total sexual compatibility. We both had a headache.

Most divorced husbands find out that sex isn't as much fun as when they used to cheat.

Never make love if you've got something better to do—but what's better?

This man wanted some old-fashioned loving. I introduced him to my grandmother.

My old girl was really patriotic. I found her number on the wall of a voting booth.

I won't say she's a lover, but she left her diaphragm to the Smithsonian.

Sex isn't half as much fun when you're a bachelor. You can't cheat.

Just because a guy asks a girl to lie down on the couch doesn't mean he's a psychiatrist.

Tom Bryce goes over to Al's house after work and tells Al's wife that Al had to work late. Then he looks at the attractive woman and says, "I'll give you five hundred dollars if you'll make love to me." Astonished, but practical, Al's wife dispenses her favors to Tom.

Later that evening, Al comes home bushed and asks, "Did Tom Bryce come by this evening? He promised to give me the five hundred he owed me."

I believe that a man should kiss and tell. Most of us need all the publicity we can get.

To me, nowadays sex is a four-letter word—help!

Sex can shorten your life. I know a guy who got killed by sex when he was thirty. A jealous husband shot him.

My sex life is terrific. Especially the one in the winter.

It's a sad story. She forgot to take a pill, so he took a powder.

When she's good, she's very good. When she's bad, she's better.

When it comes to making love, he's a winner—he always finishes first.

I'm against topless dancing. The best part of getting a gift is unwrapping it.

Chastity is its own punishment.

He prefers masturbation to regular sex, because he doesn't have to get up at four in the morning to drive his hand home.

I haven't had sex in so long, I don't remember which one gets tied up.

He's never given a girl a present, but he did give a couple a pretty good past.

Worry is the first time you can't make it the second time. Panic is the second time you can't make it the first time.

Some people love to make love to schoolteachers. Who else makes you do it over and over till you get it right?

The difference between sex for money and sex for free is that sex for money usually costs a lot less.

Romance is timing. The girl has to give in just before the guy gives up.

Sex appeal is 50 percent what you got and 50 percent what men think you've got.

Nowadays, people do things in cars they wouldn't even do in French postcards.

Sex is dirty, but only when it's done right.

A plump man boarded the bus and sat down. The woman seated opposite whispered to her friend, "If that stomach was on a woman, it would indicate that she was in a family way."

Overhearing the remark, the plump man said, "It was—and she is."

There's a lot of permissiveness nowadays. The only way to avoid sex is to get married.

My doctor recently gave me something for my sex drive—a ticket to Lourdes.

A recent survey shows that 10 percent of men interviewed liked women with thin legs. Another 10 percent liked fat legs. The rest liked something in between.

He held her close and tried to pretend a sexual interest. But finally he bellowed, "You have no boobs, and your hole's too tight."

She answered, "Get off my back!"

Three male hookers are discussing their trade. The first one says, "I kiss and nibble women on their toes. It drives them mad."

The second hooker says, "I'll show you how to drive women mad. Tickle them all over with a feather."

The third hooker shrugs off the first suggestions and says, "I make love to them, and then I wipe myself on their drapes. That really drives them wild!"

"Why is pubic hair curly?"

"It's a good thing, because otherwise it could blind you."

"What's twelve inches long and white?"

"Nothing."

Two older women meet and start to discuss their mates. The first one says, "There may be winter in my Tom's hair, but there's summer in his heart."

The second one says, "That's nice, but is there any spring in his ass?"

Then there was this young fellow who swerved to avoid a child. He fell out of bed.

Mr. Stone, a man in his sixties, went to see his physician son about impotence. After an examination, the son indicated that there were shots that would help. They were expensive, but the son would give them to his father at cost—twenty-five dollars each. A series of the shots followed.

A week later, the father returned for a second series, but insisted on paying fifty dollars per shot. The son said, "They only cost me twenty-five."

"I know," the father said, "but the other twenty-five is from your mother!"

Liz ran into her friend Marge, who was surprised to see marks on Liz's knees.

"What happened to you?" Marge asked.

"Oh, that's from making love doggie-style."

"Don't you know other ways?"

"Sure, but my dog doesn't!"

A young male driver was coasting along when he saw a nun standing on a corner. He drove toward her and stopped when he'd pulled up next to her. "Would you like a ride, Sister?" he asked.

The nun nodded, got into the car, and sat back gratefully.

After a few blocks, the young man said, "Sister, I have to tell you this—black and white really turns me on. It makes me so sexy."

A few blocks later, the young man went on, "No kidding, Sister. I'm really, really turned on. I'd love to take you up to the hills and make mad love to you."

The nun asked, "Are you a Catholic?"

"Sure."

"Then let's go up to the hills."

Stunned, the young man managed to navigate up to the hill that served as a Lovers' Lane for the town's younger people. The nun managed to satisfy him orally.

As they drove back toward the city streets, the young man said, "Sister, I have a confession to make. I'm not a Catholic."

The nun said, "I have a confession too. My name is Ralph, and I'm on the way to a costume ball!"

He makes love like a frog—he jumps on, he jumps off, and then he goes— "Ggychhhrr."

If it weren't for pickpockets, I'd have no sex life at all.

All men between fifteen and eighty have the same attitude toward sex—they like it.

You're allowed to buy anything in America. You can buy a suit, you can buy a sweater, you can buy a shirt. But you can't buy sex. What's more important—clothes or sex?

After watching a wild sex movie, Edith asked her husband, Ed, "How come you never make love to me like that?"

Ed answered, "Are you kidding? Do you know how much they pay those people to do that?"

One day, this famous womanizer felt a tickle in his throat. He turned to a friend and asked, "Do you know a cute girl I could gargle with?"

She's seen more love than a cop's flashlight.

**A** young lady at a cocktail party is bragging about her purity to another young lady, saying, "I still have my cherry."

The second says, "No kidding? Does it get in your way when you're screwing?"

**T**hree chorus girls meet in the dressing room before the show. The first has an impression of a *C* on her stomach. She explains, "My boyfriend goes to Cornell, and he forgot to take off his belt buckle."

The second has a *W* on her stomach and explains, "My date went to Wisconsin."

The third has an *F* on her stomach. The second chorus girl asks, "Your fellow go to Florida?"

The third chorus girl explains, "No. He's a fire chief and forgot to take off his hat."

**A**n American is in Paris and goes to the Left Bank for some fun and games. He asks one of the girls, "How about American Express?"

She answers, "I'll do it as fast I can, Monsieur."

**A** priest is in town for a guest sermon at the local church. He checks into a motel and, feeling a little hungry, goes down to the lobby, where he's about to put some coins in the vending machine, when a woman wrapped in a towel appears from the pool outside. As she heads for the elevator, the towel slips, and she stands there in her altogether.

Abashed, she says to the priest, "I'm so sorry, Father."

The priest says, "There's no need for forgiveness, my dear. As a priest, I do not see the outer manifestations of the body. I see only the soul. Tell me, would you happen to have two nipples for a quarter?"

**A** girl says, "I got picked up by the fuzz last night."

Her girlfriend asks, "Doesn't it hurt?"

**A** man is stopped in the street by a woman wearing tights and heavy makeup. She whispers, "For fifty dollars, I'll do anything you ask."

The man hands her the money and says, "Paint my house."

**T**he two most important things in his life are sex and laughs. Unfortunately, he gets them both at the same time.

"**S**ex is a pain."

"You're doing it wrong."

**S**ex over sixty can be dangerous, so pull over to the curb first.

**T**here's nothing I like better before a good cigarette than sex.

**A** guy who likes to lie in bed can usually find a girl who will listen to him.

**A** great way to soften up the lady: "How do you know you're not frigid?"

**T**he way I see it—a Peeping Tom is just a window fan.

A woman asks a friend, "Do you smoke after sex?"

The friend said, "Gee, I never looked."

"Were you ever in a predicament, Sue?"

"No, Alice, but I've tried."

"Is it a sin to have sex before the wedding?"

"Only if you block the aisle of the church."

On his honeymoon night, Jimmy finds that his wife is very adept at sex. Puzzled, he asks, "Have you ever done this before?"

"Just once."

"With whom?"

"The Chicago Bears."

A woman was bragging about her husband's athletic abilities. He was a local champion in many sports. The woman went on to explain he was so good at physical things, he'd do everything in the most difficult manner possible, simply out of boredom; and this helped him build his strength.

"I'd like to ask you one question," a woman said hesitantly.

"I know what you're thinking," her friend answered, smiling. "I don't mind telling you. In a hammock—standing up."

You know you ejaculate prematurely if you tell the girl, "It won't hurt, did it?"

A furrier from the United States goes to Helsinki to buy furs. As a reward for the long trip, he has a hooker sent to his room. When they are done, he says, "I'm afraid my Finnish isn't too good."

The hooker says, "Your foreplay isn't too hot either."

He was a very clumsy lover, so the girl had to put him in her place.

"Do you know how to keep a sex fiend in suspense?"

"How?"

"I'll tell you tomorrow."

I know a woman who wears a nightgown with all kinds of pleats and ruffles. Her husband has more fun looking for it than finding it.

I finally found out why Mary had a little lamb. A black sheep pulled the wool over her eyes.

"What's the problem with oral sex?"

"The view."

They met at work but had nothing in common. So they fooled around until they did.

## SEX EDUCATION

Sex education is a big thing today. I don't think kids should read books on sex. I think they should read a book or two on how to avoid it.

Be honest when you tell your kids about sex—use books, diagrams, and a laugh track.

I don't worry too much about sex education in the schools. If the kids learn it like they do everything else, they won't know how.

With sex education going strong today, many a minor becomes a major before he can spell.

Some sex-education classes are so graphic, schools are having a big drop-in problem.

## SEXY

She brings out the animal in men—mink, ermine, sable.

With her, opportunity doesn't knock. It whistles.

She's so sexy. She took up karate and now has a black garter belt.

She was quite a girl—two kids by her first husband, four by her second, three by her third. And five on her own.

They say a girl can't make the football team. She did.

I came into the world sexy. When I was born, the doctor didn't slap me. But three nurses had to.

She's an athletic girl. Will play ball with anybody.

With her shape, she wears prescription underwear.

## SHIPWRECKED

A mermaid and a sailor are on a deserted island. The sailor starts to get close to the mermaid when a giant shark's fin approaches them. The mermaid says, "You better cool it. Here comes my father."

Then there was the girl alone on a deserted island with a man. She hated being taken for granted.

A man is shipwrecked on a small island with a dog and a female pig. After a few days, the man becomes sexy and wants to go after the pig. Each time he starts to, the dog bares his fangs and growls. Several more weeks go by when, suddenly, a beautiful nude woman is washed ashore. She looks into the eyes of the man and whispers, "I'll do anything for you."
   The man says, "Great. Hold the dog."

A man is shipwrecked all alone on a deserted island. After several weeks, he sees a barrel and someone holding it to keep from going under. Closer and closer and finally ashore. The man is stunned to find a beautiful nude holding the barrel. She whispers, "I have something you want."
   The man says, "Don't tell me you've got beer in that barrel."

## SHOPPING

A man goes into a store to buy some rat poison. Handing him a packet, the storekeeper says, "You just sprinkle it around his hole."

The man says, "If I could get that close, I'd step on him."

A pretty young lady comes into a store and tells the clerk, "I want flats and the lowest-cut gown you've got."

The clerk says, "To wear with what?"

"A short, fat, bald millionaire."

My wife is a compulsive shopper. She bought me a gift the other day and then offered to buy it back from me.

My wife was in a dress shop the other day, and the salesgirl showed her a nice dress. My wife said, "It's pretty, but it's a lot less than I wanted to spend."

My wife is a magnetic woman. Everything she picks up, she charges.

A woman sees a beautiful necklace in a jewelry-store window. She goes inside and says to a clerk, "Will a small deposit hold that necklace until my husband does something unforgivable?"

A woman tried on a dozen pairs of glasses with different lenses. Nothing seemed to be right for her. To keep her from becoming unhappy, the eye doctor said, "Finding the right glasses can be very hard."

The woman said, "Especially when you're shopping for a friend!"

If my wife gets one more credit card, she'll have a complete deck.

A woman comes home with the ugliest contraption of all time. Her husband asks, "What salesman ever induced you to buy that ugly thing?"

The wife says, "One of the best in the business."

My wife'll buy anything that's marked down. Yesterday she came home with an escalator.

A man pushed his cart through the aisles of a grocery store. All the while, his baby screamed. The man kept repeating, "Keep calm, Billy. Don't yell, Billy. Don't get excited, Billy."

Finally, one woman said, "You are certainly to be commended for your patience."

"Lady," he declared, "I'm Billy!"

A man driving in southern Indiana saw a sign that read, LAST CHANCE FOR $1.25 GAS. As he was getting his change from the attendant he asked, "How much is gas in Kentucky?"

"A dollar fifteen."

They're really offering a lot of values. I saw one item that was marked down twenty-five dollars—a Rolls-Royce.

A man goes into Tiffany and asks to see some rings. The clerk shows him several.

The man points to one and asks how much it is. The clerk tells him, and the man lets out a real whistle. He then points to another ring. The clerk says, "That'll cost two whistles."

Nothing makes time go so fast as buying on it.

I went to a dime store. They had two dimes for a quarter.

A shoplifter was arrested the other day. The store detective became suspicious when she wore the same maternity dress for a year and a half.

Shoplifting may have its drawbacks, but it certainly saves you money.

One woman came up with a great way to save on grocery bills. She put her baby in the shopping cart and then filled the cart with everything in the store. By the time she got to the checkout stand, the baby had thrown out most of the food.

## SHORT

I won't say he's short, but yesterday he was unlucky. He walked under a black cat.

He's so short, his skin drags on the floor.

He's seen more knees than an orthopedic surgeon.

He's so short, his shirt collar is knee-length.

The whole world smells different to a short person.

## SHOW-OFFS

They're thinking of putting his head on Mount Rushmore. Why not, it's the right size.

"Let me tell you this, Evelyn. You're a terrible show-off. You brag. You're a snob. You think you know everything. You're the most pretentious woman I know!"

"Pretentious? *Moi?*"

I know a guy who graduated from college summa cum loudest.

## SHY

He was so shy, he used to pin his own diapers.

He was so shy—he was forty before he found out what he weighed stripped.

He's very shy. He once checked into a motel under an assumed name, and he was alone.

They recently isolated the gene for shyness. They had a hard time finding it, because it was hiding behind a couple of other genes.

They have a new sex kick for shy people who like orgies—they hump schizophrenics.

## SIAMESE TWINS

I wanted to have a date with a Siamese twin, but she couldn't get away.

A Siamese twin says to his brother, "Let's move to England so you can drive for a while."

"Have you heard about the absent-minded Siamese twin?"
"Everything went in one ear and out his brother's!"

## SILLY JOKES

The answer is: Intense.
The question is: Where do campers fool around?

"How do you get rid of a boomerang?"
"Throw it down a one-way street."

"Where's your coat?"
"I left it at the restaurant."
"Was it checked?"
"No, a solid navy."

"What's good for cold cuts?"
"Frozen Band-Aids."

"What does a bat do in the wintertime?"
"It cracks if you don't oil it."

## SKIING

The newest thing in ski equipment—a pair of skis that converts into a pair of splints!

I'm a great skier. My bones knit fast.

Skiing is a sport where you spend an arm and a leg to break an arm and a leg.

I go to a very fancy ski resort. They close down if it snows.

He had a job for a few days as a ski instructor, but he got fired.
Every time a girl fell down, he fell on top of her.

## SKYDIVING

I love to skydive. I jump out of a plane and try to land on a little black dot on the ground. But I have to remember to pull the rip cord so the black dot won't be me!

A student skydiver was being given instructions by the instructor: "You count to ten and just pull the rip cord."
The student said, "W-w-w-w-w-whhhattt w-w-w-was th-th-th-that n-n-num-m-mb-b-b-ber?"
The instructor said, "Two."

I'll never go skydiving. I'd hate to be dug up so I can be buried.

Skydiving isn't such a dangerous sport. Nobody's ever had more than one accident.

## SKYSCRAPERS

The foundation for a skyscraper is being dug when there's a cave-in, and tons of earth fill the former trench at the base. The construction boss comes over and asks a workman, "Does the foreman know about this?"

The workman: "He will as soon as we dig him out."

Three men enter the lobby of a sixty-story skyscraper only to find that the elevator isn't working. They'll have to walk up sixty stories. One says, "Look, to make it seem like less of a chore, let's each tell a sad story. It'll take our minds off the pain."

They start up. The first man tells about having lost his first love to another man. At the twenty-first story, the second man talks about how illness has plagued his family. When they start up the last twenty floors, the third man says, "I'll tell you a real sad story. I forgot the key to the office."

Due to a power outage, a man had to race down forty stories of a tall building, using the spiral staircase. He couldn't stop when he got downstairs, and ended up screwing himself into the ground!

I was riding up the elevator in a high rise. When we got to the top floor, I said, "Good Lord," and a voice answered, "Yes?"

### SLEEP

"If you're a light sleeper, try sleeping at the edge of the bed."

"Is that going to help me sleep?"

"Of course. In no time at all, you'll drop off."

Why is it that the one who snores always goes to sleep first?

"I haven't slept for six days."

"Aren't you tired?"

"No, I sleep nights."

### SMALL TOWN

No one has ever figured this out—a small town that can't afford one lawyer can always support two of them.

If you're a street cleaner, living in a one-horse town has a lot going for it.

It was a real small town. The phone book had one Yellow Page!

My hometown is so square, a playboy is anybody who's still up for the eleven o'clock news!

I stopped at a small-town garage one day. The attendant gave me the key to the bushes.

My hometown has some night life—unless she's ill that day.

My hometown was so small, the movie house was a Foto-mat.

It was a real small town. The ZIP code was a fraction.

My hometown is so small—the phone book only has first names.

Mine was a real small town. It was the only town with dead-end one-way streets!

My hometown was real small. Town drunk was an elective office.

The town was real small—the only industry was dust.

My hometown is so small, they don't even have a sanitation department—a cleaning woman comes in twice a week.

The town was so small—the local hooker was the community chest.

My hometown is so small, Second Street is in the next town.

"That guy was completely in the wrong," a man yelled from behind bars in the one-cell jail. "He was in complete violation of several traffic laws, and I had the right of way when he smashed my car! And you're holding *me*?"
    "That's right," said the cop.
    "Why?" the man asked.
    "Because that guy's father is the mayor, his brother is the chief of police, and I'm engaged to his sister."

My hometown is so small, it doesn't have a jail. When somebody does something bad, he has to stand in the corner.

I come from a very small and reserved town. It's very old-fashioned. The speed limit is zero, and you're not allowed to back up.

We didn't have any professional call girls in my hometown—just volunteers.

My hometown is so small—there's no place to go where you shouldn't.

This man was a dogcatcher in his small town, but he lost the job one day. He caught the dog.

She used to spend her time hanging around the village square—then she married him.

In a small town, if you see a girl out with someone who looks old enough to be her father, he is.

### SMOG

It's so smoggy in Los Angeles—when you eat a doughnut, you can taste the hole.

It's amazing, but in a backward country you can't drink the water, and in an advanced nation you can't breathe the air.

The air is so bad in Los Angeles, people deliberately crash their cars so they can suck on the air bag.

### SNAKES

A city dweller took himself to a mountain retreat for a weekend. Late in the evening, he returned to the hotel from a stroll in the woods. His clothes were ripped, his face bruised, his arms and legs scratched, and he looked as if he'd been in a war. The desk clerk asked what had happened.

The city soul said, "A big green snake chased me."

The desk clerk said, "The green snakes up here aren't poisonous."

The city dweller said, "If he can make me jump off a fifty-foot cliff, he doesn't have to be."

Then there was this snake that went to a psychiatrist. He claimed his friends stuck their tongues out at him.

Then there's this game of Hindu roulette. You sit next to a snake charmer with six cobras and one of them is deaf.

## SNOBS

A man is having dinner with some associates. The waiter happens to spill some water on him. The man jumps up and says, "You're not fit to serve a pig."

The waiter says, "I'm doing my best."

The only thing he ever did for a living was read his father's will.

He's living proof that stuffed shirts come in all sizes.

He spent ten thousand to have his family tree checked—five to go through it and five to hush it up.

I wouldn't say she's a snob, but she eats potato chips with a knife and fork.

One snobbish lady decided to shoot her husband, so she put on a hunting outfit.

A tourist asks a proper Bostonian the way to downtown. The Bostonian says, "Sorry, sir, but I'm afraid I can't help you. I'd have to point."

They're a colorful couple—she's in the Blue Book and he's in the Yellow Pages.

The two New Englanders were chatting. "Say, I hear you had an operation on your nose," one said.

"Sure did," said the other. "It was getting so I could hardly talk through it."

Sarah had just come into money. Taking advantage of it, she goes to the fanciest restaurant in town and tells the waiter, "Bring me some caviar, but make sure it's imported, because I don't know the difference."

A dowager goes to the hospital to visit her ailing chauffeur. The nurse asks, "Are you his wife?"

The dowager says, "Certainly not. I'm his mistress."

A Boston lady goes on a trip to Europe. When she returns, she complains, "I couldn't stand it. It was so full of foreigners."

"How do proper Bostonians know it's raining?"

"Water gets in their noses."

I know a town that's so ritzy, you can't go there without an invitation.

A very staid Bostonian lady is in a bookstore and sees a display of books. She asks the clerk what they are, and he explains that they are cookbooks from other parts of the country. The lady looks at him sternly and says, "There are no other parts of the country."

Then there was the snobbish rancher who stopped branding his cattle and sent them out to be engraved.

Two mainline Bostonian dowagers visit San Francisco in August. One says, "It's very warm here."
The other says, "What do you expect? We're three thousand miles from the ocean."

A rich lady decked out in her finest jewels and mink, heading to the opera, couldn't get a cab and was forced by time constraints to take the subway with her date. "This is the first time I've been on this smelly subway in twenty years," she said.
An old man seated nearby informed her, "Lady, we've missed you!"

I've always been interested in society, because my hometown never had any.

## SONS

My son is so good to his mother. He never comes home.

My son used to be real sloppy. He never tucked in his shirt. But my wife stopped him. She sewed lace to the bottom of it!

## SOUTH

A Yankee heads South and stops off in Mobile, Alabama. In a bar, he orders a Bama Banger, a local and potent drink. After emptying the glass, he feels a little heady and says, "The South stinks. The women are as ugly as sin, and the whole place is dull."
After a second drink, he says, "Come to think of it, this town isn't that dull."
After a third drink, he says, "I'll tell you something—the gals around here aren't bad-looking."
One final drink and he says, throwing a twenty-dollar bill on the bar, "Give me my damn change in Confederate money."

Did you ever hear of anybody retiring and moving North?

A couple heading South drop off in Charleston for a few days to visit southern friends. During a party, many of the southern gallants come over and speak to the wife.
Afterward, the wife tells her friend, "It's amazing. Every man I spoke to propositioned me."
The friend says, "In Charleston, that's only a common courtesy."

A northerner meets a southern belle and says to her, "I'm going to take you like Grant took Richmond."

The belle says, "You all mean you're going to wait foh years?"

A bus driver is conducting a tour of famous Civil War battle sites. "Here," he points out at one spot, "is where the Southern troops routed a whole regiment of Yankees. Over there, the Rebs wiped out a whole platoon of Yanks. Down about a mile, there's another valley where we captured a thousand Union soldiers."

A tourist says, "Didn't the North ever win a battle?"

"Yup. But not while I'm driving this bus."

## SPACE

The obvious fact that the planets in the solar system have never been rearranged is proof that God isn't a woman.

The young moon man held his girl and whispered, "Look, honey, there's a full earth tonight."

Some astronauts landed on a remote planet. Off in the distance, they saw what seemed to be activity. They traveled for three days and arrived at the source of the activity. They saw about a dozen little old men working away on sewing machines. One of the old men, obviously the leader, asked, "Who are you?"

The head spaceman said, "We're astronauts."

The old man shook his head sadly and said, "Astronauts they send us! Pressers we need!"

For centuries, scientists have wondered what all the blinking lights in space were. They've finally got an answer from pictures sent back by Mariner. The blinking lights say: Walk . . . Don't walk . . . Walk . . . Don't walk . . .

They've measured and found out that it's eighty sixtillion billion miles to the next nearest galaxy. So why do they make closets so small?

They finally found out who lives on the dark side of the moon—moon people who don't pay their electric bill.

How would you feel if we gave astronauts mileage?

I don't think we should try to find life on other planets. Look at all that foreign aid we'd have to come up with.

Astronauts are just like the rest of us. All they do is talk about their trip.

They just opened a new restaurant on the moon. It has great food but no atmosphere.

Feeling that astronauts got a lot of glory, two less than brilliant men built a spaceship of all the junk they could find around. Then they attached a decent-sized rocket behind it.

A friend said, "You guys are nuts. Before that thing can go fifty miles, it'll incinerate you."

One of the men said, "Not if we go at night."

"Why does the moon travel around the earth every month?"

"What else does it have to do?"

The last space satellite flew at seventy thousand miles an hour. But then, the lights were with them all the way.

The new space probe costs $2 billion. But the radio and heater are extra.

If astronauts are so smart, why do they count backward?

"What time is it when an elephant sits on a rocket?"

"Time to get a new rocket."

## SPEAKING

He has a slight impediment in his speech—his wife.

A man sat at a bar, drinking slow. On his face was the saddest hangdog expression. The bartender asked, "What's the matter? Are you having troubles with the wife?"

The man said, "We had a fight, and she told me that she wasn't going to speak to me for a month."

The bartender said, "That should make you happy."

The man said, "Not if the month is up today!"

Stage fright doesn't get to me. I pretend I'm talking to one person . . . and most of the time I am.

A speech closing: I see that my time has elapsed, so I will end with a closing you'll all like—my mouth!

If a thing goes without saying, let it!

If you stand up, you'll be seen. If you speak up, you'll be heard. If you sit down, you'll be appreciated!

To make a long story short . . .
Too late!

Repartee is what you would have said if the guy before you hadn't!

A speech is like a woman's skirt. It should be long enough to cover the subject, but short enough to make it interesting.

This is a strange audience. You look so clean, but you laugh so dirty.

That's the dirtiest laugh I've heard since I asked my wife if she was faithful to me during the war.

A stranger walked into a political rally in a town hall while a well-known local office seeker was talking away. After a while, the stranger began to fidget. He finally leaned to the man in front of him and asked, "How long has he been speaking?"

"Ten or fifteen years," the old man replied.

"Good," said the stranger. "He must be nearly through."

I'm glad you people laughed. I was all set to mark you "absent."

The difference between a good speaker and a bad speaker is a nice nap.

You're such a nice crowd. You deserve me.

An elocution teacher advised her student to practice speaking with pebbles in his mouth. A few weeks later, she asked him about his progress.

"I was doing fine," the student said, "until one day I got the hiccups. I broke the mirror and the picture window."

I goofed. How do you like that? I had my teeth fixed, now my mouth won't work.

## SPEED

"I didn't have no part in the fight, Your Honor," swore the man on the witness stand. "Just as soon as I seen there was trouble, I started runnin' as fast as I could. Then I heard two shots ring out."

"Two shots?" interrupted the judge. "The last witness said there was only one shot fired."

"Oh, no, sir," the man insisted. "I counted two shots, definitely. One when the bullet passed me, and the other when I passed the bullet!"

## SPERM BANKS

A young man went to a sperm bank to make a donation. Unable to ejaculate by himself, he asked one of the young, and very new, nurses to help him. An hour later, the young man emerged with his contribution in a small jar. The doctor asked him, "How come you had so much trouble?"

The young man said, "I'd have been out a half hour ago, but I had a hell of a time getting your nurse to cough it back up!"

A sperm bank is only a place whose come has time.

## SPIES

Two soldiers were captured by the enemy, tried for spies, and sentenced to death. As they were being led to the firing squad, one soldier yelled out, "Down with the enemy!"

The other said, "Shhh. Don't make trouble."

## SPORTS

I'm a natural athlete. I learned to ice-skate in only twelve sittings.

A gay Canadian is anybody who'd rather go out with girls than play hockey.

One sports figure was found guilty of gambling, sent to jail, and barred from his sport for life. The question is—if he gambles from his cell, can he be barred from jail for life?

I love team bobsledding, but I always have to smile when I see them so close. If it wasn't a sport, they'd be arrested!

The leader of the oarsmen in a Roman galley said to his men, "I have some good news and some bad news for you. The good news is that the captain said you can have the rest of the day off." When the cheers of the men died down, he went on, "You will also get an extra ration of bread tonight." As soon as that round of cheers ebbed, he went on, "The bad news is that tomorrow he wants to go water-skiing!"

I figured out why track stars from Eastern European countries used to run so fast. In their starting guns, they used real bullets!

I like bowling. I bowled for six hours yesterday and didn't lose one ball.

Mountain climbers say they climb mountains "because they're there." Somebody ought to let them know that that's the same reason most of us go around them!

A basketball coach decided to switch over to track and field, saying, "All you gotta do is tell them to keep turning left and get back as fast as they can."

If you can't hear a pin drop, you're a rotten bowler.

A man yells out to a drunk at the ball game, "Sit down in front."
    The drunk says, "Sorry, but I don't bend that way."

The Poles were determined to climb Mount Everest. They would have made it, too, if they hadn't run out of scaffolding.

Hockey is a war in which people keep score.

The most important rule of playing horseshoes is, first remove the horse.

Ask a gent from Idaho about the weather in the northern part of the state, and he'll tell you, "We got eleven months of winter and one month of bad skiing."

The hockey star's wife admitted to a friend, "It's really thrilling to be married to a big-time hockey player. Every time he comes home, he looks like a different person!"

People never say, "It's only a game" when they're winning.

She joined the bowling team but quit. Her first ball knocked down four pins, but they wouldn't count it because they were in the next alley.

I love domed stadiums. They're a great place for outdoor sports.

"What's the difference between two dogs in love and a soccer player who puts his socks on inside out?"
　"There's no difference. You have to turn the hose on both of them."

"Why did the ——— team install Astroturf in its stadium?"
　"To keep the cheerleaders from grazing."

Three men were turned down for seats at the Olympics. One picked up a manhole cover and walked up to the guard and said, "Discus tosser." He was allowed in.
　The second appeared with a long piece of pipe and said, "Pole vaulter." He, too, was allowed in.
　The third found some barbed wire and entered, saying, "Fencing."

You know the team isn't going to have a good season when the coach starts by saying, "This is a basketball" and somebody says, "Not so fast."

I love sports. Where else do you get a chance to boo a whole slew of millionaires to their faces?

"Where's Henry?" a neighbor asked Henry's mother.
　"I'm not sure," she replied calmly. "If the ice is as thick as he thinks it is, he's skating. If it's as thin as I think it is, he's swimming."

Back home we used to play ball in a cow pasture. One time I slid into third base and it wasn't.

Two psychiatrists are playing golf. One hits the ball and yells, "Nuts!"
　The other says, "Let's not talk shop."

## STATISTICS

Statistics are like a bikini—what shows is real, but what's hidden is vital.

## STOCKS

Most of us have a good time playing Monopoly. Stockbrokers get indicted for it.

This broker took his young son aside, sat him on his knee, and said, "Son, let me tell you about the bulls and the bears."

I had some good news in the market. My stock split. Unfortunately, so did my broker.

"How do you call your broker today?"
　"Hey, cabbie."

To make a small fortune in stocks, invest a large fortune.

In the old days, stocks split. Today, they fall apart.

Things are so bad on Wall Street, seats on the exchange now need air bags.

Wall Street has given us a new class—the nouveau poor.

I just switched brokers—from stock to pawn.

You can always tell an investor nowadays—he's smart, he's sharp, he knows the market, and he cries a lot.

Let's face it. The sound, secure investments of today are the tax losses of tomorrow.

The new name—Ow Jones.

My stockbroker was just voted the man of the year—1929.

The market today is making a comeback—to 1929.

I've lost so much money on the market, I'm even afraid to read a book, because it has margins!

I put a lot of money into National Underwear, but the bottom fell out.

Stocks no longer provide for your old age, but they do hasten its arrival.

I put half my money in paper towels and half in revolving doors. I was wiped out before I could even turn around.

The secretary answers her boss's phone and is asked where her stockbroker boss is. She replies, "He's on the phone with his wife."

"Well, tell me, is he bullish or bearish today?"
"Right now he's sheepish."

I call him "broker" because when I listen to him, that's what I am.

The market is weird. Every time one guy sells, another one buys, and they both think they're smart.

It's not the bears and bulls that get you in the stock market. It's the bum steers.

The way I feel about investing in the stock market is: There's plenty more where that went.

## STORES

One store put up a sign that said, DON'T BE FOOLED BY ALL THE BUSINESSES ON THIS BLOCK GOING OUT OF BUSINESS. WE'VE BEEN GOING OUT OF BUSINESS LONGER THAN ANY OF THEM.

The boss of the haberdashery was called away and had to leave the store in the hands of an inexperienced salesman. The boss returned an hour later and noticed a coat missing from the rack. The salesman explained, "I sold it for ninety-eight cents."
The boss said, "Ninety-eight cents? That was dollars! But don't feel too bad. We made a quarter anyway."

One store has a sign: AT OUR PRICES, THERE'S NO NEED TO SHOPLIFT.

Things must be bad. I saw a going-out-of-business sale at a store that did.

## STRENGTH

A salesman visits a farmer who's at the pigsty tending to his hog. Trying to make small talk, the salesman asks how the hog is doing. The farmer says, "Amazing story about that hog. About a month ago, he got into the toolshed and ate about a dozen sticks of dynamite I was saving. On the way out, he ran into this mean mule of mine. The mule kicked him, and there was an explosion you could hear in the next county. The shed went up, the barn went up, the mule went up, and we had a mighty sick hog for a couple of days."

He can lick his weight in wildcats, but he never tries. The fur dries out his tongue.

The first man to tear a telephone book in half probably had teenage kids.

He's so strong, he eats steak with a spoon.

## STUPID

My nephew put too many stamps on a letter, and he kept worrying that it would go too far.

"What's that on your cheek?"
"It's a birthmark."

"No kidding. How long have you had it?"

Two rather stupid gents were traveling home one night, and the driver said to his companion, "Will you stick your head out of the window and see if my blinkers are working?"
The companion stuck out his head and said, "They are, they aren't, they are, they aren't . . ."

## STUTTERING

There was this one girl who stuttered badly. Before she could say I'm not that kind of girl, she was.

He really stutters. It costs him a hundred dollars to send a ten-word telegram.

Two stutterers met at a bar and started to talk politics. One, said, "W-w-w-we d-d-d-d-don't-t-t b-b-belong in L-l-lat-t-t-t-tin Am-m-meric-c-c-ca!"
The other said, "Th-th-that's easy for y-y-y-you t-to s-s-s-s-s-say."

## STYLE

If you were wearing miniskirts the last time they came around, you shouldn't be wearing them this time.

The best thing about the latest fashions is that they won't last.

Women need hindsight, especially when they're shopping for slacks.

My date last night was wearing a real low-cut gown. I had to look under the table to see what she was wearing.

My wife finally put on a mini. She said, "If I'm going to be ugly, I might as well be this year's ugly."

Nowadays, you can't judge a woman by the clothes she wears. There's not enough evidence.

I keep my clothes a long time. The other day I shook one of my suits, and a moth with a Mondale button flew out.

She used to wear a bra that was at least two sizes too small for her. When she unhooked it, it sounded like two champagne bottles being opened.

Women are wearing shorter skirts and much lower necklines. Men don't know where it's going to end, but they'd like to be around when it does.

It isn't what a girl puts in a dress that's interesting. It's what she leaves out.

I like women who wear very short shorts. I'm behind them all the way!

They're now selling nightgowns with fur hems. That's to keep a man's neck warm.

Her neckline was real low. When she wanted to adjust it, she had to kneel.

If she wore her dress any lower, she'd be barefoot all over.

My wife doesn't like loose dresses. She thinks tents are strictly for Boy Scouts.

"What size shoe do you wear?"
"Four is my size, but I wear a six because fours hurt my feet."

There's only one thing smaller than my wife's shoes—her feet.

I'd like to know—if Batman is so smart, how come he wears his underwear outside his clothes?

Dresses are really being cut low. The other night I saw a girl with a neckline that was so low, she spilled herself all over a drink.

If her skirt was any shorter, it would be a collar.

Miniskirts are like the cost of living—neither can go much higher.

## SUBURBIA

Our new house isn't too well constructed. The termites wear parachutes.

You have to watch out. Some houses are built to last, others to sell.

I couldn't keep my basement dry, so I just had it stocked.

The suburbs are strange. A man will lend you his wife, but not his golf clubs.

When you hear an explosion coming from next door, it doesn't always mean dynamite. It could also mean a little powder on his coat.

A picture window is worth a thousand words.

Think how it evens out—your neighbors' problems aren't as bad as yours, but their kids are worse.

A builder should live in his own subdivision for the first year.

We really live far out. Our mailman has to send our mail by mail.

The golden rule in the suburbs is to love your neighbor. He may have the tools you need.

Theirs was a typical suburban marriage. They didn't get along, but they were trying to stick it out for the sake of the parakeet.

Be glad your neighbor has a nicer house than you do. When it comes time to sell, that might help.

I don't have to tell my wife anything. The neighbors do that for me.

A good neighbor is a guy who doesn't mow his lawn either.

The only thing worse than the neighbor on the right with an old car is the neighbor on the left with a brand-new one.

By the time you finish paying for your house in suburbia, it's no longer in suburbia.

The smart suburban never buys anything anybody can borrow.

SUBURBIA TENANT: This darn roof is leaking on our heads. How long is that going to continue?
LANDLORD: Whaddaya think I am, a weatherman?!

You never finish paying for a house in the suburbs. Last Christmas we got a card from the bank that said, *Merry Christmas from our house to our house.*

The widow next door is beautiful, and it takes Tom a long time to go over to her house and borrow a piece of equipment or a tool. One afternoon he's gone a particularly long time. The wife calls. The widow answers.

"Why is it taking my husband such a long time over there?" the wife asks.

The widow answers, "I don't know. And this interruption isn't helping any."

Everybody likes those split-level homes nowadays. Years ago, when you lived over a garage, you kept it to yourself.

"What words do they fear most in suburbia?"

"Señor, I be your new neighbor."

I live in one of those tiny towns in the suburbs. The biggest industry is commuting.

Suburbia now has its own bird—the extramarital lark.

Then there was the suburban housewife who called a carpenter because she had sticky drawers.

A house built at today's cost is really the home of the brave.

One suburban husband had a big fight with his wife. She wanted twin beds, and he said, "I commute five days a week. I don't want to have to at night."

I'm sorry, but you can't interest me in a new vacuum cleaner. But try the lady next door. I'm always borrowing hers and it's terrible.

Birds of a feather flock to my lawn when the car is parked.

## SUCCESS

There's a time when everything you do turns to gold. Don't worry, it'll pass.

No man is a success until his mother-in-law admits it.

He's very successful, but he hasn't forgotten his humble origins. Even though he has $10 million, he still goes back once a month to the old slum neighborhood—to visit his parents!

If at first you did succeed, it's probably your old man's business.

I've paid the price of success. I'm just waiting for the delivery.

Success is an island of envy surrounded by an ocean of envy.

Behind every successful man, you'll find somebody who says, "I went to school with him."

A salesman with a company tries to borrow a tenner from another salesman. The other salesman turns him down.
    The years go by, and the second salesman goes on to own the company. The first salesman, now long gone from the company, runs into him again. "Lend me a tenner," he says.
    "No chance."
    "Let me shake your hand. Success hasn't changed you."

A successful businessman was asked to give a speech at a graduation. "Always remember," he said, "education is a fine thing. Nothing like it. Take arithmetic, for instance. Through education we learn that two twos are four, that four fours are eight, eight eights are—and then there's geography. . . ."

Behind every successful man is a woman, declaring that she knows a man who's more successful.

## SUICIDE

The Suicide Club held a meeting last week. It'll be the only one.

When the psychiatrist determined that the man had suicidal tendencies, he made him pay in advance.

A young lady, disappointed in love and life generally, is about to jump off the bridge. Passing by, a young sailor says, "Don't do that. It's dumb. You have a lot to live for."

"Like what?"

"Like a lot of things. I tell you what. It's romantic being on a ship. Let me smuggle you onto mine, and I'll take you to Europe. I'll hide you in a lifeboat, and every night I'll bring you food, some wine, and we may even make love. Making love on a ship is special."

The young lady agrees. The sailor smuggles her aboard his ship. For the next month, they have a grand old time. After the fourth week, however, the girl is discovered by the captain of the ship. He demands an explanation.

The young girl says, "One of your sailors smuggled me aboard. He screwed me every night."

The captain says, "He certainly did. This is the Staten Island Ferry."

A man put a rope around his neck, stood up on a chair, and threw the rope around a thick overhead pipe. One jump and it would all be over. A friend walked in and found him on the chair and asked, "Why don't you put the rope around your neck tighter?"

The man answered, "I tried that, but I can't breathe!"

One guy didn't know whether he really wanted to commit suicide, so he threw himself in front of a parked car.

He called the suicide hotline, and they put him on hold!

He called the suicide hotline and told them his troubles. They asked him why he was waiting!

The other day, she felt that she'd had enough. She put a gun to her breast and pulled the trigger—shattered her kneecap!

Joe Brown is at a low ebb. His job stinks, his bills are piled high on his desk, and he has no money for rent or food. He decides to end it all. Putting a rope around his neck as he stands on a chair, he says, in preparation for jumping, "I must die. All I have given my poor wife is fourteen kids and no way of supporting them."

His wife bursts in and says, "Don't do it. You're hanging an innocent man."

## SUITS

I won't say my suit is made of cheap material, but yesterday it shrank two inches, and it was only cloudy out.

I went in for a fitting and I noticed that one shoulder was three inches higher than the other. I complained. The tailor said, "The shoulders are perfect. The floor's crooked."

Shopping for a new suit, I saw an attractive blue serge on the rack. The clerk told me that it was an expensive suit. It was genuine virgin wool.

I said, "Don't you have one from sheep that only fooled around a little?"

A man points out a swatch of fabric from which he wants a suit made. The tailor says, "You have excellent taste. That's the best fabric in the world. It comes from the rare East Andes vicuña. To get to its habitat, you have to fly to Argentina, take a train to Rosario, then a bus on a one-lane road that goes twelve thousand feet up. But—you can only make this trip between the first and fourth week in October after the second rain of the season. And—the vicuñas must be two-year-old females with a tiny patch of hair under their chins. Each hair must be plucked singly."

The man says, "But I need the suit for a wedding on the weekend."

The tailor says, "It'll be ready Friday."

## SUPERMARKETS

This morning I gave my place in the checkout line at the market to a man with only two items—a note and a gun.

The manager of a supermarket managed to hear a man bragging about how much he'd been stealing from the store. When the man came in the next day, the manager followed him around. The man loaded his cart, paid for every item, and put the groceries in his car.

In the weeks that followed, the man kept returning to shop. A dozen times he loaded his cart with groceries, and a dozen times he paid for every single item.

Finally, the manager walked over to him and said, "Mister, I've been watching you like a hawk. I've never seen you pocket one thing. You've never hidden anything under your coat. And you've paid for every item you've bought. Look, I won't prosecute or say a word. In fact, I'll give you a hundred dollars if you tell me what you're stealing."

The man said, "Shopping carts."

A woman is going through a supermarket with her six-year-old kid. The kid takes an item off the shelf and wants to put it in the cart. The mother says, "No, dear. You have to cook that."

A supermarket is a place where you spend forty minutes looking for instant coffee.

The slowest-moving item in the market is always my shopping cart.

## SURGERY

He's a great surgeon. Two hundred forty operations, and he's never cut himself once.

There was an orthopedic surgeon who had a bad rep. He always had a bone to pick with his patients.

A surgeon told his patient, "You're going to have to be out for this surgery.

Do you want sodium Pentothal or a look at our bill?''

When you're laid out on the operating table, try thinking of it this way—the man who's about to cut into you is the same bum who, only a couple of hours before, missed a two-inch putt!

My cousin the surgeon just got discharged from his fifth hospital. It wasn't the patients he lost that bothered them. It was all those deep gashes he left on the operating table!

A surgeon goes to a party and manages to drink everything but the mercury in the outdoor thermometer. By the tenth drink, he falls on the couch and is dead to the world.

Comes three in the morning, and the host wants to get to bed, so he shakes the surgeon, trying to rouse him. No luck. He shakes more and finally starts to slap the surgeon around. The surgeon's wife says, "What are you doing? Don't you know he has to operate at seven in the morning?"

I didn't have the three hundred needed to remove my tonsils, so my doctor just loosened them a little.

I have this fancy surgeon. He doesn't just charge for his surgery, he also charges for new parts.

"How many surgeons does it take to change a light bulb?"

"Why don't you just have us remove the socket? You aren't using it, and it'll only cause you problems in the future."

An operation is something that takes hours to perform and years to describe.

## SUSPICION

Always be suspicious. Even a farmhouse has something behind it.

You should be a little suspicious of your wife if she asks for her weekly household money in traveler's checks.

Greg goes to his attorney and says that he wants to divorce his wife because she's carrying on with her riding instructor.

"How do you know?" the attorney asks.

"Because when she gets back, she's winded and the horse isn't."

## SWIMMING

Two gays are at the beach. One goes out too far and starts to cry for help. The other says, "Wait a minute, I'll throw you a buoy."

"Stop joking. I'm really drowning."

A woman tells another, "I understand your husband died last month and left you five million dollars. Amazing, he couldn't even read or write."

The widow says, "He couldn't swim either."

"Can you do the Australian crawl?"

"I can't even swim in English yet."

Then there's the man who thought that he'd be different. He filled his swimming pool with club soda. People hated to swim in it. They'd go two strokes forward, belch, and go three strokes back.

One young lady was amply endowed but a little weak with the brains. When she came in late in the breaststroke competition at the school swim meet, she complained, "The other girls cheated. They used their arms!"

## SYNAGOGUES

One synagogue had a robbery the other day. Somebody broke in and stole a hundred thousand dollars' worth of pledges.

An immigrant arrived in America. Unable to read or write English, he could find no decent job. To keep him from starving, the members of the synagogue made him beadle. Soon, however, it was discovered that he had no reading or writing skills, and he was dismissed.

He took on a job as a salesman of notions door-to-door. He did so well that he was able to open a store. The store prospered. He opened a second store, and a third, and a fourth. Within ten years, he had fifty stores and was a millionaire many times over.

One day several new members of the congregation came to him. They wanted him to sign a farewell card to the rabbi. The ex-beadle hesitated. Grudgingly, he admitted that he was unable to read or write.

A member said, "Oh, dear Lord. You can't read or write yet you've amassed a giant fortune. Do you have any idea of what you would have been if you had only known how to read and write?"

He said, "Yes. A beadle."

## TACT

Poise is the ability to keep on talking while the other guy reaches for the check.

Diplomacy is the art of saying "Nice dog" until you have time to pick up a board.

If you can't be kind, at least be vague.

Two men are discussing the meaning of tact. One says, "I can explain it. I'm a plumber. Well, the other day, a woman called and told me that her bathtub was leaking. I rushed over and ran right into the bathroom. There she was, taking a bath. I said, 'Good afternoon, sir.'"

"That's just courtesy."

"The 'Good afternoon' was courtesy. The 'sir' was tact."

Diplomacy is the ability to take some and act like you're giving it away.

A diplomat is a guy who explains to his wife, "I didn't forget your birthday. It's just that I didn't want to remind you of it."

A person has the right to disagree with you. If he wants to hold on to his dumb opinions, let him!

An ambassador is an honest man sent abroad to lie for his country!

A diplomat is a man who praises marriage but remains single.

Be sincere, whether you mean it or not!

A diplomat is a guy who goes to a nudist colony, sees some women playing tennis, and asks the score.

One way to save face is to keep the bottom half shut!

A gossip columnist chiseled his way into a swank party hosted by one of the most talented and wittiest actresses. When he left, he gave her a limp handshake and thanked her for the party.

"That's quite okay," the actress said. "Next time remind me to invite you."

## TALKING

Talk is cheap unless it's lawyers talking.

They say that talk is cheap. How come I get such a big phone bill?

They have a club for compulsive talkers. It's called On-and-On Anon.

It's amazing how long my wife can talk without mentioning what she's talking about.

My wife has made a new arrangement— she can only be interrupted by appointment.

## TARZAN & JANE

Tarzan comes home and gulps down the martini Jane has ready for him. He then asks for another, drinks that, and then another. Jane says, "You've had enough."

Tarzan says, "You have to understand, honey. It's a jungle out there."

Jane asks Tarzan, "How was the traffic on the way home?"

Tarzan says, "It was impossible. Vine-to-vine all the way."

## TAXES

Who can understand taxes? With what they leave you, it means that you work like a dog to live like one.

They've never been able to improve on the greatest spot remover ever perfected—the IRS. It removes five-spots, 10-spots . . .

I've been trying to figure my adjusted gross income. I adjusted it, and it's still gross.

The Founding Fathers were wrong. They should have fought for representation without taxation.

I put all my money into taxes. They're the only thing that's sure to go up.

The IRS must need money badly. It's started selling gift certificates!

I never cheat on my taxes. I always let someone do it who knows how.

A fool and his money are soon audited.

Presidents always promise no new taxes. But they never say anything about making the old ones bigger.

In case you didn't know—taxes are due April 15, the same day *The Titanic* went down.

The government says we should be proud to be paying taxes to the country. I think I could be just as proud for about a third of the money.

I got in trouble with charitable donations last year. I gave five thousand to the family of the unknown soldier.

It's very hard to make your friends believe you earn as much as you do and the government to believe you make as little as you do.

Every time my ship comes in, the government unloads it.

A fair tax structure is one that allows everybody to cheat evenly.

Taxes are so bad nowadays, a fellow has to be unemployed to make a living.

I just discovered a great tax shelter—unemployment.

Congress wants to increase taxes on booze and tobacco. That wouldn't be necessary if people had more bad habits.

Psychiatrists say a man shouldn't keep too much to himself. So does the IRS.

I lied on my return. I listed myself as head of the house.

A fine is a tax for doing wrong. A tax is a fine for doing well.

Tax time is when the government of the people, for the people, and by the people sticks it to the people.

Why does a slight tax increase cost you two hundred dollars and a substantial tax cut save you thirty cents?

I can't understand it. The dollar is now worth thirty cents. But forty-six cents of every dollar goes to taxes.

My brother just came up with a new wrinkle. He says that the tax forms are Greek to him, and he won't pay taxes to a foreign government.

If the Founding Fathers thought taxation without representation was bad, what would they think it is today *with* representation?

On April 16, do you have the feeling that somebody flushed your wallet?

Making out your own return is like a do-it-yourself mugging.

The only things that are certain are death and taxes. Unfortunately, they don't come along in that order.

A Dutchman was describing the red, white, and blue flag of his native country. "It's symbolic of our taxes," he explained. "We turn red when we talk about them, white when we figure them, and blue when we pay them."

The American he was talking to said, "It's the same in America—only we see stars too!"

Wouldn't it be great if sex was tax-deductible?

Income taxes are something. Who says you can't get killed by a blank?

A bachelor businessman lists a dependent son on his tax forms. The tax man objects and says, "Is this a stenographic error?"

"He certainly was," says the bachelor.

I was having a lot of trouble with my taxes, so I asked my son to help me, and I promised I'd do his homework. Now I stay after school, and he'll be in San Quentin until 1995.

I owe the government a fortune. They don't know whether to throw me in jail or declare me a foreign power.

## TEENAGERS

My teenage son gets up every morning and counts his mustache.

My teenage niece is in a quandary about her latest beau. She doesn't know if it's true love, because her family likes him.

She was thirteen when she got her first love letter. She framed it, and a month later she framed the thirty-year-old guy who'd written it.

It's amazing how kids can learn to drive the car and can't master a lawn mower.

It's hard for a 5'6" father to tell a 6'4" son that junk food is no good for him.

Teenage boys and girls have it easy nowadays. They can always give one another the same gift—earrings!

A teenager can tell how good his stereo is by how many times the neighbors call the police.

Teenagers are alike in most disrespects.

Adolescence is the stage between pigtails and cocktails.

Do you remember when "Is it a boy or a girl?" only referred to babies?

It's not what a teenager knows that bothers his folks. It's how he or she found out.

My teenage niece was in tears the other night because she had nothing to wear to her prom. All her sweatshirts were in the wash!

A girl tells her teenage beau, "You know, we're just like Romeo and Juliet. My Dad says he's going to kill you."

A teenager says to his father, "Don't you have faith in my generation?"
   The father says, "Of course. Look at the debt we're leaving you to pay."

He was the typical school jock: talk, dark, and hands.

A teenager is a child old enough to dress by himself if he could only remember where he last saw his clothes.

You know your kids are growing up when your daughter starts putting on lipstick and your son starts taking it off.

My teenage niece went to a department store last night with something she'd bought earlier and told the clerk, "My parents like this outfit. Can I exchange it?"

Teenagers want to be different, so they all dress alike.

Two teenage girls were in New York for the first time. They looked around for the Empire State Building and finally had to ask someone. The other person, also a teenage girl, said, "It's about three blocks up that street. You can't miss it. It's right across the street from the record shop."

It's tough when teenagers get married. What wine goes with Twinkies?

My daughter hasn't found herself yet. She sure picks some weird places to look.

A teenage girl showed off her prom dress for her father and asked him if it was cut too low. The father answered, "Either that or you're not in it far enough."

I found a way to keep teenage girls out of hot water. Put some dishes in it.

My teenage daughter came home last night in tears. Her boyfriend had not only ruined her life, he'd also loused up the whole evening.

Recently, a teenage girl went crazy trying to look as young as her mother.

Telling your teenager the facts of life is like giving a guppy a bath.

## TELEPHONES

One psychiatrist has a great way of getting women to talk. He puts a phone in their hands.

My shrink helped me a lot. Before I went to him, I was afraid to answer the phone. Now, I answer it whether it rings or not.

There was one town that had only one phone. After a while, the man had it taken out. There was nobody to call.

A man complained to his doctor that his wife was weird, saying, "She talks to her plants."

The doctor said, "A lot of people talk to their plants."

"By telephone?"

A woman answers the phone only to hear heavy breathing at the other end. She says, "Is this an obscene phone call? If it is, let me get a drink and a cigarette."

The telephone was invented twenty-five years after the bathtub. You would have had to sit twenty-five years in the tub to wait for the phone to ring.

The telephone company has a great new service. For a dollar a week, you can call up any number in the world and get a busy signal.

The telephone rings, and Mrs. Martin, in her eighties, says hello. On the other end is an obscene caller. He waxes poetic about what he'd like to do to her. No perversion is too vile. Finally, Mrs. Martin says, "You can tell all that from one hello?"

They say talk is cheap. Baloney. I have a wife and two daughters and a phone bill to prove it.

It's easy to know when a woman gets a wrong number. She only talks for fifteen minutes.

But, Operator, the line can't be busy. I'm the only one who talks to her.

If you call 911 in Beverly Hills, you have to tell them who recommended you.

A man calls 911 and says that his cat is lost. The 911 operator says, "We only take special matters."

"You don't understand. This isn't just a cat. This cat can talk."

"You should hang up. Maybe he's trying to phone you right now."

## TEXANS

Then there's this Texan who owns a well that comes up with two hundred barrels a day—no oil, just barrels.

This pregnant Texas lass got a sudden craving for mints. So her husband ran out and bought her Fort Knox.

If God had meant Texans to ski, he would have made fertilizer white.

There's a rumor about this family in Texas that leaves Hondas all around the ranch. Once a year, they send the foreman out in a 450 SL to round them up.

One Texan kid gave his mother a Cadillac for her birthday. Cost him his allowance for two weeks.

**I** know a hotel in Texas—when you ring for a bellhop, he sends up his valet.

**A** young Texan told his dad he needed some oil for his hair. His father bought him Oklahoma.

**C**laustrophobia is a Texan in Delaware.

"**W**hat is a Texas virgin?"

"A girl who can run faster than her roommates."

**A** Texan wakes up, and next to him is the blackest black woman ever seen. He asks, "Who are you?"

She answers, "My name's Ruby, but last night I was the Yellow Rose of Texas."

**A** beautiful debutante shows her mother a picture of her new fiancé's house in town. "He is clumsy, funny-looking, and short, I'll admit. That thing behind the house is an oil well."

**A** big oilman from Texas was being shown around the Big Apple by a New Yorker. He took the Texan to the United Nations Building.

"Isn't that magnificent?" the New Yorker said.

"Hell, I got me an outhouse bigger than that in Texas!" the man replied.

The New Yorker looked him over and said, "You need it!"

**A** rich Texan decided to start collecting miniatures. He started with Rhode Island.

**T**exas has some real wide-screen theaters. They show you this week's movie and next week's too.

**T**hey don't celebrate Washington's Birthday in Texas. They figure a guy isn't worth remembering if he can't tell a lie.

**A** visitor to the noble state of Texas was asked, "What do you think of civilization out here?"

The visitor answered, "I think it would be a great idea!"

**T**exas is the only state in the Union where there are more men in high heels than women.

**A** Texan finds himself in a small town in Nevada. Lonely for affection, he goes to a small country bar. There he meets a young lady and invites her to his room. After they make love, he puts a hundred-dollar bill in her purse. The girl gasps and says, "I never got a ninety-eight-dollar tip before."

**A** Galveston man reeled in a redfish and decided it was too small to take back to show his friends. So he persuaded two deckhands to help him throw it back in the Gulf.

## THANKSGIVING

**I**'m always thankful for what I receive. I'd be in trouble if I got what I deserved.

**O**n Thanksgiving I'm grateful for all the turkeys, except in Congress.

There's a lot to be thankful for. If you can't pay your bills, be thankful that you're not one of your creditors.

We stuffed our Thanksgiving turkey with diced cardboard. We got the recipe from some airline chef.

Our turkey was a little small last Thanksgiving. Actually, it was a chicken with a gland condition.

Thanksgiving is a great big family holiday. Everybody gets together during halftime.

We had a tearful Thanksgiving. The turkey was so tender, it reached up and put its wings around me.

That's the trouble with Thanksgiving. Two days later, you're hungry again.

Our pioneer ancestors had a lot to be thankful for. When they traveled, they had it rough, but they always knew where their luggage was.

## THEATER

This show had an incredible score. Even the backers whistled all the tunes as they left their seats, climbed on the roof, and jumped.

This amateur theater group is presenting a play, and the stagehand is new to the business. With the cast in place for the opening, the star calls to the stagehand, "Okay, run up the curtain."

The stagehand says, "What do you think I am—a squirrel?"

The nouveau riche lady said, "I hope this isn't the same *Hamlet* that Shakespeare wrote. We saw that one already."

An old Shakespearean actor decided one day that he just wasn't in the mood to play Hamlet, and that he'd do Othello instead. When he told the manager of the one-horse little theater, the man hit the ceiling.

"I've got you listed outside on the billboard for Hamlet, and you're going to play Hamlet!" the manager yelled.

"Okay," said the actor, "then I need a ten-dollar advance to go get a haircut and shave."

"Ten bucks, huh?" the manager said. "Oh, hell, play Othello."

On arriving at the theater, the young girl excused herself and set off to powder her nose. The theater was built like a maze, with lots of winding corridors and spiral staircases. Finally, she located a mirrored room with nobody inside except a maid dusting furniture. The young lady adjusted the seams of her stockings, looked in the mirror, and said to the maid, "What a horrible mess. I look like hell."

Makeup restored, the young lady returned to her seat.

"What'd I miss?" she asked her date.

"Nothing much," he said. "A maid was dusting, and some girl came in and fixed her stockings and said, 'What a horrible mess. I look like hell,' then powdered her nose and left."

**A** man takes his place in the theater, but his seat is far from the stage. He whispers to an usher, "This is a mystery, and I have to watch a mystery close up. Get me a better seat, and I'll give you a handsome tip."

The usher moves him into the second row, and the man hands the usher a dime tip. The usher leans over and whispers, "The wife did it."

## THIN

**T**he tires on my car were so thin, you could see the air.

**S**he's so skinny, she can tap-dance on Jell-O.

**S**he's so skinny, she has to tease her pubic hair to keep her jeans up.

**S**he's so skinny, her striped dresses have only one stripe!

**S**he's so skinny, she has to tie knots in her stockings to make them look like knees!

**I** wouldn't say she's skinny, but when she closes one eye, she looks like a needle.

**H**e's so thin, he doesn't need a shirt. He just puts on a tie.

He's so thin, it takes two of him to make a shadow.

## THINNEST BOOKS

*Ten Thousand Years of German Humor*

*Blacks I Have Met While Yachting*

*Italian War Heroes*

*Polish Gourmet Cooking*

*White Pro Basketball Stars*

*French Celibates*

*Mexicans Not Named Jesus*

*Jewish Hockey Stars*

*How to Have Fun in Bismarck, North Dakota*

*Irish Fashions*

*Ten Thousand Years of German Humor, Volume II*

## THREATS

**T**wo black men are arguing. One says, "I'm going to beat you to a pulp, and then I'm going to beat up the pulp."

The other says, "Before you get that done, I'm gonna cut you three ways—frequent, deep, and wide."

A surgeon finds himself on the operating table about to be operated on by his son. The father says, "Son, think of it this way: If anything happens to me, your mother is coming to live with you."

## TIME

"Hurry. We're going to be late."

"Don't rush me. Haven't I been telling you for an hour that I'll be ready in a minute?"

Daylight saving time is throwing everyone off schedule. This morning, three worms mugged the early bird.

"What's the difference between a husband and a lover?"

"Thirty minutes."

"I got up at dawn to see the sun rise."

"You couldn't have picked a better time."

My kid is going to be an executive. He's only six, but already he takes two hours for lunch.

A woman applied for a divorce after ten years of marriage, explaining the marriage had never been consummated. The judge asked the husband to explain. The husband said, "To tell the truth, I didn't know she was in a hurry."

The psychiatrist told his new patient, "Now we'll see what makes you tick."

The patient said, "While you're at it, will you find out what makes me chime every half hour?"

A man has been driving a long time, so he pulls over to the side of the road for a nap. Just as he's about to doze off, a jogger stops and raps on the window, asking, "Do you have the time?"

The man tells him the time and tries to sleep again. In a few minutes, another jogger comes by, raps on the window, and asks for the time.

The man tells him the time, but now takes a piece of paper, writes on it, *I don't have the time,* and puts it in the window. He now goes to sleep again.

In ten minutes, another jogger comes up, raps on the window, and says, "It's nine-fifteen."

What's a light-year?

A year that has 40 percent less calories than a regular year.

In France at 11:00 P.M., a Frenchman asks, "It's eleven o'clock—do you know where your wife is?"

In Italy, the question is, "It's eleven o'clock—do you know where your husband is?"

In the United States, it's "It's eleven o'clock—do you know where your children are?"

In Poland, the Pole asks, "It's eleven o'clock—do you know what time it is?"

Yesterday is experience; tomorrow, hope; and today is getting from one to the other.

A rather disorganized businessman was rummaging through his desk looking for lost documents when he came across a claim check for shoes he had dropped off in 1971. He had lost the check and never gone back for the shoes. He knew the shop still existed. In fact, the owner was a proud craftsman who had inherited the business.

More or less as a joke, the man went in the next day with the claim check.

"I know this was twenty years ago," he said, "but I thought you might still have them."

"Wait here. I go see," said the cobbler.

A few minutes later, the shop owner appeared without the shoes, explaining casually, "They'll be ready Tuesday."

Every time history repeats itself, the price goes up.

Time may be a great healer, but it's a lousy beautician.

A young girl asks her grandmother how old she is.

"I'm eighty-eight," Grandma says.

The young girl's eyes widen. "Wow, you mean starting from one?"

Thirty days hath September, April, June, and November. All the rest have thirty-one. Is that fair?

Every year it takes less time to fly across the ocean and longer to drive to work.

Joe is sleeping soundly, but the phone startles him awake at three-thirty in the morning. He hears the gruff voice of the man in the house across the street. "Do something. It's three-thirty, and your dog is barking to beat the band. Shut him up!"

Joe goes back to sleep.

Twenty-four hours later, Joe dials the phone at three-thirty. When he hears the gruff hello of the man across the street, Joe says, "I don't have a dog."

The doctor tells his patient, "I have very bad news for you. Your tests came back, and you have twenty-four hours to live. But I also have worse news."

"What could be worse news?"

"I was supposed to tell you yesterday."

The amount of time between throwing something away and needing it is about two days.

A minute contains sixty seconds unless it's prefaced by "Just a . . ."

An old-timer, living up in the mountains, had no timepieces but always knew what time it was. Testing him, I asked what time it was one afternoon. The old man shifted the tobacco in his cheek, spat, and studied the shadow on his porch. Then he answered, " 'Bout four and a half planks to supper time."

The longest wait in the world is when the nurse tells you to take off your clothes and the doctor will be right with you.

Never eat a watch. It's time-consuming.

A man riding on a bus saw a clock that said 10:30. A few minutes later, he passed another clock that read 10:15. The man said, "I must be going the wrong way."

A watch is something a woman looks at to see how late she is.

"Last night I didn't get to sleep until after four."
"Really? All I need is three."

Then there was the honeymoon couple who checked into a hotel on July 4 and left a call for Thanksgiving.

Time changes a lot of things, but it can't change a light bulb.

## TOUGH

There's a motel in our neighborhood that asks for name, address, and next of kin.

He's so tough, he has concrete on his breath.

In my old neighborhood, the ice-cream wagon plays Taps.

My neighborhood is real tough. Last week, the local gun shop had a back-to-school sale.

My school was tough but decent. You had to raise your hand before you could hit a teacher.

My old neighborhood was so tough, one Christmas Santa got mugged coming down the chimney.

This one kid set fire to his desk, tore up his books, and beat up on his teacher. Naturally, the principal wasn't allowed to touch him. But he did send a stern note to the kid's shrink.

My old neighborhood was real tough. In school, they used to frisk you for your homework.

Boy, did I grow up in a tough neighborhood. I remember my mom giving my dad a dollar every morning for the holdup man!

My old neighborhood was really rough. During the Christmas pageant, all the kids wanted to play one of the three wise guys.

In my old neighborhood—if somebody raised a hand in class, you didn't know if it was to answer a question, ask for permission to leave the room, or because there was a robbery in progress.

In my old neighborhood, Dear Abby answers questions like: How do you get blood off a saw?

In my old neighborhood, the most popular form of transportation was the stretcher.

In my old neighborhood, if you get invited to a screening, it's a police lineup.

The teacher says to the class, "There's more than one way to skin a cat."

The whole class says, "How? How?"

My neighborhood was so tough—the high school newspaper had an obituary column.

My neighborhood is real tough. You go into a restaurant there, and they serve you broken leg of lamb.

In my neighborhood, one guy had a tattoo of a pit bull on his arm, and it bit him.

I live in a rough neighborhood. The other day I called the police. There was a three-year waiting list.

In my neighborhood, the school song was a police siren.

If you were sick in my school, you had to bring a note from your parole officer.

My old neighborhood is tough. When you go to a nightclub, they frisk you. If you don't have a gun, they give you one.

In my neighborhood, we had Jehovah's Alibis.

Our neighborhood was real tough. Five kids who sat in Santa's lap got their pockets picked.

In my old neighborhood, it was pretty rough. Even the confessionals had bouncers.

I was in my old neighborhood the other day. It's gotten real rough. I walked down the street, and I saw half a cop.

A biker runs into another and says, "Hey, we had a real gang bang last week. How come you weren't there?"

The second biker grins sheepishly and says, "I got hitched."

"No kidding? Is legit humping as good as the other kind?"

"About the same, but you don't have to wait in line for it."

All the kids in my neighborhood were honor students—yes, Your Honor . . . no, Your Honor . . .

In my old neighborhood, they went bowling overhand.

I went to a tough school. Once I got hit by a spitball, and the doctor gave me a 50–50 chance to live.

## TOYS

I bought my kid a kite and he went crazy. He couldn't find where to put the batteries.

I sold my married sex life to a toy company. They're going to make a game out of it!

An unbreakable toy is one a kid uses to break those that aren't.

Times are real bad. In the toy department, the dolls and the clerks are crying real tears.

**I** bought my son an indestructible toy. He left it in the driveway, and it destroyed my car.

**P**hil is having a great deal of trouble assembling his jungle gym. The instructions baffle him. Put *A* in slot *B*, add *C* to slot *A*, put *B* into slot *D* as you put *X* into *Y* and slot *L*. He's about to give up when his neighbor, old Mr. Tyler, comes over. "Let me have a go at it," says Mr. Tyler.

Phil says, "Sure."

He hands the old man the instruction manual. The old man shakes his head and says, "Can't use that. I can't read."

Two minutes later, the jungle gym is completely assembled. Phil shakes his head. "How can that be?" he asks.

"Well, when you can't read," the old man says, "you gotta think."

**W**ouldn't it be great if they came up with a robot toy that picked itself up after being played with?

**T**oys are so advanced nowadays, they can play with each other.

### TRAFFIC

**T**raffic is real bad nowadays. The other afternoon, I was passed by an abandoned car.

**A** man is going about two miles an hour when a traffic cop pulls him over. The cop says, "Do you know why I stopped you?"

The man says, "Sure. I'm the only one you could catch."

**A** man gets stopped by a cop for walking across the street against the light. The cop says, "Don't you see that sign? 'Don't Walk.' "

The man says, "Oh, I thought the bus company had put that up."

**T**raffic is really bumper-to-bumper nowadays. This morning I saw a fire engine going to last night's fire!

**T**raffic is impossible. I saw a pedestrian get hit by a car, and it was two hours before he could fall down.

**T**raffic is terrible today. If you want to get from one side of the street to the other, you have to be born there.

**I** have a great solution for the traffic problem—encourage car thefts!

**T**raffic is awful. The other day I saw a tow truck pull a car out of a spot. And right behind them was another car waiting to get in.

**T**raffic is so slow—I had to leave the car twice to make payments.

**T**he other day I went down to pay a parking ticket. It took me six hours. I couldn't find a place to park.

**T**he other day I went down to pay a parking ticket. But I couldn't find a parking place, so I double-parked. But I left a note for the cops—"Inside for a minute to pay parking ticket."

When I got back, there was another ticket and a note that said—"As long as you're in the neighborhood . . ."

It was bumper-to-bumper downtown today. I drove forty miles in neutral.

Traffic is real bad today. If you want to hit a pedestrian, you have to get out of the car.

Why do they call the time when cars are bumper-to-bumper rush hour?

## TRAINS

It was quiet in the Pullman car as people readied themselves for sleep. Then, from one upper, came a man's voice: "I'll have you know I'm a respectable man, so one of you girls will have to leave."

Amtrak isn't bad. It's only three places behind Lionel.

Kansas is as flat as a pancake, maybe even flatter. At a train station, a customer asks about the next train. The stationmaster says, "Right now, it's supposed to be in Purdock about ninety miles up the track, but I don't see it, so it must be running late."

I had a wonderful trip on Amtrak. Only two wrecks.

A boy and his grandfather are taking their first long trip by train. The train is scooting along at a good pace. It doesn't slow down as it tunnels through a mountain.

When it gets to the other side, the kid says, "Gee, Grandpa, it's a good thing the train didn't miss the hole in that mountain."

A man takes his small dog on a train. Arriving to take his ticket, the conductor says, "I'm afraid you can't keep that dog in here. You'll have to put him in the baggage car." The man argues, but the conductor won't be dissuaded.

The man heads for the baggage car, but as soon as he's in the vestibule, he loosens his belt and puts the dog in his pants. When he returns to his seat and starts to squirm as the dog moves around, the woman behind him, aware of what he'd done, decides to kid him, saying, "I'll bet he's not housebroken."

The man says, "I don't know about that, but I've got a feeling he hasn't been weaned."

A man gets off a sleeper in Pasadena. The porter hints, "You won't forget me, will you, sir?"

The man says, "Of course not. I'll write to you."

"Conductor, does this train stop in Key West?"

"If it doesn't, you're gonna hear one big splash."

The best time to miss a train is at a crossing.

A friend had a stateroom on a train. He was lonely, so he pursued a woman in the dining car. Back in his stateroom, she warned him, "I'm married."

"So am I," he told her.

A few minutes later, the conductor came in and caught them in a very compromising position.

"It's okay," my friend said, "we're married!"

It was a five-mile walk from town to the train station. Once there, the potential passenger asked the conductor, "Why did they build this station so far out of town?"

The conductor shrugged. "Wanted to get it near the railroad."

A young man huffs and puffs as he manages to jump on to the train as it's leaving the station. Another passenger looks at him scornfully and says, "At your age, young fellow, I could run like mad, catch the train with one finger, and still be as fresh as dew."

"Terrific," says the young man. "But I missed this one two stations ago."

## TRANSVESTITES

A woman comes home to find her son wearing a black dress, mesh silk stockings, and high heels. Angrily, she says, "I told you a hundred times. Don't let me catch you wearing your father's things!"

Transvestites have a great motto—Eat, drink, and be Mary.

## TRAVEL

A traveler is stopped by Customs. "Anything to declare?"

"No, sir."

"What about that elephant behind you with a piece of bread in his trunk and another one in his tail?"

The traveler says, "What I put in my sandwiches is my own business!"

He travels a lot. He's seen more strange places than a porno cameraman.

My wife and I had a terrible time in Venice. The streets were always filled with water!

While I was in Italy, I went through a monastery. It was nice, but it needed a woman's touch!

Two women were discussing trips. One said, "Last year we went to Sicily."

The other woman said, "Where's Sicily?"

The first one answered, "I'm not sure. We flew!"

Never travel to any country where they set fire to the American flag and the ambassador.

He always has trouble with those fluffy hotel towels. He can't get them in his valise!

A cruise ship sinks, and only a few men live to swim to a desert island. Time goes by and one of the men, a German, teaches the natives how to march. A Frenchman opens a restaurant. An Italian teaches the natives how to sing. An American opens a fast-food place. And the Englishman stands around waiting to be introduced.

A travel agent described the beauties of Tahiti. I asked, "When's the best time to go there?

The travel agent said, "Between twenty-one and thirty."

Some tourists were stranded on a deserted island. One said, "We're doomed. We're lost, and they'll never find us."

Another one said, "They have to. We took this cruise on the installment plan."

Why do people have to go to Egypt or India to find a dead civilization? Just go to Philadelphia.

Two fancy ladies meet, and one asks, "Where did you go on your vacation?"

The second says, "We went around the world, but next year we're going somewhere else."

When I go on a trip, I always take so many things I don't use—shirts, shoes, ties . . . my wife.

He was smart. He took one of those trips where you go now and pay later and he never came back.

My great-grandfather crossed the country in a covered wagon. It took him four

months. With today's traffic, that's not bad.

A man goes into his bathroom after a fight with his wife. He's so angry, he goes out the window without making a sound. He goes to a doctor and gets his face redone. He grows a mustache. He gets new clothes, unlike in every way those he'd worn formerly, takes a plane to South America and, after wandering around for ten years, checks into a small hotel in Rio.

His wife, meanwhile, searches for him relentlessly, spending a fortune on leads. Finally, she learns of his whereabouts. She flies to Rio and goes into his room to accost him. He happens to be washing up when she arrives, so she knocks on the bathroom door and identifies herself.

From beyond the door, the husband says, "What the heck is this? Can't a guy finish washing up in peace?"

## TRAVELING SALESMEN

Traveling salesman Joe Adams is in a hospital with a broken leg. Required to take down his history, the nurse asks, "What happened to you?"

Joe says, "It was about thirty years ago. I was a salesman and happened to come to this farmhouse where I got a room for the night. About ten minutes after I got into bed, the farmer's daughter came into my room and asked me if I wanted anything. Well, I didn't need anything. About an hour later, she walked in wearing this sheer nightie, and asked me if I wanted anything. Again I told her no. About midnight, she came in again wearing the scantiest baby dolls I ever saw and asked me if I needed anything. I told her no. The way I saw it was, I'd had a decent supper, the bed was warm, and the pillows soft. What else could I want? I couldn't even understand what she could think I wanted. Then, yesterday, as I was shingling the roof, it came to me like a bolt out of the blue. That's when I fell off the roof I was repairing."

## TROUBLE

The trouble with sex is that it takes the least time and makes the most trouble.

In certain sections of Paris, prostitutes ask prospective customers "if they want their watch fixed."

Upon being asked, a tourist says, "No, thanks. I had mine fixed last year, and it's still running."

Trouble is when a man in a blue serge suit dates a woman with an angora sweater.

Trouble is heading your way when you tell the doctor about your symptoms as he keeps backing farther and farther away from you.

Jake Burley has a few problems. His cows have died from the pox. His chickens won't lay. The drought has dried up his crops. His wife has left him, and his two sons are in jail. To ease his pain, the local minister visits him and says, "Whom the Lord loves, he chastens."

Jake says, "Yeah, but don't you think he's overdoing it in my case?"

A young man is reading a letter and seems puzzled. A friend asks what the problem is. The young man answers, "Well, I got this letter. It says that I'd better stay away from this man's wife, or he'll blow my head off."

The friend says, "That seems perfectly clear."

"The damn thing isn't signed."

Nobody wants to hear your problems unless there's a girl involved.

The strange thing about trouble is that it always starts out to be fun.

## TRUST

My wife really trusts me. After twenty years, she still believes I have a sick friend.

When somebody tells you he's laying all his cards on the table, count them.

Eighty percent of lawyers were bottle babies. Even their mothers wouldn't trust them.

There's so little trust in this country today. Yesterday I heard a politician confess that he'd lied, and I didn't believe him.

A trusting father is one who thinks his daughter has gotten religion because she came home with a Gideon Bible in her valise.

He doesn't even believe that storks bring baby storks.

Sign in a restaurant: IF YOU ARE OVER EIGHTY YEARS OLD AND ACCOMPANIED BY YOUR PARENTS, WE WILL CASH YOUR CHECK.

### TRUTH

Truth is stranger than fiction, but not nearly as popular.

An Indian chief assembled the young men of his tribe and asked, "Who threw outhouse over cliff?"

Nobody spoke up. Again the chief asked. Again there was silence.

The chief went on, "Many moons ago, George Washington cut down cherry tree. He confess. He no get whipping. So, tell me—who push outhouse over cliff?"

Running Wind, a boy of ten and the chief's son, raised his hand. "I push outhouse over cliff."

The chief wound up and smacked the kid halfway across the camp.

Running Wind said, "George Washington no get hit by father."

The chief said, "George Washington's father not in cherry tree at time."

Among the truths of the world are the beliefs that the husband is head of the household and the pedestrian has the right of way. Both of them are real safe until you try to prove them.

A defendant in a trial is told by the judge, "You will tell the truth, the whole truth, and nothing but the truth."

The defendant says, "With limitations like that, I don't figure I have anything to say."

Returning home late one night, a man told his wife he'd been out with his business manager.

"That's nice," said the wife, "but he's waiting for you in the living room."

"Well, who are you going to believe," the man said, "Me or your eyes?"

It's wrong to hold anybody to anything he says while he's in love, drunk, or running for office.

### TV

I love cable TV. I get a chance to see all those movies I walked out on twenty years ago!

A cable TV installer arrived at a house, rang the bell, and nodded pleasantly to the lady who opened the door, saying, "I came to install the set, Mrs. Thompson."

The lady said, "I'm not Mrs. Thompson. The Thompsons have been living in another state for over a year now."

The installer shook his head. "Some people are like that. They ask for service right away, and then they move."

On TV today there are so many cop shows. Every Tom and Harry is a Dick.

The way things are going, people will soon start demanding longer commercials.

There's one thing I like about a TV commercial. There are no interruptions.

TV is proof that people'll look at anything rather than one another.

A producer was auditioning women for the lead in his new one-hour dramatic show.

"You're just right," he says to a girl. "Right face, right voice, exactly what's called for in the script! By the way, what's your average salary?"

"Twenty-thousand a week," the woman answers.

"Sorry," snapped the producer. "You're too tall."

If it wasn't for the guy who invented TV, we'd still be eating frozen radio dinners!

Our local TV weatherman is so bad, he couldn't even predict yesterday's weather.

Before TV, nobody knew what a headache looked like.

Go to any movie today and you'll know what cable'll be like in ten years.

This news show hired a shapely young lady, amply endowed, put her into a low-cut gown, and had her do the weather report. She didn't last long. When she talked about cold fronts, nobody believed her.

TV is strange. The good guys win out on every program but the eleven o'clock news.

Then there was this TV producer who was doing fine with the summer replacement, but his wife found out about her.

Prime time is the time when the set is off.

Television must be bad. I came home the other night, and my kid was doing homework.

I used to watch baseball on TV, but now I watch soap operas. There's much more scoring.

I watch a lot of public TV. The other day, I saw a science show about all the galaxies pulling away from the earth at ten thousand miles a second. I keep wondering: Do they know something?

I saw a real old western on cable. Billy the Kid was played by Billy the Kid.

Forty years ago, some people thought television was impossible. Some still do.

She's an active actress. She's made more pilots than a stewardess.

I finally had to move my antenna from the top of the chimney. The picture was too smoky.

Since cable came on, my kids have seen 1,930 more pictures than I have.

He must be a TV sponsor. He watches the commercials and goes to the fridge during the show.

Television executives ought to learn that the only thing worse than no taste is having no shame.

They grounded my nephew for a week—no TV. He sat for three days watching the microwave oven.

I always used to wonder where my wife was all the time. One day the TV set broke down during a ball game, and there she was.

Television tends to take our minds off our minds.

A lot of today's shows are what they call reality shows. They show murders, assaults, cops breaking into homes. In my neighborhood, you just have to look out the window.

A television director is hit on the head and goes out like a light. When he wakes, the producer asks him, "What happened?"

The director says, "I hit my head, and suddenly everything went black-and-white."

There's a great way to end a war—put it on a bad network, and it'll be over in thirteen weeks.

Television opens a lot of doors, most of them on refrigerators.

I saw a movie on cable TV the other night that was real old. The getaway car was a chariot.

I have a TV set with only two controls—my wife and my kid.

I don't mind my wife serving TV dinners—but reruns?

Most TV dinners taste like they've been made by the TV repairman.

I have a remote control for my TV—my three kids. Chances of my getting the set are pretty remote.

One sponsor had to leave one of the big game shows. They gave away his factory.

I believe in pay TV. We should get paid for watching some of those shows.

### TWINS

My little niece saw twins and said, "Look, there's two of the same girl."

Two garment-center stalwarts are both making love to their secretary. One of them, however, keeps referring to her as "my" secretary. The other registers a strong protest: "Why must it always be *your* secretary. *Your* secretary. Why not *our* secretary?"

"All right, *our* secretary."

Accidentally, the secretary becomes pregnant and goes to the hospital. Both men pace up and down the waiting room.

Finally, a nurse emerges. The first man rushes back with her.

He returns a few moments later with a big smile on his face and says, "She had twins. Mine died."

"I'm married to twin sisters. They're alike in every way."

"How do you tell them apart?"

"Who tries!"

## UGLY

She's really ugly. I took her to the top of the Empire State Building, and she was attacked by planes.

She's so ugly—she keeps sending her mirror back for repairs.

I won't say she's ugly, but I've seen better skin on wallets.

Her beauty is down real deep. She must have a gorgeous skeleton.

I won't say she's ugly, but I took her to the dog track, and three men put her in the quiniela.

She once entered a beautiful-legs contest and was beaten out by the mike stand.

A man visited a friend's home for the first time and was let in by a very ugly woman. In the living room, he asked the friend, "Was that your wife who let me in?"

The friend answered, "Of course. Would I have a maid that ugly?"

She's ashamed of her long black hair. She always wears long gloves to cover it up.

This one woman was so ugly, during a flight the stewardess covered her face to show how the oxygen mask works, and the other passengers applauded.

She's so ugly—at night she puts her whole body up in curlers.

Nobody ever saw anything as ugly as her without paying admission.

She was such an ugly hooker, she ended up working in a doghouse.

This man is discussing marriage with a friend and tells the friend he has no feelings for his wife. The friend says, "What if you caught her cheating? You'd get angry, I'm sure of that."

The man says, "I sure would. I'd break the bastard's white cane and shoot his seeing-eye dog."

She's as ugly as homemade soap.

"Dear Lord, just look at the ugly child. He's got a face like a monkey."

"He just happens to be my son, the one who's got a face like a monkey."

"You know, on him it looks good."

She took a four-year course in ugliness and finished it in two.

She was a perfect 10. Her face was a 2, her body was a 2, her legs were a 2 . . .

"I'm going to marry an ugly girl because a beauty can run away."

"An ugly girl could run away too."

"Yeah, but who would care?"

Why don't you take your wife on a second honeymoon?

What for? Her looks loused up the first one.

She loves mosquitoes. They're the only ones who want her for her body.

She was a real rocking chick—that's what they threw at her!

She was so ugly, as a child they hired a kid actress to play her in home movies!

"What an ugly woman that hag is!"

"That happens to be my wife."

"I'm sorry."

"Not as sorry as I am!"

She's so ugly, they give her a doggie bag before she eats!

She looked like the loser in a cockfight. When she overheard somebody say that, she got insulted. She'd won!

"What does your girl look like?"

"Take the face of a movie star, the body of a pinup girl, the bosom of a stripper, and the eyes of a mascara model. What you have left—that's my girl."

## UNCLES

**M**y uncle works in a shipyard. They don't pay him a salary, but they let him lick up the champagne after a launching.

**M**y uncle has been on strike for twelve years, and he never even worked for the place.

**M**y uncle once broke his leg throwing a ball. It was chained to his ankle.

## UNEMPLOYMENT

**T**imes are very bad. A friend of mine just lost his job. He worked in the Unemployment Office.

**G**od helps those who help themselves, and Washington those that don't.

**A**fter this evening, he goes back into the family business—unemployment.

**A** man overheard a son and father having a distressing conversation.
"You're a no-good worthless bum!" the father says.
"Yeah?" answers his son. "Who brings home the unemployment checks?"

## UNIONS

**A**fter weeks of negotiating, a management representative finally gave in. "Why the sudden change?" a co-worker asked.

"This morning, two of the huskiest union members picked me up by the collar and said if I didn't sign, they'd break both my arms and my legs. I'd never had the plan explained to me so clearly before."

## UNITED NATIONS

**T**he UN might be a better outfit if there weren't so many foreigners in it.

**T**he UN does keep the peace. In all these years, there's never been a war in the building.

**T**he UN makes strange bedfellows. But then, so does prostitution.

**T**he UN is made up of countries that can't stand oppression except at home.

**T**he UN was started so everybody would act like friends. Right now they're acting more like relatives.

**A** UN delegate is a man who only has one lie to give for his country.

**M**ost Americans fight with their neighbors, scream at their families, threaten everybody, and then wonder why different countries don't get along.

**O**r as some call the UN—the Tower of Babble.

**A**t the UN they're trying to get all the countries to be like one big family. If they end up like mine, the world's in real trouble.

The UN has done more to promote peace than a divorce court.

The cannibal chief has a plan. "Let's declare war on the territory next to us. The UN will step in and ask for a cease-fire. They'll refer the matter to the Security Council. The Security Council will send an arbitrator, and we'll eat him."

Every time two countries have a fight, they call the UN. Maybe an unlisted phone number might help.

## USELESS

He's as useful as a wake-up call at Forest Lawn.

He's a jack-of-all-trades, and he's out of work in all of them.

He's as useless as an On-Off switch on a sundial.

## VACATIONS

Vacation time is when you spend days looking for a place to avoid next year.

We went sightseeing until our eyes were sore. Then they took us to a sight for sore eyes.

Vacations really aren't much fun unless you go somewhere you can't afford.

I took a vacation recently. I needed the towels.

My wife must be descended from Noah. Whenever we go anywhere, she takes two of everything.

I don't need a vacation this year. I'm already broke.

Italy was fantastic. Rome took my breath away. Venice left me speechless. And then there was Florence. She got me for five hundred in traveler's checks.

A vacation's when you spend two weeks in a motor home with people you thought you loved the most.

Does she travel? She's been in Paris more often than April.

Most people go on vacation to forget things. When they get home and open their luggage, they did.

I don't like cruises because the captain always asks me to sit at his table. I pay so much money, why should I eat with the crew?

It wasn't just Denmark. I found things rotten in six European countries.

People keep telling me to go to Europe. But where can I send my wife?

Nowadays, people vacation in places where years ago you could only go if you were shipwrecked.

We got lucky driving on our vacation. The highway was open while the detour was being repaired.

If you did all the things you really should do before you go on vacation, it would be over before you got started.

People vacation nowadays in places you could only get to in the old days if you were drafted.

My wife and I took separate vacations last year. I redid the basement, and she cleaned the attic.

I used to wonder why the English drank so much tea. Then one day I tried their coffee.

I went to a travel bureau and asked where I could go for fifty dollars. They told me.

We stayed at a great hotel. It had an eighteen-hole golf course and sheets to match.

When my wife and I go on vacation, I don't even bother to lock the front door. Everything we own is in the station wagon.

I just came back from a vacation overseas with the family.
Lindbergh had the right idea. He flew to Europe alone.

This is a guarantee: Whatever you want is in the other valise.

We went mountain climbing in the Alps. The guide was nice. He told us, "Be careful. Try not to slip. We're six thousand feet up. But if you do slip, look to the right. It's a great view!"

"I've been in Paris six days, and I haven't been to the Louvre yet."
"Maybe it's the water."

If you can't get away for a vacation, just tip every third person you see, and you'll get the same effect.

A tourist resort is a place where nobody knows how big a man you are back home.

I worry about a hotel where the bellhop takes away your belt and shoelaces.

We just returned from a trip where we saw a lot of ruins—our bank accounts.

On vacation, this family is going through a Wisconsin dairy where cheese is made. A guide explains about how the milk is set, rennet added, the whey strained off, and the curds pressed. The guide then asks if there are any questions. The little daughter says, "I have a question. Since you know so much about curds and whey, what's a tuffet?"

We took a trip to the Grand Canyon this summer. It took five days to drive and six to refold the maps.

They now have a new resort for people who limp. It's called Club Foot.

Don't vacation in any country where strip-searching is a hobby.

A vacation nowadays fills most of the year. You go away in January, you get the pictures back in February, your bills in March, your health back in April, and your luggage back in May.

My wife and I couldn't decide on whether to go to Hawaii or the West Indies, so we went to Hawaii, and our luggage went to the West Indies.

Two textile manufacturers went on a safari to Africa. While they were walking along, a hissing animal jumped out at one of them and ran off. The almost-victim asked, "Was that a leopard?"

The other one said, "How would I know? I'm not in furs."

I checked into my last resort hotel and asked them for something nice and restful. They gave me a sedative.

A man took his wife on a vacation to a swanky resort. The clerk tried to sell them the bridal suite. The man said, "Pal, we've been married fifteen years."

The clerk said, "So? If I gave you the ballroom, would you have to dance?"

Hotel employees love tips. I once called down for a deck of cards. The bellhop made fifty-two trips.

Some resorts are unbelievably plush nowadays. One vacationer checked into an elegant resort and was immediately taken by the manager to a room that had a gold telephone, a stereo, color TV, and a bar. The vacationer was delighted and said, "I'll take it."

The manager said, "Wait. We're still in the elevator."

I had a great vacation. I went through two national parks and four thousand dollars.

Vacations are when you dump your family into a car and tell everybody you're going to get away from it all.

A man decides to go on vacation with his teenage daughter. The wife is beside herself. "Why can't I go?"

"Because you have a big mouth."

The man and his daughter take off on what promises to be a wonderful train trip. After a few hours out, there is a noise, and a robber comes in. Brandishing a gun, he proceeds to relieve the passengers of their possessions.

When he's gone, the man starts to shake and sob. "We've lost everything."

The daughter says, "It's not awful, Dad. When I saw the gun, I hid all my money and jewelry in my mouth."

The man says, "Too bad your mother isn't here. We could have saved the suitcase."

**H**e's got a great gimmick. He goes to a resort and registers as an unmarried doctor.

**I** loved Venice. Where else can you get seasick crossing the street?

## VALENTINE DAY

**M**y wife sent me a nice Valentine Day card—"Guess who, and you'd better!"

**I**f you don't have a little gift for Valentine Day, the next day may be Moving Day.

## VALUE

**A** rabbi fills in for the local priest in the confessional. After hearing Mary Millicent confess to having had sex with the neighbor's son next door, the rabbi tells her to put ten dollars in the collection basket next time she goes to mass.

Mary Millicent says, "But the priest only makes us put two dollars in."

The rabbi says, "Maybe he doesn't know what that stuff is worth."

**T**his young man, to whom affluence had come suddenly, is driving, when he is sideswiped by an old truck. The young man starts to moan, "My beautiful new Mercedes. My beautiful Mercedes."

A traffic cop who had pulled up says, "Buddy, you have more to worry about than your car. Your arm is all smashed up. You need medical attention, right away."

The young man looks and starts to moan, "My Rolex, my beautiful Rolex."

**T**here are two kinds of people—the deserving and the undeserving. Unfortunately, the choosing is done by the deserving.

**I**f somebody sticks his two cents in and gives you a penny for your thoughts and a nickel for your chances, you'll have eight cents!

**L**ike most fathers, this one father is upset when a young man comes to ask for the hand of his daughter. The young man says, "Look, I know that she can't cook or clean. I know that she's impossible to control with money. I know that she has a tendency to talk too much. Still, I love her. I want to marry her in spite of all her faults."

The father arches his brows. "What faults?"

## VATICAN

I'd love to have an office job at the Vatican. You never get taken for a baby gift!

The pope is running around in the Vatican without a stitch of clothes on, yelling, "I'm invisible! I'm invisible!"

A cardinal stops him and says, "I don't want to say anything, but the word is 'infallible'!"

## VAUDEVILLE

A vaudevillian died and ended up in a warm spot beyond the horizon. He asked his escort where he was, and the escort said, "You're in hell."

The vaudevillian said, "I should have known. My agent never booked me into a good spot yet."

A ventriloquist fell on hard times. He was finally forced to go to work for a swami who ran séances. At the request of a guest, he'd throw his voice and pretend to be the departed person with whom the guest wanted to converse. At one session, he was pretending to be Mr. Brown, whose widow had paid fifty dollars for the séance.

After talking to her Mr. Brown for a long time, the widow said, "I can't believe I could talk to my husband for just fifty dollars."

The ventriloquist said, "For a hun-dred, you could talk to him while he's drinking a glass of water."

A man walks into an agent's office with his small dog. The agent says, "Another trained dog?"

"Just another trained dog? Watch." The man points off to the piano against the wall. The dog rushes to it, jumps upon the piano stool, cracks its paws, and starts to play.

After an incredibly sustained arpeggio, the dog starts to sing. Its voice is golden and rich.

The agent says, "Wow! What an act! We'll make a fortune."

Suddenly, the door swings open. A large dog runs in, grabs the little dog by the scruff of the neck and disappears.

"What's that?" the agent asks.

"She's the little dog's mommy. She wants him to be a doctor."

## VEGETARIAN

A vegetarian is somebody who won't eat anything that can have kids.

A vegetarian is halfway to an anorexic.

A vegetarian is a teenage daughter who sees that you're making roast beef.

## VIRGINS

A hillbilly married. He returned alone from the honeymoon and was asked by his father, "Where's your bride?"

The hillbilly said, "I found out she was a virgin, so I shot her."

The father said, "Serves her right. If she wasn't good enough for her own family, she sure wasn't good enough for ours."

What's the difference between a virgin and a light bulb?

You can unscrew a light bulb.

The crowd has gathered and is about to wreak havoc on Mary Magdalene. Jesus steps up and says, "Hold it. Let he who is without sin cast the first stone."

From the back of the crowd, a big rock comes flying forward. Jesus says, "Come on, Ma, cut it out."

A man has his heart set on marrying a pure young lady, so he chooses a wife who has just gotten out of twelve years in convent school. As they start out on their honeymoon, they walk toward their hotel and see some young women loitering in the street. The bride says, "Who are those ladies, dear?"

"They're prostitutes."

"What's a prostitute?"

"A woman who'll make love for large amounts of money."

"Really? At school, the priests only gave us an orange."

To the virgins of the world—thanks for nothing!

A virgin who giggles is half-taken.

A mistake is something a skydiver and a virgin can only make once.

## VIRTUE

A mature man was asked for the secret of his long and happy life.

He explained, "I never smoked, drank, or ran around with women until I was eleven years old!"

The trouble with the straight and narrow is that it runs through such dull territory.

The way I see it is that any man who doesn't drink, smoke, fool around, or gamble is either dead or senile.

The virtuous man will get to heaven first. Some unvirtuous man will knife him.

## VITAMINS

The fellow who figured out how to get 400,000 units of vitamin E in that small capsule must have been a bus driver.

They married late in life. To compensate, she takes vitamins and he takes iron. That's the trouble. When she's ready, he's rusty.

A woman called the doctor. "Doctor, my son just swallowed a whole bottle of beta carotene. What should I do?"

The doctor said, "Hide your rabbit."

They say that vitamin E is an aid to virility. In fact, one company is putting it out with the trade name Honeymoon Helper!

Now they have megavitamins. Chew one bottle, and you get enough strength to open the second bottle.

I have a friend who takes two hundred different vitamins and minerals a day. It's not the vitamins so much. He just loves all that cotton.

I take a lot of beta carotene. That's the vitamin in carrots. But the only thing I can do like a rabbit is hop.

## VOTING

This one candidate made such fantastic promises, his opponent switched his vote.

The secret ballot is great. It gives you the chance to say that you didn't vote for the guy who got in.

In one of those cities where there are often more voters than people, two men are going through a cemetery looking for names to put into the voter register. They reach a tombstone that says, HERE LIES NAVGRANEY KROFNOSVKIVANTCHINAK DRJCKANIMKCSZLIVERTAMK.

The first man says, "Let's forget about this one."

The second man says, "That's not fair. He's got as much right to vote as anybody in this cemetery."

## WAGES

**My** nephew gets paid every two weeks. That's good. He can't buy anything with one week's pay.

**The** state and the federal government take a good chunk in withholding every week. A friend of mine wanted to make a deal with them. Let them take his salary and just give him the deductions.

## WALL STREET

**It's** a little odd. People in 450 SLs drive downtown to Wall Street to get advice from a guy who came to work in a bus.

**My** cousin is half Yuppie and half Mexican. He's a migrant stockbroker.

**The** recession has hit so many people so bad that they will have to drive off a cliff in a car pool.

## WAR

A general at one of the guided-missile bases was asked about the accuracy of the weapons. He said, "From here I can get a direct hit on downtown Chicago or Cleveland."

"How about targets in Russia?" the questioner asked.

"No problem if they're near downtown Chicago or Cleveland!"

In the next war, we won't have the same old problems. For example, we won't have to worry about veterans' benefits.

Wouldn't it be funny if we fought our next war over disarmament?

Then there's the soldier who was scared about catching shrapnel. There was a lot of it going around.

There's a lot of talk about World War III, and I hate it. We can't afford to win another war right now.

## WASHINGTON

When a particularly difficult congressman opened up on newer members of the House, a colleague warned, "Getting into a debate with him is like wrestling a skunk. The skunk doesn't care; he likes the smell!"

A businessman with some government business to attend to in Washington took time off after a few weeks to go to a bar and have himself a drink. Seeing a pretty woman, he asked her, "Can I buy you a drink?"

The pretty woman said, "No!"

At her one word, the man fainted. When he was revived, someone asked him why he'd fainted, and he said, "I've been in this town for two weeks, and that was the first time I got a definite answer."

Jesus could never have been born in Washington. You couldn't find three wise men or a virgin.

Here's the newest thing—they're taking out malpractice insurance on the vice president.

The government has declared war on poverty. Last week alone, it wiped out eighteen bums and a bag lady.

This bright man wants to go to work for the government for a dollar a year. Now if the government only had that dollar.

Two congressmen went at it with words for hours. The papers reported the next day that Congressman Smith and Congressman Brown had indulged in intellectual combat and both of them were unarmed.

George Washington didn't have it easy when he ran. He couldn't complain about the previous administration.

A congressman greets a delegation from his state, one of the visitors being a pretty lady. The pretty lady says, "Sir, when my grandmother was a girl, she went to Washington. There, her congressman gave her a kiss that she remembered all her life. Could you do that for me?"

Smiling, the congressman leaned over and kissed the girl tenderly. As his lips brushed her lips, one of the other visitors took a picture in one of those cameras that develop a photo instantly. The visitor showed the picture to the congressman and pointed out that such a photo could harm his career. It would cost a thousand dollars to have the picture destroyed.

The congressman anted up and then asked, "Just tell me one thing. How much did it cost that other congressman?"

Washington wouldn't have been a biggie today. He might have been first in war and first in peace, but if he never told a lie, there went his chances to get elected.

I figured out why George Washington stood in the boat. Every time he sat down, somebody gave him an oar.

A lovely German fräulein in Washington was suspected of hanky-panky with government officials. Asked if she'd ever been away on official trips with senators, she replied, *"Nein"*—so she was deported.

Only in Washington can you find a thousand lobbyists, five hundred economists, eight hundred experts, and all of Congress working on a plan to simplify taxes.

Senate investigations are like a fishing trip. All the big ones get away.

Half the politicians in Washington are trying to start investigations. The other half are trying to get them stopped.

## WEATHER

Today's California weather report is typical: Clear today except for dense early fog, followed by heavy smog, followed by dense evening fog.

This year I didn't go to Florida for color. I went to Alaska and came back with a beauty—blue!

A TV station in a rural area has a hillbilly weatherman who reports, "Mebbe it will and mebbe it won't. Most likely, it will."

I just bought a barometer made in Yokohama. Now I know when it's raining in Yokohama.

Rain was bad enough when it only contained water.

One weatherman finally hits it on the button. He predicts rain and it rains, because he's lost his umbrella, he has a golf date, and his wife is throwing a lawn party.

I like winter. That's when my lawn looks the same way it looks the rest of the year, but now there's a reason.

We have real rotten weather. At the zoo the other day, the polar bear asked to be made into a rug.

The flooding has been fierce. The river has overflowed its banks and is now up to the second story of most of the homes. Mrs. Lewis, a pious woman, is looking out of her second-story bedroom window when a man in a rowboat comes by. The man says, "Jump in, lady. I'll save you."

Mrs. Lewis smiles and says, "Thank you, but the Lord will provide."

The waters continue to rise. Mrs. Lewis is forced to climb to the roof. A motorboat passes by, and the man in the boat says, "Jump in, lady. We'll take you to safety."

"Thank you so much, but the Lord will provide."

The waters continue to rise. Unable to keep her head above water, Mrs. Lewis drowns.

Arriving in heaven, she is irate and demands to see God. When she is brought before him, she says, "I've always been religious, I've never missed church, I've done good deeds—how come you didn't provide?"

God says, "How many boats do you want me to send for you?"

I just heard the Seattle weather report. Last week, it rained only twice—once for three days and once for four days.

It's so foggy here, on a clear day you can see the fog.

It was so cold, the farmer milked for ten minutes before he realized he was shaking hands with himself.

You don't need magic to end a drought. Just let me come to the place on a two-week vacation.

It's been real cold. The other day, I had my appendix taken out, and it was chapped.

Winter must be here. My car heater stopped working.

A tourist in the Mojave takes time out from souvenir-hunting to ask a grizzled old desert rat, "Do you think it's going to rain?"

The desert rat says, "I sure hope so. But not for me, for my son. I've seen it rain."

The best thing about rain is that you don't have to shovel it.

Into each life, some rain must fall—especially on a weekend.

"Do you think it'll snow?"
"It all depends on the weather."

I can tell rain by my corns. If they get wet, it's raining.

It was so cold the other day, I saw a man wearing his toupee upside down.

There's been flooding all over the country. Couches now come with oarlocks.

To the TV weatherman, one and one is two—probably.

It's been real dry around here. Last week I mailed a letter, and I had to pin the envelope shut.

It was 125 in the shade. I fooled them. I stayed in the sun.

It was so dry, the fish were spitting at each other to stay alive.

It was so damp in our place, the mousetraps were catching fish.

It really stormed last night. I saw the animals at the zoo going inside two by two.

It must be spring in Cleveland. They just reported their first robin-rust-breast.

I hate icy roads. It's no fun when your tires are going sixty-five but your car is backing up!

The weather in London is frightful. It's cold, dank, a freezing rain is falling, and the wind rushes through the streets like a locomotive. A man finds a cab by luck and gets in. As they start off, the man says, "Frightful weather, isn't it?"

The cabbie says, "I know. I haven't seen a butterfly in the last half hour."

It does get windy up around Chicago way. But it has its benefits. During the last storm, my car got 580 miles to the gallon.

It was raining cats and dogs. I know because I stepped in a poodle.

"When do you know it's too cold to go for a walk?"

"When your dog sticks to the fire hydrant."

Recently, a tornado hit an area where they had dairy farms and grew strawberries. The whole area became a disaster area and two malteds.

A man comes to town, checks into a hotel, and has a hooker sent up. A beautiful girl arrives. The man asks her how much she gets.

"A thousand, but I'm great."

The man says, "All right, but you have to do what I like."

"Name it."

They undress. The man gets into the bathtub and says, "Blow wind, like there's a storm."

The hooker goes, *"Whoosh, whoosh, whoosh."*

The man says, "Make waves likes there's a storm."

The hooker pummels the water until it sloshes around all over.

"Now make thunder."

The hooker bangs her shoe against the side of the tub.

"And lightning."

The hooker works her cigarette lighter on and off.

Finally, she says, "Honey, I'm a hooker, and I'm great. Isn't there something sexual I could do for you?"

"Are you kidding? In this weather?"

It was so foggy yesterday, you could chop down a tree and it wouldn't fall.

It's real cold in Minnesota. The last summer they had there was on a Monday.

There's a real drought in Kansas. One cowboy rounded up fifteen hundred head of catfish before he knew they weren't steers.

It gets windy around here. Farmers have to feed their chickens buckshot to keep them from blowing away.

It gets cold in Oregon. The trout go around with two inches of fur to keep from freezing.

It gets so cold here—one winter the mercury went through the bottom of the tube and dug a two-foot hole in the sidewalk.

California weather is terrific. The other day, it was shining cats and dogs.

If you hear it's not the heat, it's the humidity, you know it's the heat.

How did they measure hail before golf balls were invented?

We need some rain badly. Yesterday, as they were swimming upstream, the fish were kicking up the dust.

The government weatherman has been predicting rain for two months. But last night he found out his coin was two-headed.

In the Panhandle the other day, they had a terrible dust storm. It was so thick, one gopher was digging a hole ten feet in the air.

A flooded basement is no fun, but how about a flooded attic?

It's always so foggy in this part of the country. I didn't meet my parents until I was eight!

After a recent flood in Texas, a whole group of people were given shelter in a school gym. A Red Cross worker asked, "Are there any pregnant women in here?"

A woman answered, "Hell, we aren't even dry yet."

A married couple was on the outs but refused to split up just yet. They had gone a year without speaking to each other when, in the middle of a hurricane, they were both blown through the roof of their home. It saved their marriage. The wife explained, "It seemed silly for us to go out together and not be speaking."

It was real hot the other day. I caught a hummingbird trying to drink my earwax.

Nobody dares come out in North Dakota's cold weather. Sixteen women are in their twelfth month.

A woman shopping for thermometers settled on Fahrenheit because she figured it was a good brand.

## WEDDINGS

They were having their first fight, and finally he said, "When we got married, you promised to love, honor and obey."

She said, "I know. I didn't want to start an argument in front of all those people."

It was some fancy wedding. No finger bowls. After the main dish, everybody went in and took a shower.

She was such an ugly bride, all the men got in line to kiss the groom!

He was such an ugly groom, he had to wear the veil!

This one woman was married eleven times. She didn't like men, but she loved wedding cake.

The words "Love, honor, and obey" were about to be uttered by the minister. The groom leaned forward and whispered, "Padre, read those words twice, will you? I've been married before, and I want this one to get the full solemnity of the meaning."

Little Mary was at her first wedding and gaped at the entire ceremony. When it was over, she asked her mother, "Why did the lady change her mind?"

Her mother asked, "What do you mean?"

"Well, she went down the aisle with one man, and came back with another one."

It was a small wedding: just her parents, his parents, and the obstetrician.

You know the marriage is in trouble when they start walking down the aisle and the bride asks somebody for an aspirin.

A little girl is a guest at a wedding and asks her mother, "Why is the bride wearing white?"

The mother explains, "White is the color of purity and the future and happiness."

The little girl asks, "Why is the groom wearing black?"

It was a special wedding. People met who hadn't talked to one another for years, including the bride and groom!

She was really a blushing bride. The groom didn't show up.

Then there were this bride and groom who left the reception early so they could get their things together.

When we walked down the aisle, my bride took my arm. She knew the way better.

At a modern wedding, there are always three things on the cake—a bride, a groom, and a test tube.

A wedding generally means showers for the bride and curtains for the groom.

We looked like a new house. She was freshly painted, and I was plastered.

She was such a horny bride—she carried a bouquet of batteries.

I had so much fun at my bachelor dinner, I called off the wedding.

This groom received absolutely no respect at the wedding. When the minister said, "Is there anybody here who objects to this marriage?" forty people got in line.

At one wedding, a midget guest got so loaded, he attacked the bride on the wedding cake.

I was at a wedding where the groom wept for two hours. Seems the bride got a bigger piece of cake than he did.

## WEIGHT

Misery is when you break two things—your diet and your scale!

My husband says I'm too fat. So I went to a paint store. You can get thinner there.

This couple just became the proud parents of a thirty-six-pound baby. At least that's what the butcher's scale said.

After twenty-nine years of wedded bliss, a man's wife passed away, and the bereaved husband had her ashes put into a beautiful urn, which he placed on his mantel. Heedless friends took to the habit of flicking their cigarette ashes into the urn.

Months after the funeral, the man's brother was in town. Looking at the urn, he remarked, "Say, your wife is gaining weight!"

I think my butcher cheats. I put a postcard on his scale, and it weighed four pounds nine ounces.

A man stepped on a scale in a train station. A paper came out of the slot and said, "You are handsome, debonair, brilliant, and make a fortune."

His wife looked at the paper and said, "It got your weight wrong too."

## WEIGHT LIFTING

A weight lifter comes into a café with an advertising executive from a health-food company. The waitress asks if they want a drink. The weight lifter sits back and says, "I'd sooner dirty my body by having intercourse with a whore than drink this alcoholic garbage."

The advertising executive says, "Miss, as long as there's a choice . . ."

Then there was the weight lifter who tried to dial 911, but he couldn't find the 11.

## WESTERN LIFE

"Do you know the difference between a regular rodeo and a gay rodeo?"

"I'm afraid not."

"Well, at a regular rodeo, the crowd hollers, 'Ride that sucker!' "

The cowhand asked the dude, "What kind of saddle do you want—one with a horn or without?"

The dude answered "Without, I guess. I figure you don't have much traffic around here."

A young gunslinger is boring everybody to death with accounts of his exploits. Seeing that he's not making friends and influencing people, he leaves. A moment later, he returns and says, "Okay, who's the clown that painted a red line along my horse's rear end?"

A gunslinger about 6'6″ with shoulders from wall to wall, says, "I did. Why are you asking?"

The young gunslinger says, "I just wanted to tell you the first coat is dry."

A city dude bought a ranch and moves his family out West to raise cattle. He wanted to name the ranch—the Double Q. His wife wanted to call it the Double X. His son wanted to call it the Lazy Flying Y Bar Z. To keep everybody happy, the man included all the names.

Unfortunately, none of the cattle survived the branding.

A great deal of rustling was going on, but it was hard to prove. One rancher, the owner of the Bar WQ ranch, ran into another rancher, who was suspected of being a rustler, and said, "Tom, I wish you'd stop leaving your hot branding irons around where my cattle can lie down on them."

The saloon owner gave his new bartender a word of warning. "Drop everything and run for your life if ever you hear that Big John is on his way to town."

The man worked several months without any problems. Then one day, a cowhand rushed in shouting, "Big John is coming," and knocked the small bartender on the floor in his hurry to get out. Before the bartender had a chance to recover, a giant of a man with a black bushy beard rode in through the swinging doors on the back of a buffalo, using a rattlesnake for a whip. The doors tore off their hinges, tables were knocked over, and the snake was flung into the corner. The man took his massive fist and split the bar in half as he asked for a drink. The bartender nervously pushed a bottle at the man. He bit off the top of the bottle and downed the contents in one gulp. Seeing that he wasn't hurting anyone, the bartender offered the man another drink.

"I ain't got no time," the man roared. "Big John's comin' into town!"

She felt like a young colt, but she looked more like an old .45.

A cowboy brings news that Black Bart, the vicious outlaw, has died.

Somebody asks, "What was the complaint?"

"There weren't any. Everybody's satisfied."

They are in the middle of a fierce and high-stakes poker game. As one player starts to pick up a card, a second whips out a knife, pins the first player's hand to the table, and says, "If that ain't the ace of spades, I beg your pardon."

## WESTERNS

One famous Western star has started to go to a shrink. At the end of every movie, he has to kiss his horse, and lately he's been looking forward to it.

There's a very skinny movie star who wants to play a two-gun cowboy in a western. But they can't figure out how he can draw one gun without tilting.

One of these days, they're going to write a really modern western. The cowboy'll pull up to the saloon and won't be able to find a place to park his horse.

I saw a crazy western the other day. Instead of horses, they rode on a cross between a horse and a kangaroo. It was so that the cowboys could ride inside during bad weather.

I saw a modern cowboy movie. The cigarettes the cowboy rolled had filter tips.

I saw a tough sheriff in a western. He worked a nudist colony and wore his badge anyway.

I don't know why they call them "adult" westerns. Senile, maybe.

"You're shot up real bad, son."

"Ever know anybody who was shot up good?"

I saw a western about a poor western town. The posse had to ride out two to a badge.

I saw a psychological western. Instead of "How," the Indians kept saying, "Why?"

## WHOREHOUSES

A very old man goes to a brothel and asks the price. The madam tells him that the cheapest price is two hundred dollars.

The very old man says, "You're putting me on."

"All right," the madam says, "but that'll be another twenty."

A man goes to a whorehouse, hands a hundred dollars to the lady of the evening, and says, "I want a little Greek, some French, and then I'd like to spank you."

The lady of the evening says, "How

much spanking do you intend to do?"

The man says, "Just enough to get my hundred back."

**O**ne elderly man went to a whorehouse at four-thirty in the afternoon and asked, "Am I in time for the Early Bird Special?"

## WIDOWS & WIDOWERS

**T**his elderly woman is toasting her husband: "May you live to be a hundred and nine."

The husband says, "Why not a hundred and ten?"

The elderly woman says, "For one year, I want to be a widow."

**A** widow received $100,000 from a policy her husband had taken out years before. Looking at the money, the bereaved widow said, "I'd give ten thousand dollars to have him back!"

**A** man is on his knees at a tombstone, moaning, "Why did you die? Why did you die? Why did you die?"

A stranger, passing by, says, "Sir, I've never seen such passionate mourning. Please tell me who died—a parent, a child, a loved one?"

The mourner said, "No. My wife's first husband! Why did you die? Why did you die?"

**A** woman marries eight times, and each of her husbands dies. She plans on getting married again, but a friend says, "I

wouldn't get married again. Husbands just aren't lucky for you."

**I** see that God took Alvin Parker last week.

After being married to Emmy Parker for fifteen years, Al volunteered.

## WILLS

**A**fter all, a will is only a dead giveaway.

**T**ommy is bitten by a rabid dog. The doctor gives him some painful shots and tells him to wait in the reception room until it can be discerned if Tommy reacts unfavorably. The doctor comes out a few minutes later and is puzzled as he sees Tommy writing madly on a sheet of paper. The doctor says, "There's no rush to make out your will."

Tommy says, "This isn't my will. I'm just making a list of all the people I'm going to bite."

## WINTER-SUMMER ROMANCES

**A** man of ninety married a twenty-year-old girl. Unfortunately, on the third day of the honeymoon he died. It took a week just to wipe the smile off his face.

**A** man in his eighties marries a young maiden. On their honeymoon night, he joins her in bed and holds up five fingers. The bride is overwhelmed and asks, "You want to do it *five* times?"

The old man says, "Heck, no. I mean, pick a finger."

One old man solved his marriage to a young girl. Instead of going to Niagara for a honeymoon, he sent his wife to camp.

The eighty-year-old man asked his twenty-year-old bride, "Would you still love me if I lost all my money?"

The young bride answered, "Of course. And I'd miss you too."

A rich man in his late eighties marries a very young girl, the lady no doubt hoping that he won't last too long. On their honeymoon night, the bride gets into a very sheer negligee and lies down in bed to await her groom's emergence from the bathroom. He finally does appear, strangely accoutred. He has earplugs, nose plugs, and wears a condom. The bride says, "Why are you wearing all those things?"

The groom answers, "Well, if there's anything I can't stand, it's a woman screaming and the smell of burning rubber."

An eighty-year-old man marries a twenty-two-year-old girl. Two weeks after the ceremony, she finds that he's cheating on her. She says, "Why are you cheating with a fifty-five-year-old woman? What does she have that I don't have?"

He says, "Patience."

## WISHES

"You're always wishing for something you don't have."

"What else is there to wish for?"

Walking along a beach, three men find an old bottle. They wipe it, and a genie pops out. She offers each of them a wish.

The first one has an easy life and a good family, so he says, "I wish I were twice as smart as I am."

"So be it," says the genie. "You are now twice as smart."

The second man has a wealthy wife and three Rolls Royces, so he says, "I wish I were a hundred times smarter."

The genie says some magic words and concludes, "You are now a hundred times smarter."

The third man is pensive. He's married to an heiress and has money to burn. Finally, he says, "I wish I were a thousand times smarter."

The genie goes *poof* and says, "You are now a woman."

## WIVES

My wife is very angry with me. She caught me patching a tire with one of her hotcakes.

My wife likes to make things—like mountains out of molehills.

My wife is always wearing my clothes. A man could save a fortune by marrying someone his own size.

I bought my wife a membership in a bridge club. They're supposed to jump next Thursday.

Two men meet on a bench in the park. The conversation gets around to the little woman. One man says, "My wife is an angel. She doesn't drink or smoke and spends half her time in church and comes home and sings hymns all evening long."

The other man says, "My wife was like that too. I strangled her."

My wife found a way to take off wrinkles. She broke my glasses.

A woman got a letter from her husband. He sent her a million kisses, so she had the mailman cash them.

My wife tried to bake a birthday cake in the oven, but the heat melted the candles.

My wife has more clothes than any woman. Her clothes closet is so packed, there are moths inside who haven't learned how to fly.

He didn't think much of his wife. For years he placed her under a pedestal.

Gee, we must be eating out tonight. I don't smell anything burning.

My wife's TV dinners used to melt in my mouth. Now she defrosts them first.

My wife isn't neat. It's been so long since she cleaned, dogs bury their bones in our rug.

My wife was always ahead. She served frozen dinners before there was TV.

My wife just doesn't have the knack of cooking. The other day she boiled an egg for twenty minutes, and it didn't get soft.

My wife is the most wonderful woman in the world. And that's not only my opinion, it's hers.

I talk so much, my wife gets hoarse listening to me.

Every time I taste my wife's Jell-O, I get a lump in my throat.

My wife gets a strange sensation when she goes behind the curtain to vote. She wants to try on a new dress.

I met my wife in a swinging singles' bar. She should have been home with the kids.

My wife never tastes the food while cooking it. She may not have the nerve to serve it.

It took my wife three-and-a-half cars to learn how to drive.

How is it that a wife who can see a blond hair on your coat at fifty feet can't see a garage door at six inches?

I always take my wife to an after-hours club. That's the only place open when she gets dressed.

My wife doesn't quite have the knack of making coffee. This morning I was stirring, and I bent the spoon.

"What do you love most about me, darling—my great body or my beauty?"
"Your sense of humor, dear."

One day I decided to get something for my wife. But nobody would start the bidding.

I found a great way to keep my wife from driving. I tell her that if she has an accident, the papers'll print her age.

My wife found a way to keep the kitchen spotless. We eat out.

My wife has a great fantasy. She wants to watch two women—one washing, the other cleaning.

This wife tells her husband, "You certainly were an ass at the party last night. I just hope nobody knows you were sober."

A woman tells her friend, "I have the most wonderful news. My husband just had a nervous breakdown, and we have to go to Acapulco for the next three months."

My wife and I decided to level with one another, so I told her I was seeing a therapist. She told me she was seeing a therapist, two dentists, a butcher, and a plumber!

"What do most women do with their assholes every morning?"
"They kiss them and send them off to work."

My wife is always ready to listen to both sides of an argument, as long as it's coming from next door.

My wife has kept her wedding outfit—the dress, the veil, the shotgun.

My wife and I have a great relationship. I love sex, and she'll do anything to get out of the kitchen!

My wife just won a beauty contest. She fired my secretary.

There are two reasons my wife won't wear last year's clothes—she doesn't want to get into them and she can't!

Ten years ago, he put her on a pedestal. Yesterday, he put her on a diet.

The other day she made alphabet soup. It spelled "Ugh."

A woman tells her friend that she should be angry with her husband for chasing women. The woman replies, "Why? A dog always chases cars, and he can't drive."

A woman went to an attorney and asked him to obtain a divorce for her. The attorney asked, "Do you have grounds?"
"Oh, we have about an acre."

"No, no, I mean—do you have a grudge?"

"We have a carport."

"I mean—does he beat you up in the morning?"

"No, I get up first."

"Well, why do you want a divorce?"

"Because I can't carry on a decent conversation with that man!"

**I** know a man who knows a great way to get his wife home from a vacation—he sends her the local paper with something clipped out of it.

**A** domineering wife was finally convinced by her husband that she needed treatment. After her first session, she returned home, and her husband asked, "How did it go?"

"It was difficult. It took me fifty minutes to convince the guy that his couch would look better against the far wall."

**My** wife came home the other day and told me that the doctor had said she couldn't make love. I wonder how he found out.

## WOMEN

**If** you don't think women are explosive, just try dropping one.

**The** years a woman takes off her age never get lost. They're just tacked on to another woman.

**They're** all the same. I got a secretary at the office who's getting a little behind in her work, and a wife who's getting a big one at home.

**She** didn't know whether to be prim or daring, so she compromised. She wore a low-cut dress with a turtleneck slip.

**The** best twenty years of a woman's life come between twenty-eight and thirty.

**Show** me the man who understands women, and I'll show you a man who's in for a big surprise.

**Three** young women enrolled in a logic class at the local college. The professor started by asking a question. "What would you do," he asked, "if you were on a small boat and saw a ship coming at you? On board there were a thousand sex-crazed sailors. What would you do to avoid any problem?"

One young woman said, "I'd turn my boat as fast as I could and try to get away."

A second said, "I'd hold my course and pray that my pistol would keep them away."

The third, a curvaceous blonde, said, "What's the problem?"

**Women** are still the best opposite sex we have.

**One** day she showed me her true colors. She ran out of makeup.

**Two** women meet. One asks, "Do you like men with big rear ends covered with pimples?"

The second woman says, "Of course not."

"How about hairy backs and ten folds on their stomachs?"

"That sounds so gross. Why do you ask?"

"I just wanted to know why you were fooling around with my husband."

The heaviest thing in the world is the body of a woman you don't love anymore!

Women have the edge over men. If they can't get what they want because they're smart, they can get it by being dumb.

Women are lucky. They don't have to worry about getting men pregnant.

A woman only looks for a man when she's single or married.

Never start a fight with a woman if she's tired. . . . or if she's rested.

From fifteen to twenty-one, women are like the continent of Africa—part virgin, part explored.

From twenty-two to thirty-five, women are like Asia—dark and mysterious.

From thirty-six to forty-five, women are like America—high-toned and sophisticated.

From forty-six to fifty, women are like Europe—still interesting in places.

From fifty on, women are like Antarctica—everybody knows about it, but nobody goes there.

"Did you ever meet any professional women?"

"I never met any amateur ones!"

A woman never forgets her age—once she decides what it is.

A woman should hold on to her youth, but not while he's driving.

"What's the difference between a wife and a mistress?"

"About thirty pounds."

She always flirts with the butcher. She likes to play for bigger steaks.

A woman is a person who reaches for a chair when the phone rings.

It's very windy out, and Janet holds on to her hat for dear life while her skirt flies up and around. Responding to the strange looks from passing men, she says, "Fellows, what you're looking at is forty-five years old. What I'm holding on to is brand-new!"

She talks so much, her insurance is five hundred dollars debatable.

Women who want to be equal to men have no ambition.

Women are smarter than men. You never see a woman marry a man because he's big-busted.

She told her friend, "All I want is a husband who's good-looking, kind, and sensitive. I don't think that's too much to ask of a millionaire!"

The best way to tell a woman's age is in a whisper.

She's not very feminine. Her gynecologist calls her "sir."

Women, can you imagine a world without men? No crime and lots of happy fat women.

I remember when women who ran around didn't wear jogging outfits.

Some women don't have it too good. Between douches and dishes, they're always in hot water.

The incredible things women put in the handbags! Last week in New York's Central Park, a juvenile snatched a purse and got twenty-seven dollars and a hernia!

A doctor asked a female patient her age.
"I never disclose my age," the woman said, "but as a matter of fact, I have just reached twenty-five."
"Really," the doctor said. "What detained you?"

## WOMEN'S LIB

When all is said and done, men still have the last word. It's "Yes, dear."

A liberated woman is one who has sex before marriage and a job afterward.

Women's lib is right. No one should have to dance backward all the time.

A lot of men are violently against women's lib. They believe that a woman should stick to the shopping for food, cleaning, ironing, cooking, washing dishes, and taking care of the kids.
As one of these men said, "No wife of mine is going to work!"

Most women don't want equality with a man. It's a step down.

"What's the difference between a liberated woman and the garbage?"
"The garbage gets taken out once a week."

I'm glad my wife's joined women's lib. Now, she complains about all men, not just me.

Women keep saying they want to get a man's salary. Mine does.

"How many women's libbers does it take to screw in a light bulb?"
"One and there's nothing funny about it."

A fellow runs into some friends and tells them that he's really a woman trapped in a man's body, and he's going to get a sex-change operation.
Some months later, he runs into his friends. He has obviously undergone the sex-change operation. One friend says, "It must have been awful when they cut off your penis."

"No, that wasn't so bad."

The second chum says, "And when they cut off your testicles, that must have been terrible."

"That wasn't terrible."

"Well, what was the worst part?"

"When I went back to work and they cut my salary in half."

"**W**here would man be today if it weren't for women?" asked the speaker at a women's liberation meeting.

A small voice spoke out from the back of the room, "Back in the garden eating strawberries."

**W**omen want sexual harassment in the workplace stopped. They want the men to stop groping the women, and that means no ifs, ands, or butts.

## WORDS

**T**hey just came out with a dictionary for masochists. It has all the words, but they're not in alphabetical order.

**A** synonym is a word you use when you can't spell the other one.

**A** German tourist gets off a plane in Boston and says to a man, walking alongside, *"Was sagst du?"*

The man says, "They lost three to one."

## WORK

**M**y nephew learned that there was an acute shortage of elevator operators. He applied. The personnel manager at one company turned him down, telling him, "We want somebody with experience."

My nephew said, "Can't you start me off on a building with only one floor?"

**A** foreman was impossibly tough on his crew at the factory. After giving a particularly tough assignment, he adds, "I bet you guys are hoping I get killed. I bet you can't wait to spit on my grave."

A worker says, "Not me. I'm not going to get on the end of that big line."

**H**e got a job as a night watchman, but he was fired. Somebody stole two nights.

**O**ne company just came up with a brilliant incentive plan—one mistake and you're finished!

**I**t's no disgrace to work. Now if a guy could only get his wife to believe that.

**A**l is telling Tommy about losing his job. Tommy asked, "Why did the foreman fire you?"

"You know what foremen are like. They stand around watching all the other guys work."

"But why did he fire you?"

"Well, everybody thought I was the foreman."

**A** lot of men don't object to doing an honest day's work. But they want a week's pay and a lot of fringe benefits to do it.

**M**ost people have to admire their boss. If they don't, they get fired.

The government sends out one of its myriad questionnaires that go out to small businesses. On one of the questionnaires, the government asks, "How many employees do you have broken down by sex?"

The president of the company wrote, "None that I know of, but a few look pretty tired when they show up in the morning."

I don't believe I'll ever get fired by my boss. Sold, maybe.

A boss told his workers that he was planning a salary raise. One employee asked, "When does it become effective?"

The boss answered, "As soon as you do."

I hated to go in and ask my boss for a raise the other day, but my kids found out that other kids eat three times a day.

Never hire an electrician with singed eyelids.

My brother doesn't like working. To him, it's an invasion of privacy!

Ideas are funny. They won't work unless you do.

A prospective employee asked, "Do I get a raise every six months?"

The employer said, "Certainly, if you do a good job."

The prospective employee said, "I knew there was a catch to it."

The village blacksmith was breaking in a new apprentice, telling him, "I'll take the hot horseshoe out of the fire. When I nod my head, hit it."

Now the apprentice is the new village blacksmith.

"How's your new job?"
"I'm through."
"Why?"
"A lot of reasons: the shoddy work, the sloppiness, the vile language . . . they just wouldn't put up with them."

There's nothing that makes a worker get better faster than running out of sick benefits.

Joe has a terrible job. The conditions are awful, the hours terrible, and his co-workers rotten. Joe won't quit. This is the first time he's looked forward to going home.

Never hire a plumber who wears rubber boots.

People say that hard work never killed anybody, but on the other hand, did you ever know anybody who rested to death?

There's a distillery in Kentucky that pays time and a fifth for overtime.

"I know you can't get married on the money I pay you," said the boss to his new employee, "but someday you'll thank me for it!"

My company printing machinery broke down the other day. We couldn't make good on a thousand Out of Order signs.

The chairman of the board was touring his manufacturing plant, and he stopped to chat with an older worker.

"How long have you been with the company?"

"Thirty-nine years," the man said. "And in that time, I've only made one little mistake."

"Let's try to be a bit more careful," the CEO replied.

My brother always talks in the millions. He's an exterminator.

Who can forget the necrophiliac who through hard work and dedication achieved his goal of becoming a mortician?

Every day I get up and look in *Fortune* magazine to see if I'm one of the hundred richest men in the country. If my name's not there, I go to work.

A man goes to his boss and says, "I must have a raise. My mother is very ill. I have to scrape bottom to keep my kids in school. I can't afford to have my car worked on; even though I don't know much, I have to do it all. My house is falling apart. When I get home, I have a dozen chores to do."

The boss says, "You're fired. You have too many outside activities."

He just got a job at an art school—a hundred a week and all he could see.

Then there was the street cleaner who lost his job because he couldn't keep his mind in the gutter.

A harassed office manager was asked, "Who are you working for these days?"

His answer: "Same old outfit: my wife and six kids."

Sometimes all the early bird gets is up.

"We can pay you eighty dollars a week now and one hundred dollars a week in eight months," the personnel director offered.

"Thanks," the applicant said, "I'll be back in eight months!"

I don't have to do this for a living. I sell fire extinguishers to Indians as smoke-signal erasers.

I never drink coffee at work. If I do, all day long I toss and turn at my desk.

No matter how busy people are, they are never too busy to stop and talk about how busy they are.

An executive is a businessman who wears out three suits to every pair of shoes.

Everybody says they don't like yes-men, but how many no-men are working?

A young man is planning to become a mailman. As part of the test, he is asked, "How far is it from New York to Los Angeles?"

He says, "If that's going to be my route, forget it."

Then there was the labor leader who told his kids a fairy tale that began, "Once upon a time and a half . . ."

One company doesn't need a retirement plan. Nobody wants to work there that long.

A modern boy's the kind who tells his fiancée, "Our marriage won't change a thing. You hold on to your job, and I'll keep looking for one."

A young man is being interviewed for a job. The last question is, "Are you a natural-born citizen of the United States?"
"No. Cesarian."

This mother was so ashamed of her family. Her son swept the streets, and her two daughters walked them.

One young man passed his driver's test. The next day, he lost his job at the parking lot.

When a man believes in working hard, he's probably the boss.

## WORLD

I've decided that I don't mind paying taxes as long as we give the money to a nice country.

If it's such a small world, why does it cost so much to run it?

They say that there's only enough oil left in the world to last twenty-five years. Why don't they plant some more?

Things are very rough. The United States is making more money than Europe and Asia know what to do with.

I just came off a flight on one of the airlines from a Third World country. It had four bathrooms—two more than the country!

All the other countries tell us the same thing: Go home and leave us a loan.

Half the world doesn't know how the other half manages today, and neither does the other half.

A few more allies and we'll go completely broke.

We once thought the world was flat. Then we thought it was round. And now we know it's crooked.

## WRITING

A critic wrote of a writer, "He's one writer worth watching. Watching, not reading."

He just got a hundred dollars a word. He talked back to a judge!

Last month I sold four articles: two coats, a suit, and my typewriter.

A critic wrote about a writer, "Once you put down one of his books, you can't pick it up again."

It's not hard to be a writer. This morning I wrote something worth a hundred dollars—a grocery list!

A young writer sent a manuscript to a famous author, with a note saying, "Please read this manuscript and advise. Please answer as quickly as possible because I have other irons in the fire."

The noted writer sent back a brief note that said, "Remove irons. Insert manuscript."

He just wrote something that was accepted by a magazine—a year's subscription.

An editor offers a columnist a three-month vacation with pay, but the columnist turns it down. The editor says, "But it's with full pay."

"I know. But I'm afraid of two things. It might affect the circulation of the paper. The other is that it might not."

He was such a bad writer, they revoked his poetic licence.

He's written about six children's books, but not on purpose.

A terrible writer sent in a manuscript. It was returned a few days later with a note from the editor: *Am returning this paper. Somebody wrote on it.*

"When," said the publisher to the poet, "did they open up that sidewalk café I saw you in last night?"

"That wasn't a sidewalk café," the poet said. "That was my furniture."

## X

If you sign a paper with an *X*, but you change your mind, how do you *X* it out?

They just came out with a new cleaning fluid. It gets out all the *X*s that mark the spot.

Two ballplayers are talking at a sports fair. One says, "My *X* is worth five hundred dollars."

The other says, "My ex is worth ten thousand a month."

The Indian chief signed the treaty with two *X*s. The cavalry officer asked him what they meant.

The Indian chief explained, "First is name—Running Wolf. Second—Chief."

## X RAYS

**I** know of an old-fashioned doctor in a small town. He doesn't even have an X-ray machine. He just holds you up to the light.

**M**y wife has X-ray vision. She can see through anything.

**X** rays can make you sterile. I took a chest X ray in 1970, and it's just beginning to work on me.

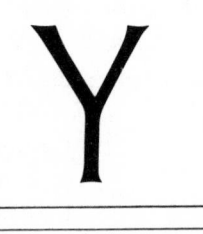

## YANKEES

A man walked into the general store in a small New England town. "Got a criminal lawyer in these parts?" he asked.

"We think we have," the man answered. "But we can't prove nothin' on him."

A traveler stops off at a general store and asks the Yankee clerk if this is the road to Murphysville. "Sure is," says the clerk.

The traveler takes off and drives on for a while, but there's no Murphysville in sight. He returns to the general store and says angrily, "You told me this was the road to Murphysville."

The clerk says, "It is, but you're on the wrong end of it."

Auctions never go well in Yankee country. People there never bid. They just watch who does bid, and then borrow the stuff the next day.

Two Yankees are sitting outside the general store when a lady, dressed to the hilt, comes out of the dress shop. One Yankee says, "Guess the riggin's worth more than the hull."

This cabbie picks up a vacationer at the railroad station and starts to drive him to the summer resort. The road is winding and leads back to a crossing a mile away. It's weed-covered and looks as if it hasn't been used for ages. But the cabbie stops and waits. The passenger says, "Why are you stopping? This crossing hasn't been used in years."

The cabbie nods and says, "Yup, but he might be coming back."

A motorist stops at a tiny gas station and asks the attendant, "What's this place called?"

The attendant says, "By whom? By the folks who live in this dang-blasted, filthy, one-horse dump? Or those who are just going to enjoy our rustic charms for a short spell?"

A city family is traveling through New England, heading for Bar Harbor, Maine. After hours on the road, they concede that they might be lost. They stop a Yankee and ask, "Is this the way to Bar Harbor?"

"Aye."

"And how far is it?"

"About twenty-five thousand miles, but I don't know how you're gonna get over all that water."

A tourist complained to the gas-station attendant in a small Yankee village, saying, "Gas in the last state was ten cents cheaper."

The attendant said, "Well, that's the place to buy it."

Two grumpy old Maine farmers met each other every morning for twenty years in the village post office without exchanging one single word. One day one of the farmers turned left instead of right as they exited.

"Where are ya going?" the other asked.

"None o' yer darn business!" the farmer said. "And I wouldn't tell you that much 'cept we've been friends so long!"

A city person goes fishing in a remote Maine town. While waiting for a bite, the city slicker explains to his guide that he comes from New York, a city with 7 million people in it. The guide shakes his head. "Shame. So many people living so far from everything."

## YOUTH

I won't say she's young, but he met her at a school crossing.

If young people were wise, they'd miss half the fun.

We spend the first half of our lives trying to understand the older generation, and the second half trying to understand the younger.

The police called the Bronsons at one in the morning. "We have your teenage son down here. He was apprehended in a stolen car going a hundred miles an hour while he was trying to get away from a store he'd just robbed."

Mrs. Bronson said, "It can't be him. He never does anything like that at home."

Mabel told her friend Alice, "Everybody said that Jimmy and I were the cutest couple on the floor."

Alice said, "I thought you weren't going to the dance."

Mabel said, "We didn't. We went to a pajama party."

If you want to recapture your youth, cut off his allowance.

There comes a time for a young man when he stops wanting to go out with girls and wants to stay home with them.

A swain asks the girl's father if he can marry the girl. The father asks, "Can you make her happy?"

The swain says, "Happy? You should have seen her last night in the back of the car."

The best way for a woman to keep her youth is not to introduce him to anybody.

He promised her the sky, the moon, and the stars. On their honeymoon, he took her to the planetarium.

The young lady was sitting around the house knitting little booties. Watching her happily, her mother said to a visitor, "I'm so glad she's interested in something besides men."

## YUPPIES

It was a Yuppie production of the Nativity. It went well until the moment when the owner of the inn denies Mary and Joseph a room. The Yuppie youngster playing the part forgot himself and said, "There's no room at the inn, but come in anyway and I'll make you a drink."

# Z

## ZEBRAS

A zebra is a sports-model jackass.

They put a stallion in a compound with a female zebra to keep him company. The next morning, the keeper sees the zebra all scuffed up and the stallion almost dead on his feet.

At the keeper's puzzled look, the stallion says, "I spent the whole night trying to get her pajamas off."

It's one of those zoos with wide-open spaces. A woman visitor reaches over and tickles a zebra with a feather. The zebra takes off a mile a minute and jumps over fences and embankments and disappears in the distance.

The zookeeper walks over to the lady and says, "You better tickle me too. I've got to catch him."

Then there was the prisoner who escaped on a zebra. Nobody could see him go.

## ZINGERS

You're in the pink of condition. Even your eyes are bloodshot!

534

**B**oy, you could give Tylenol a migraine!

**B**elieve me, if I lent you a hundred and never saw you again, it would be worth it!

**I** hear they named a hangover after you!

**I** hear you were arrested the other day for trying to suck a brewery!

**H**e brags about being a great lover, but it won't stand up!

**Y**ou know, your mouth is big enough to sing duets!

**H**e doesn't know shit from Shinola. Just look at his shoes!

**S**he's the kind of woman who bolsters her man's feelings of self-doubt!

## ZOO

**A** monkey was reading Darwin's *Origin of Species*. He wanted to find out if he was his brother's keeper or his keeper's brother.

**T**hey brought a new young female elephant into the compound. The male elephant jumped up and down with joy, saying, "Wow a perfect 290-350-290!"

**T**he leopard finished his dinner and grinned, saying to his friend the lion, "Boy, that sure hit the right spots."

**T**his woman promises to take her children to the zoo. They'll leave as soon as the maid comes home to take care of their dogs. However, the maid doesn't show up, so the woman calls the zoo and asks if she can bring her dogs along.
  The receptionist says, "I'm sorry but we don't allow animals in the zoo."

**O**ne day, I went to a zoo and saw a man-eating lion. Then I went to a deli and saw a man eating herring.

**H**e had a job throwing fish to the pelicans. It wasn't much, but it filled the bill.

**A** woman takes her son to the zoo. The kid sees the elephant and, pointing, asks, "What's that?"
  The mother says, "That's a trunk."
  "No, farther back."
  "That's his tail."
  "No, in between."
  "Oh, that's nothing. Ask your father."
  Later, the kid asks his father, "What's that thing between the trunk and the tail? Mommy says it's nothing."
  The father says, "Son, your mother's been spoiled."

**A** woman wanted to see something in fur, so her husband took her to the zoo.

**A** waiter used to go to the zoo to watch the turtles. He loved to watch them whiz by.

A zookeeper is asked, "Does that giraffe ever catch cold from standing around getting his feet wet?"

The zookeeper answers, "Yes, but not until the following week."

The female baboon had absolutely no interest in the male, and thus wouldn't mate. They asked the zookeeper to volunteer. He said, "Okay, but you have to promise me one thing—if anything happens because of this, you'll raise it Catholic."

The waiter took his young son to the zoo. It happened to be feeding time, and the zookeeper walked along, throwing slabs of meat to the animals. The young son asked, "Why don't they serve the food like you do, Daddy?"

The waiter whispered, "Confidentially, son, animals are lousy tippers."

# How to Cook Somebody
## (Milton Berle's Secret Recipe for Roasts)

To salute someone and/or raise money for a group or cause, the roast is a perfect vehicle. People love to pay money to watch a friend, co-worker, or authority figure being lampooned. They'd give their eyeteeth to sit back and relish some poor soul twisting slowly, ever so slowly, in the wind of vitriol. And thus it has always been.

The roast no doubt served the cavepeople well. When Og was retiring, giving up the dinosaur chase forever, Og, Max, and all the tenants of the cave gathered around the fire and, tongue in cheek, started to throw barbs at the re-tiree. "Og," Seymour said, "is a legend in his own mouth." And so on.

Hilary, the hide-softener, said, "Og is one of the greatest lovers of the day. But when night comes, something seems to leave him." She got a scream with that one.

Ten speeches later, the whole audience was doubled over with laughter and possibly some undercooked pterodactyl. What a night!

The evening was given a glowing review in the *Reader's Rock Digest,* cavetime's leading and heaviest periodical. Copies can still be found in the reception rooms of many dentists.

Now, several million roast routines later, with over two thousand of them delivered by me personally, this unique form of entertainment belongs to the world. The "Friars Roast" has become part of our language. It is recognized in at least one major dictionary. I heard it came within two votes of making the *Oxford English Dictionary*. What do the Oxford English people know? They don't even recognize the existence of "humongous."

Unfortunately, the roast hasn't always been crafted properly. Because I treasure perfection in any matter comedic, I am therefore making public for the first time my recipe for the basting of a roastee. There will be no undercooked or overdone roasts while Berle lives.

The ingredients follow.

Don't deviate. I'm watching!

### The Roastee

*1. Choose someone worthy.* It's no fun to throw barbs at the guy in the night crew who steals Kleenex. If money is the aim, as is often the case, you need to choose someone who can put asses in the seats: the minister, the prexy, the star of the football team, the fire chief, the local TV anchorperson. The bigger the face you can make blush, the higher the gate receipts. It'll also make for bigger laughs. A master of the roast form, George Jessel, used to say, "The more starch they have in their collars, the better the roast." Jessel knew what he was talking about. He presided at the first

Friars Roast, when Enrico Caruso was honored. Opera was never the same.

At the Friars, we've roasted the biggest stars and public officials. Our stag roast for the sheriff of Los Angeles County was a giant affair. Before we were through with him, he was shredded. The audience was rolling in the aisles. I hope the sheriff left happy. In 1990, we took on Arnold Schwarzenegger and fearlessly destroyed him. A very funny evening, about a thousand words beyond X-rated.

All of our Friars Roasts are proof that the bigger they are, the better.

*2. Marry the roastee to an event if possible.* Roast the coach of the school baseball team at the beginning of the season or when the team wins the area pennant. Occasion gives momentum, and an occasion can always be found: a birthday, an anniversary, a retirement, recovery from surgery—the fifth anniversary of recovery from surgery, you name it. I once helped a town in Kentucky roast the local doctor. I suggested it be a "Welcome Home Roast" for him, as he'd just been released from jail for income-tax evasion. Honest.

*3. Make certain the roastee has some characteristics at which fun can be poked:* He or she bets, gambles, lies, overeats, exaggerates, is shy, boorish, lazy, an eager beaver.

It's hard to roast an average Joe or Jane. A dull Joe or Jane is easier. Try it: "He's so average that ————." I'll give nineteen cents for any funny line you come up with. Try the dull person: "He's so dull that . . . a Peeping Tom looked in his bedroom last night and fell asleep." "He's so dull, he lights up a room when he leaves it." "She's so dull, she wears gray lipstick."

The difference between average and dull, for roast purposes, is that put-down comedy is a matter of extremes. Cheap is not funny. The cheapest person is. The drinker is not funny. The person "who had a blood test and it came back marked Smirnoff" is hysterical.

Also, see what physical characteristics the roastee is blessed with. Is he short, tall, thin, fat, flat-footed? Does she waddle like a duck? Does he have big lips? Is he balding? Is there some plastic surgery in the background?

Physical characteristics lend themselves easily to extremizing. (That's my word and I'm proud of it.) A man 6'5" is not exactly big enough to be a starting center for the Knicks. For roast comedy, however, he qualifies: "He's so tall, six months a year he walks around with snow on his head." "She has so many chins, she can hold six months of rain." "They're a cute couple—she's knock-kneed and he's bowlegged. When they stand together, they spell the word 'ox.' " "She's so cross-eyed—when she opens one eye, all she can see is her other eye." Find yourself a cross-eyed, bow-legged, cheap, fat, short, dumb blowhard to roast. Your affair will be a smash.

*4. A roast should last between forty minutes and an hour and a half.* At least that should be the target. Rumps start to hurt if sat on too long. (Unless you're doing a rump roast. Oh, God! Milton, have you no shame?) In all my years, I've tried to keep the time down. I've never succeeded. There must be a roast imp who fools around with the clock. But we do plan for an hour and a half, two hours at most. For nonprofessionals, the shorter the better.

Each turn (that's show biz for segment) should run between four and six minutes. Again, the shorter the better.

*5. The designer of the affair should try to ensure that each speaker cover only a specific topic or topics.* One will talk about the roastee's sex habits. Another will discuss gambling or drinking. Still another is to describe the roastee at work.

At times, obviously, it may be difficult to design the roast. When the CEO of the company is asked to speak, his time to prepare may be limited. Nor can he be ordered around. It often works in the roast's favor if the areas already to be discussed by others are brought up subtly: "Sir, if you'd like to talk about how he behaved when he first came with the company, that'll be appreciated." The CEO will take the hint. He'll get laughs anyway because he's the boss. Fear.

Obviously, in the preparation of a routine, each speaker is drawn to the easy stuff, those areas in which the roastee is most vulnerable. But this could result in an evening limited to one topic. Not good. After the first half-dozen "lazy" jokes, the audience has had it with "lazy."

There's more gold to be mined in off-beat topics. At a roast in Canada, I heard an amateur talk about a cruise he and the roastee took up to Alaska. I laughed myself sick, as did the audience. I didn't even know the speaker.

Not long ago, we roasted a comedian known for his volatile temper and anger. The biggest laughs of the evening came when one of the comics talked about having dinner with the roastee one night and how he sent back everything. Sending back food was his hobby. He became Mr. Sendback. No matter what was said, as long as "Mr. Sendback" was in the phrase, it was funny. (I'll bet that as of this moment, there are eighty-seven potential Mr./Mrs./Miss/Ms. Sendbacks in your world.) A wonderful area for a spot on a roast. Our Mr. Sendback has gotten so used to the epithet, he won't answer to his real name anymore.

Offbeat topics abound: "Marge and I were Girl Scouts together. Let me tell you about the first cookie sale. . . . You haven't lived until you've driven with Al. . . . I'm Fred's doctor, and I want to tell you about him and his last twelve diets. . . ." The number of routines is limitless.

Often, the nature and background of a speaker can be used to enhance a spot. As X's lawyer, the speaker can frame his bit in legal language and with legal forms. Thus, he can indicate that he's holding a subpoena and X is wanted for being the dullest man in town, the fattest, the baldest. At a roast in Boston, I heard a roastee's physician do a chunk in which he used medical terminology that sounded and was funny. "Let me tell you about Bill's coccyx. And his uvula." The audience was in stitches. (Why not? The speaker was a surgeon. Milton, you really have no shame.)

Probably the hardest part of assembling a dais or a group of speakers is in getting each person to commit to the chore. Many are afraid of speaking before a group. Others fear hurting the feelings of the roastee. Persistence will get them to perform. In addition, offer some assistance in the preparation of the material. It will seldom be needed. Preparing a roast spot becomes fun after a while, but to help fill your spot, I've included a few tons of insults at the end of this section.

A word of caution in assembling spots. Consider the thickness of the roastee's skin. The purpose of the roast is to "honor," not to make a roastee bleed red. The roast tells the guest of honor he or she is loved. If you want to inflict real damage, buy a gun and try another forum.

*6. The master or mistress of ceremonies need not be a born clown.* As Hal Kanter, a top writer-producer and raconteur in Hollywood has often said when acting as master of ceremonies, "My purpose isn't to bore you, but to introduce people who will." The emcee (a nonsexist term) should be at least witty. I don't believe that an emcee need get a big laugh every two seconds. Danny Thomas could weave five minutes of words together without getting a laugh. But when he went for one, he got it.

I like to start off with an opening line or two in humor: "We are gathered here to honor a man of great fame, a man who is loved, a man to whom many of us look for guidance. But enough about the pope! Let's talk about this bum here!" The roasts that close this section will give a pretty good idea of the kinds of openings that are possible.

The emcee should do a brief monologue. ("Brief" is a subjective word. It takes me thirty minutes to say hello. You'd better get there in thirty seconds. I like to cover many areas. I do that to test the waters and show the rest of the speakers where the audience is coming from. Some of my comedian friends insist that I cover every area under the sun because I'm a greedy bastard. Untrue. Well, maybe there's a smidgen of truth in that.)

The emcee should have an introductory joke for each speaker: "Our next speaker, XXY, needs no introduction, but he seems to want one." Or "XXY is here under difficult circumstances—he wasn't invited."

A wrap-up joke for after the turn is also welcomed. A favorite after a roaster who has bombed is: "That was nice, Eloise. Every roast needs a serious speaker.". . . Or: "You were never fun-nier, and it's a damn shame!". . . Or: "Sid, I told you, you have to prepare for these things."

The opening spot after the emcee's monologue is a tough spot, "a spot you wouldn't give a leopard." In early roasts, opening was someone you wanted to dump. The theory went back to theater and vaudeville. The first few minutes were vamping time, time for the audience to get to its seats.

I happen to like an opener who can score, who has a chance to beat out the busing of dishes or guests straightening their shorts. A strong speaker is needed to get the attention of the group. If not strong, at least a "weird" speaker, who can get the audience to focus on the rostrum.

At Friars affairs, we've often started with Pat McCormick. For years one of Johnny Carson's insane writers, Pat shakes up any audience with his outrageous humor. He once told us that he'd just come from the doctor, who'd given him three days to live. But not consecutively. That may be his only clean line.

The next-to-closing, what we call next-to-shut, is traditionally reserved for the hardest hitter on the dais. Because fair is only fair, this spot has come to be the space where the roasters get their comeuppances. They've ridden roughshod over the soul and reputation of the honoree, now it's time to pay for the license. I've found that revenge is called for generally because most roastees are unable to hit back with power. Where the roastee has some muscle, I prefer the next-to-closing speaker to tie up the loose ends not covered by other speakers. Otherwise, the roastee is only duplicating what the next-to-closer has said.

Since there's a big chunk of roast between opener and closer, that area shouldn't be given short shrift. (I love that term. Did anybody ever have a long shrift?) The producer, emcee, or entertainment committee should try to balance and pace the show. A weak speaker should be sandwiched between stronger speakers.

Music can be invaluable. A well-done parody gets big laughs and gives pace. Caveat: Don't stop the show to set up a musical chunk. It should be preset and ready to go at the last word of the emcee's introduction. Empty space and time hurt a roast.

Not every guest on the dais will speak. There are almost always a half-dozen VIPs who will stand up and take a bow. I like to get an index card or note to each of them, telling when they will be introduced. Reminder cards serve the speakers too.

7. *Turns need not be memorized.* There are no demerits for working from cards with key words on them. I don't even mind if the card has a whole joke on it. The purpose of the card, however, is not to provide material for a reading test. Each card is a reminder only. Don't recite the words. The poetry reading is next door.

In the first volume of my private files, I went into an extensive treatise on the "card game." Since everybody in the world has a copy of that first volume, I need merely to reiterate my fondness for three-by-five index cards. I won't leave the house without my index cards. They came in handy during my honeymoon.

8. *A good joke has a form.* It must, first of all, have an element that prepares the audience for the subject matter— "Let's talk about Joe's sex life. . . . Let's turn now to Joe the businessman—" The meat of the joke follows. It should sound as if you just thought of it. Leave space for the audience to laugh. You can control the laughter space by closing the area with a button—"Yes, that's the kind of guy Joe is . . . And that's not the half of it—" Until the phrase, "But seriously, folks," became the cliché of spoken clichés, it served well to fence in the laughter.

Each joke area is a unit. Don't trust the audience to know that. Let them know what you're going into. Let them know when you're off and running in another direction. Obscurity kills humor.

9. *Keep the faith.* Your roast is going to be a smash.

(You're in luck. We're roasting good old A.Z. [or anybody whose name you want to fill in] for the next few pages, and you've been invited.)

**MASTER OF CEREMONIES:**

Good evening . . . If you'll simmer down, we'll start our festival of frivolity!

First, let me thank —— —— for that wonderful introduction. It had all the sincerity of a Hollywood star saying "ouch" on her seventh honeymoon! . . . Just kidding, —— . . . He's such a sensitive man.

By the way, ——, you look nice in that outfit. . . . They made great suits in 1950! . . . I love the way it laces in the back.

Ladies and gentlemen, we are gathered here to pay tribute to a man known to all of us . . . a man who deserves the plaudits of every person here tonight . . . a man who is a shining example of all that is good. But enough about the pope! . . . Let's talk about this yutz here! . . . He is something, isn't he?

Before I get to the work at hand, let me say that to be chosen as master of ceremonies for this cacophony of comedy . . .

. . . Is more than an honor. It's an imposition! . . . A goddam imposition.

We had to draw lots to see who would be the master of ceremonies. I lost! . . . I never was lucky.

And to think I gave up an evening of bursitis for this!

When I first found out about this much sought-after job, I called the ——house to find out what I could say. How far could I go? Could I be a little risqué . . . off-color . . . dirty . . . filthy?!

I was told, "Don't inhibit yourself, you dumb schmuck. Use all the four-letter words you goddam want to. Give it to the bastard up the kazoo." Then *Mrs.* Z. said, "Honey, it's for *you!*" . . . You folks have no idea of how much I cleaned that up.

I'm only kidding, sweetheart. . . . Will you folks take a good look at her? You just know he only married her for her money!

A.Z. takes her everywhere. That's so he doesn't have to kiss her goodbye! Just kidding, sugar, you're gorgeous.

But they have such good-looking kids. Thank God, she cheats! . . . Stop the groaning. I only said that to be funny. A shame it didn't work.

Now on to the matter at hand . . . Good old A.Z . . . Oh, God!

I've known A.Z. a long time . . . for nigh onto . . . fifteen minutes!

Maybe seventeen if you count those two minutes in the john!

So he isn't much. . . . What can you expect for ten dollars a ticket?!

Did you like that chicken entrée? Mine tasted like it was kicked to death! . . . It wasn't that bad. Don't get me started on the salad.

Before I go on with these wonderful jokes, I'd like to acknowledge our dais. It's the kind of dais an A.Z. deserves!

I haven't seen such misfits since the day I bought two suits at Kramer's Men's Shop! . . . I got that plug in, Mr. Kramer . . . when do I come in for the free tie?

Yes, this is a devastating dais . . . It looks as if everybody on this dais made love to Amelia Earhart! Recently! . . . I did, and it wasn't bad.

Such a deplorable dais. What a tawdry group this is! The kitchen staff is honoring a busboy in the kitchen and they've got a better-looking dais in there! . . . The food was better too.

Of course, A.Z., some of your best and closest friends wanted to be here tonight, but they couldn't make it. Judge ——— wanted to be here, but he couldn't make it because of the distance. He's in the lobby! . . . That's a pretty long walk . . . three feet.

Mayor ——— thought he might make it, but he's very busy with his campaign to drive the hookers out of the city. I saw him about two hours ago, driving two of them out of town! . . . Wonderful man, the mayor.

And, A.Z., your grandfather wanted to be here, too, but something came up, and he's very proud! Right now, he's having it bronzed! . . . Look at this—his wife is explaining it to him!

Your lawyer, ——— ———, wanted to be here, too, but he's in Lourdes . . . for his practice! . . . Great lawyer.

But the people we do have here are top-drawer. I look around, and I get a warm feeling right here in my heart. I think it's gas!

Since dinner I've had so much gas, two Arabs have been following me! . . . Two Arabs . . . Oh God. Why do I volunteer for these things?

But we're not here to talk about me. We're here to pay tribute to your Outstanding Citizen of the City. Cheesus, he shouldn't even be Alien of the Block!

Actually, it's not easy to be chosen Citizen of the Year in this town. You have to be in the phone book!

A.Z. appreciates the honor because he's a very humble man, and rightfully so . . .

By the way, I have to interrupt my brilliant speech for a bulletin that came in two minutes ago. A tornado just hit the South Side of town and did $2 million worth of improvements!

But back to the helpless human we're honoring. I first met A.Z. in high school. He was the quarterback of our high school team and led us to a successful 1-and-10 season!

The best year we ever had!

A.Z. wasn't too good as quarterback. He once threw his helmet to the ground, and it was intercepted!

Who among us will ever forget when he ran ninety-eight yards against ——— High? Unfortunately, it was during a basketball game!

A.Z. was a two-letter man, only

one of which he could read when he graduated.

Both of us used to fool around with Helen in those days. But he must have been the better man, because he married her!

Oh, well, here's another joke you may not like!

Better still, let's move on. You know, it's not the toastmaster's job to come out and bore you, but to introduce people who will!

As I mentioned earlier, your lawyer couldn't be here tonight, but we do have his partner. —— —— is a brilliant attorney who recently had a parking ticket reduced to second-degree manslaughter! . . . another Clarence Darrow.

He's beyond brilliant. In a recent case some of you may have read about, he told his client, "Don't worry. The judge is my cousin. Their chief witness goes with my secretary. And I'm planning to bribe four of the jurors. Meanwhile, try to escape!"

Ladies and gentlemen, —— ——!

(Using jokes from the roast-joke section and the contents of this book, the legal beagle goes on to bedazzle, stun and overwhelm the audience with his wit as he discusses A.Z.)

(You kind souls are in more luck than you ever dreamed was possible. From the Citizen of the Year dinner, we whip you next to the opening spot for A.Z.'s stag roast. It'll demonstrate how stories can be adapted to involve the roastee.)

## MASTER OF CEREMONIES:

Thank you and welcome to our festival of filth!

As you can see, I'm your toastmaster tonight—a chore that ranks in importance with being the chairman of the Welcome Home, Amelia Earhart Committee! . . . which is a nice group, by the way.

Actually, I looked forward to being here tonight. I thought you were raffling off a prostate operation! . . . Look, six guys winced when I said "prostate."

As far as I'm concerned, it's just a pain in the ass!

Which brings me to our roastee. Yes, it has long been our tradition to honor pillars of the community, guys who have done a lot of great work, guys who deserve the plaudits of their peers. Tonight we kick the hell out of this tradition! . . . And how.

Tonight we honor a man who once went to an orgy and stole a guy's erection!

Look at Councilman —— laughing. What a pain in the ass he is! He's the kind of guy who goes to an orgy and complains about the cheese dip! But what the hell, you elected him.

Oh, before I proceed, I must explain to those of you who have never been to a roast that you will hear words like "hump" and "screw" and "crap"—all things most of the people on this dais can't do anymore!

You will also hear our roastee called a rotten lover, a lying bum, and a conniving bastard. And then there are those who will get up and *lie* about him! . . . but all in good fun.

Others will tell us about his bestiality and his acts of sodomy and describe his many perversions. But don't worry, it'll all be in good taste!

So on to our horny honoree.

A.Z. has never been popular. When he was four, he was abandoned by an orphanage!

They left him on the steps of a moving Winnebago!

The truth be known, I did some research on A.Z. I went to see his father, but his father didn't remember him. Then I went to see his mother. She didn't remember his father! . . . a forgetful family.

As a young man, A.Z. was always interested in philosophy. He used to ask: "If a light sleeper can sleep with the light on, can a hard sleeper sleep with—?" Answers, always wanted answers.

A.Z. as you all know, is of Polish extraction. He once pulled out of a hooker in Warsaw! . . .

Nature endowed A.Z. very well. When he was circumcised, they had to use power tools! *Power* tools? Power *tools*? . . . I wish you all boils on your funny bone.

And believe it or not, A.Z. is in the *Guinness Book of World Records*. He once made love to a woman for three hours and forty minutes—which was very hard, because for the last hour and ten minutes she was running for a bus! . . . and she made it.

His sex life with his wife is also something for the books. He called her the other night and said, "I wish I were there with you. I'd tear off all your clothes. I'd kiss every part of your body. I'd wrap you in my arms and make passionate love to you." And she said, "Who is this?"

The first night he spent with her was unforgettable . . . Right, A.Z.? . . . He nods like he knows what I'm talking about. . . .

Yes, the first night, A.Z. asked, "Am I the first?" And she said, "Why does everybody ask me that?" . . . By the way, he wasn't, not even for that day.

At the end of their lovemaking, she told him he was the worst lay she'd ever had. So he said, "With that attitude, you can untie yourself!"

Of course, their fifteen years of marriage have changed things. Most of the passion has been spent. Now when he begs for a little romance, she says, "Okay, but when you're finished, cover me up!" It gets cold in town.

You can't blame her. She quit smoking six months ago. Now she has nothing to look forward to after sex!

Of course, they tried to spruce up

their sex life last month on their anniversary. They went to the hotel where they'd honeymooned. They took the same suite. And she said, "Remember when we came here the first time? You couldn't wait for me to get my stockings off." And he said, "The way I feel now, you can knit a pair!"

And that, gentlemen . . . a name I call you loosely . . . is the saga of A.Z. However, we have with us some fellows who can fill in various details.

(The master of ceremonies goes on to introduce different members of the dais who will make this a night to remember, a night that will live in the anals, I mean annals, of the town.)

The following gags and one-liners are those that have served me well. They should serve you well also. They are not in order—deliberately. In other sections of the book are lines that have been collected into small groupings. Those can help you. Comedy, however, needs freedom too. The random order of this material will help you open your mind. By going off in all directions, your comedy muse will find the good stuff applicable to your roast.

If you can't find jokes to use or switch to fit in this collection, take a good look at the honoree. You may be roasting a visitor from another planet.

## The Roast Grab Bag

There's something to be said for a man like him, and *he's* usually saying it.

They finally broke off their affair. Now he's able to go back to his first love—himself.

Egotism is what makes other people think they're as great as we know we are.

He's a man of great religious convictions. And three of the other kind.

He's not too good sexually. For him, jumper cables are a marital aid.

He's dull. If he took LSD, all he'd see would be Lawrence Welk.

I just introduce the speakers, I don't guarantee them.

His is really an American success story. As a young man, he picked himself up out of the gutter, but unfortunately he left his mind there.

He's so dull—when he goes to vote, they hand him an absentee ballot.

I won't say how old he is, but rumor has it that he was a busboy at the Last Supper.

Ugly? She got picked up for indecent exposure, and only her face was showing.

**I** have the feeling that tonight his wife is going to set the electric blanket for "Headache."

**H**e's a loser. He was invited on the honeymoon with the guy who stole his wife.

**H**e made his mark in the world. That's because he can't write.

**H**e just came back from the pet cemetery. He was visiting his childhood sweetheart.

**H**er body is so ugly, she has to coax on her panties.

**S**he can walk through the park at night and reduce the crime rate.

**I**f I'd known that this dinner would be so long, I would have bought the tuxedo.

**H**e's a loser. He had Chinese food the other day. When he opened his fortune cookie, he got a summons.

**I**'ll try my best not to louse up this dinner, but it looks like I'm too late.

**N**obody likes this man. He once climbed a mountain, called out his name, and the echo said: "Jump!"

**O**ur guest of honor is very special. He's unlike most of you here tonight. For one thing, he's got a job.

**I**'m glad to be here. I'm at that age when I look forward to a dull evening.

**Y**ou've brought something into our lives—boredom.

**H**e's nobody's fool. He's a free-lancer.

**I**f the Ku Klux Klan would buy the booze, he'd drink to slavery.

**H**e reminds me of a toothache I once had.

**W**ith the right amount of training, he could be a nobody.

**H**e never opens his mouth unless he has nothing to say.

**H**e hasn't a thought in his head. He couldn't come up with an "ouch" if a shark bit his testicles.

**H**e's pretty sneaky. He can follow you into a revolving door and come out first.

**H**e's been written up many times. He's got 108 parking tickets.

**I**f ignorance is bliss, why isn't he happy?

**H**e's dumb. He'd look for a wishbone in a soft-boiled egg.

**I**f his IQ were any lower, he'd be a plant.

When he brought his girl home to meet his folks, they approved of her but hated him.

He's a real doll. He'd throw a drowning man an anchor.

She had a face that men go for—they used to call her "Gopher Face."

She dresses like she was just leaving a burning hotel.

He's on everybody's lips—like a fever blister.

She has Early American features. She looks like a buffalo.

He's indecisive. He won't even take a stand on a scale.

A terrible thing happened to her last night—nothing!

She was fat and ugly, so she went on a diet. Now she's thin and ugly.

She's pretty ugly. One day she wore feathers. She was attacked by an ostrich.

She likes to sit in the sun a lot. It's the only thing that's hot for her body.

I think she's twenty-nine. I counted the rings under her eyes.

She spends so much time in parked cars, they show her on road maps.

Sneaky? He won't even look a potato in the eye.

He never goes back on his word. Of course, he may go around it all the time.

He tried to get a job as an idiot, but he was underqualified.

She's so clumsy, her mantra is "Oops."

Even as a kid, he knew he'd go far. The other kids chased him.

He's one guy who can say absolutely nothing and mean it.

She'd have an hourglass figure, but time has shifted her sands.

I'm fond of him, but not as much as he is.

If he said what he thought, he'd be speechless.

The bags under her eyes are so big, she needs a porter to get out of bed in the morning.

She's so dull. Her computer-dating service once matched her with mayonnaise.

She was named after Betsy Ross . . . and not long afterward.

His mother loved children. She would have given anything if he'd been one.

She was born in the year of Our Lord only knows.

He wants to die with his boots on. He's got holes in his socks.

He's always trying to pass the buck except when it has Washington's picture on it.

He's pretty snappy, just like his checks.

He's had it rough recently. His organ grinder died.

Two things are important in his life—sex and laughs. Unfortunately, he gets them both at the same time.

There are a lot of fish in the ocean, but she looks like the bait.

Her face proves that love is blind.

She has the kind of face you want to tune in a little clearer.

On Mother's Day, he has to send his a sympathy card.

Is he a self-made man, or does somebody else take the rap?

He comes from Akron, the rubber capital. It's a shame his father never wore one.

He's so frightened—when he makes love, he has to wear a seat belt.

He made a fool of himself, and you can tell he's a perfect craftsman.

He was a pen pal. That's where he wrote from.

She's the salt of the earth, and people try to shake her.

When it comes to girls, he gives them all the same thing—herpes!

He thinks a chain letter is an invitation to bondage.

They just redecorated his room. They put new padding on the walls.

They just moved into a house with one bath. He can't understand why they need so many.

He's got the personality of the back wall of a handball court!

He comes from a moneyed family. His brother is worth fifty thousand dollars, dead or alive.

He's not himself today. It looks as if he got the best of the deal.

It's not his fault. He wore his beanie with the propeller inside.

He had to get a job recently. He was too nervous to steal.

He's trying. We all agree to that—he's trying!

Last Christmas, he hung up his stocking, and all he got was a note from the Health Department!

He'd park in Lovers' Lane by himself.

She likes to wear a lot of perfume. If she ever stops moving, she leaves a puddle.

She used to eat garlic just to prove she was breathing.

She never wore a necklace. She just braided her chins.

She's like a page out of *Vogue*. I never knew a woman who was more out of vogue.

He's as useful as the parsley they put on steak.

His athlete's foot won Best of the Breed.

Nothing could stop him, not even his talent!

He was born with a silver spoon in his mouth, and when he goes into a restaurant, he tries to complete the set.

Men don't trust him too far, and girls don't trust him too near.

She once tried to give a drowning man mouth-to-mouth, and he refused.

She has no taste in clothes. I've seen poultry dressed better.

He started out working for peanuts until he could prove his salt. Now, he has salted peanuts.

He left school to support his mother. He was forty-one at the time.

He was heads above anybody in his class. He was sixteen, and they were eight.

She's been around—you can tell because her telephone exchange has an 800 number.

He once looked up his family tree and found his family still living in it.

He became a father recently. They must have lowered the requirements.

His family has always served the country—some of them ten years, some of them twenty.

He comes from an alert family. His uncle was the lookout at Pearl Harbor.

Most people feel like his proctologist. They've seen enough of that asshole.

He wears a rubber when he makes love. The dampness is bad for his arthritis.

She's an exception to the Law of Gravity. It's easier to pick her up than to drop her.

He should be a good swimmer. He's been up the creek for years.

When he started out, he didn't have a nickel in his pocket. Now, after thirty years of hard work, he has a nickel in his pocket.

He was so busy learning the tricks of the trade, he forgot to learn the trade.

He could be the poster boy for vasectomies.

He's very busy with the stock market. He has a seat on the curb.

He does nothing all day, and by ten at night he's half through.

The only things that lie more than he does are falsies.

Her age is a military secret—the Civil War!

People who knew her thirty years ago say she still looks like she did then—old.

He's at the age where the only thing that gets steamed up is his glasses.

She will never be as old as she looks.

She doesn't make up her face. She assembles it.

He's not in bad shape. It's just that the parts of his body don't want to work together anymore.

He's as important as a VD doctor in a senior citizen's home.

He's very unpopular. He just bought a parrot. When he got it home, it told him to get out.

He doesn't know when he's well off because he never is.

If he disappears suddenly, it couldn't happen to a nicer guy.

He grows on you. So do warts.

You have to give him a lot of credit. He has no cash.

She's out of this world. I'm glad they don't let her in.

He's here with a girl. Must be novelty night.

She's as pure as the driven snow, although she's drifted a little lately.

There's one thing about him—he doesn't let success go to his clothes.

He's really a modest guy. And he has a lot to be modest about.

We have to forgive her. She's having husband trouble—can't get one.

He's real lazy. He'd stand with a cocktail shaker and wait for an earthquake.

Poor soul. Living proof that cousins do marry.

I can't believe her. Nobody could be that ugly without outside help.

This man is a brain. He recently opened an insurance office in the Bermuda Triangle.

Here's a man who ran into the pope at the Vatican and said, "If you're ever in America, drop in on us . . . and bring the wife and kids."

You'll hear words tonight that you'll never hear at home, unless you're married to a hooker.